Econometric Society Monographs No. 12

Advances in Economic Theory
Fifth World Congress

Econometric Society Monographs

Editors:

Jean-Michel Grandmont   *Centre de'Études Prospectives
d'Économie Mathématique Appliquées à la Planification,
Paris*
Charles F. Manski   *University of Wisconsin, Madison*

The Econometric Society is an international society for the
advancement of economic theory in relation to statistics and
mathematics. The Econometric Society Monograph Series
is designed to promote the publication of original research
contributions of high quality in mathematical economics
and theoretical and applied econometrics.

Other titles in the series:

Werner Hildenbrand, Editor   *Advances in economic theory*
Werner Hildenbrand, Editor   *Advances in econometrics*
G. S. Maddala   *Limited-dependent and qualitative variables in
econometrics*
Gerard Debreu   *Mathematical economics*
Jean-Michel Grandmont   *Money and value*
Franklin M. Fisher   *Disequilibrium foundations of equilibrium
economics*
Bezalel Peleg   *Game theoretic analysis of voting in committees*
Roger Bowden and Darrell Turkington   *Instrumental variables*
Andreu Mas-Colell   *The theory of general economic equilibrium*
James J. Heckman and Burton Singer   *Longitudinal analysis of
labor market data*
Cheng Hsiao   *Analysis of panel data*

Advances in Economic Theory Fifth World Congress

Edited by

TRUMAN F. BEWLEY
Yale University

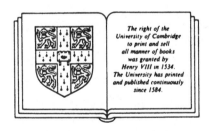

The right of the
University of Cambridge
to print and sell
all manner of books
was granted by
Henry VIII in 1534.
The University has printed
and published continuously
since 1584.

CAMBRIDGE UNIVERSITY PRESS

Cambridge
New York   Port Chester   Melbourne   Sydney

CAMBRIDGE UNIVERSITY PRESS
Cambridge, New York, Melbourne, Madrid, Cape Town, Singapore, São Paulo, Delhi

Cambridge University Press
The Edinburgh Building, Cambridge CB2 8RU, UK

Published in the United States of America by Cambridge University Press, New York

www.cambridge.org
Information on this title: www.cambridge.org/9780521389259

First published 1987
First paperback edition 1989
Re-issued in this digitally printed version 2009

A catalogue record for this publication is available from the British Library

Library of Congress Cataloguing in Publication data

Advances in economic theory.
(Econometric Society monographs ; no. 12)
Papers presented at the Fifth World Congress of the
Econometric Society in Cambridge, Mass., August 1985.
1. Economics – Congresses.   2. Economics, Mathematical –
Congresses.   3. Econometrics – Congresses.   I. Bewley,
Truman F. (Truman Fassett), 1941–   . II. Econometric
Society. World Congress (5th : 1985 : Cambridge, Mass.)
III. Series.
HB21.A329   1987   330.1   87-889

ISBN 978-0-521-34044-1 hardback
ISBN 978-0-521-38925-9 paperback

Contents

Contributors

Peter Diamond
Department of Economics
Massachusetts Institute of Technology

Avinash Dixit
Department of Economics
Princeton University

Oliver Hart
Department of Economics
Massachusetts Institute of Technology

Bengt Holmström
School of Organization and
    Management
Yale University

Paul R. Krugman
Department of Economics
Massachusetts Institute of Technology

Nimrod Megiddo
IBM Research
Almaden Research Center
San Jose, California
and School of
    Mathematical Sciences
Tel Aviv University

Paul R. Milgrom
School of Organization and
    Management
Yale University

John Roberts
Graduate School of Business
Stanford University

Alvin E. Roth
Department of Economics
University of Pittsburgh

Ariel Rubinstein
Department of Economics
Hebrew University

Robert M. Townsend
Department of Economics
University of Chicago

Robert Wilson
Graduate School of Business
Stanford University

Editor's preface

This book and the two companion volumes, *Advances in Econometrics - Fifth World Congress,* Volumes I & II, contain invited papers presented at symposia of the Fifth World Congress of the Econometric Society in Cambridge, Massachusetts, August 1985. The topics and speakers were chosen by the Program Committee. The symposia surveyed important recent developments in economic theory and econometrics. All manuscripts were received by the end of June 1986.

Truman F. Bewley
Chairman of the Program Committee of the
Fifth World Congress of the Econometric Society

CHAPTER 1

Auction theory

Paul R. Milgrom

1   Introduction

Auctions are one of the oldest surviving classes of economic institutions.
The first historical record of an auction is usually attributed to Herodotus, who reported a custom in Babylonia in which men bid for women
to wed.[1] Other observers have reported auctions throughout the ancient
world – in Babylonia, Greece, the Roman Empire, China, and Japan.[2]

As impressive as the historical longevity of auctions is the remarkable
range of situations in which they are currently used. There are auctions
for livestock, a commodity for which many close substitutes are available. There are also auctions for rare and unusual items like large dia-
monds, works of art, and other collectibles. Durables (e.g., used machinery), perishables (e.g., fresh fish), financial assets (e.g., U.S. Treasury
bills), and supply and construction contracts are all commonly bought or
sold at auction. The auction sales of unique items have suggested to some
that auctions are a good vehicle for monopolists. But it is not only those
in a strong market position who use auctions. There are also auction sales
of the land, equipment, and supplies of bankrupt firms and farms. These
show that auctions are used by sellers who are desperate for cash and willing to sell even at prices far below replacement cost.

The first draft of this paper was written while I was a Fellow at the Institute for Advanced
Studies of the Hebrew University of Jerusalem. Discussions with Charles Wilson, Motty
Perry, and, especially, Ariel Rubinstein contributed enormously to my understanding of
the relation between auctions and bargaining. Comments by Byung-Il Choi and Alvin Roth
on a previous version of this manuscript led to improvements in the exposition.

[1] Herodotus may not have been the first to publish. Some scholars interpret the biblical
account of the sale of Joseph (the great-grandson of Abraham) into slavery as being an
auction sale.

[2] For a more detailed history of auctions and a description of some of the auctions used in
the modern world, see Cassady (1967).

Indeed, the only clear common denominator for the kinds of objects that are sold at auction is the need to establish individual prices for each item sold. Used cars, whose condition varies over a wide range, are sold to dealers at auction; new cars are not. Livestock are sold at auction even though close substitutes are readily available, because individual animals differ in weight and health. The price of fresh fish needs to be determined daily, because the daily supply of fish varies so tremendously. Construction contracts are normally too complex to allow a simple pricing schedule to work; competitive bids sometimes provide a workable alternative.

In this essay, 1 review only a small part of auction theory – the part that claims to explain the long and widespread use of auctions and competitive bidding and to account for certain details of the way auctions are usually conducted. These details include the popular use of sealed-bid and ascending-bid auctions, the establishment of minimum prices, the preparation of expert appraisals of items being sold, and so forth.

Logically prior to explaining the use of auctions is defining just what an auction is. The characteristic feature of an auction is that there is an explicit *comparison* made among bids. In the ascending-bid ("English") auction, a bidder's offer remains open long enough for other bidders to make counteroffers, so that the seller can take the highest offer. In the sealed-bid auction, the bidders' offers are all made simultaneously, so that the seller can compare them directly. In the descending-bid ("Dutch") auction, the seller makes a series of price offers, declining over time. Each bidder has the opportunity to accept or reject the seller's latest price offer; this affords the seller an opportunity to compare the timing of buyers' offers, and to take the offer that is made earliest. Each of these auctions requires that all the bidding be completed within a relatively short period of time. They can be contrasted with, say, a sequential bargaining process in which the seller negotiates one-by-one with a series of buyers who make short-lived offers, so that the seller has no opportunity to compare the simultaneous offers of competing buyers. We shall develop the importance of this difference in more detail later.

The simplest explanation of the continuing popularity of auctions is that auctions often lead to outcomes that are efficient and stable. More formally, in a static deterministic model, the set of perfect equilibrium trading outcomes obtained in an auction game (as the minimum bid is varied) coincides with the set of core allocations. An outcome is in the *core* when there is no coalition of traders that can, by trading just among its members, make all coalition members better off.

To understand the significance of this conclusion, imagine a situation in which a single item is sold but the resulting allocation lies outside the core. There are two possibilities. First, the allocation may be inefficient;

in this case, the new owner will likely find it profitable to resell the item to a buyer who values it more. The second possibility is that, even though the allocation is efficient, there are other buyers around who were willing to pay a higher price (and after the auction are willing to tell the seller so). In either case, the seller may well resolve not to be so quick to sell the next time around and perhaps even to compare alternative offers – that is, to conduct some kind of auction.

A second explanation of the popularity of auctions highlights the advantages of an auction to a seller in a relatively poor bargaining position[3] (such as the owner of a nearly bankrupt firm) when the goods sold at auction can later be resold. Consider the problem of such a seller. Suppose that there are two potential buyers: Mr. 1, who has a high valuation for the item being sold, and Mr. 2, whose valuation is lower. What happens if the seller conducts an auction with a low minimum price? At the equilibrium of the auction game, the item will be sold to Mr. 1 for approximately its value to Mr. 2. With the possibility of resale, that value cannot be less than the price that Mr. 2 could get by reselling to Mr. 1. By conducting an auction, the seller expects to get about the same price as Mr. 2 would get, even though Mr. 2 may be much better positioned for face-to-face bargaining with Mr. 1. Thus, a seller in a relatively weak bargaining position can do as well as a strong bargainer by conducting an auction.

These first two explanations of the prevalence of auctions are developed in detail in Section 2, which focuses on deterministic auction models. A third explanation, reviewed in Section 3, is that even a seller in a strong bargaining position will sometimes find it optimal to conduct an auction. That is, the seller will prefer to conduct some standard auction, such as the sealed-bid or ascending-bid auction with a suitably chosen minimum price, rather than to play any other exchange game[4] with the bidders.

The three explanations just described are, of course, complementary. Together, they provide a cogent set of reasons for a seller to use an auction when selling an indivisible object over a wide range of circumstances.

In the auction models discussed so far, there is little that can be said about the details of how auctions are conducted. In those models, many kinds of auctions (including all the usual ones) lead to the same mean price. However, this "independence" result depends on the assumption that bidders have no private information about each other. Formally, the observations they make are assumed to be statistically independent. When

---

[3] That is, a poor bargaining position relative to the potential buyers.
[4] An exchange game is any game whose outcome determines an allocation and time of trade, and in which each player has a strategy of nonparticipation that leaves him with his initial allocation.

there is correlated uncertainty on the part of the bidders, different auction rules lead to different mean prices.

In Section 4, we introduce correlated uncertainty into the bidding model and focus on the strategies open even to a seller with no bargaining power, that is, one who cannot commit himself to withhold an item that attracts only low bids.[5] What strategies can such a seller adopt? For one, he can normally choose which kind of auction to offer, provided the minimum bid is kept low, because buyers will always want to participate in the auction.[6] Normally, the seller can also decide whether to reveal any information about the item being sold or about the potential buyers, because it always pays a buyer to listen if he can do so without being seen. Given these options, the seller's preferences are surprisingly systematic. In a wide range of circumstances,[7] the seller will prefer (1) to conduct an ascending-bid auction rather than a sealed-bid auction, (2) to reveal all information that he has available, and (3) to link the price to any available exogenous indicators of value.

The analysis leading to these conclusions is founded on what has been called the *Linkage Principle*. Intuitively, a bidder's expected profits from an auction are greatest when he has private information that the item being sold is quite valuable. The intuition of the Linkage Principle is that the auctions yielding the highest average prices are those that are most effective at undermining the privacy of the winning bidder's information, thereby transfering some profits from the bidders to the seller. According to the principle, privacy is undermined by linking price to information other than (but correlated with) the winning bidder's private information.

The three conclusions described above all follow from the Linkage Principle. In an ascending-bid auction, the equilibrium price depends on the information of losing bidders through the bids they place. That dependence, or linkage, is absent in the sealed-bid auction. Its presence in the ascending-bid auction leads to a higher predicted price (provided that the bidders' information is correlated).

---

[5] In Section 4, we review some game-theoretic arguments supporting the presumption that a "rational" seller cannot hold out for a high price when he is uncertain about the buyers' reservation prices.

[6] No matter what strategies the other players adopt, each buyer does at least as well by entering the minimum bid as by abstaining from the auction. For some strategies - namely, when others refrain from bidding - he does better. (This argument is transparent for the case where resale is impossible, and can be extended also to the case with resale possibilities.)

[7] The principal assumptions required include risk neutrality, symmetric uncertainty about the bidders' valuations, and a strong form of nonnegative correlation, known as *affiliation,* among the bidders' valuations.

In any kind of auction, the seller, by revealing information, influences the bids and therefore the price. So, by revealing his information, the seller links the price directly to his information. Thus, according to the Linkage Principle, a policy of revealing information raises the expected price that will result from the auction, provided that the information to be revealed is affiliated[8] with the bidders' information. Similarly, basing the price in part on ex post indicators of value creates a linkage that on average increases the expected price (if these indicators are affiliated with the bidders' information). Examples of contracts let at auction where price is determined in part by ex post indicators include construction contracts with a cost-sharing provision and petroleum drilling contracts that provide for royalty payments based on actual production.

The main theme of explaining the prevalence and robustness of auctions is continued in Section 5, where the possibility of collusion is briefly studied. Collusion is widespread in real auctions, and there is little a one-time seller can do to prevent it when the bidders have a long-term relationship. However, it is shown that ascending-bid auctions are more vulnerable to collusive agreements among bidders in a long-term relationship than are sealed-bid auctions. This is an important reason for industrial firms to solicit sealed bids from suppliers, despite the general superiority of ascending-bid auctions in one-shot competitive situations.

2   Auctions, bargaining, and the core

We begin by formulating and proving the claim that the trading outcomes of the auction game coincide with the core of the corresponding exchange game. This result provides a simple, partial answer to the question of why auction institutions are so prevalent throughout the world and throughout history.

Consider a deterministic setting with a single seller and n (potential) buyers for some item. Let s be the monetary value of the item to the seller; this means that if the seller had the option of selling for some price p or not selling the item at all, he would choose to sell for p if and only if $p \geq s$. Similarly, the buyers have monetary valuations $b_1, \ldots, b_n$. Our model is discrete: All the valuations and bids are multiples of some common unit. Here and throughout this chapter, we make the standard game-theoretic assumption that the deterministic parameters are common knowledge

---

[8] Random variables are said to be *affiliated* when they are positively correlated conditional on lying in any small rectangle. For example, any pair of positively correlated joint normal random variables are affiliated. A precise formal definition of the concept is given in Section 4.

among the buyers and the seller.[9] Without significant loss of generality, we may assume that $b_1 > \cdots > b_n$ and limit attention to the case where there are some potential gains from trade: $b_1 > s$.

Now, if the seller offers the item for sale using a sealed-bid auction with minimum price $m < b_2$,[10] what will happen? Using any sensible equilibrium concept (e.g., Nash equilibrium in undominated strategies,[11] perfect equilibrium, "rationalizable" strategies, or even correlated equilibrium), the item will be sold to bidder 1 for his bid of b_2.[12] The same trade will occur if the seller sets any minimum price not exceeding b_2. Again, the same will occur if the seller hires an auctioneer to conduct an ascending-bid auction, regardless of whether the bids are called by the bidders themselves or at a slow pace by the auctioneer.

If the seller sets a minimum price $m \in (b_2, b_1)$, the equilibrium outcome assigns the item to bidder 1 for a price of m. Of course, if $m > b_1$,

[9] In the standard theory of games, the players need to know this structure in order to compute the equilibrium and determine how to play. An alternative view, relevant to auction theory, holds that players learn from experience about the reduced form of their decision problems and select their best bids for that problem. Equilibrium is then a state where all players have correctly learned and are using optimal strategies in their decision problems. Mathematically, this leads to the same definition of equilibrium as does the standard view, but it raises different stability questions and does not require as much knowledge among the players about the overall structure of the game.

[10] We assume in this auction and all those considered hereafter that ties are broken by tossing a fair coin.

[11] Although the Nash equilibrium and its refinements are often justifiably criticized, they are particularly well suited to the analysis of auction games. A Nash equilibrium can be defined as a profile of strategies, one for each player, such that (1) each player is maximizing given his beliefs about how the others will play and (2) those beliefs are correct. The first condition is neither stronger nor weaker than the usual rationality assumption in economic models. The second ("rational expectations") condition is most plausible for institutions – such as auctions – that have existed for millennia and so for which expectations can be based on actual experience.

[12] Any perfect equilibrium (Selten, 1975) is a Nash equilibrium in undominated strategies, and in fact for this game the two concepts coincide. In the two-bidder game, the set of perfect equilibria are characterized as follows: Bidder 1 bids b_2. Bidder 2 uses any mixed strategy F that satisfies two conditions. First, $F(b_2^-) = 1$. Second, let $G(x) = [F(x) + F(x-1)]/2$; then $G(x) \le (b_1 - b_2)/(b_1 - x)$ for all $x \in (m, b_2)$. With more than two bidders, one can specify the strategies of the others arbitrarily, provided bidder j always bids less than b_j, and this remains a perfect equilibrium.

Rationalizable strategies are derived by eliminating weakly dominated strategies from the strategy set to form a reduced game. Then weakly dominated strategies are eliminated from the reduced game, and so on until the process ends. The strategies that survive are called *rationalizable*. The only such strategies for bidders 1 and 2 are to bid b_2 and $b_2 - 1$, respectively.

Correlated equilibria (Aumann, 1973) of bidding games employ only rationalizable strategies, so that concept is covered also.

no exchange takes place; in that case the seller's payoff is s and each buyer's payoff is zero. The case $m = b_1$ is somewhat degenerate; its equilibria include both the no-trade outcome and a trade at price b_1. Our earlier choice of the phrase "equilibrium trading outcomes" was intended to denote all the equilibrium outcomes except the no-trade outcome. Our claim is then justified by the following proposition.

> *Proposition 1. The set of perfect equilibrium outcomes of the auction game, as the minimum price ranges from s to b_1, consists of the core outcomes of the corresponding exchange game together with the no-trade outcome. The latter can only occur when the minimum price is b_1.*

Proof: Let $x = (x_0, x_1, \ldots, x_n)$ be the vector of payoffs that are received by the seller and the n buyers, respectively. A vector of payoffs x is called an *imputation* if it is individually rational (i.e., nonnegative) and Pareto optimal and corresponds to some feasible allocation of the goods and money among the players. These imply:

$$x_0 + x_1 + \cdots + x_n = b_1. \tag{2.1}$$

To be in the core, an imputation must also satisfy inequalities asserting that no coalition could, by agreeing to exchange among themselves, earn a higher total payoff:

$$x_0 + \sum_{i \in S} x_i \geq \max\{s, (b_i; \ i \in S)\}, \quad \text{for all } S \subset \{1, \ldots, n\}. \tag{2.2}$$

In view of the preceding discussion, the proposition asserts that the core consists entirely of points of the form

$$(x_0, b_1 - x_0, 0, \ldots, 0) \quad \text{for } \max(s, b_2) \leq x_0 \leq b_1.$$

It is easy to check that all such points satisfy (2.1) and the inequalities (2.2), and so in fact do lie in the core.

Conversely, suppose x lies in the core. From (2.1) and nonnegativity, $x_0 + x_1 \leq b_1$. From (2.2) for $S = \{1\}$, $x_0 + x_1 \geq b_1$. Hence, $x_0 + x_1 = b_1$ and, by (2.1) and nonnegativity, $x_2 = \cdots = x_n = 0$. Therefore, all points in the core are of the form $(x_0, b_1 - x_0, 0, \ldots, 0)$. Using (2.2) with $S = \{2\}$, one finds $x_0 + x_2 \geq \max(s, b_2)$; so $x_0 \geq \max(s, b_2)$. Nonnegativity of x_1 implies $x_0 \leq b_1$. ∎

The strategic equivalence of the Dutch and sealed-bid auctions and the notion of perfect equilibrium do not transfer neatly to bidding games with continuous bid spaces. For discrete bid spaces with bid increment ϵ,

8   **Paul R. Milgrom**

the only perfect equilibrium in the Dutch auction is for the highest evaluator to stop the auction when the price reaches b_2, and for each other player i to stop it at the price $b_i - \epsilon$. There are no corresponding strategies in the standard formulation of the continuous Dutch auction, because there is no possibility of bidding b_i "minus an infinitesimal." Indeed, in the standard formulation of the continuous Dutch auction, no subgame perfect equilibrium exists.

To avoid this problem, we formulate the extensive form Dutch auction game so that a bidder can claim the object whenever the price falls to p, which we call bidding p, or whenever the price falls strictly below p, which we call bidding p^-. If a player bids p, another bids p^-, and all others bid less, then the item is awarded to the one who bids p for price p. If a player bids p^- and nobody else bids more, then the item is awarded to that bidder for a price of p. This specifies a well-defined continuous Dutch auction game which suitably generalizes the game with discrete bid amounts. Moreover, like the discrete bids game, it does have a unique subgame perfect equilibrium: Player 1 bids b_2 and each $i \neq 1$ bids b_i^-.[13]

There still remains the problem that "trembling-hand" perfect equilibrium is undefined for sealed-bid auction games with a continuum of possible bids. To avoid unnecessary technical difficulties, we shall normally limit our analysis to equilibria of Dutch auctions.

From the perspective of cooperative game theory, the seller's ability to set any particular minimum price and stick to it measures his bargaining power.[14] Indeed, the case $n = 1$ is just a bargaining problem, and auction theory predicts (as does core theory) only that the outcome will be efficient and that nobody will be worse off at equilibrium than if they did not trade. Evidently, a complete auction theory must be informed to some degree by bargaining theory. This leaves open the possibility that the predictions of auction theory could be quite sensitive to the bargaining model used.

Actually, when there are several viable bidders, auction theory is surprisingly insensitive to the bargaining theory used at its foundations. To show this, we embed the auction model in a general discounted, infinite-horizon, noncooperative model of bargaining in which an owner always

13 One could, of course, define a modified sealed-bid auction game that is strategically equivalent to our continuous Dutch auction game. However, comparing the subgame perfect equilibria of the Dutch auction game (identified in the text) with the trembling-hand perfect equilibria of the corresponding sealed-bid auction (identified in note 12) shows that the two games are not equivalent for the purposes of perfect equilibrium analysis.

14 The role of commitment in bargaining has been analyzed by Crawford (1982). The associated roles of patience and risk aversion have been given a particularly penetrating analysis by Binmore, Rubinstein, and Wolinsky (1986).

has the right to resell anything he has bought. Because a single player may be sometimes a buyer and sometimes a seller, we shall designate a player's valuation by v_i rather than by s or b_i. It is assumed that $v_1 > \cdots > v_n > 0$.

Let Γ^i be a game form that is to be played when i is the owner of the durable good. Thus, $\Gamma^i = (\{\Sigma^i_j; j = 1, \ldots, n\}, f^i)$, where Σ^i_j is the set of strategies available to j in the game form and f^i is a function mapping strategy profiles into outcomes. Time is modeled as discrete. An outcome involving trade specifies a date of trade $t \geq 1$, a (nonnegative) price p, and the next owner j. There is also an outcome called "no trade" that we identify as a trade at date $t = \infty$. To interpret the results that follow, it will be useful to think of t as the period of i's ownership, rather than to associate t with any actual date.

Certain specified strategies are assumed to be available to the players in each game form Γ^i. First, the owner is permitted to keep the item for himself; that is, he may choose a strategy that always leads to no trade. Second, the owner is permitted to offer a Dutch auction with a zero minimum price. Such an offer, if made, is the first move in Γ^i and initiates an auction subgame (actually, a "subgame form"). If any non-owner bids in the auction, Γ^i ends at date 1 with the item being assigned according to the usual Dutch auction rules. Non-owners must decide simultaneously whether to bid. If no bids are made, play continues according to the continuation rules of Γ^i, whatever they may be. Each non-owner is assumed to have a strategy of refusing to be party to any trade, in which case no payment can be required of him. The assumption that the decision of whether to offer an auction immediately is the first move in Γ^i means that non-owners have no way, before an auction is offered, to commit themselves not to trade.

Using these very general game forms, which specify the rules governing trade given the owner's identity, we create a game in which the buyer can (if he chooses) resell the good. Let player i_0 be the initial owner. Then the game form Γ^{i_0} is played. If the outcome involves trade after a period of ownership of length t_0, at price p_0, and with next owner i_1, we continue with game form Γ^{i_1}, which determines a period of ownership t_1, price p_1, and next owner i_2. The outcome of this sequence of trades specifies that i_0 owns the item from date 0 to date $t_0 - 1$, i_1 owns the item from t_0 to $t_0 + t_1 - 1$, and generally i_j owns it from date $t_0 + \cdots + t_{j-1}$ to date $t_0 + \cdots + t_j - 1$. Payments are made on the dates of transfer of ownership. The number of actual times the good changes hands can be finite or infinite.

The payoff associated with any outcome for any fixed player j is the present value of the flow of benefits he receives plus the net present value of payments received minus payments made. To make this more precise, fix an outcome path. Let $1_j(t)$ be one if player j owns the item on date t and zero otherwise. (In particular, $1_j(-1) = 0$.) Let $p(t)$ be the price paid in any trade at date t, or zero if there is no trade at t. Then, j's payoff in the game is:

$$\sum_{t=0}^{\infty} \delta^t [(1-\delta)v_j 1_j(t) + p(t)[1_j(t-1) - 1_j(t)]]. \tag{2.3}$$

Thus, δ is the discount factor for the players' payoffs.

With this, the specification of the selling games is completed. Corresponding to each player i there is a game in which the identity i_0 of the initial owner is i. We shall call that game Γ_i^*.

The games Γ_i^* that can be constructed in this way for some choice of game forms Γ^i form a huge class. Included are games where the seller can conduct auctions with a positive minimum price, exclude some set of bidders, bargain effectively with some buyers, commit himself to take-it-or-leave-it offers, or do all of these. Indeed, the only important restrictions on the set of options available to a seller are that he can neither compel a non-owner to buy nor prevent a buyer from reselling the good, and that he can always offer an auction with a zero minimum price. An additional "stationarity" restriction will be imposed through the equilibria that we isolate for study.

In general, a strategy for a player specifies how to play at each date as a function of the date and the entire past history. For our analysis, we limit attention to equilibria in which the players adopt stationary strategies. A *stationary strategy* for player j is an n-tuple $\sigma_j = (\sigma_j^1, \ldots, \sigma_j^n)$ such that $\sigma_j^i \in \Sigma_j^i$. Such a strategy specifies how player j should play in each game form Γ^i (he should play σ_j^i) without regard to the earlier history of play. By a *stationary perfect equilibrium*, we mean an n-tuple of stationary strategies $(\sigma_1, \ldots, \sigma_n)$ that is a perfect equilibrium profile regardless of the identity of the initial owner (i.e., in each of the games Γ_i^*).

Given a strategy profile $(\sigma_1, \ldots, \sigma_n)$, one can define for each player i a value v_i^* associated with owning the item, that is, with playing the game Γ_i^*. With stationary strategies, v_i^* is also the continuation payoff or value of acquiring ownership at any point in the game, regardless of the previous history of play. With nonstationary strategies, that value might depend on the history of play, because future play could also depend on the history.

> **Proposition 2.** *Assume there are least three players, $n \geq 3$. Let v_i^* be the expected payoff to i at a stationary perfect equilibrium in the game Γ_i^*. Then $v_1^* = v_1 > v_i^*$ for all $i \neq 1$. Let a_i^* be the payoff to i in Γ_i^* if all players except i adhere to their equilibrium strategies while i deviates to adopt a strategy that entails conducting*

an auction and refusing to participate in any later sale. Then, for all $i, j \neq 1$, the following inequalities hold:

$$v_i^* > \delta v_j^*, \tag{2.4}$$

$$a_i^* > \delta^2 v_i^*. \tag{2.5}$$

According to Proposition 2, for δ close to 1 it is optimal or nearly optimal for any player other than the highest evaluator to offer the good at auction. Moreover, initial ownership is about equally valuable for all the players other than player 1, even though owners may differ in the strategies available to them. The proposition applies even when some owners are able to make credible take-it-or-leave-it offers while others can sell only at auction. The ability to conduct an auction allows a weak bargainer to benefit from the abilities of any stronger bargainers who may be present, forcing player 1 to bid just as if he were bargaining with a strong player.

Proof of Proposition 2: In the game Γ_1^*, player 1 can guarantee a payoff of v_1 by refusing to trade. Each other player can guarantee a payoff of zero. Hence, the equilibrium payoffs must be at least that high. But the maximum total utility from any outcome is v_1, and that can be achieved only if player 1 is the owner in every period. Hence, in Γ_1^*, any equilibrium must specify that no trade occurs.

Suppose $i \neq 1$. In the game Γ_i^*, the total payoffs to all players at equilibrium cannot exceed the total payoff $(1-\delta)v_i + \delta v_1 < v_1$ that results from an efficient exchange. Since all players' payoffs are nonnegative, this implies that $v_i^* < v_1$.

Now, in Γ_i^*, i has the opportunity to conduct an auction with minimum price 0. If he does and the non-owners refuse to participate, let the expected continuation payoffs at equilibrium be $\bar{v} = (\bar{v}_1, \ldots, \bar{v}_n)$. The auction offer will be accepted by someone with certainty (at equilibrium) unless each non-owner prefers (weakly) his continuation payoff to the payoff from placing the minimum bid of 0: $\bar{v}_j \geq \delta v_j^*$. Because the sale price cannot be negative, the seller's expected payoff can never be less than the first period flow: $\bar{v}_i \geq (1-\delta)v_i$. Thus, some bidder will participate in the auction at equilibrium unless the expected sum of payoffs when no auction takes place is at least $\delta \sum_{j \neq i} v_j^* + (1-\delta)v_i > \delta v_1 + (1-\delta)v_i$. The last expression, however, is the total payoff that results from efficient trade. Hence, there can be no strategies leading to continuation payoffs $\bar{v}$ satisfying the requisite inequality.

So the auction, if offered, will be played with certainty. Let p be the lowest price in the support of the equilibrium price distribution when an auction is offered in Γ_i^*. Let $k \notin \{1, i\}$ be such that $v_k^* = \max_{j \notin \{1, i\}} v_j^*$.

During a Dutch auction, when the price has fallen to any level $p' > p$, bidder 1 must expect a payoff of at least $\delta(v_1 - p')$ from allowing the auction to continue, and k must expect at least $\delta(v_k^* - p')$. Because the total expected payoff to all bidders in the continuation after p' is at most $\delta(v_1 - p)$ (since the price will be at least p), it follows that $\delta(v_1 - p') + \delta(v_k^* - p') \leq \delta(v_1 - p)$ for all $p' > p$. Hence, $p \geq v_k^*$. In the Dutch auction, no bidder j can benefit by bidding more than v_j^*, so bidder 1 never finds it optimal (at equilibrium) to bid strictly more than v_k^*. Hence, the highest equilibrium price cannot exceed v_k^*. Therefore the equilibrium price following an auction offer is v_k^* with probability one.

If i offers an auction in Γ_i^* and never repurchases the item, while the other players follow their stationary equilibrium strategies, i's payoff will be

$$a_i^* = (1 - \delta)v_i + \delta v_k^* > \delta v_j^*, \tag{2.6}$$

for all $j \notin \{1, i\}$. Since $v_i^* \geq a_i^*$, (2.4) follows.

Next we make two applications of (2.6),

$$a_i^* > \delta v_j^* \geq \delta a_j^* > \delta^2 v_i^*, \tag{2.7}$$

which establishes (2.5).   ∎

So far, we have allowed the game forms $(\Gamma^i; i = 1, \ldots, n)$ to be quite general. As an aid to intuition, let us now specify some simple game forms as follows. At odd-numbered dates, the owner chooses a non-owner to whom to make a price offer. The non-owner can accept the offer, in which case a trade is consummated. Or, the non-owner can reject the offer and, at the next (even) date, make a counteroffer. So far, this is the same game as used for the "telephone bargaining" model of Binmore (1983). Now comes a difference: We specify that the owner can, at time 0, offer a Dutch auction with a zero minimum price. If no buyer participates in the auction, then the seller can make a private offer at time 1, and the game continues in the Binmore fashion.

The games Γ_i^* constructed from the specified game forms differ from Binmore's telephone bargaining game in two ways: by allowing auctions and by including the possibility of resale. One can show that each Γ_i^* has a unique perfect equilibrium outcome. To describe it, define a function $B: \mathbb{R}^2 \to \mathbb{R}$ by:

$$B(x, y) \equiv x + (y - x)/(1 + \delta). \tag{2.8}$$

In the telephone bargaining model, if $i \neq 1$ then the perfect equilibrium outcome is that the item is sold to player 1 for the price $B \equiv B(v_i, v_1)$. Note that for δ close to one, the bargainers split the surplus almost equally. Note too that the price is not at all sensitive to the presence of additional bargainers. For the games Γ_i^*, however, the equilibrium outcomes are quite different.

> **Proposition 3.** *If the initial owner is $i = 1$, then no trade ever occurs at equilibrium. If the initial owner is any other player, then at equilibrium the item is sold at date 1 to player 1 and never resold. The sale is by private offer if the private offer price of $B(v_i, v_1)$ is larger than the auction price of $(1 - \delta)v_2 + \delta B(v_2, v_1)$. Otherwise, the sale is by auction.* [15]

The game has been structured so that the owner makes the first offer. Because delays are costly, this gives the owner some advantage in the bargaining. When the time between successive offers is long and delay costs are high, the advantage of making the first offer in negotiations is large, and it is not optimal then for the owner to give up that advantage by conducting a low minimum-price auction.

Probably more common is the situation where the time between offers is small enough that δ is nearly one. [16] In this case, the auction price will exceed the private offer price if and only if there are at least two non-owners with higher valuations than the initial owner i. That is, at equilibrium the owner bargains if and only if there is only one real potential buyer. Otherwise, he conducts an auction!

Together, Propositions 2 and 3 provide a strong case for the desirability of conducting an auction.

3   Expected price-maximizing auctions

So far, we have shown that auctions lead to core outcomes and that when resale is possible and trading costs are low, it is almost optimal for almost every seller to conduct an auction with a low minimum price. This near optimality holds regardless of the other alternatives available to the seller, provided only that the buyers cannot be compelled to buy. However, the specific example with which we ended Section 2 establishes that conducting an auction with a low minimum price is not generally the best strategy for a seller in a strong bargaining position.

We therefore turn to the question: What is the best strategy for a seller with a hegemony of bargaining power? What we have in mind is a situation in which the seller, for some unspecified reason, has the power to

[15] The proof is omitted. It follows the now familiar lines for alternating offer bargaining models (see Rubinstein, Chapter 5, this volume).

[16] For example, if the annual real interest rate were as much as 5% and it took a week to arrange an auction, δ would be .999.

select any institution he likes for conducting trade. The seller assumes that the buyers will agree to participate if their expected payoffs are non-negative – the buyers are too weak to demand more. In the deterministic setting, the seller's optimal strategy is obvious: make a take-it-or-leave-it offer to the highest valuation buyer that extracts all the surplus from him. If buyers' valuations are private information, however, then the seller cannot implement such a strategy; he does not know what offer to make. What, then, should an expected price–maximizing seller do?

Let us begin with the simplest case. We suppose that there is only one buyer whose valuation V ($V \geq 0$) for the item is unknown and has distribution F. Suppose the seller's valuation is s, corresponding to a flow benefit from ownership of $(1-\delta)s$. These valuations mean that if the buyer acquires the item at date t for a price of p, his payoff (in von Neumann–Morgenstern utility) is $(V-p)\delta^t$ and the seller's is $p\delta^t + s(1-\delta^t)$.[17] If no trade occurs, the buyer's payoff is zero and the seller's is s. Following Vickrey's style of formulation, let us suppose that the buyer observes private information X and has a valuation $V = u(X)$, where X is uniformly distributed on $(0, 1)$ and u is a nondecreasing function.[18] For simplicity, we take u to be strictly increasing and continuously differentiable.

If the seller makes a take-it-or-leave-it offer at a price of $p = u(x)$, the buyer will accept if his valuation exceeds $u(x)$. The probability of that is $1-x$. The seller's expected payoff is then $(1-x)u(x) + xs$. Of course, the seller has other strategies available. He could require the buyer to play a game in which the buyer's choices determine a probability distribution over outcomes. An outcome specifies whether a trade occurs, when it occurs, and what payments are made at which dates. The content of the next result is that a simple take-it-or-leave-it offer is as good or better than any such game.[19]

> **Proposition 4.** *Let x^* solve $\max(1-x)u(x) + xs$. Then making an immediate take-it-or-leave-it offer to sell at the price $u(x^*)$, with a commitment never to make another offer, maximizes the seller's expected payoff (over the class of all exchange games).*

---

[17] The assumption of identical discount rates can be weakened to an assumption that the seller is no more patient than the buyers, without upsetting any of our results.

[18] This involves no loss of generality. One can reproduce any distribution F essentially by taking $u = F^{-1}$.

[19] Propositions 4 and 5 synthesize results of Harris and Raviv (1982), Milgrom (1985), Myerson (1981), Riley and Samuelson (1981), and Rubinstein, Wilson, and Wolinsky (private communication, 1985). Rubinstein, Wilson, and Wolinsky were the first to extend the optimal auction results to models in which the seller could use the threat of delays to extract a higher price from the buyer. Their analysis makes clear that Proposition 5 depends on the assumption that the seller is no more patient than the buyers.

Moreover, if $(1-x)u(x)$ is strictly concave, then the seller's payoff is maximized only by games that sell at time 0 to all buyers for whom $X > x^*$ and do not sell to other buyers at any date.

The most surprising part of this conclusion is that it does not, in general, pay the seller to use time and uncertainty for purposes of price discrimination. As a corollary, the seller cannot benefit from private information about his own valuation; he would make the same take-it-or-leave-it offer as a function of s regardless of whether s is known ex ante.

The method of analysis used to prove Proposition 4 is important and worthy of detailed study. The heart of the method is the observation that it is possible to place substantive restrictions on the allocation that can result from any Nash equilibrium of any Bayesian game. The first restriction is the so-called *incentive compatibility* constraint: Each player must prefer his own equilibrium allocation to anything he could get by pretending to be a player of another type. A second type of restriction, the *participation constraint,* reflects the assumption that the buyer cannot be forced to participate: The buyer must actually prefer participation to nonparticipation. As applied to the problem at hand, the incentive compatibility constraint means that the seller cannot extract a higher price from a buyer with a higher valuation unless he gives that buyer something of corresponding value in return, such as a higher probability of receiving the item or the opportunity to receive it sooner. The participation constraint means that the buyer's expected payoff must be nonnegative, regardless of his valuation of the item. These constraints imply a bound on what the seller can expect to receive at any Bayesian–Nash equilibrium of any game. The proof of Proposition 4 amounts to computing the bound and showing that it is achieved by a take-it-or-leave-it offer.

This method is most fruitful when applied to a model in which the incentive constraints take a particularly simple form. In the problem at hand, the buyer cares only about the expected discounted date at which he acquires the item $E[\delta^T]$ (where $T = \infty$ if he makes no acquisition) and the expected discounted payments $\bar{e}$ to be made. The payoff to a buyer of valuation v is $vE[\delta^T] - \bar{e}$, a linear function of the relevant variables. The seller cares about the same things; his payoff is $\bar{e} + s(1 - E[\delta^T])$. A proof of Proposition 4 using these ideas is given in the appendix to this chapter.

Next, we introduce multiple potential buyers into the environment. Assume that there are n bidders, and that bidder i's private information is represented by the random variable X_i. Bidder i's valuation $V_i = u(X_i)$ depends only on his private information. Assume that u is nondecreasing and that the X_i's are independently uniformly distributed on $(0, 1)$. This combination of assumptions defines the *independent private values model* adopted by Vickrey (1961, 1962), Griesmer, Levitan, and Shubik (1967), and Ortega-Reichert (1968) in their pioneering studies of auction theory. The independence assumption is particularly important for the results of this section; it means that an outside observer (or the seller) can never infer anything about X_1 by observing $(X_2, ..., X_n)$. We relax this assumption in Section 4.

The analysis in the multiple buyer case follows the same lines as in the single buyer case. The conclusion, however, is even more striking.

> **Proposition 5.** Assume that $(1-x)u(x)$ is concave and let x^* denote a maximizer of $(1-x)u(x)+xs$. Then among all possible games that the bidders might agree to play, the sealed-bid and ascending-bid auctions with minimum price $u(x^*)$ maximize the seller's expected payoff.[20]

Proposition 5 as stated applies only to a very limited set of auction environments. However, it can be (and has been) extended in many different directions. The case of risk-averse buyers has been treated by Matthews (1983) and Maskin and Riley (1984a). Cremer and McLean (1985b) have studied a variation involving some statistical dependence. Milgrom (1985) allowed the seller to have many objects for sale, subject to some convex cost of production. Other variants can also be found. Most often, the optimal selling strategies for these more complicated environments are not recognizable auctions nor, indeed, recognizable institutions of any kind. Thus, the optimal auction theory is inadequate, by itself, to explain why auctions are used.

What is perhaps most missed in the theory of optimal auctions is some indication of which institutions for selling an object are robust – that is, optimal or nearly so in a range of environments, or at least not weakly dominated across a range of environments. Also missing is some formalization of the idea that auctions are "simple" – for example, in most auctions, all the bids that can be made actually are made with positive probability at equilibrium in several simple environments. Properties like simplicity and robustness are interesting to think about but hard to formulate; almost nothing is known about this topic.

4   Strategies for a weak seller

The models of Sections 2 and 3 go a long way toward explaining the continuing widespread use of auctions for selling many goods. However,

---

[20] As shown in Section 4, other standard auctions with the same minimum price lead to the same expected price.

these theories tell us almost nothing about the details of auctions. The deterministic models predict that all the usual sorts of auction mechanisms lead to the same outcome. Vickrey, who first introduced and used the independent private values model of Section 3, found that all the common auctions lead to the same allocation of the item and the same average price for the seller. One of the main puzzles of auction theory since Vickrey's pioneering work has been to explain when different auctions can be expected to lead to substantially different outcomes. Our purpose in this section is to review a theory that offers such an explanation.

Our analysis is based on the symmetric auction model introduced by Milgrom and Weber (1982a), which extends and unifies the earlier models of Vickrey (1961, 1962) and Wilson (1977). In the Milgrom–Weber model, each bidder i observes some private information variable X_i in $(\underline{x}, \bar{x})$ before bidding. These observations are assumed to be drawn from some symmetric joint distribution. The value of the item to bidder i is denoted by $V_i = u(X_i, X_{-i}, S)$, where X_{-i} is the list of valuations of the other bidders and S is some vector of unobserved random variables. It is assumed that u is nondecreasing in all its arguments and is a symmetric function of the components of X_{-i}. It is also assumed that the bidders are risk-neutral.

We have already seen in Section 2 that the value of the item at auction to any bidder can depend on the valuations of other bidders when there is a possibility for resale. The vector variable S, which generally represents unknown attributes of the item, could be interpreted as the valuations of bidders not present at the auction. Another interesting interpretation of the variable S is that it represents some unknown physical attributes of the item. For example, if the item being sold is the rights to timber on a tract of land in Oregon, then the potential yield of the tract in board feet of each species of timber is normally unknown. If the right to drill for oil on some underwater tract off the north coast of Alaska is being auctioned, the value will depend on the amount and grade of the oil, its depth, future oil prices, availability of transport facilities such as pipelines (which in turn depends on the productivity of nearby tracts), and so forth.

The presence of unknown attributes (physical or otherwise) gives rise to a curious phenomenon known as the *Winner's Curse*. The idea of the curse is that inexperienced bidders will often lose money, or earn less than expected, because a bidder is much more likely to place the highest bid when he has overestimated the value of the item than when he has underestimated it. Of course, experienced bidders are aware of this phenomenon and adjust their bids accordingly, which makes studying the bidding problem an interesting exercise. Before giving a more formal account of the Winner's Curse, we must finish specifying our modeling assumptions.

We shall assume that the variables (S, X) are pairwise positively correlated on all rectangles in $\mathbb{R}^{n+m}$. That is, they are positively correlated conditional on any information of the form $S_i \in (s_i, \bar{s}_i)$ and $X_j \in (x_j, \bar{x}_j)$, $i = 1, \ldots, m$, $j = 1, \ldots, n$. Such random variables are called *affiliated*. Some key facts about affiliated random variables are briefly summarized in the next paragraph. A complete treatment, including proofs, is given in Milgrom and Weber (1982a).

Suppose the random variables $Z \equiv (S, X)$ have a joint density $f(Z)$. Then affiliation can be expressed as a property of the density f as follows:

$$f(z)f(z') \leq f(z \wedge z')f(z \vee z'), \tag{4.1}$$

where $z \wedge z'$ is a vector whose ith component is $\min(z_i, z_i')$ and $z \vee z'$ is a vector whose ith component is $\max(z_i, z_i')$. Note, in particular, that independent random variables are affiliated. If f is smooth and everywhere positive, affiliation is equivalent to the requirement that the $\partial^2 \ln f / \partial z_i \partial z_j \geq 0$ for all $i \neq j$. A fact about an affiliated random vector Z which is used repeatedly in auction theory is that for any nondecreasing function g, the function G defined by

$$G[(\underline{z}_i, \bar{z}_i; i = 1, \ldots, n)] \equiv E[g(Z) \mid \underline{z}_i < Z_i \leq \bar{z}_i; i = 1, \ldots, n] \tag{4.2}$$

is nondecreasing. In particular, if (Z_1, Z_2) is affiliated then $P\{Z_1 \leq x \mid Z_2 = y\}$ is decreasing in y.[21]

Given our assumptions about the bidders' information, there is an especially nice way to formalize the Winner's Curse. Suppose all the bidders $j \neq 1$ choose bids in a sealed-bid auction as functions $\beta_j(X_j)$ of their information. Suppose each β_j is increasing. Finally, suppose that bidder 1 submits a bid of b and wins. When the bidder learns that he has won, how should he evaluate his winnings? The answer is that he should always revise his estimate of value downward from his initial estimate:

$$E[V_1 \mid X_1, \max_j \beta_j(X_j) < b] \leq E[V_1 \mid X_1, \max_j \beta_j(X_j) < \infty]$$
$$= E[V_1 \mid X_1] \tag{4.3}$$

[where we have used the fact (4.2) that conditional expectations of monotone functions of affiliated variables are monotone functions of the conditioning variables]. In simple English, learning that others have bid less than b is bad news about the value of the item being acquired [see Milgrom (1981) for a more complete analysis]. Of course, at equilibrium, bidders will take this fact into account in advance when choosing their strategies.

---

[21] That probability is equal to $1 - E[1_{\{Z_1 > x\}} \mid Z_2 = y]$ which, by (4.2), is decreasing in y.

Consider a sealed-bid auction with a zero minimum price. We wish to represent this formally as a game. The players are the n bidders. Each bidder i observes X_i and decides what to bid. A strategy is therefore a function $\beta_i(X_i)$ specifying how much to bid as a function of what the bidder knows. Given any realization of the vector X, the item will be sold for the price $\max_i \beta_i(X_i)$ to the player who submits that bid.

Next, consider a Dutch auction game. In a Dutch auction, the auctioneer starts the price at some very high level, and reduces it until some bidder shouts "Mine!" to claim the item. Although there are complicated ways to describe any bidder's strategic options, all amount to saying that, as a function of X_i, player i must decide how far to let the price fall before shouting "Mine!" Suppose that bidder i's strategy is to let the price fall to $\beta_i(X_i)$ and then shout "Mine!" Then, the item will be sold for a price of $\max \beta_i(X_i)$ to the bidder who chose that maximum level. Remarkably, *in strategic form, the Dutch and sealed-bid auctions are the same game!*

It was Vickrey (1961, 1962) who first noted this equivalence; he also claimed that the standard ascending-bid auction is equivalent to a particular sealed-bid auction. He reasoned as follows. Suppose that in the ascending-bid auction bidder i decides to bid up to the level $\beta_i(X_i)$, which we shall call i's "bid." Then the item will be sold for the second highest bid to the high bidder. This is the same as conducting a sealed-bid auction in which the item is awarded to the high bidder for the second highest bid. Actually, this analysis is not quite correct, because the bidders in an ascending-bid auction have additional strategies available: They can make their bids depend on the previous bids of the other bidders. Nevertheless, in the interest of brevity and simplicity, we shall adopt Vickrey's "second price auction" as a model of the ascending-bid auction. The results we obtain are not affected in any essential way by this modeling. [22]

One can show for the model we have described that there are unique increasing strategies β_S and β_A such that $(\beta_S, \ldots, \beta_S)$ is an equilibrium of the sealed-bid auction game, and $(\beta_A, \ldots, \beta_A)$ is an equilibrium of the ascending-bid auction game, and that these strategies are characterized by solutions to first-order conditions. [23]

---

[22] Milgrom and Weber (1982a) distinguish the Vickrey second price sealed bid auction from the English ascending-bid auction. In the latter, they assume, bidders can base their bidding decisions on the levels where other bidders ceased to be active. Such strategies require making complicated inferences in real time, and in any case their equilibria share many of the same properties as those studied here.

[23] Here, I ignore the possibility of multiple equilibria, and focus attention exclusively on a monotone, symmetric equilibrium. The uniqueness problem and related issues are taken up by Milgrom (1981), Maskin and Riley (1983), and Harstad and Levin (1985).

How is one to compare the expected revenues from these two kinds of auctions? How can one evaluate the impact of revealing information on the expected selling price in either kind of auction? The main tool for this analysis is the Linkage Principle.

The sealed-bid and ascending-bid auctions are examples of what we shall call *standard* auctions – auctions in which (at equilibrium in the specified environments) the highest evaluator wins and pays a nonnegative price, and in which losers always pay zero. Given a standard auction A, let P^A be the resulting price; in general P^A might depend on all the bids. Let $\pi^A(z, x)$ be the expected payment by a bidder, say bidder 1, who bids in auction A as if his estimate were z when his actual estimate is x. Letting $Y = \max_{i \neq 1} X_i$, we may write $\pi^A(z, x) = E[P^A \cdot 1_{\{Y < z\}} \mid X_1 = x]$.

> **Proposition 6 (The Linkage Principle).**[24] *Let A and B be standard auctions. Suppose that for all x, if $\pi^A(x, x) < \pi^B(x, x)$ then $\pi_2^A(x, x) \geq \pi_2^B(x, x)$ (where the subscripts denote partial derivatives with respect to the second argument). Then, $\pi^A(x, x) \geq \pi^B(x, x)$ for all x, and the expected price is higher in auction A than in auction B.*

Proof: Let $R(z, x) = E[V_1 \cdot 1_{\{Y < z\}} \mid X_1 = x]$, that is, the expected value received in a standard auction when player 1 observes $X_1 = x$ and bids as if he had observed $X_1 = z$, assuming that the other bidders adhere to their equilibrium strategies. At equilibrium, a bidder with estimate x cannot improve his payoff by bidding as if his estimate were some $z \neq x$. Hence, for any standard auction A, $R_1(x, x) - \pi_1^A(x, x) = 0$. Because this holds also for the standard auction B, $\pi_1^A(x, x) = \pi_1^B(x, x)$ for all x.

Now consider the function $\Delta(x) = \pi^A(x, x) - \pi^B(x, x)$. Since $\pi^A(\underline{x}, \underline{x}) = \pi^B(\underline{x}, \underline{x}) = 0$ (because $P\{Y < \underline{x}\} = 0$), $\Delta(\underline{x}) = 0$. For $x > \underline{x}$, by hypothesis either $\Delta(x) \geq 0$ or

$$\Delta'(x) = \frac{d}{dx}[\pi^A(x, x) - \pi^B(x, x)] = \pi_2^A(x, x) - \pi_2^B(x, x) \geq 0.$$

If there were some $\hat{x} > \underline{x}$ such that $\Delta(\hat{x}) < 0$, then by the mean value theorem there must be some $\tilde{x} \in (\underline{x}, \hat{x})$ with $\Delta(\tilde{x}) < 0$ and $\Delta'(\tilde{x}) < 0$, which contradicts our last conclusion. ∎

The Linkage Principle derives its name from the fact that it makes comparisons of revenues across auctions using the statistical linkages that exist

---

[24] The Linkage Principle was originally introduced by Milgrom and Weber (1982a), who described it as "the common thread running through" their results (pp. 110–11). The mathematics of the principle, which is buried in their arguments, was first made explicit in a second (unpublished) paper, "A Theory of Auctions, Part II."

between a bidder's private information and any information on which the price is based. The partial derivative π_2 measures how much the expected price increases with increases in the bidder's private evaluation, holding his bidding behavior constant; that is, it measures changes in π that result from changes in the bidder's beliefs about how others will bid. When statistical linkages are used to align the price more closely to the buyer's willingness to pay, the rents associated with private information fall and the average price rises.

Our first application of the Linkage Principle is to explain the equivalence in expected prices that Vickrey first observed among the standard auctions in his model.

> **Proposition 7 (Revenue Equivalence).** *Assume that the bidders' observations $X_1, \ldots, X_n$ are independent. Then the expected price in any standard auction is the same as in the ascending-bid auction.* [25]

Proof: By independence, for any auction mechanism M:

$$\pi^M(z, x) = E[P^M \cdot 1_{\{Y < z\}} \mid X_1 = x] = E[P^M \cdot 1_{\{Y < z\}}].$$

Hence, for all auction games, $\pi_2^A(z, x) = \pi_2^B(z, x) = 0$. The result then follows from the Linkage Principle. ∎

When we replace the hypothesis of statistical independence by one of affiliation, the Linkage Principle provides a powerful tool for making comparative statements about the expected prices under various alternative arrangements. For a first example, we can now compare the expected price in the sealed- and ascending-bid auctions.

> **Proposition 8.** *The expected price (at equilibrium) in the ascending-bid auction is never less, and is sometimes more, than for the sealed-bid auction.*

Proof: Let A be the ascending-bid auction and B the sealed-bid auction, with equilibrium bidding strategies α and β, respectively. These auctions are standard, because α and β are increasing (Milgrom and Weber, 1982a). Now $\pi^B(z, x) = E[\beta(z) \cdot 1_{\{Y < z\}} \mid X_1 = x] = \beta(z) P\{Y < z \mid X_1 = x\}$, which we write as $\beta(z) F(z \mid x)$. Also,

$$\pi^A(z, x) = E[\alpha(Y) \cdot 1_{\{Y < z\}} \mid X_1 = x] = E[\alpha(Y) \mid X_1 = x, Y < z] F(z \mid x).$$

---

[25] For a more general revenue equivalence result and a helpful discussion of its implications, see Riley and Samuelson (1981).

Hence:

$$\frac{\partial}{\partial x}[\pi^A(z,x) - \pi^B(z,x)] = [\pi^A(z,x) - \pi^B(z,x)]\frac{F_2(z\,|\,x)}{F(z\,|\,x)}$$

$$+ F(z\,|\,x)\frac{d}{dx}E[\alpha(Y)\,|\,X_1 = x, Y < z].$$

By affiliation, $(d/dx)E[\alpha(Y)\,|\,X_1 = x, Y < z]$ is nonnegative and $F_2(z\,|\,x)$ is nonpositive, so the partial derivative is nonnegative unless $\pi^A(z,x) > \pi^B(z,x)$. Apply the Linkage Principle.   ∎

In the sealed-bid auction, the price the winning bidder pays depends only on his own bid; there is no direct or indirect linkage to other variables. In the ascending-bid auction, the price is an increasing function of the second highest bidder's observation, which is affiliated with the winning bidder's observation. This provides the price-increasing linkage.

When the seller has a private estimate that he can provide, the equilibrium price may be an increasing function of that estimate, providing yet another price-increasing linkage. Of course, this assumes that the seller can both provide information in a verifiable way and commit to a policy for revealing information.

> **Proposition 9.** *Verifiably revealing any information variable S_0 raises the expected price both in the sealed-bid auction and in the ascending-bid auction. Among all policies for full or partial revelation of information, the policy of full revelation maximizes the expected price.*

Partial proof: For the sealed-bid auction A without information revealed and B with information revealed, the expected prices are

$$\pi^A(z,x) = E[\alpha(z)\cdot 1_{\{Y<z\}}] \quad \text{and} \quad \pi^B(z,x) = E[\beta(z,S_0)\cdot 1_{\{Y<z\}}],$$

where α and β are the equilibrium bidding strategies. As before,

$$\frac{\partial}{\partial x}[\pi^B(z,x) - \pi^A(z,x)] = [\pi^B(z,x) - \pi^A(z,x)]\frac{F_2(z\,|\,x)}{F(z\,|\,x)}$$

$$+ F(z\,|\,x)\frac{d}{dx}E[\beta(z,S_0)\,|\,X_1 = x, Y < z].$$

This is nonnegative whenever $\pi^B(z,x) < \pi^A(z,x)$. Thus, by the Linkage Principle, revealing information raises the average price.

Applying this result to the case where only partial information is revealed, the expected price can be raised by revealing the remaining information. Hence, no policy can be better than the policy of full revelation of the available information.

For the ascending bid auction, the price depends on both Y and S_0. The proof given by Milgrom and Weber (1982a) uses the characterization of the equilibrium strategies to show that the linkage is greater when information is revealed than when it is withheld (even though the linkage to Y may be weakened). ∎

The policy of full revelation can also be expected to emerge when the seller cannot commit to an information policy.

> **Proposition 10.** *If a seller must decide, after observing S_0, whether to report it, and if his report is verifiable, then at a perfect equilibrium he always reports S_0 regardless of its value.*

Proof sketch: Suppose that a seller observes S_0 and then decides whether to report it. At equilibrium, the buyers' bids (when the seller makes no report) depend on their beliefs about the value of S_0. For any beliefs the buyers may have, one can show that the seller's best reponse is to make a report whenever S_0 is in fact sufficiently favorable; thus any equilibrium must have the property that the seller reports whenever $S_0 > s^*$. But then, when the seller reports nothing, at equilibrium the buyers must believe that $S_0 \leq s^*$ and bid accordingly. They would bid strictly more if they had the "more favorable" [in the sense of Milgrom (1981)] belief that $S_0 = s^*$, so it would be in the seller's interest to report S_0 even when it is slightly lower than s^*. Hence there can be no perfect equilibrium at which s^* exceeds the lower bound $\underline{s}$ of the support of S_0. Because $P\{S_0 > \underline{s}\} = 1$, the proposition is proved. ∎

In a further application of the Linkage Principle, Riley (1985) argues that when value can be observed ex post (even imperfectly), the expected price is higher when part of the price is a royalty based on the observed value. McAfee and McMillan (1986) make the same observation in connection with incentive contracting, where bidding and moral hazard issues arise together. Consider a situation in which a buyer must select one of several contractors for, say, a construction project. Including a cost-sharing provision in a contract yields a lower price at the bidding stage (apply the Linkage Principle), but that must be balanced against the weakened incentive for cost control that such contracts may create. This examination of the relation between bidding and contract incentives is one of the most promising recent developments in bidding theory.

Even when a seller has little ability to enforce a high minimum price, he can still choose any auction with a zero minimum price because, as noted in Section 2, rational buyers cannot refuse to participate. If the bidders behave noncooperatively, the seller does better by using an ascending-bid auction than by soliciting sealed bids. This accords well with Cassady's (1967) observation that ascending-bid auctions are by far the most popular kind worldwide. The seller also does well to provide any information he may have, since that, too, creates a price-increasing linkage.

In terms of incentive theory, the Linkage Principle is based on the observation that *a bidder's profits depend upon his ability to conceal information*. Linking the price to variables that are affiliated with the bidder's private information diminishes his ability to conceal information effectively, and so lowers his profits. When comparing auctions (with risk-neutral bidders and a risk-neutral seller) that allocate the good efficiently, any reduction in the bidders' payoffs is a gain to the seller.

Clearly, this reasoning depends on the assumption that bidders are risk-neutral. With risk aversion, there can be efficiency gains from making the bidders' payoffs less random. This idea has heretofore been studied only in connection with the independent private values model. For that model, Matthews (1980) noted that if the bidders' observations are statistically independent and the valuation function is $V_i = X_i$, then the sealed-bid auction is always preferred by the seller when either he or the buyers (or both) are risk-averse [see also Holt (1980)].

In the independent private values model, linkages inefficiently increase the randomness in the payoffs. In other models, however, linkages reduce the randomness in the payoffs. For example, suppose the observations are independent and the valuation function is $V_i = \min(X_i, \max X_j)$. Then the ascending-bid auction is always preferred by the seller when the bidders are risk-averse. In this example, the linkage of the price to other bidders' information reduces the fluctuations in the winning bidder's payoffs and makes him willing to pay more, to the seller's benefit. In general, in the presence of risk aversion, linkages may or may not enhance revenue and efficiency.

Finally, we turn to the question of whether uncertainty about the bidders' valuations makes it harder or easier for the seller to achieve commitment in his efforts to maintain a high minimum price. Consider a model in which the seller conducts a series of auctions, specifying any minimum price he chooses, and the buyers are limited to bidding in the auction; they cannot make extraneous offers. In the deterministic case, the seller can extract all the surplus from the highest valuation buyer by insistently setting the minimum price equal to that valuation. Indeed, in the discrete time version of this game model, the equilibrium just described is the only perfect equilibrium.

With uncertainty, however, the situation is quite different. The case of a single buyer and offers made by the seller has been analyzed by Stokey (1982), and by Gul, Sonnenschein, and Wilson (1986). In the discrete time game where offers are made by the seller, there is a unique perfect equilibrium. If the buyer's reservation value is uncertain to the seller and distributed over an interval that includes the seller's reservation value, then at equilibrium the seller must sell for nearly his own reservation price: Uncertainty is the enemy of commitment. Gul and Sonnenschein (1985) have proved a variant of this result for the case where both the seller and the buyer can make offers.

Here we make a simple extension of this conclusion to the case of many buyers. Suppose that the seller can conduct an auction at each moment of time, and can vary the minimum price $m(t)$ over time. For technical convenience, we require that the seller choose a path $m(t)$ that is right continuous. A buyer's strategy specifies whether to bid and an amount to bid, for each moment in time, as a function of the path of minimum prices announced by the seller up to that point. We limit the bidders to strategies that determine a first moment to bid (possibly $+\infty$) for any feasible strategy of the seller. For example, the buyer cannot specify that he will make a bid whenever the minimum is below \$5 and has been below \$5 before, because that does not specify a first moment to bid if the seller sets a minimum of \$4 at all times. Finally, suppose that payoffs from trades conducted at any date $t > 0$ are discounted to time zero at the same rate for buyers and the seller.

> *Proposition 11. An equilibrium of the continuous auction game is described as follows: The seller sets a minimum price equal to his reservation price s at every point in time. A buyer with observation $X_i = x$ bids $\beta_S(x)$ at the first moment that $m(t) \leq \beta_S(x)$, where β_S is the symmetric equilibrium strategy for the (static) sealed-bid auction.*

During the play of the game, if the seller sets a minimum price other than s, a player using the prescribed strategy will bid if and only if his planned bid exceeds that minimum. Therefore, by watching the game progress, the seller and the other bidders could learn about the bidders' valuations – specifically, that they are too low to justify bidding at the prices named by the seller. This sort of learning is perfectly analogous to what occurs in a Dutch auction. As with Dutch auctions, no matter what upper bound on valuations a bidder may learn during the course of the auction, it will always be optimal for him to adhere to his equilibrium strategy, "because" he expects the seller to reduce the price to s very soon.

It is easy to see that the optimal auction, which requires that the seller make a once-and-for-all take-it-or-leave-it offer, is not a perfect equilibrium of this continuous time game. Suppose that the seller expects the bidders to adhere to the optimal auction equilibrium strategies. The optimal auction offer always entails setting a minimum price in excess of the seller's reservation price. Hence, if the seller makes the optimal auction offer and no bidder bids, it will always pay the seller to make another, better offer to the buyers. Hence, the seller can conduct an optimal auction only if he can commit himself to refrain from making a profitable offer later. Such commitment is proscribed by the perfect equilibrium solution concept.

By imposing a plausible restriction on the buyers' strategy spaces, one can eliminate much more than just the optimal auction equilibrium in this continuous time game. Indeed, if the bidders are limited to strategies that satisfy the Gul and Sonnenschein (1985) stationarity property, then the equilibrium of Proposition 11 is the unique symmetric (among buyers) equilibrium. The stationarity property requires that a buyer's current decision depend only on his own type and on the "common knowledge" distribution of buyer types (which, at equilibrium, can be inferred from past bidding behavior); in particular, the behavior does not depend on the time nor on how those beliefs were reached. When the buyers are limited to stationary strategies, if all trading does not take place at time zero then it will always be in the seller's interest to "speed up the clock," replacing his strategy $m(t)$ by $\hat{m}(t) = m(2t)$. This stratagem makes all trades occur earlier, without reducing the price obtained by the seller. Therefore, at any equilibrium in stationary strategies, all trading occurs at time zero. Then, because the seller cannot adhere to a minimum price above his reservation price of s, the uniqueness result follows.

Thus, with uncertainty about the buyers' valuations, the seller's ability to achieve commitment is severely reduced. Whatever power the seller retains comes from his ability to generate competition among bidders by conducting an auction.

5   Collusion

Only recently has any theoretical attention been devoted to the problem of collusion in auctions. The fact that the outcome of auctions in deterministic settings lies in the core of the exchange game does not mean that auctions are immune to collusion; it means only that no subset of players could improve their lot by going off and trading among themselves. Auctions with low minimum prices are vulnerable to collusion among bidders. Graham and Marshall (1985), beginning with that observation and a claim that collusion is rampant in real auctions, have studied a variation of the independent private values model of Section 3 in which the bidders may have formed a cartel or *ring*. They find that the optimal minimum price to be set by a seller is an increasing function of the likelihood that a ring has formed.

My purpose here is simply to examine the hypothesis that auction forms differ in their degrees of susceptibility to collusion. I will focus on Mead's (1967) hypothesis that ascending-bid auctions are more susceptible to collusion than are sealed-bid auctions. Such a conclusion would explain why a seller might choose a sealed-bid auction in preference to an ascending-bid auction, despite the latter's theoretical superiority when bidders behave competitively. The simplest model (not involving side payments) that I have found to study collusion is the following; it exploits the existence of multiple Nash equilibria in ascending-bid auctions to construct collusive perfect equilibria in repeated ascending-bid auctions.[26]

The model is deterministic. We suppose that two bidders bid periodically against one another in an auction for items that both bidders value at x. Suppose they agree to take turns winning at a price of $b < x$. The discount factor that reflects the frequency of these periodic interactions is some number $\delta < 1$. How frequent must the interactions be to support this collusive arrangement? That is, how large must δ be to allow collusion of this sort to survive at an equilibrium?

In the case of a sealed-bid auction, suppose it is an equilibrium for the players to alternate bidding b, while the other bidder makes a show of it by bidding $b - \epsilon$. To be an equilibrium, it must be unprofitable for the scheduled loser to bid just more than b today and forgo future profits:[27]

$$x - b < \delta \frac{x - b}{1 - \delta^2},$$

which reduces to $\delta > (\sqrt{5} - 1)/2$ or, approximately, $\delta > .62$. One corresponding collusive agreement in the ascending-bid auction has the scheduled winner bid x and the scheduled loser bid b. For the scheduled loser to find a deviation unprofitable requires only that $\delta > 0$.

Thus, collusion is easier to support in an ascending-bid auction than in a sealed-bid auction. The intuition for this result is a familiar one: Collusion is hardest to support when secret price concessions are possible, and easiest to support when all price offers must be made publicly.

---

[26] Bikhchandani (1984) has exploited the fact that the one-shot ascending bid auction has multiple equilibria to construct a repeated bidding game in which the equilibria have a collusive flavor. Robinson (1985) has also exploited the multiple equilibrium idea. He analyzes a simple one-shot game model, but the analysis assumes that colluders can share information verifiably – an assumption that naturally favors the formation of collusive rings.

[27] There are some minor issues here about whether the inequalities given below should be strict or weak. These depend on the solution concept used, and are not a matter of great importance here.

6   Conclusion

I have organized this paper around two central questions. Why do auction institutions continue to be so popular after thousands of years? And what accounts for such particular details as the popularity of sealed- and ascending-bid auctions? The answers to these questions were summarized in the introduction. The answers are plainly incomplete; indeed, they rely on fundamentally different models of the auction environment. It would be much better to have a single consistent model that explained both the use of auctions (in preference to other mechanisms when individual items are unique) as well as the widely observed preference for ascending-bid auctions over sealed-bid auctions.

There are large segments of auction theory that I have omitted from my review, partly because a surveyor must draw lines. One could survey very different territory by asking questions such as the following. (1) How do experimental subjects behave in auctions? Such a survey would feature the work of Vernon Smith and his colleagues, who have led the way in the study of bidding behavior with controlled laboratory experiments.[28] It would also cover studies of the implications of alternative models of choice under uncertainty for bidding behavior.[29] (2) What insights does auction theory offer into the problems of price discrimination by a monopolist? Many researchers who have contributed to the theory of expected price–maximizing auctions have extended their results to the problem of optimal price discrimination [Cremer and McLean (1985a), Harris and Raviv (1981), Maskin and Riley (1984b)]. (3) What are the relationships between bargaining theory, auction theory, and competitive equilibrium theory? Wilson's companion survey gives an introduction to this new and lively area of research (see Chapter 2, this volume), sometimes called the

[28] An excellent example of this line of research is the work reported in Cox, Smith, and Walker (1984).

The proper interpretation of their experimental results is controversial. The experimenters generally regard it to be evidence concerning how actual bidders behave in auctions. However, I tend to regard it as another kind of model: the subjects (instead of rational maximizers) are the model of actual bidders. This is analogous to comparing mathematical models of air foils with corresponding scale models tested in wind tunnels; often, the mathematical models are better predictors.

In auctions for mineral rights, the bidders (oil company executives) normally have access to professional consultants who can conduct formal analyses with much more proficiency than the typical subject in an experiment. It seems likely that these executives bid much more rationally than typical experimental subjects, although this supposition is of course subject to empirical refutation.

For a carefully articulated view of the role of experiments in economics, see Roth (Chapter 7, this volume).

[29] For example, Karni and Safra (1985) have a model of bidding behavior in which the bidders may behave differently in strategically equivalent games.

theory of market microstructure. Our Propositions 2, 3, and 11 introduce some of the main issues studied in that connection. (4) How are auctions used in contracting environments, where the risk of cost overruns may need to be shared and the bidder's performance in the contract properly motivated? This is a new subject of study that so far has limited itself mostly to private value auction models, but which is evidently generalizable to many important bidding situations.

The list of possible questions is endless, but this survey is not.

Appendix

Proof of Proposition 5: Suppose the seller designs some game Γ in which, at equilibrium, trade takes place at some date T that may depend (possibly probabilistically) on some choice made by the buyer. If no trade takes place, let us say that $T = \infty$. Suppose Σ is the set of strategies available to the buyer. For each $\sigma \in \Sigma$, let $p(\sigma) = E_\sigma[\delta^T]$ be the expected present value of 1 unit paid at the time of trade. This expectation depends, of course, on the strategy σ chosen by the buyer. Similarly, let $e(\sigma)$ be the expected present value of net payments made by the buyer over the course of the game. If the buyer's information is X, his expected payoff using σ is $u(X)p(\sigma) - e(\sigma)$. Let $\sigma^*(x)$ and $\Pi^*(x)$ denote, respectively, the buyer's optimal strategy and the maximum payoff in the game when $X = x$. Define $p^*(x) \equiv p(\sigma^*(x))$ and $e^*(x) \equiv e(\sigma^*(x))$. Then,

$$\Pi^*(x) = u(x)p^*(x) - e^*(x). \tag{A.1}$$

As Vickrey originally argued, $p^*(x)$ must be nondecreasing; otherwise the buyer must be using a dominated strategy $\sigma^*(x)$. He could increase his ex ante expected payoff by rectifying his strategy to make $p^*(x)$ nondecreasing while holding the distribution of $\sigma^*(X)$ fixed, since that leaves his expected payment and probability of winning unchanged while increasing the expected value received. By the Envelope Theorem, $d\Pi^*/dx = u(x)p^*(x)$, using equation (A.1), $de^*(x) = u(x)dp^*(x)$. Hence, $e^*(x) = e^*(0) + \int_0^x u(t)\,dp^*(t)$. Now the seller's expected cash receipts, conditional on x, are $(1 - p^*(x))s + e^*(x)$. Because X is uniformly distributed on $(0, 1)$, the corresponding unconditional expectation is:

$$\int_0^1 e^*(x)\,dx = e^*(0) + \int_0^1 \int_0^x u(t)\,dp^*(t)\,dx$$

$$= e^*(0) + \int_0^1 \int_t^1 dx\,u(t)\,dp^*(t)$$

$$= e^*(0) + \int_0^1 (1 - t)u(t)\,dp^*(t). \tag{A.2}$$

In addition, the seller obtains value from keeping the item:

$$s \int_0^1 (1-p^*(x))\,dx = s \int_0^1 \left[1-p^*(1)+\int_x^1 dp^*(t) \right] dx$$

$$= s \left[1-p^*(1)+\int_0^1 \int_0^t dx\,dp^*(t) \right]$$

$$= s \left[1+p^*(1)+\int_0^1 t\,dp^*(t) \right]. \tag{A.3}$$

The seller's total expected payoff is therefore:

$$e^*(0)+s[1-p^*(1)]+\int_0^1 [(1-t)u(t)+st]\,dp^*(t). \tag{A.4}$$

Because the buyer must have a strategy σ of nonparticipation, which leads to a payoff of zero, we may conclude:

$$e^*(0) \le p^*(0)u(0). \tag{A.5}$$

Inequality (A.5) constrains the seller in designing a game. Another constraint that (by Vickrey's argument cited earlier) must hold at equilibrium is:

$$p^*: [0,1] \to [0,1] \text{ is nondecreasing.} \tag{A.6}$$

Because the objective (A.4) is linear in p^* and $e^*(0)$, and because the constraint set (A.5)–(A.6) is convex, the maximum must occur at an extreme point of the constraint set. Thus, at a maximum, (A.5) must hold with equality. Also, the optimal p^* function must be everywhere 0 or 1. So, by (A.6), there is a point x^* such that $p^*(x)$ is 0 for $x < x^*$ and 1 for $x \ge x^*$. The maximized value of the seller's payoff (A.4), subject to (A.5)–(A.6), is $sx^* + (1-x^*)u(x^*)$.

This maximum, which bounds what the seller can get at any equilibrium of any game, can be achieved by making the take-it-or-leave-it offer $u(x^*)$. Moreover, if $(1-x)u(x)$ is strictly concave, there is a unique x^* that maximizes $sx+(1-x)u(x)$. Hence, the unique $p^*(\cdot)$ function that attains the maximum is $p^*(x) = 0$ for $x < x^*$ and $p^*(x) = 1$ for $x \ge x^*$. Any institution as good as making a take-it-or-leave-it offer must lead to the same trading outcome. ∎

References

Aumann, Robert. 1973. "Subjectivity and Correlation in Randomized Strategies." *Journal of Mathematical Economics* 1: 67–96.

Bikhchandani, Sushil. 1984. "Reputations in Repeated Second-Price Auctions." Working paper, Graduate School of Business, Stanford University.

Binmore, Ken. 1983. "Bargaining and Coalitions I." London School of Economics, International Centre for Economics and Related Disciplines, Theoretical Economics Discussion Paper Series, 83/71.

Binmore, Ken, Ariel Rubinstein, and Asher Wolinsky. 1986. "The Nash Bargaining Solution in Economic Modelling." *Rand Journal of Economics* 17: 176–88.

Cassady, R. 1967. *Auctions and Auctioneering.* Berkeley: University of California Press.

Cox, James, Vernon Smith, and James Walker. 1984. "Theory and Behavior of Multiple Unit Discriminative Auctions." *The Journal of Finance* 39: 983–1010.

Crawford, Vincent. 1982. "A Theory of Disagreement in Bargaining." *Econometrica* 50: 607–38.

Cremer, Jacques, and Richard McLean. 1985a. "Optimal Selling Strategies Under Uncertainty for a Discriminating Monopolist When Demands Are Interdependent." *Econometrica* 53: 345–61.

1985b. "Full Extraction of Surplus in Bayesian and Dominant Strategy Auctions." CARESS Working Paper #85-17, University of Pennsylvania.

Graham, Daniel, and Robert Marshall. 1985. "Collusive Bidder Behavior at a Single Object English Auction." Department of Economics Working Paper No. 85-01, Duke University.

Griesmer, J., R. Levitan, and M. Shubik. 1967. "Toward a Study of Bidding Processes: Part IV: Games with Unknown Costs." *Naval Research Logistics Quarterly* 14: 415–33.

Gul, Faruk, and Hugo Sonnenschein. 1985. "One-Sided Uncertainty Does Not Cause Delay." Mimeo, Stanford University.

Gul, Faruk, Hugo Sonnenschein, and Robert Wilson. 1986. "Foundations of Dynamic Monopoly and the Coase Conjecture." *Journal of Economic Theory* 39: 155–90.

Harris, Milton, and Arthur Raviv. 1981. "A Theory of Monopoly Pricing With Uncertain Demand," *American Economic Review* 71: 347–65.

1982. "Allocation Mechanisms and the Design of Auctions." *Econometrica* 49: 1477–99.

Harstad, Ronald, and Dan Levin. 1985. "A Dominant Strategy Argument for a Class of Common Value Auctions." *Review of Economic Studies* 52: 525–8.

Holt, Charles A., Jr. 1980. "Competitive Bidding for Contracts Under Alternative Auction Procedures." *Journal of Political Economy* 88: 433–45.

Karni, Edi, and Zvi Safra. 1985. "English and Vickrey Auctions in the Theory of Expected Utility With Rank-Dependent Probabilities." Working Paper, Tel-Aviv University.

McAfee, Preston, and John McMillan. 1986. "Bidding for Contracts: A Principal-Agent Analysis." *Rand Journal of Economics* 17: 326–38.

Maskin, Eric, and John Riley. 1983. "Uniqueness of Equilibrium in Open and Sealed Bid Auctions." Unpublished manuscript.

1984a. "Optimal Auctions with Risk Averse Buyers." *Econometrica* 52: 1473–1518.

1984b. "Monopoly With Incomplete Information." *Rand Journal of Economics* 15: 171–96.

Matthews, Steven. 1980. "Risk Aversion and the Efficiency of First and Second Price Auctions." Unpublished manuscript, Northwestern University.

　　1983. "Selling to Risk Averse Buyers with Unobservable Tastes." *Journal of Economic Theory* 30: 370–400.

Mead, Walter. 1967. "Natural Resource Disposal Policy – Oral Versus Sealed Bids." *Natural Resource Planning Journal* M: 195–224.

Milgrom, Paul. 1981. "Rational Expectations, Information Acquisition, and Competitive Bidding." *Econometrica* 49: 921–43.

　　1985. "The Economics of Competitive Bidding: A Selective Survey." In L. Hurwicz, D. Schmeidler, and H. Sonnenschein (eds.), *Social Goals and Social Organization: Essays in Memory of Elisha Pazner,* pp. 261–89. Cambridge: Cambridge University Press.

Milgrom, Paul, and Robert Weber. 1982a. "A Theory of Auctions and Competitive Bidding." *Econometrica* 50: 1089–1122.

　　1982b. "A Theory of Auctions: Part II." Unpublished manuscript.

Myerson, Roger. 1981. "Optimal Auction Design." *Mathematics of Operations Research* 6: 58–73.

Ortega-Reichert, Armando. 1968. "Models for Competitive Bidding Under Uncertainty." Technical Report No. 8, Department of Operations Research, Stanford University.

Riley, John. 1985. "Ex Post Information in Auctions." Department of Economics Working Paper #367, University of California–Los Angeles.

Riley, John, and William Samuelson. 1981. "Optimal Auctions." *American Economic Review* 71: 381–92.

Robinson, Marc. 1985. "Collusion and the Choice of Auction." *RAND Journal of Economics* 16: 141–5.

Selten, Reinhard. 1975. "Reexamination of the Perfectness Concept for Equilibrium Points in Extensive Games." *International Journal of Game Theory* 4: 25–55.

Stokey, Nancy. 1982. "Rational Expectations and Durable Goods Pricing." *Bell Journal of Economics* 12: 112–28.

Vickrey, William. 1961. "Counterspeculation, Auctions, and Competitive Sealed Tenders." *Journal of Finance* 16: 8–37.

　　1962. "Auctions and Bidding Games." In *Recent Advances in Game Theory,* pp. 15–27. Princeton: Princeton University Press.

Wilson, Robert. 1977. "A Bidding Model of Perfect Competition." *Review of Economic Studies* 4: 511–18.

CHAPTER 2

Game-theoretic analyses of trading processes

Robert Wilson

Abstract: Three topics are discussed. The first is a research program to establish whether the familiar trading rules, such as sealed-bid and oral double auctions, are incentive efficient over a wide class of economic environments. The second is a review of recent studies of dynamic trading processes, and particularly the effects of impatience and private information on the timing and terms of trade; the main emphasis is on models of bilateral bargaining. The third considers prospects for embedding bargaining and auction models in larger environments so as to endogenize traders' impatience as a consequence of competitive pressures; models of dispersed matching and bargaining and a model of oral bid–ask markets are mentioned.

Introduction

My aim in this chapter is to describe some developments in the theory of exchange. The topics I describe share a common focus, namely the determination of the terms of trade. They also share a common methodology: the application of game theory to finely detailed models of trading processes. The aim of this work is to establish substantially complete analyses of markets taking account of agents' strategic behavior. Typically the results enable two key comparisons. One is the effect of altering the trading rules, and the other is the effect of alterations in the environment, such as changes in the number, endowments, preferences or information of the participants. Beyond these comparisons, however, the results are building blocks in the construction of a genuine theory of price forma-

I am indebted to many colleagues for their interest, and to Peter Cramton, Drew Fudenberg, John Roberts, and Ariel Rubinstein for their specific comments on an earlier draft. I especially thank Faruk Gul and Hugo Sonnenschein for the pleasure of working together. Errors and omissions are mine. Research support from the National Science Foundation (SES-83-08-723) and the Office of Naval Research (N00014-79-C-0685) is gratefully acknowledged.

tion. There are also important welfare consequences: The choice of trading rule determines the magnitude and distribution of gains from trade among the agents.

I mention two caveats. One is that the many contributors to this work are not a team with a unified research program; rather, I perceive a shared belief that advances in game theory enable direct approaches to the problem of price formation. The other is that I address only a few topics with which I have been recently engaged, without any attempt to survey the field or mention all the relevant contributions. In particular, I confine attention to some exchange models with explicit trading rules. This excludes, for example, the field of industrial organization, which has enjoyed the most progress from application of game-theoretic methods (see Roberts, Chapter 4, this volume). I regret omitting the work on markets mediated by specialists (e.g., Rubinstein and Wolinsky [41]), particularly the contributions that examine the role of traders with inside information (see Glosten and Milgrom [19], Hagerty [25], and Kyle [29]). And for some topics I do discuss, such as auctions and bargaining, I defer to other contributors of this volume for more complete treatments (see Milgrom, Chapter 1, and Rubinstein, Chapter 5).

The game-theoretic method is usually interpreted as employing models that specify explicitly the contingencies in which economic agents take actions. I agree, but place the emphasis on the role of common knowledge. As Sergiu Hart has remarked, the common knowledge comprises the rules of the game. In practice, however, there may be little that is common knowledge. Game theory has a great advantage in explicitly analyzing the consequences of trading rules that presumably are really common knowledge; it is deficient to the extent it assumes other features to be common knowledge, such as one agent's probability assessment about another's preferences or information. I foresee the progress of game theory as depending on successive reductions in the base of common knowledge required to conduct useful analyses of practical problems. Only by repeated weakening of common knowledge assumptions will the theory approximate reality. But game theory as we presently know it cannot proceed without the fulcrum of common knowledge.

I have chosen three themes. The first is the matter of the efficiency of trading rules. I discuss the prospect that the familiar trading rules found in established markets can be verified to be incentive efficient in the sense of Holmström and Myerson [27]. If successful this effort would establish results comparable to those established for the Walrasian model, but in this case with explicit attention to strategic behavior and private information. The second theme is the role of time in exchange processes. Presently we know little about dynamics, but already the study of bargaining models has revealed that intertemporal features combined with asymmetries of information can greatly affect the terms of trade and that efficiency can be adversely affected by delay costs. On the other hand, if traders are patient or offers are rapid these costs can be eliminated, but only by skewing the distribution of the gains from trade; this is the Coase [8] conjecture that plays a central role in this theory. My final theme is a speculative essay on the prospects for synthesizing a theory of complex markets from simpler ingredients. I mention recent contributions that build models of exchange from particular models of bargaining and auctions.

Throughout, I restrict attention to situations in which traders have inelastic demands or supplies for a single unit of consumption at a valuation or reservation price that may be privately known. No risk aversion or wealth effects are included. Probability distributions are always taken to be common knowledge among the traders. By an equilibrium I shall always mean a sequential equilibrium, for which a subgame-perfect equilibrium suffices if there is complete information. Not all of the assumptions are specified for the models considered; hopefully they are clear from the context but in any case consult the references mentioned. The appendix includes several brief specifications of models mentioned in the text.

1 Incentive efficiency of trading processes

By a trading rule, I mean a specification of the actions available to the agents in each contingency, together with a function specifying the outcome (an allocation) resulting from each combination of the agents' actions. Given a trading rule, a strategy for an agent specifies which action to take in each contingency, depending for example on his preferences and other private and public information. Thus, each trading rule induces a game among the agents – a game of incomplete information (Harsanyi [26]) if the agents have private information. To predict the outcome of this game we rely on a selection of one of the sequential equilibria (Kreps and Wilson [28]). For welfare comparisons, assume that one trading rule dominates another if all agents prefer the outcome of the first to the outcome of the second, and assume that an undominated trading rule is efficient. When the agents have private information this notion must be amplified (cf. Holmström and Myerson [27] and Wilson [47]): One rule dominates a second if it is common knowledge among the agents that all agents prefer the first to the second, as measured by their conditional expected utilities of outcomes. This definition yields the efficiency criterion called *interim* or incentive efficiency; the strong criterion of *ex ante* efficiency evaluates the agents' preferences before they receive their private information, in terms of their unconditional expected utilities. In the use of this criterion it is important to identify the feasible set of trading rules: Each outcome must be an allocation, and each agent must have an (interim) incentive to participate. In particular this restriction excludes rules developed by Groves [22] and d'Aspremont and Gerard-Varet [11].

The study of efficient trading rules originated with Myerson's [32] study of bargaining and his [33] characterization of auctions that are optimal for the seller, and subsequent work has successfully characterized trading rules in other environments.[1] The key technique in this work has been the revelation principle (cf. Myerson [32], among others). Essentially this uses the fact that to every trading rule and equilibrium corresponds another trading rule with the same outcomes, for which an equilibrium specifies only that the agents report truthfully their private information. The revised trading rule is simply the composition of the original trading rule and its equilibrium strategies. Thus, among the efficient trading rules is one inducing a "direct revelation game." The power of this approach is seen most clearly in the results of Gresik and Satterthwaite [20], showing for a class of environments the construction of ex ante efficient trading rules whose expected unrealized gains from trade decrease inversely with the number of agents – in inverse proportion to the square of the number of agents in the case of uniformly distributed valuations. Their results indicate that surprisingly few agents are required to obtain most of the gains from trade realized by perfect competition or with complete information.

This brings me to a point I wish to emphasize: The optimal trading rule for a direct revelation game is specialized to a particular environment. For example, the rule typically depends on the agents' probability assessments about each other's private information. Changing the environment requires changing the trading rule. If left in this form, therefore, the theory is mute on one of the most basic problems challenging the theory. I refer to the problem of explaining the prevalence of a few simple trading rules in most of the commerce conducted via organized exchanges. A short list – including auctions, double auctions, bid–ask markets, and specialist trading – accounts for most organized exchange. Indeed, bid–ask markets (such as those conducted in the commodities pits) have long been economists' paradigms for the nearly perfect markets addressed by the Walrasian theory of general equilibrium. The rules of these markets are not changed daily as the environment changes; rather they persist as stable, viable institutions. As a believer that practice advances before theory, and that the task of theory is to explain how it is

---

[1] See especially Myerson and Satterthwaite [35] and Gresik and Satterthwaite [20]. For surveys see Myerson [34] and Wilson [49].

that practitioners are (usually) right, I see a plausible conjecture: These institutions survive because they employ trading rules that are efficient for a wide class of environments. The experimental evidence, moreover, reinforces this view (cf. Plott [36] and Smith [43]).

A useful next step in the study of trading processes is to verify the efficiency of the several familiar trading rules. This research program poses an analytical task that is the reverse of the approach derived from the revelation principle. Using the revelation principle one can construct for each environment a direct revelation game that is efficient. Unfortunately, the trading rule obtained this way depends on the common knowledge structure of the environment. In contrast, the familiar trading rules specify procedures that are independent of such data; typically they merely process bids and offers. The task is to show that some rule, or a specific candidate rule, of this special kind is efficient – and not just for one environment, but uniformly over a wide class of environments.

This task is actually a familiar one, at least in spirit. The analyses of the Walrasian model in the 1950s specified a particular trading rule and then showed that it yielded efficient outcomes for a wide class of environments (characterized mainly by convexity properties). We often ignore the trading rule underlying the Walrasian model, but it is clearly there: If the distribution of preferences and endowments is common knowledge then the market clearing price is computed and announced, and the agents receive their reported preferred net trades. Sonnenschein [45] develops an axiomization of rules that rely on a public signal followed by private responses, and shows that such rules are essentially equivalent to a Walrasian price system.

I have attempted this task for the case of a double auction, where buyers and sellers submit sealed bids and offers and a market clearing price is selected. I can report that it is quite complex (cf. [52]). No simple argument based on a separating hyperplane suffices as in the Walrasian model; apparently, novel mathematical aspects are involved. The key tool available is Myerson's [33, 34] condition: An efficient rule must maximize the gains from trade that would result were the agents' valuations replaced by their *virtual* valuations, in which each agent's valuation is modified by a term reflecting incentive constraints. This term depends endogenously on the common knowledge structure of the trading game as well as on the trader's valuation, so it is generally difficult to compute. Fortuitously, however, the trading rule for a double auction maximizes the gains from trade that would result were the agents' valuations replaced by their submitted bids and offers. Thus, it has a form quite similar to the one required for efficiency, except that the way in which imputed gains are measured differs; moreover, the maximization of these gains is an operation that depends only on ordinal properties, so any ordinally equivalent representation of the gains from trade yields the same allocation. The proof of efficiency reduces, therefore, to a demonstration that the agents' bids and offers are related by a monotone transformation to their virtual valuations. Some details are described in Section A.1 of the appendix. In my work I employed an ad hoc guess to construct such a transformation, and the conclusion was consequently rather weak: With various restrictive assumptions (e.g., independently and identically distributed valuations), a double auction is interim efficient if the number of buyers and sellers is sufficiently large. A corollary is that with symmetric equilibria all of the agents' welfare weights converge to unity as the number of buyers and sellers increases, and the double auction trading rule is asymptotically ex ante efficient. A more precise examination of the conditions for existence of the requisite transformation might yield a stronger result. I know of no mathematical tools that address this problem directly.

What we know about auctions and double auctions suggests an interesting speculation. Each of these trading rules selects the allocation that would be efficient (maximizing the gains from trade) if the agents' submitted bids and offers were their true valuations, as would be the case, for example, were the numbers of buyers and/or sellers infinite. It would be nice if, fairly generally, the rule that maximizes the apparent gains from trade (as measured by submitted bids and offers) were efficient. Such a rule is a natural candidate for a uniformly efficient rule, because it works when there is complete information and also when there is incomplete information if there are infinitely many agents. This hypothesis would say that, with finite numbers, the agents' equilibrium strategies for submitting bids and offers take account of the incentive constraints in precisely the way required to realize efficiency. A counterexample would be equally interesting.

I summarize these remarks as follows. The program that demonstrated the existence of equilibrium for the Walrasian model, and established the efficiency of the resulting allocation for a large class of environments, has a current counterpart in a program to establish the existence of equilibrium and the uniform efficiency of the trading rule for some of the familiar market mechanisms, including explicit procedures for price formation based on agents' submitted bids and offers. The success of such a program would establish a cornerstone for economic theory; its failure (say, by significant counterexamples) would raise challenges to either theory or practice. As suggested in Section 2, extension of this program to dynamic trading processes will be important; an interesting recent contribution by Gale [16–18] will be discussed later.

2   Time and impatience in dynamic trading processes

The theory of efficient trading processes developed in a static framework relies heavily on the assumption that repetitions are precluded. For example, the design of an auction that is optimal for the seller (as derived in Myerson [34]) includes an optimal reservation price that exceeds both the seller's valuation and the buyers' least possible valuation. Thus there is a chance that the buyers' valuations are insufficient to elicit acceptable bids, yet gains from trade are present. In this case, if no acceptable bid is received then the seller and the buyers share an incentive to reopen the bidding with a lower reservation price.[2] Another way to see this is to consider a Dutch auction in which the seller reduces the asking price until some buyer accepts or the seller terminates the auction. In any sequential equilibrium of this game, the seller continues to reduce his asking price so long as a chance remains of gains from trade. Similarly, in the double auctions studied by Myerson and Satterthwaite [35], Chatterjee and W. Samuelson [7], and Wilson [50], there is a chance that not all the gains from trade are realized, and consequently there is an incentive to reopen trading. Cramton [9] has emphasized, therefore, the importance of studying so-called perfect market games that allow continuation (e.g., repetition) so long as gains from trade remain likely. Models that allow such continuation have the advantage of avoiding a priori presumptions that commitments to terminate trading are credible. Assured continuation is a significant restriction (e.g., a seller cannot make a final "take-it-or-leave-it" offer) but it gains realism. It also has important distributional consequences, since the gains from trade are usually allocated quite differently and there may be substantial costs of delay incurred; on the other hand, all gains from trade are eventually realized.

In this section I offer remarks about several recent studies of market games allowing endless continuation. Mainly I comment on the role of time in trading processes and the important effects of agents' impatience to conclude trades. I divide the discussion between market games with and without complete information.

2.1   *Dynamic market games with complete information*

The key contribution is Rubinstein's [38] study of a bargaining game in which a buyer and a seller of an indivisible item alternate bids and offers

---

[2] That this is a practical concern is evidenced by the Department of Interior's policy for setting reservation prices on oil leases: The calculation is based on the costs of delay until the lease can be reoffered in a subsequent auction.

until one accepts. Rubinstein shows that, for a restricted class of preferences exhibiting stationarity and impatience, this game has a unique subgame-perfect equilibrium. Trade occurs immediately at a price that divides the gains from trade according to the parties' relative impatience, measured by, say, their discount factors as will be assumed hereafter.[3]

Rubinstein's formulation allows many extensions, one [51] with many buyers and sellers each with one unit to buy or sell. Suppose that the sellers simultaneously each offer an ask price; then buyers simultaneously respond, with each either accepting any seller's offer or making a counteroffer of a bid price; and so forth with the buyers and sellers alternating roles. Assume that tied acceptances are resolved to maximize the realized gains from trade. Then again there is a subgame-perfect equilibrium in which the outcome is efficient: All trade occurs immediately and gains from trade are exhausted. Also, all accepted prices are the same, and this price is a Walrasian market-clearing price.[4]

Variants of Rubinstein's model have been useful in studying other market structures. Notable instances in industrial organization theory are the models analyzed by Maskin and Tirole [31], where firms alternate in making two-period commitments to their production plans.

In Gul, Sonnenschein, and Wilson [24] we study the case of a single seller and a continuum of buyers. Assume that the seller has a constant unit cost of supply and that the distribution of the buyers' valuations (each for a single unit of consumption) is known to the seller; assume also that all buyers (and, for simplicity, the seller) have the same discount rate. In a fashion similar to Rubinstein's bargaining model, allow the seller to offer a price each period – which each buyer can accept or reject – but in this model exclude counteroffers by the buyers. Again, focus attention on the subgame-perfect equilibria of this game. This formulation provides a basic model of monopoly when the seller cannot restrain his output rate nor commit to a particular path of prices. Some technical aspects of the formulation are described in Section A.2 of the appendix.

The analysis of this game divides into two cases depending on whether the seller's cost is less than all the buyers' valuations. If it is, then when sufficiently few buyers remain the seller offers the maximum price that will clear the market. This feature allows a construction of the equilibrium by backward induction much as in dynamic programming. As shown by Fudenberg, Levine, and Tirole [13] and in [24], the market is cleared

---

[3] And their risk aversion, and nonlinear preferences for gains, both of which I exclude; cf. Roth [37].

[4] This result depends on the rule of public offers; private offers directed to particular agents can yield non-Walrasian prices. See [51] for an example.

after a finite number of offers from the seller, and there is a unique subgame-perfect equilibrium. A novel feature is that the buyers expect the seller to use a nonstationary randomized strategy off the equilibrium path. However, an important simplifying feature is that the buyers have strategies that are pure and stationary: Each buyer's strategy specifies a reservation price and he waits to accept until that price or one lower is offered. Also, the seller makes only serious offers: each is accepted by some buyers.

If the seller's cost is not less than all the buyers' valuations then the matter is more complicated. Even for the simple case that the buyers' valuations are uniformly distributed (i.e., a linear demand function), we exhibit a continuum of equilibria in stationary strategies; moreover, these can be pieced together to generate equilibria in nonstationary strategies. All of these equilibria have different price paths. Thus in this case the game-theoretic analysis reveals much more indeterminancy and complexity than is often ascribed to monopoly behavior. The source of this phenomenon is that there are many price paths that can be anticipated by buyers and that are optimal for the seller, since the infinite continuation of the game precludes pinning down a unique equilibrium by working backward from the terminus. Even with complete information, indeterminancy of rational expectations is possible.

A major result in [24] is a general verification, for the case that buyers' strategies are stationary, of a conjecture due to Coase [8]. (Here, stationarity means that each buyer's maximal acceptance price is independent of the seller's previous history of offers.) As the duration between the seller's offers shrinks to zero, along the equilibrium path the seller's ask prices converge to the maximum of his cost and the minimum among the buyers' valuations. That is, with frequent offers the outcome is approximately Walrasian: All trades occur early at prices near the maximum Walrasian market-clearing price. As Coase conjectured, when a monopolist can neither commit to future prices nor limit his production rate, his market power is severely eroded if either buyers are patient or the rate of offers is high.

It is not easy to develop an intuitive appreciation of this result, but here is an attempt. The key consideration is that (since the buyers' strategies are stationary) the seller has the option at any time to accelerate the process by offering tomorrow's price today, thereby advancing the acceptance dates of subsequent buyers. The cost of doing so is the forgone higher profit on those buyers accepting today, whereas the benefit is the interest on the seller's present value of continuation, which arrives a day earlier. Because an equilibrium requires that exercising this option must be disadvantageous for the seller, we know that the cost must exceed the benefit. But the cost is approximately the price cut times the number of buyers who accept today's price, and the benefit is the daily interest on the continuation value. Consequently, the daily interest on the continuation value is bounded approximately by the day-to-day price drop times the number accepting per day. Fix the interest rate per unit time to be 100%, and divide this inequality through twice by the length of a day: Then the continuation value divided by the length of a day is bounded by the product of the rates (per unit time) at which prices decline and buyers accept (see Section A.2 for details). As the length of a day shrinks, the rate of price decline must be bounded or buyers would prefer to wait rather than accept the current price. If the rate of acceptance is also bounded, then as the length of a day shrinks the continuation value must also shrink to zero – if opportunities remain for the seller to reduce his price. If the continuation value shrinks to zero then the seller's later prices must all be converging to his unit cost, and therefore his present prices too: Otherwise, if the day is sufficiently short then the buyers all prefer to delay purchasing. If no opportunities for further price reductions remain then the price must already be at its minimum, which is the minimal valuation among the buyers. The remaining case, therefore, is that the rate of acceptances is unbounded. But in this case also the prices offered by the seller must all be converging downward to his unit cost (or to the buyers' least valuation), because this is the only way that a positive fraction of the buyers will accept in each of several days when their interest cost of delay is small; that is, the sequence of prices must become flat in the limit, yet the sequence is tied down at the end. In outline, this is one interpretation of the arguments supporting the Coase conjecture.[5] The complete proof is much more complicated, of course.

The exploration of these ideas has been a central topic in the literature on the durable-good monopoly problem, which is essentially equivalent to the one posed here (cf. Bulow [4] and Stokey [46]). They are also discussed briefly in Maskin and Newbery [30]. As we shall discuss later, the Coase conjecture also has important ramifications for the study of bargaining with incomplete information.

2.2   *Dynamic market games with incomplete information*

Extensions of Rubinstein's bargaining model to situations with private information is currently the most active research topic in this area. Here I mention briefly a few recent results that raise issues of general interest.

---

[5] For the reader who prefers a one-line explanation, go directly to the continuous-time limit: If the schedule of prices over time were not flat, then the seller would prefer to accelerate the process by rescaling time so that the clock runs twice as fast.

For simplicity, assume that the seller and the buyer have the same discount rate. Also, assume throughout that the buyer's valuation is privately known, and distributed independently of the seller's according to a distribution that is common knowledge. As in Cramton [9, 10], say that an offer is serious if it has a positive probability of being accepted.

Among the possible trading rules with possibly endless continuation, three of interest are the following:

(S) Only the seller makes offers and the buyer merely waits to accept some ask price;

(B) Only the buyer makes offers and the seller waits to accept some bid price; and

(A) The seller and the buyer alternate making offers until one accepts the other's offer.

2.2.1 *Bargaining with private information on one side*

First consider the case where the seller's valuation is common knowledge and the buyer's valuation is privately known.

Trading rule (S), in which only the seller makes offers, has been studied by Sobel and Takahashi [44], Fudenberg, Levine, and Tirole [13], Cramton [9, 10], and Gul, Sonnenschein, and Wilson [24]. The key observation is that the characterization of the sequential equilibria of this game and the characterization of the subgame-perfect equilibria of the monopoly game are formally equivalent (see Section A.2). That is, the situation of a seller repeatedly making offers to sell a single item to a single buyer with privately known valuation is equivalent to the situation of a seller repeatedly making offers to sell many units to a population of many buyers, with valuations known to be distributed according to the same distribution function for the privately known valuation of the buyer in the bargaining situation. Thus, all the results described above for the monopoly game apply to this bargaining game, including (for example) the verification of the Coase conjecture for equilibria with stationary strategies for the buyer. Also, if the buyer's valuation surely exceeds the seller's then there is a unique equilibrium, obtained by backward induction from the final offer of the seller, that the buyer is sure to accept.

Trading rule (B), in which only the buyer makes offers, presents a game with significantly different features, because the buyer's offers potentially reveal his valuation. I cannot recall an exposition in the literature, but the main ideas are implicit in Cramton [9, 10]. There are many sequential equilibria, because the variety of responses by the seller to disequilibrium offers by the buyer can support an equal variety of equilibrium-signaling strategies by the buyer. One salient class of equilibria comprises those in which the buyer signals his valuation by his willingness to delay making a serious offer. Typically, these require nonstationary strategies for both parties as a way of coping with the buyer's incentive to defect from the seller's prediction of his behavior (see Section A.4 for more details). When offers are made continuously, an extreme case is the trivial equilibrium in which the buyer offers only the price zero and the seller accepts any price that is at least zero. This is apparently the only equilibrium in stationary strategies: Given stationarity, it is always in the interest of the buyer to accelerate the process so as to avoid interest costs. In view of the result obtained for trading rule (S) – that with stationarity and frequent offers the informed party captures all the gains from trade – this equilibrium has special significance. It shows that the same result can obtain if the informed party makes all the offers.

Trading rule (A), in which the seller and the buyer alternate offers, has been studied by Grossman and Perry [21] and Gul and Sonnenschein [23], among others. The principal result is a theorem of Gul and Sonnenschein about equilibria in which the buyer's strategy is stationary.[6] Informally, their theorem states that the probability of a trade not being concluded within any initial time interval can be made arbitrarily small by making the period between offers sufficiently short. To see the ramifications of this theory, consider the case where the least possible valuation v_* of the buyer exceeds the seller's valuation of zero. Let Δ be the period length and let $n(\Delta)$ be the maximum number of periods that can transpire before trade is concluded along the equilibrium path: Then the theorem states that $\Delta n(\Delta) \rightarrow 0$ as $\Delta \rightarrow 0$. Thus, the time required to complete the transaction is small if the period length is short, and in the limit trade occurs immediately; moreover, the limit price is necessarily no more than v_*. We see again that the informed party obtains most of the gains from trade if the period length is short – another version of the Coase conjecture.

In [48] I develop some further consequences of this striking result for equilibria of the form studied by Grossman and Perry. In some examples of their construction a serious counteroffer by the buyer is the Rubinstein offer for the least among the buyer types making that offer in equilibrium. That is, along the equilibrium path, if a serious counteroffer is made by buyer types with valuations in the interval $[x, y]$, after a history that enables the seller to restrict the support to $[v_*, y]$, then this offer is $p°(x) \equiv \delta x/(1+\delta)$, where $\delta = e^{-r\Delta}$ is the discount factor. For equilibria of this

---

[6] Also imposed are a monotonicity and a "no free screening" assumption. Here, stationarity means essentially that the buyer's response to the seller's current offer does not depend on features of the history that do not affect the seller's equilibrium prediction of the set of buyer types who would accept; in turn, this prediction depends only on the seller's current offer and his probability assessment that motivated this offer.

Table 1

δ	α	β	A
.80	.692	.679	.306
.83	.668	.908	.342
.8392867552	.6477988713	1.000	.3522011287
.84	.64826		.35174
.90	.69643		.30357
.95	.76205		.23795
.99	.87637		.12363

type, the theorem of Gul and Sonnenschein implies that for any particular valuation v, if the period length is sufficiently short then the buyer makes no serious counteroffers except possibly the minimal one $p^{\circ}(v_*)$. This suffices to explain why Grossman and Perry find that an equilibrium of the kind they specify can exist only if the discount factor is sufficiently small.[7]

To illustrate these features, consider the example in which the buyer's valuation is uniformly distributed between zero and one. In this example the Grossman–Perry equilibrium does not exist if $\delta > .8393$. More interesting, however, is the way in which their equilibrium behaves as the discount factor increases toward this critical level: The length of the interval of buyer types making a particular counteroffer shrinks to zero. At this critical level of the discount factor, the equilibrium changes continuously to one where the buyer of any type always counteroffers with the nonserious offer of zero. Thus, for larger discount factors, only the seller makes serious offers; the buyer waits to accept a price that is sufficiently low considering his valuation. In such a game we know [24] that the Coase conjecture is satisfied for any equilibrium with a stationary strategy for the buyer. This seems to be a main explanation for the Gul–Sonnenschein theorem. See Section A.3 of the appendix for more details.

The main parameters of the equilibria for this example are tabulated in Table 1, using the following notation. When the support of the buyer's valuation is $[0, x)$ the seller's offer is $p(x) = Ax$, which is accepted by the buyer if his valuation is in the interval $[\alpha x, x)$ and rejected otherwise, whereupon the buyer makes the serious counteroffer $p^{\circ}(\alpha\beta x)$ if his valuation is in the interval $[\alpha\beta x, \alpha x)$ and this offer is accepted by the seller. Note that a counteroffer is possible only if $\beta < 1$, which occurs only if

---

[7] The nonexistence result in [21] depends on the presumption that the buyer makes counteroffers no matter how large the discount factor.

$\delta < .8392867552$. From the support $[0,x)$ the seller's expected present value of continuation is $\frac{1}{2}Ax$; that is, $2A$ is the fraction of the expected profit the seller could obtain were he able to make a final take-it-or-leave-it offer. We omit here the description of the off-the-equilibrium-path behavior, except to note that in one version the seller employs a randomized acceptance strategy in response to a counteroffer in an interval below the one expected in equilibrium; Grossman and Perry [21] suggest another version.

There are several main conclusions to be drawn from the known results about trading rules (S), (B), and (A) when the seller's valuation is common knowledge. One is surely the strong confirmation of the Coase conjecture when the seller makes offers and the buyer has a stationary strategy. The seller's bargaining power is severely eroded if the buyer has private information, has the option to pass, and is patient – at least if the buyer's strategy is stationary. This prediction from the game-theoretic analysis has important practical applications, and it is a prediction that is suitable for experimental testing. On the other hand, the key role of stationarity in the buyer's strategy suggests caution. Stationarity is necessary only for trading rule (S) and only for the case where the existence of positive gains from trade is common knowledge. We know little about the equilibria with nonstationary strategies, yet (as we shall see later) they can play an important role in bargaining with uncertainty about the existence of gains from trade.

Trading rule (A) has also been studied in a different context by Rubinstein [39] and by Bikhchandani [1]. These authors consider the case where the gains from trade are common knowledge (say, the seller's valuation is zero and the buyer's is one) but the seller is uncertain about the buyer's discount factor. Both study a model in which it is common knowledge that the seller's discount factor is δ and the buyer's is either δ_s or $\delta_w < \delta_s$ with specified probabilities that are common knowledge; of course the buyer knows his own discount factor. Noting that this game has many sequential equilibria, Rubinstein imposes a set of conditions that are sufficient to identify a unique equilibrium where, in the interesting case, the seller makes an initial offer that the impatient buyer accepts but that the patient buyer rejects, counteroffering with a bid that the seller accepts. Because these results are described by Rubinstein in Chapter 5, I will not explore his construction further here, except to endorse Bikhchandani's observation that the key feature of disequilibrium behavior is possibly worrisome: The probability assigned by the seller to the prospect of the buyer's impatience after seeing a counteroffer is neither continuous nor monotone in this counteroffer. In particular, the expected counteroffer is conclusive evidence that the buyer is patient (by Bayes's rule), whereas a slightly smaller counteroffer leaves the seller's prior assessment unchanged. To alleviate this difficulty, Bikhchandani constructs an alternative equilibrium that can be described briefly as follows for the case where $\delta_s^2 < \delta_w$.[8] Each time it is the buyer's turn he offers the seller his expected value of continuation, to which the seller responds with a randomized acceptance rule. At his turn, the seller similarly offers a price that the impatient buyer is indifferent about accepting, and he too responds with a randomized acceptance rule (the patient buyer surely rejects). Both the buyer's and the seller's prices decline over time, but of course at any time the seller asks more than the buyer bids. As the process continues without an acceptance the seller's probability assessment that the buyer is impatient becomes increasingly pessimistic, until after a finite number of periods the seller asks or surely accepts the Rubinstein offer were the buyer known to be patient.[9] This equilibrium is qualitatively different than Rubinstein's in that the bargaining can extend over numerous periods and the gains from trade can be split in numerous ways – mainly because of the randomized acceptance rules used by both the seller and the impatient buyer.

I see the two dramatically different equilibria proposed by Rubinstein and Bikhchandani as an interesting test case for experimental studies. A persistent difficulty in the study of bargaining is the plethora of equilibria when there is incomplete information. Here we have a model simple enough for an experimental design and two quite different equilibria with plausible merits that appear susceptible to definitive empirical confirmation or rejection. As we make headway in choosing among these two equilibria and others, we will learn better how to select among plausible equilibria in more complicated problems.

2.2.2   *Bargaining with private information on both sides*

I turn now to bargaining games in which both parties have private information. Any approach to this subject must contend with the ramifications

---

[8] This equilibrium is analogous to the unique subgame-perfect equilibrium for the monopoly problem with a population of buyers having two types (cf. [51]). Bikhchandani's equilibrium has a further desirable property: Unlike Rubinstein's, it is preserved under the insertion of dummy moves by the seller after the buyer rejects but before the buyer counteroffers. The addition of dummy moves of this sort allows the seller to revise his beliefs about the buyer's type more frequently; in the present example it excludes an equilibrium in pure strategies, provided that (as both Rubinstein and Bikhchandani assume) zero probabilities can never be revised to be positive. Preservation of an equilibrium under irrelevant transformations, such as the addition of dummy moves, is a central requirement for the equilibrium to be stable.

[9] However, as the initial probability tends to 1 that the buyer is impatient, it becomes certain that the seller and impatient buyer trade immediately at the Rubinstein price were the buyer known to be impatient.

of the Coase conjecture that has been established for the case where only one party has private information. Essentially this says that if the period between offers is short then, in any reasonable equilibrium with a stationary strategy for the informed party, the other party with inferior information captures little of the gains from trade – essentially because of the incentive to accelerate the process. In bargaining with both sides having private information, therefore, if periods are short and the equilibrium is stationary then each party is deterred from making an offer that might reveal his valuation – doing so would substantially eliminate his gains from trade. Thus, the dilemma has two horns: One can either have a separating equilibrium using nonstationary strategies to avoid the Coase conjecture, or some kind of pooling equilibrium using stationary strategies. So far, the latter approach has not been pursued except (in a version with strategies restricted to stopping times) by Chatterjee and L. Samuelson [5], but suggestions are included in Gul and Sonnenschein [23]. Cramton [9] has developed the former approach using strategies in which delay in making or accepting a serious offer is a trader's means of credibly signaling his valuation. In the equilibria he constructs, the nonstationarity is localized in the process by which beliefs are revised off the equilibrium path.

First consider trading rule (S), in which only the seller makes an offer in each period. Assume for simplicity that both parties have the same discount factor and that the seller's and buyer's privately known valuations are uniformly distributed on the same interval. Although Fudenberg and Tirole [15] and Cramton [9] establish in two-period models that a partially pooling equilibrium can be advantageous for the seller, in the infinite-period model discussed here a separating equilibrium is analyzed. In such an equilibrium, along the equilibrium path the seller initially delays making a serious offer, in order to signal that his cost is not very low, until he makes a serious offer that enables the buyer to infer his cost precisely. This first serious offer has positive probability of being accepted; the buyer accepts if his valuation is sufficiently high. If this first serious offer is not accepted then a second phase ensues in which the seller continues with successively lower offers (declining to his cost), as in a Dutch auction, until the buyer accepts (if there are gains from trade) at a price depending monotonically on his valuation and the discount rate. In this second phase, the seller is deterred from accelerating the process by nonstationary responses of the buyer: Unexpectedly low offers are interpreted as convincing evidence that the seller's cost is lower than originally inferred, and if the seller's inferred cost is zero then the buyer expects to obtain a price of zero and thereafter insists on it. Given this anticipation of the second phase, the seller's strategy in the first phase is supported by two considerations. First, assuming that all nonserious offers are equally uninformative to the buyer, the seller can make any offer (sufficiently above the buyer's acceptable level) in order to effect the delay signaling that his cost is not very low. Second, contemplating a serious offer, the seller trades off two considerations. Making an immediate serious offer brings a chance that it will be accepted, or in any case obtains the value of continuation in the Dutch auction based on his true cost while following the strategy were his cost the lower one inferred by the buyer, depending on which of the possible serious offers the seller makes; hence the seller assesses an interest cost on this forgone continuation value that is immediately accessible. On the other hand, delaying another period signals that his cost is higher and induces a higher continuation value in the second phase. Balancing these two considerations and choosing an optimal offer when the time comes, with both the time and the offer depending on his cost, the seller eventually makes a serious offer that reveals his cost precisely.

The feature of such a construction that makes the equilibrium work is the seller's signaling motive: At any time a serious offer is higher than the price he would offer were his cost common knowledge, because it must be high enough to be credible by assuring that if his cost were lower then he would have no incentive to imitate such an offer. Of course, this signaling is expensive for the seller: It reduces the chance the buyer will accept. As a result of this signaling incentive, serious offers are a sharply increasing function of the seller's cost, and the range of prices at any time has an upper bound beyond which there is no chance the buyer will accept. The buyer can do better than accepting an exorbitant (i.e., nonserious) offer by waiting one period for a lower offer from the seller, because in the next period the seller, having a diminished signaling motive (since a range of lower possible costs is now excluded from the buyer's assessment of the seller's cost), can be expected to make a serious offer less inflated by the pressure to signal credibly. This bound establishes the range of serious offers and thus assures the existence of nonserious offers that the seller can make to effect delay. The net result is that, along the equilibrium path, at successively later times successively higher intervals of costs induce the seller to make a serious offer. These serious offers are increasing in the seller's cost and therefore are revealing, but they are not monotone over time because (for each particular cost) the pressure to signal credibly diminishes with time, as the buyer truncates from below the support of his assessment as the history of nonserious offers is extended.

The plausibility of this equilibrium clearly depends on the central issue of whether the second phase's reliance on nonstationary responses by the buyer off the equilibrium path – and thereby the circumvention of the Coase conjecture's implications when the discount factor is large – can reflect actual behavior. If the second phase is accepted then the seller's incentive to signal by delay and to make a revealing offer follows convincingly. If stationary behavior by the buyer is assumed, on the other hand, then with short periods the seller is deterred from making a revealing offer by the anticipation that there will be little gains from trade realized in the second phase. There is, however, the possibility that partially revealing offers by the seller (also studied by Cramton [9]) should come into play in this case: For the two-period examples studied by Cramton these yielded very small benefits to the seller, but in many-period models with short periods one can expect that these benefits will loom large.

Cramton has extended his construction to trading rule (A), involving alternating offers, by employing a continuous-time model interpreted as the limit of such a process. This interpretation is invoked by assuming that if at any time both parties' valuations stand revealed (by inference from serious offers), then gains from trade are split immediately in proportions specified by Rubinstein's model with alternating offers and complete information. From this assumption, the construction works backward much as before. If one trader's (say, the seller's) valuation is revealed then he conducts a Dutch auction, now in continuous time with offers declining continuously to his revealed cost. The novel feature is that in the initial phase both parties use delay followed by a serious offer to signal their valuations.[10] Of course, in considering a first serious offer a trader now sees a further advantage to waiting: There is a chance that the other will make a serious offer first, which is advantageous to the one who waits. The equilibrium conditions derived from this construction yield differential equations that in special cases can be solved to obtain the traders' strategies explicitly. I defer elaboration of Cramton's construction to Section 3, where I describe some of its implications in the context of bid–ask markets.

An equilibrium of this form poses clearly the dilemma in the second phase between nonstationarity and stationarity. Using a nonstationary construction for off-the-equilibrium-path behavior, Cramton's equilibrium has the unrevealed trader making no serious offers until he accepts or offers the Rubinstein offer, which is itself strongly dependent on the alternation of serious offers. In contrast, with stationarity the Gul–Sonnenschein theorem precludes the revealed trader from obtaining any of the gains from trade, and in particular for the Grossman–Perry equilibrium we have seen, in the example reported in Table 1, that if the period length is short (zero for a continuous-time model) then the unrevealed trader makes no serious offers. My conclusion is that nonstationary equilibria fare poorly in this comparison; the best hope is that stationary equilibria with partial pooling can be developed to provide more plausible insights into the bargaining process, and I endorse the suggestions along

---

[10] Also interesting is that if the seller's cost exceeds the buyer's valuation then in finite time one or the other can conclude that no gains from trade exist and so cease bargaining.

this line by Gul and Sonnenschein [23]. In the meantime, it remains true that Cramton's two equilibria for the trading rules (S) and (A) remain the only ones known (other than trivial equilibria enforced by extremely optimistic beliefs off the equilibrium path) and therefore provide our only developed analyses of bargaining with both parties having private information.[11] The search for stationary equilibria appears formidable, and it may take considerable effort to explore fully its many complexities.

In summary of this section, I offer the following conclusions. First, it is abundantly clear that dynamic market processes, even the simplest cases of monopoly and bargaining, reveal awesome complexities and startling results. "Rational expectations" is found to pervade even monopoly with complete information. With incomplete information, central to what we know so far are the myriad possibilities for signaling, delay, and the like. In dynamic processes, asymmetries of information interact strongly with traders' impatience. Most extraordinary is the Coase conjecture: Asymmetries of information in trading processes that proceed rapidly can skew the terms of trade completely in favor of the informed party. Because this result depends heavily on stationarity, it calls attention to the critical behavioral role of stationarity and throws into perspective the role of nonstationarity assumptions so often invoked in earlier models.

3   Synthesizing theories of markets

Much of economics concerns the theory of markets. Often we assess the contributions of this theory in terms of the analyses of models that it offers. Equally important, I believe, are the models themselves. Models are designed to capture succinctly various salient features of practical situations. The formulation of models is an art form requiring insight and skill, as well as a sensitive appreciation of the features amenable to tractable analysis. Translating aspects of actual markets into consistent mathematical representations demands both keen perceptions of reality and mastery of the craft of construction.

[11] Cramton's equilibria rely on two special features that future research could usefully investigate. One is the assumption that when both parties' valuations are revealed trade occurs at the Rubinstein price were their valuations common knowledge and the trading rule one of alternating offers; whereas when only one has revealed, revisions of beliefs remain possible if the revealed trader deviates by attempting to accelerate the process. Thus, "probability one" events are taken to be equivalent to common knowledge in the one case and not in the other. The second is that deviation by the seller with the revealed valuation that is the minimal one possible is deterred by the optimistic belief of the buyer that he can expect minimal prices in the future; thus, at the seller's minimal possible valuation, beliefs are not continuous in the seller's offer. It is unclear whether these assumptions can be weakened while retaining the form of Cramton's equilibria. Perhaps more detailed study of trading rule (A) in a discrete time model can clarify these issues.

There is also a meta-level of model formulation that deserves attention. At this level, the task is to assemble several models into a unified structure that describes a wider variety of economic environments according to a consistent scheme. Sometimes unification is achieved by generalization. The prominent example is the Walrasian model, which has been vastly generalized. I doubt that the game-theoretic analysis of markets will take this form. Presently the special structure of particular models must be exploited to obtain significant results; indeed, the comparative advantage of game theory is its elaboration of the fine structure of equilibria. An alternate path, however, relates to modeling the way that urban design relates to architecture. Progress on this path requires assembling large structures from smaller ones whose fine structure is modeled in detail.

There are now models describing market structures along a spectrum that ranges from perfect competition with many agents to bargaining between two agents. Along the spectrum are special cases such as (omitting the full list) the following.

- Auctions: a single seller offering a single item to several buyers.
- Double Auctions: many traders, each demanding or supplying a single unit.
- Monopoly: a single seller offering many units to several buyers.

The models formulated to examine these markets emphasize the structure implied by their particular features, expressed mainly in terms of the numbers, preferences, endowments, and/or information of the agents. A theory of markets gains explanatory power if these ad hoc formulations are knit together consistently, so that a single construct can be specialized to address any particular market structure along the spectrum. A truly successful endeavor would have comparable explanatory power in elucidating both bargaining and perfectly competitive markets, and would provide basic principles revealing how competition becomes perfect as the number and attributes of the participants change.

3.1   Bargaining models of decentralized exchange

An interesting contribution of this kind is the construction by Rubinstein and Wolinsky [40] and Wolinsky [53]. These papers build on the bargaining model of Rubinstein [38] based on alternating offers and complete information, and imbed it in the fabric of a larger economy with many traders. To induce the feature of impatience so essential to the bargaining model, without imposing it exogenously, these authors develop a version of the "competitive pressure" hypothesis (more on this below) by imposing on each bargainer a risk that his partner will find comparable (or, in [53], at some cost better) bargaining opportunities elsewhere. Thus in equilibrium each pair trades immediately at a price determined from their relative risks of losing their partner – much as in the basic Rubinstein model, but with the novel feature that the gains from trade are computed relative to the traders' alternative continuation values if their bargaining sequence were to be interrupted.

In [40] the authors envision a market with dispersed (identical) buyers and (identical) sellers who randomly encounter each other and then bargain together over the price via alternating offers. The stochastic assignment process that matches the traders for bargaining is exogenous and stationary. Most important, having found a partner for bargaining, each trader runs a continuing risk that his partner may find another. If his partner leaves in some period, then the trader is left without a bargaining relationship for at least that period, after which he again stands a chance of finding a new partner. Thus failure to trade immediately imposes both the usual interest cost plus the risk of incurring a further delay if the partner departs next period – this delay is the expected time until a new partner is found. The gist of this model, therefore, is that to the traders' direct impatience (represented by the interest rate) is added an additional term reflecting the competitive pressure that one's bargaining partner may find another and leave one in the lurch until a new partner can be found. In equilibrium, of course, each pair trades immediately, at a price that reflects each one's relative total impatience as measured by the sum of these two terms.

As the interest rate or the length of a period shrinks to zero, the predicted price at which each pair trades converges to a price that is not a Walrasian price for the economy as a whole – namely, a price that equates the totality of demand and supply. This result differs from the corresponding result for the basic Rubinstein model, which yields a Walrasian price. The reasons for this deviation from the usual Walrasian prediction are explored in Binmore and Herrero [2, 3]. The essential technical feature is the fact that in a bargaining relationship the gains from trade are computed relative to the traders' continuation values: If there are more sellers than buyers then the buyers have a proportionately greater chance of successfully finding another partner while the sellers have a proportionately greater chance of being left without a partner for a while. The end result is that the price at which they trade lies between their two valuations, in proportions that reflect these relative chances. In contrast, the only Walrasian price is equal to the sellers' valuation, which can result from a Rubinstein model only if the buyers' impatience is infinitesimal compared to the sellers'. Here their relative impatience is bounded, so the equilibrium price is not Walrasian.

As Binmore and Herrero [2, 3] emphasize, this feature arises from the assumed stationarity of the process. To maintain stationarity, any initial disparity among the numbers of buyers and sellers must be sustained by arrivals of new traders in numbers equal to those departing with completed trades; hence, the surplus of traders on one side of the market is maintained at every time and there is no possibility that the market can actually clear in the Walrasian sense. Gale [16–18] also concludes that stationarity is the essential ingredient. Both exhibit nonstationary processes that lead to Walrasian outcomes; one such model has a fixed population of traders.[12]

I view these results as possibly realistic for the case of trade among dispersed, impatient agents who direct their offers to particular partners. For such cases, Rubinstein and Wolinsky effectively demonstrate that the continuing existence of asymmetries in the pool of unmatched traders can affect the terms of trade to the extent of yielding non-Walrasian outcomes if market clearing is perpetually delayed. Their model reveals the underlying assumption of the Walrasian model that eventually the market can clear, usually by the imposed structure that eventually all traders get to take equal advantage of the trading opportunities. On the other hand, the analyses of Gale and of Binmore and Herrero suggest that with market clearing and nil delay costs, Walrasian outcomes are to be expected.

Based on a seemingly comparable (though much generalized) model, Gale [17] argues that any equilibrium outcome must be Walrasian if markets clear and delay costs are nil. His formulation differs from the others we have discussed in that preferences are such that a Walrasian equilibrium is characterized by equality of the traders' marginal rates of substitution. (Thus the Rubinstein–Wolinsky model is excluded, but in [18] Gale follows Binmore and Herrero in arguing that this is inessential.) Gale assumes outright that the interest rate is zero. In this case, he argues that any trader will continue trading – offering and accepting net trades according to a trading rule where one trader is randomly selected to make a single take-it-or-leave-it offer – so long as his marginal rate of substitution differs from the Walrasian price; because by continuing he obtains a positive chance of encountering another with whom an advantageous trade can be made. Thus, if the process stops at all it stops at a Walras-

---

[12] On the other hand, Gale [18] points out that the Rubinstein–Wolinsky result is Walrasian if market clearing is interpreted in a flow sense: Given the equal arrival rates of buyers and sellers (even though the "stocks" of buyers and sellers are unequal), any price between their two valuations induces departures at a rate equal to the arrival rate. In this interpretation, the unequal stocks of buyers and sellers and the matching process are relevant mainly to the determination of which price (in the interval of flow-clearing prices) is selected. This points out that interpretations of Walrasian models depend on whether market clearing is interpreted in a stock or flow sense.

ian outcome. Assuming that endless continuation yields no consumption value, and that the stochastic matching process by which traders encounter each other is sufficient to ensure that the process stops after some finite time, Gale therefore argues that equilibrium outcomes are Walrasian.[13]

Unlike the previous models, Gale's model does not elucidate in detail the role of impatience. In particular, the role of competitive pressure is diminished to a search for the partners (several, if multilateral trades are required) who will provide the anticipated Walrasian net trades – partners who are assumed to be found eventually with no real delay cost. Strategic behavior is reduced to the mutual anticipation of each pair that only the predicted Walrasian net trade is acceptable, and each partner is willing to wait indefinitely to obtain that trade or to wait for a comparably good opportunity from a substitute. Though Gale's formulation seems somewhat displaced from the spirit of the other game-theoretic treatments, I find it particularly interesting as a fundamentally new motivation for the standard Walrasian model of exchange. Absent impatience, the Walrasian model can be justified as the net result of bilateral bargaining among dispersed agents who encounter each other randomly, but with full knowledge of the terms of trade they can demand and should accept. As we have seen with the Rubinstein–Wolinsky model, this need not be the case if balanced departures and arrivals in the market prevent the market from ever clearing; there is therefore no Walrasian clearing price that identifies unique marginal rates of substitution that can guide the agents in their searches for trades. But in other cases Gale's model, and the related ones of Binmore and Herrero, likely set a standard against which to compare the limits of other models as the interest rate or period length shrinks to zero.

3.2 Competitive pressure in auctions and bid–ask markets

The principle that competitive pressure induces impatience that affects the terms of trade can be further illustrated with the simple example of a Dutch auction conducted in real time. Suppose that there is a single seller and several potential buyers for an item. The seller's value is zero, whereas each buyer's valuation is privately known but distributed according to a probability distribution that is common knowledge. In a Dutch auction conducted over a fixed time interval of duration 1, the seller starts with an asking price possibly as high as the highest possible valuation among the buyers, and then the asking price is reduced continuously to reach zero at time 1 (stopping at a price above zero cannot be a sequential equilibrium

---

[13] Part of this assumption is that traders' endowments are sufficiently diverse. The finite stopping time is ensured by requiring the total measure of the agents to be finite; this precludes a stationary matching process.

strategy for the seller). The first buyer to announce acceptance of the current asking price receives the item by paying that price. In such an auction, equilibrium strategies for the buyers specify for each buyer, depending on his privately known valuation, the highest asking price (or the earliest time) that he will accept. The optimization of this acceptance price by a buyer involves the following tradeoff. At any instant, waiting a little longer reduces the price paid but incurs two charges against his present profit (the difference between his value and the price): One charge is the interest on the delay in receiving the profit, and the other is the hazard rate of the risk that some other buyer will intervene and accept the asking price first. Thus, the interest rate and the hazard rate of a competitor intervening occur additively in determining the optimal strategy. The interesting consequence of this observation is that even if the interest rate is zero, so that seemingly all buyers are patient enough to wait for the final price of zero, in fact the competitive pressure induces impatient behavior endogenously. As a result, a buyer with a high valuation accepts early. The case where the interest rate is zero, at least for the seller, is particularly interesting because it enables the seller to be unconcerned about delay costs in conducting a Dutch auction; if the interest rate is positive and the buyers' strategies are stationary, then the seller has an incentive to accelerate the process. For more details see Section A.5 of the appendix.

The principle that competitive pressure induces impatience is, I think, an important explanation of behavior in more complicated real-time markets with many buyers and sellers. The prominent examples are markets with orally announced bids, offers, and acceptances. Such bid–ask markets are familiar in commodity trading, and indeed scenes of eager traders gathered around a pit in Chicago or a ring in London are a staple of economics textbooks illustrating "perfectly competitive" markets. Such markets have also been studied experimentally, and typically the results strongly confirm the predictions that most of the gains from trade are realized and that prices tend to approximate the Walrasian market clearing price – especially if repetition of the market enables traders to learn from experience (cf. Plott [36], Smith [43], and Easley and Ledyard [12]).

In [52] I attempt to synthesize a construction of sequential equilibria for bid–ask markets, using elements already known from previous studies of bargaining, auctions, and monopoly. The key idea is to envision the market as a process by which sellers and buyers are endogenously matched into bargaining pairs, and impatience to trade is induced mainly by competitive pressure; in turn, the induced impatience determines the terms of trade, much as in the Dutch auction described above.[14] Using this ap-

---

[14] In [52] the exposition assumes for simplicity that the agents' discount rate is zero, but this leads to an incomplete determination of the strategies for the endgame in which only

proach I establish that at least the necessary conditions associated with the corresponding direct revelation game can be satisfied; the full sufficient conditions for verification of an equilibrium remain to be studied.

The matching and bargaining process works as follows. As in Cramton's bargaining model [9, 10] using nonstationary strategies, say that an offer is serious if according to the equilibrium it has a positive probability of acceptance. For a continuous-time model, one anticipates the existence of a separating equilibrium in pure strategies for which a trader's first serious offer reveals his valuation. Moreover, at any time only the buyer with the highest valuation or the seller with the lowest valuation possibly finds it optimal to make or accept a serious offer. Along the equilibrium path, therefore, the play of the game transpires as follows. The game opens with an initial phase in which no trader makes a serious offer – waiting is the means of signaling that the buyer's valuation is not very high and the seller's valuation not very low. When a serious offer is made but not accepted, the game enters a second phase in which the revealed trader continues with serious offers (as in a Dutch auction) until one is accepted, thereby revealing the valuation of the acceptor to be the highest if he is a buyer or the lowest if he is a seller. Completion of this second phase with a trade removes the highest-valuation buyer and the lowest-valuation seller from the market; consequently, the ensuing subgame is like the original game, except that one less buyer (and seller) are present and the probability distributions of the remaining traders' valuations are truncated – by the inference that the remaining buyers have valuations lower than the one last revealed while the remaining sellers have valuations higher than the one last revealed. Of course, if the Dutch auction runs its course with no acceptance then the game concludes; in this case one can infer that no gains from trade remain. Similarly, if the initial phase produces no serious offer then no gains from trade are present.[15]

In more detail, the second phase runs as follows. Suppose that the lowest-valuation seller has made a serious offer that has not been accepted. Along the equilibrium path, the buyers are able to infer from this serious offer the seller's valuation, whereas this seller remains uncertain about the buyers' valuations. The continuation game therefore consists of a single-seller, many-buyer bargaining game in which the seller's valuation is presumed known. Generalizing from the one-buyer case with frequent alter-

a single buyer or seller remains (because a single trader on one side of the market has no induced impatience from competitive pressure). Making the discount rate positive removes this indeterminacy, but of course then one requires nonstationary strategies to sustain the equilibrium against deviations in which a trader would prefer to accelerate the process.

[15] In [52] I assume a finite allowed time and a zero interest rate, in which case the initial phase could end with a small positive probability of gains from trade remaining.

nating offers, we expect in this case an equilibrium in which only the seller makes serious offers and the buyers wait until the seller's ask price declines sufficiently before one accepts.[16] Thus the seller is effectively in the position of conducting a Dutch auction against the several remaining buyers who have not yet traded and whose valuations have not been revealed by any serious bid. Intervention by other sellers is precluded by the revelation that the revealed seller's valuation is the lowest and therefore that he can undercut any competitive offer. As the seller continuously reduces his offer towards his (revealed) valuation, each buyer follows a Dutch auction strategy specifying how low the seller's offer must get before accepting.[17] Of course this acceptance level depends on the buyer's valuation, on the sum of the discount rate and his perceived hazard rate that some other buyer will accept first, and on his expected value of continuation in the ensuing subgame should he fail to trade with the presently revealed seller. Acceleration of the process by the seller is forestalled by the anticipation that this would induce the buyers to reassess a lower estimate of the seller's cost.[18]

Thus, the seller's value of continuation from making a serious offer is his expected discounted profit from the ensuing Dutch auction, with offers descending to his valuation. Similarly, the value of continuation for a buyer who contemplates making a first revealing bid is his expected discounted profit from the ensuing Dutch auction, with bids ascending to his valuation.

With this construction of the consequences of making a revealing bid or offer, we can address the determination of the traders' strategies in the initial phase. Consider the case of a seller. At any time the equilibrium predicts how low an ask price must be to have a chance that some buyer will accept; this required level of serious ask prices increases over time, because it is associated with the inferred valuation of a seller making such a serious offer. At any instant, a seller's decision whether to wait or to make the maximum serious offer trades off two considerations, each the sum of several terms. First, by waiting he obtains a chance that some buyer will enter a serious bid, which is advantageous because his expected profit is greater if he is on the receiving end of the ensuing Dutch auction.

---

[16] That is, an equilibrium with serious counteroffers by the buyers cannot be sustained, for such bids reveal the buyer's valuation and are therefore disadvantageous for the buyers, compared to the opportunity to wait for further reductions in the seller's ask price.

[17] A serious counteroffer is excluded here because, as we have seen in Section 2, it is advantageous for the buyers to let the seller make all the offers.

[18] As previously mentioned, unfortunately a special treatment is required for the case that the seller's cost is the minimal one: As in Cramton [9], for this case invoke the Coase conjecture in the form that buyers expect to obtain all the gains from trade.

Moreover, by waiting and offering a higher serious ask price, his profit is increased if it is accepted. Waiting also induces in the buyers the inference that his valuation is higher, and this inference increases their acceptance prices in the ensuing Dutch auction. Second, however, the seller incurs two costs. One is the hazard that another seller will intervene with a serious offer and conclude an advantageous trade with the highest-valuation buyer, who will then be unavailable in the ensuing subgame. The second is the forgone interest on his expected profit were he to conclude a trade by making a serious offer immediately. Both of these costs might in principle be negligible were it not for a particular feature of the equilibrium: There is a positive probability that the initial serious offer is accepted outright. That is, some buyers find it advantageous to accept the first serious ask price. This is because they have been waiting partly in hopes that some seller will make the first serious offer; when a seller does make a first serious offer this incentive is removed and they accept.

I am quick to acknowledge that this construction has deficiencies, although I tend to view them less as refutations and more as challenging topics for research. First, it is abundantly clear that the whole approach needs to be substantiated via a corresponding discrete-time model. Second, the off-the-equilibrium-path beliefs that sustain a sequential equilibrium of this type are less than fully convincing: In the Dutch auction, ask prices that are higher than buyers expect are ignored, but lower ones are interpreted as convincing evidence that the seller's valuation is lower than originally estimated from the first serious offer; as a consequence the buyers' acceptance strategies are necessarily nonstationary, because they depend on the history of the seller's offers after the first serious one. This feature is central to the equilibria constructed by Cramton [9, 10] for his bargaining model. The device is not uniformly successful, moreover, as it does not deter the lowest-cost seller from accelerating the Dutch auction; for this case Cramton requires a special treatment, in effect reverting to stationarity by assuming that thereafter the buyers expect to be able to capture all the gain from trade. In contrast, from Fudenberg, Levine, and Tirole [13] and from Gul, Sonnenschein, and Wilson [24] we know that, for the bargaining problem in the discrete-time case, if the seller's valuation is common knowledge (rather than inferred from a serious offer) then equilibria with stationary strategies for the buyers not only exist (uniquely if the seller's valuation is low enough), but – most crucially – also satisfy the Coase conjecture: If the interval between offers is short (e.g., continuous time) then the buyer captures most of the gains from trade. Presently, my view is that this difficulty would be most satisfactorily resolved by relaxing two features of the model: that delay is the sole signaling mechanism, and that serious offers are perfectly revealing (more on this later).

Suffice it to say here that an equilibrium with considerable pooling might be possible. In such an equilibrium a serious offer might be made by a clump of buyer or seller types, and the subsequent refinement of this clump into more finely identified intervals of types might proceed piecemeal, with alternation between the refinements of the sellers' and buyers' identified clumps.

The third deficiency of this construction has practical ramifications for the conduct and analysis of experiments with bid–ask markets. The hypothesis that there are precise serious offers anticipated at each time, and that these offers fully reveal traders' valuations, derives partly from the assumption that the traders' probability assessments are common knowledge. Such common knowledge is rarely present in experiments and never in practice; the equilibrium depends moreover on unrealistic computational abilities and therefore such common knowledge, even if present initially, erodes with time. This difference between assumptions and reality is reflected, I believe, by the absence in experimental protocols of any clear evidence that the predicted signaling and Dutch auction phases are actually occurring. Presently, my conclusion is that the equilibrium described above, even if mathematically correct, is simply one of many possible equilibria, one that (perhaps unfortunately) is implausible as a positive predictive theory. I suggest therefore that we take it mainly as an instructive exercise, and an indication that as more robust models of bargaining are developed they can be used to develop corresponding models of the intricate behavior that occurs in bid–ask markets.

For experimental purposes, the likely prediction of any model based on endogenous bargaining is that parties will trade in order of their valuations (if no risk aversion intervenes), that in any transaction the imputed gains from trade are measured relative to the continuation values in an ensuing subgame, and that these gains will be split in proportions reflecting competitive pressures on the two parties. As a practical matter, the continuation values might be estimated (rather than computed from theoretical considerations) from the data obtained from replications of the market, so that the main test of the theory is internal consistency – rather than relying on absolute predictions that depend crucially on the common knowledge structure and the participants' computational abilities.

This brings me back to the theme which opened this section. I believe that developments in the theory of bargaining, auctions, and other finely structured market processes can be viewed also as steps toward synthetic theories of complex markets. The device I have proposed and illustrated is to interpret complex markets as a heirarchy of imbedded bargaining and auction games with endogenous processes of signaling and competitive pressure. These supplant the simplistic assumptions of exogenously specified matching processes and impatience parameters used in bargaining models. I view this approach as a way to develop useful positive hypotheses about realistically complex markets using simple, tractable models from which the structural features of equilibria can be derived.

This may also be the only way that the key role of delay and impatience in simple models can be reconciled with the key observation that most markets operate quickly. Indeed, if costly delays (and impatience un-augmented by competitive pressure) were crucial to the operation of markets, then the delay costs would render such markets inefficient quite apart from the realized gains from trade. Alternatively, if trading is rapid and strategies are stationary then informed traders have no incentive to make revealing offers, or when they do they forgo most of the gains from trade. What we see in practice is that gains from trade are identified and realized quickly and efficiently, and apparently gains are distributed fairly evenly. My hypothesis is that this success reflects the power of competitive pressure to greatly magnify traders' impatience and thereby to realize the signaling and price-determination functions without significant real delay costs.

Central to this thesis, of course, is the belief that identification of the possibility of gains from trade is crucially important. Were gains from trade known to be present, as for example might be the case in labor negotiations, most models (Rubinstein [38]; Gul, Sonnenschein, and Wilson [24]; etc.) predict that simply accelerating the rate of offers achieves a quick and efficient determination of the terms of trade – although possibly to the disadvantage of a trader with a commonly known valuation, as in the case of the Coase conjecture. For this reason, current work on bargaining models with incomplete information on both sides has special importance; in contrast to the genre of models that assume foreknowledge of gains from trade and focus exclusively on the terms of trade, these models can reveal more about the possible equilibria that include revelation of the existence of gains from trade.

4 Conclusion

I have discussed three main topics: incentive efficiency of trading rules, equilibria of dynamic trading games, and assembling models of complex markets from simpler ingredients. These topics are linked by the theme that it is worthwhile to study the trading rules found so prominently in practice, a theme that happily is shared by those using experimental methods. The familiar trading rules are likely efficient, both individually and as endogenous components of larger assemblies. I think too that we can learn from studying the structural features of the equilibria of models based on the familiar trading rules. The fine details of equilibria evidence the constraints imposed by logical consistency in reconciling the optimal strategies of several interacting agents. These details are possibly reflections of practical aspects of behavior in actual markets; moreover they provide hypotheses that are specific enough to be testable. Certainly this has been true in the case of auctions – witness the role of the Winner's Curse – and I believe that elementary bargaining models are already contributing to a better understanding of negotiations. Game-theoretic formulations have also been helpful in revealing the deficiencies in previous theories that ignored some of the aspects of strategic behavior; industrial organization has been the main turf for this encounter. Ultimately I would like to see a reconstruction of economic theory to take full account of strategic behavior in dynamic situations with incomplete information. In this endeavor, the exploration of the properties of trading rules is one step in a broader program to construct a convincing theory of price formation.

For the audience of non-economists beyond this Congress, the study of trading rules and other realistic aspects of the micro-structure of markets is likely welcome. Bargaining, auctions, bid–ask markets, and brokered and specialist markets are important economic institutions. Laymen expect economists to say something interesting about these institutions, something more useful than that demand equals supply. When we attain an explanatory theory that encompasses these institutionalized markets, elucidates oligopolistic behavior, and explains the many forms of discriminatory pricing, then economics will have better tools to be a practical science at the micro level.

Appendix

This appendix amplifies several of the models mentioned in the text by presenting explicit, although very brief, formulations. For complete expositions see the references mentioned.

A.1   Conditions for incentive efficiency of double auctions

A criterion sufficient to establish the incentive efficiency of a trading rule is that there exist welfare weights $\alpha_i(v_i)$ for each trader i in the event his valuation is v_i, such that no other trading rule achieves a higher value of the welfare measure

$$\mathcal{W} \equiv \mathcal{E}\left\{ \sum_i \alpha_i(v_i) U_i(v_i) \right\},$$

where (for some selection of the equilibrium) $U_i(v_i)$ is trader i's expected gain from trade if his valuation is v_i, and $\mathcal{E}$ indicates the expectation over the traders' valuations. From the analysis of the associated direct revelation game, Myerson and Satterthwaite [35] have shown that such a measure can be written as

$$\mathcal{W} = \mathcal{E}\left\{ \sum_{i \in T} k_i u_i(v_i) \right\} + \text{constants},$$

where the indicated constants depend only on the participation constraint. T is the (random) set of traders who trade, and each k_i is plus or minus one as the trader is a buyer or seller, so feasibility requires that $\sum_{i \in T} k_i = 0$. In the formula, $u_i(v_i)$ is what Myerson calls trader i's *virtual* valuation. For example, if the sellers' valuations are distributed i.i.d. according to the distribution function F then

$$u_i(v_i) = v_i + \bar{\alpha}_i(v_i) F(v_i)/F'(v_i),$$

where

$$\bar{\alpha}_i(v_i) \equiv \mathcal{E}\{\alpha_i(\tilde{v}_i) \mid \tilde{v}_i \le v_i\}.$$

In a double auction, by comparison, the set T of traders who trade is selected to maximize $\sum_{i \in T} k_i \sigma_i(v_i)$, where σ_i is the strategy that specifies trader i's submitted bid or ask price depending on the valuation v_i. Since this maximization depends only on ordinal comparisons, a double auction is therefore incentive efficient if there is some increasing function ψ such that $\psi(\sigma_i(v_i)) = u_i(v_i)$. One such function is constructed in [50] that has the required properties if the number of buyers and sellers is sufficiently large.

A.2   Characterization of the monopoly problem

Consider a seller with zero unit cost and a population of buyers with types in the interval $[0, 1]$ such that a buyer of type x has the valuation $f(x)$, where f is increasing. The seller and all buyers use the discount factor δ. If the seller expects that a buyer of type x uses the stationary strategy that accepts any price not exceeding $P(x)$, then along the equilibrium path his value of continuation $V(x)$ when the set of buyers remaining is the interval $[0, x]$ must satisfy the dynamic programming relation:

$$V(x) = \max_{y \le x} P(y)[x - y] + \delta V(y),$$

and if $y(x)$ is the (maximal) optimal choice here then his optimal price is $p(x) = P(y(x))$. For the buyer of type x, on the other hand, it is optimal to accept a price p only if waiting for a lower price is not preferable. Along the equilibrium path this reduces to the condition that:

$$f(x) - P(x) = \delta[f(x) - p(x)].$$

Characterizations of the equilibria determined by these conditions are obtained in [13] and [24]. As noted there, randomization by the seller may be necessary off the equilibrium path. An elaborate example is in [51] and others are described in [24].

In order to amplify the intuitive argument for the Coase conjecture given in the text, let $y = y(x)$ and $z = y(y(x))$. Then, in addition to the above conditions, we have

$$V(x) \geq p(y)[x - z] + \delta V(z)$$

and

$$V(y) = p(y)[y - z] + \delta V(z).$$

Together these three conditions imply that

$$[p(x) - p(y)][x - y] \geq \delta[1 - \delta]V(z) + [1 - \delta]p(y)[y - z]$$
$$\geq \delta[1 - \delta]V(z),$$

which we write in the form

$$\left[\frac{p(x) - p(y)}{\Delta}\right]\left[\frac{x - y}{\Delta}\right] \geq e^{-r\Delta}\left[\frac{1 - e^{-r\Delta}}{\Delta}\right]\left[\frac{V(z)}{\Delta}\right],$$

where $\delta = e^{-r\Delta}$ expresses the discount factor in terms of the length Δ of the period between offers. The discussion in the text uses this inequality to justify the Coase conjecture, interpreting the two factors on the left as the rates (per unit time) at which prices decline and buyers accept. The terminology is abbreviated by relying on two approximations,

$$\left[\frac{1 - e^{-r\Delta}}{\Delta}\right] \approx r \quad \text{and} \quad \frac{p(x) - p(y)}{\Delta} \approx r[f(y) - p(y)],$$

that are valid if Δ is small; the interest rate is set at $r = 1$.

In the case of bargaining, let x indicate the buyer's type, uniformly distributed on $[0,1]$; then $f(x)$ is the buyer's valuation if his type is x. Let $\hat{V}(x)$ be the seller's expected discounted value of continuation after a history that enables the seller to infer that the buyer's type lies in the restricted interval $[0, x]$. If only the seller makes offers then the same conditions, with $V(x) = \hat{V}(x)x$, characterize equilibria with a stationary strategy for the buyer. If both can make offers but the buyer finds it preferable to make only nonserious offers that the seller is sure to reject, then replace δ by δ^2 since the seller makes offers only every other period.

A.3   *An equilibrium of a bargaining game*

Assume that the seller and buyer alternate offers, and as before the seller's cost is zero and the buyer's valuation is $f(x)$ if his type is $x \in [0,1]$, where x is uniformly distributed. Consider an equilibrium with a stationary strategy for the buyer with the reservation price $P(x)$ if his type is x. Along the equilibrium path, if the buyer finds it optimal to make a nonserious counteroffer then the seller's continuation value satisfies the dynamic programming relation specified above (using δ^2). Otherwise, it satisfies

$$V(x) = \max_{y \le x} P(y)[x - y] + \delta W(y),$$

where $W(y)$ is his continuation value after rejection of the offer $P(y)$ when it is the buyer's turn to counteroffer. In turn, this must satisfy

$$W(y) = q(z)[y - z] + \delta V(z),$$

if he expects the buyer to make the serious acceptable counteroffer $q(z)$ if his type is in the interval $[z, y]$. In this case the buyer's reservation price necessarily satisfies

$$f(y) - P(y) = \delta[f(y) - q(z)].$$

In some examples the counteroffer is $q(z) = \delta f(z)/(1 + \delta)$, which is the Rubinstein offer by the buyer expecting that any lower price will be countered by the seller with the acceptable offer $f(z)/(1 + \delta)$, since the seller can now infer that the buyer's type lies in the interval $[z, y]$. Moreover, the lowest type z for which the counteroffer is optimal satisfies

$$f(z) - q(z) = \delta[f(z) - p(z)],$$

where $p(z)$ is the seller's optimal offer when he infers that the buyer's type is in the interval $[0, z]$ if the counteroffer $q(z)$ is not forthcoming.

The example in the text uses the assumption that $f(x) = x$ so that the buyer's valuation is uniformly distributed. As shown in Table 1, if the discount factor is sufficiently high then the buyer makes no serious counteroffers. Thus, the Coase conjecture applies and the buyer obtains most of the gains from trade if the discount factor is large. This is an instance of the more general theorem of Gul and Sonnenschein [23], which addresses also the case where the buyer makes counteroffers if his valuation is sufficiently small; also, these authors allow a more general class of equilibria than allowed by Grossman and Perry.

A.4   *Bargaining with offers only by the informed trader*

Consider, for example, the simplified version of the game in continuous time in which both parties use the discount rate r, the seller's valuation is 0, and the continuous distribution function of the buyer's valuation is F on an interval $[v_*, 1]$. Along the equilibrium path, if the buyer's valuation is v then he bids 0 until he makes his first serious offer $p(v)$ at time $t(v)$. The seller immediately accepts because he expects the bid thereafter to increase toward the buyer's revealed valuation at a rate less than the discount rate, which is also optimal for the buyer given the expectation that the seller will accept such bids. The buyer's delay in making a serious offer is sustained by the seller's strategy. Along the equilibrium path the seller rejects bids of 0, but at any time $\hat{t}$ he accepts bids $\hat{p}$ not less than the predicted serious offer level, as specified above: $\hat{p} \geq p(t^{-1}(\hat{t}))$. Off the equilibrium path, if at $\hat{t}$ the buyer offers $\hat{p} < p(t^{-1}(\hat{t}))$ then the seller rejects, and continues with a strategy that is optimal for the subgame with the support of the buyer's distribution truncated to some interval $[a, b]$, where $b = t^{-1}(\hat{t})$ by inference from the previous absence of a serious offer. There are, however, many feasible choices for the lower bound $a = a(\hat{p}, \hat{t})$ that satisfy the natural constraints that $a(p(v), t(v)) = v$ and that rejection of $\hat{p}$ is optimal for the seller:

$$\hat{p} < \frac{\int_a^{t^{-1}(\hat{t})} p(x) e^{-r[t(x) - \hat{t}]} \, dF(x)}{F(t^{-1}(\hat{t})) - F(a)}.$$

For example, a plausible choice of a is one that satisfies

$$a - \hat{p} = [a - p(a)] e^{-r[t(a) - \hat{t}]},$$

so that $[a, b]$ is the interval of buyer types preferring that the seller accept $\hat{p}$ at $\hat{t}$ rather than waiting to make their equilibrium offers at later times. Cramton uses the simpler convention that $a = b = p^{-1}(\hat{p})$. Either way, a special treatment is required for the case that $\hat{p} \leq p(v_*)$ because in this case a low-value buyer is not necessarily deterred by the seller's revised assessment, and such a buyer has an incentive to accelerate the process: Cramton's device is to assume that in this case the seller expects and only accepts prices of v_* thereafter.

The possibility that this variety of disequilibrium assessments by the seller induces a comparable variety of equilibria is clear from the fact that the buyer's anticipation that the seller will not accept prices lower than $p(v)$ before $t(v)$ implies (for an optimal strategy) only the necessary condition that

$$p'(v)/t'(v) = -r[v - p(v)].$$

This condition determines only one of the two functions p and t given the other; it remains to fix the equilibrium by specifying the seller's interpretation of the signaling significance of the buyer's delay. Thus, although delay is an effective signal for the buyer, various equilibria are possible depending on the seller's prediction of the delay that each buyer type will use to signal his valuation.

A.5   *Impatience in an auction*

Consider a Dutch auction in which a bidder with the valuation v obtains the discounted profit $[v - p(t)]e^{-rt}$ if he is the first to accept the ask price $p(t)$ at the time t. Suppose the $n+1$ bidders' valuations are distributed i.i.d. such that $F(\hat{v})$ is the probability that one's valuation is less than $\hat{v}$. If one expects another bidder with the valuation $\hat{v}$ to accept at time $t(\hat{v})$, then he will choose his acceptance time s to maximize his expected discounted profit:

$$[v - p(s)]e^{-rs}F(t^{-1}(s))^n.$$

A symmetric equilibrium requires that the optimal choice is $s = t(v)$. A necessary condition for this optimum is that:

$$|p'(t(v))| = [v - p(t(v))]\{r + nF'(v)/F(v)|t'(v)|\}.$$

As mentioned in the text, the second term in the curly brackets is the hazard rate that another bidder will intervene with an earlier bid. The interest rate r and this hazard rate add to impute the bidder's impatience in delaying receipt of the immediate profit $v - p(t)$ rather than waiting for the price to decline further before accepting. Either a positive interest rate or a positive hazard rate suffices to induce early acceptance by the bidder. If there are many bidders then the hazard rate is the dominant term; this is an instance of the competitive pressure mentioned in the text.

References

[1] Bikhchandani, Sushil. 1985. "A Bargaining Model with Incomplete Information." Working Paper, Stanford Business School. Appears in "Market Games with Few Traders," Ph.D. dissertation, 1986.

[2] Binmore, Kenneth G., and Maria J. Herrero. 1984. "Frictionless Non-Walrasian Markets." Technical Report 84/103, ICERD, London School of Economics. First part superseded by "Matching and Bargaining in Steady State Markets," 1985.

[3] Binmore, Kenneth G., and Maria J. Herrero. 1985. "Matching and Bargaining in Dynamic Markets." Technical Report 85/117, ICERD, London School of Economics.

[4] Bulow, Jeremy. 1982. "Durable-Goods Monopolists." *Journal of Political Economy* 90: 314-32.

[5] Chatterjee, Kalyan, and Larry Samuelson. 1984. "Infinite Horizon Bargaining with Alternating Offers and Two-Sided Incomplete Information." Working Paper, Pennsylvania State University.

[6] Chatterjee, Kalyan, and Larry Samuelson. 1985. "Bargaining under Incomplete Information: the Continuum of Offers Case." Working Paper, Pennsylvania State University.

[7] Chatterjee, Kalyan, and William F. Samuelson. 1983. "Bargaining under Incomplete Information." *Operations Research* 31: 835-51.

[8] Coase, Ronald H. 1972. "Durability and Monopoly." *Journal of Law and Economics* 15: 143-9.

[9] Cramton, Peter C. 1984. "The Role of Time and Information in Bargaining." Ph.D. Thesis, Stanford University.

[10] Cramton, Peter C. 1984. "Bargaining with Incomplete Information: An Infinite Horizon Model with Continuous Uncertainty." *Review of Economic Studies* 167: 579-93.

[11] d'Aspremont, Claude, and Louis-André Gerard-Varet. 1979. "Incentives and Incomplete Information." *Journal of Public Economics* 11: 25-45.

[12] Easley, David, and John O. Ledyard. 1983. "A Theory of Price Formation and Exchange in Oral Auctions." Technical Report 249, Cornell University.

[13] Fudenberg, Drew, David Levine, and Jean Tirole. 1985. "Infinite Horizon Models of Bargaining with One-Sided Incomplete Information." In Alvin Roth, *Game-Theoretic Models of Bargaining*, pp. 73-98. Cambridge: Cambridge University Press.

[14] Fudenberg, Drew, David Levine, and Jean Tirole. 1985. "Sequential Bargaining with Many Buyers." Unpublished manuscript, University of California–Berkeley. Forthcoming in *Quarterly Journal of Economics*.

[15] Fudenberg, Drew, and Jean Tirole. 1983. "Sequential Bargaining with Incomplete Information." *Review of Economic Studies* 161: 221-47.

[16] Gale, Douglas. 1984. "Bargaining and Competition." Working Paper 84-23, CARESS, University of Pennsylvania. Revision included in [17].

[17] Gale, Douglas. 1986. "Bargaining and Competition." *Econometrica* 54: 785-818.

[18] Gale, Douglas. 1985. "Limit Theorems for Markets with Sequential Bargaining." Working Paper 85-15, CARESS, University of Pennsylvania.

[19] Glosten, Lawrence, and Paul R. Milgrom. 1985. "Bid, Ask, and Transaction Prices in a Specialist Market with Heterogeneously Informed Traders." *Journal of Financial Economics* 14: 71-100.

[20] Gresik, Thomas A., and Mark A. Satterthwaite. 1983. "The Numbers of Traders Required to Make a Market Competitive: The Beginnings of a Theory." Technical Report 551, MEDS, Northwestern University. See also "The Rate at which a Simple Market Becomes Efficient as the Number of Traders Increases," Technical Report 641, 1985.

[21] Grossman, Sanford J., and Motty Perry. 1986. "Sequential Bargaining under Asymmetric Information." *Journal of Economic Theory* 39: 120-54.

[22] Groves, Theodore. 1973. "Incentives in Teams." *Econometrica* 41: 617-31.
[23] Gul, Faruk, and Hugo Sonnenschein. 1985. "Uncertainty Does Not Cause Delay." Working Paper, Stanford Business School. Forthcoming in *Econometrica*.
[24] Gul, Faruk, Hugo Sonnenschein, and Robert B. Wilson. 1986. "Foundations of Dynamic Monopoly and the Coase Conjecture." *Journal of Economic Theory* 39: 155-90.
[25] Hagerty, Kathleen M. 1985. "Equilibrium Bid-Ask Spreads in a Dealership Market." Ph.D. Thesis, Stanford University.
[26] Harsanyi, John C. 1967. "Games with Incomplete Information Played by Bayesian Players, I-III." *Management Science* 14: 159-83, 320-34, 486-502.
[27] Holmström, Bengt R., and Roger B. Myerson. 1983. "Efficient and Durable Decision Rules with Incomplete Information." *Econometrica* 51: 1799-1820.
[28] Kreps, David M., and Robert B. Wilson. 1982. "Sequential Equilibrium." *Econometrica* 50: 863-94.
[29] Kyle, Albert. 1985. "Continuous Auctions and Insider Trading." *Econometrica* 53: 1315-35.
[30] Maskin, Eric, and David Newbery. 1978. "Rational Expectations with Market Power: The Paradox of the Disadvantageous Tariff on Oil." Working Paper 227, Churchill College, Cambridge University.
[31] Maskin, Eric, and Jean Tirole. 1982. "A Theory of Dynamic Oligopoly: I, II, III." Technical Reports 320, 373, et seq., Massachusetts Institute of Technology.
[32] Myerson, Roger B. 1979. "Incentive Compatibility and the Bargaining Problem." *Econometrica* 47: 61-73.
[33] Myerson, Roger B. 1981. "Optimal Auction Design." *Mathematics of Operations Research* 6: 58-73.
[34] Myerson, Roger B. 1985. "Bayesian Equilibrium and Incentive Compatibility: An Introduction." In Leonid Hurwicz, David Schmeidler, and Hugo Sonnenschein (eds.), *Social Goals and Social Organization: Essays in Memory of Elisha Pazner,* pp. 229-59. Cambridge: Cambridge University Press.
[35] Myerson, Roger B., and Mark A. Satterthwaite. 1983. "Efficient Mechanisms for Bilateral Trading." *Journal of Economic Theory* 28: 265-81.
[36] Plott, Charles R. 1982. "Industrial Organization Theory and Experimental Economics." *Journal of Economic Literature* 20: 1485-1527.
[37] Roth, Alvin E. 1985. "A Note on Risk Aversion in a Perfect Equilibrium Model of Bargaining." *Econometrica* 53: 207-12.
[38] Rubinstein, Ariel. 1982. "Perfect Equilibrium in a Bargaining Model." *Econometrica* 50: 97-110.
[39] Rubinstein, Ariel. 1985. "A Bargaining Model with Incomplete Information about Preferences." *Econometrica* 53: 1151-72.
[40] Rubinstein, Ariel, and Asher Wolinsky. 1984. "Equilibrium in a Market with Sequential Bargaining." Technical Report 84/91, ICERD, London School of Economics. Appears in *Econometrica* 53 (1985): 1133-50.
[41] Rubinstein, Ariel, and Asher Wolinsky. 1985. "Middlemen." Working Paper, Hebrew University of Jerusalem.

[42] Samuelson, William. 1984. "Bargaining under Asymmetric Information." *Econometrica* 52: 995–1006.

[43] Smith, Vernon L. 1982. "Microeconomic Systems as an Experimental Science." *American Economic Review* 72: 923–55.

[44] Sobel, Joel, and I. Takahashi. 1983. "A Multi-Stage Model of Bargaining." *Review of Economic Studies* 162: 411–26.

[45] Sonnenschein, Hugo. 1974. "An Axiomatic Characterization of the Price Mechanism." *Econometrica* 42: 425–34.

[46] Stokey, Nancy. 1982. "Rational Expectations and Durable Goods Pricing." *Bell Journal of Economics* 12: 112–28.

[47] Wilson, Robert B. 1978. "Information, Efficiency, and the Core." *Econometrica* 46: 807–16.

[48] Wilson, Robert B. 1985. "An Example of Alternating-Offers Bargaining with Private Information on Both Sides." Note, Stanford Business School.

[49] Wilson, Robert B. 1985. "Efficient Trading." In George Feiwel, *Issues in Contemporary Microeconomics and Welfare*, pp. 169–208. Macmillan Press.

[50] Wilson, Robert B. 1985. "Incentive Efficiency of Double Auctions." *Econometrica* 53: 1101–16.

[51] Wilson, Robert B. 1985. "Notes on Market Games with Complete Information." Working Paper, Stanford Business School.

[52] Wilson, Robert B. "On Equilibria of Bid-Ask Markets." In George Feiwel (ed.), *Arrow and the Ascent of Economic Theory: Essays in Honor of Kenneth J. Arrow*. Forthcoming from Macmillan Press. Distributed as IMSSS Technical Report 452, November 1984.

[53] Wolinsky, Asher. 1985. "Matching, Search, and Bargaining." Research Paper 151, Hebrew University.

CHAPTER 3

The theory of contracts

Oliver Hart and Bengt Holmström

Introduction

The past decade has witnessed a growing interest in contract theories of various kinds. This development is partly a reaction to our rather thorough understanding of the standard theory of perfect competition under complete markets, but more importantly to the resulting realization that this paradigm is insufficient to accommodate a number of important economic phenomena. Studying in more detail the process of contracting – particularly its hazards and imperfections – is a natural way to enrich and amend the idealized competitive model in an attempt to fit the evidence better. At present it is the major alternative to models of imperfect competition; we will comment on its comparative advantage below.

In one sense, contracts provide the foundation for a large part of economic analysis. Any trade – as a quid pro quo – must be mediated by some form of contract, whether it be explicit or implicit. In the case of spot trades, however, where the two sides of the transaction occur almost simultaneously, the contractual element is usually downplayed, presumably because it is regarded as trivial (although this need not be the case; see Section 3). In recent years, economists have become much more interested in long-term relationships where a considerable amount of time may elapse between the quid and the quo. In these circumstances, a contract becomes an essential part of the trading relationship.

Of course, long-term contracts are not new in economics. Contingent commodity trades of the Arrow–Debreu type are examples par excellence of such contracts. What does seem new is the analysis of contracts written

We would like to thank Jonathan Feinstein, Paul Joskow, John Moore, Sherwin Rosen, Jean Tirole, and Andy Weiss for comments on an earlier draft. Financial support from NSF and the Sloan Foundation is gratefully acknowledged.

by and covering a small number of people. That is, there has been a move away from the impersonal Arrow–Debreu market setting where people make trades "with the market," to a situation where firm A and firm B, or firm C and union D, write a long-term contract. This departure is not without economic significance. Williamson (1985), in particular, has stressed the importance of situations where a small number of parties make investments which are to some extent relationship-specific; that is, once made, they have a much higher value inside the relationship than outside. Given this "lock-in" effect, each party will have some monopoly power ex post, although there may be plenty of competition ex ante before investments are sunk. Since the parties cannot rely on the market once their relationship is underway, the obvious way for them to regulate (and divide the gains from) trade is via a long-term contract. Until the advent of contract theory, economists did not have the tools to analyze ex ante competitive, ex post noncompetitive relationships of this type via formal models.

Research on contracts has progressed along several different lines, each with its own particular interests. It may be useful to begin by mentioning some of these directions before outlining the subjects we will concentrate on in this chapter.

One strand of the literature has focused on the internal organization of the firm, viewing the firm itself as a response to failures in the price system. Questions of interest include structuring incentives for members of the firm, allocating decision authority, and choosing decision rules to be implemented by suitable reward structures. Of course, the objective is partly to gain insight into organization theory as such. But perhaps more importantly, one is interested in knowing whether organization theory matters in the aggregate – that is, to what extent the conduct of firms will be different from the assumed profit-maximizing behavior; and, if it differs, what ramifications follow for market outcomes and overall allocations in the economy.

Another prominent line of research has explored the workings of the labor market. A plausible hypothesis is that contingent claims for labor services are limited for reasons of opportunism. This invites innovation of other types of contracts that can be used as substitutes. The research has centered on the structure of optimal bilateral labor contracts (under various assumptions about enforcement opportunities), on the properties contractual equilibria will have, and in particular on whether these equilibria will exhibit the commonly claimed inefficiencies associated with real-world adjustments in employment.

Inspired by the possibility that long-term contracts may embody price and wage sluggishness, a related body of work has explored their macroeconomic implications [see, e.g., Fischer (1977) and Taylor (1980)]. Unlike most contract analysis this literature has taken the form of contracts as given, typically with nominal wage and price rigidities. This is not as satisfactory as working from first principles, but it has made policy analysis quite tractable.

Financial markets offer another arena of substantial potential for contract theoretic studies that is beginning to be recognized. The importance of limited contracting for the emergence of financial services and institutions has been suggested by D. Diamond (1984), Gale and Hellwig (1985), and Townsend (1980). This line of research also offers prospects for a careful modeling of the role of money and the conduct of monetary policy [see Townsend, Chapter 11 this volume, and D. Diamond (1985)].

As the field is progressing, it becomes harder to place models in specific categories. Initially, models of organizational design ignored market forces, or at least treated them in a very primitive fashion. In contrast, the theory of labor contracts started out without consideration for organizational incentives. More recent models, however, treat both incentive and market issues concurrently. Such crossbreeding is fruitful, but it makes the task of organizing this chapter much harder. Since we have been unable to come up with a natural classification that would avoid this problem, we will employ an outline that follows the historical progress rather closely.

We begin in Section 1 with agency theory as a representative paradigm for the organization-theoretic aspects of contracting. From there we go on to labor contracting (Section 2). Finally, we turn to incomplete contracts and the aforementioned lock-in effects (Section 3). This work, representing more recent methodological trends in contract research, has not advanced very far yet, and our discussion will be correspondingly more tentative in nature.

Needless to say, we will not attempt a comprehensive survey of the large number of contractual models that have appeared to date. Some subjects (e.g., models relating contracts to macroeconomic policy) are left out entirely. So are models of financial contracting. Our intention has been to be selective and critical rather than comprehensive. Although we allow ourselves a rather opinionated tone, we trust this chapter still gives a good idea of the general nature of the ongoing research and a reasonably fair assessment of its main contributions.

Despite our selective approach, the chapter has grown very long. In order that it may be more readily digestible, we have written it so that the three parts can be read essentially independently; each part has a concluding section that sums up its major points.

A word about methodology

Most contract theories are based on the assumption that the parties at some initial date (say, zero) design a Pareto optimal (for them) long-term contract. Optimality is not to be understood in a first-best sense, but rather in a constrained or second-best sense. Indeed, informational and other restrictions that force the contract to be second-best are at the heart of the analysis – without them one would quickly be back in the standard Arrow–Debreu paradigm where contractual form is inessential. Because informational constraints will play a particularly important role in the ensuing discussion, let us note right away that throughout we will restrict attention to cases in which informational asymmetries arise only subsequent to contracting. In the typical language of the literature, we will not consider adverse selection models.

The design of a Pareto optimal contract proceeds by maximizing one party's expected utility subject to the other party (or parties) receiving a minimum (reservation) expected utility level. Which party's utility level is taken as a constraint does not usually matter, because most analyses are partial equilibrium. When there is perfect competition ex ante, this reservation utility can be interpreted as that party's date-zero opportunity cost determined in the date-zero market for contracts. When ex ante competition is imperfect, the parties will presumably bargain over the ex ante surplus from the relationship, and so the reservation expected utility levels become endogenous.

The literature has often been cavalier about the determinants of the reservation utility, because valuable insights have emerged from the general characteristics of Pareto optimality alone. On the other hand, the fact that market forces reduce to simple constraints on expected utilities greatly facilitates equilibrium analysis. Equilibration in expected utilities is usually trivial. This gives the contractual approach its main methodological advantage relative to models of imperfect competition, for instance. The analytical core of contract theory is an optimization problem, whereas in imperfect competition it is an equilibrium problem. Methods for solving optimization exercises are substantially more advanced than methods for solving equilibrium problems.

Of course, substituting an optimization analysis for an equilibrium analysis is not always economically meaningful (for instance, we are not implying that imperfect competition should be studied in this way). Indeed, the economic credibility of the contractual approach may be called into question when, as often happens, optimal contracts become monstrous state-contingent prescriptions. How are such contracts written and enforced?

Three responses to this question can be offered. The first one is to appeal to the powers of the judicial system and its ability to enforce certain explicitly agreed-upon contractual terms. The assumption is that sufficient penalties, either pecuniary or nonpecuniary, will be imposed for breach and hence rational parties will not breach. This assumption makes a model internally consistent, but is unsatisfactory on two accounts. It maintains an artificial dichotomy between those contractual provisions that are assumed to be infinitely costly to enforce and those that are assumed to be completely costless to enforce. Also, it often predicts (by assumption) explicit terms that are much more complex than those we observe and in that sense is no answer to what prodded the enforcement question above.

The second response is a pragmatic one: One could argue that qualitative and aggregate features, rather than contractual detail, are the relevant ones for judging the success of a model. In support of this view one can allude to the implicit nature of contracts in the real world; in other words, suggest that equilibrium outcomes in the real world mimic optimal, complex state-contingent contracts despite the relative simplicity of the explicit agreements we observe. The difficulty with this response is that we do not understand well how implicit contracts of this type are sustained as equilibrium phenomena.

Ideally, one would like to know what determines the division between explicit and implicit enforcement of a contract. This leads to the third approach, which is to confront the enforcement issue explicitly by including realistic legal penalties for breach as well as indirect costs that affect equilibrium behavior, for instance through reputational concerns. Whereas much of the extant literature rests on a combination of the first two responses to the enforcement issue, the present trend is toward the more ambitious, but also more satisfactory, third approach. This will be discussed at some length in Section 3.

1   Agency models

1.1   *Introduction*

Agency relationships are ubiquitous in economic life. Wherever there are gains to specialization there is likely to arise a relationship in which agents act on behalf of a principal, because of comparative advantage. Examples abound: workers supplying labor to a firm, managers acting on behalf of owners, doctors serving patients, lawyers advising clients. The economic value of decision making made on behalf of someone else would easily seem to match the value of individual consumption decisions. In this light the attention paid to agency problems has been relatively slight. Moreover, there are some less obvious instances of the same formal agency structure – the government taxing its citizens, the monopolist price-discriminating customers, the regulator controlling firms – all of which are substantial problems in their own right.

If agents could costlessly be induced to internalize the principal's objectives, there would be little reason to study agency. Things become interesting only when objectives cannot be automatically aligned. So what is it that prevents inexpensive alignment? The most plausible and commonly offered reason is asymmetric information, which of course ties closely to the source of agency: returns to specialization. The sincerity of a worker's labor input is often hard to verify, leading to problems with shirking. Informational expertise permits managers to pursue goals of their own such as enhanced social status or improved career opportunities. Private information about individual characteristics causes problems for the government in collecting taxes.

Thus, underlying each agency model is an incentive problem caused by some form of asymmetric information. It is common to distinguish models based on the particular information asymmetry involved. We will use the following taxonomy. All models in which the agent has precontractual information we place under the heading of *adverse selection;* except for an occasional reference, we will not deal at all with this category. Our models will assume symmetric information at the time of contracting. Within this category, which we refer to as *moral hazard,* a further distinction is useful: the case where the agent takes unobservable actions, and the case where his actions (but not the contingencies under which they were taken) may be observed. Arrow (1985) has recently suggested the informative names Hidden Action Model and Hidden Information Model for these two subcategories. The worker supplying unobservable effort is the prototypical hidden action case, while the expert manager making observable investment decisions leads to a typical hidden information model.

As will become clear shortly, the hidden action case formally subsumes the hidden information case. (This rationalizes our use of moral hazard as a joint label.) Nevertheless, it is meaningful to keep the two distinct, because they differ in their economic implications as well as in their solution techniques. In this section we focus on the hidden action case. Section 2, on labor contracting, will illustrate the hidden information case.

The general objective of an agency analysis is to characterize the optimal organization response to the incentive problem. Typically, the analysis delivers a second-best reward structure for the agent, based on information that can be included in the contract. Characterizing the optimal incentive scheme is important but not the prime economic purpose. What is more interesting is the allocational distortions that come with the incentive solution. Although one could often design incentive schemes that induce the agent to behave as if no information asymmetry were present, that is rarely second-best. Instead, some of the costs of the information asymmetry are borne by distortions in decision rules, task assignments, and other costly institutional arrangements. This is what gives the theory its main economic content.

The agency paradigm has indeed been quite successful in shedding light on institutional phenomena that are beyond received microeconomic theory. The second-best nature of incentive efficient solutions admits a host of arrangements that would be inexplicable if information flows were costless. Examples abound in the literature and we could easily use up our allotted space by describing some of them. However, we have chosen not to follow this line, but rather to be more methodologically oriented. Agency models are not without problems, and this is best brought home by going into the details of a generic structure.

We will begin with three different formulations of the agency problem, each with its own merits. Next we go on to discuss a simple version of hidden action that will suffice to sum up the main insights of that type of model. An economic assessment and critique follow, which in turn lead us to a discussion of recent improvement efforts. These include the role of robustness in simplifying incentive schemes and the use of dynamic models to arrive at richer predictions. Finally, we provide a summary of what agency theory has to offer as well as what (in our view) its shortcomings are.

1.2   Three formulations

Let A be the set of actions available to the agent and denote a generic element of A by a. Let θ represent a state of nature drawn from a distribution G. The agent's action and the state of nature jointly determine a verifiable outcome $x = x(a, \theta)$ as well as a monetary payoff $\pi = \pi(a, \theta)$. The verifiable outcome x can be a vector and may include π. The monetary payoff belongs to the principal. His problem is to construct a reward scheme $s(x)$ that takes outcomes into payments for the agent.

The principal values money according to the utility function $v(m)$ and the agent according to the utility function $u(m)$. The agent also incurs a cost from taking the action a, which we denote $c(a)$. We assume initially that the agent's cost of action is independent of his wealth, that is, that his total utility is $u(s(x)) - c(a)$. The principal's utility is $v(\pi - s(x))$.

The agent and the principal agree on the distribution G, the technology $x(\cdot, \cdot)$, and the utility and cost functions.

This is the *state-space formulation* of the agency problem as initiated by Wilson (1969), Spence and Zeckhauser (1971), and Ross (1973). Its main advantage is that the technology is presented in what appear to be the most natural terms. Economically, however, it does not lead to a very informative solution.

There is another, equivalent way of looking at the above problem that yields more economic insights. By the choice of a, the agent effectively chooses a distribution over x and π, which can be derived from G via the technology $x(\cdot, \cdot)$. Let us denote the derived distribution $F(\pi, x; a)$ and its density (or mass function) $f(\pi, x; a)$. This *parameterized distribution formulation* was pioneered by Mirrlees (1974, 1976) and further explored in Holmström (1979). For later reference, we state the principal's problem mathematically in parameterized distribution terms. His problem is to

$$\text{Max} \int v(\pi - s(x)) f(\pi, x; a)\, dx \quad \text{over } a \in A, \; s(\cdot) \in S, \quad (1.1)$$

subject to

$$\int u(s(x)) f(\pi, x; a)\, dx - c(a) \ge \bar{u}, \quad (1.2)$$

$$\int u(s(x)) f(\pi, x; a)\, dx - c(a) \ge \int u(s(x)) f(\pi, x; a')\, dx - c(a'),$$
$$\forall a' \in A. \quad (1.3)$$

In this program the principal is seen as deciding on the action he wants the agent to implement and picking the least cost incentive scheme that goes along with that action. It is worth noting that because the principal knows the agent (his preferences), he also knows what action the agent will take even though he cannot directly observe it. Constraint (1.3) assures that the incentive scheme is consistent with the action the principal wants the agent to choose, while constraint (1.2) assures the agent a minimum expected utility level $\bar{u}$, presumably determined in the marketplace.

A solution to the principal's program is not automatically assured; in fact simple examples can be given in which no optimal solution exists. We will encounter a non-existence example shortly, but otherwise we merely assume that a solution exists.[1]

The third, most abstract, formulation is the following. Since the agent in effect chooses among alternative distributions, one is naturally led to take the distributions themselves as the actions, dropping the reference

---

[1] Grossman and Hart (1983a) offer a set of sufficient conditions for existence. A key condition is that the probabilities controlled by the agent are bounded away from zero.

to a. Let p denote a chosen density (or mass) function over π and x, and let P be the set of feasible densities from which the agent can choose. Because the agent can randomize among actions, P can be assumed convex. In the case (π, x) takes on a finite number of values, P is a simplex. The cost function in this formulation is written as $C(p)$, which also will be convex because of randomization.

Of course, the economic interpretation of the agent's action and the incurred cost is obscured in this *general distribution formulation,* but in return one gets a very streamlined model of particular use in understanding the formal structure of the problem.

This way of looking at the principal's problem is also very general. It covers situations where the agent may observe some information about the cost of his actions, or the expected returns from his actions, before actually deciding what to do; in other words, cases of hidden information. To see this, simply note that whatever strategy the agent uses for choosing actions contingent on information he observes, the strategy will in reduced form map into a distribution choice over (π, x). Thus, ex ante strategic choices are equivalent to distribution choices in some P (properly restricted, of course). Note also that the primitive cost function for actions, $c(a)$, could be stochastic without affecting the general formulation. Taking expectations over costs $c(a)$ would still translate into a cost function $C(p)$, because the agent's utility function is separable.

1.3 *The basic hidden action model*

Much of the general insights obtained from studying hidden action models can be conveyed in the simplest setting, where the agent has only two actions to choose from. For concreteness, let us identify them with working hard, H, and being lazy, L. Also, assume for the moment that x coincides with the monetary payoff to the principal and that the principal is risk-neutral. If the agent works hard, the distribution over x is $f_H(x)$, while if he is lazy, the distribution is $f_L(x)$. In view of this language it is natural to assume that f_H dominates f_L in a first-order stochastic dominance sense; that is, the cumulative distribution functions satisfy $F_H(x) < F_L(x)$, for all x, and the cost of hard work, c_H, is greater than the cost of being lazy, c_L.

Substituting these simplifying assumptions into (1.1)–(1.3) yields a straightforward program that can be easily solved. First, note that if the principal wants to implement L then he should pay the agent a constant, because that yields optimal risk-sharing. The problem therefore assumes interest only if the principal wishes to implement H, because now some risk-sharing benefits have to be sacrificed in order to provide the agent with the right incentives. Letting λ and μ be the Lagrangian multipliers for constraints (1.2) and (1.3), respectively, we see that the optimal sharing rule must satisfy:

$$1/u'(s(x)) = \lambda + \mu[1 - f_L(x)/f_H(x)] \quad \text{for a.e. } x. \tag{1.4}$$

This is a particular version of Mirrlees's (1974, 1976) formula, analyzed and interpreted further in Holmström (1979). Let us discuss its revealing message.

First, note that if $\mu = 0$ then we have first-best risk sharing ($s(x)$ constant), and the agent picks L in violation of the incentive constraint. Therefore, $\mu > 0$. With μ positive, $s(x)$ will vary with the outcome x, trading off some risk-sharing benefits for incentive provision; more precisely, it will vary with the likelihood ratio $f_L(x)/f_H(x)$. To understand why, a few words on the likelihood ratio are in order.

The likelihood ratio is a concept familiar from statistical inference. It reflects how strongly x signals that the true distribution from which the sample was drawn is f_L rather than f_H. A high likelihood ratio speaks for L and a low for H; a value of one is the intermediate case in which nothing new is learned from the sample, because it could equally as well have come from either of the two distributions.

The agency problem is not an inference problem in a strict statistical sense; conceptually, the principal is not inferring anything about the agent's action from x, because he already knows what action is being implemented. Yet, the optimal sharing rule reflects precisely the principles of inference. This can be seen even more transparently by rewriting (1.4) formally in terms of a posterior distribution derived from updating a "prior" on H. Let the prior be γ ($=$ probability of H) and denote the posterior $\gamma'(x)$. Then by Bayes's rule and (1.4), we have:

$$1/u'(s(x)) = \lambda + \mu\{(\gamma'(x) - \gamma)/\gamma'(x)(1 - \gamma)\}. \tag{1.4'}$$

From (1.4') we see that the agent is punished for outcomes that revise beliefs about H downward ($\gamma'(x) < \gamma$), and rewarded for outcomes that revise beliefs upward. Moreover, the sharing rule is a function of x only through the posterior assessment $\gamma'(x)$; outcomes that lead to the same posterior imply the same reward. As in statistical decision theory, the posterior is a sufficient statistic about the experimental outcome.

The fact that we can interpret the optimal sharing rule in standard statistical terms is important. It is intuitively appealing and it will yield some interesting predictions. At the same time it will reveal the main weakness of the model: As we will see, very few restrictions can be placed on the shape of the sharing rule.

To begin with, consider the issue of monotonicity. One might think that $s(x)$ should always be increasing in x given that f_H stochastically dominates f_L. Somewhat surprisingly, this is not true in general. The reason is that higher output need not always signal higher effort despite stochastic dominance. For instance, suppose $f_H(x) = f_L(x+1)$ and $f_L(x)$ is not unimodal (say, it has two humps). Then there will exist two values of x such that the higher one has a larger likelihood ratio $f_L(x)/f_H(x)$ than the smaller one, implying that the larger outcome would speak more strongly for a low choice by the agent than the smaller outcome. Just as statistical intuition would suggest, we should pay the agent less in the high outcome state. However, to the extent one thinks this is not descriptive of the economic situation considered, one can add the assumption that the likelihood ratio is monotone in x. Because [from (1.4)] the sharing rule is monotone in the likelihood ratio, this assumption will assure a monotone sharing rule. Not surprisingly, the Monotone Likelihood Ratio Property (MLRP) is a well-known concept from statistics. It was introduced into economics by Milgrom (1981), on which the above discussion is based.

What about other questions concerning the shape of $s(x)$? For example (anticipating an upcoming discussion), are there natural restrictions on the model that yield linear sharing rules? The answer is No. The problem is that the connection between x as physical output and as statistical information is very tenuous. In fact, the physical properties of x are rather irrelevant for the solution; all that matters is the distribution of the posterior (or likelihood ratio) as a function of the agent's action. To highlight the problem, note that x would not even have to be a cardinal measure for its information content to be the same. Since it is the information content of x that determines the shape of the optimal incentive scheme, it is hard to come up with natural economic assumptions that connect the agent's reward in any particular way to the physical measures of x.

There are cases for which linear rules are optimal; in fact, almost any shape of $s(x)$ is consistent with optimality, because output can be endowed with rather arbitrary information content. To illustrate this, suppose we want an optimal rule that is linear. Start with any example with two actions, MLRP and a continuous outcome space. As argued above, the optimal sharing rule will be monotone for such an example; call it $s^*(x)$. Now transform the example by redefining output as $x' = \alpha s^*(x) + \beta$, where α and β are constants to be determined. Because this transformation is monotone, the information content of x' is the same as the information content of x. It follows that the optimal way of implementing H in this revised example is to pay the agent $s(x') = \alpha^{-1}x' - \alpha^{-1}\beta$, which is a linear function of the output x'. With $s(x')$ the agent is paid $s^*(x)$ whenever x' corresponds to x, since we know this is the cheapest way of implementing H. Or, put into statistical terms, this scheme pays the agent the same function of the posterior as the optimal scheme in the initial example. The role of α and β is to assure that H remains the optimal action to implement in the transformed example.

The same idea can be used to prove the optimality of other shapes as well. Some very weak restrictions apply. For instance, as proved in Grossman and Hart (1983a), $s(x)$ cannot be decreasing everywhere and on average $s(x)$ cannot be increasing too rapidly either. More generally, one can show that $s(x)$ has to satisfy $0 < \int s'(x) f_H(x)\, dx < 1$, but that is about all. This inability to place natural restrictions on the model that yield commonly observed sharing rules should be contrasted with the theory of risk sharing, where linear schemes (for instance) arise from simple restrictions on preferences alone.

Although the model puts few constraints on the sharing rule, it yields very sharp predictions about the measures that should enter the contract in the first place. To illustrate this, suppose initially that $x = \pi$ and next introduce some other source of information, y, that could potentially be used in the contract. This could be information about the general economic conditions under which the agent operates, or direct monitoring of his performance, or indirect evidence from the performance of agents in stochastically related technologies. When would it be the case that y is valuable in the sense that a contract based on the vector $x = (\pi, y)$ Pareto dominates all contracts based on π alone?

The answer is evident from our earlier discussion and equation (1.4). The additional signal y will necessarily enter an optimal contract if and only if it affects the posterior assessment of what the agent did; or, perhaps more accurately, if and only if y influences the likelihood ratio. Conversely, $s(x)$ will not depend on y precisely when

$$f_L(x)/f_H(x) = h(\pi) \text{ a.e.} \tag{1.5}$$

If (1.5) is true then y will be worthless, but if (1.5) is false then y will have some strictly positive value because $s(x)$ will depend on it. This necessary and sufficient condition can be translated into a more familiar form:

$$f_i(x) = A(x) B_i(\pi) \text{ a.e.}, \quad i = L, H. \tag{1.5'}$$

In this form the condition says that π is a sufficient statistic for $x = (\pi, y)$. Thus, we have the simple but strong result that y is valuable if and only if it contains some information about the agent's action that is not already in π [Holmström (1979, 1982a) and Shavell (1979)].

This *sufficient statistic condition* underlines again the close analogy between the strategic principal–agent game and classical statistical decision theory, which describes a game against nature. Blackwell's celebrated result, which states that optimal single-person decision rules can be based on sufficient statistics alone, is very similar. Some differences should be noted, however. First, although (1.5′) states that randomization has no value (just as in Blackwell's theorem), this conclusion depends on the separable form of the agent's utility function, as Gjesdal (1982) has shown. [Of course, this randomization could be carried out without an exogenous costly signal, so in this sense it still remains true that y has no value if (1.5′) holds.] Second, that any signal with some information about the agent's action has strictly positive value is a fact without counterpart in Blackwell's theorems.

An alternative way of expressing the sufficient statistic condition is to say that it partially orders various information systems [see Grossman and Hart (1983a) and Gjesdal (1982)]. If x and x' are two different information signals (possibly vectors) that can be ordered by Blackwell's notion of informativeness, so that (say) x is more informative than x', then it is true that x' is not preferred to x. In fact, if the ordering is strict then x is strictly preferred to x' in almost all agency problems. The qualifier "almost all" is needed to take care of exceptional situations in which x' is equal to the optimal sharing rule $s(x)$ for a particular problem, which of course is as much information as one would ever want from x. We leave the qualifier deliberately vague to avoid straying too far from our main course.

The sufficient statistic result gives the model its main predictive content, as we will indicate shortly.[2]

1.4   *The general case*

Let us consider briefly what happens when one moves beyond the two-action case studied above. Economically, not much new will come out, but it is worth understanding why.

Consider the common case where the agent's action is a continuous, one-dimensional effort variable. The agent's incentive constraint (1.3) is in this case problematic, and it has been standard practice to replace it with the more manageable first-order condition:

---

[2] Our discussion of the optimal incentive scheme would not materially change by assuming that the principal is risk-averse; only the left-hand side of equation (1.4) would change to $v'(x-s(x))/u'(s(x))$. We could also have imposed constraints on the agent's wealth, so that $s(x) \geq w$ and (1.4) would remain intact with this constraint effective whenever $s(x) \leq w$ in (1.4). The case of a wealth constraint is of some economic interest, however. If the wealth constraint is binding it may force the agent to receive more than $\bar{u}$. The economic intuition is that if the agent cannot be punished sufficiently to induce him to choose H, then a bribe – extra rewards for good outcomes – will be the only alternative. These rewards may well lead to slack in (1.2), as Becker and Stigler (1974) first noted. Subsequently, Shapiro and Stiglitz (1984) have used this feature to study the efficiency wage hypothesis, a theory of underemployment arising from the difference between compensation and opportunity cost.

$$\int u(s(x))f_a(x;a)\,dx - c'(a) = 0. \tag{1.6}$$

Relaxing (1.3) in this way is referred to in the literature as *the first-order approach*. It is easy to proceed to a characterization of the optimal scheme, provided the relaxation embedded in (1.6) is appropriate. The result is as follows:

$$v'(x-s(x))/u'(s(x)) = \lambda + \mu f_a(x;a)/f(x;a) \quad \text{for a.e. } x. \tag{1.7}$$

Here f_a/f is the continuous counterpart of the likelihood ratio. It is increasing when MLRP holds. Thus, when this characterization is correct, we obtain the same qualitative insights as from the simple two-action case above, including the sufficient statistics results.

Unfortunately, the first-order approach does not always work, in the sense that it will sometimes pick out a scheme that in the end does not satisfy the global incentive constraint (1.3) even though it does satisfy the first-order condition (1.6). Mirrlees (1975) was the first to recognize this dilemma. Subsequently, Grossman and Hart (1983a) and Rogerson (1985b) worked out conditions that ensure the validity of the first-order approach. It is of some interest to understand the resolution, because the issue has received considerable attention.

First, consider a simple extension of the two-action case. Assume the agent controls the following family of distributions:

$$f(x;a) = af_H(x) + (1-a)f_L(x), \quad a \in [0,1]. \tag{1.8}$$

In other words, the agent determines by his effort a convex combination of two fixed distributions. This was called the Spanning Condition by Grossman and Hart; we will refer to it as the Linear Distribution Function Condition (LDFC). Note that by randomizing in the two-action model the agent has access to the family described by (1.8).

With LDFC it is evident that the first-order approach is valid. The reason is that no matter what schedule the principal offers to the agent, the first-order condition will coincide with the agent's global incentive constraint (for a fixed action), because the integral in (1.3) is linear in a.

When we treat the general case using the first-order approach, we are effectively taking a linear approximation of the true family of distributions $f(x;a)$ around the particular action (say, a^*) that the principal wants to implement; in other words, we are treating the problem as if the agent were choosing from the hypothetical family:

$$f'(x;\alpha) = f(x;a^*) + \alpha f_a(x;a^*), \quad \alpha \text{ small}, \tag{1.9}$$

using a cost function

$$\tilde{c}(\alpha) = c(a^*) + \alpha c'(a^*).$$

The family in (1.9) is linear in the same sense as LDFC, and there is no problem in obtaining a proper characterization. (Note that since $\int f_a = 0$, f' is a legitimate distribution for small α, provided f_a is bounded.) However, it may be that once we have induced the agent to choose $\alpha = 0$ (i.e., to choose the desired a^*) among the distributions in (1.9), he would actually want to go to another distribution in the true family $\{f(x; a)\}$ that he is controlling. This involves a discrete jump in the effort level and is the source of the potential problem with the first-order approach.

So the question is what distributions we can add to (1.9) and still be assured that the agent would not want to deviate to any of them. Here is the class proposed originally by Mirrlees and later verified by Rogerson (1985b): Assume that $\{f(x; a)\}$ satisfies MLRP and that it additionally satisfies the Convexity of Distribution Function Condition (CDFC):

$$F(x; \lambda a + (1 - \lambda)a') \leq \lambda F(x; a) + (1 - \lambda)F(x; a'),$$

$$\forall a, a', \; \lambda \in (0, 1). \qquad (1.10)$$

What (1.10) states is that the agent always has an action available yielding a distribution that stochastically dominates the distribution he could achieve by randomizing between the two actions a and a' (in other words, a peculiar sort of diminishing stochastic returns to scale); LDFC is obviously a special case of (1.10).

Now, let us see why this restriction will do the job. The optimal scheme that obtains with the local family of distributions (1.9) is differentiable. From this it follows, using integration by parts, that

$$\int u(s(x))f(x; a)\, dx - c(a) = K - \int u'(s(x))s'(x)F(x; a)\, dx - c(a), \quad (1.11)$$

where K is an integration constant. Because of MLRP, $s'(x) > 0$ and so (by CDFC) the right-hand side is a concave function in a. Consequently, none of the distributions in the original family will be as appealing to the agent as the action the principal is implementing from the local family (1.9). Hence, $s(x)$ remains optimal in the extended family as well.

This argument is illustrated in Figure 1. The triangle represents the simplex of all distributions in the case where there are only three possible outcomes x_1, x_2, and x_3, which we assume for ease of diagramming. One axis measures p_1, the other p_2; the third, $p_3 = 1 - p_1 - p_2$, does not appear in the figure. The curved line CBA is the one-dimensional manifold of distributions $f(x; a)$ [here represented as $\{(p_1(a), p_2(a)) \mid a \in A\}$]; this set is one-dimensional, because the action a is a scalar. Any straight line in the simplex represents a family satisfying LDFC. The shaded region is the set P of all distributions that the agent has access to when randomized strategies are included (cf. the general distribution formulation in

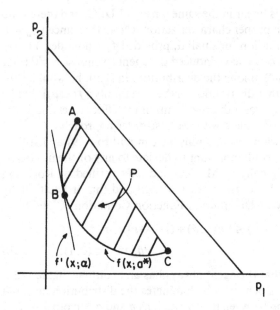

Figure 1

Section 1.2). The figure does not show the cost function or the incentive scheme. With a third dimension measuring costs and rewards, the incentive scheme would be a hyperplane and the cost function a convex manifold in R^3.

Assume the principal wants to implement the distribution at point B (representing the earlier a^*). Corresponding to the argument above, he starts by designing a cost-minimizing scheme that implements B when the agent's hypothetical alternatives are the distributions along the tangent to B [the tangent represents the distributions in the linear family (1.9)]. This cost-minimizing scheme is characterized by (1.7). Next, CDFC and MLRP assure [using (1.7) and (1.11)] that none of the distributions along the curved line (or in P for that matter) is as attractive to the agent as point B given the scheme in (1.7). Thus, B is indeed implemented in the actual set of feasible distributions P. Without CDFC and MLRP, the agent might want to jump across, for instance to C, when B is being implemented from the tangent set. Then (1.7) would not be valid.

As might be expected, MLRP and CDFC are very restrictive conditions and economically rather peculiar. Particularly, CDFC seems to rule out a number of "natural" families, because few of those we might think of are closed under convex combinations. For instance, there is no family we know of that satisfies both conditions and is generated from the technology $x = a + \theta$ (or $x = a\theta$). This does not mean that the set of families satisfying both CDFC and MLRP is small. There is an easy way of generating sample families with both properties. Simply start with any two distributions and extend this family by LDFC as in (1.8). If the two initial distributions can be ordered by MLRP, the extended family will have this property. Note that the role of MLRP here is simply to obtain an increasing schedule and not to assure the validity of the first-order approach, which is already guaranteed by LDFC.[3]

The fact that LDFC appears to be the main instrument for constructing families with CDFC and MLRP leaves open the question of whether there are any interesting cases that do not satisfy LDFC but only CDFC. Except for added convenience in studying examples, this issue is not very interesting either. We already saw how the two-action case was rather rich in generating a variety of optimal incentive schemes. This richness obviously carries over to the LDFC case.

From the preceding discussion one should infer that the first-order approach works in the case where the family of distributions controlled by the agent is one-dimensional in distribution space (LDFC). It also works in cases which are effectively one-dimensional, in the sense that their solution is equivalent to a problem with a one-dimensional family (CDFC plus MLRP). Notice that it is one-dimensionality in distribution space that makes things simpler, not one-dimensionality in the underlying economic variable (effort). Even though effort is taken to be one-dimensional, the curve it traces will generally (when convexified) generate a higher-dimensional P, making matters complex.

What is meant above by "the first-order approach works" also needs a bit of elaboration. Its precise meaning is that the optimal scheme is characterized by (1.7), which is a narrower statement than the claim that one can describe the agent's choice by first-order conditions. Viewing things in distributional terms, we note that the agent in Figure 1 has two decision variables: p_1 and p_2. If the cost function over P were strictly convex and the optimal distribution to implement were interior to P (because, say, the cost goes to infinity toward the boundary), then a first-order approach in the traditional sense would work perfectly well. Normally a single first-order condition would not be enough to describe the agent's behavior, but two would always do. One would then obtain a characteri-

---

[3] Alternatively, of course, one can work with any one-parameter family (for which a solution is known to exist) and then interpret the characterization as referring not to this family necessarily, but to the tangent space of distributions described by (1.9).

zation like (1.7), but with two multipliers μ_1 and μ_2 rather than one. This dilutes the information content of the characterization; the sufficient statistic results will not be as crisp (in particular, optimal incentive schemes may aggregate more than what the earlier sufficient statistic result indicated; see Section 1.6) and statements about monotonicity will be hard to make. Needless to say, when one goes to higher-dimensional cases, the value of a general characterization along these lines quickly disappears.[4,5]

We conclude that models with a continuous effort variable allow a simple characterization when they look much like the two-action case discussed before. In that case the solution, as far as the optimal reward structure is concerned, exhibits the same features and the same variety. One difference is worth stressing, though. In the two-action model it is difficult to say anything about the agent's choice of action, because it is not determined by a continuous trade-off. One has to compare the solution that implements H with the solution that implements L directly. On the other hand, if effort is a continuous variable and the first-order approach works, then it can be proved (Holmström, 1979) that the optimal level of effort to implement is such that the principal would like to see it go even higher. In other words, in equilibrium we should see principals desiring more effort from their workers. Because this enrichment can be obtained already, by moving from the two-action case to the LDFC case, there appears to be little reason ever to go beyond LDFC in a model that wants to exploit the characterization in (1.7).

1.5   An intermediate assessment

The main predictive content of the basic agency model is in the sufficient statistic result, which tells what information should enter into a contract in the first place. Simple as it seems, this result turns out to have quite a bit of economic scope. One trivial implication is that agency relationships create a demand for monitoring. This has generated substantial interest

---

[4] Grossman and Hart (1983a) study cases in which the first-order approach may not be applicable. Even with MLRP, incentive schemes need not be monotone. On the other hand, the result that sufficient statistics are sufficient for designing optimal incentive schemes does not depend on the first-order approach. Also, a more informative system (in the Blackwell sense) is strictly better than a less informative one, assuming that the garbling matrix that connects the two systems has full rank. However, signals that provide additional information about the agent's strategy may not be valuable when the first-order approach fails.

[5] Hidden Information Models, viewed in distribution space, are typically of high dimension, because contingent strategies result in rich distributional choices for the agent (see Section 1.6). This is why the analyses of Hidden Information Models proceed along quite different lines than the analysis of Hidden Action Models.

in the accounting literature and has led to various refinements in predicting the usefulness of different monitoring schemes [for a survey, see Baiman (1982)].

A more significant implication concerns the use of relative performance evaluation [Baiman and Demski (1980), Holmström (1982a)]. Agents who work on tasks that are related – in the sense that one task provides information about the other – should not be compensated solely on individual output, but partly on the output of others. Note that the reason for this (according to the sufficient statistic result) is not that one would like to induce competition for incentive purposes, because if the agents' technologies are not stochastically related then relative performance evaluation is useless at best. Rather, competition is a consequence of the desire to extract information about the circumstances under which the agents performed. This information is used to filter out as much of the exogenous uncertainty as possible, allowing more weight to be placed on individual performance.

A further consequence of the sufficient statistic result is that sometimes aggregate information will do as well as detailed information in relative performance schemes. For instance, if technologies have normal noise then weighted averages of peer performance will suffice as a basis for an optimal scheme. The weights are proportional to the information content of the signals from peers.

Predictions like these accord at least broadly with stylized facts. Relative performance evaluations are commonplace, particularly in the form of prizes (e.g., promotions) awarded to top performers in an organization. Indeed, the labor market as a whole forms a grand incentive structure in which relative evaluations implicitly or explicitly play a dominant role. The literature on rank order tournaments, initiated by Lazear and Rosen (1981), has studied in more detail the performance and design of such contests [see also Green and Stokey (1983) and Nalebuff and Stiglitz (1983)]. We note that the use of rank order as a basis for payment is rarely optimal in the basic agency model; one could usually do better with schemes sensitive to cardinal measures. However, there may be other advantages to rank-order payments not captured by the standard agency model. One reason is that rank is easier to measure in many circumstances. Another argument – suggested by Carmichael (1984), Malcomson (1984a), and Bhattacharya (1983) – is that tournaments provide the principal with incentives to honor promised awards even in cases where legal enforcement is difficult, because performance can be observed but not verified. In tournaments the total amount paid by the principal remains constant and payment should therefore be easy to verify.

Explicit relative performance schemes have recently emerged in executive compensation packages as well. Typically, they relate managerial performance to companies within the industry, which fits the notion that stochastically closer technologies have more value as a basis for optimal rewards. Antle and Smith (1986) have studied more broadly the degree of relative performance evaluation in executive compensation, measuring implicit (as well as explicit) contractual elements. Their statistical tests show that the data in fact exhibit a component of relative compensation, but not to the extent predicted by the basic theory. This seems puzzling at first, but two explanations can be suggested for the evidence. First, executives may be diversifying their portfolio through personal transactions in the market, which do not show up in the data; in fact, Section 1.6 discusses a model with precisely the property that no relative performance payments are necessary because the executive can manufacture them himself. The other, more plausible, reason is that relative performance evaluations distort economic values and thereby decision making (e.g., an executive completely insulated from systematic risk will disregard such risk in evaluating investment decisions). In the one-dimensional agency models normally studied, such decisions are excluded. Including more decision dimensions in the model seems essential for gaining a better fit with the data and a better understanding of the merits of relative performance schemes.

Given that the basic agency model is so general, it is perhaps surprising that it has any predictive value at all. To this can be added the value of having a paradigm within which one may begin considering in more precise terms such subjects as the managerial theory of the firm. Jensen and Meckling's (1976) pioneering work is an example of what insights can be derived from the mere recognition that managers need to be provided with incentives against shirking; another (more explicit) model on the same subject is in Grossman and Hart (1982). Both papers derive the capital structure of the firm from the underlying incentive problems (with opposite hypotheses about the manager's options to dilute the firm's resources). Although these studies beg the question of why capital structure needs to be used for incentive purposes when direct incentive schemes appear to be cheaper, they still open the door for further investigations into a subject that surely is of substantial economic importance.

Let us next turn to the problems with the basic agency model. The main one is its sensitivity to distributional assumptions. It manifests itself in an optimal sharing rule that is complex, responding to the slightest changes in the information content of the outcome x. Such "fine-tuning" appears unrealistic. In the real world incentive schemes do show variety, but not to the degree predicted by the basic theory. Linear or piece-wise linear schemes, for instance, are used frequently and across a large range of environments.[6] Their popularity is hardly explained by shared properties of the information technology, as the basic model would have it. It is clear that other technological or organizational features, excluded from the simple model, must be responsible for whatever regularities in shapes we do observe empirically.

Fine-tuned, complex incentive schemes also stand in the way of serious extensions and applications. One can say little about comparative statics properties of the model and it is also hard to introduce additional variables into the analysis. This is a critical drawback, because the unobservable variable in the model (say, effort) is not of primary interest precisely because it cannot be observed. Instead one would be interested in what consequences the agency model has for such observable variables as investment decisions and task assignments, for example. Little has been done in this regard, due to the complexity of the basic solution. [For one attempt that reveals these difficulties, see Lambert (1986).]

Thus casual empiricism, as well as the desire to include decision variables of allocational and aggregate significance, strongly point to a need to refine agency models in the direction of predicting simpler incentive schemes. We turn next to such an effort.

1.6   *Robustness and linear sharing rules*

The prevalence of relatively simple incentive schemes could partly be explained by the costs of writing intricate contracts.[7] But that is hardly the whole story. A more fundamental reason is that incentive schemes need to perform well across a wider range of circumstances than specified in standard agency models. In other words, incentive schemes need to be robust.

One way of expressing the demand for robustness is to allow the agent a richer set of actions or strategies. Intuitively, the more options the agent has, the more poorly intricate schemes will perform. To give a familiar example: If there is a secondary market for goods, arbitrage will take away all opportunities for price discrimination. Linear schemes are optimal, because they are the only ones that are operational.[8]

---

[6] Sharecropping rules are almost exclusively linear, despite great variations in stochastic environments.

[7] We remind the reader of our discussion of explicit versus implicit incentive schemes in the introduction. Some would argue that real-world schemes are quite complex when viewed as equilibrium phenomena.

[8] This could be one reason for the prevalence of linear sharing rules in sharecropping. It may also explain why corporate tax schemes are more linear than income tax schemes;

Another elementary example of how added options contribute to simplifications can be given in the context of our basic agency model. We noted that an optimal incentive scheme need not be monotone in general unless MLRP holds. On the other hand, if the agent is allowed free disposal of output, then the only operational schemes are monotone no matter what the stochastic technology looks like. This illustrates the kind of nondistributional considerations that one is led to look for in understanding more universal properties of incentive schemes.

Recently, Holmström and Milgrom (1985) have proposed a simple agency model in which linear schemes are optimal because the agent is assumed to have a rather rich action space. The main idea can best be grasped by describing an example, due to Mirrlees (1974), in which no optimal solution exists. Mirrlees's example has a risk-neutral principal, an agent with unbounded marginal utility for consumption, and a technology with output $x = a + \theta$, where θ is a normally distributed error term with zero mean and a is the agent's labor supply. In other words, the agent controls the mean of a normally distributed output. This technology is the most obvious candidate for an agency analysis, and it is quite a shock to learn that the problem has no solution. The reason is that first-best can be approximated arbitrarily closely by step-function schemes that offer first-best risk sharing (a flat reward) for almost all outcomes except the extremely bad ones for which a severe punishment is applied. This approximation result is in fact easy to understand using the statistical intuition that the basic model offers. The normal technology has a likelihood ratio f_a/f that is unbounded below (it is linear in x). Therefore, very low x values will be very informative about the agent's action, and one can act on that information almost as if it revealed compliance perfectly. The step functions approximate forcing contracts, which are well known to be optimal if there are outcomes that reveal deviations with certainty.[9]

The example is clearly unrealistic and there are ways to patch it (e.g., bound utility or bound the likelihood ratio). But this would be misleading, because the example points to a more fundamental flaw. Step functions come close to first-best only under the unrealistic assumption that one knows exactly the parameters of the problem (utility functions, technology, etc.), and they will generally perform poorly as soon as one introduces slight variations or uncertainty into the model. In other words, the example represents the extreme case of fine-tuning discussed earlier.

Footnote 8 *(cont.)*
presumably, corporations can circumvent nonlinearities in tax schemes more easily than individuals. (Some would argue that individuals can do a lot of arbitrage as well, making income tax a lot less progressive than it appears.)
[9] Harris and Raviv (1979) study optimal forcing contracts.

For instance, think of a dynamic context, where the agent is paid (say) at the end of the week, and assume he can observe his own performance during the week so that he can adjust his labor input as a function of the realized path of output. Then step functions will induce a path of effort that will be both erratic and, on average, low (generally, the agent will bide his time to see if there is any need to work at all). In contrast, a linear scheme, which applies the same incentive pressure no matter what the outcome history, will lead to a more uniform choice of effort. This suggests that the optimality of step functions is highly sensitive to the assumption that the agent chooses his labor input only once. [10]

This intuition can be made precise by considering a dynamic version of the normal example. Specifically, let the agent control the drift rate μ of a one-dimensional Brownian motion $\{x(t); t \in [0,1]\}$ over the unit time interval. Formally, the process $x(t)$ is defined as the solution to the stochastic differential equation:

$$dx(t) = \mu(t)\,dt + \sigma dB(t), \quad t \in [0,1]. \tag{1.12}$$

Here B is standard Brownian motion (zero drift and unitary variance). Note that the instantaneous variance, $\sigma^2 dt$, is assumed to be constant.

The agent in the model is assumed to have an exponential utility function, and the cost of effort (unlike in our earlier model) is assumed to be independent of the agent's income. In other words, the agent's payoff is:

$$u\left(s(x) - \int c[\mu(t)]\right) = -\exp\left\{-r\left(s(x) - \int c[\mu(t)]\right)\right\} \tag{1.13}$$

as evaluated at the end of the horizon, where $x = x(1)$ is the final position of the process (the profit level at time 1, say), $c(\mu)$ is a convex (instantaneous) cost function, and r is the coefficient of absolute risk aversion. The particular form of the utility function assures that a linear scheme will indeed apply the same incentive pressure over time. In general, income effects would cause distortions.

Notice that if the agent were unable to observe the path $x(t)$, then it would be optimal for him to choose a constant drift rate $\mu(t) = \mu$ [because $c(\cdot)$ is convex], and the end-of-period position x would be normally distributed with mean μ and variance σ. In other words, we would have a model identical to our previously discussed one-period example that had

---

[10] This can be simply illustrated in the case of a risk-neutral agent, where an infinity of schemes will be first-best. They include a linear scheme with unitary slope as well as the aforementioned step function. However, if the agent receives some noisy information about the technology before choosing his effort, the linear scheme will be uniquely optimal. This idea is used in Laffont and Tirole (1986).

no optimal solution, because step functions approximate first-best. When the agent can observe $x(t)$ and base his choice $\mu(t)$ on the history of the path of $x(t)$ (which we denote x^t), the situation is significantly changed. Instead of being constrained to a one-parameter family of outcome distributions, the rich set $\{\mu(x^t); \; t \in [0,1]\}$ of contingent strategies permits a vastly wider choice. The enormous expansion of the agent's opportunity set limits the principal's options dramatically; in fact, for each strategy that the principal wants to implement there is essentially a unique incentive scheme that he must use, which stands in sharp contrast to the usual flexibility in choice that the principal has in one-dimensional static models.

The one-to-one mapping between strategies and sharing rules makes the model solvable technically (recall the discussion in Section 1.4). The relationship can be written out explicitly, after which it is easy to show that the optimal rule is linear. The interested reader is referred to the original paper (Holmström and Milgrom, 1985) for details.

Intuitively the result can be seen as follows. Consider a discrete version of the Brownian model, one in which the agent controls a Bernoulli process. Because of exponential utility it is easy to see that the optimal compensation scheme, if it could be made contingent on the whole path of periodic outcomes, would be to pay the agent the same bonus each time he has a "success"; the problem is stationary, because there are no income effects. Viewed as an end-of-period payment scheme, this rule pays the agent a constant plus the number of successes times the bonus, which amounts to a linear scheme in end-of-period profits. The Brownian model – being the limit of a Bernoulli process – should therefore be expected to have a linear optimum as well, and indeed it does.

Notice that this line of reasoning shows that the principal need not use the detailed information of the path of the outcome process even if he has access to it. This is a case where an insufficient statistic with respect to the agent's distributional choice (the end-of-period level of profits) is still enough for constructing an optimal rule; in other words, a case where the principal uses more aggregated information than the sufficient statistic results of one-dimensional models would suggest. The reason is that there is no conflict of interest in the timing of effort, only in the aggregate level of effort; hence information about timing is of no value.[11]

---

[11] We venture the guess that (in multidimensional agency models) additional signals are valuable precisely when they give information about dimensions of choice in which there is a conflict of interest. In one-dimensional models there is a conflict of interest always (by assumption). The result that additional signals have value if they are informative is always true in that case.

The remarkable thing about this model is that by making the incentive problem apparently much more complicated (the rigorous proof that a linear scheme is optimal is nontrivial), it delivers in the end a much simpler solution. In fact, once we know that the optimal incentive scheme is linear it is trivial to solve for its coefficients. A linear scheme will induce the agent to choose a constant level of effort. Therefore we can treat the problem as a static one (cf. the discussion above) in which the agent chooses the mean of a normal distribution, but this time with the constraint that the principal is only allowed to use linear rules. The dynamics rationalizes an ad hoc restriction to linearity in the static model and in the process resolves the nonexistence problem that Mirrlees originally posed!

Computational ease gives the model substantial methodological value. In contrast to general agency models it is easy to conduct comparative statics exercises. More importantly, one can use the model as a building block in studying richer applications of moral hazard. Such applications are further facilitated by the fact that the linearity results extend to situations in which the agent controls the vector of drift rates of a multidimensional Brownian process; or, in static terms, chooses the mean vector of a multivariate normal distribution.

As a brief illustration, let us discuss the effects of agency costs on investment decisions, assuming that investments are made jointly by the principal and the agent. (We cannot let the agent make the choice privately, because that would amount to having him control the variance, which would upset the linearity results.) Suppose there is a collection of projects available for investment. Each project returns $x = \mu + \theta$, where θ is a normally distributed variable with mean m and variance σ^2 and μ is the agent's effort. For a closed-form solution, assume the cost of effort to be quadratic: $c(\mu) = \mu^2/2$. To make the example a bit richer, assume in addition that there is a market index z, normally distributed with variance γ^2 and zero mean, that correlates with x. Then each project can be characterized by the triple (m, σ^2, ρ), where ρ is the correlation coefficient between z and x.

To determine the best investment one solves first for the optimal incentive scheme and net return to the principal, given a particular project. The optimal scheme is linear in x and z – that is, of the form $s(x, z) = \alpha_1 x + \alpha_2 z + \beta$. The best coefficients are easy to calculate. One finds that the principal should set

$$\alpha_1 = (1 + r\sigma^2(1 - \rho^2))^{-1}, \tag{1.14}$$

$$\alpha_2 = -\alpha_1(\sigma/\gamma)\rho. \tag{1.15}$$

The constant coefficient β is determined by the agent's participation constraint. If he has to be assured a zero certain equivalent, then the principal will be left with an expected net return equal to

$$\pi = m + \tfrac{1}{2}(1 + r\sigma^2(1 - \rho^2))^{-1}. \tag{1.16}$$

Note that the optimal incentive scheme exhibits relative performance evaluation. The agent is not merely rewarded based on the project outcome x, but also on the market outcome z. The sign of α_2 is the opposite of ρ as one would expect. This is in accordance with the general result that an optimal design should filter out as much uncontrollable risk as possible. Using z as a filter reduces uncontrollable risk by the factor $(1 - \rho^2)$. If x and z happen to be perfectly correlated, all risk can be filtered out and first-best can be achieved. (In first-best, $\alpha_1 = 1$ and $\pi = m + \tfrac{1}{2}$.) [12]

The best project is the one that maximizes (1.16). Because of the agency problem, we see that project choice depends on the degree of idiosyncratic risk as measured by $\sigma^2(1 - \rho^2)$ (which is the conditional variance of x given z). The price of that risk is a function of the agent's risk aversion (and in general also the cost of effort). There is no price for systematic risk, because the principal is risk-neutral. One could allow a risk-averse principal (with exponential utility) without altering the linearity result; then systematic risk would also enter the decision criterion. But the main point is that, unlike standard portfolio theory, idiosyncratic risk will play a role in investment decisions.

Because idiosyncratic risk carries a price, diversification will generally have value [see Aron (1984) for the same point]. Also, a concern for idiosyncratic risk will give rise to a market portfolio that is more concentrated than under full information. Firms will find value in choosing projects that are more heavily correlated with the market, because that will enable a better incentive design. (This assumes all projects are positively correlated.) Thus, agency costs could amplify aggregate swings in the economy.

This discussion is merely suggestive of what one might be able to do when linear schemes are optimal. It appears that linearity has the potential to take us toward some livelier and more serious economic analyses. [For some other illustrative examples, see the original paper (Holmström and Milgrom, 1985).] On the other hand, the Brownian model is quite

---

[12] It is worth noting that in this example the agent could privately manufacture the optimal degree of relative performance evaluation by trading in other firms' assets. In other words, the principal could equally well pay the agent based on x alone and leave it up to the agent to filter out uncontrollable risk. (Of course, the agent must not be allowed to trade stock in his own firm.)

special. The technological options are very limited; for instance, the fact that the agent cannot be allowed to make private investment decisions is an unfortunate constraint for applications. The effectiveness of the Brownian model is restricted, because it does not capture the demand for robustness in the most intuitive way. Presumably, one will have to go outside the Bayesian framework and introduce bounded rationality in order to capture the true sense in which incentive schemes need to be robust in the real world.

1.7 *Dynamic extensions*

Dynamic extensions of the basic agency model are of interest for two rather opposite reasons. One has to do with the relevance of the incentive issues portrayed in the static models, the other with the added predictions that might be had from introducing dynamics. In the former category we have theoretical studies that suggest that time may resolve agency problems costlessly. This has been argued both from the perspective of supergames, in which all cooperative gains can be realized between two parties, and in terms of reputation effects created by the market. While we do not concur in either case with the conclusion that incentive problems disappear, it is worth understanding the arguments. They will take us to dynamic models that can expand and sharpen the predictions from the static theory.

The first studies of dynamic agency were those by Radner (1981) and Rubinstein (1979). Both show that in an infinitely repeated version of the basic one-period model, the first-best solution (complete risk-sharing together with correct incentives) can be attained if utilities are not discounted. The analysis does not offer an optimal solution, but rather a class of contracts within which first-best can be reached. These contracts operate like control charts, punishing the agent for a period of time if his aggregate performance falls sufficiently below expectations. Over time, as uncertainty is filtered out by the law of large numbers, the punishments become more severe and the control region tighter. The assumption of no discounting assures that only events in the distant future, where the control is tight and few violations occur, matter.

These models appear to formalize the intuition that in long-term relationships one can cope more effectively with incentive problems, because time permits sharper inferences about true performance.[13] The fact that

---

[13] This interpretation is disputed in Fudenberg et al. (1986). There it is argued that repetition changes the agent's preferences rather than improves monitoring accuracy.

first-best can be achieved is more incidental and a consequence of the unrealistic assumption of no discounting paired with infinite repetition. Even though Radner (1981) has subsequently shown that with some discounting one can still get close to first-best, there is little reason to believe that incentives are costless in reality. The main question then is whether dynamics alters the insights and results from one-period models. In the studies above, as well as in subsequent work by Rogerson (1985a) and Lambert (1983) [see also Roberts (1982) and Townsend (1982)], memory plays a key role, suggesting that an optimal long-term contract might look rather different from a sequence of short-term contracts.

Jumping to such a conclusion is premature, however. The models discussed above assume that the agent cannot borrow and save, in which case long-term contracts substitute in part for self-insurance that would in fact be available to agents (saving is certainly a real option and limited borrowing as well). Could it be true that the gains to long-term contracting identified in the early models are in fact due to restrictions on borrowing and savings?

Recent studies by Allen (1985), Malcomson and Spinnewyn (1985), and Fudenberg et al. (1986) show that this may indeed be the case. More specifically, if one goes to the other extreme and assumes that the agent can access capital markets freely and on the same interest terms as the principal, then long-term contracts will be no better than a sequence of short-term contracts in the (independently) repeated model.

For instance, Allen noted that if there is no discounting, then one can simply appeal to Yaari's (1976) early work on consumption under uncertainty to conclude that a first-best solution can be achieved by having the agent rent the production technology from the principal at a fixed price. The agent, by borrowing or saving, need not be concerned about fluctuations in income, since they can be smoothed out at no cost. In this case self-insurance is perfect and risk carries no premium.

Allen also studies the finite horizon case, but in a pure insurance context [specifically, Townsend's (1982) model], which is simpler than the agency model we have been discussing. Here also he finds that long-term contracts do not dominate short-term contracts. The same results for the agency model are established by Malcomson and Spinnewyn and by Fudenberg et al. These two papers differ in that the former assumes that the agent's borrowing and saving decisions can be verified (and hence his consumption can be controlled contractually), whereas the latter treats these decisions as private to the agent. The basic idea of the argument is very similar, however. The key observation is that long-term contracts can be duplicated by a sequence of short-term contracts by rearranging the payment stream to the agent without altering its net present value along any realized path. Roughly speaking, the rearrangement works so that the principal clears his balance with the agent in utility terms each period. Because there is a capital market, the timing of payments does not matter. The agent returns to the consumption stream implied by the long-term contract by borrowing and saving appropriately.

Of course, the assumption that the agent can borrow and save freely in the capital market is rather unrealistic. (In addition, the Fudenberg et al. model asumes that the agent can consume negative amounts, which certainly is unrealistic.) Nevertheless, the models do make clear that one should not rush to the conclusion that long-term contracts, at least in repeated settings, have substantial benefits; in some situations, the insights of the one-period models remain unaltered with the introduction of dynamics. More importantly, however, these findings suggest that – because we do observe long-term relationships and long-term contracts – some forces other than income smoothing are likely to be behind the benefits.

There are many potential forces one could think of. Informational linkages between periods are discussed in Fudenberg et al., and some other reasons will be taken up in Section 3. Here we want to stress that when contingences are hard or impossible to verify, so that explicit contracts cannot be easily enforced, long-term relationships are likely to provide major advantages. They can implicitly (via reputation effects) support contracts that may be infeasible to duplicate in short-term relationships. Bull (1985) offers a model of this variety, which we will come back to in Section 3. Radner's and Rubinstein's models are also best interpreted in this fashion; both have self-enforcing equilibria that do not require outside enforcement. Lazear's (1979) model on mandatory retirement is in the same vein. Lazear argues that age-earnings profiles slope upward [as an abundance of empirical evidence corroborates; see, however, Abraham and Farber (1985) for contradicting evidence], because that way incentives for work are maintained over the agent's employment horizon. The implication is that termination of employment should be mandatory, because marginal product will be below pay at later stages in the career. Although the argument needs some refinement, Lazear's model serves well as an illustration of how introducing dynamics can yield additional predictions into the basic agency set-up.

As a related example of reputation modeling, let us consider Fama's (1980) argument that incentive problems, particularly managerial incentive problems, are exaggerated in the agency literature, because in reality time will help alleviate them. His reasoning is different from Radner's and Rubinstein's in that it focuses on the power of the market to police managerial behavior, rather than on the theory of supergames. Fama coins the term "ex post settling up" for the automatic mechanism by which managers' market values, and hence their incomes, are adjusted over time in response to realized performance. If there is little or no discounting, then the manager will be held fully responsible for his deeds through his lifetime income stream and, Fama claims, induced to perform in the stockholders' interest.

Fama's intuitive argument has been formalized in Holmström (1982b). We will sketch the construction partly to indicate that the first-best result hinges on very special assumptions, but also because the model offers the simplest illustration of reputation formation and suggests some interesting extensions.

Consider a risk-neutral manager who operates in a competitive market for managerial labor. Assume the market can follow the manager's performance over time by observing his periodic output. At the same time, assume that the manager's fee cannot be made contingent on output, because enforcing third parties cannot verify the output. Therefore the manager will be paid his expected marginal product in each period.

Obviously, if the world only lasted for one period, the manager would have no incentives to put out extra effort. But if he wishes to stay in the profession longer, matters are different. Prospective employers will follow the manager's performance and forecast his future potential from past behavior. Logically, this means that there must be some characteristic of the manager that is not fully known to the market and that is being signaled by past performance. For managers, competence or talent is a natural candidate for what is being signaled, though many other alternatives could also be considered.

Let us now see how the uncertainty about the manager's competence will induce effort even though there is no explicit contract.

In the simplest setting the manager controls a linear technology:

$$x_t = a_t + \eta_t + \theta_t,$$

where x_t is output in period t, a_t is the manager's effort, η_t is a quantified measure of managerial competence, and θ_t is a driftless i.i.d. sequence of stochastic shocks. Managerial competence progresses over time according to a simple auto-regressive process:

$$\eta_{t+1} = \eta_t + \epsilon_t, \tag{1.17}$$

which is independent of the θ sequence.

In each period the manager will be paid his expected marginal product. This is the sum of his expected competence as assessed on the basis of past performance and the value of his effort a_t. Because the market is assumed to know the utility function of the manager, it can forecast the manager's choice of a_t.

To find out what the manager will do in equilibrium and what he will be paid, one has to solve a rational expectations equilibrium. This is relatively easy if the shock terms θ and ϵ are normal and the prior on competence is also normal. Then the market will be monitoring a standard normal learning process [see DeGroot (1970)] in which assessments about competence are updated based on a weighted average of present beliefs and the last observation of output. If we denote by m_t the expected value of η_t based on history, the m_t progresses as:

$$m_{t+1} = \alpha_t m_t + (1 - \alpha_t)(x_t - a_t). \tag{1.18}$$

Note that the market in updating beliefs about competence will subtract from output the present level of effort, which it can infer in equilibrium. This filters out time-varying transient effects.

The weights α_t are deterministic functions of time, and converge to some equilibrium value $\alpha \in [0, 1]$ in the long run. The value of α depends on the distribution of the stochastic shock terms. If competence remains constant (i.e., $\mathrm{var}(\epsilon_t) = 0$) then $\alpha = 1$. In general α is smaller the more noisy the competence process is relative to the noise in the output process; that is, the higher the ratio is of signal to noise.

Given that the market updates beliefs according to (1.18) and pays the manager in proportion to m_t each period t, it is easy to calculate the return from managerial effort in period t. In a stationary state the marginal return will be given by

$$k = \beta(1 - \alpha)/(1 - \alpha\beta), \tag{1.19}$$

where β is the manager's discount factor and α is the aforementioned long-run value of the updating weight. From this we can see that if β is close to 1, then marginal returns to effort will be close to 1 both in the manager's objective function and the production technology, so incentives will be right. In general, though, effort will fall short of first-best. It will be lower the lower the discount factor is and the lower the ratio is between the variances of ϵ and θ – that is, the more noise there is in the output process and the less innovation there is in the competence process. This is all in line with intuition. If output is very noisy, returns from effort will be distributed further into the future and will have less value. On the other hand, variation in competence will raise the need to reestablish one's reputation and therefore increase effort. Without (1.17), the manager's effort would converge to zero deterministically.

As in the case of Radner's and Rubinstein's models, the result that first-best can sometimes be achieved is of little interest per se. It requires very special and implausible assumptions, in particular that the manager is risk-neutral and does not discount future payoffs. The main point with the model is rather to illustrate that reputation can indeed enforce an implicit contract of some form, when learning about characteristics is a key factor as it often would seem to be. In the particular example, the implicit contract performs exactly like an explicit contract would (in a world with known competence) if that contract were of the form $s(x) = kx + b$, where k is given in (1.19). It is important to note, however, that when relying on reputation effects (at least as determined in the market) there is little freedom to design the contract in desirable ways.

Wolfson (1985) has conducted an empirical study of the returns to reputation in the market for general partners of oil-drilling ventures. The results conform broadly with the implications of the example. In the market for oil-drilling ventures myopic behavior would dictate that general partners complete fewer wells than limited partners desire (because of the tax code). However, because new ventures come up frequently and new partnerships are formed, one might expect general partners to take into account their reputation and complete more wells than would be optimal in the short run. Indeed, Wolfson finds statistically significant evidence for that to be the case. Reputation is priced in the market much as in the model described. The results correspond to a case where $k < 1$, because Wolfson also finds that residual incentive problems remain and that these are reflected in the price of the shares of limited partners.

These empirical findings give reason to explore further the workings of reputation and learning. The general idea can be pursued in many directions and some interesting work has already been done. Gibbons (1985) has considered what organizations can do to align reputation incentives more closely with true productivity. It is evident from the model described that there need not be a very close relationship, particularly in the early periods, between the returns to reputation for a manager and his present marginal product. Indeed, if we think of young managers in lower positions, their returns from effort may vastly exceed the actual product of what they do, because the future value of being considered competent multiplies in general through enhanced responsibility. One way of coping with the problem, suggested by Gibbons, is to control the flow of information about performance potential so that the initial impact of performance is diminished. Perhaps the phenomenon of young professionals joining larger partnerships before establishing their own firms can be seen as a way of protecting oneself against overly strong reactions by the market if mistakes happen in the early career.

Another paper that elaborates on this simple learning model is Aron (1984). She uses the learning effects to derive a number of implications concerning the correlation between the growth rate of firms, the degree of diversification within firms, and the size of firms.

Although our example supported the common intuition that incentive problems are alleviated by long-term considerations, it is important to stress that this is by no means true universally. In fact, career concerns can themselves be a source of incentive problems. For instance, in Holmström and Ricart-Costa (1986) a model is analyzed in which incongruities in risk-taking between managers and shareholders arise purely because of reputation effects. The reason is that managers look upon investments as experiments that reveal information about their competence, while shareholders of course view them in terms of financial returns. The main point is that there is no reason for a project's human capital return to be closely aligned with its financial return; hence the problem requires explicit incentive alignment. For those who distrust incentive models that rely on effort aversion, such a model provides a new channel for analyzing managerial risk-taking incentives.[14]

Finally, we want to mention the work of Murphy (1986) as an example of how dynamics can help discriminate between competing theories of compensation. Murphy compares two hypotheses for why age–earnings profiles tend to be upward-sloping. One is the earlier mentioned model of Lazear. The other theory suggests that the upward slope comes from learning about productivity and the contracting process associated with insurance against that risk [see e.g. Harris and Holmström (1982)]. Murphy argues that if the incentive hypothesis were true then the variance in individual earnings should increase with tenure due to income smoothing. The reverse should be true if the learning hypothesis held, because then the effects of performance information are strongest in the early years. Murphy tests these competing positions on panel data for executive compensation drawn from prospectuses. His results are rather inconclusive, perhaps because both effects are really present. But the main point is that in principle dynamic models allow discrimination that is plainly unavailable from single-period studies.

1.8   *Summary and conclusions*

Despite the length of this section we have covered only a few dimensions of the extensive literature on principal–agent models. Before summing up

---

[14] A related reputation model concerning risk-taking, which derives very interesting predictions about the nature of debt contracts and credit rating in capital markets, is in D. Diamond (1985).

we want to mention two important omissions. One is the lack of examples of Hidden Information Models, which have played a visible role in the literature, often under the name of Mechanism Design [see Harris and Townsend (1981) and Myerson (1979) for seminal contributions and Green (1985) for a unified look at the field]. We will partly make up for this omission in Section 2, where a model of hidden information is analyzed in connection with labor contracting. The mechanism design approach has been quite successful in explaining a range of institutions that are beyond the scope of standard theory, and it has also offered insights into normative problems such as taxation [Mirrlees (1971)], auction design [Harris and Raviv (1981), Myerson (1981), and Maskin and Riley (1984)], and regulation [Baron and Myerson (1982), Baron and Besanko (1984), and Laffont and Tirole (1986)]. In the same way as the models we have discussed here, these models are plagued by an excessive sensitivity to informational assumptions, which makes it hard to go beyond qualitative conclusions.

The other major omission is that we have not discussed at all the general equilibrium effects from contracting, an area in which Stiglitz has been particularly active. As Stiglitz has noted in a variety of different contexts [see, e.g., Arnott and Stiglitz (1985)], the imperfections of second-best contracts will have external effects that may be important. The general idea, familiar from second-best theory, can be described as follows. In all economies, contracting between two parties will have some equilibrium effect on the rest of the economy. However, in the idealized Arrow-Debreu world, equilibrium occurs at a social optimum and so the impact of marginal changes in a bilateral contract will have zero social costs. In contrast, when we are in a second-best world (for whatever reason), marginal changes in contracts will have a first-order effect on the social welfare function, which is not accounted for by the contracting parties.[15] Perhaps one relevant example would be the consequences of nominal contracts in one part of the economy on the use of indexed contracts in other parts.

Naturally, such externalities could give reason for government intervention. However, one should be careful in making sure that there is an improving policy that acts solely on information that the government has available. As a modeler it is easy to spot improvements, because the modeler sees all the relevant information. But that does not imply automatically that the government can improve things, particularly if the more stringent notions of efficiency that are associated with incomplete infor-

---

[15] A somewhat different dimension of the same problem appears when a party contracts with many independent agents in a decentralized fashion. This has been recently looked at by Cremer and Riordan (1986), but it deserves much more attention.

mation models are applied. Operational welfare schemes in this sense seem to have been little explored in the literature to date.

To summarize:

1. In reduced form all agency models have the agent choose from a family of distributions over observable variables, such as output. A key simplification in Hidden Action Models is to assume that the agent controls a one-dimensional family of distributions. This leads to a simple and intuitive characterization of an optimal scheme. One-dimensionality does not refer here to any economic variable, like effort, but to the set of distributions that the agent can choose from. Understanding this is important for resolving the confusions associated with the validity of the characterization of the optimal rule, which is sometimes (but misleadingly) referred to as the validity of the first-order approach.

2. The main insight of the basic Hidden Action Model is that the optimal incentive scheme looks like one based on an inference about the agent's action from observable signals. This implies that the optimal scheme is highly sensitive to the information content of the technology that the agent controls, which has only loose ties with the physical properties of that technology. Consequently, fiddling with the information technology will accommodate almost any form of incentive schedule and the theory is really without predictive content in this regard.

What does have some predictive content, however, is the result that a contract should use all relevant information that is available up to a sufficient statistic. Among other things, it leads to statements about the use of relative performance evaluation that seem to match empirical evidence at least broadly.

3. However, the extreme sensitivity to informational variables that comes across from this type of modeling is at odds with reality. Real-world schemes are simpler than the theory would dictate and surprisingly uniform across a wide range of circumstances (e.g., linear schemes are quite common in a variety of situations). The conclusion is that something other than informational issues drives whatever regularities one might observe. One possibility that has recently been suggested is that the usual agency models are overly simplistic and fail to account for the need to have schemes that perform well in a variety of circumstances – that is, schemes that are robust. We gave one example of a model in which robustness issues lead to linear schemes. It seems that research in this direction could have high payoffs in the future.

Another reason why schemes in reality are simpler and less sensitive to environmental differences is that exotic contracts are hard to evaluate in terms of both their implied performance and their value for the parties involved. This is not something which we addressed, because it seems to fall outside the common Bayesian paradigm; but that is not to say it is unimportant. Research along these lines may also have high payoffs.

4. The common Hidden Action Models are rather weak predictively. One reason is that complex incentive schemes make it hard to say anything about distributional choices. The other reason is that the actions in the model are not observable economic variables. (In this regard Hidden Information Models are more useful, because actions - e.g., levels of investment or employment - are usually observable; see Section 2.) Modeling efforts should be directed more toward including interesting economic quantities that focus on allocational consequences of agency. Robustness arguments that predict simpler schemes should be helpful in this endeavor, as indicated in Section 1.6.

5. Another useful direction for sharpening predictions from agency models is to go to dynamic formulations. These bring to bear time series and panel data that allow discriminations that are impossible to make in static models. Dynamic models also bring attention to reputation effects and long-term explicit and implicit contracting that may well be at the center of real-world incentive problems.

2   Labor contracts

One of the first applications of contract theory was to the case of contracts between firms and workers [the seminal papers are by Azariadis (1975), Baily (1974), and Gordon (1974)]. Section 2 is concerned with this work and various extensions, including the introduction of asymmetric information and macroeconomic applications. We begin with the Azariadis–Baily–Gordon model itself. [For an excellent recent survey of labor contract theory with a rather different focus from the present one, see Rosen (1985).]

2.1   The Azariadis–Baily–Gordon (ABG) model

The ABG model was developed to explain non-Walrasian employment decisions, particularly layoffs, and to understand deviations between wages and the marginal product of labor. It is based on the idea that a firm offers its risk-averse workers wage and employment insurance via a long-term contract.

The model can be described as follows. Imagine a single firm that has a long-term relationship with a group of workers.[16] Presumably a lock-in

[16] On the empirical importance of such relationships, see Hall (1980).

effect of some sort explains why the relationship should be long-term, although this is not modeled explicitly. To simplify, assume that the relationship lasts two periods. At date 0, the firm and workers sign a contract while employment and production occur at date 1. ABG stress the idea of an implicit contract; we postpone discussion of this until Section 3.4 and rely on the contract being explicit and legally binding.

Let the firm's date-1 revenue be $f(s, L)$, where s represents an exogenous demand or supply shock, and L is total employment at date 1. Assume that the date-0 workforce consists of m identical workers, where m is given.[17] Each worker has an (indirect) von Neumann–Morgenstern utility function $U(I, \ell; p)$, where I represents income or wages received from the firm, ℓ is employment in the firm, and p refers to a vector of consumption goods prices. We shall suppose that p is constant and therefore suppress it in what follows.[18] We assume that $U_I > 0$, $U_\ell < 0$, and U is concave in I and ℓ with $U_{II} < 0$ (i.e., workers are risk-averse). The firm, on the other hand, is supposed to be risk-neutral. We shall assume that ℓ is a continuous variable, in contrast to ABG who suppose that it equals 0 or 1.

In the ABG model, the state s is taken to be publicly observable at date 1, although unknown to both parties at date 0. In this case, a contract can be contingent in the sense of making I and ℓ functions of s: $I = I(s)$, $\ell = \ell(s)$. Since ℓ is smooth and U is concave in ℓ, it is desirable to have work sharing at date 1; that is, $\ell(s) = (L(s)/m)$ (so this version of ABG does not explain layoffs; see, however, Section 2.4B). Therefore, an optimal date-0 contract solves:

$$\text{Max } E_s[f(s, m\ell(s)) - mI(s)] \quad \text{subject to } E_s[U(I(s), \ell(s))] \geq \bar{U}, \quad (2.1)$$

where both expectations are taken with respect to the objective probability distribution of s, which is assumed to be common knowledge at date 0. We are adopting the assumption that the firm gets all the surplus from the contract while the workers are held down to their date-0 reservation expected utility levels $\bar{U}$. Nothing that follows depends on this ex ante division of the surplus, however.

The solution to (2.1) is very simple. Under the usual interiority assumptions, it is characterized by

$$\frac{\partial f}{\partial L}(s, m\ell(s)) = -\left(\frac{\partial U}{\partial \ell}(I(s), \ell(s)) \middle/ \frac{\partial U}{\partial I}(I(s), \ell(s))\right) \quad \text{for all } s, \quad (2.2)$$

[17] In a more general model, the size of the workforce would be a choice variable.
[18] Two assumptions are embodied here. First, that p is independent of the shock s hitting the firm; and, second, that the firm and workers are sufficiently small that their actions do not affect prices. We shall maintain both assumptions throughout Sections 2 and 3.

$$\frac{\partial U}{\partial I}(I(s), \ell(s)) = \lambda \quad \text{for all } s, \tag{2.3}$$

$$E_s U(I(s), \ell(s)) = \bar{U}, \tag{2.4}$$

where λ is a Lagrange multiplier. Equation (2.2) tells us that the marginal rate of substitution between consumption and employment equals the marginal rate of transformation in each state; (2.3) tells us that a worker's marginal utility of income is constant across states. It is the condition for optimal insurance between a risk-averse agent and a risk-neutral agent. [Note that (2.3) implies that if $\ell(s_1) = \ell(s_2)$ then $I(s_1) = I(s_2)$; that is, wages vary only if employment does.]

Several observations can be made. First, it follows from (2.2) that employment decisions will be ex post Pareto efficient in each state. Hence to emphasize what is by now well known, the ABG model does not explain inefficient employment levels. Although there was some initial confusion about this result, it is not exactly surprising given that an ex ante optimal contract should exploit all the gains from trade ex post (under symmetric information). Employment levels, however, although efficient, are not generally the same as in a standard Walrasian spot market, where the wage $w(s)$ in state s satisfies

$$\frac{\partial f}{\partial L}(s, m\ell(s)) = w(s) = -\frac{\partial U}{\partial \ell}(w(s)\ell(s), \ell(s)) \bigg/ \frac{\partial U}{\partial I}(w(s)\ell(s), \ell(s)). \tag{2.5}$$

The point is that the possibility of income transfers across states permits a divergence between $(I(s)/\ell(s))$ and $w(s) = (\partial f/\partial L)(s, m\ell(s))$. In fact, if labor is a normal good and the Walrasian labor supply is upward-sloping, Rosen (1985) has pointed out that employment will generally vary more in a contractual setting than in a Walrasian spot market.[19]

An important special case is where labor causes no disutility for a worker per se, but simply deprives him of outside earning opportunities at date 1. This can be represented by

$$U(I, \ell) = \hat{U}(I + R(\bar{\ell} - \ell)), \tag{2.6}$$

where $\bar{\ell}$ is the worker's total endowment of labor and R is the wage in alternative date-1 employment [in (2.6), labor is neither normal nor inferior]. Equations (2.2) and (2.5) both then become

---

[19] The reason is the following. In a spot market, a worker's incentive to work hard in a good state where the wage rate is high (the substitution effect) will be offset by his desire to consume a lot of leisure given that his income is high (the income effect); and conversely in a bad state. In a contractual setting, the income effect is reduced in size because the firm provides income insurance across different states of the world.

$$\frac{\partial f}{\partial L}(s, m\ell(s)) = R; \tag{2.7}$$

that is, employment levels will be exactly the same in a contract as in a Walrasian spot market. Equation (2.3), on the other hand, implies that

$$I(s) + R(\bar{\ell} - \ell(s)) = \text{a constant.} \tag{2.8}$$

That is, optimal insurance leads to the equalization of a worker's (real) income across states of the world (relative to the prices p), a very different outcome from what one would see in a spot market.

The ability to explain the divergence between workers' wages and their marginal (revenue) product of labor is the principal achievement of the ABG model. In fact, the model provides a striking explanation of sticky (real) wages or incomes, which is in notable contrast to that provided by, say, disequilibrium theory.[20]

Let us examine the underlying assumptions of the ABG model. A key assumption is that firms are less risk-averse than workers, and are therefore prepared to act as insurers. To the extent that the shock s is idiosyncratic to the firm (we have essentially assumed this anyway in regarding goods prices p as independent of s), this is reasonable since it is probably easier for a firm's owners to diversify away idiosyncratic profit risk via the stock market than it is for workers to diversify away human capital risk. However, the assumption is less convincing in a macroeconomic setting where firms' shocks are correlated.[21]

Even when the shock is idiosyncratic, it is not obvious that a worker must look to his own firm for insurance. Why not go to an insurance company? In the ABG world, where s is publicly observable, there should be no difficulty in making payments to and from the insurance company conditional on s. However, if the model is complicated, some justification for the firm as insurer can be given.

First, it may be the case that, while s is observable to the firm and the workers, it is not observable to the insurance company. If the insurance company relies on a worker to report s, the worker will, of course, have an incentive to announce an s that maximizes his transfer from the insurance company. Now it is possible that the insurance company can learn s by getting independent reports on it from the firm and the workers, but there is the danger that the firm and workers may collude. The whole pro-

---

[20] We have assumed that the firm is risk-neutral, but the main results generalize to the case of firm risk aversion. In particular, as long as the firm is sufficiently less risk-averse than the workers, workers' incomes will be stabilized relative to the spot market outcome. Note also that equation (2.2) continues to hold when the firm is risk-averse.

[21] Although the Knightian argument can be made that entrepreneurs are, by self-selection, less risk-averse than workers. For a formalization, see Kihlstrom and Laffont (1979).

cess may involve considerable costs relative to the case of insurance by the firm.

In fact, to provide optimal insurance, it is not necessary that the insurance company observe s, only that it observe wages $I(s)$ and employment $\ell(s)$. However, even if it can observe these variables, new problems arise if some aspect of a worker's performance is unobservable to the insurance company. For example, suppose that to make employment productive it is necessary that a worker exert effort, e. Then the optimal risk-sharing contract would insure a worker's wage subject to the worker exerting effort. If the insurance company – which cannot observe s or e – offers insurance, the worker may exert no effort and claim that his low wage was a result of a bad s. Again this problem is reduced if the firm, which does observe e, acts as insurer.

The reader may wonder how, if s and e are not observable to outsiders such as insurance companies, a contract between the firm and workers making I and ℓ functions of s and e can be enforced. This is an important question, to which two answers can be given. First, it may be the case that the firm and workers each have enough evidence to establish to an outsider what s and e really are; that is, in the event of a dispute between them "the truth will come out" (whereas in a three-party contract involving an insurance company, collusion between the firm and the workers may prevent this). Second, if the contract is implicit rather than explicit, then it may be enforced by reputational considerations; that is, the firm will not deny that the worker exerted effort if he really did, because this would ruin its reputation with future workers (for more on this, see Section 3.4).

2.2   The possibility of worker quits

The ABG model is based on the idea that firms insure workers against fluctuations in their real income. This means that workers will receive more than their marginal (revenue) product in some states and less in others. A difficulty that has been raised with this is that a worker may quit in the latter states – that is, simply walk away from the contract. This will, of course, be a problem only if the worker's marginal product outside the firm is comparable to that inside; that is, if the lock-in effect that is responsible for the long-term relationship in the first place is small. If it is small, however, the insurance element of the contract will be put under severe pressure.

To see this, suppose that there is a single worker ($m = 1$) who can work either in the firm ($L = 1$) or outside ($L = 0$). To simplify, assume that the worker's marginal (equals average) product, denoted by s, is the same inside and outside the firm (i.e., there is no lock-in at all), and that the worker cares only about total income: $U = \hat{U}(I)$ [as in (2.6)]. Then, in order to stop the worker from quitting at date 1, the firm must pay him at least s in every state. However, in order to break even on the worker, the firm cannot pay him more than s. The conclusion is that the firm will pay the worker exactly his marginal product in each state, which is, of course, the spot market solution.

In this extreme case of no lock-in, then, the insurance element is completely destroyed. Holmström (1983) has argued that this conclusion is no longer valid when employment and production take place at more than one date. The argument is the following. In the above example, the firm could provide complete insurance at date 1 and at the same time avoid quits by agreeing to pay the worker $\bar{s} = \text{Max } s$ in every state. Of course, the firm takes a loss on this, but if the worker also has a nonstochastic productivity s_0 at date 0, the firm can offset this loss by paying the worker less than s_0 at date 0. There is a cost of doing this because, assuming that the worker cannot borrow, his consumption path will be more steeply sloped over time than he would like. [If the worker's utility function is $\hat{U}(I_0) + \delta\hat{U}(I_1)$, where $1/\delta - 1$ is the market rate of interest, then the first-best contract would have $I_0 = I_1(s) = \bar{I}$ (say) for all s; i.e., complete income smoothing.] It is easy to show that when this cost is traded off optimally against the insurance benefit, the outcome is incomplete insurance of the following sort: The firm puts a floor on date-1 income by guaranteeing the worker at least $\hat{s} < \bar{s}$; however, in states where $s > \hat{s}$, the firm agrees to pay the worker his full marginal product s.

One benefit of the quit model is that it provides an explanation of the back-end loading of earnings (the worker gets less than his marginal product at date 0 and at least his marginal product at date 1).[22] However, the model is based on a number of fairly strong assumptions. First, it is supposed that, while the firm is bound to the contract, the worker can simply walk away. One may ask why the contract cannot specify either that a worker cannot quit at all, or (less extremely) that a quitting worker must compensate the firm by paying an "exit fee." In answering this question, some have appealed to the idea that the courts will not enforce involuntary servitude of this sort (although note that we are really talking about voluntary servitude insofar as the worker presumably agrees to the contract at date 0). While historically this may have been the case, it is interesting to note that attitudes seem to be changing; the use of exit fees (e.g., repayment of training or transportation costs by leaving workers) seems to be on the increase, with recent indications being that the courts are prepared to enforce them (*New York Times*, October 30, 1985). In

---

[22] There is an obvious parallel between Holmström's model and Becker's (1964) analysis of worker training.

particular, there seems to be a move to apply to labor contracts the basic principle of common law that the victim of a breach of contract is entitled to compensatory damages – that is, to be put in as good a position as if the breach had not occurred. In the quit model, compensatory damages correspond to the quitting worker paying the firm $s - I(s)$ in state s, where $I(s)$ is his wage if employed by the firm. In this case, however, the worker never desires to quit and the first-best $I_0 = I_1(s) = \bar{I}$ can be achieved.[23]

The quit model also assumes, like the ABG model, that the firm must provide workers' insurance. We have given some justifications for this above, but they become less plausible when the lock-in effect is small. The reason is that, if s is the amount that the worker can earn inside or outside the firm, the assumption that an insurance company cannot observe s is perhaps less convincing (although there may still be problems in enforcing a contract based on s if s is not "verifiable"; see Section 3). Even if outsiders cannot observe s, the worker could still rely on the firm for insurance by borrowing a fixed amount from a bank and depositing it with the firm; the worker would receive it back only if he did not quit (i.e., the worker could post a bond). Such an arrangement would again achieve the first-best, although it may of course stretch to the limit the assumption that the firm will not default on its part of the contract.[24] (Note that this arrangement does involve a form of back-loading.)

One case where these criticisms do not apply is where the worker can simply "disappear." If this is so, then the firm knows that it will never be able to collect any exit fee and no bank will be prepared to lend to the worker. Another reason for the absence of exit fees or bond posting is that the worker may sometimes quit for reasons other than a high alternative wage; for example, work in the firm may become intolerable or the worker may become sick. These states are likely to be bad for the worker and so for reasons of risk-aversion he will be unwilling to forfeit a substantial amount in them. (We are assuming that the reason for quitting is not publicly observable and so the exit fee cannot be made contingent upon it.) Considerations such as these seem likely to lead to a not insignificant complication of the model, however, and it is unclear how robust the back-end loading result is to their introduction.

2.3   Asymmetric information

Let us return to the case where all parties to the contract are bound. As we have seen, the ABG model can explain sticky (real) wages or incomes,

---

[23] It is also worth pointing out that various forms of disguised exit fees may actually be quite common; consider, e.g., non-vested pensions.

[24] Note that deposits are used in some contexts; consider, for instance, rental deposits.

but not ex post inefficient employment. Because of this, various attempts have been made to enrich the ABG model. An important development has been the introduction of asymmetric information. The first set of models along these lines considered the case where the firm's revenue shock s is observed only by the firm at date 1 [see Calvo and Phelps (1977) and Hall and Lilien (1979)]. This "hidden information" assumption, as Kenneth Arrow has termed it, has force when the party with private information is risk-averse.[25] It is this supposition that underlies the models of Azariadis (1983) and Grossman and Hart (1981, 1983b): The firm is identified with its risk-averse manager.

A consequence of managerial risk aversion is that it is no longer optimal for the firm to provide workers with complete income insurance as in the basic ABG model; rather, the manager will now want to obtain some insurance himself. The manager's ability to obtain insurance, however, is limited by his private information. For example, an insurance contract that pays the manager $\$\alpha > 0$ in state one and taxes the manager $\$\beta > 0$ in state two cannot be implemented if the insurer must rely on the manager to report which of the two states has occurred (the manager will always report state one). However, the manager's incentive to report the wrong state can be lessened by introducing a production inefficiency: The manager will be less inclined to report state one if, as well as receiving $\$\alpha$, he must choose a production plan that is inefficient and (moreover) relatively unprofitable if the true state is indeed two. We shall see that the second-best optimal insurance contract includes production inefficiencies of this kind; furthermore, under certain conditions the inefficiencies take the form of underemployment of labor in bad states of the world.

It turns out that the case where the manager and workers must provide each other with insurance is quite complicated to analyze. A considerable simplification is possible, however, if it is supposed that each group can get insurance from a risk-neutral third party (this is, of course, a departure from the idea that the firm has a comparative advantage in insuring the workers; or vice versa). Although the existence of such a third party may at first sight seem farfetched, it can be argued that in the case of a public company the firm's shareholders play this role, acting as a financial wedge between the manager and the workers (moreover, risk-neutrality of the shareholders may be reasonable to the extent that they hold well-diversified portfolios).[26]

If workers can get insurance from a third party, the long-term contract between the firm and workers becomes much less important, and in fact a simple case (which we follow) is where this contract is ignored altogether,

---

[25] If the party with private information is risk-neutral, the first-best can be achieved by making this party the residual income claimant.

[26] The analysis below follows Hart (1983).

with the firm being assumed to make all input purchases in the date-1 spot market. That is, we now focus on a risk-averse manager with private information, who insures himself with a risk-neutral third party and buys all his inputs in the date-1 spot market. (Below we discuss the implications of putting the worker–firm contract back into the analysis, particularly when the firm has a comparative advantage in insuring the workers.)

The main implications of asymmetric information can be understood from the special case where there are only two states of the world [we follow Holmström and Weiss (1985)]. We now interpret f to be the manager's benefit function (measured in dollars). This benefit is supposed to be private; that is, it does not show up in the firm's accounts and so payments cannot be conditioned on it. We write $f = f(s, L)$, where we are now more general in allowing $L \geq 0$ to be a vector of inputs or managerial decisions. It is assumed that, while s is observed at date 1 only by the manager, L (which is chosen after s is observed) is publicly observable. It is in fact convenient to regard f as the manager's net benefit in state s after all inputs have been purchased in the date-1 spot market.

Let the two states be $s = s_1, s_2$ with probabilities π_1, π_2 respectively ($\pi_1, \pi_2 > 0$, $\pi_1 + \pi_2 = 1$). The manager signs a contract with a risk-neutral third party. The contract says that in state s_i, $i = 1, 2$, the third party will pay the manager I_i and the manager must choose L_i. An optimal contract solves

$$\text{Max } \pi_2 V(f(s_2, L_2) + I_2) + \pi_1 V(f(s_1, L_1) + I_1), \qquad (2.9)$$

subject to the following constraints:

$$f(s_2, L_2) + I_2 \geq f(s_2, L_1) + I_1,$$
$$f(s_1, L_1) + I_1 \geq f(s_1, L_2) + I_2,$$
$$\pi_2 I_2 + \pi_1 I_1 \leq 0.$$

Here V is the manager's von Neumann–Morgenstern utility function, where $V' > 0$, $V'' < 0$. The third constraint says that the third party is prepared to participate in the contract (we give the firm all the surplus from the transaction). The first and second constraints are the well-known truth-telling constraints [see, e.g., Myerson (1979)]. Because the third party cannot observe s directly it must rely on the manager to report s. Constraints 1 and 2 say that the manager will report $s = s_2$ when s_2 occurs and $s = s_1$ when s_1 occurs.[27]

Another interpretation of the contract is that, instead of asking him to report s, the contract gives the manager the choice of the pairs (I_1, L_1)

---

[27] A more general contract would make the outcome (I_i, L_i) depend stochastically on the report s_i. Such random contracts are more complicated to analyze and, at least for the two-state case considered here, do not lead to substantially different results. On random schemes, see Maskin and Riley (1984) and Moore (1985).

and $(I_2, \mathbf{L}_2)$. The first and second constraints then say that the manager will choose $(I_i, \mathbf{L}_i)$ in state s_i.

We shall assume that s_2 is the good state and s_1 the bad state, in the sense that total benefits are higher in s_2 than in s_1:

$$f(s_2, \mathbf{L}) \geq f(s_1, \mathbf{L}) \quad \text{for all } \mathbf{L} \geq 0, \text{ with strict inequality if } \mathbf{L} \neq 0. \quad (2.10)$$

We suppose also that

$f(s, \mathbf{L})$ is strictly concave in $\mathbf{L}$, and the (unique) maximizer $\mathbf{L}(s)$ of $f(s, \mathbf{L})$ exists and satisfies
$$\mathbf{L}(s) \neq 0 \text{ and } \mathbf{L}_1^* \equiv \mathbf{L}(s_1) \neq \mathbf{L}(s_2) \equiv \mathbf{L}_2^*. \quad (2.11)$$

That is, the maximizer of $f(s, \mathbf{L})$ is sensitive to s. Statements (2.10) and (2.11) imply immediately that the first-best – the solution to (2.9) without the truth-telling constraints – cannot be achieved under asymmetric information. The first-best has the property that $\mathbf{L}$ is chosen to maximize f in each state and the manager is perfectly insured; that is,

$$f(s_2, \mathbf{L}_2) + I_2 = f(s_1, \mathbf{L}_1) + I_1, \quad (2.12)$$

where

$$\pi_2 I_2 + \pi_1 I_1 = 0 \quad \text{and} \quad \mathbf{L}_2 = \mathbf{L}_2^*, \ \mathbf{L}_1 = \mathbf{L}_1^*.$$

But given (2.10)–(2.11), this violates the first truth-telling constraint (i.e., the manager will *under-report* s in state s_2).[28] This observation suggests that only the first truth-telling constraint will be binding in the solution to the second-best. This turns out to be true, as is proved in the appendix. (It is interesting to note that in the two-state case we can establish this even in the absence of a Spencian single-crossing property on marginal benefit.) It follows that the first-order conditions for (2.9) are

$$\pi_2 V_2' - \mu \pi_2 + \lambda = 0,$$

$$(\pi_2 V_2' + \lambda) \frac{\partial f}{\partial L_k}(s_2, \mathbf{L}_2) = 0 \quad \text{for all } k,$$

$$\pi_1 V_1' - \mu \pi_1 - \lambda = 0,$$

$$\pi_1 V_1' \frac{\partial f}{\partial L_k}(s_1, \mathbf{L}_1) - \lambda \frac{\partial f}{\partial L_k}(s_2, \mathbf{L}_1) = 0 \quad \text{for all } k, \quad (2.13)$$

where $V_i \equiv V(f(s_i, \mathbf{L}_i) + I_i)$, and similarly V_i'; $\lambda \geq 0$ is the Lagrange multiplier for the first constraint, $\mu \geq 0$ for the third, and the second constraint has a zero multiplier. In fact, $\lambda > 0$ because $\lambda = 0$ gives us the first-best, which we know violates constraint 1.

---

[28] The first-best could be achieved if the manager were risk-neutral, because in this case no insurance is required at all; i.e., $I_1 = I_2 = 0$ and $\mathbf{L}_i = \mathbf{L}(s_i)$, $i = 1, 2$, which satisfies the truth-telling constraints.

From the second equation in (2.13), we see that

$$\frac{\partial f}{\partial L_k}(s_2, \mathbf{L}_2) = 0 \quad \text{for all } k \quad (\text{i.e., } \mathbf{L}_2 = \mathbf{L}_2^*), \tag{2.14}$$

while the third and fourth equations imply that

$$\mu\pi_1 \frac{\partial f}{\partial L_k}(s_1, \mathbf{L}_1) + \lambda\left(\frac{\partial f}{\partial L_k}(s_1, \mathbf{L}_1) - \frac{\partial f}{\partial L_k}(s_2, \mathbf{L}_1)\right) = 0 \quad \text{for all } k. \tag{2.15}$$

It follows that $(\partial f/\partial L_k)(s_1, \mathbf{L}_1)$ can be zero only if $(\partial f/\partial L_k)(s_2, \mathbf{L}_1)$ is also zero. Therefore, we cannot have $(\partial f/\partial L_k)(s_1, \mathbf{L}_1) = 0$ for all k because this would imply that $\mathbf{L}_1 = \mathbf{L}_1^*$ maximizes $f(s_2, \mathbf{L})$, which contradicts (2.11). Hence we have established

$$\mathbf{L}_1 \neq \mathbf{L}_1^*. \tag{2.16}$$

Equations (2.14) and (2.16) comprise the main result of this (two-state) asymmetric information model: The optimal second-best contract has efficient production in the good state, but inefficient production in the bad state. The intuition behind this is that if production in the bad state were efficient, an improvement could be made by perturbing $\mathbf{L}_1$ slightly so as to reduce $f(s_2, \mathbf{L}_1)$; this would have only a second-order effect on $f(s_1, \mathbf{L}_1)$ by the envelope theorem but would relax the truth-telling constraint with a positive multiplier (in contrast, perturbations in $\mathbf{L}_2$ do not relax this constraint). In fact, we will in general have a distortion in *each* of the firm's input decisions in the bad state. For (2.15) tell us that

$$\frac{\partial f}{\partial L_k}(s_1, \mathbf{L}_1) = 0 \Rightarrow \frac{\partial f}{\partial L_k}(s_2, \mathbf{L}_1) = 0; \tag{2.17}$$

that is, L_k is undistorted in the second-best only if its marginal product does not depend on s. To put it another way, in general, *the manager's contract with the third party will constrain every observable dimension of action that the manager takes in the bad state.*

To identify the direction of the distortion in L_k, we must put further restrictions on f. Assume that

$$\frac{\partial f}{\partial L_k}(s_2, \mathbf{L}) > \frac{\partial f}{\partial L_k}(s_1, \mathbf{L}) \quad \text{for all } \mathbf{L}; \tag{2.18}$$

that is, the marginal product of each input is higher in the good state for all $\mathbf{L}$. Then

$$\frac{\partial f}{\partial L_k}(s_1, \mathbf{L}_1) > 0 \quad \text{for all } k, \tag{2.19}$$

since the term after λ in (2.15) is negative, and so the first term must be positive. So (2.19) tells us that each input L_k is underemployed, given other input choices. It does not necessarily follow that $\mathbf{L}_1 < \mathbf{L}_1^*$, although this will be so if either (i) **L** is one-dimensional, (ii) **L** is two-dimensional and $f_{12} > 0$, or (iii) f is Cobb–Douglas. In these cases, we may conclude [using also (2.14)] that *input use varies more across states in the second-best than in the first-best*.

Unfortunately, these results do not generalize easily to the case of more than two states (although there will still generally be distortions). The reason is that it becomes much harder to know which of the many truth-telling constraints will be binding. One case where progress can be made is when there is only one input and, as in (2.18), the marginal product of this input can be ranked across all states. Then only the downward truth-telling constraints are binding and the underemployment result holds. For a discussion of this case, see Hart (1983).

As we have noted, the above model emphasizes the idea of a risk-averse manager trying to get insurance against fluctuations in his net income.[29] In order to maintain the assumption of informational asymmetry it must be supposed that this income is private (it doesn't show up in the firm's accounts). A generalization of the above model would have part of net income observed and part not; for example, $f = f_1 + f_2$, where f_1 is the firm's profit and $-f_2$ represents the manager's effort cost in realizing this profit (or f_2 represents managerial "perks"). The only difference now is that the manager's insurance payment I can be conditioned on f_1 so that f_1 becomes like one of the observable inputs **L**. This case is analyzed in Holmström and Weiss (1985).

The above model completely deemphasizes the role of the long-term contract between the firm and its workers. This can be reintroduced without significant change if it is supposed that the workers, like the manager, can receive wage insurance from a third party; on this, see Hart (1983). If, however, for reasons discussed in Section 2.1, the manager has a comparative advantage in providing insurance, then matters become more complicated. The reason is that the manager is a "flawed" insurer, even if he is risk-neutral, because he has private information. As Chari (1983) and Green and Kahn (1983) have shown, this leads to a further distortion in production. For example, if $U(I, \ell) = \alpha(I) - \ell$, where ℓ is employment and $\alpha'' < 0$, the solution to (2.2)–(2.3) has $I(s) = $ constant and $\ell(s)$ increasing when the manager is risk-neutral. This, however, gives the manager an incentive always to report the highest employment state. That is, in the two-state example of this section, the manager now has an incentive to report s_2 when the true state is s_1. To overcome this, the second-best will have $I(s)$ increasing with $\ell(s)$. In addition, in the two-state example,

---

[29] Some versions of the model assume instead that the manager is risk-neutral but cannot have negative net income [see, e.g., Farmer (1985)]. This amounts to a form of risk aversion, however, since it is equivalent to supposing that negative net income gives the manager a utility of minus infinity.

the optimal second-best contract will have the property that the *second* truth-telling constraint is binding, and (2.2) holds with *equality* in the bad state and the left-hand side of (2.2) is *less* than the right-hand side in the good state. This has been called "overemployment" in the good state, although the inequality in (2.2) does not necessarily imply that $\ell(s_2)$ is higher in the second-best than in the first-best. In fact, this overemployment result holds whenever the manager is risk-neutral, as long as $U(I, \ell)$ has the property that leisure is a normal good [see Chari (1983), Green and Kahn (1983)].

If the manager is risk-averse, this desire to over-report s comes into conflict with the desire to under-report s effect discussed above. To put it another way, the manager's desire to obtain insurance for himself comes into conflict with his role as insurer for the workers. Which effect "wins" depends in some sense on how risk-averse the manager is in comparison with how normal leisure is [see Cooper (1983)]. One case where there is no conflict is when, as in (2.6), the cost of supplying labor comes entirely from missed outside opportunities; or, more generally, when $U(I, \ell) = \hat{U}(I - g(\ell))$.[30] Under these conditions, the overemployment effect disappears and we unambiguously have underemployment [see Azariadis (1983), Grossman and Hart (1981, 1983b)]. As we have noted, another case where underemployment is the outcome is when the workers can obtain income insurance elsewhere.

The fact that some asymmetric information models predict underemployment while others predict overemployment has caused some to conclude that this is not a fruitful approach for analyzing employment distortions. This seems unfortunate for several reasons. First, the models all have the property that there is ex post inefficient employment. This is of considerable interest given that most neoclassical models of the labor market – those, say, that treat it as a spot market or analyze wage–employment decisions as a symmetric information bargaining process – predict ex post efficiency. Second, the underemployment and overemployment models may not be in quite as much conflict as is sometimes thought. Because one model refers to underemployment in bad states and the other to overemployment in good states, both in fact suggest increased employment variability compared to the spot market (the word "suggest" is important here since, as we have noted, "overemployment" refers to the relative size of marginal rates of substitution and transformation rather than to differences in labor). From a macroeconomic point of view, this may be the most important conclusion. Third, the question of whether the

---

[30] In this case, where labor is neither normal nor inferior, the manager's desire to over-report s vanishes. This follows from the fact that the solution to (2.2)–(2.3) has $I - g(L) =$ constant when the manager is risk-neutral. Since the manager is the residual income claimant, he has no incentive to misreport s.

overemployment effect is likely to dominate the underemployment effect in a particular context is one that empirical work can shed light on. Most empirical analyses of the labor market find that participation decisions of prime-age males are highly income inelastic [see Killingsworth (1983)]. This suggests that the normality of leisure effect is likely to be very small with respect to significant employment changes that are more than temporary (e.g., severances). To put it another way, outside earning opportunities are likely to swamp leisure as an opportunity cost of labor in such cases, which provides some support for the utility function $\hat{U}(I - g(\ell))$ and for the underemployment effect. On the other hand, the overemployment effect may be more relevant in the case of temporary layoffs or short-run variations in hours.[31]

Finally, mention should be made of a body of literature that considers other asymmetries of information. Some papers have analyzed the case where workers have private information about their opportunity costs [see, e.g., Kahn (1985) and Moore (1985)] while others have studied situations where firms and workers each possess some private information. This last "two-sided" case is very complex, and only limited progress has so far been made in its analysis [see, e.g., d'Aspremont and Gerard-Varet (1979); Riordan (1984); and, particularly, Moore (1984)].

2.4   Extensions of the labor contract model

A   Macroeconomic applications

The original labor contract model was developed with an eye to macroeconomic applications. The discovery that employment decisions are ex post efficient [and, under (2.6), the same as in the Walrasian model] perhaps dampened enthusiasm, but the advent of the asymmetric information models has stimulated some new work in this direction.

A simple way to incorporate the model of Section 2.3 into a macroeconomic setting is to suppose that the economy consists of many identical managerial firms, with perfectly correlated demand or supply shocks s. Given (2.14) and (2.19), this would seem to give us an explanation of why an aggregate down shock would lead to a greater fall in employment in each firm than would be expected in a spot market.

Unfortunately, this is too simple. If all firms reduce employment, one would surely expect this to be observable to workers (and third parties); moreover, since presumably no firm has an influence on aggregate employment and aggregate employment is perfectly correlated with s, the asymmetry of information will disappear if payments are conditioned on this variable.

---

[31] Feldstein's (1976) work suggests that surprisingly many layoffs are in fact temporary.

Two ways of overcoming this problem have been attempted. One is to suppose that the aggregate shock causes a change in the variance of the distribution of s, as well perhaps as its mean [see Grossman, Hart, and Maskin (1983)]. Suppose that there are two states of the economy: one, α_1, in which the variance of s is very small and the other, α_2, in which it is large. Consider the special case where the Walrasian aggregate employment levels are the same in α_1 and α_2. Then, under asymmetric information, a shock that moves the economy from α_1 to α_2, *even if it is publicly observed* (say, through changes in aggregate employment), will reduce total employment. This is because the asymmetry of information will be (almost) irrelevant in the low-variance state $\alpha = \alpha_1$ (where a firm's profitability can essentially be deduced from macro variables), but will have force in the high-variance state $\alpha = \alpha_2$. Hence aggregate employment will be close to the Walrasian level in α_1, but will be below the Walrasian level in α_2; the latter because low-s firms have lower employment levels under asymmetric information [by (2.19)] while high-s firms do not have higher employment levels [by (2.14)]. Together these arguments yield the conclusion that total employment will be lower in α_2 than in α_1 under asymmetric information. In fact, the same logic generalizes to show that if Walrasian aggregate employment falls when the economy is hit by a variance-increasing shock, this fall will be amplified under asymmetric information.

Farmer (1984) exploits a similar idea. Suppose that a publicly observable macroeconomic shock increases the cost of firms' inputs, for example by raising the real rate of interest. Then, although the distribution of s may not change, firms' net profits fall. If managers have decreasing absolute risk aversion, this is like an increase in managerial risk aversion. This will increase the distortion found in low-s firms (which is a function of risk aversion), without there being offsetting effects in high-s firms [by (2.14)]. Hence an aggregate increase in unemployment will again be amplified under asymmetric information.

A second approach is to suppose that s consists of a component common to all firms and an idiosyncratic component [see Holmström and Weiss (1985)]. The common component will presumably again show up in the aggregate employment figures, and so wages can be conditioned on it. But suppose these figures are published with a lag – after managers learn their s and employment decisions must be made. A low-s manager will then be unsure if his is one of many adversely affected firms (i.e., if there has been an aggregate down shock), or if he is in a minority (i.e., if he has had a bad idiosyncratic shock).[32] In the first case, he will be able to reduce the wage rate (with a lag), whereas in the second case he will not (it is not incentive-compatible to allow a firm with a bad idiosyncratic

---

[32] This is of course the same confusion that Lucas (1972) exploited.

shock to reduce wages). A risk-averse manager will put relatively high weight on the second possibility and so will cut back on employment as a second-best way of reducing the wage bill. As above, this is not compensated for by an increase in employment in high-s firms [by (2.14)]. The result can be shown to be greater aggregate employment variability between economywide up shocks and down shocks than would occur in a spot market.

The conclusion that aggregate employment levels can be inefficient raises the question of whether there is a role for government intervention. In a version of the Grossman–Hart–Maskin (1983) model, where s reflects a relative demand shock, it can be shown that a policy that stabilizes demand across different firms can be welfare-improving. This is because demand shifts have an externality effect via their impact on the extent of the asymmetry of information between firms and workers and/or third parties. Because externalities like this seem to be a fairly pervasive feature of asymmetric information/moral hazard models (see Section 1), it seems likely that there will be a role for government intervention in other models too (of course, the usual qualification that the government may require very good information to improve things should be borne in mind). Work on this topic is still in its infancy, however, and general results on the nature of macroeconomic externalities and the way to correct them are not yet available.

B *Involuntary unemployment*

We have focused on whether contract theory can explain ex post inefficient allocations. A related question which has received attention is whether the theory can explain involuntary layoffs. The results here have been rather disappointing.

To understand the issues, let us return to the ABG model, but drop the assumption of work-sharing. Instead we suppose that $\ell = 0$ or 1 for each worker at date 1. A contract will now specify a number of workers $n(s) \leq m$ who should work in state s, a payment $I_e(s)$ to each of these and a payment $I_u(s)$ to each of the laid-off workers. The total wage bill $W(s)$ in state s then equals

$$W(s) = n(s)I_e(s) + (m - n(s))I_u(s). \tag{2.20}$$

Since the firm cares only about the size of this wage bill and not how it is divided, an optimal contract must *in each state* solve:

$$\text{Max}\left[\frac{n(s)}{m} U(I_e(s), 1) + \left(1 - \frac{n(s)}{m}\right) U(I_u(s), 0) \right] \tag{2.21}$$

subject to

$$W(s) = W.$$

Here the maximand is the expected utility of each worker, given that layoffs are chosen randomly. The first-order conditions for (2.21) are

$$\frac{\partial U}{\partial I}(I_e(s), 1) = \frac{\partial U}{\partial I}(I_u(s), 0); \tag{2.22}$$

that is, retained and laid-off workers should have the same marginal utility of income.[33] It is not difficult to show that this implies that laid-off workers are better off than retained workers if leisure is a normal good, worse off if it is inferior, and equally well off if $U = \hat{U}(I - g(\ell))$; that is, if the demand for leisure is income-inelastic.

Since it is hard to argue empirically that leisure is inferior, this model gives us the perverse result that there will be ex post involuntary retentions. Various attempts have been made to get away from this.[34] One approach is to drop the assumption that the utility function $U(I, \ell)$ is publicly known at date 1. For example, suppose that $U(I, \ell) = \hat{U}(I + \tilde{R}(\bar{\ell} - \ell))$, where $\tilde{R}$, the outside reservation wage at date 1, is a random variable. A simple case is where neither the firm nor the workers know $\tilde{R}$ when the layoff decision is made (but both know its distribution). Under these conditions, Geanakoplos and Ito (1982) have shown that the optimal contract will involve involuntary layoffs only if $\hat{U}$ exhibits increasing absolute risk aversion (which is usually regarded as implausible).

A second case is where $\tilde{R}$ is known to the workers but not to the firm. If workers' $\tilde{R}$'s are correlated and there are many of them, it is likely that the firm will be able to elicit the common component, and so the natural case to study is where the $\tilde{R}$'s are independently drawn from a known distribution. In this case, however, Moore (1985) has shown that the utility function $\hat{U}$ gives rise to involuntary *retentions* if $\ell < \bar{\ell}$.[35] One disturbing feature of any contract where retention is involuntary is that it gives workers an incentive to be fired. Several papers have built on this, developing models in which involuntary layoffs are part of an incentive scheme to encourage the firm's work force to work hard [see Malcomson (1984b),

---

[33] This is the wage bill argument of Akerlof and Miyazaki (1980). Note that the conclusion that an optimal contract must satisfy (2.21) generalizes to the case where the firm is risk-averse, because a risk-averse firm also cares only about the size and not about the division of the wage bill in a particular state.

[34] Azariadis was able to explain involuntary layoffs in his original (1975) paper, but only by making the arbitrary assumption that layoff pay is zero.

[35] A third approach is to focus on the costly search process that laid-off workers must engage in to find a new job [see, e.g., Arnott, Hosios, and Stiglitz (1985)]. It is clear that workers will not be provided with the right incentives to search if they are guaranteed a fixed income level, independently of whether they find new employment. However, since a firm can preserve incentives by giving a departing worker a lump-sum payment, it does not follow from this that laid-off workers will be worse off than retained workers. In fact the results on this are ambiguous.

Hahn (1984), and Eden (1985)]. These models may apply to situations where employers have discretion about whom to lay off, but in practice this appears usually not to be the case – in union contracts, for example, layoffs are almost always by seniority.

It should be emphasized that none of these theories explains involuntary unemployment at the contract date. The reason is that, if there is a competitive labor market at date 0, an optimal contract will have the property that each employed worker's expected utility equals $\bar{U}$, the market clearing level. In particular, it cannot be an equilibrium for employed workers to receive more than $\bar{U}$ and employment to be rationed, because individual firms could then increase profit by reducing wages, $I(s)$, in each state (without distorting incentives). This conclusion is subject to some qualifications. First, it may be impossible to reduce wages in some states because workers are at the boundary of their consumption set. Second, in models involving worker effort, if a worker's utility function $U(e, I)$ is appropriately nonseparable in effort and income, then a reduction in I may have a sufficiently adverse effect on a worker's desire to work to be unprofitable for the firm [see, e.g., Malcomson (1981); a similar incentive effect underlies much of the efficiency wage literature; see, e.g., Shapiro and Stiglitz (1984)]. In both of these cases, employed workers may receive more than $\bar{U}$. Third, involuntary unemployment at the contract date is possible in models where there is adverse selection at date 0, an important case that falls outside the scope of this survey [see Weiss (1980) and Stiglitz and Weiss (1981)].

C   *Long-term (repeated) contracts*

Labor contracts, whether implicit or explicit, have been regarded as most important in long-term relationships. To formalize these relationships as a "one-shot" situation (as in Sections 2.1–2.3) does not seem very satisfactory. Nevertheless, there are dynamic versions for which the preceding analysis applies essentially intact. A particular example that precisely fits the structure of (2.9) is in Fudenberg et al. (1986).

Consider an infinitely (and independently) repeated version of the one-period model studied above. The manager's utility over a consumption stream $\{c_t\}$ is given by $\Sigma - \delta^t \exp(-rc_t)$, where δ is the discount factor and r is the manager's coefficient of absolute risk aversion. The manager can borrow and save freely at the interest rate $(1-\delta)/\delta$. This is not observed by the principal.

As discussed in Section 1.7, an optimal long-term contract can in this situation be duplicated by a sequence of short-term contracts – with exponential utility and independent shocks a sequence of identical short-term contracts. Note, however, that an optimal one-period contract in the dynamic model is not the same as in the static model, because the manager can smooth consumption. Instead, the one-period solution in the dynamic case is the same as if the manager worked just once, but consumed forever. (Because there are no income effects and shocks are independent, contracts across periods do not affect each other.) This program can be reduced to the form (2.9) as follows.

Assume the manager consumes after he is paid in the single period he works (this is the reverse of Fudenberg et al., but of no consequence for the decomposition result). Let w_i be the manager's net wealth if s_i occurs in that period [i.e., $w_i = f(s_i, L_i) + I_i$, $i = 1, 2$, in our earlier notation]. With no further income, the manager will consume the interest on his wealth in all future periods; that is, he will consume $(1 - \delta)w_i$ forever. This implies a lifetime utility $V(w_i) = -\exp\{-r(1 - \delta)w_i\}/(1 - \delta)$. Consequently, using this V as the manager's utility function in (2.9), we obtain the optimal short-term contract for the dynamic case.

Notice that the only difference between the static problem and the dynamic (short-term) problem is that the manager's risk-aversion coefficient is smaller in the latter. In the dynamic case the coefficient is $r(1 - \delta)$, while in the static case it is r. The reduction in risk aversion comes from self-insurance in the dynamic model. In the limit, as δ goes to one and there is no discounting of the future, the manager effectively acts in a risk-neutral fashion. One optimal (and first-best) solution in that situation is to rent out the technology to the manager and let him carry all the risk. (Recall our earlier comment on Yaari's work in Section 1.7.)

Since the introduction of dynamics in this example only changes the manager's risk-aversion coefficient, the earlier static analysis applies directly. We conclude that while there will be a smaller allocational distortion in the multi-period situation than in the one-period situation, in both cases the distortion will be qualitatively the same.

It is also worth noting that not all long-run relationships are subject to independent shocks. With serial correlation of the s_i's, however, the gains from self-insurance may be substantially reduced. For instance, in the extreme case of a single shock that persists forever, there are no self-insurance gains at all, and the optimal long-term contract will be the repeated static contract from (2.9). More generally, with positive correlation, repetition will have a smaller effect in reducing the level of second-best inefficiency than with independent shocks (but see Section 2.4D below).

D   Enforcement of the contract

The asymmetric information contract models are sometimes criticized on the ground that "while the parties may agree in advance to have unemployment in bad states of the world, they will surely change their mind once such a state is realized." To understand this, consider a firm that signs a contract with a single worker. Suppose that $\ell = 0$ or 1, that there are two states $s = s_2$ or $s = s_1$ ($s_2 > s_1$), and that the ex post opportunity cost of labor is zero. An optimal second-best contract might have the property that $\ell = 1$ when $s = s_2$ and $\ell = 0$ when $s = s_1$. But suppose now that $s = s_1$ is realized and the firm lays off the worker. Then the argument goes that the firm and worker will recontract at this stage since they will recognize that there are some unexploited gains from trade (assuming that $s_1 > 0$).

Such recontracting can only make the parties worse off in ex ante terms (assuming it is anticipated) – otherwise the original contract would not have been an optimal one. The question therefore is whether the parties can precommit themselves not to renegotiate; in the static model of Section 2.3, the answer seems to be yes. Presumably there is a last moment at which employment decisions must be made. Let the original contract state that the firm can change its mind about whether to employ the worker up to this last moment. Then any threat to lay off the worker before the last moment is not credible because the worker knows that the firm can costlessly change its mind, while a threat at the last moment is, of course, useless to the firm since by that time it is too late to renegotiate.

The recontracting criticism does not therefore seem to be valid when there is only one employment date. However, it does have force in a dynamic context. Change the above example so that the worker can work or not work on each of T days (but suppose, in contrast to Section 2.4C, that the shock s is the same for all days). The optimal second-best contract might call for the worker to be laid off for $1 < T_1 \leq T$ days in the bad state $s = s_1$. However, it is hard to see what is to stop the parties from renegotiating such a contract after one day of unemployment, given that there are clearly unexploited gains from trade at this point and that the only irreversible decision which has been made concerns the first day's layoff.[36]

In future work it would be interesting to investigate the constraints that such renegotiation puts on dynamic contracts.[37] We shall return to the issue of ex post renegotiation in Section 3.

---

[36] A similar phenomenon arises in a dynamic bargaining context where a seller would like to commit himself to make a single take-it-or-leave-it offer to a buyer, but cannot do so since he cannot constrain himself not to make a second offer if his first offer is rejected. See, e.g., Fudenberg and Tirole (1983). Note that there is a fundamental difference between all the parties agreeing to tear up the contract and one party repudiating the contract – something which we have implicitly assumed never occurs, e.g. because the resulting damage payment is so large.

[37] A start on this has been made by Dewatripont (1985).

2.5   Summary and conclusions

There seem to be two major conclusions from the labor contract literature. First, in an optimal contract, there will be systematic discrepancies between wages and the marginal product of labor. Second, under asymmetric information, there will be ex post inefficiencies.

Both these conclusions have important implications for the way we think about labor markets. In almost all empirical work on the labor market, for instance, it is taken for granted that wages measure the opportunity cost of labor, and that firms will be on their demand curves or workers on their supply curves or both. In a contracting framework, as Rosen (1985) has stressed, none of these suppositions is valid. To take another example, it is often assumed that the following is a good model of union behavior: The union chooses the wage rate to maximize the representative worker's utility subject to the constraint that the firm will be on its labor demand curve. According to the contracting framework, however, such behavior is irrational because both the firm and the union can make themselves better off by agreeing on a wage–employment pair that lies on the efficiency frontier.

In view of the strong implications of the labor contract approach, it is important to know how well the theory matches up with the facts. Serious econometric work on this topic is only just beginning, but some interesting papers by Brown and Ashenfelter (1986) and by Card (1985) are already available. These papers test the prediction of the ABG model that ex post employment levels can be explained by opportunity costs rather than actual wages [as in (2.7)]. The results obtained so far suggest little support for this hypothesis, but it is possible that some of the explanatory power of actual wages found by Brown and Ashenfelter and by Card can be traced to asymmetries of information (as in the model of Section 2.3), rather than being a rejection of the optimal contracting approach per se. Unfortunately, testing the asymmetric information contract model directly is a very difficult task, and we are not aware of any attempts so far in this direction.

A much less formal empirical approach, which has been adopted by Oswald (1984), is to examine actual labor contracts to see whether they contain the features that one might expect from the theory. The results here have again been less than favorable to the contracting approach. First, most non-union contracts are surprisingly rudimentary, sometimes consisting of as little as a verbal statement that an employee has a job at a particular (current) wage. Second, union contracts, although frequently lengthy and complex, do not contain a number of the provisions that the theory suggests they should. For example, it is rare to find joint agreements on wages and employment; typically wage rates are specified over the course of the contract, but employment decisions are left to the firm. [Although this is not inconsistent with the model of Section 2.3, in more general asymmetric information models (where, e.g., workers and firms both have private information) an optimal contract will involve joint determination of employment by firms and workers.] Other anomalies are the lack of indexation of wages to retail prices or to variables such as firm employment or firm sales, and the limited provisions for layoff pay.

Of course, one possible escape for the contract theorist is to argue that whatever does not appear in the explicit contract is simply part of an implicit contract (see the introduction). This is akin to the proposition that a theory should be judged by its predictions (e.g., whether employment levels are determined solely by opportunity costs) rather than by its assumptions (whether a particular contractual provision is physically present). Although there is surely something to this idea, it seems a considerable act of faith to rely on the notion of an implicit contract, given that so little is presently known about how implicit agreements are enforced (but see Section 3.4). In fact, in view of the current ignorance about this, it seems curious – and unfortunate – that the whole field often goes under the name of Implicit Labor Contracts.

Given that empirical support for the labor contract model is at present rather limited, the question arises whether the contracting approach is worth pursuing. Not surprisingly, we feel strongly that the answer is yes. The main reason is that there appears to be no serious alternative available for analyzing this class of problems. For example, the wage-setting-union model described above may fit some of the facts better, but it is based on the assumption that the parties fail to exploit all the gains from trade, which (in theoretical terms) seems unacceptable. Rather than abandoning the contracting framework, therefore, it seems desirable to try to modify it so as to make it more realistic, for example by incorporating further moral hazards or asymmetries of information or – and perhaps this is most important – by introducing the costs of writing contracts (see Section 3). It should also be noted that firm/worker relationships are only one application of the contracting framework. In Section 3, we argue that other applications (e.g., to input supply contracts between firms) may in the long run be at least as fruitful, as well perhaps as being more consistent with the facts.

2.6   *Appendix*

It is easy to show that, if f is continuous, a solution to (2.9) exists. Denote it by $(\hat{L}_1, \hat{L}_2, \hat{I}_1, \hat{I}_2)$. Clearly, $\pi_2 \hat{I}_2 + \pi_1 \hat{I}_1 = 0$. Furthermore, at least one of the truth-telling constraints must be binding (otherwise a Pareto improvement could be made by moving in the direction of the first-best). We consider three cases.

Case 1 (both truth-telling constraints are binding):

$$f(s_2, \hat{\mathbf{L}}_2) + \hat{I}_2 = f(s_2, \hat{\mathbf{L}}_1) + \hat{I}_1,$$
$$f(s_1, \hat{\mathbf{L}}_1) + \hat{I}_1 = f(s_1, \hat{\mathbf{L}}_2) + \hat{I}_2. \tag{1}$$

In this case the manager is indifferent between the two states. Hence $\hat{I}_1 = \hat{I}_2 = 0$ since, if $\hat{I}_i < \hat{I}_j$, a Pareto improvement could be achieved by replacing the old contract by a new contract $(\hat{\mathbf{L}}_i, \hat{I}_i, \hat{\mathbf{L}}_i, \hat{I}_i)$. But, if $\hat{I}_1 = \hat{I}_2 = 0$, it is optimal to set $\mathbf{L}_i$ equal to its first-best value, $\mathbf{L}_i^*$, $i = 1, 2$, which contradicts (1). Therefore Case 1 is impossible.

Case 2 (only the second truth-telling constraint is binding):

$$f(s_1, \hat{\mathbf{L}}_1) + \hat{I}_1 = f(s_1, \hat{\mathbf{L}}_2) + \hat{I}_2,$$
$$f(s_2, \hat{\mathbf{L}}_2) + \hat{I}_2 > f(s_2, \hat{\mathbf{L}}_1) + \hat{I}_1. \tag{2}$$

The second inequality, together with (2.10), implies that $f(s_2, \hat{\mathbf{L}}_2) + \hat{I}_2 > f(s_1, \hat{\mathbf{L}}_1) + \hat{I}_1$; that is, the manager prefers s_2 to s_1. In this case, however, by a standard risk-sharing argument, a Pareto improvement can be made by lowering I_2 and raising I_1, keeping $\pi_2 I_2 + \pi_1 I_1$ constant (the truth-telling constraints will continue to be satisfied). Hence Case 2 is ruled out.

We are left with Case 3, where only the first truth-telling constraint is binding; this case was analyzed in the text.

3   Incomplete contracts

3.1   *The benefits of writing long-term contracts*

The literature on labor contracts focuses on income-shifting as the motivation for a long-term contract; that is, on the gains the parties receive from transferring income from one state of the world or one period to another. In the ABG model, the worker wants to insure his income. This is also the case in the quit model, where in addition the worker wants to smooth his consumption over time. Finally, in the Azariadis–Grossman–Hart model, it is the entrepreneur/manager who desires insurance.

In all these models, the rationale for the contract would disappear if the agents were risk-neutral and faced perfect capital markets. Even if risk aversion and imperfect capital markets are present, the ABG and

Holmström explanations of labor contracts rely on the assumption that firms have a comparative advantage in providing insurance and income-smoothing opportunities to workers.

It is perhaps unfortunate that so much attention has been devoted to "financial" contracts of this type. As we noted in the introduction, a fundamental reason for long-term relationships is the existence of investments that are to some extent party-specific. Although this lock-in effect is often used to motivate the long-term relationship between workers and firms in labor contract models, it then tends to be ignored. Yet this lock-in effect can explain the existence and characteristics of long-term contracts even in the presence of risk neutrality and perfect capital markets. Moreover, in the case (say) of supply contracts involving large firms, risk neutrality and perfect capital markets may be reasonable assumptions in view of the many outside insurance and borrowing/lending opportunities available to such parties.

The importance of a long-term contract when there are relationship-specific investments can be seen from the following example [based on Grout (1984); see also Crawford (1982)]. Let B and S be, respectively, the buyer and seller of (one unit of) an input. Suppose that in order to realize the benefits of the input, B must make an investment a which is specific to S; for example, B might have to build a plant next to S. Assume that there are just two periods: The investment is made at date 0, while the input is supplied and the benefits are received at date 1. S's supply cost at date 1 is c, while B's benefit function is $b(a)$ (all costs and benefits are measured in date-1 dollars).

If no long-term contract is written at date 0, the parties will determine the terms of trade from scratch at date 1. If we assume that neither party has alternative trading partners at date 1 then there is, given B's sunk investment cost a, a surplus of $b(a)-c$ to be divided up. A simple assumption to make is that the parties split this 50:50 (this is the Nash bargaining solution). That is, the input price p will satisfy $b(a)-p=p-c$. This means that the buyer's overall payoff, net of his investment cost, is

$$b(a)-p-a=\frac{b(a)-c}{2}-a. \tag{3.1}$$

The buyer, anticipating this payoff, will choose a to maximize (3.1), that is, to maximize $\frac{1}{2}b(a)-a$.

This is to be contrasted with the efficient outcome, where a is chosen to maximize total surplus, $b(a)-c-a$. Maximizing (3.1) will lead to underinvestment; in fact, in extreme cases, a will equal zero and trade will not occur at all. The inefficiency arises because the buyer does not receive the full return from his investment - some of this return is appropriated by the seller in the date-1 bargaining. Note that an up-front payment from S to B at date 0 (to compensate for the share of the surplus that S will receive later) will not help here, because it will only change B's objective function by a constant (it's like a lump-sum transfer). That is, it redistributes income without affecting real decisions.

Efficiency can be achieved if a long-term contract is written at date 0 specifying the input price p^* in advance. Then B will maximize $b(a) - p^* - a$, yielding the efficient investment level a^*. An alternative method is to specify that the buyer must choose $a = a^*$ (if not, he pays large damages to S); the choice of p can then be left until date 1, with an up-front payment by S being used to compensate B for his investment. The second method presupposes that investment decisions are publicly observable, and so in practice may be more complicated than the first (see Section 3.3).

This example – formalizing arguments contained in Williamson (1975, 1985) and in Klein, Crawford, and Alchian (1978) – illustrates the role of a long-term contract when there are relationship-specific investments. The word "investment" should be interpreted broadly; the same factors will apply whenever one party is forced to pass up an opportunity as a result of a relationship with another party (e.g., A's "investment" in the relationship with B may be not to lock into C). That is, the crucial element is a sunk cost (direct or opportunity) of some sort. (An effort decision is one example of a sunk cost.) Note that the income-transfer motive for a long-term contract is completely absent here; there is no uncertainty and everything is in present-value terms.

In spite of their importance, the analysis of "real" contracts of this type ("real," rather than "financial," because their rationale comes from the existence of real decisions such as investments) is in its infancy. A notable early reference is Becker's (1964) analysis of worker training. More recently, Williamson (1975, 1985) and Klein, Crawford, and Alchian (1978) have emphasized the difficulty of writing contracts that induce efficient relationship-specific investments as an important factor in explaining vertical integration.

Section 3 of this survey will be concerned primarily with the analysis of such real contracts. At this stage, however, it may be useful to summarize the general benefits of writing long-term contracts. We have discussed the income-transfer and "real" motives. Let us note three further benefits. First, if a relationship is repetitive, it may save on transaction costs to decide in advance what actions each party should take rather than to negotiate a succession of short-term contracts. Second, if asymmetries of information arise during the course of the relationship, letting the parties negotiate as they go along may lead to ex post bargaining inefficiencies [as in, e.g., Fudenberg and Tirole (1983)], which can be avoided by a long-term contract.[38] Third, a long-term contract may be useful for screening purposes – for example, a firm may attract a productive worker by offering a high future reward in the event that the worker is successful. [This is an example drawn from the adverse selection literature; see, e.g., Salop and Salop (1976).]

Given the many advantages of long-term contracts, the question that obviously arises is why we don't see more of them, and why those we do see seem often to be limited in scope. To this question we now turn.

3.2   *The costs of writing long-term contracts*

Contract theory is sometimes dismissed because "we don't see the long-term contingent contracts that the theory predicts." In view of the benefits of long-term contracts, this statement (even if true) needs to be explained.

The first point to make is that there is no shortage of complex long-term contracts in the world. Joskow (1985), for example, in his recent study of transactions between electricity generating plants and mine-mouth coal suppliers, finds that some contracts between the parties extend for fifty years, and a large majority for over ten years. The contractual terms include quality provisions, formulas linking coal prices to costs and prices of substitutes, indexation clauses, and so forth. The contracts are both complicated and sophisticated. Similar findings are contained in Goldberg and Erickson's (1982) study of petroleum coke.

At a much more basic level, a typical contract for personal insurance, with its many conditions and exemption clauses, is not exactly a simple document. Nor for that matter is a typical house rental agreement. On the other hand, as we noted in Section 2, labor contracts are often surprisingly rudimentary, at least in certain respects.

Given that complex long-term contracts are found in some situations but not others, it is natural to explain any observed contract as an outcome of an optimization process in which the relative benefits and costs of additional length and complexity are traded off at the margin. We have

---

[38] For example, suppose that B does not have to make any investment, but that his benefit from the input is stochastic: $b = 10$ with probability $1/2$ and 3 with probability $1/2$. Assume that B learns the exact value of b at date 1 while S does not, that $c = 0$ for sure, and that both parties are risk-neutral. Then if bargaining occurs from scratch at date 1, and S has the power to make take-it-or-leave-it offers, he will set a price of 10 (obviously S will not find it profitable to set a price other than 10 or 3; the price of 10 gives him higher expected profit). But this means that a mutually beneficial trade will not be made in the event $b = 3$. On the other hand, the first-best can be achieved by a long-term contract specifying that the buyer can insist on supply of the input in all circumstances at some predetermined price.

given some indication of the determinants of the benefits of length and complexity. But what about the costs? These are much harder to pin down because they fall under the general heading of "transactions costs," a notoriously vague and slippery category. Of these, the following seem to be important: (1) the cost to each party of anticipating the various eventualities that may occur during the life of the relationship; (2) the cost of deciding, and reaching an agreement about, how to deal with such eventualities; (3) the cost of writing the contract in a sufficiently clear and unambiguous way so that the terms of the contract can be enforced; and (4) the legal cost of enforcement.

One point to note is that all these costs are present also in the case of short-term contracts, although presumably they are usually smaller. In particular, since the short-term future is more predictable, the first cost is likely to be much reduced, and so possibly is the third. However, it certainly is not the case that there is a sharp division between short-term contracts and long-term contracts, with (as is sometimes supposed) the former being costless and the latter being infinitely costly.

It is also worth emphasizing that, when we talk about the cost of a long-term contract, we are presumably referring to the cost of a "good" long-term contract. There is rarely significant cost or difficulty in writing *some* long-term contract. For example, the parties to an input supply contract could agree on a fixed price and level of supply for the next fifty years; they do not, because (presumably) such a rigid arrangement would be very inefficient.[39]

Due to the presence of transaction costs, the contracts people write will be incomplete in important respects. The parties will quite rationally leave out many contingencies, taking the point of view that it is better to wait and see what happens than to try to cover a large number of individually unlikely eventualities. Less rationally, the parties will leave out other contingencies that they simply do not anticipate. Instead of writing very long-term contracts the parties will write limited-term contracts, with the intention of renegotiating these when they come to an end. Contracts will often contain clauses that are vague or ambiguous, sometimes fatally so.

---

[39] In some cases, the courts will not enforce such an agreement, taking the point of view that the parties could not really have intended it to apply unchanged for such a long time. A clause to the effect that the parties really do mean what they say should be enough to overcome this difficulty, however. In other cases, it may be impossible to write a binding long-term contract because the identities of some of the parties involved may change. For example, one party may be a government that is in office for a fixed period, and it may be impossible for the government to bind its successors. This latter idea underlies the work of Kydland and Prescott (1977) and of Freixas, Guesnerie, and Tirole (1985).

Anyone familiar with the legal literature on contracts will be aware that almost every contractual dispute that comes before the courts concerns a matter of incompleteness. In fact, incompleteness is probably at least as important empirically as asymmetric information as an explanation for departures from "ideal" Arrow–Debreu contingent contracts. In spite of this, relatively little work has been done on this topic, the reason (presumably) being that an analysis of transaction costs is so complicated. One problem is that the first two transaction costs referred to above are intimately connected to the idea of bounded rationality [as in Simon (1982)], a concept that has not yet been successfully formalized. As a result, perhaps, the few attempts that have been made to analyze incompleteness have concentrated on the third cost, the cost of writing the contract.

One approach, due to Dye (1985), can be described as follows. Suppose that the amount of input q traded between a buyer and seller should be a function of the product price p faced by the buyer: $q = f(p)$. Writing down this function is likely to be costly. Dye measures the costs in terms of how many different values q takes on as p varies; in particular, if $\#\{q \mid q = f(p) \text{ for some } p\} = n$ then the cost of the contract is $(n-1)c$, where $c > 0$. This means that a noncontingent statement "$q = 5$ for all p" has zero cost; the statement "$q = 5$ for $p \leq 8$, $q = 10$ for $p > 8$" has cost c; and so forth.

The costs Dye is trying to capture are real enough, but the measure used has some drawbacks. It implies, for example, that the statement "$q = p^{1/2}$ for all p" has infinite cost if p has infinite domain, and does not distinguish between the cost of a simple function like this and the cost of a much more complicated function. As another example, a simple indexation clause to the effect that the real wage should be constant (i.e., the money wage $= \lambda p$ for some λ) would never be observed because, according to Dye's measure, it too has infinite cost. In addition, the approach does not tell us how to assess the cost of indirect ways of making q contingent; for example, the contract could specify that the buyer (having observed p) can choose any amount of input q he likes, subject to paying the seller σ for each unit.

There is another way of getting at the cost of including contingent statements. This is to suppose that what is costly is describing the state of the world ω rather than writing a statement per se. That is, suppose that ω cannot be represented simply by a product price, but is very complex and of high dimension – for example, it includes the state of demand, what other firms in the industry are doing, the state of technology, and so on. Many of these components may be quite nebulous. To describe ω ex ante in sufficient detail for an outsider (e.g., the courts) to verify that a particular state $\omega = \hat{\omega}$ has occurred, and so enforce the contract, may be prohibitively costly. Under these conditions, the contract will have to omit some (in extreme cases, all) references to the underlying state.

Similar to this is the case where what is costly is describing the characteristics of what is traded, or the actions (e.g., investments) the parties must take. For example, suppose that there is only one state of the world, but that q now represents the quality of the item traded rather than the quantity. An ideal contract would give a precise description of q. However, quality may be multidimensional and very difficult to describe unambiguously (and vague statements to the effect that quality should be "good" may be almost meaningless). The result may be that the contract will have to be silent on many aspects of quality and/or actions.

Models of this sort of incompleteness have been investigated by Grossman and Hart (in press) and Hart and Moore (1985) for the case where the state of the world cannot be described, and by Bull (1985) and Grossman and Hart (1986; in press) for the case where quality and/or actions cannot be specified. These models do not rely on any asymmetry of information between the parties. Both parties may recognize that the state of the world is such that the buyer's benefit is high or the seller's cost is low, or that the quality of an item is good or bad or that an investment decision is appropriate or not. The difficulty is conveying this information to others; that is, *it is the asymmetry of information between the parties on the one hand, and outsiders (such as the courts) on the other hand, which is the root of the problem.*

To use the jargon, incompleteness arises because states of the world, quality, and actions are *observable* (to the contractual parties) but not *verifiable* (to outsiders). We describe an example of an incomplete contract along these lines in Section 3.3.

3.3   Incomplete contracts: an example

We will give an example of an incomplete contract for the case where it is prohibitively costly to specify the quality characteristics of the item to be exchanged or the parties' investment decisions. Similar problems arise when the state of the world cannot be described. The example is a variant of the models in Grossman and Hart (1986; in press) and in Hart and Moore (1985).

Consider a buyer B who wishes to purchase a unit of input from a seller S. B and S each make a (simultaneous) specific investment at date 0 and trade occurs at date 1. Let I_B, I_S denote (respectively) the investments of B and S, and to simplify assume that each can take on only two values, H or L (high or low). These investments are observable to B and S, but are not verifiable (they are complex and multidimensional, or represent effort decisions) and hence are noncontractible. We assume that at date 1 the seller can supply either satisfactory input or unsatisfactory input. "Unsatisfactory" input has zero benefit for the buyer and zero cost for the seller (so it's like not supplying at all). "Satisfactory" input yields benefits and costs that depend on ex ante investments. These are indicated by

	$I_B = H$	$I_B = L$
$I_S = H$	(10, 6)	(9, 7)
$I_S = L$	(9, 7)	(6, 10)

The first component refers to the buyer's benefit v, and the second to the seller's cost c. So if $I_S = H$ and $I_B = H$ then $v = 10$ and $c = 6$ (if input is satisfactory). From these gross benefits and costs must be subtracted investment costs, which we assume to be 1.9 if investment is high and zero if it is low (for each party). (All benefits and costs are in date-1 dollars.) Note that there is no uncertainty and so attitudes to risk are irrelevant.

Our assumption is that the characteristics of the input (e.g., whether it is satisfactory) are observable to both parties, but are too complicated to be specified in a contract. The fact that they are observable means that the buyer can be given the option to reject the input at date 1 if he does not like it. This will be important in what follows.

An important feature of the example is that the seller's investment affects not only the seller's costs but also the buyer's benefit and the buyer's investment affects not only the buyer's benefit but also the seller's cost. The idea here is that a better investment by the seller increases the quality of satisfactory input; and a better investment by the buyer reduces the cost of producing satisfactory input - that is, input that can be used by the buyer.

For instance, one can imagine that B is an electricity generating plant and S is a coal mine that the plant sites next to. I_B might refer to the type of coal-burning boiler that the plant installs and I_S to the type of mine the coal supplier develops. By investing in a better boiler, the power plant may be able to burn lower quality coal, thus reducing the seller's costs, while still increasing its gross (of investment) profit. On the other hand, by developing a good seam, the mine may raise the quality of coal supplied while reducing its variable cost.

The first-best has $I_B = I_S = H$, with total surplus equal to $10 - 6 - 3.8 = .2$ (if $I_B = H$ and $I_S = L$ or vice versa then surplus $= .1$; if $I_B = I_S = L$ then no trade occurs and surplus is zero). This could be achieved if either investment or quality were contractible as follows. If investment is contractible, an optimal contract would specify that the buyer must set $I_B = H$ and the seller $I_S = H$ and give the buyer the right to accept the input at date 1 at price p_1 or reject it at price p_0. If $10 > p_1 - p_0 > 6$, the seller will be induced to supply satisfactory input (the gain $p_1 - p_0$ from having the input accepted exceeds the seller's supply cost) and the buyer to accept it (the buyer's benefit exceeds the incremental price $p_1 - p_0$). If, on the other hand, quality is contractible, then the contract could specify that the seller must supply input with the precise characteristics that make it satisfactory when $I_B = I_S = H$. Each party would then have the socially correct investment incentives because, with specific performance, neither party's investment affects the other's payoff (there is no externality).

We now show that the first-best cannot be achieved if investment and quality are both noncontractible. A second-best contract can make price a function of any variable that is verifiable. Investment and quality are not verifiable (nor is v or c), but we shall suppose that whether the item is accepted or rejected by the buyer is verifiable; thus the contract can specify an acceptance price p_1 and a rejection price p_0. In fact, p_0, p_1 can also be made functions of (verifiable) messages that the buyer and seller send each other, reflecting the investment decisions that both have made [as in Hart and Moore (1985)]. The following argument is unaffected by such messages and so, for simplicity, we ignore them (but see note 44).

Can we sustain the first-best by an appropriate choice of p_0, p_1? The seller always has the option of choosing $I_S = L$ and producing an item of unsatisfactory quality, which yields him a net payoff of p_0. In order to induce him not to do this, we must have

$$p_1 - 6 - 1.9 \geq p_0 \quad \text{(i.e., } p_1 - p_0 \geq 7.9). \tag{3.2}$$

Similarly, the buyer's net payoff must be no less than $-p_0$ since he always has the option of choosing $I_B = L$ and rejecting the input. That is,

$$10 - p_1 - 1.9 \geq -p_0 \quad \text{(i.e., } p_1 - p_0 \leq 8.1). \tag{3.3}$$

Hence $(p_1 - p_0)$ must lie between 7.9 and 8.1.

Now the seller has an additional option. If he expects the buyer to set $I_B = H$, he can choose $I_S = L$ and, given that $8.1 \geq p_1 - p_0 \geq 7.9$, still be confident that trade of satisfactory input will occur under the original contract at date 1 (the buyer will accept satisfactory input since $v = 9 > p_1 - p_0$, while the seller will supply it since $p_1 - p_0 > 7 = c$). But if the seller deviates, his payoff rises from $p_1 - 6 - 1.9$ to $p_1 - 7$. (The example is symmetric and so a similar deviation is also profitable for the buyer.) Hence the equilibrium of $I_B = I_S = H$ will be disrupted.

We see, then, that the first-best cannot be sustained if investment and quality are both noncontractible. The reason is that it will be in the interest of the seller (respectively, the buyer) to reduce investment because, although this reduces social benefit by lowering the buyer's (seller's) benefit, it increases the seller's (buyer's) own profit. The optimal second-best contract will instead have $I_B = H$, $I_S = L$ (or vice versa), which will be sustained by a pair of prices p_0, p_1 such that $9 > p_1 - p_0 > 7$. Total surplus will be .1 instead of the first-best level of .2.[40]

The conclusion is that inefficiencies can arise in incomplete contracts even though the parties have common information (both observe investments and both observe quality). The particular inefficiency that occurs in the model analyzed is in ex ante investments. Ex post trade is always efficient relative to these investments since p_1, p_0 can and will be chosen so that $v > p_1 - p_0 > c$; that is, the seller wants to supply and the buyer to receive satisfactory input. The example can be regarded as formalizing the arguments of Williamson (1975, 1985) and of Klein, Crawford, and Alchian (1978) that relationship-specific investments will be distorted due to the impossibility of writing complete contingent contracts – note that this result is achieved without imposing arbitrary restrictions on the form of the permissible contract.[41]

The above example can be modified to illustrate an interesting possibility that can arise in an incomplete contract. Suppose we change the $I_S = H$, $I_B = L$ payoffs from (9, 7) to (9, 8.2) and the $I_S = L$, $I_B = H$ payoffs to (7.8, 7). The first-best stays the same. But now it can be sustained *as long as renegotiation of the contract is impossible at date 1*. In particular, choose $p_1 - p_0 = 8$. Then if either the buyer or seller deviates from the first-best, $v \geq p_1 - p_0 \geq c$ will be violated and so the deviating party's profit will fall to p_0 (for the seller) or $-p_0$ (for the buyer).

---

[40] It is worth pointing out why we have assumed that both the buyer and seller make investments. If only the buyer (respectively, the seller) invests, the first-best can be achieved by choosing $p_1 - p_0$ between 6 and 7 (9 and 10): Any deviation by the buyer (seller) will then be unprofitable since it will lead to no trade. This argument depends on the assumption of no renegotiation of the contract at date 1, an issue we deal with below. However, even if renegotiation is allowed, the first-best can be achieved with one-sided investment by a contract that fixes p_0 but gives the investing party the power to choose any p_1 he wants. This party then faces the social net benefit function because he extracts all the surplus.

[41] The inefficiency that we have identified may not seem so surprising given that our model resembles that found in the literature on moral hazard in teams [see, e.g., Holmström (1982a)]. In that literature, each agent takes a private action that affects total benefits; in our model, investment decisions have this property. However, there are some differences between the frameworks. First, in our context, the agents observe each other's actions. Second, the externality in investments only materializes in the event that trade occurs, and so the terms of trade can be used to mitigate the externality. In any case, our purpose is not the development of a new model, but rather the application of it to a new context – the analysis of the consequences of incomplete contracting.

However, the first-best may not be sustainable if renegotiation is possible. The previous argument showing that $7.9 \le p_1 - p_0 \le 8.1$ still applies. Without loss of generality, set $p_0 = 0$ in the following. Suppose the seller chooses $I_S = L$, while $I_B = H$. Then at date 1, the parties will realize that, because $7.8 = v < p_1$, trade – although mutually beneficial – will not occur under the original contract (the buyer will reject the input). Hence they will presumably lower the price p_1 to lie between 7 and 7.8. But as long as the new price $p_1' > 7.2$, the seller's net payoff will be higher than if he does not deviate (because his first-best surplus $p_1 - 7.9 < 0.2$). Hence the seller will deviate unless his power to keep p_1 up in the renegotiation is rather limited. (If the parties split the gains from renegotiation 50:50, $p_1' = 7.4$ and the seller will certainly deviate.)[42] If the seller is a poor bargainer, however, the buyer will presumably deviate; that is, he will set $I_B = L$, anticipating that $I_S = H$ – the parties will then agree to raise the price p_1 to lie between $c = 8.2$ and $v = 9$, and the buyer's net payoff will rise as long as the new price $p_1'' < 8.8$.

In this modified example, then, the buyer and seller can do better if they can precommit themselves not to renegotiate the contract! We have encountered this possibility before in Section 2.4D, but note that the method proposed there for preventing renegotiation (in the static case) will not work here (that method depended on the worker not knowing what the firm was going to do until the last moment, whereas here both parties will recognize the need for renegotiation as soon as investment decisions are made). Simply putting in renegotiation penalties in the original contract (e.g., the buyer must pay the seller a million dollars if there is renegotiation) is unlikely to be effective because the parties can always agree to rescind the old contract, thereby voiding the penalties [see Schelling (1960)].[43]

---

[42] In fact, Hart and Moore (1985) give an argument that the seller will be strongly advantaged in a renegotiation involving a price decrease, and that $p_1' = p_0 + 7.8$.

[43] The inclusion of a third party in the contract – with the initial two parties promising to pay the third party a large sum of money if they ever renegotiate – also does not overcome the problem because, if there are ex post gains from renegotiation, the third party can be persuaded at date 1 to give up his claim to this large sum in exchange for a sidepayment. The inclusion of a third party may help, however, to the extent that it makes renegotiation more costly; e.g., because it is known that the third party will be unavailable at a crucial moment during the renegotiation process.

It should be noted that third parties have uses beyond their ability to make renegotiation more difficult. A third party can act as a financial wedge between the initial contracting parties, so that the amount the seller receives in a particular state (p_1 or p_0) differs from the amount the buyer pays, with the third party making up the difference. Also, whenever actions or states are observable but not verifiable, it may be possible to get the initial parties to reveal their information to outsiders by inducing them to make reports to the third party, with a penalty due if their reports don't match (equilibria other than

If renegotiation cannot be prevented, the condition that there are no ex post Pareto improvements from recontracting must be imposed as a constraint in the original contract [as in Hart and Moore (1985); recall that, in the present context, information is symmetric and so it is clear what a Pareto improvement is]. We have already noted that such a constraint may be important in dynamic asymmetric information labor contract models, and it seems to apply to other contexts too. For instance, a firm may wish to convince a customer that it is not going to reduce its price in the future, but a binding contract to that effect may be infeasible since the firm and customer know that they will agree to rescind it at a later date (an agreement not to raise the price, on the other hand, may not suffer from the same difficulty). Other examples in the same spirit may be found in Schelling's (1960) interesting discussion of the difficulties of making commitments.[44]

Returning to our example, we may illustrate a theory of ownership presented in Grossman and Hart (1986; in press). It is sometimes suggested that when transaction costs prevent the writing of a complete contract, there may be a reason for firm integration [see Williamson (1985)]. Consider the payoffs of our diagram (page 135) and suppose that B takes over S. The control that B thereby gains over S's assets may allow B to affect S's costs in various ways, and this may reduce the possibility of opportunistic behavior by S. To take a very simple (and contrived) example, suppose that if S chooses $I_S = L$ then B can take some action α with respect to S's assets at date 1 so as to make S's cost of supplying either satisfactory or unsatisfactory input equal to 9. (In the coal–electricity example, α might refer to the part of the mine's seam the coal is taken out of; note that we now drop the assumption that the cost of supplying unsatisfactory

the truth-telling one may be a problem here). A difficulty with either of these arrangements is that there may be a great incentive for two of the three parties to collude; e.g., one of the initial two parties can deliberately report the wrong information, having (secretly) agreed with the third party to divide up the penalty that will result. If such collusion is possible, it can be shown in the present context that a three-party contract offers no advantage over a two-party one [see Hart and Moore (1985), Eswaran and Kotwal (1984)].

[44] In our earlier discussion we mentioned, but did not analyze, the possibility that the parties might send (verifiable) messages to each other at date 1, reflecting their jointly observable investment decisions, with the contract specifying how final prices p_1 and p_0 should depend on these messages. It should be noted that the use of such messages does not allow the first-best to be achieved in the original example, at least if renegotiation is possible. This is because if $v = 9$ and $c = 7$ then trade will occur at date 1 at some price (say, p_1') that depends on the messages sent. Hence to make a deviation from the first-best $I_B = I_S = H$ unprofitable for the buyer, we must have $10 - p_1 - 1.9 \geq 9 - p_1'$, where p_1 is the trading price when $v = 10$ and $c = 6$. On the other hand, to make it unprofitable for the seller, we must have $p_1 - 6 - 1.9 \geq p_1' - 7$. These inequalities are inconsistent.

input is zero.) Imagine furthermore that this action increases B's benefit, so that B will indeed take it at date 1 if S chooses L. Then with this extra degree of freedom, the first-best can be achieved. In particular, if $p_1 = p_0 + 6.1$ then $I_S = I_B = H$ is a Nash equilibrium because (by the above reasoning) any seller deviation will be punished, whereas a buyer deviation will induce the seller to supply unsatisfactory input, given that $p_1 < p_0 + 7$.[45]

Note that if action α could be specified in the initial contract then there would be no need for integration: The initial contract would simply say that B has the right to choose α at date 1. Ownership becomes important, however, if (i) α is too complicated to be specified in the date-0 contract and therefore qualifies as a residual right of control; and (ii) residual rights of control over an asset are in the hands of whomever owns that asset. The point is that, under incompleteness, the allocation of residual decision rights matters because the contract cannot specify precisely what each party's obligations are in every state of the world. To the extent that ownership of an asset guarantees residual rights of control over that asset, vertical and lateral integration can be seen as ways of ensuring particular – and presumably efficient – allocations of residual decision rights. [Although in the above example integration increases efficiency, this is in no way a general conclusion. In Grossman and Hart (1986; in press), examples are presented where integration reduces efficiency.]

Before concluding this section, we should emphasize that for reasons of tractability we have confined our attention to incompleteness that is due to a very particular sort of transaction cost. In practice, some of the other transactions costs we have alluded to are likely to be at least as important, if not more so. For example, in the type of model we have analyzed, although the parties cannot describe the state of the world or quality characteristics, they are still supposed to be able to write a contract that is unambiguous and anticipates all eventualities. This is very unrealistic. In practice, a contract might (say) have B agreeing to rent S's concert hall for a particular price. But suppose S's hall then burns down. The contract will usually be silent about what is meant to happen under these conditions (there is no hall to rent, but should S pay B damages and if so how much?), and so, in the event of a dispute, the courts will have to fill in the missing provision. (A situation where it becomes impossible or extremely costly to supply a contracted-for good is known in the legal literature as one of "impossibility" or "frustration.") An analysis of this sort of incompleteness is, though extremely difficult, a very important topic

---

[45] This assumes that the contract cannot be renegotiated at date 1. However, even if renegotiation is possible, the buyer's deviation will be unprofitable. This is because the renegotiated price for satisfactory input, p_1', will satisfy $p_1' \geq p_0 + 7$, and hence the buyer's net profit if he deviates is $9 - p_1' \leq 8.1 - p_1$.

for future research. It is likely to yield a much richer and more realistic view of the way contracts are written and throw light on how courts should assess damages [this latter issue has begun to be analyzed in the law and economics literature; see, e.g., Shavell (1980)].[46]

3.4 Self-enforcing contracts

The previous discussion has been concerned with explicit binding contracts that are enforced by outsiders, such as the courts. Even the most casual empiricism tells us that many agreements are not of this type. Although the courts may be there as a last resort (the shadow of the law may therefore be important), these agreements are enforced on a day-to-day basis by custom, good faith, reputation, and so on. Even in the case of a serious dispute, the parties may take great pains to resolve matters themselves rather than go to court. This leads to the notion of a self-enforcing or implicit contract [the importance of informal arrangements like this in business has been stressed by Macaulay (1963) and Ben-Porath (1980), among others].

People often bypass the legal process, presumably because of the transaction costs of using it. The costs of writing a good long-term contract (discussed in Section 3.2) are relevant here. So also is the skill with which the courts resolve contractual disputes. If contracts are incomplete and contain missing provisions as well as vague and ambiguous statements, appropriate enforcement may require abilities and knowledge (what was in the parties' minds?) that many judges and juries do not possess. This means that going to court may be a considerable gamble – and an expensive one at that. (This is an example of the fourth transaction cost noted in Section 3.2.)

Although the notion of implicit or self-enforcing contracts is often invoked, a formal study of such agreements has begun only recently [see, e.g., Bull (1985)], with a considerable stimulus coming from the theory of

---

[46] Mention should also be made of a theory of damages developed by Diamond and Maskin (1979). Diamond and Maskin consider a situation where a buyer and seller plan to trade with each other, but recognize that it may be efficient in some states of the world for one of them to trade instead with another party; for instance, the seller may find another buyer with a higher willingness to pay. Under these conditions, the buyer and seller can use the breach damages in their initial contract as a way of extracting surplus from this new party. For example, the bargaining position of a new buyer will be weakened if he must compensate the seller for breaching his contract with the original buyer. (This argument assumes that the new party cannot negotiate ex post with the buyer and seller together to waive the damage payment.) This idea has been used in an interesting paper by Aghion and Bolton (1985) to explain how long-term contracts can deter entry in an industry.

repeated games (cf. the model in Section 1.7). This literature has stressed the role of reputation in "completing" a contract. That is, a party may behave "reasonably," even if he is not obliged to do so, in order to develop a reputation as a decent and reliable trader. In some instances such reputational effects will operate only within the group of contractual parties – this is sometimes called *internal* enforcement of the contract – while in others the effects will be more pervasive. The latter will be the case when some outsiders to the contract (e.g., other firms in the industry or potential workers for a firm) observe unreasonable behavior by one party and as a result are more reluctant to deal with it in the future. In this case the enforcement is said to be *external* or *market-based*. (The model of Section 1.7 uses the idea of external enforcement.) Note that there may be a tension between this external enforcement and the reasons for the absence of a legally binding contract in the first place – the more people can observe the behavior, the more likely it is to be verifiable.

The distinction between an incomplete contract and a standard asymmetric information contract should be emphasized here. It is the former that allows reputation to operate, since the parties have the same information and can observe whether reasonable behavior is being maintained. In the latter case, it is unclear how reputation can overcome the asymmetry of information between the parties that is the reason for the departure from an Arrow–Debreu contract.

The role of reputation in sustaining a contract can be illustrated using the following model [based on Bull (1985) and Kreps (1984); this is an even simpler model of incomplete contracts than that of the last section]. Assume that a buyer B and a seller S wish to trade an item at date 1 that has value v to the buyer and cost c to the seller, where $v > c$. There are no ex ante investments and the good is homogeneous, so quality is not an issue. Suppose, however, that it is not verifiable whether trade actually occurs. Then a legally binding contract which specifies that the seller must deliver the item and the buyer must pay p, where $v > p > c$, cannot be enforced. The reason is – assuming (as we shall) that simultaneous delivery and payment are infeasible – that if the seller has to deliver first then the buyer can always deny that delivery occurred and refuse payment, while if the buyer has to pay first, the seller can always claim later that he did deliver even when he did not. As a result, if the parties must rely on the courts, a gainful trading opportunity will be missed.

The idea that not even the level of trade is verifiable is extreme, and Bull (1985) in fact makes the more defensible assumption that it is the quality of the good that cannot be verified (in Bull's model, S is a worker and quality refers to his performance). Bull supposes that quality is observable to the buyer only with a lag, so that take-it-or-leave-it offers of the type considered in Section 3.3 are not feasible. As a result, the seller always has an incentive to produce minimum quality (which corresponds in the above model to zero output). Making quantity nonverifiable is a cruder but simpler way of capturing the same idea [this is the approach taken in Kreps (1984)].

Note that in the above model incompleteness of the contract arises entirely from transaction cost (3), the difficulty of writing and enforcing the contract.

To introduce reputational effects one supposes that this trading relationship is repeated. Bull (1985) and Kreps (1984) follow the supergame literature and assume infinite repetition in order to avoid unraveling problems. This approach, as is well known, suffers from a number of difficulties. First, the assumption of infinite (or, in some versions, potentially infinite) life is hard to swallow. Second, "reasonable" behavior (i.e., trade) is sustained by the threat that if one party behaves unreasonably so will the other party from then on. Although this threat is credible (more precisely, subgame perfect), it is unclear why the parties could not decide to continue to trade after a deviation; that is, to "let bygones be bygones." [See Farrell (1984); this is another example where the ability to renegotiate ex post hurts the parties ex ante.]

It would seem that a preferable approach is to assume that the relationship has finite length, but introduce asymmetric information, as in Kreps and Wilson (1982) and in Milgrom and Roberts (1982). The following is based on some very preliminary work that we have undertaken along these lines.

Suppose that there are two types of buyers in the population, honest and dishonest. Honest buyers will always honor any agreement or promise that they have made, whereas dishonest ones will do so only if this is profitable. A buyer knows his own type, but others do not. It is common knowledge that the fraction of honest buyers in the population is π ($0 < \pi < 1$). In contrast, all sellers are known to be dishonest. All agents are risk-neutral.

Assume for simplicity that a single buyer and seller are matched at date 0, with neither having any alternative trading partners at this date or in the future (we are here departing from the ex ante perfect competition story that we have maintained for most of the chapter). Consider first the one-period case. Then a date-0 agreement can be represented as follows:

$$
\begin{array}{c|c|c|c}
\text{|}\underline{\qquad}\text{|} & \underline{\qquad}\text{|} & \underline{\qquad}\text{|} \\
p_1 & S & p_2 \\
\text{I} & \text{II} & \text{III}
\end{array}
$$

The interpretation is that the buyer promises to pay the seller p_1 before date 1 (stage I); in return, the seller promises to supply the item at date 1 (stage II); and in return for this, the buyer promises to make a further payment of p_2 (stage III).

We should mention one further assumption. Honest buyers, although they never breach an agreement first, are presumed to feel under no obligation to fulfill the terms of an agreement that has already been broken by a seller (interestingly, this theory of buyer psychology has parallels in common law). Note that if a buyer ever breaks an agreement first, he reveals himself to be dishonest, with the consequence that no further self-enforcing agreement with the seller is possible and hence trade ceases.

What is an optimal agreement? Consider the preceding diagram. The seller knows that he will receive p_2 only with probability π since a dishonest buyer will default at the last stage. Since the seller is himself dishonest, he will supply at stage II only if it is profitable for him to do so; that is, only if

$$\pi p_2 - c \geq 0. \tag{3.4}$$

Assume for simplicity that the seller has all the bargaining power at date 0 (nothing that follows depends on this). Then the seller will wish to maximize his overall payoff

$$p_1 + \pi p_2 - c, \tag{3.5}$$

subject to (3.4), which makes it credible that he will supply at stage II, and subject also to the constraint that he does not discourage an honest buyer from participating in the agreement at date 0. Because [with (3.4) satisfied] buyers know for certain that they will receive the item, this last condition is

$$v - p_1 - p_2 \geq 0. \tag{3.6}$$

Note that a dishonest buyer's payoff $v - p_1$ is always higher than an honest buyer's payoff given in (3.6), so there is no way to screen out dishonest buyers. In the language of asymmetric information models, the equilibrium is a pooling one.

Because the seller's payoff is increasing in p_1, (3.6) will hold with equality (the buyer gets no surplus). (More generally, changes in p_1 simply redistribute surplus between the two parties without changing either's incentive to breach.) If we substitute for p_1 in (3.5), the seller's payoff becomes $v - p_2(1 - \pi) - c$, which - when maximized subject to (3.4) - yields the solution $p_2 = c/\pi$. The maximized net payoff is

$$v - \frac{c}{\pi} \tag{3.7}$$

which is less than the first-best level, $v - c$.

We see then that the conditions for trade are more stringent in the absence of a binding contract. If $c/\pi > v > c$, there are gains from trade that will not be realized in a one-period relationship.

Suppose now that the relationship is repeated. Consider a two-period version of the above and assume no discounting. Now the following diagram applies:

$$
\begin{array}{ccccc}
|\underline{}| & \underline{}| & \underline{}| & \underline{}| & \underline{}| \\
p_1 & S & p_2 & S & p_3 \\
\text{I} & \text{II} & \text{III} & \text{IV} & \text{V}
\end{array}
$$

That is, the agreement says that the buyer pays, the seller supplies the first time, the buyer pays more, the seller supplies a second time, and the buyer makes a final payment. Rather than solving for the optimal arrangement, we shall simply show that the seller can do better than in the one-period case. Let $p_3 = c/\pi$, $p_2 = c$, and $p_1 = 2v - c - c/\pi$. Then (i) the seller will supply at stage IV (if matters have gone that far), knowing that he will receive p_3 with probability π; (ii) both honest and dishonest buyers will pay p_2 at stage III, the latter because (at a cost of c) they thereby ensure supply worth $v > c$ at stage IV; (iii) the seller will supply at stage II because this gives him a net payoff of $p_2 + \pi p_3 - 2c \geq 0$, while if he does not the arrangement is over and his payoff is zero; (iv) an honest buyer is prepared to participate since his surplus is nonnegative (actually, zero). The seller's overall expected net payoff is

$$
p_1 + p_2 + \pi p_3 - 2c = 2v - c - \frac{c}{\pi}, \tag{3.8}
$$

which exceeds twice the one-period payoff. Hence trade is more likely to take place in a two-period relationship than in a one-period one. In fact, it can be shown that the above is an optimal two-period agreement.

Repetition improves things by allowing the honest buyer to pay less the second time (stage III) than the third time (stage V). That is, the arrangement *back-loads* payments. This is acceptable to the seller because he knows that even a dishonest buyer will not default at stage III since he has a large stake in the arrangement continuing. To put it another way, the dishonest buyer does not want to reveal his dishonesty at too early a stage.

The same arrangement can be used when there are more than two periods: The buyer promises to pay c at every stage except the last, when he pays (c/π). In fact, the per-period surplus of the seller from such an arrangement converges to the first-best level $(v - c)$ as the number of periods tends to infinity (assuming no discounting, of course).

Although the above analysis is extremely provisional and sketchy, we can draw some tentative conclusions about the role of reputation and indicate some directions for further research. First, the notion of a psychic cost of breaking an agreement seems to be a useful – and not unrealistic – basis for a theory of self-enforcing contracts. It is obviously desirable to drop the assumption that some agents are completely honest and others completely dishonest, and assume instead that the typical trader has a finite psychic cost of breaking an agreement, where this cost is distributed in the population in a known way. In other words, everybody has their price, but this price varies. Preliminary work along these lines suggests that the above results generalize; in particular, repetition makes it easier to sustain a self-enforcing agreement.

Of course, asymmetries of information about psychic costs are not the only possible basis for a theory of reputation. For example, the buyer and seller could have private information about v and c, and might choose their trading strategies to influence perceptions about the values of these variables. A theory of self-enforcing contracts should ideally generate results which are not that sensitive to where the asymmetry of information is placed. However, the work of Fudenberg and Maskin (1986) in a related context suggests that this may be a difficult goal to achieve.[47]

There are a number of other natural directions in which to take the model. One is to introduce trade with other parties. For example, the seller may trade with a succession of buyers rather than a single one. The extent to which repetition increases per-period surplus in this case depends on whether new buyers observe the past broken promises of the seller. (This determines the degree to which external enforcement operates; more generally, a new buyer may observe that default occurred in the past but be unsure about who was responsible for it.) If new buyers do not observe past broken promises then repetition achieves nothing, which gives a very strong prediction of the possible benefits of a long-term relationship between a fixed buyer and seller. Even if past broken promises are observed perfectly, it appears that, ceteris paribus, a single long-term agreement may be superior to a succession of short-term ones. The reason is that in the latter case the constraint is imposed that each party must receive nonnegative surplus over *their* term of the relationship, whereas in the former case there is only the single constraint that surplus must be nonnegative over the whole term [see Bull (1985) and Kreps (1984)].

Probably the most important extension is to introduce incompleteness

---

[47] The role of uncertainty about v and c in determining reputation has been investigated by Thomas and Worrall (1984).

due to other sorts of transaction costs, such as the bounded rationality costs (1) and (2) discussed in Section 3.2. The problem is that the same factors that make it difficult to anticipate and plan for eventualities in a formal contract apply also to informal arrangements. That is, an informal arrangement is also likely to contain many missing provisions. But then the question arises, what constitutes "reasonable" or "desirable" behavior (in terms of building a reputation) with regard to states or actions that were not discussed ex ante? Custom, among other things, is likely to be important under these conditions: Behavior will be reasonable or desirable to the extent that it is generally regarded as such [for a good discussion of this, see Kreps (1984)]. This raises many new and interesting (as well as extremely difficult) questions.

Even though our analysis of reputation is very preliminary, it can throw some light on the ABG implicit contract model. There the firm insures the workers against fluctuations in their marginal product of labor. Uncertainty and risk aversion will obviously complicate the analysis of self-enforcing agreements considerably, but the above results suggest that a long-term agreement that stabilizes the workers' net income may be sustainable even in the absence of a binding contract, particularly if trade is repeated. Moreover, this can be so even if the marginal product of labor is (perfectly) correlated over time (in the above model it is constant), suggesting that an implicit contract may be sustained also for the asymmetric case studied in Section 2.3 (correlation of the marginal product is important because, in its absence, the asymmetry of information may disappear asymptotically; see Section 2.4C). With strong correlation, however, the conditions for an implicit contract will be more stringent, since a firm that has had a bad draw – and knows that this is permanent – will have a stronger incentive to breach [see Newbery and Stiglitz (1983)]. More generally, the fact that a contract must be self-enforcing will impose constraints on the form that it can take. An analysis of the precise conditions under which implicit contracts can be sustained (and of their resulting characteristics), when there is risk aversion and asymmetric information, is an interesting and important topic for future research.

3.5   *Summary and conclusions*

The vast majority of the theoretical work on contracts to date has been concerned with what might be called complete contracts. In this context, a complete contract is one that specifies each party's obligations in every conceivable eventuality, rather than a contract that is fully contingent in the Arrow–Debreu sense. According to this terminology, the asymmetric information labor contracts of Section 2.3 are just as complete as the symmetric information ones of Section 2.1.

In reality it is usually impossible to lay down each party's obligations completely and unambiguously in advance, and so most actual contracts are seriously incomplete. In Section 3, we have tried to indicate some of the complications of such incompleteness. Among other things, we have seen that incompleteness can lead to departures from the first-best even when there are no asymmetries of information among the contracting parties (and, moreover, the parties are risk-neutral).

More important perhaps than this is the fact that incompleteness raises new and difficult questions about how the behavior of the contracting parties is determined. To the extent that incomplete contracts do not specify the parties' actions fully (i.e., they contain "gaps"), additional theories are required to tell us how these gaps are filled in. Among other things, outside influences such as custom or reputation may become important under these conditions. In addition, outsiders such as the courts (or arbitrators) may have a role to play in filling in missing provisions of the contract and resolving ambiguities, rather than in simply enforcing an existing agreement. Incompleteness can also throw light on the importance of the allocation of decision rights or rights of control. If it is too costly to state precisely how a particular asset is to be used in every state of the world, it may be efficient simply to give one party "control" of the asset, in the sense that he is entitled to do what he likes with it, subject perhaps to some explicit (contractible) limitations.

Although the importance of incompleteness is very well recognized by lawyers, as well as by those working in law and economics, it is only beginning to be appreciated by economic theorists. It is to be hoped that work in the next few years will lead to significant advances in our formal understanding of this phenomenon. Unfortunately, progress is unlikely to be easy since many aspects of incompleteness are intimately connected with the notion of bounded rationality, a satisfactory formalization of which does not yet exist.

As a final illustration of the importance of incompleteness, consider the following question. Why do parties frequently write a limited term contract, with the intention of renegotiating this when it comes to an end, rather than writing a single contract that extends over the whole length of their relationship? In a complete contract framework such behavior cannot be advantageous, because the parties could just as well calculate what will happen when the contract expires and include this as part of the original contract. It is to be hoped that future work on incomplete contracts will allow this very basic question to be answered.

References

Abraham, K., and H. Farber. 1985. "Job Duration, Seniority, and Earnings." Mimeo, Massachusetts Institute of Technology.

Aghion, P., and P. Bolton. 1985. "Entry-Prevention Through Contracts with Customers." Mimeo, Massachusetts Institute of Technology.

Akerlof, G., and H. Miyazaki. 1980. "The Wage Bill Argument Meets the Implicit Contract Theory of Unemployment." *Review of Economic Studies* 47: 321-38.

Allen, F. 1985. "Repeated Principal–Agent Relationships with Lending and Borrowing." *Economic Letters* 17: 27-31.

Antle, R., and A. Smith. 1986. "An Empirical Investigation of the Relative Performance Evaluation of Corporate Executives." *Journal of Accounting Research* 24: 1-39.

Arnott, R., and J. Stiglitz. 1985. "Labor Turnover, Wage Structures, and Moral Hazard: The Inefficiency of Competitive Markets." *Journal of Labor Economics* 3: 434-62.

Arnott, R., A. Hosios, and J. Stiglitz. 1985. "Implicit Contracts, Labor Mobility and Unemployment." Mimeo, Queen's University, Canada.

Aron, D. 1984. "Ability, Moral Hazard, and Firm Diversification, Parts I and II." Mimeo, University of Chicago.

Arrow, K. 1985. "The Economics of Agency." In J. Pratt and R. Zeckhauser (eds.), *Principals and Agents: The Structure of Business,* pp. 37-51. Boston: Harvard Business School Press.

Azariadis, C. 1975. "Implicit Contracts and Underemployment Equilibria." *Journal of Political Economy* 83: 1183-1202.

1983. "Employment with Asymmetric Information." *Quarterly Journal of Economics (Supplement)* 98: 157-73.

Baily, M. 1974. "Wages and Employment Under Uncertain Demand." *Review of Economic Studies* 41: 37-50.

Baiman, S. 1982. "Agency Research in Managerial Accounting: A Survey." *Journal of Accounting Literature* 1: 154-213.

Baiman, S., and J. Demski. 1980. "Economically Optimal Performance Evaluation and Control Systems." *Supplement to Journal of Accounting Research* 18: 184-220.

Baron, D., and D. Besanko. 1984. "Regulation, Asymmetric Information, and Auditing." *Rand Journal of Economics* 15: 447-70.

Baron, D., and R. Myerson. 1982. "Regulating a Monopolist with Unknown Costs." *Econometrica* 50: 911-30.

Becker, G. 1964. *Human Capital.* New York: Columbia University Press.

Becker, G., and G. Stigler. 1974. "Law Enforcement, Malfeasance and Compensation of Enforcers." *Journal of Legal Studies* 3: 1-18.

Ben-Porath, Y. 1980. "The F-Connection: Families, Friends, and Firms and the Organization of Exchange." *Population and Development Review* 6: 130.

Bhattacharya, S. 1983. "Tournaments and Incentives: Heterogeneity and Essentiality." Research Paper No. 695, Graduate School of Business, Stanford University.

Brown, J., and O. Ashenfelter. 1986. "Testing the Efficiency of Employment Contracts." *Journal of Political Economy* 94: 540–87.

Bull, C. 1985. "The Existence of Self-Enforcing Implicit Contracts." C. V. Starr Center, New York University.

Calvo, G., and E. Phelps. 1977. "Employment Contingent Wage Contracts." *Journal of Monetary Economics* 5: 160–8.

Card, D. 1985. "Efficient Contracts and Costs of Adjustment: Short-Run Employment Determination for Airline Mechanics." Mimeo, Princeton University.

Carmichael, L. 1984. "Firm-Specific Human Capital and Promotion Ladders." *Rand Journal of Economics* 14: 251–8.

Chari, V. 1983. "Involuntary Unemployment and Implicit Contracts." *Quarterly Journal of Economics (Supplement)* 98: 107–22.

Cooper, R. 1983. "A Note on Overemployment/Underemployment in Labor Contracts Under Asymmetric Information." *Economic Letters* 12: 81–7.

Crawford, V. 1982. "Long-Term Relationships Governed by Short-Term Contracts." ICERD DP, London School of Economics.

Cremer, J., and M. Riordan. 1986. "On Governing Multilateral Transactions with Bilateral Contracts." Discussion Paper No. 134, Studies in Industry Economics, Stanford University.

D'Aspremont, C., and L. Gerard-Varet. 1979. "Incentives and Incomplete Information." *Journal of Public Economics* 11: 25–45.

DeGroot, M. 1970. *Optimal Statistical Decisions.* New York: McGraw-Hill Book Company.

Dewatripont, M. 1985. "Renegotiation and Information Revelation Over Time: The Case of Optimal Labor Contracts." Mimeo, Harvard University.

Diamond, D. 1984. "Financial Intermediation and Delegated Monitoring." *Review of Economic Studies* 51: 393–414.

1985. "Reputation Acquisition in Debt Markets." Mimeo, University of Chicago.

Diamond, P., and E. Maskin. 1979. "An Equilibrium Analysis of Search and Breach of Contract, 1: Steady States." *Bell Journal of Economics* 10: 282–316.

Dye, R. 1985. "Costly Contract Contingencies." *International Economic Review* 26: 233–50.

Eden, B. 1985. "Labor Contracts, Enforcement and Fluctuations in Aggregate Employment: The Case of No Severance Payments." Working Paper, University of Iowa.

Eswaran, M., and A. Kotwal. 1984. "The Moral Hazard of Budget-Breaking." *Rand Journal of Economics* 15: 578–81.

Fama, E. 1980. "Agency Problems and the Theory of the Firm." *Journal of Political Economy* 88: 288–307.

Farmer, R. 1984. "A New Theory of Aggregate Supply." *American Economic Review* 74: 920–30.

1985. "Implicit Contracts with Asymmetric Information and Bankruptcy: The Effect of Interest Rates on Layoffs." *Review of Economic Studies* 52: 427–42.

Farrell, J. 1984. "Renegotiation-Proof Equilibrium in Repeated Games." Mimeo, Massachusetts Institute of Technology.

Feldstein, M. 1976. "Temporary Layoffs in the Theory of Unemployment." *Journal of Political Economy* 84: 937–57.

Fischer, S. 1977. "Long Term Contracts, Rational Expectations, and the Optimal Money Supply Rule." *Journal of Political Economy* 85: 191–205.

Freixas, X., R. Guesnerie, and J. Tirole. 1985. "Planning Under Incomplete Information and the Ratchet Effect." *Review of Economic Studies* 52: 173–92.

Fudenberg, D., B. Holmström, and P. Milgrom. 1986. "Repeated Moral Hazard with Borrowing and Saving." Draft, School of Organization and Management, Yale University.

Fudenberg, D., and E. Maskin. 1986. "The Folk Theorem in Repeated Games with Discounting and with Incomplete Information." *Econometrica* 54: 533–54.

Fudenberg, D., and J. Tirole. 1983. "Sequential Bargaining with Asymmetric Information." *Review of Economic Studies* 50: 221–48.

Gale, D., and M. Hellwig. 1985. "Incentive Compatible Debt Contracts: the One Period Problem." *Review of Economic Studies* 52: 647–64.

Geanakoplos, J., and T. Ito. 1982. "On Implicit Contracts and Involuntary Unemployment." Cowles Foundation Discussion Paper #640, Yale University.

Gibbons, R. 1985. "Essays on Labor Markets and Internal Organization." Unpublished dissertation, Stanford University.

Gjesdal, F. 1982. "Information and Incentives: The Agency Information Problem." *Review of Economic Studies* 49: 373–90.

Goldberg, V., and J. Erickson. 1982. "Long-Term Contracts for Petroleum Coke." Department of Economics Working Paper Series No. 206, University of California-Davis.

Gordon, D. 1974. "A Neo-Classical Theory of Keynesian Unemployment." *Economic Inquiry* 12: 431–59.

Green, J. 1985. "Differential Information, the Market and Incentive Compatibility." In K. Arrow and S. Honkapohja (eds.), *Frontiers of Economics,* pp. 178–99. Oxford: Basil Blackwell.

Green, J., and C. Kahn. 1983. "Wage Employment Contracts." *Quarterly Journal of Economics (Supplement)* 98: 173–88.

Green, J., and N. Stokey. 1983. "A Comparison of Tournaments and Contracts." *Journal of Political Economy* 91: 349–64.

Grossman, S., and O. Hart. 1981. "Implicit Contracts, Moral Hazard and Unemployment." *American Economic Review (Papers and Proceedings)* 71: 301–8.

1982. "Corporate Financial Structure and Managerial Incentives." In J. McCall (ed.), *The Economics of Information and Uncertainty,* pp. 107–37. Chicago: University of Chicago Press.

1983a. "An Analysis of the Principal–Agent Problem." *Econometrica* 51: 7–45.

1983b. "Implicit Contracts Under Asymmetric Information." *Quarterly Journal of Economics (Supplement)* 71: 123–57.

1986. "The Costs and Benefits of Ownership: A Theory of Vertical and Lateral Integration." *Journal of Political Economy* 94: 691–719.

In press. "Vertical Integration and the Distribution of Property Rights." In A. Razin and E. Sadka (eds.), *Economic Policy in Theory and Practice*. New York: Oxford University Press.

Grossman, S., O. Hart, and E. Maskin. 1983. "Unemployment with Observable Aggregate Shocks." *Journal of Political Economy* 91: 907–28.

Grout, P. 1984. "Investment and Wages in the Absence of Binding Contracts: A Nash Bargaining Approach." *Econometrica* 52: 449–60.

Hahn, F. 1984. "Implicit Contracts and Involuntary Unemployment." Discussion Paper No. 71, Cambridge University.

Hall, R. 1980. "Employment Fluctuations and Wage Rigidity." *Brookings Papers on Economic Activity* 1: 91–123.

Hall, R., and D. Lilien. 1979. "Efficient Wage Bargains Under Uncertain Supply and Demand." *American Economic Review* 69: 868–79.

Harris, M., and B. Holmström. 1982. "A Theory of Wage Dynamics." *Review of Economic Studies* 49: 315–33.

Harris, M., and A. Raviv. 1979. "Optimal Incentive Contracts with Imperfect Information." *Journal of Economic Theory* 20: 231–59.

1981. "Allocation Mechanisms and the Design of Auctions." *Econometrica* 49: 1477–99.

Harris, M., and R. Townsend. 1981. "Resource Allocation Under Asymmetric Information." *Econometrica* 49: 33–64.

Hart, O. 1983. "Optimal Labour Contracts Under Asymmetric Information: An Introduction." *Review of Economic Studies* 50: 3–35.

Hart, O., and J. Moore. 1985. "Incomplete Contracts and Renegotiation." Working Paper, London School of Economics.

Holmström, B. 1979. "Moral Hazard and Observability." *Bell Journal of Economics* 10: 74–91.

1982a. "Moral Hazard in Teams." *Bell Journal of Economics* 13: 324–40.

1982b. "Managerial Incentive Problems – A Dynamic Perspective." In *Essays in Economics and Management in Honor of Lars Wahlbeck*. Helsinki: Swedish School of Economics.

1983. "Equilibrium Long-Term Labor Contracts." *Quarterly Journal of Economics (Supplement)* 98: 23–54.

Holmström, B., and P. Milgrom. 1985. "Aggregation and Linearity in the Provision of Intertemporal Incentives." Cowles Discussion Paper No. 742.

Holmström, B., and J. Ricart-Costa. 1986. "Managerial Incentives and Capital Management." *Quarterly Journal of Economics* 101: 835–60.

Holmström, B., and L. Weiss. 1985. "Managerial Incentives, Investment and Aggregate Implications: Scale Effects." *Review of Economic Studies* 52: 403–26.

Jensen, M., and W. Meckling. 1976. "Theory of the Firm: Managerial Behavior, Agency Costs, and Capital Structure." *Journal of Financial Economics* 3: 305–60.

Joskow, P. 1985. "Vertical Integration and Long-Term Contracts." *Journal of Law, Economics and Organization* 1: 33–80.

Kahn, C. 1985. "Optimal Severance Pay with Incomplete Information." *Journal of Political Economy* 93: 435–51.

Kihlstrom, R., and J. Laffont. 1979. "A General Equilibrium Entrepreneurial Theory of Firm Formation Based on Risk Aversion." *Journal of Political Economy* 87: 719–48.

Killingsworth, M. 1983. *Labor Supply.* Cambridge University Press.

Klein, B., R. Crawford, and A. Alchian. 1978. "Vertical Integration, Appropriable Rents and the Competitive Contracting Process." *Journal of Law and Economics* 21: 297–326.

Kreps, D. 1984. "Corporate Culture and Economic Theory." Mimeo, Stanford University.

Kreps, D., and R. Wilson. 1982. "Reputation and Imperfect Information." *Journal of Economic Theory* 27: 253–79.

Kydland, F., and E. Prescott. 1977. "Rules Rather Than Discretion: The Inconsistency of Optimal Plans." *Journal of Political Economy* 85: 473–92.

Laffont, J-J., and E. Maskin. 1982. "Theory of Incentives: An Overview." In W. Hildenbrand (ed.), *Advances in Economic Theory,* pp. 31–94. Cambridge: Cambridge University Press.

Laffont, J-J., and J. Tirole. 1986. "Using Cost Observation to Regulate Firms." *Journal of Political Economy* 94: 614–41.

Lambert, R. 1983. "Long-Term Contracting and Moral Hazard." *Bell Journal of Economics* 14: 441–52.

1986. "Executive Effort and Selection of Risky Projects." *Rand Journal of Economics* 16: 77–88.

Lazear, E. 1979. "Why is There Mandatory Retirement?" *Journal of Political Economy* 87: 1261–84.

Lazear, E., and S. Rosen. 1981. "Rank-Order Tournaments as Optimum Labor Contracts." *Journal of Political Economy* 89: 841–64.

Lucas, R. 1972. "Expectations and the Neutrality of Money." *Journal of Economic Theory* 4: 103–24.

Macaulay, S. 1963. "Non-Contractual Relations in Business: A Preliminary Study." *American Sociological Review* 28: 55–67.

Malcomson, J. 1981. "Unemployment and the Efficiency Wage Hypothesis." *Economic Journal* 91: 848–66.

1984a. "Rank-Order Contracts for a Principal with Many Agents." Working Paper No. 8405, Universite Catholique de Louvain.

1984b. "Work Incentives, Hierarchy, and Internal Labor Markets." *Journal of Political Economy* 92: 486–507.

Malcomson, J., and F. Spinnewyn. 1985. "The Multiperiod Principal Agent Problem." Discussion Paper No. 8511, University of Southampton.

Maskin, E., and J. Riley. 1984. "Optimal Auctions with Risk-Averse Buyers." *Econometrica* 52: 1473–1518.

Milgrom, P. 1981. "Good News and Bad News: Representation Theorems and Applications." *Bell Journal of Economics* 12: 380–91.

Milgrom, P., and J. Roberts. 1982. "Predation, Reputation and Entry Deterrence." *Journal of Economic Theory* 27: 280–312.

154   Oliver Hart and Bengt Holmström

Mirrlees, J. 1971. "An Exploration in the Theory of Optimum Income Taxation." *Review of Economic Studies* 38: 175–208.

1974. "Notes on Welfare Economics, Information and Uncertainty." In M. Balch, D. McFadden, and S. Wu (eds.), *Essays in Economic Behavior Under Uncertainty,* pp. 243–58. Amsterdam: North-Holland.

1975. "The Theory of Moral Hazard and Unobservable Behavior – Part I." Mimeo, Nuffield College, Oxford.

1976. "The Optimal Structure of Authority and Incentives Within an Organization." *Bell Journal of Economics* 7: 105–31.

Moore, J. 1984. "Contracting Between Two Parties With Private Information." Working Paper, London School of Economics.

1985. "Optimal Labour Contracts When Workers Have a Variety of Privately Observed Reservation Wages." *Review of Economic Studies* 52: 37–67.

Murphy, K. 1986. "Incentives, Learning and Compensation: A Theoretical and Empirical Investigation of Managerial Labor Contracts." *Rand Journal of Economics* 17: 59–76.

Myerson, R. 1979. "Incentive Compatibility and the Bargaining Problem." *Econometrica* 47: 61–74.

1981. "Optimal Auction Design." *Mathematics of Operations Research* 6: 58–73.

Nalebuff, B., and J. Stiglitz. 1983. "Prizes and Incentives: Towards a General Theory of Compensation and Competition." *Bell Journal of Economics* 13: 21–43.

Newbery, D., and J. Stiglitz. 1983. "Wage Rigidity, Implicit Contracts and Economic Efficiency: Are Market Wages Too Flexible?" Economic Theory Discussion Paper 68, Cambridge University.

New York Times. 1985. "The Two-Tier Wage Impact." October 30.

Oswald, A. 1984. "Efficient Contracts Are on the Labour Demand Curve: Theory and Facts." Mimeo, Oxford University.

Radner, R. 1981. "Monitoring Cooperative Agreements in a Repeated Principal–Agent Relationship." *Econometrica* 49: 1127–48.

1985. "Repeated Principal–Agent Games with Discounting." *Econometrica* 53: 1173–98.

Riordan, M. 1984. "Uncertainty, Asymmetric Information and Bilateral Contracts." *Review of Economic Studies* 51: 83–93.

Roberts, K. 1982. "Long-Term Contracts." Mimeo, Warwick University.

Rogerson, W. 1985a. "Repeated Moral Hazard." *Econometrica* 53: 69–76.

1985b. "The First-Order Approach to Principal–Agent Problems." *Econometrica* 53: 1357–68.

Rosen, S. 1985. "Implicit Contracts: A Survey." *Journal of Economic Literature* 23: 1144–75.

Ross, S. 1973. "The Economic Theory of Agency: The Principal's Problem." *American Economic Review* 63: 134–9.

Rubinstein, A. 1979. "Offenses That May Have Been Committed by Accident – An Optimal Policy of Retribution." In S. Brams, A. Shotter, and G. Schwödiauer (eds.), *Applied Game Theory,* pp. 406–13. Wurtzburg: Physica-Verlag.

Salop, J., and S. Salop. 1976. "Self-Selection in the Labor Market." *Quarterly Journal of Economics* 90: 619-27.

Schelling, T. 1960. *The Strategy of Conflict.* Harvard University Press.

Shapiro, C., and J. Stiglitz. 1984. "Equilibrium Unemployment as a Worker Incentive Device." *American Economic Review* 74: 433-44.

Shavell, S. 1979. "Risk Sharing and Incentives in the Principal and Agent Relationship." *Bell Journal of Economics* 10: 55-73.

1980. "Damage Measures for Breach of Contract." *Bell Journal of Economics* 11: 466-90.

Simon, H. 1982. *Models of Bounded Rationality.* MIT Press.

Spence, M., and R. Zeckhauser. 1971. "Insurance, Information and Individual Action." *American Economic Review (Papers and Proceedings)* 61: 380-7.

Stiglitz, J., and A. Weiss. 1981. "Credit Rationing in Markets with Imperfect Information." *American Economic Review* 71: 393-410.

Taylor, J. 1980. "Aggregate Dynamics and Staggered Contracts." *Journal of Political Economy* 88: 1-24.

Thomas, J., and T. Worrall. 1984. "Self-Enforcing Wage Contracts." Mimeo, University of Cambridge.

Townsend, R. 1980. "Models of Money With Spatially Separated Agents." In J. Kareken and N. Wallace (eds.), *Models of Monetary Economics.* Minneapolis: Federal Reserve Bank.

1982. "Optimal Multiperiod Contracts and the Gain from Enduring Relationships Under Private Information." *Journal of Political Economy* 90: 1166-86.

Weiss, A. 1980. "Job Queues and Layoffs in Labor Markets with Flexible Wages." *Journal of Political Economy* 88: 526-38.

Williamson, O. 1975. *Markets and Hierarchies: Analysis and Antitrust Implications.* New York: Free Press.

1985. *The Economic Institutions of Capitalism.* New York: Free Press.

Wilson, R. 1969. "The Structure of Incentives for Decentralization under Uncertainty." *La Decision* 171.

Wolfson, M. 1985. "Empirical Evidence of Incentive Problems and Their Mitigation in Oil and Tax Shelter Programs." In J. Pratt and R. Zeckhauser (eds.), *Principals and Agents: The Structure of Business,* pp. 101-25. Boston: Harvard Business School Press.

Yaari, M. 1976. "A Law of Large Numbers in the Theory of Consumer's Choice Under Uncertainty." *Journal of Economic Theory* 12: 202-17.

CHAPTER 4

Battles for market share: incomplete information, aggressive strategic pricing, and competitive dynamics

John Roberts

In the last five years, economists have begun to apply the theory of games of incomplete information in extensive form to problems of industrial competition. As a result, we are beginning to get a theoretical handle on some aspects of the rich variety of behavior that marks real strategic interactions but that has previously resisted analysis. For example, the only theoretically consistent analyses of predatory pricing available five years ago indicated that such behavior was pointless and should be presumed to be rare; now we have several distinct models pointing in the opposite direction. These not only formalize and justify arguments for predation that had previously been put forward by business people, lawyers, and students of industrial practice; they also provide subtle new insights that call into question both prevailing public policy and legal standards and various suggestions for their reform. In a similar fashion, we now have models offering strategic, information-based explanations for such phenomena as price wars, the use of apparently uninformative advertising, limit pricing, patterns of implicit cooperation and collusion, the breakdown of bargaining and delays of agreement, the use of warranties and service contracts, the form of pricing chosen by oligopolists, the nature of contracts between suppliers and customers, and the adoption of various institutions for exchange: almost all of this was unavailable five years ago.

The development of such theory would seem to be a major event in the study of industrial organization. This field arose fifty years ago because scholars studying actual market behavior found received microeconomic theory to be of little value in understanding many of the phenomena that they observed and believed to be crucial. For its first thirty-plus years,

The comments of Drew Fudenberg, George Mailath, Ariel Rubinstein, Hugo Sonnenschein, Jean Tirole, and Bob Wilson, the financial support of the National Science Foundation (Grant SES 83-08723), and the hospitality of the Institute of Advanced Studies of the Hebrew University are gratefully acknowledged.

the field developed through case studies and statistical investigations with little reliance upon – and little contribution to – theory. Then, as Schmalensee (1982) has documented, in the 1970s theoretical models of some of the classical issues of industrial organization began to emerge. Increasingly over this decade it was realized that a satisfactory modeling of industrial competition must involve treating all the participants as rational, strategic actors. This inevitably led to the use of formal game-theoretic methods. The first such work assumed complete information. Research in this mold has provided and continues to yield important insights on several fundamental issues, including product differentiation, R&D races, and strategic investment as a means of creating entry barriers. However, it was only with the recognition of informational asymmetries that game-theoretic models began to generate some of the richness that the founders of the field of industrial organization saw in the world and found missing in the theory.

Although the use of incomplete information game theory in industrial organization is a recent development, it has already generated too large a volume of work to survey adequately here. Given the necessity of limiting the range of material covered, I have chosen to concentrate on a group of models aimed at explaining various sorts of "aggressive" pricing behavior that I call "battles for market share." In these models, firms operating under incomplete information depart systematically from standard, Cournot- or Bertrand-like oligopolistic behavior in an attempt to gain market share from current rivals or to protect it from potential competitors. By making this selection I am leaving aside a vast range of important, strikingly interesting applications to other questions in industrial organization. Still, the models I consider focus on central questions in the field and yield answers suggesting the sort of changes that these new methods are working more broadly.

I hope this paper will be useful to nonspecialists who may be interested in what all the recent excitement in theoretical industrial organization has been about. I have been quite informal in presenting this work, focusing on examples and the cases of central interest, and ignoring hard technical problems. I hope this approach will give some intuitive feel for the methods and some understanding of the nature of the results in the field. Of course, this means that many readers will be profoundly dissatisfied. For those, I can recommend the original papers and also the excellent surveys by Fudenberg and Tirole (1986a) and Kreps and Spence (1985).

1   Limit pricing

A major focus of industrial organization research has been potential competition and its impact on conduct and performance. Of particular interest have been the issues of whether incumbent firms can limit or prevent entry by strategic behavior, of the methods they might adopt, and of the resultant welfare effects.

Bain's (1949) concept of limit pricing suggested that pre-entry pricing might be the instrument of such a strategy. His idea was that if there were a monotone relationship between the pre-entry price and the probability, speed, or amount of new entry, then incumbents would have an incentive to protect their markets from entry by charging lower prices. During the '60s and '70s, a series of authors produced increasingly sophisticated models which suggested that limit pricing would, in fact, be used. This theory was important in two ways. First, it explained the observation that firms have apparently selected prices in the range of inelastic demand. Moreover, it also suggested a policy problem: Limit pricing would result in lower pre-entry prices, but would defer (perhaps indefinitely) the realization of the even lower prices that follow entry.

These models assumed that entry would be an increasing function of the incumbent's price. The validity of the resultant conclusions thus depended on whether entrants actually would respond to pre-entry prices as assumed.

As Bain himself accentuated, the entry decision should be determined by expectations of profitability. The profitability of entry in turn will depend on cost and demand conditions and the nature of competition in the post-entry world. Unless these in turn depend on the pre-entry price (as they would with learning curves or customer loyalty), the pre-entry price is, per se, irrelevant. Thus, the only way that this price might influence entry is if it somehow influenced *expectations* of profitability, as opposed to profitability itself.

How then might the current price influence these expectations? This issue was typically not addressed explicitly in the early literature, and when it was, some exogenous specifications of the relationship between profit expectations and pre-entry prices was given. For example, the widely used "Sylos postulate" had entrants believe that the pre-entry price would be maintained after entry. Clearly a more satisfactory procedure would model the post-entry competition, assume rational expectations, and then use these to investigate the nature of optimal pre-entry pricing. However, as James Friedman (1979) noted, there is a fundamental problem here. Suppose we make the standard (but usually implicit) assumptions that potential entrants and the established firm are equally well informed about the determinants of post-entry profitability and that pre-entry price is not directly one of these determinants. Then the rational expectation of post-entry profitability – and the entry decision – will be independent of the pre-entry price. Consequently, if all firms are treated as equally well informed rational maximizers, limit pricing would not emerge.

However, suppose that markets differ in their post-entry profitability in a way that is not observable to potential entrants. Entrants would want to identify and avoid the unprofitable markets. Suppose too that incumbents are informed about the parameters determining the profitability of entry, and that this private information affects their decision making so that the pre-entry price and the profitability of entry are positively correlated. Then entrants, in trying to infer the private information from prices, would avoid entry if price were low. One would thus have a basis for the previously assumed price–entry relationship. Further, by charging lower prices, an incumbent could hope to bias entrants' inferences and thereby prevent their entry.

This sort of idea is in Bain's work (1949), but the first full game-theoretic equilibrium modeling based on it, with both incumbent and entrant treated as rational strategic actors, was offered by Milgrom and Roberts (1982a).[1] Because this model was one of the first treatments of industrial organization using the methods that are our focus here, because it has been the basis for a significant volume of other work, and because it is a useful vehicle for discussing many of the characteristic features of analyses using these methods, we will give it a rather extended treatment.

1.1   Limit pricing as signaling

Consider a monopolist faced with a single potential entrant. The monopolist must set the price at which it will sell in the pre-entry period. The entrant observes this price, then makes its entry decision. If entry occurs, the two firms share the market; if it does not, the monopolist is not threatened further. This is a classic context for examining limit pricing.

Suppose the monopolist is initially better informed about some argument of the function giving the entrant's equilibrium post-entry profits than is the entrant. To use the specific example from Milgrom and Roberts (1982a), suppose the monopolist knows its (constant per-unit) costs of production c_I, but this information is not available to the entrant at the time of its entry decision. If entry occurs the entrant will learn the value of c_I and the two firms will then play the usual full-information Cournot game.[2] Assume that the entrant's profits are an increasing func-

---

[1] For a brief review of some earlier work in this spirit, see Salop (1979).

[2] This assumption can be relaxed in various ways without disrupting the principal conclusion that the incumbent will adopt limit pricing; see below. One important complication would arise if the post-entry game were a Bertrand one. When competition is in prices, each firm wants the other to set a high price, and each firm will optimally set its price higher the higher is its estimate of the other's costs. Thus, *conditional on entry,* the incumbent would prefer the entrant believed c_I were higher than its true value [see Bulow, Geanakoplos, and Klemperer (1985), Fudenberg and Tirole (1986a), and Mailath (1985)]. This could complicate the first-stage incentives to signal low costs and thereby deter entry.

tion of c_I. Suppose that if c_I is high then the entrant would profit from entry, while if c_I is low then the entrant's profits from entry are less than what it can earn elsewhere. Meanwhile, the monopolist's profits are those accruing to it in the pre-entry period plus (the present value of) either its duopoly or its monopoly profits in the second period, depending on whether entry occurred or not. Assume that, other things being equal, the incumbent would prefer to remain a monopolist than to share the market, no matter what its costs.

If c_I were common knowledge, we would have a simple extensive form game whose unique solution would be for the entrant to come in if and only if it were profitable, and for the incumbent to charge the simple monopoly price corresponding to the actual value of c_I. (This is Friedman's point.) In actuality, we have one such game for each possible value of c_I, and the entrant does not know which of these it is playing. It thus faces a real problem. If c_I is high, it wants to enter. If c_I is low, it wants to stay out. But it does not know what c_I actually is, and so it does not know what is optimal to do.

In fact, game theory gives no way to analyze directly such situations of *incomplete information,* because it is a fundamental assumption of game theory that players know the game they are playing. However, Harsanyi (1967/68) gives a resolution of this problem: Given such a collection of games representing a situation of incomplete information, associate with it a single game of *complete* but *imperfect* information and identify equilibria of this well-defined game as the solutions of the original game of incomplete information. To do this, assume here that the entrant is a Bayesian and has a prior distribution over the possible values of c_I, which lie in some set C_I. Now introduce a dummy player, "Nature," that picks c_I according to this distribution. For each possible realization of c_I, the incumbent learns the realization but the entrant does not, then the game corresponding to the particular value of c_I is played.

This construct is a game of complete information, because there is a single game tree (beginning with Nature's move) and the tree and the payoffs along each path in the tree are common knowledge. It is also one of imperfect information, because the entrant must move without being perfectly informed about the results of other players' previous moves: It knows the incumbent's price choice, but not Nature's choice of c_I. Thus, it can condition its entry decision on the pre-entry price, but not on the incumbent's actual cost.

The incumbent, however, knows its realized cost and can condition its price choice on the cost realization. Thus, a strategy for the entrant is a specification of the action it will take for each possible price it might observe, while a strategy for the established firm is a specification of its price for each possible cost level.

Note that, although the incumbent actually has a particular given cost level, its strategy must specify the prices it would charge for each possible cost level and not just for the one that actually obtains. Although this stricture is imposed on us by the method we are using to solve the game, it has a natural interpretation. The entrant does not know the incumbent's actual cost, but its optimal action depends on the value of this variable. It will thus try to infer the unobservable cost from the observable price. To do so, it must have a conjecture regarding the price the established firm would charge for each possible cost level; that is, it must have a conjecture as to the incumbent's strategy.

A pure-strategy Nash equilibrium of this game consists of a pair of strategies, one for each player, with the mutual best response property: each player's strategy maximizes its expected payoff,[3] given that the other player adopts its equilibrium strategy. Alternatively, in line with the discussion in the last paragraph, we can think of the equilibrium as a strategy for each player and a conjecture for each regarding the other's strategy. We then require that each player's strategy maximizes its expected profits given its conjecture as to the other's strategy, and that the conjectures are correct.

To see how limit pricing could emerge in equilibrium, suppose that the possible values of c_I are distributed on $C_I = [\underline{c}_I, \bar{c}_I]$ according to a distribution function F_I. Suppose too that the costs of the entrant are private information to the entrant when the first-period price is set, but will become common knowledge if entry occurs.[4] Let the prior beliefs regarding these be given by a distribution F_E. Finally, let $\Pi_M(p, c_I)$ denote the incumbent's monopoly profits as a function of price and its cost, let $M(c_I)$ be the monopoly price, and let $\Pi_I(c_I, c_E)$ and $\Pi_E(c_I, c_E)$ be the incumbent's and the entrant's Cournot duopoly profit functions respectively.

Suppose that the established firm plays its simple monopoly strategy $M(c_I)$, that this function is invertible, and that the entrant's strategy is the best response to this; that is, enter only if profits would be positive

---

[3] We follow the usual procedure of assuming that players select their strategies before the start of the game, i.e., before Nature's move determines c_I. Thus, the expectations in the profit calculations are, inter alia, over the possible values of c_I. However, this means that the choice for the incumbent must be optimal, given the entrant's strategy, for almost all c_I and, in particular, for any value of c_I which could obtain with positive probability. Thus, we can usually think of the informed party as maximizing separately for each value of its private information.

[4] Given that we have already assumed that the incumbent's costs become common knowledge before the post-entry competition takes place, the assumption of private cost information for the entrant serves only to generate pure strategy equilibrium (because the entrant's choice will be random from the incumbent's point of view). If costs remained private information after entry, this informational asymmetry would have an effect on strategic behavior, but would not eliminate limit pricing; see below.

given that $c_I = M^{-1}(p)$. Is is then easily seen that this situation with no limit pricing cannot be an equilibrium. Let $\gamma(c_I)$ be the cost level c_E at which the entrant's profits are zero – that is, $\Pi_E(c_I, \gamma(C_I)) = 0$ – and assume γ is strictly increasing. Thus, entry occurs if $c_E < \gamma(M^{-1}(p))$. If, when its costs are c_I, the incumbent were to charge a lower price $p' = M(c_I) - \epsilon$ for some small ϵ (where $p' = M(c_I')$, $c_I' < c_I$), this would have a zero first-order effect on the value of Π_M. However, given the entrant's strategy, the probability of entry would fall from $F_E(\gamma(M^{-1}(M(c_I)))) = F_E(\gamma(c_I))$ to $F_E(\gamma(M^{-1}(p'))) = F_E(\gamma(c_I'))$. This increases the second-period expected profit by

$$\int_{\gamma(c_I')}^{\gamma(c_I)} [\Pi_M(M(c_I), c_I) - \Pi_I(c_I, c_E)] \, dF_E(c_E)$$

for each c_I, and this term is positive and of order ϵ rather than ϵ^2 so long as M^{-1} has a nonzero derivative (see below). Thus, such a deviation is worthwhile and, if equilibrium exists, it must involve pricing at other than the simple monopoly level in an attempt to reduce entry.

To characterize equilibrium further, consider the strategies $P(c_I)$ and $E(p, c_E)$, where $P: C_I \to R_+$ and $E: R_+ \times C_E \to \{\text{in, out}\}$. Define $C_I(p)$ as the set of c_I levels that select $P(c_I) = p$, $C_E(p, 1)$ as the set of c_E levels that enter when they see price p, and $C_E(p, 0)$ as those who stay out in response to p. In equilibrium the strategies must satisfy the following: For each $c_I \in C_I$, $p = P(c_I)$ maximizes

$$\Pi_M(p, c_I) + \int_{C_E(p,0)} \Pi_M(M(c_I), c_I) \, dF_E(c_E)$$
$$+ \int_{C_E(p,1)} \Pi_I(c_I, c_E) \, dF_E(c_E) \tag{1}$$

subject to $p \geq 0$; and, for each $c_E \in C_E$ and each $p \in R_+$,

$$c_E \in C_E(p, 1) \text{ if } \int_{C_I(p)} \Pi_E(c_I, c_E) \, dF_I(c_I) > 0 \quad \text{and}$$
$$c_E \in C_E(p, 0) \text{ if } \int_{C_I(p)} \Pi_E(c_I, c_E) \, dF_I(c_I) < 0. \tag{2}$$

The first term in (1) is to the incumbent's pre-entry profit, which depends on its price and costs. Together the other two terms represent its second-period expected profit when it charges p and the entrant responds according to E. The first of these is just its monopoly profit multiplied by the probability that the entrant stays out when price p is charged. The second gives the contribution to expected profit when entry occurs. Because the incumbent's duopoly profit depends on the entrant's costs, we take the expectation over the set of cost levels that yield entry in response to the price p.

The conditions in (2) state that an entrant with costs c_E comes in if its expected profit is positive when competing against an incumbent whose costs are such that (using P) it charges p, and that it stays out if entry brings expected losses. Note that we have not specified the behavior when expected profit is exactly zero. With a non-atomic continuum of entrant types, this is immaterial. On the other hand, if some c_E values have strictly positive probability (as they must in a finite model) then the specification would influence the incumbent's payoff and behavior, and so is important. Also note that we have not specified what happens when $C_I(p)$ is empty – that is, what the entrant does after observing a price it knows it should not have seen in equilibrium. This specification of what happens "off the equilibrium path" is crucial. Because the entrant assigns probability zero to such events, it is indifferent about its behavior after such a price is observed. However, this behavior determines the payoff to the incumbent from such a price and so affects its behavior. We shall return to this issue below.

Two important points follow from these relationships. First, if the entry decision depends on the observed price p then $P(\cdot)$ will typically differ from the simple monopoly price. In particular, if $C_E(p, 1)$ is expanding in p [as it would be if $P(c_I)$ is increasing], then $P(c_I) < M(c_I)$ for almost all values of c_I, so standard limit pricing is practiced.

Second, the entrant correctly interprets the incumbent's behavior, entering only if doing so is rationally expected to be profitable. Thus, although the incumbent forgoes pre-entry profit to deter entry, in equilibrium this behavior does not systematically reduce the probability of entry. In fact, if the equilibrium $P(\cdot)$ is monotonic then entry occurs precisely when it would have under complete information – that is, only if

$$\Pi_E(P^{-1}(P(c_I)), c_E) = \Pi_E(c_I, c_E) > 0.$$

This second point is representative of a fundamental general phenomenon. Equilibrium involves players accurately accounting for each other's motives and correctly forecasting behavior. They thus do not draw inferences that are systematically biased, and attempts to influence behavior by biasing inferences must fail. We will see this same result several times in other models.

Then why not charge the simple monopoly price? We have already argued that this cannot be an equilibrium, but we can put the argument somewhat differently. If a firm with cost c_I were to charge $M(c_I)$ instead of $P(c_I)$, the entrant would see only the resultant price. It would then interpret this observation as the choice of a firm with costs $c_I' = P^{-1}(M(c_I))$

whose equilibrium limit pricing led to its charging this particular price. Such a firm would have higher costs than c_I. This results in an increased threat of entry that offsets the gain in pre-entry profits.

A difficulty with the Milgrom–Roberts theory (and, more generally, with models of signaling as games of incomplete information) is that it admits a large set of Nash equilibria of several kinds. First, there may be many separating equilibria; that is, ones in which P is an invertible function of c_I. As well, there may be equilibria with partial or complete pooling, so that some or all of the possible types of incumbent select the same price with positive probability. These equilibria do share some common features, however. Any separating equilibrium must involve reduced prices as long as it would ever be worthwhile to charge the monopoly price of a lower-cost type if this led to being perceived by entrants as having this lower cost. Any equilibrium with pooling must also involve at least some types deviating from simple monopoly pricing, although this might take the form of raising prices. Moreover, in either case there is no systematic reduction in the probability of entry as a result of this limit pricing. However, one would like sharper predictions.

There are two approaches to obtaining greater specificity. Both begin from the observation that the multiplicity of equilibria can be viewed as arising from the failure of the Nash equilibrium concept to limit behavior off the equilibrium path, that is, in situations that occur in equilibrium with probability zero. This behavior is crucial, because it determines the attractiveness of a deviation from the prescribed strategies and thus whether the strategies constitute an equilibrium. However, because it occurs with probability zero, this behavior does not influence the equilibrium expected utility of the player in question and so the best-response condition does not limit it.

One approach to obtaining sharper predictions is to introduce some noise into the model to expand the set of prices that might be observed in equilibrium. With fewer probability-zero events, Nash equilibrium then has more "bite." This approach was pioneered by Matthews and Mirman (1983) and independently by Saloner (1982). The second approach is to use a stronger notion of equilibrium. We will consider this first, then return to the noisy limit-pricing models in the context of discussing extensions of the basic model.

1.2   Refining the equilibrium concept

Some of the multiplicity of equilibria can be eliminated by considering only sequential equilibria, a strengthening of Nash equilibrium due to Kreps and Wilson (1982b). The key innovation in sequential equilibrium lies in specifying explicitly the beliefs that entrants have about the incumbent's private information conditional on seeing any particular price, and requiring these to be derived from the initial prior. Sequentiality also involves the "perfectness" condition that continued play of the given strategies must be optimal, given the beliefs, from each point forward. This serves to eliminate many strategy combinations that can be viewed as depending on incredible threats or unrealizable fears. Moreover, being explicit about beliefs facilitates consideration of the reasonableness of the beliefs supporting an equilibrium, and thus permits the formal analysis of further restrictions on beliefs.

The chief force of sequential equilibrium here is to guarantee that the highest-cost type of incumbent always selects its monopoly price in any separating equilibrium, essentially because whatever price it chooses leads to maximal entry and so there is no reason to forgo first-period profits. Without sequentiality, we might have the highest-cost firm deviating from its monopoly price because it fears that it would otherwise attract even more entry than it already experiences. This in turn would force even greater deviations by lower-cost types seeking to distinguish themselves and signal that their markets are relatively unprofitable targets for entry.

With a continuum of types for the incumbent, differentiability, and concavity, the incumbent's problem (1) yields a differential equation. Sequentiality then provides a boundary condition that $P(\bar{c}_I) = M(\bar{c}_I)$, and thereby picks out a single element from the family of curves defined by the equation. However, the first-order condition for (1) does not directly yield p as a function of c. Instead it gives dp/dc in terms of an expression with $\partial \Pi_M / \partial p$ in the denominator, and this denominator goes to zero at $(M(c_I), c_I)$. It does, however, give c_I as a (non-invertible) function of p with zero slope at $p = M(c_I)$. There are thus two solutions for p as a function of c_I that satisfy the equation and the boundary condition: one with $P(c_I) \geq M(c_I)$ and the other with prices below their monopoly levels. [Both "go vertical" at $\bar{c}_I$, which is why the earlier argument for the attractiveness of deviating from $M(c_I)$ does not apply at this point.] However, as shown by Mailath (1985, pp. 19–20), only the upward-sloping branch – on which prices are below their monopoly levels – actually gives an equilibrium. Thus there is a unique separating equilibrium, and it involves limit pricing.[5]

---

[5] Mailath gives general conditions for existence and uniqueness in signaling models. Ramey (1985) also gives conditions on the profit functions to eliminate the upper branch of the differential equation as an equilibrium in the limit-pricing model. In the present context, these are that the isoprofit curves in the space of prices and "extent of entry" are steeper the higher is c_I. This same condition is used by Engers and Schwartz (1984). They derive

However, with a discrete set $\{c_I^1 = \underline{c}_I, ..., c_I^n, ..., \bar{c}_I = c_I^N\}$ of types of the incumbent, where $c_I^n < c_I^{n+1}$, sequentiality can still leave a continuum of separating equilibria. This happens if the cost levels are close enough that some relatively high-cost type would select the monopoly price of a lower-cost type if, in so doing, it would be perceived as having this low cost; that is, so long as the full information choices do not constitute a Nash equilibrium.

One of these equilibria seems most natural because it involves minimal signaling, with $\bar{c}_I$ picking its monopoly price and each lower-cost type lowering its price just enough to distinguish itself from the next-higher-cost type. To define these "natural equilibrium" prices, begin with the highest-cost type, $\bar{c}_I = c_I^N$. It chooses $P(c_I^N) = M(c_I^N)$. With concavity of Π_M in p, there will be a pair of prices $\underline{p}_n^N$ and $\bar{p}_n^N$ for each $n < N$ that, if taken as signaling c_I^n, yield the same profit to c_I^N as does $M(c_I^N)$. Of these, the lower one, $\underline{p}_n^N$, always yields higher profits to the c_I^n type when its cost is correctly perceived by the potential entrants. Now define $\underline{p}_n^{N-1}$ and $\bar{p}_n^{N-1}$ in parallel fashion, using $\underline{p}_{N-1}^N$ as the reference price. Again, $\underline{p}_n^{N-1}$ yields higher profits to type n than does $\bar{p}_n^{N-1}$. Proceed iteratively to define $\underline{p}_n^m$ for all $n < m \le N$ and note that $\underline{p}_j^m < \underline{p}_j^n$ for $j < m < n$. Then, assuming that all the resultant prices are nonnegative, the natural separating equilibrium price schedule is $P(c_I^n) = \underline{p}_n^{n+1}$, $n < N$, and $P(c_I^N) = M(c_I^N)$.[6] Note that the unique separating equilibrium in the case of a continuum of types would be the limit of this equilibrium as N becomes large.

When $N = 2$, a simple condition eliminates all separating equilibria except the one with minimal signaling. This condition is that the equilibrium remain one when strategies that are dominated for a type are eliminated for that type. Any price above $\bar{p}_1^2$ or below $\underline{p}_1^2$ represents play of a dominated strategy for the high-cost c_I^2 type: The best that can happen when it charges such a price is that it is thought low-cost, but this is worse than charging $M(c_I^2)$ and being recognized as high-cost. If such dominated strategies are eliminated, then any price outside $(\underline{p}_1^2, \bar{p}_1^2)$ must be taken as indicating that the firm has low costs, and then $P(c_I^1) = \underline{p}_1^2$ is the unique optimal choice for the low-cost type.

This approach – considering only equilibria that are immune to elimination of dominated strategies – has been studied by Milgrom and Roberts (1984) in another signaling context. However, even when $N = 2$ it may

---

conditions on the parameters of an example with linear demand and two possible values for each of c_I and c_E that yield this relative steepness condition for prices below the monopoly price of the high-cost incumbent.

[6] No separating equilibrium can involve less deviation from monopoly pricing than this, for then some type would be willing to mimic the choice of a lower-cost type.

still leave the possibility of pooling equilibria, and moreover when $N > 2$ it also permits multiple separating equilibria.

To obtain the natural separating equilibrium (the one with minimal signaling) as the unique equilibrium, a still stronger notion of equilibrium is thus needed. Recent attention has focused on using the concept of stability introduced by Kohlberg and Mertens (1986).

This latter concept is too complex to discuss here, but Kreps (1984) has shown that it implies an "intuitive condition" on out-of-equilibrium beliefs. The spirit of this condition is that, if we consider an equilibrium and any price (not being charged in the equilibrium) with the property that the low-cost firm would prefer charging this price (and being recognized as low-cost) to adhering to the equilibrium, then the high-cost firm should also be willing to make the same deviation if it too would thereby be considered low-cost. Otherwise, the low-cost firm should be able to distinguish itself by selecting this price, and would profit by doing do.

With $N = 2$, if the low-cost firm is willing to reduce price more than would the high-cost firm to secure a given decrease in the probability of entry, the Kreps criterion eliminates all pooling equilibria where the probability of entry is higher than it would be if the incumbent were known to have low costs. Because this criterion also rules out equilibria that would not survive elimination of dominated strategies, the only equilibrium that survives in this case is the efficient separating one.[7]

However, with $N > 2$, the Kreps criterion does not suffice; in particular, with $N = 3$, any price p between $\underline{p}_1^3$ and $\underline{p}_2^3$ could be the choice in separating equilibrium of the c_f^2 type – with the lowest-cost type then picking the highest price such that the middle type (weakly) prefers charging p, and being correctly recognized, to imitating the low-cost type's price – and the Kreps criterion would still be met. The problem is that even though the high-cost type would not imitate p to be thought to have the intermediate cost level c_f^2, it would pick p if it could thereby be thought to be low-cost, and the Kreps criterion does not apply in this circumstance. Moreover, the same sorts of difficulties allow pooling, although the lowest-cost type must be separated.

Cho and Kreps (1985) have developed further implications of stability that do the job here. For example, with $N = 3$ and the condition on rela-

---

[7] Note, however, that if there is the same probability of entry in pooling equilibrium as when the incumbent is known to have low costs, pooling at prices below the low-cost monopoly price does survive. Also, the nonnegativity constraints on prices could well be binding and this means that fully separating equilibria cannot exist (see Ramey 1985). In such cases, equilibrium must involve pooling. (Fortunately, stability does not overthrow these and lead to nonexistence.) We will assume away these possible complications in what follows.

tive willingness to lower price, these criteria rule out entrants' believing that the choice of $p \in [\underline{p}_1^3, p_2^3]$ could possibly have been made by the low-cost type. Thus any such choice can signal only medium or high costs. But the high-cost firm will not make such a choice in this circumstance, and all separating equilibria but the natural one are eliminated. These conditions, including "universal divinity" [Banks and Sobel (1985)], also eliminate pooling.[8]

Thus, the strengthening of the equilibrium concept by imposing stability serves to generate fairly sharp predictions. There is often a unique equilibrium, and this equilibrium is separating and involves each type lowering its prices just enough to distinguish itself. Even when there is pooling, it too involves lowered prices. Moreover, in neither case is entry systematically reduced by the limit pricing, so the welfare implications are quite straightforward.

One final point here: In these models it would clearly be in the interest of all but the highest-cost type of incumbent to reveal its costs if it could do so in a credible fashion. Yet one rarely sees firms producing audited cost data and making such reports public. Of course, there might be costs to such revelation that are not part of our model and that prevent its being done, but there is a general point here. In situations such as this, where rational actors are involved in a losing game, there are incentives to change the game!

1.3 *Extensions of the basic model*

The basic idea – that informational asymmetries can lead to deviations from otherwise optimal pre-entry pricing in an attempt to signal this information – has been developed by a number of authors. Here we briefly summarize some directions this work has taken and suggest some open problems.

A natural first step, which largely remains to be taken, would put the analysis in a general equilibrium context in which multiple markets might be entered. For example, each market might be monopolized by a distinct incumbent with private information about that market, and potential entrants, limited in the resources they have available, would choose which market(s) to attack. A crucial difference between such a model and the basic set-up is that entrants would observe a vector of prices, one for each

---

[8] Engers and Schwartz (1984) have demonstrated that, even when pooling is inconsistent with stability, all types of incumbent might prefer to pool at a common price than be separated. (This might occur if low costs are very likely a priori, so there is little gain for the low-cost type in distinguishing itself, and signaling is quite costly for the low-cost firm.) Thus, we might question the application of stability here.

incumbent, rather than just a single price [see Rogerson (1981)]. Thus strategies such as "enter the market where price is highest" now are available. At present, the only work in the spirit of the basic limit-pricing analysis that involves multiple markets are a paper by Rogerson (1981) and some examples due to Lutz (1983).[9] The former works with the set-up of the basic model, while the latter involves a multiproduct monopolist faced with entry into one of its interrelated markets. Both generate limit pricing.

A related problem is the situation where there are already several incumbent oligopolists in the market. In this regard, Harrington (1985b) has considered a model with several incumbents where the pre-entry price signals the likelihood of post-entry collusion.

One natural extension that has been studied involves allowing imperfect observability of the incumbent's choice. It seems plausible that, even in separating equilibrium, observation of the pre-entry price should not remove all doubt about the incumbent's private information, and adding noise between the incumbent's choice and the entrant's observation is one way to incorporate this. For example, the incumbent might choose a quantity that determines the probability distribution of the price observed by the entrant, or it might choose an unobservable wholesale price while the observed retail price varies randomly with retail market conditions. Note that this randomness is environmental, not strategic: The firms do not control the noise terms. This contrasts with a situation where the firms can decide on the amount of noise to add to their actions.

This idea was studied by Matthews and Mirman (1983) and Saloner (1982). Although this work can be justified on grounds of realism, it is also important methodologically because it leads to sharper predictions from the theory. In particular, if the entrant knows the distribution of the noise conditional on the incumbent's choice, and if the support of the resultant distribution of possible observations in equilibrium is all of R_+, then there are none of the zero-probability events that bedevil the model without noise. The entrant will then have uniquely defined beliefs about the incumbent's private information conditional on any given observation. In this case (i.e., if there is enough noise), under reasonable conditions one obtains a unique equilibrium. This equilibrium is separating in that different types make different choices. Of course, the presence of the noise means that there is no simple functional relationship between the incumbent's private information and the observed price; rather, one sees a draw from a distribution that depends on the true information and is

---

[9] Gal-Or (1981) has considered a model with many of these features, but she focused on other issues.

shifted down (in the sense of first-order stochastic dominance) as a result of the limit pricing/signaling.

As Saloner (1982) noted, with price observations giving only statistical information there may be natural incentives to delay entry and gain additional observations that refine the estimate of the incumbent's private information. [10] These considerations led Saloner to consider a repeated version of the Milgrom–Roberts model with noise. If entry has not occurred by some stage, the incumbent picks its price anew. The entrant observes a noisy version of the price and has another opportunity to enter. If entry does occur at some stage, the game ends with the two firms receiving the present value of their full information Cournot payoffs in the ensuing duopoly.

The entrant's decision now involves trading off the profits from entering immediately against the expected gain from better information, which reduces the chance of making a mistaken decision to enter. Saloner gives conditions under which, in parallel with the nonrepeated version, the optimal strategy for the entrant at each date is to enter if the observed price at that date is sufficiently high. This in turn guarantees limit pricing at each stage. Of course, the equilibria are nonstationary because both sides of the market are learning about one another over time: The entrant learns from observing prices, the incumbent from the fact that the entrant has not found entry profitable after viewing the given history of prices.

The equilibrium of this model involves entry being delayed relative to the full information benchmark. Yet, as before, the limit pricing itself does not bias the entry decision. Most strikingly, however, the probability of eventual entry is greater in this model than it would be if the incumbent's costs were known: A sequence of randomly high prices may induce mistaken entry, but the law of large numbers ensures that the entrant in a separating equilibrium ultimately has full information and so can correctly infer the profitability of entry.

A further natural extension allows for more general forms of private information. This line was suggested by Milgrom and Roberts but was first developed by Matthews and Mirman (1983), who considered rather general models with either a finite or a one-dimensional ordered set of types representing the incumbent's private information. Interestingly, although any private information for the incumbent that is payoff-relevant to the entrant might lead to signaling if the costs of signaling differ with the private information, various natural candidates lead to surprising forms

[10] Note that such incentives would not automatically arise in the absence of noise, because simple repetition of the one-shot game would presumably have, among its equilibria, repetition of the equilibrium price function from the original game. If this equilibrium is in pure strategies, there would be no informational gain from additional observations.

of deviations from full-information behavior. For example, Salop (1981) has suggested that if the private information is about demand elasticity and if high elasticity is conducive to entry (because it means that a given increase in quantity can be accommodated by a lower price reduction), then incumbents want to persuade entrants that their markets have low-elasticity demand. Because monopoly markups are inversely related to elasticity, the natural way to try to deter entry is then to charge higher prices! Although this suggestion has apparently not been verified by derivation of an equilibrium in such a set-up, Harrington (1985a) has shown that if the entrant is unsure about its own costs but believes they are positively correlated with those of the incumbent, then signaling aimed at entry prevention takes the form of pricing above the monopoly level.

To date, no work has investigated models of this sort where the private information is multidimensional, even though this would seem empirically important. However, recent work by Kohlleppel (1983a, b) and by Quinzii and Rochet (1984) on labor-market signaling provides the basis for such research. On a related line, one might wonder whether incumbents would use signals other than price of their private information. The only work directly addressing this issue appears to be a paper by Bagwell (1985),[11] who builds on an analysis of signaling product quality by Milgrom and Roberts (1986) to investigate the possibility of using advertising as a signal of cost. Bagwell shows that with two possible cost levels advertising can arise in sequential equilibrium but not in equilibria meeting the additional criteria discussed in Section 1.2. Whether there are other potential signals that might be used in such circumstances – and, more generally, whether there is some other more profitable game that real economic agents might find and play when faced with the informational asymmetries posited here – remains an important open question. In this regard, it might be especially useful to integrate the sort of analysis discussed here with the work alluded to above on strategic use of capital investment as an entry barrier.

Finally, the discussion in Section 1.1 assumed that the cost levels of both firms became common knowledge if entry occurred. This might be a fairly realistic assumption in modeling industries where there is frequent movement of employees between firms, but it is not generally appropriate. However, it can be relaxed without altering the fundamental conclusions of the analysis.

Consider first the case in which c_E is known a priori but c_I does not become public after entry. The only fundamental change in the conditions for equilibrium is that the profits after entry are no longer the full-information Cournot profits. Instead, they are those that result when the

---

[11] The examples due to Lutz (1983) mentioned above are also relevant here.

entrant believes that c_I has whatever value(s) would have given rise to the observed price if the incumbent used the strategy that the entrant conjectures for it and the firms maximize accordingly. However, with c_E known, the only place this change matters is in checking that no cost-type of the incumbent prefers to deviate to the price charged by another cost-type. The effect of such a deviation on entry remains the same. However, because the entrant's output will increase with its perception of c_I, the incumbent's profits conditional on entry fall if it is perceived to have higher costs and rise if its perceived costs fall. Thus, the incentive to imitate types with lower costs increases. Consequently, if separating equilibrium exists it still involves limit pricing.

If the value of c_I is initially private information and neither c_I nor c_E are known ex post, the analysis is slightly more complicated. In addition to the above effect of influencing outputs conditional on entry, any change in the perception of c_I will also typically affect the set of c_E levels which choose to enter. Moreover, even if we have a separating equilibrium and consider only play along the equilibrium path, the post-entry competition involves incomplete information because all that I can infer from the fact of entry is that c_E is below some cutoff. This can affect I's second-period output and thus the incentives for entry. Still, the incentives for I to depart from simple monopoly pricing remain.

The conclusion that remains is that limit pricing should be expected to occur but should not be expected to reduce entry in any systematic way. Given the empirical fact of frequent entry into various markets, this is a fortunate conclusion to reach.

2   Predatory pricing

Few topics in industrial economics have been more controversial than predatory pricing. Clearly, large numbers of business people, lawyers, and legislators are sure that low prices are adopted for predatory reasons and that such pricing can be successfully used to destroy, discipline, or deter the entry of competitors. Many industrial economists seem to agree. Standard texts [e.g., Scherer (1980); Greer (1980)] describe various episodes of apparently predatory behavior and then go on to discuss the motives for predation and the circumstances in which it might be expected to occur and succeed. Moreover, prominent economists have joined the debate in the law journals on selecting evidentiary tests for establishing predation. [See Easley, Masson, and Reynolds (1985) for references and a discussion of this work.]

Other economists hold exactly the opposite view. For example, McGee (1958, 1980) has argued on theoretical grounds that predatory pricing is unlikely to succeed; that even if it were successful, there are more profitable strategies that would achieve the same ends; and that, as a consequence, instances of firms' adopting predatory strategies are likely to be quite rare. Moreover, he has suggested that predation in fact played little role in some of the classic examples of supposedly predatory pricing. The policy implication of McGee's arguments is that prohibitions against predation should be eliminated because their main effect is to provide inefficient firms with a legal protection against the normal, desirable effects of competition.

These arguments against predation are compelling, once one accepts the implicit assumption that there are no important informational asymmetries. It turns out, however, that this assumption is crucial: Several recent analyses have shown that relaxing these information assumptions can lead to predatory behavior. This is in some sense fortunate, because the historical record does indeed provide several examples of firms that followed pricing policies apparently aimed at imposing losses on rivals – policies that would have been profit-maximizing only if they either induced rival firms to leave (or, at least, to compete less aggressively) or prevented the future entry of other firms.

Here we discuss several of these models. Although they could be classified according to the nature of the informational asymmetry that permits the predation to arise, we classify them according to the objective of the behavior.

Before turning to these models, however, it is worth noting that one can obtain (at least the threat of) predation in full-information models, but not in a very satisfactory fashion. In particular, it is easy to construct a game in which one of two firms first decides whether or not to be active in a market where the other is active, and then if both are active they play the Cournot game. If the first firm has positive fixed costs in the second stage and if (for large enough quantities) price is below this firm's minimum average cost, then the two-stage game has Nash equilibria in which the threat of below-cost prices at the second stage leads the firm to stay out. The problem is that this equilibrium is not perfect (or sequential): The threat of predation would not be carried out if the first firm called the other's bluff by entering or refusing to exit. Moreover, even if one is willing to put aside this objection, we still note that predation does not actually occur under equilibrium play.

By moving to the framework of repeated games without discounting and by invoking the Folk theorem [see Aumann (1981)], one could overcome this latter problem and generate equilibria in which predation could occur. For example, consider an infinitely repeated Cournot game where either firm can drive price to or below the level of minimum average cost. Suppose the firms evaluate their profit streams according to the long-run average criterion.[12] Then it is easy to obtain as equilibrium play a pattern where price is low for some finite number of periods because one firm produces a large amount, after which the other firm produces zero in all succeeding periods while the successful predator produces its monopoly output.

The possibility of obtaining such behavior is not due to the use of any questionably credible threat of forcing price below cost if the prey does not produce zero: There is a Perfect Folk theorem that applies here as well [see Rubinstein (1979); Fudenberg and Maskin (1986)]. Moreoever, even if we relax the hypermetropia assumption and have the firms discount their future profits in the usual fashion, it might still be possible to obtain perfect equilibria that would bear an interpretation in terms of predation.[13] The problem is instead that such models admit too many equilibria. For example, in the no-discounting case, the set of perfect equilibrium outcomes (in payoff space) of the repeated game would be all the nonnegative profit levels that are feasible in a single round of play. Thus the theory, by admitting so many equilibria, fails to have predictive power.[14]

The point of this discussion is that we are interested in models where predation emerges as a perfect or sequential equilibrium and where there are not too many other equilibria.

2.1   Predation to induce exit

The classic story of predation involves a (big) firm cutting prices in order to impose losses on a (smaller) rival and induce its exit, at which point the predator will raise prices and enjoy its monopoly position.

A first criticism of this idea is that if the prey understands the price cutting is temporary then it should not leave. Instead, it should stay in business, wait out the price cutting (which cannot go on forever if it is predatory in the usual sense), then share in the profits that will ultimately be available.

The response to this criticism has been the "deep-pocket" or "long-purse" story. The idea is that staying in business when prices are low involves absorbing losses (if only from one's fixed costs), and if the resources available to the prey to cover such losses are sufficiently limited relative to

---

[12] That is, a stream Π_t ($t = 1, 2, \ldots$) is assigned the value $\lim \inf_{T \to \infty} (\sum_{t=1}^{T} \Pi_t / T)$. Note that this means the values of Π_t at any finite set of dates are irrelevant!

[13] See Abreu (1983) for perfect equilibria of repeated games with discounting.

[14] Recent work by Benoit and Krishna (1985) establishes a version of the "Perfect Folk theorem" for finitely repeated versions of situations where the basic stage game has multiple equilibria. See also Friedman (1985). One might thus possibly hope to build a finite-horizon, full-information model in which predatory behavior might occur, but the above criticism would apply here as well.

those of the predator, then the strategy of waiting out the storm is not feasible if the predator is willing to hold prices low enough for long enough. This story has been formalized by Benoit (1984). He considers an infinite-horizon model with two firms, an incumbent I and an entrant E. In each period, I decides whether to fight or cooperate and then E decides whether to be in the market for that period or to leave it forever. If E stays in and I has chosen to fight then both firms suffer losses, while both make profits if I has chosen to cooperate. Leaving nets E a payoff of zero while I receives an immediate payoff for that period plus the present value of its monopoly profits. Finally, it is assumed that E can withstand only a finite number of periods of fighting before it must leave.

If I earns more from fighting in one period and inducing immediate exit than from cooperating forever, then there is a unique perfect equilibrium for this game. In it, I fights in every period until E leaves and E exits immediately. The proof is inductive. If the game reaches a point where E can stand only one more fight, then I will be willing to fight and E will exit to save itself the cost of the last fight. Thus, if E can stand two more fights and I fights, E leaves immediately because staying in costs money and leads to a subgame in which E will leave anyway. Given this, I fights at this stage. The argument thus is clear: If E (but not I) is financially constrained, E knows that it will experience predation until it is bankrupted and must leave; so E exits immediately.[15]

The problem is to explain why the prey has limited access to capital. Presumably, if bankers understood the structure of the game, they would know that if they were willing to lend money to the prey against its future profits, so that it could survive any predatory episode, then in fact the prospective predator would understand that it could not gain from predation and would not attempt it in the first place. Thus, if the deep-pocket story is to survive, we must justify limited access to capital markets in the face of positive expected profits.

Fudenberg and Tirole (1985) provide the start of such a justification. They build on work by Gale and Hellwig (1985) and others on equilibrium in capital markets under informational asymmetries. The Gale–Hellwig model concerns a firm that has a project with random return Π and known cost K, which must be paid before Π can be realized. The expected value of Π exceeds K, but K in turn exceeds R, the resources available to the

---

[15] Benoit (1984) has also considered a version of this model in which it is private information to E whether the game is as above or whether instead E is commited to staying in until bankrupt. In the unique sequential equilibrium of this game (which involves mixed strategies for both firms), E may stay in, pretending to be committed, while I may fight in hope of inducing exit. The game thus may generate extended periods of predation that may or may not end in exit.

firm. Thus the firm must seek outside financing. The informational problem is that the realization of Π is not observable by outsiders except at a cost M. Thus, the firm is free to misrepresent (understate) its realized return if it so chooses.

It turns out that when the source of outside funding is a risk-neutral competitive (zero-profit) capital market and when the amount that can be recovered from the firm ex post is limited by the realized value of Π, the optimal one-period contract is a debt contract. The lender offers to lend $K - R$ in return for a payment of $P > K - R$. If the firm claims that Π is less than P and thus that it cannot repay its debt, the lender may then pay the cost M of driving the firm into bankruptcy and receive the actual realization of Π. In equilibrium the firm pays P so long as $\Pi \geq P$, while if $\Pi < P$ the lender seizes Π, receiving a net return of $\Pi - M$.

It can be shown that the existence of a payment P that allows both the firm and the lender at least a zero expected return under the optimal contract depends on the size of R, with no such P existing if R is too small. This provides the basis for Fudenberg and Tirole's version of the long-purse story.

In particular, suppose two firms I and E compete in quantities in each of two periods, that costs are incurred in each period before the random demand and consequent returns are realized, that firm E's resources are limited, and that the conditions in the capital market are as above. Then, by producing a large quantity in the first period, I can deplete E's resources relative to what they would have been under normal Cournot behavior. Then, at least for some realizations of demand, E may not be able to obtain financing for the second period, even though it could have absent predation. Thus, although perfectness arguments ensure that there will be no deviation from standard noncooperative pricing in the second period so long as E is active (i.e., that the price cutting is temporary), predatory behavior will be adopted and, with positive probability, will succeed.

As Fudenberg and Tirole note, the analysis depends on the financing being for a single period at a time and it is not obvious that, if E were able to contract with lenders at the outset for financing to cover both periods, the optimal two-period contract would still give I the incentive to prey. Absent a theory of such contracts, the question is open. They also remark that the unobservability assumption on Π is extreme and that, because we also lack a theory of contracts when the moral hazard problem is less intense, the possibility of generating predation when this assumption is relaxed is also unclear. In this regard it is worth noting that, even given unobservability by outsiders, there still may be a way around their analysis by recognizing the institution of the venture capitalist. These firms provide financing for new firms, which Fudenberg and Tirole suggest are most likely to have the limited resources that are key in their model. The venture capitalists also take positions on the boards of the firms in which they invest and, very commonly, become heavily involved in the day-to-day activities of the firms. This means that the venture capitalists are, in terms of the Gale–Hellwig model, no longer "outsiders": They are in an excellent position to monitor the realization of Π and thereby overcome the moral hazard problem that underlies this model of predation.

Even if the long-purse story should not survive relaxation of the assumptions in Fudenberg and Tirole, informational incompleteness about cost or demand conditions can still give rise to incentives for predation aimed at inducing exit. This effect can come about in two somewhat distinct ways. Both involve situations where two firms will compete in at least two periods, and where one of the firms has the option of exiting before the second period. In one version, explored in Roberts (1986), a determinant of the profits of the firm having the exit decision is private information to the other firm. As in the Milgrom–Roberts limit-pricing analysis, the uninformed firm attempts to infer this information from observables (e.g., price) in the first period so that it can be better informed in making its exit decision. This behavior gives the informed firm an incentive to reduce price to lower the other's estimate of second-period profits and thus induce its exit. The model is thus one of signaling. The second approach is studied by Fudenberg and Tirole (1985), who refer to it as "signal jamming." The set-up is similar except that neither firm knows the determinant of profitability. Thus there is no private information of the sort leading to signaling. Still, the same incentives arise because the entrant still must make an inference about profitability and the incumbent hopes to bias this inference by setting a low price. Because both analyses share many of the features of the Milgrom–Roberts limit-pricing analysis, we can be relatively brief in discussing them.

The Roberts analysis of predatory signaling considers an example with two firms, denoted I for incumbent and E for entrant, who may compete over two periods. In each period, price is given by $a - Q_I - Q_E$, and firms select quantities. The intercept term is assumed to be known to I, but E knows only that it might take on (say) one of two values, a_H or a_L, where $a_H > a_L$. Crucial to the analysis is that E is not able to observe Q_I, though it does observe the price and thus can calculate the value of $a - Q_I$.

Assume that each firm has zero marginal costs, but that in each period E faces fixed costs such that if demand were known to be high ($a = a_H$) then E's Cournot profits would be positive, while if a were known to be a_L then E would lose money. Then, if E believes after the first period that

$a = a_L$, E will leave and I will enjoy its monopoly profits in the second period. These are $(a_H/2)^2$ if $a = a_H$. If E believes that $a = a_H$, it will stay in and the two firms will share the market. If $a = a_H$, this yields I operating profits of $(a_H/3)^2$. Thus, when $a = a_H$, the incumbent can gain $(a_H^2/4) - (a_H^2/9)$ by inducing exit, and it will be willing to deviate from otherwise optimal behavior in the first period if it can thereby convince E that $a = a_L$.

Two factors complicate the analysis of the first period relative to the limit-pricing case. First, unlike most signaling models, the signaler's action is not directly observed. Rather, E sees only $p + Q_E = a - Q_I(a)$. For the value of the private information to be inferable from this observation (as in separating equilibrium), $a - Q_I(a)$ must be invertible, rather than $Q_I(a)$ itself. Second, because E selects Q_E in the first period at the same time that I is selecting its output, there is a simultaneity problem that does not arise in more standard signaling models. This in turn means that, in contrast to more standard models, the priors held by the uninformed agent are determinants of the separating equilibrium choices.

Despite these complications, the analysis yields the expected results. When demand is high, the incumbent has an incentive to increase its quantity to make the observed price match that which would arise if a were a_L. Then, to be able to signal credibly that demand actually is low, the firm must increase its quantity when $a = a_L$ enough that mimicry is unprofitable. Thus, I lowers price in an attempt to persuade E that continued operation will be unprofitable and thereby to induce E's exit.

Of course, in separating equilibrium, E is not fooled: It correctly infers the value of a and exits only if $a = a_L$. Thus, predation occurs, but induces no additional exit.

When there are more than two values for a, I has another incentive to increase output in hopes of lowering E's estimate of a. This incentive exists even when it is not worthwhile to lower price enough to induce exit. If E does not exit, its second-period output increases with its estimate of demand, so I's duopoly profits increase if E estimates a lower value of a. The resulting expansion of output might be interpreted as predation aimed at "disciplining" a rival. Of course, E is not fooled in equilibrium, so no effective disciplining takes place.

Note that private information about marginal costs, as in the original Milgrom–Roberts model, would lead to the same sort of analysis.

The Fudenberg–Tirole analysis does not rely on private information about market conditions. As a result, the analysis is less complicated because firms do not condition their actions on private information. However, unobservability of actions still provides an informational asymmetry.

The model involves a two-period game in which the incumbent and entrant sell imperfect substitutes and compete in prices. Neither firm can observe the other's price, although both know the functions relating operating profits to prices. The potential prey E has fixed costs f whose level is unknown and unobservable to either firm: In particular, E observes only the difference between its operating profits and its fixed costs.[16] If these costs were known to be sufficiently high, E would want to exit after the first period; otherwise it would want to stay in. With the goods being substitutes, I prefers that E exit.

In these circumstances, E will attempt to infer the level of its fixed cost from observing its first-period net profits $(\Pi(p_I, p_E) - f)$. To do so, it must form a conjecture regarding p_I. As should now be familiar, the single-period duopoly value of p_I is not optimal. A lower value of p_I would, given the conjecture that p_I is at the simple duopoly level, bias E's estimate of its fixed costs upwards and so increase the probability that it will exit. Thus, I pushes down its price but (again) in equilibrium fails to fool the entrant, which allows for this behavior, correctly interprets the observed profit level, and exits only if it would do so with complete information.

In both these analyses, predation aimed at inducing exit by biasing profit estimates occurs but fails to induce exit above what would occur if the predator could commit itself not to prey. This does not imply, however, that this pricing behavior is innocuous. For once we allow for an initial stage at which E decides whether or not to enter, the fact that the first period will involve below-normal prices may make entry unprofitable. Thus, even though there is no extra inducement of exit, there is deterrence of entry. (Note that this effect would also be present in the deep-pocket story.)

Before concluding the discussion of predation aimed at inducing exit, a further criticism should be noted. It is simply that in many circumstances merger of the two firms or acquisition of E by I would yield the monopoly situation that was I's objective in preying and would do so at less cost to I [McGee (1958)]. This of course represents another instance of the general idea that when faced with playing a losing game, players will change the game.

One response to this suggestion is that adopting a policy of buying out rivals invites entry by firms whose sole object is to be bought out. In this case there may be reasons to impose losses on an entrant before acquiring

---

[16] Fudenberg and Tirole suggest a justification for these assumptions based on managerial moral hazard. This, of course, involves an informational asymmetry between owners and managers.

it, so that the overall payoff to an entrant is negative. This idea has not been modeled formally, although some of the work discussed below is relevant.

A more fundamental objection to the merger suggestion is that, unless the process leading to merger and the result of failure to achieve merger are modeled, there is no clear basis for the claim that simple merger will be a more profitable strategy.

In fact, Scherer (1980) has suggested that predation might play a role in "softening up" a takeover target, so that the merger would be executed on a more favorable basis for the predator, and Saloner (1985) investigated a model that allows for these possibilities. The final stage involves Cournot competition if no merger is consummated. The second-to-last stage involves bargaining to determine if a takeover of E by I will occur and if so, on what terms. Finally, the first stage involves competition prior to the merger. In this model I's production costs are private information. Saloner shows that because of the effect of the level of these costs on the profits of the firms if no merger occurs, a higher probability that they are low will allow I to acquire E at a lower price. This in turn will give it incentives to price low in the first period in order to attempt to shift these perceptions. (Reducing E's output if merger does not occur provides an additional incentive for such behavior.) Thus Scherer's point is validated; even with the merger option, predation can be part of a rational strategy.

2.2   Predation to deter entry

Scherer (1980) and Yamey (1972) have argued that predation might be adopted against a particular challenger not because the aggressor hopes to profit directly from eliminating this rival, but rather because the treatment accorded to this firm may influence the behavior of other potential rivals. This is an important idea, because one of McGee's fundamental criticisms of predatory pricing is that, even if the prey can be eliminated, predation can be worthwhile only if it permits eventual super-competitive prices, and such prices would attract entry.

In fact, the first information-based models of predatory behavior were aimed at formalizing this idea. These models are of two basic types. One, originated by Kreps and Wilson (1982a) and Milgrom and Roberts (1982b), models firm's building a "reputation for toughness" by preying. This reputation leads other potential entrants to expect predation and so tends to deter their entry. Moreover, the legitimate fear of being the subject of reputation-building predation also causes early entrants to be less aggressive. The second approach is due to Easley, Masson, and Reynolds (1985).

In it, incumbents with markets that are attractive targets for entry attempt, via unobservable predatory actions, to make these markets appear unattractive and so cause potential entrants to avoid them.

The Kreps–Wilson and Milgrom–Roberts analyses both address a famous example in game theory, Selten's (1978) "Chain Store Paradox." In this example, an incumbent I operates in a finite number M of markets. Associated with each market m is a potential challenger E_m. In each market m, beginning with $m = M$ and working down to 1, E_m must decide whether to challenge (i.e., enter) or not. If it does, I must respond either aggressively (by preying) or cooperatively. The payoffs to E_m are 0 if it does not challenge, $-1/2$ if it challenges and meets an aggressive response, and $+1/2$ if its challenge is met by cooperation. The parallel payoffs to I are $+2$, -1, and 0. The overall payoff to I is the sum over the individual markets (discounted if one wishes) of the payoffs at each stage.

Note that if $M = 1$ there are two pure-strategy Nash equilibria to the game. One has E stay out and I respond to entry with predation; the second has E enter and I respond cooperatively. However, the first is a classic example of an imperfect equilibrium: E stays out only because it believes that entry will result in predation, while I is willing to threaten to prey only because E is staying out and so I need never actually accept the -1 payoff that results from preying instead of the 0 it could get by cooperating. Of course, I's threat is not credible in the sense that if E entered, I would then optimally select cooperation. Only the second equilibrium is perfect (or sequential) in that each player's strategy (and I's in particular) calls for it to act optimally from *each* point forward. Thus, with $M = 1$, we would predict that the outcome of such a competitive situation would be entry met with cooperation.

With a larger number of threatened markets, however, one might expect that any early challenges would be met aggressively. The incumbent would thereby gain a reputation for predation that would lead potential challengers to expect an aggressive response. Thus they would not enter, and the gain to I from preventing these later challenges would justify the costs of fighting early entrants.

If M were actually infinite, one could obtain an equilibrium with some of these features, though no entry would occur: I's strategy would be to prey against every entrant, while each entrant stays out if every previous entry met predation and enters if any entry ever met cooperation. However, *for any finite M,* there is a unique perfect equilibrium that involves uncontested entry at each stage [Selten (1978)]. To see this, consider the last stage, where E_1 may enter. If it does, it is optimal for I not to prey, and so it is optimal for E_1 to enter. Now consider the next-to-last stage. If E_2 were to enter and if (by fighting) I could deter E_1, then there might be some reason to fight. But we already know that E_1 will enter, independent of what happens at stage 2. Thus I gets 0 in the continuation no matter what it does here. Consequently, it is optimal for I to acquiesce and for E_2 to enter. The induction seems inexorable.

Thus, it appears that the reputation story does not stand scrutiny and that repetition has no effect in finite-horizon models. However, Kreps and Wilson and Milgrom and Roberts saw that the argument leading to this conclusion depends crucially on its being common knowledge that cooperating is better for I individually at each round than is fighting. They then developed versions of the Chain Store game in which there was some small initial probability that I was committed to meeting all entry attempts with predation (Milgrom–Roberts) or had payoffs that made fighting a dominant strategy in a single stage (Kreps–Wilson) and in which it was private information to I whether or not it was a normal maximizing agent with the usual payoffs or one of the alternate types.[17] The rationale behind these particular modifications was that real economic agents are unlikely to be absolutely certain of their opponents' options, motivations, or behavior, although they might well be expected to know their own.

With such uncertainty, the argument given above breaks down because it is no longer certain that there will not be predation against the last entrant. In fact, the nature of the game is radically changed by this addition of a small amount of incomplete information. Now entrants have to worry that they might be facing an incumbent who enjoys or is committed to fighting, and this leads them to make inferences about the incumbent's type from the observed history of play. This in turn could affect the behavior of the "normal" type of incumbent, since by preying it can keep alive the possibility that it is the "crazy" type which will prey again, while failing to prey will suggest that it finds preying costly and will acquiesce to other challenges. There is thus potentially room for reputation, because the behavior of the incumbent may depend on its type and entrants will try to infer this type (and thus behavior they should expect in the future) from observed actions.[18]

In fact, this is what happens in both the Kreps–Wilson and Milgrom–Roberts models. Although the two differ in a number of details, with the former tending to be somewhat simpler and more easily understood, the principal result is the same. It is that, for any given (small but positive) prior probability that cooperating is not the best response to entry in the

---

[17] More generally (see Milgrom–Roberts), what one wants is a model where it is not common knowledge that preying is dominated at each stage.

[18] The incomplete information version of the model in Benoit (1984), which was discussed above, is also a reputation model of this general type except that E rather than I carries the reputation.

stage games, there is an m^* such that if $M > m^*$ then both the normal and crazy types of I prey against any entry into markets $M, ..., m^*$. (In Kreps and Wilson there are other patterns of sequential equilibrium behavior; in Milgrom and Roberts this is the unique such pattern.)

To see how this works, suppose $N = 2$, that the crazy type must prey, and that the prior on the crazy type is $\delta > 1/2$. If E_2 enters and the normal type I^N does not prey, it will be revealed as normal. Because I^N will (by perfectness) not prey against E_1, E_1 will then surely enter. Thus, failure to prey against E_2 yields I^N a payoff of zero. Suppose, on the other hand, that I^N is expected to prey on E_2 with probability p. Then if E_1 sees predation against E_2, it will assign posterior probability $\rho = \delta/[\delta + (1-\delta)p]$ to the incumbent being crazy, and will definitely enter or not as (respectively) ρ exceeds or falls short of $1/2$.

Now consider $M = 3$ with the same value δ for the prior probability of the crazy type I^C. If E_3 enters and I^N does not prey then I^N gets 0 in each round. If I^N is expected to prey and does, it gets -1 in this period and goes into market 2 with E_2 believing it still might be I^C with probability δ and thus expecting predation with probability of at least δ. Thus E_2 stays out, as does E_1. Consequently, preying in market 3 yields $-1 + 2 + 2$, so I^N strictly prefers to prey at this stage or any earlier stage.

This example is extremely simple but somewhat misleading in two ways. First, the prior on I^C is unreasonably high, but this is unnecessary. Generally, with the specified payoffs the critical value for the number of markets that must remain for preying to be uniquely optimal is given by the smallest value of m with $(1/2)^m < \delta$. Thus, for example, if δ is as small as 1 in 100,000, predation is worthwhile if 17 or more potential challenges remain (see Kreps and Wilson). The second misleading aspect of the example is that it suggests that entry will not occur and thus that predation will not be observed. However, even in this simple framework, entry typically does occur near the end of the game and is probabilistically fought (see Kreps and Wilson). Moreover, the richer modeling given by Milgrom and Roberts generates early tests of the incumbent as well as occasional later entry by entrants who are not too badly hurt by predation relative to their outside opportunities.

The story that goes with the Kreps–Wilson and Milgrom–Roberts models involves having the aggressive response to entry be observed by potential challengers. Although having other players understand that predation is being practiced is not the same as predation being verifiable by third parties or (in particlar) by courts working under rules of evidence, if instances of predation conforming to this story actually occur they will presumably be most likely when predation is not illegal. In fact, some of the episodes from the nineteenth-century liner shipping industry do seem to be well modeled in terms of building a reputation for toughness. Still, in the context of legal prohibitions on predation, building such a reputation without risking legal problems might be difficult.

Easley, Masson, and Reynolds (1985) suggest that in such cases a monopolist operating in several identical markets might rather build a reputation for weakness, in the sense that it would like entrants to believe that conditions in its markets render entry unprofitable even when post-entry behavior is not predatory. If the profitability of entry is not directly observable to outsiders but is known to the incumbent, and if the incumbent's price choices are not directly observable, then the incumbent with profitable markets would have an incentive to protect its remaining markets from entry by making its markets indistinguishable from ones that are unprofitable targets.

We have already seen, in the discussion of Roberts (1986), how this sort of incentive can lead to predation. There, however, we focused on separating equilibrium, whereas in the Easley–Masson–Reynolds model (as with the Kreps–Wilson and Milgrom–Roberts models) pooling is the natural outcome. Still, the result is the same: Predation emerges in the context of informational asymmetries when realized profits in one market can influence perceptions of profitability in other markets.

A major strength of the Easley–Masson–Reynolds paper is that it provides a very rich model whose equilibria can involve quite complicated but realistic patterns of entry behavior. It also gives a very useful discussion of the ongoing debate in the law journals regarding predation, and draws out the implications of their model for the various proposals that have been put forward as tests for predation. This discussion is especially valuable because so many of the other models of predation lead to similar conclusions.

In summary, we see that the presumption toward which the profession seemed to be moving five years ago – that predation does not make sense – does not hold up if one believes that the sort of informational asymmetries considered here are present in real markets. Instead, predation can easily be part of a rational strategy, even when all concerned recognize that the price cuts are temporary, when there is no differential access to resources, and when everyone understands the incentives in the situation at hand. However, this does not mean that the policy conclusion to which the McGee arguments led – that predation probably ought not to be illegal – is necessarily wrong.[19] First, as we have seen, some forms of predation are (apart from effects on entry) apparently without social cost because they do not succeed in inducing exit. In these circumstances, an

---

[19] For reasons I will elaborate below, I am reluctant to suggest that the theory as yet justifies drawing clear policy implications. However, the following discussion is more in the line of noting problems for others' policy proposals, and I am more confident of the theory's value here.

effective prohibition of predation would simply raise prices without affecting the set of firms that remain active. Second, even when predation is not ineffective, it need not involve below-cost pricing, post-entry output expansion, or any of the other patterns of behavior that are easily recognizable and have been proposed as tests for predation. Instead, establishing that a particular pattern of behavior was in fact predatory may involve determination of intent, plus a very detailed reconstruction of informational conditions. Although prosecuting predation under such a standard of law might represent a bonanza for lawyers and expert economic witnesses, it would not obviously be more desirable socially than simply allowing predation.

3   Symmetric battles for market shares

Limit pricing and predatory pricing are inherently asymmetric phenomena, where one firm takes a leading role. However, strategic information-based methods have also had application to more symmetric problems that may again be interpreted as battles for market share. We discuss two basic sorts of such models here. The first involves price wars and focuses on the intensity of competition. The models in the second class resemble a war of attrition or "chicken" in that the issue is how long to fight.

3.1   *Price wars*

Early stages of an industry's history (or periods following some fundamental change in market or technological conditions) seem often to be marked by intense price competition. This competition is often interpreted in the business press as a battle for market share. Although learning curves [Spence (1981), Fudenberg and Tirole (1983)] and customer loyalty/switching costs [Klemperer (1984)] would both generate such price wars, two recent analyses [Riordan (1985); Mailath (1985, Chapter 3)][20] give an informational basis for such behavior. A striking prediction of these analyses is that, given the set of competing firms, the price wars will not affect the ultimate equilibrium shares, which will be determined solely by market fundamentals. This sort of conclusion should, of course, be familiar by now.

Mailath's analysis involves a signaling model with many similarities to the Milgrom–Roberts limit-pricing model and the later Roberts model of predation. Two firms will compete in each of two periods. The constant per-unit costs of each firm are private information to that firm. Suppose,

---

[20] The results from this chapter were circulated in 1984.

for simplicity, that quantities are choice variables,[21] that demand in each period is given by $p = a - q$, where $q = q_1 + q_2$, and that beliefs about costs are given by smooth distributions F_1 on $[\underline{c}_1, \bar{c}_1]$ and F_2 on $[\underline{c}_2, \bar{c}_2]$.

After observing the first-period price, each firm can calculate the other's first-period quantity and, given a conjecture as to the other's strategy, will update its prior on the other's costs. Let $F_1(\cdot \mid q_1^1)$ and $F_2(\cdot \mid q_2^1)$ be these updated priors. Then, sequential equilibrium requires that the second-period choices satisfy, for each c_i and each q_j^1, $j \neq i$, $i, j = 1, 2$, $Q_i^2(c_i, q_j^1)$ solves

$$\text{maximize}_q \int_{\underline{c}_j}^{\bar{c}_j} (a - q - Q_j^2(c_j, q_i^1) - c_i) q \, dF(c_j \mid q_j^1)$$

or, assuming concavity,

$$a - 2Q_i^2(c_i, q_j^1) - \int_{\underline{c}_j}^{\bar{c}_j} Q_j^2(c_j, q_i^1) \, dF(c_j \mid q_j^1) - c_i = 0.$$

Thus, firm i's second-period output is decreasing in its estimate of j's second-period output, and so the residual demand facing j increases in i's estimate of q_j^2. At the same time, the equilibrium value of q_j^2 decreases in c_j. Thus, each firm has an incentive to try to make the other believe that its costs are low.

From this, it is clear that the simple duopoly output functions given by $D_j(c_j) = [2a + 2E(c_i) - E(c_j) - 3c_j]/6$, $j \neq i$, $i, j = 1, 2$, do not constitute an equilibrium for first-period play. The argument should be familiar: If these were believed to be the strategies being played, then each player would enter the second period with point expectations about the other's costs. The expectations held by j would be decreasing in i's actual output. Thus, a slight increase in q_i, which has a zero first-order effect on first-period expected returns, causes a downward shift in the estimated value of c_i. This in turn increases i's second-period profits by an amount that is, to a first approximation, strictly positive.

The natural separating equilibrium here accounts for the incentives to raise quantities to lower estimates of costs, and in expectation price is lowered by this signaling. However, price is not lowered with probability one. As usual, the highest-cost types, $\bar{c}_1$ and $\bar{c}_2$, simply maximize expected first-period profits in any sequential equilibrium. But, with the expected output of firm j increased by signaling, we have $q_i^1(c_i) < D_i(c_i)$ for all c_i close to $\bar{c}_i$. Thus, this simultaneity of choices means that the realized price

[21] Note that Mailath's analysis actually centers on price competition. In this case (see note 2), the incentives can be for each to raise prices to signal higher costs, because such perceptions tend to raise the opponent's second-period prices and thus the firm's residual demand.

can, with positive probability, be above the level that would obtain absent a signaling motive. Nevertheless, we expect to see a price war, with prices depressed in an attempt to gain future market share. Of course, because the equilibrium strategies are invertible, in equilibrium both firms correctly infer one another's costs and the second-period outputs are simply $q_i(c_i, c_j) = (a - 2c_i + c_j)/3$; that is, they are fully determined by costs and demands and are equal to the full-information solution.

Riordan's model does not rely on signaling private information but rather on what Fudenberg and Tirole (1985) call "signal jamming." The idea again is that if some market variable is determined jointly by the realization of a random variable and the actions taken by the firms, if the value of the random variable is not observed by either firm but is relevant for later decisions, and if the firms' actions are not observed by their rivals, then each may have an incentive to alter its action from its short-run optimum so as to try to bias others' estimates of the random variable and so influence their future behavior. For example, consider the sort of set-up discussed above, but suppose that costs are known to all and that the demand intercept a is a random variable not observed by either firm. Suppose that the same value of a prevails in both periods and that individual quantity choices are unobservable.

In the second period, each firm will have an estimate of a based on its conjectures concerning first-period quantities – namely, $\tilde{a}_i = p - q_i - \tilde{q}_j$, where $\tilde{q}_j$ is i's estimate of j's first-period quantity. Because a lower value of $\tilde{a}_i$ reduces i's second-period best-response function and thereby increases j's profits, it is in j's interest to have i adopt a low estimate of a. As should now be familiar, this gives each firm an incentive to increase its first-period output beyond its simple duopoly level; yet, in equilibrium, both recognize that the other has this incentive, make appropriate allowances for it, and are not fooled. Again, low prices result in the first period as the firms battle to gain future market share, yet second-period outputs are just what would have arisen under full information.

The policy implications are clear, and reinforce those drawn from the study of predatory pricing. At various times different industries have sought regulation or antitrust exemption because (they argued) they were subject to destructive price competition. We already knew that, to the extent these price wars were responses to price levels far above marginal costs in times of excess capacity, the claims that they were socially undesirable were very suspect. The current analysis points to the same conclusion when the price war is aimed at influencing long-run market shares. To the extent that prices do not fall too far below marginal costs, price wars for market share are without social cost.

3.2   *Battles for dominance*

The models in the previous section focus on the intensity of price competition in a contest where, given the other firm's behavior, the prize to lower prices is a somewhat larger future market share. We now consider two related models where the issue is how long to fight and the prize to fighting longer can be total domination. Both feature two firms, with each having private information about its payoffs. The games that emerge are wars of attrition.

The first model is due to Kreps and Wilson (1982a). They consider a version of the Chain Store model discussed above in which a single incumbent monopolizes M markets that may be entered in sequence by a single entrant. As in their predation model, the incumbent's private information is whether or not aggressive competition is the optimal response to entry in a single period. Meanwhile, the entrant has private information as to whether entry is a dominant strategy in each market or instead is only best if it will meet cooperation.

The equilibrium on which Kreps and Wilson focus involves reputations for both firms. The strong (or crazy) incumbent always follows its single-period dominant strategy and fights any entry, while the strong/crazy entrant does likewise and enters at each opportunity. The normal types play mixed strategies, where pure strategies consist of how long to go on fighting or entering (as the case may be), given that the opponent has not given up. These mixed strategies amount to choosing randomly at each stage between the two options – that is, between giving up the battle and thereby revealing one's true type, or continuing and thereby further building one's reputation for toughness. If the entrant gives up first then succeeding play duplicates that in the Kreps–Wilson version of the Chain Store game so that, if enough markets remain, the normal incumbent will be willing to fight entry to maintain its reputation and consequently entry is deterred. If the incumbent gives up first and reveals itself then all remaining markets are entered without further opposition. However, as long as neither has given up, the game evolves with a battle in each market. In each of these battles, each firm suffers losses but is willing to absorb them in the hope of gaining the prize that comes if the other capitulates first.

It has been suggested that this pattern models the attempt to expand the marketing of Folgers coffee into the Eastern U.S. markets dominated by Maxwell House. Proctor & Gamble, the makers of Folgers, chose to introduce the brand into different local markets sequentially. In each, fierce price wars erupted as the price of Maxwell House was cut in the face of the new entry. The final upshot was that P&G gave up the fight and did not attempt to introduce Folgers into the New York City market. In this context, however, one must wonder about P&G's decision to move sequentially rather than to enter all of the target markets simultaneously, because the sequential strategy presumably encouraged an aggressive response aimed at protecting later markets.

The second battle-for-dominance model involving information asymmetries is due to Fudenberg and Tirole (1986b).[22] They consider two firms that have both entered a single market. The price–output decisions are not modeled: there are simply commonly known, instantaneous operating profit flows accruing to each as a duopolist or as a monopolist. However, the instantaneous fixed cost of each firm, and thus its net payoff, is private information to that firm and is not observed by the other. We can assume that each firm's fixed cost is low enough that the firm would be profitable as a monopolist, but unless cost is very low, duopoly operation is unprofitable. Neither observes the other's payoff. Each firm can exit at any time (with subsequent re-entry forbidden).

In this context, each firm must decide how long to stay in the market. A strategy for either firm then gives the time it will exit as a function of its fixed cost, given that the other has not already quit. It is clear that the strategies of giving up immediately do not constitute an equilibrium, because then either firm would gain by staying in and becoming the monopolist. Thus, a fight ensues.

This model may be a reasonable representation of new industries based on a technological advance, such as automobiles in the late nineteenth and early twentieth centuries or personal computers more recently. Such industries are often marked by the initial entry of more firms than (probably) can survive in the long run. Over time, various competitors drop out until the industry population stabilizes.

If it were common knowledge that both firms found duopoly operations unprofitable, the game would be essentially the classic war of attrition that has been used by theoretical biologists to study such phenomenon as "wasteful competition" between animals of a species to win a particular mate. In this version of the game there would be a continuum of equilibria satisfying a boundary condition that the only firm to drop out immediately at the start of the game is one whose costs are such that it earns zero profits as a monopolist. This indeterminacy arises because the differential equations that should determine the equilibrium are not

---

[22] In a sense, this model does not belong here because it does not explicitly involve any pricing decision and the phenomenon it captures can arise under complete information. Still, the informational asymmetry here yields sharp predictions that are not otherwise possible, and the phenomenon modeled is important.

Lipschitz at time zero: their right-hand sides involve dividing by the value of being a monopoly, which is zero at zero with this boundary condition. However, with some low-cost types enjoying positive duopoly profits, one gets another boundary condition at infinity – namely, that these types will never drop out. Satisfying four boundary conditions on a pair of differential equations would not typically be possible, but the non-uniqueness of the behavior at time zero permits it, and Fudenberg and Tirole obtain a unique equilibrium. This equilibrium involves firms staying in longer the lower are their fixed costs, so that the more efficient of any pair of firms is the survivor (unless both are profitable as duopolists). Of course, the longer a firm fights the lower is its opponent's estimate of its costs, so this model bears a reputation interpretation as well.

An open question that relates to both these war-of-attrition models is whether this behavior would change radically if the pricing decision were modeled. In this case, price rather than just willingness to persist in absorbing losses could possibly become a signal for efficiency in Fudenberg and Tirole, and in Kreps and Wilson the tough types might find an incentive to distinguish themselves by pricing. (This question also is relevant regarding the reputation models of predation.) If this occurred, the costly delays of exit or persistence of entry and fighting might disappear.

4   Conclusions

I have discussed three sorts of aggressive pricing aimed at maintaining or increasing market share: limit pricing, predation, and price wars or wars of attrition. Each of these phenomena have been noted and discussed by students of industrial behavior, but have not been explained satisfactorily – if at all – by standard microeconomic theory. However, over the last five years game-theoretic methods involving informational asymmetries have been applied to provide theoretical explanations of each. These models not only help us understand phenomena that before were beyond the scope of our analyses, they also suggest novel welfare implications.

This discussion, despite its length, has been quite incomplete in at least two dimensions. First, I have not been careful about spelling out details of the models, I have avoided formal statements of theorems and ignored proofs, and I have worked with the simplest versions of the models and specific examples rather than with the full richness that was often present. My hope in this has been to interest readers in studying the original papers rather than in trying to render such study unnecessary. Second, I have touched on only a small part of the literature on incomplete information and strategic behavior in industrial organization. Striking advances have been made on such issues as implicit collusion and the detection of cheating in cartels; advertising, warranties, and other signals for unobservable product quality; reputations and the incentives to maintain quality; and the optimal regulation of firms. This work is fundamentally altering the way we understand industrial behavior.

Still, these models are not yet rich enough to capture many important phenomena, let alone to provide a firm basis for policy recommendations to either government or business. It is not that these models are notably more special or limited than those traditionally used by economists; they are not. Further, models need not capture everything in order to be useful; indeed, their role must be to guide and test our intuition about real problems, and they cannot do so unless they involve simplifications.

Instead, the problem is that our intuition about the impact of informational asymmetries is (at least for me) not yet strong enough to trust very far. We know now that the results of our models can vary discontinuously with the inclusion of even small amounts of informational incompleteness. Moreover, the nature of the behavior that arises and the resulting welfare implications can depend crucially on the variables that are included in the model[23] or on the particular form of the informational asymmetry [Fudenberg and Maskin (1986)]. All this means that – to be confident about policy prescriptions derived from such models – we must be very sure we have the right model and that it is robust. I, for one, doubt that we have reached a state of understanding that would justify such confidence. Nevertheless, it is reasonable to hope that we can gain such an understanding. Moreover, doing so is sure to be fun!

References

Abreu, Dilip. 1983. "Repeated Games with Discounting: A General Theory and an Application to Oligopoly." Ph.D. dissertation, Department of Economics, Princeton University.

Aumann, Robert. 1981. "Survey of Repeated Games." In R. Aumann et al., *Essays in Game Theory and Mathematical Economics*. Zurich: Bibliographisches Institut.

Bagwell, Kyle. 1985. "Advertising and Limit Pricing." Mimeo, Department of Economics, Stanford University.

Bain, Joe. 1949. "A Note on Pricing in Monopoly and Oligopoly." *American Economic Review* 39: 448–64.

Banks, Jeffrey, and Joel Sobel. 1985. "Equilibrium Selection in Signalling Games." Discussion Paper No. 85-9, University of California–San Diego (forthcoming, *Econometrica*).

[23] For example, in a signaling context, the ability to destroy resources in a publicly observable way may result in welfare gains for both the signalers and the signal recipients (Milgrom and Roberts 1986).

Benoit, Jean-Pierre. 1984. "Financially Constrained Entry in a Game with Incomplete Information." *Rand Journal of Economics* 15: 490–9.

Benoit, Jean-Pierre, and Vijay Krishna. 1985. "Finitely Repeated Games." *Econometrica* 53: 905–22.

Bulow, Jeremy I., John D. Geanakoplos, and Paul D. Klemperer. 1985. "Multimarket Oligopoly: Strategic Substitutes and Complements." *Journal of Political Economy* 93: 488–511.

Cho, In Koo, and David Kreps. 1985. "Signalling Games and Stable Equilibria." Mimeo, Graduate School of Business, Stanford University (forthcoming, *Quarterly Journal of Economics*).

Easley, David, Robert Masson, and Robert Reynolds. 1985. "Preying for Time." *Journal of Industrial Economics* 33: 445–60.

Engers, Maxim, and Marius Schwartz. 1984. "Signalling Equilibria Based on Sensible Beliefs: Limit Pricing Under Incomplete Information." Discussion Paper No. 84-4, Economic Policy Office, U.S. Department of Justice (Antitrust Division).

Friedman, James. 1979. "On Entry Preventing Behavior." In S. J. Brams, A. Schotter, and G. Schwodiauer, *Applied Game Theory*, pp. 236–53. Vienna: Physica-Verlag.

1985. "Cooperative Equilibria in Finite Horizon Noncooperative Supergames." *Journal of Economic Theory* 35: 390–8.

Fudenberg, Drew, and Eric Maskin. 1986. "The Folk Theorem for Repeated Games with Discounting and with Incomplete Information." *Econometrica* 54: 533–54.

Fudenberg, Drew, and Jean Tirole. 1983. "Learning-by-Doing and Market Performance." *Bell Journal of Economics* 14: 522–30.

1985. "Predation without Reputation." Working Paper No. 377, Department of Economics, Massachusetts Institute of Technology.

1986a. *Dynamic Models of Oligopoly.* Chur, Switzerland: Harwood.

1986b. "A Theory of Exit in Duopoly." *Econometrica* 54: 943–60.

Gale, Douglas, and Martin Hellwig. 1985. "Incentive Compatible Debt Contracts: The One-Period Problem." *Review of Economic Studies* 52: 647–63.

Gal-Or, Esther. 1981. "Deterrence Strategies – The Strategic Behavior of the Potential Entrant." Mimeo, Graduate School of Business, University of Pittsburgh.

Greer, Douglas. 1980. *Industrial Organization and Public Policy.* New York: Macmillan.

Harrington, Joseph. 1985a. "Limit Pricing When the Potential Entrant Is Uncertain of His Cost Function." Mimeo, Department of Political Economy, The Johns Hopkins University.

1985b. "Noncooperative Behavior by a Cartel as an Entry-Deterring Signal." *Rand Journal of Economics* 15: 426–33.

Harsanyi, John. 1967/68. "Games of Incomplete Information Played by 'Bayesian Players', Parts I, II and III." *Management Science* 14: 159–82, 320–4, 486–502.

Klemperer, Paul. 1984. "Collusion via Switching Costs: How 'Frequent Flyer' Programs, Trading Stamps, and Technology Choices Aid Collusion." Research Paper No. 786, Graduate School of Business, Stanford University.

Kohlberg, Elon, and Jean-François Mertens. 1986. "On the Strategic Stability of Equilibria." *Econometrica* 54: 1003–37.

Kohlleppel, Laurenz. 1983a. "Multidimensional Market Signalling." Discussion Paper #125, Institut für Gesellschafts- und Wirstschaftwissenschaften, Universität Bonn.

    1983b. "Properties of Sorting Equilibria." Discussion Paper #133, Institut für Gesellschafts- und Wirstschaftwissenschaften, Universität Bonn.

Kreps, David M. 1984. "Signalling Games and Stable Equilibria." Research Paper No. 758, Graduate School of Business, Stanford University.

Kreps, David M., and A. Michael Spence. 1985. "Modelling the Role of History in Industrial Organization and History." In G. Feiwel, *Issues in Contemporary Microeconomics and Welfare*. London: Macmillan.

Kreps, David M., and Robert Wilson. 1982a. "Reputation and Imperfect Information." *Journal of Economic Theory* 27: 253–79.

    1982b. "Sequential Equilibria." *Econometrica* 50: 863–94.

Lutz, Nancy. 1983. "Equilibrium Limit Pricing for a Multiproduct Firm." Unpublished manuscript, Graduate School of Business, Stanford University.

McGee, John. 1958. "Predatory Price Cutting: The Standard Oil (N.J.) Case." *Journal of Law and Economics* 1: 137–69.

    1980. "Predatory Pricing Revisited." *Journal of Law and Economics* 23: 289–330.

Mailath, George. 1985. "Separating Equilibria in Signaling Games: Incentive Compatibility, Existence with Simultaneous Signalling, Welfare and Convergence." Ph.D. thesis, Department of Economics, Princeton University.

Matthews, Steven, and Leonard Mirman. 1983. "Equilibrium Limit Pricing: The Effects of Private Information and Stochastic Demand." *Econometrica* 51: 981–96.

Milgrom, Paul, and John Roberts. 1982a. "Limit Pricing and Entry under Incomplete Information: An Equilibrium Analysis." *Econometrica* 50: 443–59.

    1982b. "Predation, Reputation, and Entry Deterrence." *Journal of Economic Theory* 27: 280–312.

    1986. "Price and Advertising Signals of Product Quality." *Journal of Political Economy* 94: 796–821.

Quinzii, Martine, and Jean-Charles Rochet. 1984. "Multidimensional Signalling." Technical Report No. 453, Economics Series, Institute for Mathematical Studies in the Social Sciences, Stanford University.

Ramey, Garey. 1985. "Limit Pricing Equilibria." Mimeo, Department of Economics, Stanford University.

Riordan, Michael. 1985. "Imperfect Information and Dynamic Conjectural Variations." *Rand Journal of Economics* 16: 41–50.

Roberts, John. 1986. "A Signalling Model of Predatory Pricing." *Oxford Economic Papers* 38, supplement: 75–93.

Rogerson, William. 1981. "Competitive Limit Pricing." Mimeo, Department of Economics, Stanford University.

Rubinstein, Ariel. 1979. "Equilibrium in Supergames with the Overtaking Criterion." *Journal of Economic Theory* 21: 1-9.

Saloner, Garth. 1982. "Dynamic Equilibrium Limit-Pricing." Ph.D. dissertation, Graduate School of Business, Stanford University.

    1985. "Predation, Mergers and Incomplete Information." Working Paper No. 383, Department of Economics, Massachusetts Institute of Technology.

Salop, Steven. 1979. "Strategic Entry Deterrence." *American Economic Review, Papers and Proceedings* 69: 335-8.

    1981. Personal communication.

Scherer, Frederick Michael. 1980. *Industrial Market Structure and Economic Performance,* 2nd ed. Chicago: Rand McNally.

Schmalensee, Richard. 1982. "The New Industrial Organization and the Economic Analysis of Modern Markets." In W. Hildenbrand, *Advances in Economic Theory.* Cambridge: Cambridge University Press.

Selton, Reinhardt. 1978. "The Chain-Store Paradox." *Theory and Decision* 9: 127-59.

Spence, A. Michael. 1981. "The Learning Curve and Competition." *Bell Journal of Economics* 12: 49-70.

Yamey, B. S. 1972. "Predatory Price Cutting: Notes and Comments." *Journal of Law and Economics* 15: 129-42.

CHAPTER 5

A sequential strategic theory of bargaining

Ariel Rubinstein

1   Introduction

The purpose of this survey is to review the development of the sequential strategic approach to the bargaining problem, and to explain why I believe that this theory may provide a foundation for further developments in other central areas of economic theory.

John Nash started his 1950 paper by defining the bargaining situation:

> A two person bargaining situation involves two individuals who have the opportunity to collaborate for mutual benefit in more than one way. . . . The two individuals are highly rational, . . . each can accurately compare his desire for various things . . . they are equal in bargaining skill.

Given a bargaining situation, we look for a theoretical prediction of what agreement, if any, will be reached by the two parties.

I began with this clarification because of the existing confusion in some of the literature among the above problem and the following (nonexclusive) ethical questions: "What is a just agreement?" "What is a reasonable outcome for an arbitrator's decision?" and "What agreement is optimal for society as a whole?" These questions differ from the current one mainly in that they allow derivation of an answer from a social welfare optimization. An a priori assumption that a solution to the bargaining problem satisfies collective rationality properties seems inappropriate.

The survey was prepared while I visited the Department of Economics at the University of Western Ontario, and the IMSSS, Stanford University. I would like to thank Ken Binmore and Asher Wolinsky for their encouragement and for the insights I got from them during the past five years. Asher Wolinsky, Maria Herrero, Christopher Harris, Motty Perry, Stephen Turnbull, and in particular Ken Binmore provided many useful comments on an earlier draft of the paper.
The list of references in this paper does not purport to be comprehensive. It includes mainly papers in which the infinite-alternating-offers, sequential-bargaining model is used.

The bargaining problem was presented by Edgeworth (1881) who considered it the most fundamental economic situation. Edgeworth did not go beyond identifying the entire "contract curve" (the set of individually rational and Pareto optimal agreements) as the set of possible agreements. For years economists tended to agree that further specification of a bargaining solution should depend on the vague notion of the "bargaining ability" of the players. Among the exceptions are Zeuthen (1930) and Hicks (1932), but their models assumed patterns of concession behavior that were not derived from rational behavior assumptions.

The theory of von Neumann and Morgenstern inspired Nash to suggest two approaches to solving the bargaining problem: first, the axiomatic approach [see Nash (1950); for a survey of the axiomatic approach literature see Roth (1979)]. The axiomatic method is explained in Nash (1953):

> One states as axioms several properties that it would seem natural for the solution to have and then one discovers that the axioms actually determine the solution uniquely.

The drawback of the axiomatic approach is that it is too general. The general, abstract terms it uses and the minimal information it assumes make it hard to check the reasonableness of the axioms. In particular, Nash's axioms of Pareto optimality and Independence of Irrelevant Alternatives (IIA) have the flavor of "collective rationality" and are therefore controversial.

Nash (1953) describes the second approach to the bargaining problem, namely the strategic (noncooperative) approach:

> . . . one makes the players' steps of negotiation . . . become moves in the non-cooperative model. Of course, one cannot represent all possible bargaining devices as moves in the non-cooperative game. The negotiation process must be formalized and restricted, but in such a way that each participant is still able to utilize all the essential strength of his position.

The main difficulty with the strategic approach lies in the need to specify the moves in the game. Bargaining situations do not have a unique procedure. Therefore any bargaining game can be accused of being too special.

Nash himself felt the need to complement his axiomatic solution by a strategic model. He suggested a static strategic model in which the players make simultaneous, once-and-for-all demands. If the demands are compatible, they form the terms of the agreement; incompatible demands cause disagreement. Every agreement on the contract curve is an equilibrium outcome for this game; however, by requiring some sort of stability related to uncertainty about the compatibility of demands near the Pareto frontier, Nash established that his solution is the only necessary limit of equilibrium outcomes when the uncertainty becomes negligible. [For a clearer modification of Nash's demand game, see Binmore (1986a).] Some other pioneering strategic models of bargaining were studied by Harsanyi and Selten and are not in the scope of this survey.

Nash (1950) created the standard informational framework for the axiomatic bargaining approach. The approach is based solely on information about the bargaining preferences over lotteries in which the outcomes are taken from among the set X of possible agreements and the disagreement outcome D. These preferences are assumed to satisfy the von Neumann–Morgenstern (VM) assumptions. Nash's symmetry axiom excludes any information, other than the attitude toward risk, from being relevant to the solution.

The sequential strategic approach to bargaining is motivated by the desire to construct a bargaining theory built on information about the time preferences of the players. However, as will be explained later, it leads to unexpected support for the Nash bargaining solution. This linkage supports Nash's (1953) assertion that "the two approaches to the problem, via the negotiation model or via the axioms, are complementary; each helps to justify and clarify the other."

Let us start by reviewing the sequential bargaining model of Rubinstein (1982), which is the basis for the current survey.

2   A sequential bargaining model

2.1   *The bargaining situation*

The cornerstone of the model is the following bargaining situation: Two players, named 1 and 2, are bargaining over the set of feasible agreements $X = [0, 1]$. The players have opposing preferences over X. If $x > y$, player 1 prefers x to y and player 2 prefers y to x.

Classical economic situations that fit this bargaining situation include:

1. Two people would like to divide 1 dollar that they own jointly. An element $x \in X$ is the portion of the dollar that player 1 receives.
2. A seller of one unit of a good with reservation price 0 wishes to sell the good to a buyer with reservation price 1. A number $x \in X$ stands for the price the buyer pays the seller.
3. An employer faces a stream of profits. A member $x \in X$ is the proportion of the profits that is given to the employees.
4. Two agents in a bartering economy own initial bundles $(1, 0)$ and $(0, 1)$. The contract curve of the proper Edgeworth box can be made equivalent to X by identifying $x \in X$ with the point on the curve where 1 is left with x units of his initial commodity.

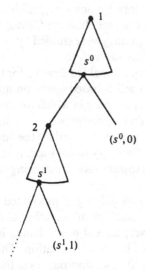

Figure 1

Remark: Note that x and $1 - x$ are not necessarily to be identified with VM utilities. In fact, by varying the associated VM utility functions, the situation can be mapped onto any Nash bargaining problem.

2.2   *The bargaining procedure*

Events in the bargaining procedure are confined to times in the set $N = \{0, 1, 2, 3, \ldots\}$. Each bargainer, in turn, offers a possible agreement and his opponent may agree to the offer, "Y," or reject it, "N." Acceptance ends the bargaining. Rejection leads to the next period when the rejecting player makes a counteroffer, and so on, without any predetermined limit on the number of repetitions of the process. There are no rules that bind the players to previous offers they made. It is assumed that the players are indifferent to the path of rejected offers made during the negotiation. An outcome of the process might be either an agreement $x \in X$ at stage n, denoted by (x, n), or perpetual disagreement, denoted by D. A diagram of the extensive form of the game is shown in Figure 1 (a radius of an arc is a choice from among the set X).

The alternating offers model was first studied (with finite horizon and fixed bargaining costs) by Ingolf Stahl (1972). An advantage of this procedure is that although it is a game form with perfect information (no simultaneous moves), the game form is "almost" symmetric. The only asymmetry arises because of the need to specify who is the first player to make an offer. Stipulating a "small" period of negotiation will eliminate this asymmetry.

2.3 *Time preferences*

The new informational element that does not appear in the Nash bargaining theory is the parties' attitudes toward time. Let $\gtrsim_i$ be player i's preference on the set of possible outcomes $X \times N \cup \{D\}$. The preferences are assumed to satisfy the following assumptions:

(A-1) The preferences extend the preferences in the basic bargaining situation: For all n_0,

$$(x, n_0) \gtrsim_1 (y, n_0) \text{ iff } (x, n_0) \lesssim_2 (y, n_0) \text{ iff } x \geq y.$$

(A-2) Time is valuable: For all $1 > x > 0$ and $n_1 > n_2$,

$$(x, n_2) >_i (x, n_1).$$

(A-3) Continuity: $\gtrsim_1$ has a closed graph in the product topology.
(A-4) Stationarity: For all $x, y \in X$ and $n \in N$,

$$(x, n) \gtrless_i (y, n+1) \text{ iff } (x, 0) \gtrless_i (y, 1).$$

By the above assumptions, $\gtrsim_i$ is determined uniquely by i's preference on the outcomes in the two first periods. These assumptions guarantee the existence of a utility representation $u_i(x)\delta^n$ for all arbitrary δ [see Fishburn and Rubinstein (1982)]. They are sufficient for the existence part of Theorem 1 below. However, for the uniqueness result it will be assumed further that:

(A-5) Existence of present value: For all $x \in X$ there exists a $v_i(x) \in X$ such that $(v_i(x), 0) \sim_i (x, 1)$.
(A-6) Increasing compensation for delay: The difference $x - v_i(x)$ is a strictly increasing function of x.

Remark: One should be careful not to apply Theorem 1 automatically to all the examples listed in Section 2.1. Assumption (A-6) is quite strong in some contexts, particularly in the bartering economy example.

A leading family of time preferences that satisfies the above assumptions includes the preferences represented by the utility functions $x\delta_i^n$ and $(1-x)\delta_2^n$ (δ_i is referred to as a fixed discounting factor).

The time preferences represented by the utility functions $x - c_1 n$ and $1 - x - c_2 n$ do not satisfy (A-5) and (A-6), but will be used to illustrate the theorems because they are covered by the original paper's conditions. For a discussion of the model without (A-4), see Binmore (1986c).

2.4   *The solution*

The Nash equilibrium concept is a very weak notion of a solution to the sequential bargaining model. Every outcome (x, n) is a Nash equilibrium outcome. As usually happens in sequential games, a Nash equilibrium analysis admits the use of incredible threats; for example, a player may insist forever on a particular large demand. Such possibilities allow the support of a large class of Nash equilibria. Using a stronger concept – such as Selten's (subgame) Perfect Equilibrium (P.E.) – would not be sufficient without the assumptions in Section 2.3 about the time preferences. Both notions are necessary for Theorem 1.

> **Theorem 1** [Rubinstein (1982)]. *Let* (x^*, y^*) *be the (unique!) solution for the pair of equations*
>
> $$(y, 0) \sim_1 (x, 1), \qquad (x, 0) \sim_2 (y, 1).$$
>
> *Then the* unique *perfect equilibrium of the game is the pair of strategies in which player 1 (player 2) always makes the offer* x^* (y^*), *accepts any offer which leaves him better off than* y^* (x^*), *and rejects any offer which is strictly worse for him than* y^* (x^*).

We refer to the two equations of Theorem 1 as the *fundamental equations*.

Remark: Under somewhat weaker assumptions [dropping (A-5) and weakening (A-6)] it was originally shown that the P.E. agreements are those $x^* \in X$ and $y^* \in X$ satisfying

$$y^* = \min\{y \mid (x^*, 1) \lesssim_1 (y, 0)\}$$

and

$$x^* = \max\{x \mid (y^*, 1) \lesssim_2 (x, 0)\}.$$

2.5   *Proofs for Theorem 1*

It is easy to verify that the pair of strategies described in the theorem is a P.E. [Just note that player 2 behaves optimally when he rejects an offer x made by player 1 if $x > x^*$, because $(x, 0) <_2 (x^*, 0) \sim_2 (y^*, 1)$.]

It is also easy to show that, given the assumptions about the preferences, the fundamental equations have a unique solution. The diagram (Figure 2) of the indifference curves $(y, 0) \sim_1 (x, 1)$ and $(x, 0) \sim_2 (y, 1)$ is useful in illustrating this fact.

The more interesting part of the proof is to show the uniqueness of the P.E. In what follows, two proofs are sketched. They reveal different in-

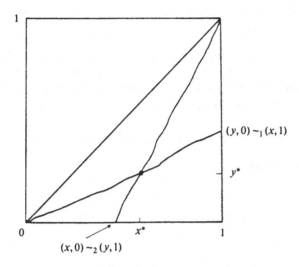

Figure 2

sights into the theorem and provide useful techniques for proving other theorems as well.

Outline of Proof 1 [this is essentially Shaked and Sutton's (1984a) simplification of the original proof]: Given an outcome (x, n), denote by $v_i^n(x)$ player i's present value of (x, n); that is, $(v_i^n(x), 0) \sim_i (x, n)$. Let M_i be the supremum of $v_i^n(x)$ over all the outcomes (x, n) of P.E. in the game where i makes the first move. Similarly, define m_i as the infimum of the same set. Note that all the subgames after a rejection of an offer are equivalent to one of the two game that start with one of the bargainers making an offer.

Step 1 $(M_2, 0) \lesssim_1 (M_1, 1)$. By perfection, whenever it is player 1's turn to react, he accepts any $y \in X$ that satisfies $(y, 0) >_1 (M_1, 1)$. If $(u_2, 0) >_1 (M_1, 1)$ and u_2 is 2's present value of a P.E. starting by 2's offer, then 2 will do better by offering some y satisfying $u_2 > y$ and $(y, 0) >_1 (M_1, 1)$.

Step 2 $(M_2, 0) \gtrsim_1 (M_1, 1)$. For any $u_1 \leq M_1$ that is 1's present value of a P.E. starting with 1's offer, it is easy to construct a P.E. that starts with player 2 making an offer y satisfying $(y, 0) \sim_1 (u_1, 1)$. Therefore, $(M_2, 0) \gtrsim_1 (M_1, 1)$.

Step 3 $(M_1, 0) \gtrsim_2 (M_2, 1)$. If player 1 demands more than $v_2(M_2)$, player 2 rejects the offer. Player 2 will never offer more than $v_1(M_1) =$

M_2, which is less than $v_2(M_2)$. Therefore, $M_1 \leq v_2(M2)$ and $(M_1, 0) \gtrsim_2 (M_2, 1)$.

By the construction of the P.E. with the outcome $(x^*, 0)$, $x^* \leq M_1$. By steps 1 and 2, $(M_1, 1) \sim_1 (M_2, 0)$. It follows from Figure 2 that $x^* \leq M_1$, $(M_1, 1) \sim_1 (M_2, 0)$, and $(M_1, 0) \gtrsim_2 (M_2, 1)$ imply that $M_1 = x^*$ and $M_2 = y^*$. Similarly, $m_1 = x^*$ and $m_2 = y^*$. ∎

Outline of Proof 2 [this proof is essentially Binmore's (1986c)]:

Step 1	Define the sequences:

$$x_0 = 1 \qquad\qquad y_0 = 0$$
$$\text{for } n \text{ odd} \quad x_n = v_1(x_{n-1}), \qquad y_n = v_2(y_{n-1}),$$
$$\text{for } n \text{ even} \quad x_n = v_2(x_{n-1}), \qquad y_n = v_1(y_{n-1}).$$

On the even numbers, $x_n \to x^*$. On the odd numbers, $y_n \to x^*$. (In Figure 2, the sequences converge to a solution of the fundamental equations.)

Step 2	There is no P.E. in which player 1's present value exceeds any of the x_N (for N even) or falls below any of the y_N (for N odd).

Step 3	By steps 1 and 2, the only present value of a P.E. of the game for player 1 is x^* and the rest follows easily. ∎

Remark: Let G_N be the bargaining game with finite horizon which ends at the end of period N. Then, for N odd (even) the only P.E. of G_N is one in which player 1 offers y_N (x_N) in the first period and player 2 accepts.

### 2.6	*Examples and remarks*

#### A	*The bargaining ends immediately*

There is no inefficiency in the P.E. characterized by Theorem 1 because the bargaining ends immediately. [This is not a mere consequence of the perfectness. Unless the fundamental equations have a unique solution, this is incorrect. See Binmore (1986c) for a discussion of the circumstances under which the bargaining does not end immediately.] Thus the model cannot explain the fact that sometimes we observe long negotiations between parties. I do not find this fact disturbing because the existence of prolonged interchanges during negotiation is more naturally attributed to problems of incomplete information.

B   *Pareto optimality*

If we extend the set of possible agreements to $X = \{(x_1, x_2) \mid 0 \le x_i$ and $x_1 + x_2 \le 1\}$ and assume that player i cares only about x_i, then the proofs of Theorem 1 validate the conclusion that in the unique P.E., player 1 offers Pareto optimal outcome $(x^*, 1 - x^*)$. Thus, even without assuming Pareto optimality, we are led to an efficient outcome.

C   *It pays to be more patient*

Define $\succsim_1$ to be *more impatient* than $\succsim_1'$ if whenever $(y, 0) \succsim_1' (x, 1)$ then $(y, 0) \succsim_1 (x, 1)$. A glance at Figure 2 reveals that $x^*(\succsim_1', \succsim_2) \ge x^*(\succsim_1, \succsim_2)$. Thus, as expected, being more patient pays in this model.

D $x^* > y^*$

The asymmetry between the players in the bargaining procedure gives player 1 an advantage over player 2 in the sense that, given the players' time preferences, player 1 is better off if he starts the bargaining ($x^* > y^*$). In particular, if the players' attitudes toward time is identical – that is, if

$$(y_1, n_1) \sim_1 (y_2, n_2) \quad \text{iff} \quad (1 - y_1, n_1) \sim_2 (1 - y_2, n_2)$$

– then $x^* > 1/2$ and $y^* < 1/2$.

E   *The P.E. of the game as a limit of the P.E. of G_N*

Binmore's proof of Theorem 1 reveals an interesting property of the game: The unique P.E. outcome is a limit of the sequence of P.E. outcomes of the finite-horizon games G_N. For more general conditions under which an infinite extensive form game is the limit of finite games, see Fudenberg and Levine (1983) and Harris (1985a).

F   *Example: fixed discount rates*

Assume that the players have time preferences induced from the utility functions $x\delta_1^t$ and $(1 - x)\delta_2^t$. Then the P.E. partition is

$$x^* = (1 - \delta_2)/(1 - \delta_1\delta_2).$$

Notice the limit cases like $\delta_1 = 1$ and $1 > \delta_2$. Although the case $\delta_1 = 1$ does not satisfy all the assumptions, it is easy to see that the limit of the above formula ($x^* = 1$) is indeed the unique P.E. outcome for this case.

G   *Accelerating the bargaining process*

Assume that players have the continuous-time, present-value formula $xe^{-r_1 t}$ and $(1 - x)e^{-r_2 t}$, where t denotes "real time." Given that the length of one period of negotiation is Δ, then $\delta_i = e^{-r_i \Delta}$. Fixing the rates r_1 and r_2, the formula $(1 - \delta_2)/(1 - \delta_1 \delta_2)$ becomes a function of Δ, $x^*(\Delta)$. If we accelerate the bargaining, we obtain

$$\lim_{\Delta \to 0} x^*(\Delta) = \lim_{\Delta \to 0} y^*(\Delta) = r_2/(r_1 + r_2).$$

In the limit we see no asymmetry: The solution depends only on time preferences, not on who moves first.

H   Example: fixed bargaining costs

Assume that player i bears a fixed bargaining cost per bargaining round, c_i. If $c_1 < c_2$ (player 1 is the stronger) then in the P.E., player 1 achieves his best outcome, "1." If $c_1 > c_2$ then the outcome is c_2. When $c_1 = c_2 = c$, for every x in the interval $c \leq x \leq 1$, $(x, 0)$ is a P.E. outcome. Furthermore, in this case the bargaining may continue beyond the first period. In Rubinstein (1982), an example is constructed where the P.E. agreement is reached in the second round. In that example, the first move by player 1 could be viewed as a signal to player 2 about the P.E. that they are playing in the subgame starting with 2's offer.

3   The axiomatic and strategic approaches to the bargaining problem

3.1   The Nash program

The Nash bargaining solution has dominated bargaining theory since 1950. The solution is attractive; it is simple, it requires little information, and it has a beautiful axiomatization. However, the drawbacks of the Nash solution are clear as well: (1) Some of the axioms are not easily defended in the abstract. (2) Additional information, such as the negotiation time preferences, seems to be relevant to the solution. This information is excluded by the axioms of Symmetry and Invariance under Affine Transformations of Utility Scales. Underlying these axioms is the assumption that the only relevant information is the players' VM utilities. (3) As economists we often find the Nash set-up too abstract to guide us in the selection of the disagreement point from among several available options.

   This is the point where the strategic approach provides insight into the bargaining process.

   The idea of supporting cooperative solutions by noncooperative models and solutions is now called the "Nash program." Nash presented this task and executed it by the demand game mentioned in the introduction. Binmore (1986b) was the first to observe that the sequential model of Section 2 has a strong relationship to the Nash solution [see also McLennan

(1982)]. This discovery seemed paradoxical because the bases for the two models were very different. This paradox was resolved in Binmore, Rubinstein, and Wolinsky (1986), which is the source for most of the rest of this section.

3.2 Nash-(VM)-bargaining solution and Nash-(time preference)-bargaining solution

The primitives of Nash bargaining theory are $(X, D, \gtrsim_1, \gtrsim_2)$, where X is the set of possible agreements, D is the "disagreement point," and $\gtrsim_i$ are the preferences of player i over the set of lotteries where the certain outcomes are elements of X. Assume that $\gtrsim_i$ satisfies the VM assumptions (i.e., is represented by the expectation of a utility function $u_i \colon X \to R$). Assume that the players are risk-averse in the sense that they prefer the average $px + (1-p)y$ to a lottery that awards prizes x and y with probabilities p and $(1-p)$, respectively. Now we fit to $(X, D, \gtrsim_1, \gtrsim_2)$ a Nash bargaining problem (S, s^0):

$$S = \{(u_1, u_2) = (u_1(x), u_2(x)) \mid \text{for some } x \in X\}$$

and

$$s^0 = (u_1(D), u_2(D)).$$

Define the Nash-VM-bargaining solution,

$$x^{\mathrm{VM}}(\gtrsim_1, \gtrsim_2) = \arg \max_{x \in X}(u_1(x) - u_1(D))(u_2(x) - u_2(D)).$$

Clearly $x^{\mathrm{VM}}(\gtrsim_1, \gtrsim_2)$ is well-defined, because Nash solution is invariant to the choice of the utility representations and the risk aversion assures that S is a convex set.

For the Nash-time preference (TP)-bargaining solution, define the primitives of the model as above with the only change that $\gtrsim_i$ is i's preference over the set $X \times T$, where $T = [0, \infty]$ is the time space. Assume that $\gtrsim_i$ satisfies the assumptions made in Section 2 about time preferences (adjusted to the change in the time space). Assume that both players are indifferent to the time dimension with respect to D; that is, $(D, t) \sim_i (D, 0)$ for all t. It was shown in Fishburn and Rubinstein (1982) that for δ large enough there exist concave functions $u_1(x)$ and $u_2(x)$ such that $u_i(x)\delta^t$ represent the time preferences. Notice that $u_1(D) = u_2(D) = 0$. Now let us fit to $(X, D, \gtrsim_1, \gtrsim_2)$ a Nash bargaining problem (S, s^0) and define the Nash-TP-bargaining solution

$$x^{\mathrm{TP}}(\gtrsim_1, \gtrsim_2) = \arg \max_{x \in X} u_1(x)u_2(x).$$

It is easy to check that $x^{\mathrm{TP}}(\gtrsim_1, \gtrsim_2)$ is well-defined. [Notice that if $v_i(x)\epsilon^t$ also represents $\gtrsim_i$ then there exists $k > 0$ such that $v_i(x) = ku_i(x)^{\log \epsilon/\log \delta}$.]

3.3   Nash-TP solution and the strategic models

We are ready to describe the exact sense in which the sequential strategic model (Section 2) is related to the Nash solution. The strategic model uses the same information as the Nash-TP solution, and indeed the strategic model approaches the Nash-TP solution and not the regular Nash-VM solution.

The exact relationship is as follows: Assume that the real time length of one period of bargaining is Δ, where $\Delta > 0$. The time preferences on the set $X \times T$ induce preferences on $X \times N$ by $(x_1, n_1) \succsim_i (x_2, n_2)$ if $(x_i, n_1 \Delta) \succsim_i (x_2, n_2 \Delta)$. For a given Δ, the sequential bargaining game has a unique P.E. outcome $(x^*(\Delta), 0)$ or $(y^*(\Delta), 0)$ depending on the identity of the player who starts the bargaining.

The following theorem is essentially due to Binmore (1986b) and was modified in Binmore, Rubinstein, and Wolinsky (1986).

Theorem 2

$$\lim_{\Delta \to 0} x^*(\Delta) = \lim_{\Delta \to 0} y^*(\Delta) = x^{TP}(\succsim_1, \succsim_2).$$

Proof: Choose concave functions $u_i(x)$ such that $u_i(x)\delta^t$ represents $\succsim_i$ $(i = 1, 2)$. Let $u_2 = \Psi(u_1)$ be the function describing the frontier of the set S. By Theorem 1, the pair $x^*(\Delta)$, $y^*(\Delta)$ is the solution to the equations:

$$u_1(y^*(\Delta)) = \delta^\Delta u_1(x^*(\Delta)), \qquad u_2(x^*(\Delta)) = \delta^\Delta u_2(y^*(\Delta)).$$

Denote $u_i^\Delta = u_i(x^*(\Delta))$. Then

$$\Psi(u_1^\Delta) = \delta^\Delta u_2(y^*(\Delta)) = \delta^\Delta \Psi(u_1(y^*(\Delta))) = \delta^\Delta \Psi(\delta^\Delta u_1^\Delta).$$

Let $u_1^{\Delta(n)}$ be a sequence that converges to $\bar{u}_1$. Then

$$\lim_{n \to \infty} \frac{\Psi(u_1^\Delta) - \Psi(\delta^\Delta u_1^\Delta)}{u_1^\Delta - \delta^\Delta u_1^\Delta} = \lim_{n \to \infty} \left(-\frac{(\delta^\Delta - 1)\Psi(\delta^\Delta u_1^\Delta)}{(\delta^\Delta - 1)u_1^\Delta} \right) = -\frac{\Psi(\bar{u}_1)}{u_1}$$

and thus $\bar{u}_1$ is the arg max of $u_1 \Psi(u_1)$. ∎

Remark: Shortening the period of negotiation eliminates the asymmetry in the bargaining procedure. In the limit, there is no difference between the game outcomes when players 1 or 2 are the first to move.

Figure 3 summarizes Section 3.3.

3.4   Nash-VM solution and the strategic models

Carrying out the Nash program for the Nash-VM solution requires modification of the model's basic strategic structure. A change suggested in

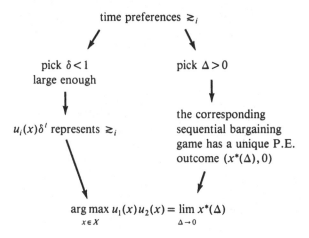

Figure 3

Binmore, Rubinstein, and Wolinsky (1986) is to introduce an exogenous risk of breakdown in the negotiations. At the beginning of every period, before an offer is made, the bargaining will end without an agreement with an exogenous positive probability p. In case of a breakdown, the outcome is D. Time is not valuable directly $[(x_1, n_1) \sim_i (x_1, n_2)$ for all n_1 and $n_2]$ but the longer the players plan to negotiate the larger the chances of a breakdown. To complete the description of the modified game, we must specify the players' preferences on the set of lotteries in which the pure outcomes are elements in X. Let $\gtrsim_1$ and $\gtrsim_2$ be extensions of the preference ordering on X to preferences on the set of lotteries over elements in X. We assume that the preferences satisfy the VM assumptions and that they display risk aversion. Formally, the strategic model with risk of breakdown closely resembles the model presented in Section 2. A pair of strategies in the bargaining determine a lottery of the type in which an outcome x is agreed with probability $(1-p)^n$ and disagreement, D, is achieved by probability $1-(1-p)^n$. Such a lottery is denoted $\langle x, n \rangle$. The game has a unique P.E. that is determined as before by the unique solution to the fundamental equations of Theorem 1, $\langle x^*, 1 \rangle \sim_1 \langle y^*, 0 \rangle$ and $\langle y^*, 1 \rangle \sim_2 \langle x^*, 0 \rangle$. Denote the solution by $x^*(p)$, $y^*(p)$. The following theorem then provides a noncooperative foundation for the Nash-VM bargaining solution.

Theorem 3. (a) The sequential game with a risk of breakdown has a unique P.E. The outcome is $x^*(p)$ if 1 starts the game and $y^*(p)$ if 2 starts the bargaining.

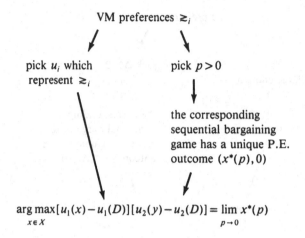

VM preferences $\gtrsim_i$

pick u_i which
represent $\gtrsim_i$

pick $p > 0$

the corresponding
sequential bargaining
game has a unique P.E.
outcome $(x^*(p), 0)$

$$\underset{x \in X}{\arg\max}\,[u_1(x) - u_1(D)]\,[u_2(y) - u_2(D)] = \lim_{p \to 0} x^*(p)$$

Figure 4

(b) $\displaystyle \lim_{p \to 0} x^*(p) = \lim_{p \to 0} y^*(p) = x^{\text{VM}}(\gtrsim_1, \gtrsim_2).$

Figure 4 summarizes Section 3.4.

Remark: The analysis of the strategic games with time preferences and with risks of breakdown can be unified and extended in several directions. For example, in Wolinsky (in press) the probability of breakdown depends on the choice of search intensities.

3.5   *The choice of disagreement point and the outside option principle*

Theorems 2 and 3 help us to identify the proper disagreement point in Nash bargaining theory for those cases where it is reasonable to regard the Nash solution as an approximation to the equilibrium outcome of an appropriate strategic model. If time impatience is the significant friction in the model, we ought to take the status quo agreement (the time-indifferent partition) as the disagreement point. Thus, if a strike is in progress during which the workers and the firm negotiate about the value of the post-strike wage stream, then the disagreement point is taken to be the consequence of prolonging the negotiations forever – that is, at the disagreement point, each negotiator is assigned the income stream he receives as long as the dispute continues. When the friction in the model is due to the risk of an exogenous breakdown of the negotiation, we ought to take as D the event that a breakdown occurs. Thus if two parties bargain over the gain from a business opportunity that they are able to exploit together, then D is the event that a third party will snatch the opportunity away.

Another natural candidate for indentification with the element D in Nash's framework is the outside option outcome, denoted by e. By the outside option outcome, we refer to an outcome that results if a party withdraws from the negotiation (a more general definition will allow the outcome to depend on the identity of the player who withdraws). In many applications of the Nash solution, e has been identified with D. The strategic approach suggests that this is wrong.

Outside options may be incorporated into the strategic model by modifying the strategic games, that of Section 2 (time impatience) and of Section 3.4 (a risk of a breakdown). At each node in which a player must respond to an offer, we add the alternative of withdrawing and forcing e. Binmore (1986c) and Shaked and Sutton (1984b) discovered that including an outside option does not alter the solution to the game without outside option, if both x^* and y^* are preferable to e by both parties. Thus, adopting the sequential strategic model leads to the conclusion that it is not proper to identify D with e. The presence of e merely restricts the domain under which the Nash-TP or VM bargaining solutions – with the choice of D as the status quo or the breakdown event – approximate the strategic models when friction elements become negligible.

4 Bargaining with incomplete information

4.1 *The role of incomplete information in the model*

A critical assumption of the sequential bargaining model as developed so far is that each player has complete information about the other player's preferences. Hence it is not surprising that in P.E. the bargaining ends immediately, and it is natural to try to explain the prolongation of the bargaining process by a game with incomplete information.

When incomplete information exists, the series of offers and reactions become a communication system between the players. Each player tries to conclude from the other's moves who his opponent is, and each may try to mislead the other to believe that he has a better bargaining position than he actually has. A player's readiness to delay an agreement may be interpreted as a signal about the unknown information. Impatience is an incentive to compromise, but introducing delays is the only means a player has under his control to test the credibility of what the opponent says.

Following Harsanyi (1967), the situation is modeled as a Bayesian game. The sequential structure of the strategic bargaining game calls for an extension of the subgame perfectness notion to games with incomplete information. Kreps and Wilson's (1982) Sequential Equilibrium (S.E.) is a natural convenient solution concept for extending the analysis of Section 2 to incomplete information situations. However, in contrast to the usefulness of perfectness in bargaining games with complete information, the set of S.E. is enormously large. Let us demonstrate this point by an example taken from Rubinstein (1985b). [A more general discussion appears in Rubinstein (1985a).]

4.2   *An example of a bargaining game with incomplete information*

Assume that the players' utility functions are $x - c_1 t$ and $1 - x - c_2 t$ (the case of fixed bargaining costs) and that these functions are the players' VM utility functions as well. Player 1's cost $c_1 = c$ is common knowledge. Player 2's cost c_2 is known only to player 2. Both parties are aware of the random process which selects c_2. With probability ω_0, $c_2 = c_w > c$. In such a case, it is said that player 2 is the weak type, 2_w, because if player 1 were in possession of exact information about 2's cost then the outcome of the bargaining would be the worse one for player 2. With probability $1 - \omega_0$, $c_2 = c_s < c$ and it is said that 2 is 2_s, the stronger type.

Candidates for equilibrium are triples (f, g, h), where f is a strategy for player 1 and g and h are strategies for types 2_w and 2_s respectively. A candidate for S.E. is a four-tuple (f, g, h, ω), where the added element ω is a function that assigns a number to every possible history after which 1 has to move. This number is interpreted as player 1's belief that 2 is of the weak type. To the assumptions on S.E. we add the requirement that if 1 concludes with certainty that he is playing against a certain type, he continues to hold this belief forever and therefore uses his unique P.E. strategy in the complete information game against this type.

The concept of S.E. requires that the solution specify the players' new beliefs after a zero-probability event occurs. The belief that a player adopts after a zero-probability event is called a conjecture. The S.E. concept allows great freedom in selecting conjectures to support strategies as best responses and thereby to rationalize threats. Player 1's most severe credible threat is that a deviation by player 2 will lead him to play the game as if he were playing against type 2_w. To support this threat, player 1 may use the rule that a deviation by player 2 is an indication that he belongs to type 2_w. These "optimistic conjectures" support many S.E. In Rubinstein (1985b) it is shown that for all ω_0 and all $1 - c + c_s \geq x^* \geq c_w$, there is a S.E.

in which the bargaining ends immediately with the agreement x^* or lasts for two periods, where in the first period 2_w agrees to x^* and in the second period player 1 accepts player 2_s's offer $x^* - c_w$. In the S.E., any move of player 2 which was not expected from either of the two types makes player 1 believe that he plays against 2_w. A deviation of 2_s is prevented by player 1's threat to believe that he plays against 2_w.

Thus the set of S.E. is very large. The perfectness notion eliminates incredible threats in the model with complete information, but the severe threats return through the back door in the game with incomplete information, in that the freedom to select conjectures is left open.

4.3   Selection of S.E.

When presenting and analyzing the concept of S.E., Kreps and Wilson (1982) wrote: ". . . the formulation [of S.E.] in terms of players' beliefs gives the analyst a tool for choosing among S.E." The idea is to impose additional restrictions on the beliefs, restrictions that are reasonable at least in the special context of bargaining games. As things stand, I do not feel that we have a firm enough theory to justify the selection of one particular S.E. from among the many. Let me mention just one approach, suggested in Rubinstein (1985a, b). No claims are made that this is the only viable approach.

Three additional requirements are imposed on S.E. The first is quite straightforward. If player 1 makes an offer s^{t-1} that is rejected and followed by 2's offer s^t satisfying $s^t > s^{t-1} - c_w$, then player 1 does not strictly strengthen his belief that he is playing against 2_w. The second assumption is a tie-breaking assumption. If an offer has been made and the receiver is indifferent between accepting it or continuing the bargaining, then he accepts the offer. The third requirement is the crucial one: Assume that 1 offers s^{t-1}, and that player 2 rejects it and makes a counteroffer s^t. Assume that 2's reaction was not an expected one from any type. If $s^t \leq s^{t-1} - c_s$ and $s^t > s^{t-1} - c_w$, it is required that player 1 conclude that 2 is 2_s. Thus, it is assumed that 2_s can sort himself out by rejecting s^{t-1} and making an offer that, if accepted in the next period, is better for 2_s and worse for 2_w than accepting s^{t-1}. The idea is that player 2_s is implicitly saying "you ought to believe that I am 2_s because if you do then your consequent outcome will make me better off, whereas if 2_w sent the same message he would be worse off." Under the above circumstances, if 1 believes the message "I am 2_s" then he accepts s^t. Indeed, it is rational for 2_s to reject s^{t-1} and offer $s^t \leq s^{t-1} - c_s$ in the following period; it is not rational for 2_w to do so because, for 2_w, $(s^{t-1}, 0)$ is preferred to $(s^t, 1)$.

A sequential equilibrium satisfying the above three assumptions is referred to as a *bargaining sequential equilibrium* (B.S.E.). The next theorem [Rubinstein (1985a, b)] is a characterization of the B.S.E. outcomes.

Theorem 4. *In any B.S.E.,*

if $w_0 > 2c/(c + c_w)$, the outcome is $(1, 0)$ if 2 is 2_w and $(1 - c_w, 1)$ if 2 is 2_s;

if $2c/(c + c_w) > w_0 > (c + c_s)/(c + c_w)$ the outcome is $(c_w, 0)$ if 2 is 2_w and $(0, 1)$ if 2 is 2_s;

if $(c + c_s)/(c + c_w) > w_0$ the outcome is $(c_s, 0)$ whatever 2's type.

The B.S.E. of Theorem 4 has some attractive features: The negotiation does not end immediately and it satisfies the expected comparative statics properties. However, the foundations for the approach remain shaky. One can bring arguments against the strong inference assumptions made in Theorem 4; for instance, the belief functions are not continuous. There are other intuitive arguments that can restrict the beliefs of an uninformed player. For example, Bikhchandani (1985) assumes that if only one of the two types of player 2 is supposed to reject a given offer, then the rejection reveals the informed player's type independently of whether his counteroffer is consistent with this type or not. This change enables Bikhchandani to build an example of S.E. (with mixed strategies) that is qualitatively different than Rubinstein's (1985a). In particular, in Bikhchandani's equilibrium the bargaining process may last for an arbitrarily large finite number of periods if player 1 assesses probability close to 1 that player 2 is of the weak type.

Extending the notion of B.S.E. to the case where the number of player-2 types is larger than 2 requires new ideas. Grossman and Perry (1986) suggest (for a buyer–seller model) such an extension leading to a unique play of the game in which the negotiation continues for many periods. However, for some parameters of the model, the requirements are too strong and lead to non-existence problems.

4.4   *The state of the art*

The topic of bargaining with incomplete information has received a lot of attention in the last five years. It was inspired by development of the "economics of information" and attempts to refine the S.E. concept. Recent surveys of the vast literature are Fudenberg, Levine, and Tirole (1985) and Cramton (1984). Among the works within the infinite alternating-offers model, let me mention especially Grossman and Perry (1986) as well as Chatterjee and Samuelson (1985), Cramton (1984), Harris (1985b), and Perry (1986). Most of the other literature simplifies the bargaining procedure to avoid too many zero-probability events. Often it has been done by giving the ability to make offers only to one party.

Recall the feature of the model with complete information that there is no delay in reaching an agreement. A central target of the literature on bargaining with incomplete information is to check the hypothesis that empirically observed delays are due to the lack of complete information. Achieving this target seems now less plausible; very recently Gul and Sonnenschein (1985) showed that, for a large class of S.E., if the length of a period of negotiation is small then it is almost certain that the bargaining ends almost instantaneously.

In my opinion, we are far from having a definitive theory of bargaining with incomplete information for use in economic theory. The problems go deeper than bargaining theory and appear in the literature on refinements of S.E., an issue explored thoroughly in the last few years. My intuition is that something is basically wrong in our approach to games with incomplete information and that the "state of the art" of bargaining reflects our more general confusion.

5 Markets and bargaining

5.1 *Bargaining as the central activity in a market*

Bargaining theory provides the building blocks for models of markets in which the transactions are made within small groups (like pairs), in the absence of trading institutions like auctioneers. The process of determining the terms of any particular contract is a bargaining situation influenced by the market environment (outside options) and by the process that matches the agents. The study of those markets where the basic activity is bargaining has the aim of providing a mini–micro foundation for market analysis and for investigation of the economic phenomena that underly price formation. In particular, we look for clarification of the sense, if any, in which the market solution approximates the competitive outcome in the case of many small agents.

5.2 *The static approach*

Diamond (1981, 1982), Mortensen (1982a, 1982b), and Diamond and Maskin (1979) have studied static models of the economy in a steady state. The next model follows their approach: There are two types of agents in the market, 1 and 2. A pair of agents of opposite types can agree on one element from among the set X. A pair of agents that is matched and reaches an agreement leaves the market. The probabilities of agents in the market being matched are kept constant. Each agent of type 1 or 2 has a probability, α or β, of meeting an agent of type 2 or 1. The players have a common discount rate δ, that is, the functions $x\delta^t$ and $(1-x)\delta^t$ are the players' VM utility functions of an agreement x at the tth period of life.

Whenever a pair of agents is matched, it is assumed that they reach an agreement $\bar{x}$. This agreement is the Nash bargaining solution with respect to the threat point $(\delta V_1, \delta V_2)$, where V_i is type i's expected value of existing in the market at the point of his arrival to the market and before it is known whether the agent is matched. Thus,

$$V_1 = (1-\alpha)\delta V_1 + \alpha \bar{x}, \qquad V_2 = (1-\beta)\delta V_2 + \beta(1-\bar{x}),$$

and

$$\bar{x} = \delta V_1 + \frac{1 - \delta V_1 - \delta V_2}{2}.$$

Therefore,

$$\bar{x} = \frac{1 - \delta + \delta \alpha}{2(1-\delta) + \delta \alpha + \delta \beta}.$$

This formula has two interesting limit cases. When the impatience element is small, we obtain

$$\lim_{\delta \to 1} \bar{x} = \frac{\alpha}{\alpha + \beta}.$$

When we take $\alpha = a\Delta$, $\beta = b\Delta$, and $\delta = e^{-r\Delta}$, and shrink the length of one period to zero, we obtain

$$\lim_{\Delta \to 0} \bar{x} = \frac{r+a}{r+a+b}.$$

Essentially, the constant elements in the market are the probabilities α and β. Diamond and Mortensen took α and β to be functions of a constant number of agents in the market, N_1 and N_2. The matching technology, which is the specification of the functional relationship between α, β and N_1, N_2, is needed for a comparison between the above results and a competitive market outcome. Specifically, for the matching technology, when $\alpha = M/N_1$ and $\beta = M/N_2$ we have

$$\lim_{\delta \to 1} \bar{x} = \frac{N_2}{N_1 + N_2},$$

and if $\alpha(\Delta) = (M/N_1)\Delta$ and $\beta(\Delta) = (M/N_2)\Delta$ then

$$\lim_{\Delta \to 0} \bar{x} = \frac{(rN_1 N_2/M)+N_2}{(2rN_1 N_2/M)+N_1+N_2}.$$

Diamond and Mortensen assumed that whenever a pair of agents is matched, they immediately agree on the Nash bargaining solution with the disagreement point $(\delta V_1, \delta V_2)$. The foundations for this assumption were not clear. If it is assumed that the bargaining is separated from the matching and occurs sequentially in the interval between any two matching periods, then Section 3 casts doubts on the plausibility of this use of the Nash bargaining solution. A better assumption is that the bargaining and matching processes are simultaneous. Then, whenever a pair of agents is matched, they take into account both the time impatience and the possibilities that one of them will pass to a new match and abandon the bargaining process. An agent's evaluations of the event that he or an opponent cease bargaining are affected by the equilibrium in the market. A priori there is no reason for the bargaining outcome in the environment to be identified with the Nash solution with a disagreement point $(\delta V_1, \delta V_2)$.

5.3 *The sequential approach*

In Rubinstein and Wolinsky (1985), we tried to look into the bargaining "black box" in this market. We specified in detail the order of events in the market and derived the market equilibrium from noncooperative behavioral assumptions. In the construction of the model we adhered as closely as possible to the spirit of competitive analysis.

We keep the assumptions of Section 5.2 except with respect to the bargaining process. The time periods of the bargaining are the same as the periods in which the random element matches the agents. A particular bargaining situation between a pair of agents is a modified version [see Binmore (1986c)] of the model of Section 2. At each stage, one of the bargainers is selected (with equal probabilities for the two agents) to make a proposal. Before the random draw selects the player who will make the proposal, the players may meet new partners and abandon the old partners. Any agent of type 1 (independently of any other element in the model) abandons his opponent with probability α. With probability $(1-\alpha)\beta$ he is abandoned and is left without a partner until he finds a new member of the opposite type. With probability $(1-\alpha)(1-\beta)$ both partners continue the bargaining. An agent cannot bargain simultaneously with more than one opponent. The decision to replace an opponent is not strategic in this model, but will apparently be a rational choice in equilibrium.

We carefully avoid calling this model a game, because the set of players is not specified. An agent in the model is born and participates in the matching and in the bargaining process until he reaches an agreement with an agent of the opposite type. Then he leaves the market. He has a perfect recall of his personal history. A strategy for an agent is a rule for how to behave after any possible personal history.

Consider a pair of strategies, one for each type, that prescribes the same bargaining tactics for every player of a particular type against any opponent. [The last restriction seems unnecessary; see Binmore and Herrero (in press a).] The pair is a Market Equilibrium (M.E.) if no agent can gain by deviating from his strategy after some personal history (assuming that all agents of the opposite type follow their original strategy). Notice that the probabilities α and β are fixed in the model independently of the outcomes of the agents.

> **Theorem 5** [Rubinstein and Wolinsky (1985)]. *There is a unique Market Equilibrium. In the equilibrium, an agent of type 1 (or 2) always makes the offer x^* (or y^*) which is accepted.*

The numbers x^* and y^* were calculated and it was shown that

$$\lim_{\Delta \to 0} x^* = \lim_{\Delta \to 0} \bar{x}, \qquad \lim_{\delta \to 1} x^* = \lim_{\delta \to 1} \bar{x},$$

and furthermore that $\bar{x} = \frac{1}{2}x^* + \frac{1}{2}y^*$.

Thus, the sequential model leads to the same outcome as in Section 5.2: The M.E. outcome is the Nash bargaining solution relative to the expected values of being in the market unmatched. This seems a "razor's edge" result. Wolinsky (in press) reveals that the coincidence is due to the assumption that a bargainer's matching options are unaffected by him being matched or not. If these matching options are not the same, the limit M.E. outcome is the Nash bargaining solution relative to a convex combination of the values of being unmatched and being matched with a partner who is not ready to make an agreement.

Before comparing the M.E. with the competitive equilibrium, I would like to mention several economic models in which the sequential bargaining model is a cornerstone and which are not mentioned later. Shaked and Sutton (1984a) assume a market where one employer can hire one worker from a pool of n workers. Once the employer starts to bargain with a worker, he must continue the negotiation for T periods; only then can he move on to a new worker. In the limit, diminishing the impatience factor of the players results in the employer's share of the surplus being $(T+1)/2T$.

Binmore (1985) is an attempt to extend the two-bargainer sequential model to an n-player situation in which different coalitions of players are to divide different surpluses. Binmore explored several bargaining procedures where an agreement requires agreement of a group containing more than two players. Wilson (1985) studied one of those procedures more extensively. In an economy with many buyers and sellers, each period has all the sellers or all the buyers making public offers to the opposite kind of agents, who must respond by accepting one of the offers or rejecting all of them. Wilson finds that in the subgame P.E. all the accepted prices are Walrasian.

Other game-theoretic analyses of trading processes are surveyed intensively by Wilson in this volume. [A pioneering work in this direction is an unpublished paper by Butters (1980).]

5.4   The strategic approach and the competitive equilibrium

Unless there is an auctioneer in the market, the competitive equilibrium analysis does not specify a mechanism that forms prices. The competitive solution is often justified by the so-called competitive conditions. These include smallness of the agents, negligible transactions costs, full rationality, symmetric information, and so on. It is usually claimed that under almost frictionless conditions, any reasonable mechanism of price formation will approximately implement the competitive equilibrium prices. The construction of our model in Section 5.3 maintained these characteristics. Therefore, it seems meaningful to compare the competitive equilibrium with the M.E. when the frictions in the model (the time impatience) become negligible.

The comparison may be made in the following example: In the market for an indivisible good, there are two types of agents, sellers (type 1) and buyers (type 2). Each seller holds one unit of the good and his reservation value is 0. Each buyer is interested in buying one unit and his reservation value is 1. The market is in a steady state, in the sense that there is a constant number N_i of agents of type i. There is a linear matching technology; that is, $\alpha(\Delta) = (M/N_1)\Delta$ and $\beta(\Delta) = (M/N_2)\Delta$, where Δ is the length of one period and M is the fixed number of matches that occur per unit of time. When the time discount factor approaches one, the M.E. price is $N_2/(N_1 + N_2)$. In contrast, it looks as if the competitive equilibrium price is 0 or 1 according to the relative size of N_1 and N_2. This observation leads us [Rubinstein and Wolinsky (1985)] to conclude that there is a difference between the competitive and the sequential strategic solutions even when the market's frictions are negligible.

This statement seems puzzling to some; others claim that this is a misuse of the concept of competitive equilibrium. Recent works of Binmore, Herrero, and Gale shed light on this result and further identify conditions under which the competitive equilibrium is approached by the strategic approach. In all these models, the set of players is specified, and is identified with the continuum set.

In their main result, Binmore and Herrero (in press b) examine a market with $N_1(0)$ sellers and $N_2(0)$ buyers at time 0 who remain in the market until all the agents of one of the types make a transaction. A trade outcome at time t is shown [in Binmore and Herrero (in press a)] to be a Nash bargaining solution as the values of being in the market matched and unmatched at time t. Most important is the assumption of a linear technology; the probabilities of being matched are endogenous and vary over time. This leads to the competitive price result: The short side collects all the surplus. If $N_1(0) = N_2(0)$ then each pair splits the surplus equally.

In one of his results, Gale (in press) extends Binmore and Herrero (in press b) to the case where sellers' and buyers' reservation values are distributed in the interval $[0, 1]$. Gale obtains the competitive result – the price is at the intersection of demand and supply curves. This result depends on a simplification of the bargaining process; one of the bargainers is randomly selected to make a take-it-or-leave-it offer, and if the offer is rejected the pair return to the pool of unmatched agents. An important assumption in Gale's model is that the agents who are matched have full information on their reservation values.

In Gale (1986) each agent is coming to the market with an initial bundle. Gale allows each agent to make a series of transactions until he decides to consume his bundle. He assumes that the bargaining procedure has the take-it-or-leave-it form. Time impatience is eliminated; the players are indifferent about the timing of their consumption. Finally, Gale assumes that the support of the set of agents is very diverse both in terms of utility functions and the initial bundles, and that this diversity remains forever.

In the second part of Gale (in press), Rubinstein and Wolinsky (1985) is extended in the following sense: Assume that each instant each seller has probability α_i of matching a buyer of type i with reservation value x_i, and that each buyer has probability β_j of being matched with a seller who has reservation price y_j. Let p be a number such that

$$\sum \alpha_i \max\{(x_i - p), 0\} = \sum \beta_j \max\{(p - y_j), 0\}.$$

Then p is the limit of the M.E. when $\delta \to 1$. If α_i and β_j are proportional to N_{1i} and N_{2j} (the steady-state numbers of buyers and sellers of types i and j, accordingly), then the above formula is transformed to

$$\sum N_{1i} \max\{(x_i - p), 0\} = \sum N_{2j} \max\{(p - y_j), 0\},$$

which has the interpretation that buyer surplus is equal to seller surplus. Thus Gale (in press) shows that a price exists even where the supply and demand curves have the regular monotonicity properties; this is what Gale calls the "stock equilibrium" price.

The main insight of Gale (in press) is the following observation: Assume that N_{1i} and N_{2j} reflect the flow rates of agents who consider entering the market. There is a small positive entrance fee. Let p be the price at the intersection of the demand and supply curves induced by these numbers. Gale calls this a "flow price." This is the only price that can be supported with a stock equilibrium when the flow of agents leaving the market is equalized by the flow of agents entering the market. As before, Gale assumes the take-it-or-leave-it bargaining procedure; the search technology is linear and a matched agent has complete information about his opponent's reservation value.

The primitives of the standard economic models are the individuals in the market and those of their characteristics relevant to their behavior in the market. A description of the strategic behavior of individuals in the framework of a game requires that information about the players operating in the game be common knowledge. This is a very strong assumption in a world where even econometricians find it hard to get a rough estimate of supply and demand. It seems that a shopkeeper bases his price strategy more on the frequency with which shoppers enter his shop than on the size of the population of the world or his town.

In contrast, the model of Section 5.3 – as well as the models of Diamond, Mortensen, and Gale – take the primitives to be the stochastic processes of arrivals of new opportunities. It is this arbitrary assumption about the search technology that makes it seem as if the Diamond–Mortensen–Gale results refer to the standard demand and supply structure. I believe that it may often be useful to analyze economic environments using information about the streams of personal opportunities, rather than confining attention to data about the flows of potential entrants to the market.

At present, I do not think that this question is settled: Under what conditions will the strategic bargaining approach generate the competitive outcome? The works surveyed above provide new insights for understanding the competitive assumption. It seems that the extensive form game-theoretic approach provides tools for analyzing exciting issues that could not be studied by other means – money, inflation, and unemployment [see Shaked and Sutton (1984a)]; as well as trading processes [see Rubinstein and Wolinsky (in press)]. The economic insights derivable from such such market models are the chief goal of sequential strategic models.

References

Bikhchandani, S. 1985. "A Bargaining Model with Incomplete Information." Working Paper, Business School, Stanford University.

Binmore, K. G. 1985. "Bargaining and Coalitions I." In A. Roth (ed.), *Game Theoretic Models of Bargaining*, pp. 269–304. Cambridge: Cambridge University Press.

1986a. "Nash Bargaining Theory, I." In K. Binmore and P. Dasgupta (eds.), *Economics and Bargaining*. Oxford: Blackwell.

1986b. "Nash Bargaining Theory, II." In K. Binmore and P. Dasgupta (eds.), *Economics and Bargaining*. Oxford: Blackwell.

1986c. "Perfect Equilibria in Bargaining Models." In K. Binmore and P. Dasgupta (eds.), *Economics and Bargaining*. Oxford: Blackwell.

Binmore, K. G., and M. J. Herrero. In press a. "Matching and Bargaining I." *Review of Economic Studies*.

In press b. "Matching and Bargaining II." *Review of Economic Studies*.

Binmore, K. G., A. Rubinstein, and A. Wolinsky. 1986. "The Nash Bargaining Solution in Economic Modelling." *Rand Journal of Economics* 17: 176–88.

Butters, G. 1980. "Equilibrium Price Distribution in a Random Meetings Market." Mimeo, Princeton University.

Chatterjee, K., and L. Samuelson. 1985. "Bargaining Under Incomplete Information: The Continuum of Offers Case." Working Paper, The Pennsylvania State University.

Cramton, P. C. 1984. "The Role of Time and Information in Bargaining." Ph.D. thesis, Stanford University.

Diamond, P. A. 1981. "Mobility Costs, Frictional Unemployment and Efficiency." *Journal of Political Economy* 89: 798–811.

1982. "Wage Determination and Efficiency in Search Equilibrium." *Review of Economic Studies* 49: 217–27.

Diamond, P. A., and E. Maskin. 1979. "An Equilibrium Analysis of Search and Breach of Contract." *Bell Journal of Economics* 10: 282–316.

Edgeworth, F. Y. 1881. "Mathematical Psychics: An Essay on the Applications of Mathematics to the Moral Sciences." Series of Reprints on Economics and Political Sciences, No. 10, London School of Economics.

Fishburn, P. C., and A. Rubinstein. 1982. "Time Preference." *International Economics Review* 23: 677–94.

Fudenberg, D., and D. Levine. 1983. "Subgame Perfect Equilibria of Finite and Infinite Horizon Games." *Journal of Economic Theory* 31: 251–68.

Fudenberg, D., D. Levine, and J. Tirole. 1985. "Infinite Horizon Models if Bargaining with One-Sided Incomplete Information." In A. Roth (ed.), *Game Theoretic Models of Bargaining*, pp. 73–98. Cambridge: Cambridge University Press.

Gale, D. 1986. "Bargaining and Competition Part I: Characterization." *Econometrica* 54: 785–806.

In press. "Limit Theorems for Markets with Sequential Bargaining." *Journal of Economic Theory.*

Gul, F., and H. Sonnenschein. 1985. "Uncertainty Does Not Cause Delay." Working Paper, Stanford Business School.

Grossman, S., and M. Perry. 1986. "Sequential Bargaining Under Asymmetric Information." *Journal of Economic Theory* 39: 120–54.

Harris, C. 1985a. "A Characterization of the Perfect Equilibria of Infinite Horizon Games." *Journal of Economic Theory* 37: 99–125.

1985b. "An Alternative Solution to Rubinstein's Model of Sequential Bargaining Under Incomplete Information." *The Economic Journal, Conference Papers*, 102–12.

Harsanyi, J. C. 1967. "Games with Incomplete Information Played by 'Bayesian Players'." *Management Science* 14: 159–82, 320–34, 486–502.

Hicks, J. R. 1932. *The Theory of Wages.* London: Macmillan.

Kreps, D. M., and R. Wilson. 1982. "Sequential Equilibrium." *Econometrica* 50: 863–94.

McLennan, A. 1982. "A Noncooperative Definition of Two Person Bargaining." Working Paper No. 8303, University of Toronto.

Mortensen, D. T. 1982a. "Property Rights and Efficiency in Mating, Racing and Related Games." *The American Economic Review* 72: 968–79.

1982b. "The Matching Process as a Noncooperative Bargaining Game." In J. J. McCall (ed.), *The Economics of Information and Uncertainty.* Chicago: University of Chicago Press.

Nash, J. F. 1950. "The Bargaining Problem." *Econometrica* 18: 155–62.

1953. "Two-person Cooperative Games." *Econometrica* 21: 128–40.

Perry, M. 1986. "Who Has the Last Word? A Bargaining Model with Incomplete Information." *Econometrica* 54: 313–22.

Roth, A. E. 1979. "Axiomatic Models of Bargaining." *Lecture Notes in Economics and Mathematical Systems,* No. 170. Berlin: Springer-Verlag.

Rubinstein, A. 1982. "Perfect Equilibrium in a Bargaining Model." *Econometrica* 50: 97–109.

1985a. "A Bargaining Model with Incomplete Information." *Econometrica* 53: 1151–72.

1985b. "The Choice of Conjectures in a Bargaining Game with Incomplete Information." In A. Roth (ed.), *Game Theoretic Models of Bargaining*, pp. 99–114. Cambridge: Cambridge University Press.

Rubinstein, A., and A. Wolinsky. 1985. "Equilibrium in a Market with Sequential Bargaining." *Econometrica* 53: 1133–50.

In press. "Middlemen." *Quarterly Journal of Economics.*

Selten, R. 1965. "Spieltheoretisch Behandlung eines Oligopolmodels mit Nachfragetragheit." *Zeitschrift für die Gesamte Staatswissenschaft* 12: 301–24, 667–89.

1975. "Reexamination of the Perfectness Concept for Equilibrium Points in Extension Games." *International Journal of Game Theory* 4: 25–53.

Shaked, A., and J. Sutton. 1984a. "Involuntary Unemployment as a Perfect Equilibrium in a Bargaining Model." *Econometrica* 52: 1351–64.

1984b. "The Semi-Walrasian Economy." Working Paper No. 98, London School of Economics.

Stahl, I. 1972. *Bargaining Theory*. Stockholm: Stockholm School of Economics.

Wilson, R. B. 1985. "Notes on Market Games with Complete Information." Working Paper, Stanford Business School.

Wolinsky, A. In press. "Matching, Search and Bargaining." *Journal of Economic Theory*.

Zeuthen, F. 1930. *Problems of Monopoly and Economics*. London: Routledge.

CHAPTER 6

On the complexity of linear programming

Nimrod Megiddo

Abstract: This is a partial survey of results on the complexity of the linear programming problem since the ellipsoid method. The main topics are polynomial and strongly polynomial algorithms, probabilistic analysis of simplex algorithms, and recent interior point methods.

1   Introduction

Our purpose here is to survey theoretical developments in linear programming, starting from the ellipsoid method, mainly from the viewpoint of computational complexity.[1] The survey does not attempt to be complete and naturally reflects the author's perspective, which may differ from the viewpoints of others.

Linear programming is perhaps the most successful discipline of Operations Research. The standard form of the linear programming problem is to maximize a linear function $c^T x$ ($c, x \in R^n$) over all vectors x such that $Ax = b$ and $x \geq 0$. We denote such a problem by (A, b, c). Currently, the main tool for solving the linear programming problem in practice is the class of simplex algorithms proposed and developed by Dantzig [43]. However, applications of nonlinear programming methods, inspired by Karmarkar's work [79], may also become practical tools for certain classes of linear programming problems. Complexity-based questions about linear programming and related parameters of polyhedra (see, e.g., [66]) have been raised since the 1950s, before the field of computational complexity

The author thanks Jeffrey Lagarias, David Shmoys, and Robert Wilson for helpful comments.

[1] The topic of linear programming has been interesting to economists not only due to its applicability to practical economic systems but also because of the many economic insights provided by the theory of linear programming. However, in this chapter we discuss linear programming from a point of view of theoretical computer science.

started to develop. The practical performance of the simplex algorithms has always seemed surprisingly good. In particular, the number of iterations seemed polynomial and even linear in the dimensions of problems being solved. Exponential examples were constructed only in the early 1970s, starting with the work of Klee and Minty [85].

The field of computational complexity developed rapidly during the 1970s. The question of the complexity of linear programming was formalized in a new and more precise sense. A specific question remained open for several years until finally solved by Khachiyan [83, 84] in 1979. He showed that linear programming, as a problem of recognizing a formal language, is in the class $\mathcal{P}$; that is, it can be solved in polynomial time relative to the length of the binary encoding of the input. Khachiyan's result was also applied in a very elegant way to problems of combinatorial optimization by Grotschel, Lovasz, and Schrijver [64].

Khachiyan's result was widely misinterpreted for a while, mainly because of popular articles claiming that a substitute had been found for the simplex algorithm. However, it was not long before it became clear that the ellipsoid algorithm (that was used by Khachiyan to prove his nice result) is not useful for solving linear programming problems in practice. This was quite a disappointment to those who believed complexity theory could be relied on in practice. It became clear that some exponential algorithms (namely, variants of the simplex method) were very efficient in practice, while a polynomial algorithm for the same problem (the ellipsoid method) was very inefficient. It was only natural that interest in the field started to increase in two directions: (i) analyzing the behavior of the simplex method from a different viewpoint, and (ii) searching for other methods.

A breakthrough in the analysis of the simplex method was independently made by Borgwardt [26, 27, 28] and Smale [144, 145]. In Section 4 we review further work in this field.

At least from a theoretical viewpoint, it is interesting to settle the computational complexity of linear programming under different models of computation. Khachiyan's result relies on the so-called logarithmic-cost model [9]. It is still an open question whether a system of linear inequalities can be solved in a number of arithmetic operations that is polynomially bounded by the dimensions of the system, independently of the magnitudes of the coefficients. In [107] such an algorithm is given for systems with at most two variables per inequality (whereas the general case can be reduced to at most three variables per inequality). Questions about the model are discussed in Section 2. So far, only partial results are known. Eva Tardos [147, 148] obtained a general linear programming algorithm whose number of elementary operations is independent of the magnitudes of coefficients in the objective-function and the right-hand-side vectors, but depends on the coefficients in the matrix A. This implies that many combinatorial optimization problems, including the minimum cost-flow problem, can be solved in "strongly" polynomial time. This work of Tardos is reviewed in Section 5.

Theoretical research on algorithms in recent years focused on the direction of estimating the asymptotic worst-case complexity of problems in $\mathcal{P}$. For instance, knowing that a certain problem can be solved in polynomial time, it is of interest to find exact (asymptotic) upper and lower bounds on the time it should take any algorithm to solve the problem in the worst case. There has been much research done in this direction in the related field of computational geometry [95]. For example, it is known that the complexity of computing the convex hull of a set of n points in the plane is $\theta(n \log n)$.[2] A surprising result was obtained in [109]; namely, for any fixed d, linear programming problems with d variables and n constraints can be solved in $O(n)$ time as n tends to infinity. This extended previous independent work ([48, 108]) that showed the same for $d \le 3$. This area of research is reviewed in Section 6.

Linear programming was again in the news in the fall of 1984: Karmarker developed a new polynomial-time algorithm for linear programming that is in fact practical. It improves the upper bound on the complexity of linear programming, again under the logarithmic-cost model. Karmarkar has claimed very strongly [80] that his algorithm is superior by far to the simplex method. However, at the time of this writing there is no publicly available evidence to support clear superiority. This work inspired renewed interest in applying methods of nonlinear programming to the linear programming problem. The algorithm is reviewed in Section 7. Recent related work is reviewed in Section 8.

Regarding the worst-case complexity of the simplex method, it is only known that specific variants of the method require exponential time in the worst case. It is a major open question whether every variant[3] requires exponential time in the worst case. The complexity of the randomized simplex algorithm is not known. Results have been obtained about the worst-case complexity of certain variants of the simplex method when applied to special classes of linear programming problems. Of special interest are assignment problems and the more general minimum cost-flow problem. This topic is discussed in Section 9.

We conclude the paper with some discussion in Section 10 on theory versus practice.

---

[2] This means that there is an algorithm that finds the convex hull in $C_1 n \log n$ time and there is a constant C_2 such that any algorithm for the convex hull requires in the worst case at least $C_2 n \log n$ time.

[3] We have not defined what a variant is. Clearly, the effort per pivot step must be restricted because otherwise any algorithm can be stated as a variant of the simplex method.

2   On complexity and models of computation

Complexity of computations is a central area of research in theoretical computer science. One of the common measures of complexity of an algorithm is the *asymptotic worst-case running time*. Here we discuss this concept on a rather informal level. The interested reader may refer to [9] for exact definitions. Any measure of complexity must be defined relative to a specific model of computation. The meaning of a statement like "Problem P has complexity $O(f(n))$" is roughly as follows. First, P is understood to be a class of instances with a well-defined measure of length of an instance. Second, there is an "algorithm" and there is a constant C such that any instance of P of length n is solved by the algorithm within $Cf(n)$ time units. The notion of an algorithm, and the amount of time it takes to execute the basic operations in the algorithm, must be defined. It is customary among theoretical computer scientists to think of a problem as tractable if it has polynomial time complexity, and intractable otherwise. The advantage of this approach is that the property of polynomial time is robust in the sense that (to a certain extent) it does not depend on the model of computation.

Practitioners usually have different points of view. First, they are not interested so much in the worst-case performance of an algorithm. They usually like to have an idea about the *distribution* of running times, although they usually do not have a definite idea about the distribution of instances.[4] Also, practitioners are less interested in asymptotic complexity. The advantage of the asymptotic approach is that it is more amenable to mathematical analysis. When a theoretician says he has improved an algorithm he usually means he has designed an algorithm of lower asymptotic worst-case time complexity. Practitioners may then wonder at what size of an instance the asymptotically better algorithm becomes more favorable (yet in the sense of the worst case). Moreover, practitioners are interested in factors such as space (also of interest to theoreticians), program length and simplicity, numerical characteristics, and versatility.

In the context of linear programming, the size of an instance can be defined in different ways. Usually the complexity is expressed in terms of the numbers of rows and columns of the system. Assuming exact computation on real machines, the cost of performing arithmetic operations must depend also on the sizes of numbers involved. However, in practice most problems are being solved in floating-point arithmetic and the cost

---

[4] It remains a challenge to theoreticians to come up with models for predicting the efficiency of algorithms in practice. Results that depend on an exact probability distribution of instances are often not satisfactory. Because the distribution is not known, analysis should be done about *classes* of distributions characterized by weakest possible assumptions (see [7] for further discussion of this issue).

is uniform (if numbers do not get out of range). On the other hand, the known polynomial algorithms for linear programming require in the worst case a number of steps that depends on the sizes of the coefficients. To relate theoretical complexity results to the practical performance of the algorithm, one needs to specify the precision under which a solution must be obtained. Matters are then complicated even further by the need to specify the measure of approximation to be used.

Another point related to linear programming is the sparsity of the matrix. Most of the theoretical work on linear programming measures the complexity relative to the dimensions or the length of the binary representation of the problem. Of course, sparse problems have shorter representations even if each zero coefficient is given explicitly. However, sparse systems are being solved much more efficiently in practice, essentially because the necessary linear algebraic steps are carried out more efficiently. For polynomial worst-case complexity, sparsity helps only because of a shorter binary representation. Theorists pay little attention to the cost of performing single iterations, whereas practitioners have a goal of making the cost of a single step as low as possible. The initial attitude of theoreticians is to look at the general problem, first ignoring any structure. When any complexity measure is expressed in terms of several parameters rather than just a single input size, it becomes more difficult to compare algorithms, because the result of the comparison may depend on the particular combination of parameter values.

The problem of linear programming has more than one level of abstraction. The original problem is usually stated and solved over the field of the reals. Actually, for the traditional model of complexity, as well as for most practical computations, the field of the rationals is the appropriate one. There also exist combinatorial abstractions of linear programming in the context of "oriented matroids" (see, e.g., [22]). This area will not be discussed here.

From an algebraic point of view, the problem can be posed relative to any "ordered field." An ordered field is a field where the nonzero elements are classified as positive (when an element a is positive we write $a > 0$) or negative ($a < 0$) subject to the following axioms: (i) If a and b are positive then so are $a + b$ and ab. (ii) If a nonzero element a is not positive then $-a$ is. It is obvious that the simplex algorithm solves the linear programming problem over any ordered field. Interesting observations on resolving degeneracy in real problems via the use of larger ordered fields, as well as solutions to asymptotic problems, are given in [77] and the references thereof. A more recent paper on this subject is [51].

The term "ordered field" is justified by the fact that positivity induces a total order: An element a precedes an element b ($a < b$) if $b - a > 0$. The relations $\leq$ and $\geq$ are defined in the natural way. Obvious consequences are as follows: (i) $1 > 0$; (ii) $a + 1 > a$; (iii) $a, b < 0$ implies $a + b < 0$ and $ab > 0$. It thus follows that an ordered field *cannot be finite*. Moreover, it must contain the field of rationals. This containment is in the strong sense of ordered fields; that is, for any ordered field F there is an isomorphism of ordered fields from the ordered field of the rationals, Q, into F. Let F be any ordered field. Since F contains the field of rationals Q, we can define a mapping ρ from F into the extended real line $R^* = R \cup \{-\infty, \infty\}$ as follows. For any $a \in F$ let $\rho(a) = \text{Sup}\{r \in Q : r < a\}$. (We use r to denote both a rational number and its corresponding element in F.) By $\rho(a) = -\infty$ (respectively, $\rho(a) = \infty$) we mean $a < r$ ($a > r$) for all rational r. It is easy to check that $\rho(a) > \rho(b)$ implies $a > b$ while $a > b$ implies $\rho(a) \geq \rho(b)$. The mapping ρ is not necessarily one-to-one; for example, F may contain "infinitesimal" elements – that is, elements a such that $0 < a < r$ for every positive rational r. However, ρ is a "homomorphism" from the subfield $F_R = \{a \in F : \rho(a) \in R\}$; that is,

$$\rho(0) = 0, \quad \rho(1) = 1, \quad \rho(\alpha + \beta) = \rho(\alpha) + \rho(b) \quad \text{and} \quad \rho(ab) = \rho(a)\rho(b).$$

It follows that many useful theorems on real systems of inequalities can be generalized to abstract ordered fields, even when the proof relies on properties of the real numbers. For example, vector spaces over ordered fields are not necessarily normed but some useful properties related to norms extend to such spaces. The following proposition is one such example, which turns out to be related to Karmarkar's algorithm.

> **Proposition 2.1.** *Let $u \in F^n$ be an n-dimensional vector over an ordered field F and let $H \subseteq F^n$ be a linear subspace. Suppose $v^* \in H$ is such that $(u - v^*)^T w = 0$ for every $w \in H$. Under these conditions, v^* minimizes the "squared distance" function $f(v) = (u - v)^T (u - v)$ for $v \in H$.*

Proof: Let $v \in H$ be any vector and denote $w = v - v^*$. Then

$$(u - v)^T (u - v) = (u - v^* - w)^T (u - v^* - w) = (u - v^*)^T (u - v^*) + w^T w.$$

The claim follows from the fact that $w^T w \geq 0$.   ∎

At least from a theoretical viewpoint, the following (loosely stated) question is important for understanding linear programming: Can linear inequalities be decided in a polynomial number of field operations over any ordered field?[5] More precisely, is there a polynomial $p(m, n)$ and an

---

[5] The same question can be asked with respect to real closed fields. A field F is *real closed* if it satisfies: (i) $\sum \alpha_i^2 \neq 0$ unless $\alpha_i = 0$ for all i, and (ii) all the nontrivial algebraic extensions of F do not satisfy (i). It is known that any real closed field can be ordered uniquely.

algorithm[6] that decides any system $Ax \le b$ of dimension $m \times n$ after performing no more than $p(m, n)$ field and other machine operations? The simplex method is valid over any ordered field but several variants of it are known to run in exponential time in the worst case.

There is still a problem with the formulation of the question in the preceding paragraph. It seems that multiplication and division are quite powerful operations. Complicated computational tasks can be performed by generating large numbers. For example, given a set S of n field elements $a_1, \ldots, a_n$, one can generate in $O(n)$ additions and multiplications an element A of the form $A = \sum_{j=1}^{2^n} \alpha_j M^j$, where $\alpha_1, \ldots, \alpha_{2^n}$ are all the sums over subsets of S, and $M > \sum a_i$ is another element. Operations on elements of the form of A can simulate simultaneous operations on all the subsets of S. This suggests that a polynomial number of multiplications involving large elements may suffice for solving real problems that require exponential time under a model of logarithmic cost. So it seems reasonable to include in a definition of a "strongly" polynomial algorithm [147, 148] also the requirement that when the input consists of rational numbers, the sizes of the numbers occurring in the computation are bounded by a polynomial in the input size. In other words, an algorithm is strongly polynomial if (first) it is polynomial and (second) the number of arithmetic operations is polynomial in the dimensions of the problem. Over an abstract field, because the size of an element is not well defined, we might require that the height[7] [110] of multiplications and divisions be bounded by $p(\log m, \log n)$ for some polynomial p. The simplex algorithm satisfies this requirement about heights, since each iteration can start from inputs and only has to solve a system of linear equations. Systems of linear equations can be solved over any ordered field in a polynomial number of field operations with small height of multiplications [53, 30, 134].

3 The ellipsoid method

The question that was settled by Khachiyan [83, 84] can be stated as follows. Given a system of linear inequalities $Ax \le b$ ($A \in R^{m \times n}$, $b \in R^m$) with integral coefficients,[8] let L denote the total number of bits in a binary representation of the coefficients a_{ij} and b_i. The question is whether there

---

[6] We still assume here that an "oracle" can be used to perform the field operations – that is, the arithmetic operations and comparison.

[7] The height $h(a)$ of an input element a is 1. In general, for any elements generated by the algorithm, $h(a+b) = \max(h(a), h(b))$ and $h(ab) = h(a)h(b)$; subtraction and division are handled like multiplications and divisions, respectively.

[8] The extension to rational coefficients is trivial.

exists an algorithm for deciding feasibility (i.e., the existence of a solution to the system) that takes no more than $p(L)$ bit operations, where p is a polynomial. The answer is yes, and the proof relies on an algorithm by Yudin and Nemirovsky [161].

Before sketching the algorithm, we find it helpful to describe an abstract scheme of establishing a time bound for an algorithm that generates a sequence of objects O_i ($i = 0, 1, 2, \ldots$) (e.g., points, intervals, ellipsoids). Suppose g is a criterion function from the set of objects into the positive reals. Assume the algorithm makes progress in terms of g, with a lower bound on the rate of improvement, so that there is a $\delta < 1$ such that for every i, $g(O_{i+1}) \leq \delta g(O_i)$. Furthermore, suppose the algorithm terminates when $g(O_i) \leq \epsilon$ for some prespecified $\epsilon > 0$. Obviously, an upper bound on the number of steps of the algorithm can be stated in terms of $g(O_o)$, δ, and ϵ. A bound N on the number of steps is derived from the equation $g(O_o)\delta^N = \epsilon$, so that $N = (\log g(O_o) - \log \epsilon)/(-\log \delta)$. Thus, if $\log g(O_o)$, $-\log \epsilon$, and $-1/(\log \delta)$ are each bounded by a polynomial function of the input size then the algorithm terminates in polynomial time.

The objects generated by the "ellipsoid" algorithm are n-dimensional ellipsoids. A suitable criterion function maps n-dimensional ellipsoids to their n-dimensional volumes. It is easier to state the algorithm for the problem of deciding feasibility of a set of strict inequalities whose solution set is guaranteed to be bounded: $Ax < b$, $|x_j| < \lfloor 2^L/n \rfloor$. For proving a polynomial upper bound, this form is equivalent to the original one. The algorithm generates a sequence of ellipsoids with the following properties: (i) Each ellipsoid contains all the *basic* feasible solutions of the system $Ax \leq b$. (ii) The factor by which the volume of the current ellipsoid decreases during a single step satisfies $\delta < 2^{-1/(2(n+1))}$. Interestingly, this factor depends only on the smaller dimension n and does not depend on the number of constraints m or the numerical values of the coefficients. This allows for many elegant applications of the method to combinatorial optimization problems with exponentially many constraints [64]. The efffect of L on the time bound is via the volumes of the first and last ellipsoids.

The first ellipsoid is a ball of radius $n2^L$ centered at the origin. Thus its volume is not greater than $(2n^2 2^{2L})^n$. This ball is guaranteed to contain all the basic feasible solutions of $Ax \leq b$ if there are any. A step of the algorithm starts by checking whether the center of the current ellipsoid solves the system $Ax < b$. If so, then the algorithm terminates with the center as solution; otherwise, a (volume-wise) smaller ellipsoid is constructed. It can be proved that if the volume of the current ellipsoid is less than $\epsilon = 2^{-(n+1)L}$ then there can be no basic feasible solutions and hence no feasible solutions at all. Polynomiality of the algorithm follows from the preceding discussion.

The original algorithm relies on the square-root operation. It is known that finite precision suffices [146, 155]. It follows that the ellipsoid algorithm can run over any ordered field; that is, the iterations can be performed. However, if infinitesimals are involved then the algorithm may not solve the problem. For example, the algorithm may never reach a point where infeasibility is evident. Similarly, if the volume of the initial ellipsoid is infinite then all the following ellipsoids have infinite volume. Thus, the ellipsoid algorithm does not solve the problem over general ordered fields. A good survey of the ellipsoid method is given in [24].

An algorithm by Levin [99] was shown by Yamnitsky and Levin [159] to run in polynomial time, using a similar analysis. Levin's algorithm works with simplices rather than ellipsoids. Hence, it can be run over any ordered field but does not solve the problem in general.

4   Probabilistic analyses of simplex algorithms

The number of pivot steps performed by simplex algorithms in practice is widely considered surprisingly small. The "surprise" is due to observations as follows. Every simplex algorithm visits bases of the underlying system of linear equations. It is known how to guarantee that no basis is visited more than once – that is, how to avoid "cycling." Because there are a finite number of bases, it follows that any noncycling simplex algorithm is finite. Moreover, this number is bounded (from above) by an exponential function of the dimensions of the system. It is not known whether there exists a simplex[9] algorithm whose (worst-case) number of steps is bounded by a polynomial function of the dimensions. Furthermore, for some simplex algorithms there have been constructed examples on which these algorithms perform an exponential number of steps. The first such example was designed by Klee and Minty [85]. Related examples were later designed for several simplex algorithms [78, 13, 119, 120, 63, 163]. It is customary to say that "the simplex algorithm is exponential," meaning that it requires in the worst case an exponential number of steps. However, this qualification is unfair because it has not been proven that for every variant of the method (in any precise sense) there exists an exponential example. There are in fact variants whose worst-case analysis seems very difficult. On the other hand, even for the (worst-case) exponential variants, practitioners report numbers of steps that are far smaller than

[9] We have stated earlier in this chapter that the concept of a simplex algorithm or variant is not well defined.

the numbers suggested by the worst-case complexity. The wide gap calls for mathematical analysis to explain it.

Many simplex algorithms can be described as generating simple paths in the one-dimensional skeleton of some polytope. In other words, in one step they move from a vertex[10] to an adjacent one, visiting no vertex more than once. This suggests that such variants would perform better on polytopes with fewer vertices. Thus, first attempts to explain the good performance of simplex algorithms in practice were based on estimating numbers of vertices of random polytopes. We will not review the results here. For analysis in linear programming it is interesting to consider random polytopes generated by picking half-spaces at random. Under most of the models investigated, it turned out that in a fixed dimension the expected number of vertices increased slowly with the number of half-spaces. However, the expected number of vertices was exponential in both the dimension and the number of half-spaces. Obviously, an approach based on estimating numbers of vertices of polytopes cannot demonstrate that a simplex algorithm is more efficient than an algorithm that enumerates all the vertices of a polytope. Such an approach ignores the particular way a specific algorithm chooses the next vertex in the path. Also, many simplex algorithms generate paths on which some linear function is monotone. The essence of the intuitive argument for the efficiency of monotone simplex algorithms is as follows. We think that if v^1 and v^2 are adjacent vertices then, on the average, there are many vertices w where the value of the objective function is between the values at v^1 and v^2. Thus, such vertices w are "skipped" when the algorithm moves from v^1 to v^2.

The works of Borgwardt [26, 27, 28] and Smale [144, 145] constituted a breakthrough in the probabilistic analysis of simplex algorithms. In these works, for the first time, the particular choice of the algorithm was taken into account. Both identified closely related variants of the simplex method, where it was possible to write closed-form formulas for the expected number of steps of the variant, in terms of the probability distribution over the set of problem instances. It is surprisingly easy to obtain formulas for these variants. The algorithms that can be analyzed in this way are based on parameterization in some form: The algorithm follows solutions to a parameterized family of problems. The number of steps corresponds to the number of certain cones met by a certain straight line. The hard part in this research is the analysis of the resulting formula.

---

[10] In the presence of degeneracy this statement is not accurate. The method actually visits *bases* of a linear system and may change the basis many times before moving to a new vertex. Furthermore, every linear programming problem can be reduced to a problem where all the algorithm has to do is move from the second-best vertex to the best one (but through many changes of the basis).

Borgwardt and Smale worked with closely related probabilistic models. However, their models differ in a very significant way. Under Borgwardt's model only feasible problems with known feasible solutions are generated. Under Smale's model most of the problems are either infeasible or unbounded, depending on whether we consider the primal or the dual problem. On the other hand, the questions that arise in the analyses of the formulas are very closely related. Borgwardt succeeded in proving that under his model the expected number of steps was bounded by a polynomial in both the dimension and the number of half-spaces. Smale proved that under his model if one of the parameters (i.e., either the dimension or the number of half-spaces excluding the nonnegativity constraints) was fixed then the expected number of steps was bounded by a polynomial in the logarithm of the other parameter. Megiddo [115] showed that in this case the expected number of steps was bounded by a function of the smaller parameter; that is, for any fixed m the poly-log function of n can be replaced by a constant. However, it is still an open question whether this constant depends polynomially on the smaller parameter. It is reasonable to conjecture that the ideas and methods used by Borgwardt would help in proving polynomiality here as well. Blair [20] obtained a result close to Smale's for a large set of algorithms. Blair's result is based on estimating the expected number of undominated columns. This is closely related to the expected number of vertices of random polyhedra.

Haimovich [67] and Adler [1] obtained a result related to the analysis of a similar simplex variant. They consider a model that was previously looked at in [31, 118, 2, 3, 104, 4]. In this model all the hyperplanes are fixed in a nondegenerate manner. A cell of the induced partition of space is picked at random. Suppose any two vectors c and c' are given. Consider the family of vectors of the form $c_t = tc + c'$, where t varies over the reals. For each cell of the partition consider a path of optimal solutions determined by minimizing the linear function $c_t^T x$ over the cell. Haimovich and Adler prove that the average length of such a path (i.e., the number of vertices on the path) is linear. However, this result applies neither directly to a specific algorithm for linear programming nor even to Phase II of an algorithm, since the "auxiliary" direction c' depends on the vertex of the cell that is produced in Phase I. Thus, it is hard to justify an assumption that the direction is independent of the cell. However, this result is surprisingly good and provides much insight into average lengths of parametric paths on random polyhedra.

Adler, Karp, and Shamir [5] show that for constraint-by-constraint algorithms (this does not include the self-dual method considered by Smale), the probabilistic model of "sign-invariance" (i.e., where the probability distribution is invariant under changes in the directions of inequalities) implies that the expected number of steps is bounded by a function of the smaller dimension. However, in that paper all the upper bounds are still exponential. The result in [115], of a bound depending only on the smaller dimension, is not covered by the result in [5].

Polynomial upper bounds depending only on the smaller dimension were obtained in [149, 7, 6, 8]. In these papers the analytic difficulties encountered in [144, 145, 115] are avoided. The mathematical analysis is considerably simplified if the starting point of the algorithm is changed from $(1, \ldots, 1)$ to $(\epsilon, \epsilon^2, \epsilon^3, \ldots)$. Furthermore, the assumptions of the probabilistic model can be relaxed. An upper bound of $O(\min(m^2, n^2))$ can be proved under assumptions of sign-invariance and nondegeneracy. A quadratic upper bound is proved in [7] for any assignment of powers of ϵ to rows and columns of the system. Moreover, [7] also proves a quadratic lower bound under a stronger model, which implies that even under the weaker model one cannot prove a subquadratic upper bound. It should also be noted that the algorithms in these papers are all special cases of the self-dual algorithm with various starting points (see [113]). It is not clear what is the best starting point for the average performance of the self-dual method for linear programming. The question of the starting point in the context of the general linear complementarity problem is tackled in [70, 140, 114, 149]. It is known that $(1, \ldots, 1)$ is worst for the average case of the general problem. However, the author conjectures that for the linear programming problem this point is best among all the nonnegative starting points. The model under which the $O(\min(m^2, n^2))$ result is obtained may be criticized for allowing unboundedness (or infeasibility) with increasing probability. However, at least for the case $m = n$ (i.e., for a system with n linear inequalities in n nonnegative variables) it implies that the conditional expectation of the number of steps, given that the problem is feasible and bounded, is only $O(m^{2.5})$, while the conditional expectation of the number of vertices is exponential.

5   Strongly polynomial algorithms

People have been interested in the computational complexity of linear programming since the development of the simplex method. The fundamental question concerned the dependence of the number of pivot steps on the dimensions m and n of the problem. The number of pivot steps is a natural measure of complexity for simplex algorithms, provided the effort per step is reasonable. The search for polynomial algorithms for linear programming was intensified in the 1970s because of two developments: (i) the discovery that several simplex algorithms required exponential numbers of pivot steps in the worst case, and (ii) the growing interest among computer scientists in polynomial-time algorithms. It seems that the concept of a polynomial algorithm was understood by the mathematical programming community differently. The mathematical programming community is a little more inclined toward practice. In practice, linear programming problems are usually solved in floating-point arithmetic and the numbers are limited to some finite range. The cost of performing arithmetic operations is constant provided the numbers stay in this range. The space occupied by a number is bounded provided it is in this range. Hence, for the mathematical programming community, the natural question was the existence of an algorithm that required only a polynomial number $p(m, n)$ of arithmetic operations. In theoretical computer science the common approach is that machines work with bits, and hence the size of the input has to be measured in bits and the running time in bit operations. This means that the size of the input for a linear programming problem depends not only on m and n but also on the coefficients themselves. The difference between the two approaches led to a surprise within the mathematical programming community when Khachiyan's result was announced. The presence of the parameter L (the number of bits in the binnary representation of the input) in the polynomial upper bound was not expected. Of course, this parameter must appear in any bit-operations estimate of the running time, because it takes unbounded time to carry out arithmetic operations on unbounded numbers. However, it is not clear that the number of arithmetic operations should depend on the magnitudes of the numbers. The distinction between the two approaches can also be explained as a difference between models of computation. Theoretical computer scientists like to work with complexity classes that are robust against changes in the model of computation. The class P of problems solvable in polynomial time is a good example. However, the complexity of a problem is actually the complexity of a formal language that encodes it, and hence depends on the encoding. The question is: What is a reasonable model for discussing problems with numerical inputs? Suppose the input in a problem is a sequence of n numbers and the required output is another number. Is it reasonable to use the number n as the input size? The answer depends on the problem. Many computational number-theoretic problems have only one or two numbers as input (e.g., primality testing, greatest common divisor), and the difficulty of the problem depends on the magnitudes of the numbers. It is hard to imagine that such problems can be solved in a bounded number of arithmetic operations. On the other hand, it seems reasonable to measure the input to a problem of solving linear equations by the number of coefficients in the system. Moreover, the number of arithmetic operations needed for solving linear equations is bounded by a polynomial in the number of coefficients.

Naturally, there is interest in settling the complexity of linear programming under this alternative model. Results are known only for special classes of linear programming problems. It is known that systems of linear inequalities with at most two variables per inequality can be decided in strongly polynomial time [107]; that is, the number of arithmetic operations is bounded by a polynomial in m and n. In fact, a linear function with at most two nonzero coefficients can be optimized subject to such inequalities. The algorithm is also polynomial in the usual sense.

Desire for a strongly polynomial algorithm for the minimum cost-flow problem was expressed by Edmonds and Karp [54] in the same paper that proposed the first polynomial algorithm to the problem. A strongly polynomial algorithm for the minimum cost-flow problem was recently developed by Tardos [147], who also obtained [148] an algorithm for the general linear programming problem. In the rest of this section we review this nice result on linear programming in strongly polynomial time (with respect to the objective function and the right-hand-side vector) recently obtained by Tardos. Work related to Tardos's algorithm was done by Orlin [127] and Fujishige [58]. Another extension is the work by Frank and Tardos [56] mentioned at the end of this section.

The main result of Tardos [148] can roughly be described as follows. Linear programming problems (A, b, c) with rational coefficients can be solved in a number of arithmetic operations bounded by a polynomial in m, n and the number of bits in the binary representation of the matrix A (regardless of the magnitudes of coefficients in b and c). For any matrix of rational numbers, the length of the binary representation of the matrix is called the *size* of the matrix. Thus, the time-complexity of Tardos's algorithm depends only on the size of A and not on the sizes of b and c, whereas in the other polynomial-time algorithms [83, 84, 79] the complexity does depend on these sizes. However, the claim about polynomial dependence on the size of A is possible due to the existence of polynomial-time algorithms for linear programming, but Tardos's result should be appreciated independently of these results. It provides strongly polynomial algorithms for numerous problems of combinatorial optimization without relying on polynomial algorithms for the general linear programming problem.

The number of elementary operations used in Tardos's algorithm is independent of large numbers occurring in the objective function and the right-hand-side vectors.[11] It is linear programming duality that allows one to deal with these vectors in a symmetric way. We first consider the objective function vector. The essence of the method is as follows. Given

---

[11] If one assumes that the cost of an operation depends on the magnitudes of the operands then the performance is affected by the existence of large numbers anywhere.

any objective function vector, one can replace it by another with "moderate" coefficients. The optimal solution relative to the revised objective function identifies at least one constraint that is tight at the optimum relative to the original objective function. Thus, instead of solving a problem with arbitrarily large coefficients, one can solve a sequence of problems (each identifying at least one additional tight constraint) with moderate coefficients in the objective function. Each of these problems may still have arbitrarily large coefficients in the right-hand-side vector. However, with the help of duality, the same trick can be applied to the subproblems.

The main ideas of the algorithm can be explained in the case where one needs to maximize a linear function $c^T x$ over a nonempty polyhedral set P, given in the form $\{x : Ax = b, x \geq 0\}$, where the dimensions of the system are $m \times n$. The algorithm is stated for an integer matrix A. Obviously, any problem with rational A can be handled too. A modified direction $\bar{c}$ is computed as follows. First, any linear combination of rows of A can be added to c^T without changing the set of optimal solutions. Choosing an appropriate combination, we can replace c by a vector $c' = c - A^T y$ such that $Ac' = 0$. The case $c' = 0$ is trivial. Otherwise, c' is replaced by $c'' = (n^2 \Delta / \|c'\|_\infty) c'$, where Δ is an upper bound on the absolute value of any minor of A. The size of Δ can be bounded by a polynomial in the size of A. Obviously, $\|c''\|_\infty = n^2 \Delta$ and the set of c''-optimal solutions still equals the set of the c-optimal ones. Now, c'' is replaced by a vector $\bar{c}$ consisting of the integral values of the coordinates of c''. The set of $\bar{c}$-optimal solutions is no longer the same as the set of c-optimal solutions. However, important information can be obtained by solving the dual problem with $\bar{c}$. Suppose y is an optimal solution to this dual problem – that is, the problem of minimizing $b^T y$ subject to $A^T y \geq \bar{c}$ and $y \geq 0$. It can be proved that, for any column A_j of A such that $y^T A_j \geq c_j'' + n\Delta$, necessarily $x_j = 0$ for any optimal solution x of the original primal problem (maximize $c^T x$ subject to $Ax = b$ and $x \geq 0$). The interesting fact is that there is at least one such column. Such a column can be dropped from the system and the same process repeated with a smaller system. After at most n steps we identify the set of all j's such that $x_j = 0$ for any optimal solution x.

Each step in the above procedure requires the solution of the dual problem whose right-hand-side vector is $\bar{c}$ (consisting of moderate coefficients, i.e., integers of absolute values not greater than $n^2 \Delta$), but whose objective function vector b may still consist of large numbers. The idea is to solve this problem with the same basic trick but note that feasibility is not guaranteed. Also, the description so far applies only to problems that are guaranteed to be feasible.

The feasibility of any system $Ax \leq b$ can be decided in polynomial time in the size of A as follows. An objective function c_o is introduced: $c_o = \sum (\Delta + 1)^i a_i$, where a_i is the ith row of A. Consider the problem of maximizing $c_o^T x$ subject to $Ax \leq b$. The dual problem of the latter is to minimize $b^T y$ subject to $A^T y = c_o$ and $y \geq 0$. We first note that this dual problem is feasible (e.g., $y_i = (\Delta + 1)^i$ is feasible). Moreover, the size of its right-hand-side vector c_o is bounded by a polynomial in the size of the matrix A. The basic trick applies here (consider maximizing $-b^T y$), and any polynomial algorithm can be used to solve the subproblems because the right-hand-side vector is of moderate size. If the dual problem is unbounded then the primal is infeasible; otherwise, the primal here is feasible since the dual is. In the latter case the basic algorithm identifies all the (dual) constraints that are tight at the (dual) optimum. Any polynomial linear programming algorithm can be used to select a dual optimal solution; it takes polynomial time in the size of A only, because the dual objective b is not required once the optimal face is known and the size of c_o is polynomially bounded by the size of A anyway. Once a dual optimal solution $\bar{y}$ is found, a primal feasible solution $\bar{x}$ is computed by solving the system $a_i \bar{x} = b_i$ for all i such that $\bar{y}_i > 0$. The validity of the last step follows from the particular choice of c_o and the complementary slackness theorem.

The complete algorithm for linear programming now works as follows. Given the problem of maximizing $c^T x$ subject to $Ax = b$ and $x \geq 0$, the algorithm first checks the feasibility of the system $\{Ax = b, x \geq 0\}$. If feasible then the feasibility of the dual system $A^T y \geq c$ is checked. If the dual is also feasible then the basic algorithm is applied to the primal problem. The subproblems here are solved as follows. First, feasibility of the dual system $A^T y \geq \bar{c}$ is checked (this may be done by any polynomial linear programming algorithm because $\bar{c}$ is of moderate size). If this dual is feasible then Tardos's algorithm can be called recursively to find an optimal solution to the problem of minimizing $b^T y$ subject to $A^T y = \bar{c}$ and $y \geq 0$. Specific optimal primal and dual solutions can then be found by the procedure described above for detecting feasibility.

In the way stated in [148], Tardos's algorithm is not well-defined for a general matrix A of real numbers, even though the vectors c and b may be real. In fact, the coordinates of b and c can be elements of any ordered field. Normalization eliminates all the infinite elements and then infinitesimal elements are rounded down to zero. Recall that the basic trick of the algorithm is to replace c by a vector whose coordinates are integers with absolute values not greater than $n^2 \Delta$, where Δ is determined by the matrix A. When A has integral entries, Δ has to be an upper bound on the absolute value of any minor of A. The natural generalization for real matrices is to choose Δ as an upper bound on the absolute value of the *ratio* of any two nonzero minors of A. The given problem is then reduced to a polynomial number (in m and n) of problems with modified objective functions. More precisely, the vector c is replaced by $\bar{c}$, where

$$\bar{c}_j = \lfloor (n^2 \Delta / \|c'\|_\infty) c'_j \rfloor \quad \text{and} \quad c' = c - A^T y$$

so that $Ac' = 0$. This raises two questions. First, it is not known whether such an upper bound Δ can be found in a polynomial number (in m and n) of elementary operations on real numbers. It is easy to compute an upper bound on the absolute value of any minor: namely, $n! \Lambda^n$, where Λ is the maximum absolute value of entries of A. However, it is not known how to compute a positive lower bound for the absolute value of any non-zero minor of A in a polynomial number of real number operations. Even if an appropriate Δ could be found in polynomial time, it is not clear that the optimization problem with the modified objective function vector $\bar{c}$ is easier than the original one.

It is interesting to examine the existence of a Tardos-type result over general ordered fields. However, we have to be careful in phrasing the question. Consider the following question: Can we solve the problem (A, b, c) using a number of field operations that depends only on A? The answer is (trivially) yes, because the problem can be solved by enumerating all the bases. This procedure has an upper bound on the number of field operations that depends only on m and n. The more general interesting question is of course the existence of polynomial bounds (in m and n) but this is the fundamental question rather than what we would call a Tardos-type question. A more reasonable question can be asked as follows. Does there exist a function g that assigns to any field element a a positive integer $g(a)$, and does there exist an algorithm that solves the problem in $g(A)p(m, n)$ field operations, where $g(A)$ is the maximum of $g(a)$ over entries of A, and p is a polynomial?

Frank and Tardos [56] extend Tardos's algorithm to certain combinatorial optimization problems with exponentially many constraints. This extension applies the simultaneous approximation algorithm of [97] for computing an equivalent objective function vector with moderate coefficients. Most of the combinatorial optimization problems can be formulated as linear programming problems (possibly with exponentially many constraints), where the coefficients in the matrix are 0, 1, or -1. If the number of constraints is polynomial in the size of the original problem (e.g., the minimum cost-flow problem) then Tardos's method provides a strongly polynomial algorithm. Linear programming problems with an exponential number of constraints (given implicitly) can be solved in polynomial time by the ellipsoid algorithm, provided a polynomial-time algorithm is available for proving feasibility of a given point or else providing a violated constraint. The Frank and Tardos algorithm makes such polynomial algorithms strongly polynomial by modifying the objective function into an equivalent one whose size is polynomial. It replaces a given objective function vector c by a vector c^* of integers of polynomial size such that, for any vector $u \in \{-1, 0, 1\}^n$, $u^T c \geq 0$ if and only if $u^T c^* \geq 0$. The components of c may be elements of any ordered field. The computation of c^* relies on the simultaneous approximation algorithm.

6   Linear programming in fixed dimension

Questions about the asymptotic worst-case time complexities of various problems became very popular during the 1970s. In particular, questions of computational geometry (see [95] for a survey) attracted much attention. It has been known that the complexity of finding the extreme points of the convex hull of a set of n points in the plane is $\theta(n \log n)$. This suggested that the complexity of the two-variable linear programming problem was the same. However, it was shown in [108, 48] that this problem could be solved in $O(n)$ time. The idea is quite simple. For any two constraints of the form $y \geq a_i x + b_i$ $(i = 1, 2)$, there is a value x' (namely, where $a_1 x' + b_1 = a_2 x' + b_2$, assuming a nondegenerate case) so that on each side of the line $\{x = x'\}$ one of the constraints dominates the other (in the weak sense). Thus, if at some point it becomes known that the search for a solution may be restricted (say) to the half-plane $\{x \geq x'\}$, then at that point one of the constraints may be eliminated. The algorithm is based on finding good values of x that allow for the elimination of "large" sets of constraints. Suppose, for simplicity, we have $n = 4k$ constraints of the form $y \geq ax + b$ and they are paired arbitrarily; that is, we have arranged them in $2k$ disjoint pairs. Let x_m denote the *median* of the intersection values $x'_1, \ldots, x'_{2k}$ of these pairs (assuming a nondegenerate case). It is easy to decide in $O(n)$ time whether the search may be restricted to $\{x \leq x_m\}$ or to $\{x \geq x_m\}$. This decision then allows for the elimination of k constraints, namely, one dominated constraint from each pair of constraints that do not intersect on the side of the line $\{x = x_m\}$ to which the search may be restricted. It follows that in Cn time (where C is some constant) about a quarter of the set of constraints can be eliminated. This implies that by repeating the process about $\log_{4/3} n$ times the set of constraints is exhausted and eventually two critical constraints are identified. The total time is of the form $Cn(1 + (3/4) + (3/4)^2 + (3/4)^3 + \cdots)$ and is hence linear in n. The linear upper bound relies on the result that the median can be found in $O(n)$ time (see [9]) and this algorithm can be considered as an extension of the linear-time median-finding algorithm.

Three-variable linear programming problems can also be solved in $O(n)$ time [108, 48] but the algorithm is more involved and the resulting constant is larger. It turns out that only about one-sixteenth of the constraints can be eliminated during one iteration. The elimination is based on knowledge that the search may be restricted to a certain quadrant of the plane, determined in two median-finding steps. The generalization of this result to dimensions higher than three [109] is not trivial. The algorithm works according to the same principle of eliminating dominated constraints. In a fixed dimension (i.e., when the number of variables is fixed and the number of constraints is n), a fixed fraction of the set of remaining constraints is eliminated. However, the fraction tends to zero very fast with the number of variables. In the construction of [109] the fraction is doubly exponential, yielding an $O(2^{2^d}n)$ algorithm for d variables and n constraints. Improved constructions that provide a bound of $O(3^{d^2}n)$ were suggested in [50, 36].

Linear-time algorithms using similar methods also appear in [49, 112, 116, 164]. Although the basic algorithm for two variables is extremely fast (using "approximate" medians obtained by sampling, rather than exact medians), the algorithm in [109] is clearly not a serious tool for solving general linear programming problems in practice. However, considering asymptotic worst-case complexity, it is optimal for any fixed number of variables.

7   Karmarkar's algorithm and related work

Karmarkar [79] developed another polynomial-time algorithm for linear programming that generates a sequence of interior points converging to an optimal solution. Interior point methods are usually used in nonlinear programming [55, 61] and have been proposed for linear programming as well (see [60]), but no one before Karmarkar had identified a method that provably ran in polynomial time. To analyze the time-complexity of an algorithm, one usually needs a measure of the progress (a "merit function") that the algorithm makes toward the solution. However, it is usually not easy to identify good measures of the progress. The naive measures – like the amount of improvement in the objective function or the distance to the solution – usually do not suffice for proving nice bounds, simply because it is impossible to prove a good lower bound on the progress *per iteration*. Of course, efficient methods do not have to make much progress in every single step and thus, to prove their efficiency, one needs to understand how they make good progress in the long run.

A common technique in nonlinear programming is the *barrier-function* method. The goal is to solve constrained optimization problems with the tools of unconstrained optimization. A sequence of points is generated, starting in the interior of the feasible domain. The objective function is replaced by another function that is coherent with the original objective, and yet has a "barrier" ingredient that prevents the algorithm from getting out of the feasible domain. To specify a barrier-function method, one needs to construct such a function and also specify an unconstrained optimization algorithm.

Karmarkar's algorithm is easy to state with respect to the following form of the linear programming problem: minimize $c^T x$ subject to (i) $Ax = 0$, (ii) $\sum_k x_k = 1$, and (iii) $x \geq 0$, where A is of dimension $m \times n$; it is also assumed that the problem has an optimal solution and that the optimum of $c^T x$ equals zero. A vector x is called *interior* if it satisfies (i) and (ii) and if $x > 0$. It is assumed that an interior point x^0 is available in the beginning. Any linear programming problem can be reduced to such a form. This is accomplished if the program is formulated so that the primal and dual problems are combined. The algorithm can be stated with the following barrier function:

$$ F(x) = \frac{c^T x}{(\prod_k x_k)^{1/n}}, $$

which is well-defined for interior points x. Obviously, the value of $F(x)$ tends to infinity when x tends (from the interior) to a boundary point z such that $c^T z > 0$. Also, unless $c^T x$ is constant over the feasible region, $F(x) > 0$ for every interior point x. On the other hand, if x tends from the interior *along any straight line* to an optimal point x^* on the boundary then $F(x)$ tends to zero; this is true because $c^T x$ approaches zero faster than $(\prod_k x_k)^{1/n}$, given that $\sum_k x_k = 1$. It follows that while $F(x)$ is sought to be minimized over the interior of the feasible domain, a minimum of $c^T x$ over the feasible domain is approached. However, we have not yet explained how an optimum is actually reached in polynomial time.

The algorithm (to be described below) generates a sequence $x^0, x^1, x^2, \ldots$ of interior points along which the function $F(x)$ decreases monotonically. Moreover, the rate of decrease is provably good enough to imply the desired result. Notice that the infinite process of optimizing $F(x)$ does not produce a boundary point. One needs to apply a stopping rule, and then either leave the problem with the current point as an approximate solution or run a procedure that produces an exact solution from the current approximate one. In practice, one can sometimes guess the optimal basis and then verify that it is optimal. In theory, if $F(x)$ is sufficiently close to zero then an optimal solution can be easily computed from x. Thus, in theory, the stopping rule is based on a sufficiently small value of $F(x)$.

The upper bound on the running time of Karmarkar's algorithm is polynomial in terms of the length of the binary representation of all the numbers involved. Let L denote this input length. An argument that appears in the analysis of the ellipsoid algorithm is as follows. For some constant κ, if x^1 and x^2 are basic solutions such that $c^T x^1 \neq c^T x^2$ then $|c^T x^1 - c^T x^2| > 2^{-\kappa L}$. This implies that if x is any feasible solution such that $0 < c^T x < 2^{-\kappa L}$, then – by modifying x into a basic feasible solution while improving the objective function value (a standard procedure sometimes called "purification") – we obtain an optimal solution. Thus a valid stopping rule is $c^T x \leq 2^{-\kappa L}$. Note also that $F(x) > c^T x$ for any interior x, so $F(x) < 2^{-\kappa L}$ is also a valid stopping rule. The barrier function $F(x)$ is also a suitable criterion function in terms of the discussion in Section 3, with the iterates x^i playing the roles of the objects. The initial interior point x^0 can be chosen so that $\log F(x^0)$ is bounded by a polynomial in L. The parameter ϵ here is equal to $2^{-\kappa L}$ so that $-\log \epsilon$ is also polynomial in L. It remains to show (see below) that the rate of improvement δ is also such that $-1/(\log \delta)$ is polynomial in L. From a theoretical viewpoint, this characteristic is perhaps the most significant contribution of [79].

Let x^i be an interior point. We would like to move from x^i to a point x^{i+1} such that $F(x^{i+1})/(F(x^i)$ is sufficiently small. Karmarkar's step is related to the fact that the barrier function is, in a certain sense, invariant under a *projective rescaling transformation* P defined as follows. Given a point $a = x^i$, let $x' = P(x)$ be defined for any feasible x. First, for convenience of notation let $D = \operatorname{diag}(a_k)$ denote a diagonal matrix of order n, where the diagonal entries are the components of the vector a. Also, let e denote an n-vector of 1's. The vector x' is equal to $(D^{-1}x)/(e^T D^{-1}x)$. The sense of invariance can be explained as follows. First note that $x = (Dx')/(e^T Dx')$. Thus,

$$F(x) = \frac{c^T Dx'}{e^T Dx'} \bigg/ \frac{(\prod_k a_k x_k')^{1/n}}{e^T Dx'} = \frac{c^T Dx'}{(\prod_k a_k x_k')^{1/n}}.$$

Denote $c' = Dc$ and $F'(x') = (c')^T x'/(\prod_k x_k')^{1/n}$. It follows that for any two points x, y, if $x' = P(x)$ and $y' = P(y)$ then

$$\frac{F(x)}{F(y)} = \frac{F'(x')}{F'(y')}.$$

This equality allows us to work in the space transformed under P so that a (relative) improvement in F', while taking a step from $a' = P(a)$, is the same as that of the corresponding step from a.

The natural question at this point is what is the benefit from the transformation P. The answer is that it reveals a good way to take a step from a', as we explain below. Note that in fact $a_k' = 1/n$ for every k. Also, the linear subspace $\{x : Ax = 0\}$ is transformed under P into a subspace $\{x : A'x = 0\}$ while the simplex $\{x : e^T x = 1, x \geq 0\}$ is mapped onto itself. The situation is now as follows. There are two balls, B_1 and B_2, both centered at the current point a', with the following properties: (i) B_1 is contained in the (transformed) feasible domain while the latter is contained in B_2. (ii) The ratio of the radius of B_2 to that of B_1 is $n-1$. The balls are simply the intersections of $\{x: A'x = 0\}$ with the largest inscribed and the smallest circumscribing balls of the simplex $\{x: \sum x_j = 1, x \geq 0\}$. This construction is reminiscent of Lenstra's construction [98] for a polynomial integer programming algorithm in a fixed dimension. The step of Karmarkar's algorithm in the transformed space is made in the direction of the projection of the vector c' on the subspace $\{x: A'x = 0\}$; its length is equal to one-quarter of the radius of B_1. The minimum of the linear function $(c')^T y$ over the (transformed) feasible domain is zero. It follows from the ball inclusion relations that the value of this function is multiplied during this step by a factor not greater than $1 - 1/4n$. However, we are interested in the improvement of the function F' so we must consider the change in $(\prod_k x_k)^{1/n}$ during the step. This is the reason a step of only one-quarter rather than the full radius of B_1 is taken. It is shown that this guarantees that the denominator of the (transformed) barrier function does not decrease too much. The result is that the value F' (and hence also of F) is multiplied during a step by a factor not greater than $e^{-1/8n}$. The latter quantity plays the role of δ in the discussion of Section 3. Polynomiality follows from the fact that $-1/(\log \delta)$ here equals $8n$. Thus, as in the ellipsoid algorithm, the factor of improvement depends (polynomially) only on the dimension[12] and not on the numerical values of the coefficients. Blair [21] showed that a step of length $(n-1)/(2n-3)$ of the radius of B_1 was possible with a corresponding $\delta = (4/(3\sqrt{e}))^{1/n}$.

Karmarkar's algorithm provides the strongest upper bound known concerning the worst-case complexity of the linear programming problem under the logarithmic cost model. The number of arithmetic operations in the worst case is bounded by[13] $O(n^{3.5}L^*)$ if the matrix operations are carried out in a specific way described in [79].

Interestingly, the iterative step of Karmarkar's algorithm can be adapted to work over any ordered field. Moreover, the guaranteed rate of improvement prevails. It is easy to get rid of the logarithms and roots in the analysis of the algorithm. Thus, for example, one can easily obtain the following from Proposition 2.1.

Proposition 7.1. *Under the conditions of Proposition 2.1, if $H = \{x \in F^n: Ax = 0\}$, where $A \in F^{m \times n}$ is of rank m, then the vector $v^* = [I - A^T(AA^T)^{-1}A]u$ minimizes the function f over H.*

---

[12] Interestingly, in the ellipsoid algorithm the factor depends on the smaller dimension of the system, and this allows for the nice applications to combinatorial optimization problems with exponentially many constraints. This is not so with Karmarkar's method.

[13] The parameter L^* is usually smaller than L and reflects a better estimate of the distances between basic solutions using minors of the matrix A.

We also have the following.

> **Proposition 7.2.** *Let* $u = (n^{-1}, \ldots, n^{-1}) \in F^n$ *and let* $H \subseteq F^n$ *be determined by* $\sum_{i=1}^{n-1} x_i = 1$ *and* $x_n = 0$. *Under these conditions, the vector* $v^* = ((n-1)^{-1}, \ldots, (n-1)^{-1}, 0) \in F^n$ *minimizes the function* $f(v) = (u-v)^T(u-v)$ *for* $v \in H$.

The following proposition extends [21, Lemma 5], and justifies the choice of the step length so that the barrier component deterioration is controlled.

> **Proposition 7.3.** *Let* F *be an ordered field,* $n \geq 2$ *a natural number, and let* $\{x_1, \ldots, x_n, \alpha\} \subseteq F$ *be such that*
>
> $$\sum_{k=1}^{n} \left(x_k - \frac{1}{n} \right)^2 \leq \frac{\alpha}{n(n-1)} \quad \text{and} \quad \sum_{k=1}^{n} x_k = 1.$$
>
> *Under these conditions,*
>
> $$\prod_{k=1}^{n} x_k \geq \frac{1-\alpha}{n} \left(\frac{1+\alpha/(n-1)}{n} \right)^{n-1}.$$

Using a criterion function that avoids nth roots, $f(x) = (c^T x)^n / \prod_k x_k$, one can see that during each step the value of this function is multiplied by a factor that is less than and bounded away from 1. If the problem is solved over the rationals then this implies a polynomial time bound. However, despite a guaranteed rate of improvement, the algorithm does not solve the problem over general ordered fields because it is not guaranteed to reach infinitesimally close to an optimum. It can be used as an approximate method though, where the approximation is in terms of the objective function value. Recall that the simplex method works over any ordered field.

The computation of the projection of c' dominates the effort involved in a single iteration of the algorithm. The projection problem of a vector c' on a subspace $\{x : A'x = 0\}$ is equivalent to the minimization of $\|A'x - c'\|$. This is known as a *least-squares* problem for which there are several techniques available. Further development in the numerical solution least-squares problems should improve the performance of Karmarkar's algorithm.

It should be noted that the practical implementations of Karmarkar's algorithm may be quite different from the theoretical algorithm. Deviations from the theoretical algorithm can be in several ways: (i) Problems may be solved not in the combined form of the primal and the dual. (ii) Instead of a fixed step length, the proposed direction of movement may be searched for a best step. Moreover, even the direction of movement itself may be selected after a search of a low-dimensional subspace. (iii) The theoretical stopping rule is not practical so heuristic rules may be developed for stopping. (iv) The least-squares subproblems may be solved only approximately (especially if iterative methods are selected for them), and there may be a certain degree of heuristicism involved in the choice of the level of precision. (v) Some effort may be invested in frequent checking for optimality of a guessed basis. (vi) Variables and constraints may sometimes be eliminated on the basis of both theoretical and heuristic arguments. The significance of an algorithm running in polynomial time diminishes in practice if it is no longer clear that the particular implementation is guaranteed to run in polynomial time. On the other hand, it is easy to run any algorithm in "parallel" to a polynomial-time algorithm, so that at least one of the algorithms is guaranteed to terminate in polynomial time.

Since the first publication of Karmarkar's algorithm there have been several papers written on variants of the method [11, 19, 32, 33, 59, 101, 111, 103, 151, 156, 160]. It is not clear what qualifies an algorithm as a variant of Karmarkar's algorithm. Karmarkar's algorithm is classified in [60] as one member of a family of methods that have been experimented with in the past and also recently at Stanford. The claim is that Karmarkar's algorithm can be reproduced as a projected Newton search method applied to a certain barrier function with a certain rule for updating the barrier parameter. Also, resemblances between Karmarkar's barrier function, Frisch's barrier function [57], and Huard's method of centers [71] are mentioned in [151]. Resemblance to Lawson's algorithm [94, 136, 38, 39] was pointed out by Walter Murray. Here, an l_∞-approximation problem is solved by a sequence of weighted l_2-approximation problems with a rule for updating the weights. However, the formal equivalence shown in [60] does not degrade the significance of Karmarkar's result. It seems reasonable to conjecture that under suitable weak conditions *any* interior-point method can be formulated as a barrier-function method. The interesting problem is to identify good methods. Karmarkar provided the first polynomial one; his algorithm is based on sensible principles that do not hold for the barrier-function algorithms in general. On the other hand, it is still not clear whether his algorithm is in fact better in practice than other variants of the barrier-function idea.

In Section 8 we discuss recent applications of nonlinear programming methods to linear programming that were inspired by Karmarkar's work. Besides the references mentioned above, further work related to Karmarkar's algorithm can be found in [21, 25, 34, 45, 60, 75, 76, 81, 87, 91, 123, 130, 131, 137, 152, 156]. Todd and Burrell [151] and Anstreicher [11] show how to extract dual variables without having to run the problem in the combined primal–dual form. This resolves the difficulties with a "sliding" objective function mechanism that was described in an earlier version of Karmarkar's paper.

Other recent iterative methods, independent of Karmarkar's work, are [102, 117, 121, 122, 133]. It is expected that more papers will appear soon in this field. Unfortunately, it is not easy to assess the practical significance of newly proposed algorithms because of insufficient computational experience. Moreover, an acceptable format for testing software for mathematical programming has not been decided yet. Some related questions are discussed in Section 10.

8   Recent interior-point methods

Methods of nonlinear programming have been tried in the past for solving linear programming problems (see [60] for references). However, the simplex method has been accepted as the most practical general-purpose method for linear programming. Practitioners often try to linearize a nonlinear problem, but not to "unlinearize" a linear one. The ellipsoid algorithm is in fact a theoretical application of nonlinear programming to linear programming. Interest in nonlinear methods for linear programming was recently revived with the strong claims about the practicality of Karmarkar's algorithm. In this section we review some of the recently proposed algorithms.

We have explained the notion of a barrier-function method in Section 7. Given a valid barrier function for a linear programming problem, it is usually a good idea to use the Newton search method for finding the optimum of the function, especially if the latter is convex. The method is usually applied to unconstrained optimization problems but can easily be extended to handle linear equality constraints. A single iteration of the Newton search method amounts to searching a direction. The direction is obtained by optimizing a quadratic function that approximates the given function. Suppose we need to minimize a convex function $F(x)$ subject to $Ax = b$, and assume we have already computed a point a. Let ∇ and H denote the gradient and Hessian, respectively, of the function F at the point a. The approximate optimization problem at a is to minimize $Q(x) = F(a) + \nabla^T(x-a) + \frac{1}{2}(x-a)^T H(x-a)$ subject to $Ax = b$. The search direction v is obtained by minimizing $\frac{1}{2}v^T Hv + \nabla^T v$ subject to $Av = 0$. This direction can also be obtained by linear optimization over an ellipsoid as follows. The inequality $(x-a)^T H(x-a) \le \rho^2$ ($\rho \ne 0$) describes an ellipsoid centered at a. An approximate linear optimization problem at a is to minimize $\nabla^T(x-a)$ subject to $(x-a)^T H(x-a) \le \rho^2$ and $Ax = b$. The direction to the optimum of the latter is independent of ρ and coincides with the direction obtained by Newton's method. There is yet another way to obtain the search direction by transforming the space. The gradient direction is not invariant under linear transformations of the space. Thus, this direction depends on the representation. It is possible to transform the space, choose the gradient direction in the transformed space, and return to the original space, so that the resulting direction is the same as the one supplied by Newton's method. If the Hessian is symmetric and positive-definite then $H^{-1} = WW^T$ for some real matrix W. In that case the transformation is $v' = W^{-1}v$. The approximate quadratic optimization problem at a is to minimize $\frac{1}{2}\|v'\|^2 + \nabla^T Wv'$ subject to $AWv' = 0$. Equivalently, v' is determined by minimizing the linear function $\nabla^T Wv'$ over a ball that can be described as the intersection of the full-dimensional ball $\{x': \|x' - a'\| \leq \rho\}$ with the affine subspace $\{x': AWx' = b\}$. Obviously, the direction v' is obtained by projecting the transformed gradient $W^T\nabla$ on the linear subspace $\{v': AWv' = 0\}$. The projection of a vector u on a subspace $\{z: Mz = 0\}$ (assuming M has a full row rank) is given by $[I - M^T(MM^T)^{-1}M]u$ (see Proposition 7.1). Thus, $v = Wv' = W[I - W^T A^T(AWW^T A^T)^{-1}AW]W^T\nabla$. In the applications the matrix W usually has a special structure that allows for more efficient ways to compute the search direction.

It is interesting to note that Newton's method for nonlinear optimization is not invariant under monotone transformations of the objective function. Thus, one obtains different search directions if the objective function is replaced by its logarithm or its nth power. On the other hand, the search directions corresponding to all possible monotone transformations of the same objective function form a two-dimensional linear space. Thus the different algorithms are closely related.

Gill, Murray, Saunders, Tomlin, and Wright [60] propose an algorithm for linear programming where they apply the Newton search method to a traditional form of a barrier function. They obtain an unconstrained optimization problem (but still with equality constraints) with an objective function of the form $F_\mu(x) = c^T x + \mu B(x)$. Here $B(x)$ is the barrier component that tends to infinity as x approaches the boundary of the feasible domain, and μ is a positive scalar that is driven by the algorithm to zero. For the linear programming problem of minimizing $c^T x$ subject to $Ax = b$ and $x \geq 0$, the proposed barrier function is $B(x) = -\sum_k \ln x_k$, so the unconstrained optimization problem with the parameter μ is to minimize $c^T x - \mu \sum_k \ln x_k$ subject to $Ax = b$. Let us use the notation of Section 7. Thus, let a denote the current point, $D = \text{diag}(a_k)$, and e is a vector of 1's. The gradient of this barrier function at a is $c - \mu D^{-1}e$ and the Hessian is μD^{-2}. For comparison, consider Karmarkar's potential function $F(x) =$

$n \ln c^T x - \sum_k \ln x_k$. Thus, in Karmarkar's algorithm, the gradient at the current point a is equal to $(n/c^T a)c - D^{-1}e$ and the Hessian is equal to $D^{-2} - n(c^T a)^{-2}cc^T$. Thus, if $\mu = (c^T a)/n$ then the directions of the gradients in both cases are formally the same. Note that if the optimal value of $c^T x$ is zero then by taking $\mu = (c^T a)/n$ we drive μ to zero. It is shown in [60] that there is a choice of μ that yields the same search direction. The Hessian in Karmarkar's function contains an extra term, attributable to the dependence of μ on x. Because the Hessian in the [60] algorithm is equal to μD^{-2}, it follows that the matrix W in that case equals $\sqrt{\mu} D$. The search direction is hence $D[I - \mu D A^T (AD^2 A^T)^{-1} AD]D(c - \mu D^{-1}e)$. To compute the search direction, there is no need to invert the matrix $AD^2 A^T$ or even to generate it. What we have to do is essentially solve a system of equations of the form $(AD^2 A^T)\xi = \beta$. Thus, we can expand the system in the form

$$\eta - DA^T\xi = 0 \qquad AD\eta = \beta,$$

so that sparsity of A can be exploited.

Iri and Imai [76] propose an algorithm that can also be described as a Newton search direction method applied to a barrier function. They work on the problem of minimizing $c^T x$ subject to inequality constraints $Ax \geq b$, where the optimal value of the objective function is zero and an initial interior point is known. The barrier function is

$$F(x) = (c^T x)^{m+1} \Big/ \prod_k (A_k^T x - b_k),$$

where m is the number of rows in the matrix A and A_k^T denotes the kth row of A. This function is based on the ideas behind the potential function used by Karmarkar for the analysis of his algorithm. The function $F(x)$ is convex. The algorithm iterates as follows. Given an interior point x^i, it finds the minimum x' of the quadratic approximation to $F(x)$ based on the Hessian at x^i. It then searches the feasible segment of the line determined by x^i and x' for a minimum x^{i+1} of $F(x)$. It is interesting to consider an analogous algorithm for the problem in the form we have used in this chapter, namely: minimize $c^T x$ subject to $Ax = b$ and $x \geq 0$. The barrier function of Iri and Imai would be $f(x) = (c^T x)^{n+1}/(\prod_k x_k)$, where $x \in R_+^n$. The gradient ∇ of F at a point a satisfies, for every j, $\nabla_j = f(a)[(n+1)(c^T a)^{-1}c_j - a_j^{-1}]$. It follows that the Hessian H of f at a satisfies, for every i and j,

$$H_{ij} = \nabla_i \nabla_j - f(a)[(n+1)(c^T a)^{-2}c_i c_j - \delta_{ij} a_i^{-2}],$$

where $\delta_{ij} = 1$ if $i = j$ and $\delta_{ij} = 0$ otherwise. It follows that

$$\frac{H_{ij}}{f(a)} = \left((n+1)\frac{c_i}{c^T a} - \frac{1}{a_i}\right)\left((n+1)\frac{c_j}{c^T a} - \frac{1}{a_j}\right) - (n+1)\frac{c_i c_j}{(c^T a)^2} + \frac{\delta_{ij}}{a_i^2}$$

$$= n(n+1)\left(\frac{c_i}{c^T a} - \frac{1}{na_i}\right)\left(\frac{c_j}{c^T a} - \frac{1}{na_j}\right) + \frac{\delta_{ij}}{a_i^2} - \frac{1}{na_i a_j}.$$

In matrix notation,

$$\frac{1}{f(a)}H = n(n+1)uu^T + D^{-1}\left(I - \frac{1}{n}ee^T\right)D^{-1},$$

where $u_k = (c^T a)^{-1}c_k - (na_k)^{-1}$ and $D = \text{diag}(a_k)$. It is now clear that H is positive semidefinite at any $a \in R_+^n$ so F is convex over R_+^n. Interestingly, Karmarkar's potential function $(c^T x)^n / (\prod_k x_k)$ is not convex. For example, let $n = 2$, $c = (1, 0)^T$, and $a = (\frac{1}{2}, \frac{1}{2})^T$. Then the Hessian of this function at a is proportional to the 2×2 matrix $I - ee^T$, which is indefinite. On the other hand, Karmarkar's algorithm works within the subspace $\{x: \sum_k x_k = 1\}$. The restriction of Karmarkar's function to the latter subspace *is* convex. The proof of this claim follows by eliminating x_n. Consider the function $G(x)(c^T x)^n / ((1 - \sum_k x_k)\prod_k x_k)$, where $x \in R_+^{n-1}$. The Hessian of the latter can be represented as the sum of the Hessian of $F(x) = (c^T x)^n / \prod_k x_k$ (also with $x \in R_+^{n-1}$) and a positive multiple of ee^T, so the Hessian of G is positive definite.

The difference between the [60] and the [76] algorithms is that the former has a parameter that is updated by the algorithm, so that the Newton step is computed with respect to a different function in each iteration; the latter applies Newton's method to a fixed function. Because the rule for updating the parameter is incorporated into the barrier function in [76], the Hessian matrix is naturally a little more complicated. On the other hand, it is still amenable to sparse matrix computation. The search direction is obtained by solving (for v) an optimization problem of the form: minimize $\frac{1}{2}v^T Hv + g^T v$ subject to $Av = 0$. With a vector λ of Lagrange multipliers, this amounts to the following system of equations:

$$Hv - A^T\lambda = -g \qquad Av = 0.$$

In [60], H is diagonal so the sparsity of the latter system is essentially determined by the sparsity of the matrix A. In the algorithm analogous to [76] the matrix H is dense but has a nice structure: $H = D^{-2} - ww^T$ for a certain vector w. Thus, the system of equations (in v and λ) is

$$D^{-2}v - A^T\lambda = (w^T v)w - g \qquad Av = 0.$$

The latter can be solved by taking a linear combination of solutions for two systems with a diagonal matrix in the upper left-hand corner:

$$D^{-2}v^1 - A^T\lambda^1 = w \qquad Av^1 = 0$$

and

$$D^{-2}v^2 - A^T\lambda^2 = -g \qquad Av^2 = 0.$$

The solution is $(v, \lambda) = t(v^1, \lambda^1) + (v^2, \lambda^2)$, where t is determined by the equation $w^T(tv^1 + v^2) = t$.

Vanderbei, Meketon, and Freedman [156] propose an algorithm that, in a certain sense, can be derived by dropping the projective ingredient from Karmarkar's algorithm. This algorithm (which we refer to as the VMF algorithm) can be described as follows. Suppose the problem is to minimize c^Tx subject to $Ax = b$ and $x \geq 0$. Let a denote the current interior point. Thus, $Aa = b$ and $a > 0$. The direction that the VMF algorithm takes is computed as follows. It is convenient to describe this direction using an affine scaling transformation. Given a, any point x is mapped into x' where $x'_k = x_k/a_k$. In particular, the current point a is mapped into the n-vector e consisting of n 1's. Let D denote the same diagonal matrix used above; that is, $D = \text{diag}(a_k)$. Thus, the problem is transformed into an equivalent one: minimize c^TDx' subject to $ADx' = b$ and $x' \geq 0$.

The equivalence holds in general regardless of the vector b and the optimal value of the objective function. For comparison, consider Karmarkar's transformation. The latter is applied when the problem is to minimize c^Tx subject to $Ax = 0$, $e^Tx = 1$, and $x \geq 0$. Given an interior point a, the projective rescaling transformation takes x into $x' = (D^{-1}x)/(e^TD^{-1}x)$ so the problem is transformed into the following: minimize c^TDx'/e^TDx' subject to $ADx'/e^TDx' = 0$, $e^Tx'_j = 1$, and $x' \geq 0$. However, because $b = 0$ and the optimal value of the objective function is also equal to 0, it follows that the latter is equivalent to minimizing c^Tx' subject to $ADx' = 0$, $e^Tx'_j = 1$, and $x' \geq 0$.

In the transformed space the direction v' is obtained by projecting the direction Dc on the space $\{v': ADv' = 0\}$. Thus, in this space the VMF algorithm moves from e to a point of the form $e + \alpha v'$, where α is chosen so that the new point is still interior. This step can be interpreted in two ways: (i) It is a *rescaled* steepest descent method; the algorithm moves (in the transformed space) in the direction opposite to the projected gradient. (ii) The algorithm considers (in the transformed space) a ball, contained in the feasible region and centered at the current point. It takes a direction that passes through the point where the objective function is minimized over that ball.

The VMF direction is computed as follows. First, the projection of any vector u on a subspace $\{z: Mz = 0\}$ is given by $(I - M^T(MM^T)^{-1}M)u$. Thus the projection of the vector Dc on the subspace $\{v': ADv' = 0\}$ is given by $(I-(AD)^T(AD^2A^T)^{-1}AD)Dc$. The inverse image of the latter (i.e., the VMF direction in the original space) is obtained by multiplying by D. Thus, this direction is $D^2(I-A^T(AD^2A^T)^{-1}AD^2)c$.

Interestingly, the VMF direction can be derived from the [60] algorithm as the limit of the search direction when the parameter μ tends to zero. It is instructive to consider analogous algorithms for the problem in inequality constraints form, since it seems that in this form projections on subspaces may not be needed and insight into duality may be gained. Consider the problem of minimizing c^Tx subject to $Ax \geq b$ (where $A \in R^{m \times n}$ is of rank n). An adequate barrier function for the problem in this form would be $F(x) = c^Tx - \mu \sum_k (A_k^Tx - b_k)$, where A_k^T denotes the kth row of the matrix A. Suppose that a is an interior feasible point; that is, $A_k^Ta > b_k$ $(k=1, \ldots, m)$. Let $D = \text{diag}(A_k^Ta - b_k) \in R^{m \times m}$. The gradient of F at a is equal to $c - \mu A^TD^{-1}e$ (where e is an m-vector of 1's). The Hessian of F at a is proportional to $A^TD^{-2}A$ so the Newton search direction at a with parameter μ is equal to $(A^TD^{-2}A)^{-1}(c - \mu A^TD^{-1}e)$. When μ tends to zero this direction tends to $v = (A^TD^{-2}A)^{-1}c$. Note that, as in the other algorithms, v is convenient for sparse matrix computation if A is sparse. It can be computed as the solution of $(A^TD^{-2}A)v = c$, which can be solved as an expanded sparse system in the unknowns u and v:

$$u - D^{-1}Av = 0 \qquad A^TD^{-1}u = c.$$

The latter arises in the solution of a familiar least-squares problem: minimize $\|u\|$ subject to $A^TD^{-1}u = c$, where the nearest point to the origin in the affine subspace $\{u : A^TD^{-1}u = c\}$ is sought. The components of v serve as Lagrange multipliers in this least-squares problem. Thus, the effort per iteration here is also dominated by a least-squares problem of the same size and structure. Interestingly, the dual linear programming problem can be represented in the form: maximize $b^TD^{-1}u$ subject to $A^TD^{-1}u = c$ and $u \geq 0$. This representation reflects a scaling transformation on the dual problem which is similar but not identical to the VMF transformation. The dual problem in the original form is to minimize b^Ty subject to $A^Ty = c$ and $y \geq 0$. The VMF transformation would be to divide each y_k by its current value, whereas here we multiply each y_i by the corresponding current value of $A_k^Tx - b_k$.

The algorithm proposed by Barnes [19] turns out to produce the same direction of movement as the VMF algorithm, even though it is stated differently. Given a, Barnes considers a certain ellipsoid E centered at a and contained in the feasible domain. He chooses as the direction of movement the one where the minimum of the linear function c^Tx over E is found. The ellipsoid E can be described as the intersection of the full-dimensional ellipsoid $\bar{E} = \{x : \|D^{-1}x - e\| \leq 1\}$ (where $D = \text{diag}(a_k)$, as above) with the affine space $\{x: Ax = b\}$. It is easy to verify that $\bar{E}$ is contained in the nonnegative orthant, hence E is contained in the feasible domain. The equivalence to the VMF direction is by substituting $x = Dx'$. The Barnes direction in the transformed space is obtained by minimizing the function $c^T Dx'$ over the ball E' defined as the intersection of the full-dimensional ball $\bar{E}' = \{x': \|x' - e\| \le 1\}$ with the subspace $\{x': ADx' = b\}$. Obviously, this direction is independent of the radius of the ball. In other words, the same direction is obtained if the ellipsoid $\bar{E}$ is replaced by an ellipsoid $\bar{E}(t) = \{x: \|D^{-1}x - e\| \le t\}$ for any positive t. Thus, the property that the ellipsoid E is contained in the feasible domain is irrelevant.

A variation on Karmarkar's algorithm, proposed in [111], can be explained as follows. Karmarkar's algorithm is based on a projective transformation that maps the linear objective function into a fractional one. If the optimal value is zero then the function may be replaced by its numerator. However, the minima of the fractional function and its numerator over the inner ball usually do not coincide. In the original space, the inverse image of the inner ball is an ellipsoid (assuming the feasible domain is bounded, as in Karmarkar's formulation). If that ellipsoid is indeed a good approximation to the feasible domain then a good direction should be obtained by minimizing the objective function $c^T x$ over it. Thus, the problem of minimizing $c^T x$ subject to $Ax = b$ and $x \ge 0$ is approximated by the problem of minimizing $c^T x$ subject to $Ax = b$ and $x^T D^{-1}[I - (n-1)^{-1}ee^T]D^{-1}x \le 0$. With a vector λ of Lagrange multipliers for the linear equations and a scalar multiplier η attributed to the boundary of the ellipsoid, we obtain the following system of equations:

$$(D^{-2} - ww^T)x - A^T\lambda = \eta c \qquad Ax = b$$
$$x^T(D^{-2} - ww^T)x = 0,$$

where $w = (n-1)^{-1/2}D^{-1}e$. This system can be solved using ideas already described in this section for the analogue of the [76] algorithm.

9 Simplex methods for network problems

The simplex algorithm has been used extensively and very successfully to solve network problems in practice. We will not review practical experience here. On the theoretical side, it was shown in [162] that exponential cases exist within the class of network problems. However, in recent years there have been identified simplex algorithms that perform only a polynomial number of pivot steps when applied to certain network problems. This direction is presumed to lead to better understanding of the simplex method. It may help finding a polynomial simplex variant or a proof that no such one exists.

Interesting work on network simplex algorithms was done by Cunningham [41, 42] (who, according to [73, 17], has done further unpublished work on polynomial simplex network algorithms). Roohy-Laleh [138] uses a primal simplex method for the assignment problem that runs in $O(n^3)$ pivot steps. Hung [72] obtains a number of pivots that is polynomial in the size of the problem (i.e., taking the numerical values of the costs into account). Balinski [17] develops a "signature" method that solves – in $O((n-1)(n-2)/2)$ pivot steps – the assignment problem as a dual simplex algorithm. Additional works on this problem are [10, 62, 154]. Ikura and Nemhauser [74] derive a dual simplex algorithm for the more general (but yet the uncapacitated) transportation problem. Their algorithm solves a sequence of scaled problems (using ideas from [54]). It is not strongly polynomial because the upper bound on the number of pivots depends on the numerical values. A polynomial dual simplex algorithm for the minimum cost-flow problem was presented in [128]. So far, it is not known whether a strongly polynomial simplex algorithm for the transportation problem exists. However, Orlin [126] claims that the original Edmonds and Karp scaling algorithm [54] can be made strongly polynomial with minor modifications. It should be noted that Tardos's algorithm for the transportation problem [147] is strongly polynomial, although it is not clear whether a strongly polynomial simplex algorithm can be derived from it.

10   Theory versus practice

Complexity theory in 1985 does not provide enough insight into the practical efficiency of algorithms for linear programming. Even if the issue of the distribution of inputs is resolved, the efficiency of an algorithm even on a single instance is determined by too many factors. The word "algorithm" usually refers to the underlying method and not to the detailed implementation. Thus, for example, the particular method of solving linear equations during a single iteration is not part of the algorithm. However, the efficiency of an algorithm in practice depends very heavily on the implementation. Obviously, different implementation strategies may be efficient for some inputs while others may be efficient for other inputs. Thus, when comparing different algorithms, one has to specify what part of the implementation strategy is to be considered a part of the algorithm. An interesting question at the present is whether interior-point methods will prove better for linear programming than the simplex algorithms. First, the concepts are not at all well defined. However, the answer will probably depend on the development of methods for analyzing the density structure of the matrices involved. It became apparent during the 12th International Symposium on Mathematical Programming (1985) that various interior-point methods converge in a small number of iterations. The numbers of pivot steps of simplex algorithms are also predictable to a certain extent. The potential for improvement in interior-point methods is in the reduction of the effort per iteration. Regarding the simplex method, the question of the effort per iteration seems to be better understood than the question of reducing the number of steps.

Reported computational experience is used by practitioners as an indicator for the efficiency of an algorithm. This approach suffers from many known disadvantages. Here we mention briefly only a few of them.

It is often said that there is a need for a standard set of test problems. The idea is that whenever a new algorithm is proposed for a problem, people would be able to compare it with previous methods by running it (or letting the proposer run it for them) on the test problems. However, one should be very careful to separate the research and development of the algorithm from the test problems. If there is a fixed small set of test problems, there is always the danger that we will improve the implementation by choosing the values of parameters to fit the test problems. Software packages typically have a certain degree of heuristicism involved. There are simple parameters – such as step sizes, accuracy in performing single iterations, and the like – that require some arbitrary choice of value by the designer. The choice should not depend on the test problems. Whenever sparse matrix computations are involved there is always the question of factorization and preconditioning; the performance of an implementation depends very much on the success of these operations, success that may be attributable to heuristic techniques having nothing to do with the theory of linear programming. It is natural that the person who models a real-life problem for solution as a linear programming problem understands the structure of the problem better than any heuristic computer program that must analyze this structure.

During the development of an algorithm, the designer sometimes likes to see his algorithm performing well and therefore enjoys running successful instances rather than unsuccesful ones. This distortion of proportion should not be projected to the phase of testing the final algorithm on independent test problems.

Obviously, a test of a final algorithm should be performed like any other controlled experiment. However, even this is not enough. There is a fundamental difficulty with testing algorithms that makes this field less exact than the classical exact sciences. When results of a computational experiment are reported, we usually cannot tell whether there have been prior experiments that produced contradicting results. Thus, the reported results may be easily reproducible yet not particularly instructive if the experiment itself was selected from a larger concealed set of experiments. An even more problematic issue is proprietary material. We may refer to [40] for recommendations:

> Occasionally, the solution of a proprietary problem may shed light on some aspect of the algorithm which could not be seen otherwise. Nonetheless, we believe that these problems should be referred to in the report only under special circumstances and with adequate justification. . . . Experiments involving the use of proprietary programs should only be published because of the presentation of a new strategy or of new theoretical developments. Authors should be willing to reproduce their experiments for the referees. Where necessary, referees should exercise this right. (pp. 199, 201)

References

[1] Adler, I. 1983. "The Expected Number of Pivots Needed to Solve Parametric Linear Programs and the Efficiency of the Self-Dual Simplex Method." Technical Report, Department of Industrial Engineering and Operations Research, University of California–Berkeley.

[2] Adler, I., and S. E. Berenguer. 1981. "Random Linear Programs." Technical Report ORC 81-4, Operations Research Center, University of California–Berkeley.

[3] Adler, I., and S. E. Berenguer. 1981. "Duality Theory and the Random Generation of Linear Programs." Technical Report, Department of Industrial Engineering and Operations Research, University of California–Berkeley.

[4] Adler, I., and S. E. Berenguer. "Generating Random Linear Programs." Technical Report, Department of Industrial Engineering and Operations Research, University of California–Berkeley.

[5] Adler, I., R. M. Karp, and R. Shamir. 1983. "A Family of Simplex Variants Solving an $m \times d$ Linear Program in Expected Number of Pivots Depending on d Only." Report UCB CSD 83/157, Computer Science Division, University of California–Berkeley.

[6] Adler, I., R. M. Karp, and R. Shamir. 1983. "A Simplex Variant Solving an $m \times d$ Linear Program in $O(\min(m^2, d^2))$ Expected Number of Pivot Steps." Report UCB CSD 83/158, Computer Science Division, University of California–Berkeley.

[7] Adler, I., and N. Megiddo. 1985. "A Simplex Algorithm Whose Average Number of Steps Is Bounded between Two Quadratic Functions of the Smaller Dimension." *Journal of the Association for Computing Machinery* 32: 871-95.

[8] Adler, I., N. Megiddo, and M. J. Todd. 1984. "New Results on the Behavior of Simplex Algorithms." *Bulletin of the American Mathematical Society* 11: 378-82.

[9] Aho, A. V., J. E. Hopcroft, and J. D. Ullman. 1974. *The Design and Analysis of Computer Algorithm.* Reading, Mass.: Addison-Wesley.

[10] Akgul, M. 1985. "A Genuinely Polynomial Primal Simplex Algorithm for the Assignment Problem." Presented at the 12th Symposium on Mathematical Programming, Cambridge, Mass.

[11] Anstreicher, K. M. 1985. "Analysis of a Modified Karmarkar Algorithm for Linear Programming." Working Paper Series B#84, School of Organization and Management, Yale University.

[12] Aspvall, B., and Y. Shiloach. 1980. "A Polynomial Algorithm for Solving Systems of Linear Inequalities with Two Variables per Inequality." *SIAM Journal on Computing* 9: 827–45.

[13] Avis, D., and V. Chvatal. 1978. "Notes on Bland's Pivoting Rule." *Mathematical Programming Study* 8: 24–34.

[14] Baathe, O., and P. O. Lindberg. 1985. "Studies on the Efficiency of the Stochastic Simplex Method." Presented at the 12th Symposium on Mathematical Programming, Cambridge, Mass.

[15] Balinski, M. L. 1984. "The Hirsch Conjecture for Dual Transportation Polyhedra." *Mathematics of Operations Research* 9: 629–33.

[16] Balinski, M. L. 1984. "A Good (Dual) Simplex Method for the Assignment Problem." Report AD 275.07.84, C.N.R.S., Laboratoire d'Econometrie, de l'Ecole Polytechnique, Paris.

[17] Balinski, M. L. 1985. "Signature Methods for the Assignment Problem." *Operations Research* 33: 527–36.

[18] Balinski, M. L., Th. M. Leibling, and A.-E. Nobs. 1985. "On the Average Length of Lexicographic Paths." RO 850415, Department de Mathematiques, Ecole Polytechnique Federale de Lausanne, CH-1015 Lausanne-Ecublens, Switzerland.

[19] Barnes, E. R. 1985. "A Variation on Karmarkar's Algorithm for Solving Linear Programming Problems." Research Report No. RC 11136, IBM T. S. Watson Research Center, Yorktown Heights, New York.

[20] Blair, C. E. 1983. "Random Linear Programs with Many Variables and Few Constraints." Faculty Working Paper No. 946, College of Commerce and Business Administration, University of Illinois–Champaign-Urbana.

[21] Blair, C. E. 1985. "The Iterative Step in the Linear Programming Algorithm of N. Karmarkar." Unpublished manuscript, College of Commerce and Business Administration, University of Illinois–Champaign-Urbana.

[22] Bland, R. G. 1977. "A Combinatorial Abstraction of Linear Programming." *Journal of Combinatorial Theory* 23 (B): 33–57.

[23] Bland, R. G. 1978. "New Finite Pivoting Rules." *Mathematics of Operations Research* 3: 103–7.

[24] Bland, R. G., D. Goldfarb, and M. J. Todd. 1981. "The Ellipsoid Method: A Survey." *Operations Research* 29: 1039–91.

[25] Blum, L. G. 1985. "Towards an Asymptotic Analysis of Karmarkar's Algorithm. Extended abstract.

[26] Borgwardt, K.-H. 1977. "Untersuchungen zur Asymptotik der mittleren Schriftzahl von Simplexverfahren in der Linearen Optimierung." Disserta-

tion, Universität Kaiserlautern.

[27] Borgwardt, K.-H. 1982. "Some Distribution-Independent Results about the Asymptotic Order of the Average Number of Pivot Steps of the Simplex Method." *Mathematics of Operations Research* 7: 441-62.

[28] Borgwardt, K.-H. 1982. "The Average Number of Steps Required by the Simplex Method Is Polynomial." *Zeitschrift für Operations Research* 26: 157-77.

[29] Borgwardt, K.-H. 1985. "Average Behavior of the Simplex Algorithm: Some Improvements in the Analysis of the Rotation-Symmetry-Model." Presented at the 12th Symposium on Mathematical Programming, Cambridge, Mass.

[30] Borodin, A., J. von zur Gathen, and J. E. Hopcroft. 1982. "Fast Parallel Matrix and GCD Computations." *Information and Control* 52: 241-56.

[31] Buck, R. C. 1943. "Partition of Space." *American Mathematical Monthly* 50: 541-4.

[32] Cavalier, T. M., and A. L. Soyster. 1985. "Some Computational Experience and a Modification of the Karmarkar Algorithm." Presented at the 12th Symposium on Mathematical Programming, Cambridge, Mass.

[33] Chandru, V., and B. P. Kochar. 1985. "A Class of Algorithms for Linear Programming." Presented at the 12th Symposium on Mathematical Programming, Cambridge, Mass.

[34] Charnes, A., T. Song, and M. Wolfe. 1984. "An Explicit Solution Sequence and Convergence of Karmarkar's Algorithm." Unpublished manuscript, University of Texas–Austin.

[35] Chvatal, V. 1983. *Linear Programming*. New York: W. H. Freeman and Co.

[36] Clarkson, K. 1984. "Linear Programming in $O(n(5/2)^d 3^{d^2})$ Time." Unpublished manuscript, Department of Computer Science, Stanford University.

[37] Clausen, J. "Recent Results on the Complexity of the Simplex Algorithm." Presented at the 12th Symposium on Mathematical Programming, Cambridge, Mass.

[38] Cline, A. K. 1970. "Uniform Approximation as a Limit of L_2 Approximations." Ph.D. thesis, University of Michigan.

[39] Cline, A. K. 1972. "Rate of Convergence of Lawson's Algorithm." *Mathematics of Computation* 26: 167-76.

[40] Crowder, H., R. S. Dembo, and J. M. Mulvey. 1979. "On Reporting Computational Experience with Mathematical Software." *ACM Transactions on Mathematical Software* 5: 193-203.

[41] Cunningham, W. H. 1976. "A Network Simplex Method." *Mathematical Programming* 11: 105-16.

[42] Cunningham, W. H. 1979. "Theoretical Properties of the Network Simplex Method." *Mathematics of Operations Research* 4: 196-298.

[43] Dantzig, G. B. 1963. *Linear Programming and Extensions*. Princeton, N.J.: Princeton University Press.

[44] Dantzig, G. B. 1980. "Expected Number of Steps for a Linear Program with a Convexity Constraint." Technical Report SOL 80-3, Systems Optimization Laboratory, Department of Operations Research, Stanford University.

[45] de Ghellinck, G., and J.-Ph. Vial. 1985. "An Extension of Karmarkar's Algorithm for Solving a System of Linear Homogenous Equations on the Simplex." Discussion Paper No. 8538, C.O.R.E., Catholic University of Louvain, Belgium.

[46] Dobkin, D. P., and S. P. Reiss. 1980. "The Complexity of Linear Programming." *Theoretical Computer Science* 11: 1–18.

[47] Dunham, R., D. G. Kelly, and J. W. Tolle. 1977. "Some Experimental Results Concerning the Expected Number of Pivots for Solving Randomly Generated Linear Programs." Report TR 77-16, Operations Research and Systems Analysis Department, University of North Carolina–Chapel Hill.

[48] Dyer, M. E. 1984. "Linear Time Algorithms for Two- and Three-Variable Linear Programs." *SIAM Journal on Computing* 13: 31–45.

[49] Dyer, M. E. 1984. "An $O(n)$ Algorithm for Multiple-Choice Knapsack Linear Program." *Mathematical Programming* 29: 57–63.

[50] Dyer, M. E. 1984. "On a Multidimensional Search Technique and Its Application to the Euclidean One-Center Problem." Department of Mathematics and Statistics, Teesside Polytechnic, Middlesbrough, Cleveland TS1 3BA, United Kingdom.

[51] Eaves, B. C., and U. G. Rothblum. 1985. "A Theory of Extending Algorithms for Parametric Problems." Technical Report RE5685, Department of Operations Research, Stanford University.

[52] Eaves, B. C., and H. Scarf. 1976. "The Solution of Systems of Piecewise Linear Equations." *Mathematics of Operations Research* 1: 1–27.

[53] Edmonds, J. 1967. "Systems of Distinct Representatives and Linear Algebra." *Journal of Research of the National Bureau of Standards* 71B: 241–5.

[54] Edmonds, J., and R. M. Karp. 1972. "Theoretical Improvements in Algorithmic Efficiency for Network Flow Problems." *Journal of the Association for Computing Machinery* 19: 248–64.

[55] Fiacco, A. V., and G. P. McCormick. 1968. *Nonlinear Programming: Sequential Unconstrained Minimization Techniques.* New York: J. Wiley and Sons.

[56] Frank, A., and E. Tardos. 1985. "An Application of Simultaneous Approximation in Combinatorial Optimization." In *Proceedings of the 26th Annual IEEE Symposium on Foundations of Computer Science (1985),* pp. 459–63. Los Angeles: IEEE Computer Society Press.

[57] Frisch, K. R. 1955. "The Logarithmic Potential Method of Convex Programming." Unpublished manuscript, University Institute of Economics, Oslo, Norway.

[58] Fujishige, S. 1985. "An $O(m^3 \log m)$ Capacity-Rounding Algorithm for the Minimum-Cost Circulation Problem: A Dual Framework of the Tardos Algorithm." Technical Report No. 254 (85-3), Institute of Socio-Economic Planning, University of Tsukuba, Sakura, Ibaraki 305, Japan.

[59] Gay, D. M. 1985. "A Variant of Karmarkar's Linear Programming Algorithm for Problems in Standard Form." Presented at the 12th Symposium on Mathematical Programming, Cambridge, Mass.

[60] Gill, P. E., W. Murray, M. A. Saunders, J. A. Tomlin, and M. H. Wright. 1985. "On Projected Newton Barrier Methods for Linear Programming and an Equivalence to Karmarkar's Projective Method." Technical Report SOL 85-11, Systems Optimization Laboratory, Department of Operations Research, Stanford University.

[61] Gill, P. E., W. Murray, and M. H. Wright. 1981. *Practical Optimization.* New York: Academic Press.

[62] Goldfarb, D. 1985. "Dual Simplex Algorithms for the Assignment Problem." Presented at the 12th Symposium on Mathematical Programming, Cambridge, Mass.

[63] Goldfarb, D., and W. Sit. 1979. "Worst Case Behavior of the Steepest Edge Simplex Method." *Discrete Applied Mathematics* 1: 277–85.

[64] Grotschel, M., L. Lovasz, and A. Schrijver. 1981. "The Ellipsoid Method and Its Consequences in Combinatorial Optimization." *Combinatorica* 1: 169–97.

[65] Grotschel, M., L. Lovasz, and A. Schrijver. 1984. "Corrigendum to Our Paper 'The Ellipsoid Method and Its Consequences in Combinatorial Optimization'." *Combinatorica* 4: 291–5.

[66] Grunbaum, B. 1967. *Convex Polytopes.* New York: Wiley.

[67] Haimovich, M. 1983. "The Simplex Algorithm Is Very Good! – On the Expected Number of Pivot Steps and Related Properties of Random Linear Programs." Technical Report, Columbia University.

[68] Haverly, C. A. 1985. "Behavior of the Simplex and Karmarkar Algorithms." Presented at the 12th Symposium on Mathematical Programming, Cambridge, Mass.

[69] Hoffman, A. J., M. Mannos, D. Sokolowsky, and N. Wiegmann. 1953. "Computational Experience in Solving Linear Programs." *J. Soc. Indust. Applied. Math.* 1: 17–33.

[70] Howe, R. 1983. "Linear Complementarity and the Average Volume of Simplicial Cones." Cowles Foundation Discussion Paper No. 670, Yale University.

[71] Huard, P. 1967. "Resolution of Mathematical Programming with Nonlinear Constraints by the Method of Centers." In J. Abadie (ed.), *Nonlinear Programming,* pp. 207–19. Amsterdam: North-Holland.

[72] Hung, M. S. 1983. "A Polynomial Simplex Method for the Assignment Problem." *Operations Research* 31: 595–600.

[73] Ikura, Y., and G. L. Nemhauser. 1982. "An Efficient Primal Simplex Algorithm for Maximum Weighted Vertex Packing on Bipartite Graphs." *Annals of Discrete Mathematics* 16: 149–68.

[74] Ikura, Y., and G. L. Nemhauser. 1983. "A Polynomial-Time Dual Simplex Algorithm for the Transportation Problem." Technical Report No. 602, School of Operations Research and Industrial Engineering, Cornell University.

[75] Iri, M. 1985. "Another 'Simple and Fast' Algorithm for Linear Programming." Presented at the 12th Symposium on Mathematical Programming, Cambridge, Mass.

[76] Iri, M., and H. Imai. 1985. "A Multiplicative Penalty Function Method for Linear Programming – Another 'New and Fast' Algorithm." Research Memorandum RMI 85-04, Department of Mathematical Engineering and Instrumentation Physics, University of Tokyo, Tokyo, Japan.

[77] Jeroslow, R. G. 1973. "Asymptotic Linear Programming." *Operations Research* 21: 1128–41.

[78] Jeroslow, R. G. 1973. "The Simplex Algorithm with the Pivot Rule of Maximizing Criterion Improvement." *Discrete Mathematics* 4: 367–77.

[79] Karmarkar, N. 1984. "A New Polynomial-Time Algorithm for Linear Programming." In *Proceedings of the 16th Annual ACM Symposium on Theory of Computing (1984)*, pp. 302–11. New York: ACM. Revised version in *Combinatorica* 4: 373–95.

[80] Karmarkar, N. K. 1985. "Further Developments in the New Polynomial Time Algorithm for Linear Programming." Presented at the 12th Symposium on Mathematical Programming, Cambridge, Mass.

[81] Karmarkar, N. K., and L. P. Sinha. 1985. "Application of Karmarkar's Algorithm to Overseas Telecommunications Facilities Planning." Presented at the 12th Symposium on Mathematical Programming, Cambridge, Mass.

[82] Karp, R. M., and C. H. Papadimitriou. 1980. "On Linear Characterizations of Combinatorial Optimization Problems." In *Proceedings of the 21st Annual IEEE Symposium on Foundations of Computer Science (1980)*, pp. 1–9. Los Angeles: IEEE Computer Society Press.

[83] Khachiyan, L. G. 1979. "A Polynomial Algorithm in Linear Programming." *Soviet Math. Dokl.* 20: 191–4.

[84] Khachiyan, L. G. 1980. "Polynomial Algorithms in Linear Programming." *USSR Computational Mathematics and Mathematical Physics* 20: 53–72.

[85] Klee, V., and G. J. Minty. 1972. "How Good Is the Simplex Algorithm?" In O. Shisha (ed.), *Inequalities III*, pp. 159–75. New York: Academic Press.

[86] Klee, V., and D. W. Walkup. 1967. "The d-Step Conjecture for Polyhedra of Dimension $d < 6$." *Acta Math.* 117: 53–78.

[87] Kojima, M. 1985. "Determining Basic Variables of Optimum Solutions in Karmarkar's New LP Algorithm." Research Report No. B-164, Department of Information Sciences, Tokyo Institute of Technology, O-Okayama, Meguro-ku, Tokyo, Japan.

[88] Kolata, G. 1979. "Mathematicians Amazed by Russian's Discovery." *Science* (2 November): 545–6.

[89] Kolata, G. 1982. "Mathematician Solves Simplex Problem." *Science* (2 July): 39.

[90] Kolata, G. 1984. "A Fast Way to Solve Hard Problems." *Science* (21 September): 1379–80.

[91] Kortanek, K. O., D. N. Lee, and M. Shi. 1985. "An Application of a Hybrid Algorithm for Semi-Infinite Programming." Presented at the 12th Symposium on Mathematical Programming, Cambridge, Mass.

[92] Kozlov, M. K., S. P. Tarasov, and L. G. Khachiyan. 1979. "Polynomial Solvability of Convex Quadratic Programming." *Dokl. Akad. Nauk SSSR* 5: 1051–3.

[93]   Kuhn, H., and R. E. Quandt. 1963. "An Experimental Study of the Simplex Method." *American Mathematical Society, Proc. Symp. Appl. Math.* 15: 107-24.

[94]   Lawson, C. L. 1961. "Contributions to the Theory of Linear Least Maximum Approximation." Ph.D. thesis, University of California–Los Angeles.

[95]   Lee, D. T., and F. F. Preparata. 1984. "Computational Geometry – A Survey." *IEEE Transactions on Computers* C-33: 1072-1101.

[96]   Lemke, C. E. 1965. "Bimatrix Equilibrium Points and Mathematical Programming." *Management Science* 11: 681-9.

[97]   Lenstra, A. K., H. W. Lenstra, Jr., and L. Lovasz. 1982. "Factoring Polynomials with Rational Coefficients." *Math. Ann.* 26: 515-34.

[98]   Lenstra, H. W., Jr. 1983. "Integer Programming with a Fixed Number of Variables." *Mathematics of Operations Research* 8: 538-48.

[99]   Levin, A. Yu. 1965. "On an Algorithm for Convex Minimization." *Soviet Mathematics Doklady* 160.

[100] Liebling, Th. M. 1973. "On the Number of Iterations of the Simplex Method." In R. Henn, H. Kunzi, and H. Schubert (eds.), *Methods of Operation Research* 17: 284-64.

[101] Lustig, I. 1985. "A Practical Approach to Karmarkar's Algorithm." Technical Report SOL 85-5, Systems Optimization Laboratory, Department of Operations Research, Stanford University.

[102] Mangasarian, O. 1984. "Normal Solutions of Linear Programs." *Mathematical Programming Study* 22: 206-16.

[103] Marsten, R. E., and D. F. Shanno. 1985. "On Implementing Karmarkar's Algorithm." Presented at the 12th Symposium on Mathematical Programming, Cambridge, Mass.

[104] May, J., and R. Smith. 1982. "Random Polytopes: Their Definition, Generation, and Aggregate Properties." *Mathematical Programming* 24: 39-54.

[105] Megiddo, N. 1982. "Is Binary Encoding Appropriate for the Problem-Language Relationship?" *Theoretical Computer Science* 19: 337-41.

[106] Megiddo, N. 1982. "Polylog Algorithms for LP with Application to Exploding Flying Objects." Unpublished manuscript, Carnegie-Mellon University.

[107] Megiddo, N. 1983. "Towards a Genuinely Polynomial Algorithm for Linear Programming." *SIAM Journal on Computing* 12: 347-53.

[108] Megiddo, N. 1983. "Linear-Time Algorithms for Linear Programming in R^3 and Related Problems." *SIAM Journal on Computing* 12: 759-76.

[109] Megiddo, N. 1984. "Linear Programming in Linear Time When the Dimension Is Fixed." *Journal of the Association for Computing Machinery* 31: 114-27.

[110] Megiddo, N. 1984. "Dynamic Location Problems." To appear in *Proceedings of the Third International Symposium on Locational Decisions.* Thompson's Island, Mass.

[111] Megiddo, N. 1984. "A Variation on Karmarkar's Algorithm." Unpublished manuscript.

[112] Megiddo, N. 1985. "Partitioning with Two Lines in the Plane." *Journal of Algorithms* 6: 430-3.

[113] Megiddo, N. 1985. "A Note on the Generality of the Self-Dual Simplex Algorithm with Various Starting Points." *Methods of Operations Research* 49: 271-5.

[114] Megiddo, N. 1986. "On the Expected Number of Linear Complementarity Cones Intersected by Random and Semi-Random Rays." *Mathematical Programming* 35: 225-35.

[115] Megiddo, N. 1986. "Improved Asymptotic Analysis of the Average Number of Steps Performed by the Self-Dual Simplex Algorithm." *Mathematical Programming* 35: 140-72.

[116] Megiddo, N., and T. Ichimori. 1985. "A Two-Resource Allocation Problem Solvable in Linear-Time." *Mathematics of Operations Research* 10: 7-16.

[117] Mitra, G., M. Tamiz, J. Yadegar, and K. Darby-Dowman. 1985. "Experimental Investigation of an Interior Search Algorithm for Linear Programming." Presented at the 12th Symposium on Mathematical Programming, Cambridge, Mass.

[118] Motzkin, T. S. 1955. "The Probability of Solvability of Linear Equalities." In H. A. Antosiewicz (ed.), *Proceedings of the Second Symposium in Linear Programming,* pp. 607-11. USAF: National Bureau of Standards and Directorate of Management Analysis.

[119] Murty, K. G. 1978. "Computational Complexity of Complementary Pivot Methods." *Mathematical Programming Study* 7: 61-73.

[120] Murty, K. G. 1980. "Computational Complexity of Parametric Linear Programming." *Mathematical Programming* 19: 213-19.

[121] Murty, K. G. 1985. "A New Interior Variant of the Gradient Projection Method for Linear Programming." Technical Paper 85-18, Department of Industrial and Operations Engineering, University of Michigan.

[122] Murty, K. G., and Y. Fathi. 1984. "A Feasible Direction Method for Linear Programming." *Operations Research Letters* 3: 121-7.

[123] Nazareth, J. L. "Karmarkar's Method and Homotopies with Restarts." Manuscript, CDSS, P.O. Box 4908, Berkeley, Calif. 94704.

[124] Orden, A. 1976. "Computational Investigation and Analysis of Probabilistic Parameters of Convergence of a Simplex Algorithm." In *Progress in Operations Research II,* pp. 705-15. Amsterdam: North-Holland.

[125] Orden, A. 1980. "A Step Towards Probabilistic Analysis of Simplex Convergence." *Mathematical Programming* 19: 3-13.

[126] Orlin, J. B. 1984. "Genuinely Polynomial Simplex and Nonsimplex Algorithms for the Min-Cost Flow Problem." Working Paper 1615-84, Sloan School of Management, Massachusetts Institute of Technology.

[127] Orlin, J. B. 1985. "A Dual Version of Tardos' Algorithm for Linear Programming." Working Paper 1686-85, Sloan School of Management, Massachusetts Institute of Technology.

[128] Orlin, J. B. 1985. "A Polynomial Time Dual Simplex Algorithm for the Minimum Cost Flow Problem." Presented at the 12th Symposium on Mathematical Programming, Cambridge, Mass.

[129] Orlin, J. B. "On the Simplex Algorithm for Networks and Generalized Networks." *Mathematical Programming,* to appear.

[130] Padberg, M. W. 1985. "A Different Convergence Proof of the Projective Method for Linear Programming." Unpublished manuscript, New York University.

[131] Padberg, M. W. 1985. "Solution of a Nonlinear Programming Problem Arising in the Projective Method for Linear Programming." Unpublished manuscript, New York University.

[132] Padberg, M. W., and M. R. Rao. 1980. "The Russian Method and Integer Programming." GBA Working Paper, New York University.

[133] Pan, V. Y. 1983. "On the Computational Complexity of Solving a System of Linear Inequalities." Department of Computer Science, State University of New York.

[134] Pan, V., and J. Reif. 1985. "Efficient Parallel Solution of Linear Systems." In *Proceedings of the 17th Annual ACM Symposium on Theory of Computing (1985),* pp. 143–52. New York: ACM.

[135] Pickel, P. F. 1985. "Implementing the Karmarkar Algorithm Using Simplex Techniques." Presented at the 12th Symposium on Mathematical Programming, Cambridge, Mass.

[136] Rice, J. R., and K. H. Usow. 1968. "The Lawson Algorithm and Extensions." *Mathematics of Computation* 22: 118–27.

[137] Rinaldi, G. 1985. "The Projective Method for Linear Programming with Box-Type Constraints." Report R.119, Instituto di Analisi dei Sistemi ed Informatica del CNR, Viale Manzoni 30, 00815 Roma.

[138] Roohy-Laleh, E. 1981. "Improvements to the Theoretical Efficiency of the Network Method." Ph.D. thesis, Carleton University.

[139] Ross, S. M. 1981. "A Simple Heuristic Approach to Simplex Efficiency." Department of Industrial Engineering and Operations Research, University of California–Berkeley.

[140] Saigal, R. 1983. "On Some Average Results for Random Linear Complementarity Problems." Department of Industrial Engineering, Northwestern University.

[141] Saigal, R. 1983. "An Analysis for the Simplex Method." Preliminary Report, Department of Industrial Engineering, Northwestern University.

[142] Shamir, R. 1984. "The Efficiency of the Simplex Method: A Survey." Department of Industrial Engineering and Operations Research, University of California–Berkeley.

[143] Shostak, R. 1981. "Deciding Linear Inequalities by Computing Loop Residues." *Journal of the Association for Computing Machinery* 28: 769–79.

[144] Smale, S. 1983. "On the Average Number of Steps of the Simplex Method of Linear Programming." *Mathematical Programming* 27: 241–62.

[145] Smale, S. 1983. "The Problem of the Average Speed of the Simplex Method." In A. Bachem, M. Grotschel, and B. Korte (eds.), *Mathematical Programming: The State of the Art,* pp. 530–9. Berlin: Springer-Verlag.

[146] Stone, R. E. 1980. "Khachiyan's Algorithm with Finite Precision." Working Paper SOL 80-1, Department of Operations Research, Stanford University.

[147] Tardos, E. 1984. "A Strongly Polynomial Minimum Cost Circulation Algorithm." Report No. 84356-OR, Institut fur Oconometrie und Operations Research, University of Bonn. Forthcoming in *Combinatorica*.

[148] Tardos, E. 1985. "A Strongly Polynomial Algorithm to Solve Combinatorial Linear Problems." Report No. 84360-OR, Institute for Econometrics and Operations Research, University of Bonn.

[149] Todd, M. J. 1983. "Polynomial Expected Behavior of a Pivoting Algorithm for Linear Complementarity and Linear Programming Problems." Technical Report No. 595, School of Operations Research and Industrial Engineering, Cornell University.

[150] Todd, M. J., and B. P. Burrell. 1985. "The Ellipsoid Algorithm Generates Dual Variables." *Mathematics of Operations Research* 10: 688–700.

[151] Todd, M. J., and B. P. Burrell. 1985. "An Extension of Karmarkar's Algorithm for Linear Programming Using Dual Variables." Technical Report No. 648, School of Operations Research and Industrial Engineering, Cornell University.

[152] Tomlin, J. A. 1985. "An Experimental Approach to Karmarkar's Projective Method for Linear Programming." Report, Ketron, Inc., Mountain View, Calif. 94040.

[153] Traub, J. F., and H. Wozniakowski. 1982. "Complexity of Linear Programming." *Operations Research Letters* 1: 59–62.

[154] Tufecki, S. 1985. "A Polynomial Dual Simplex Algorithm for Assignment and Transportation Problems." Manuscript, University of Florida.

[155] Ursic, S. 1982. "The Ellipsoid Algorithm for Linear Programming in Exact Arithmetic." In *Proceedings of the 23rd Annual IEEE Symposium on Foundations of Computer Science (1982)*, pp. 321–6. Los Angeles: IEEE Computer Society Press.

[156] Vanderbei, R. J., M. J. Meketon, and B. A. Freedman. 1985. "A Modification of Karmarkar's Linear Programming Algorithm." Report, AT&T Bell Laboratories, Holmdel, N.J. 07733.

[157] Vershik, A. M., and P. V. Sporyshev. 1983. "An Estimate of the Average Number of Steps in the Simplex Method, and Problems in Asymptotic Integral Geometry." *Soviet. Math. Dokl.* 28: 195–9.

[158] Wan, Y.-H. 1983. "On the Average Speed of the Lemke's Algorithm for Quadratic Programming." Department of Mathematics, State University of New York–Buffalo.

[159] Yamnitsky, B., and L. A. Levin. 1982. "An Old Linear Programming Algorithm Runs in Polynomial Time." In *Proceedings of the 23rd Annual IEEE Symposium on Foundations of Computer Science (1982)*, pp. 327–8. Los Angeles: IEEE Computer Society Press.

[160] Ye, Y. 1985. "K-Projection and the Cutting-Objective Methods for Linear Programming." Presented at the 12th Symposium on Mathematical Programming, Cambridge, Mass.

[161] Yudin, D. B., and A. S. Nemirovsky. 1976. "Informational Complexity and Effective Methods for Solving Convex Extremum Problems." *Economica i Mat. Metody* 12.

[162] Zadeh, N. 1973. "A Bad Network Problem for the Simplex Method and Other Minimim Cost Flow Algorithms." *Mathematical Programming* 5: 255–66.

[163] Zadeh, N. 1980. "What Is the Worst Case Behavior of the Simplex Algorithm?" Technical Report No. 37, Department of Operations Research, Stanford University.

[164] Zemel, E. 1984. "An $O(n)$ Algorithm for Multiple Choice Knapsack and Related Problems." *Information Processing Letters* 18: 123–8.

CHAPTER 7

Laboratory experimentation in economics

Alvin E. Roth

1   Introduction

Controlled experiments conducted by economists under laboratory conditions have a relatively short history. Only in the last ten years has laboratory experimentation in economics completed the transition from being a seldom-encountered curiosity to a well-established part of the economic literature. (The *Journal of Economic Literature* has this year initiated a separate bibliographic category for "Experimental Economic Methods.") How this came to pass makes for an interesting episode in the history and sociology of science. In this chapter, however, we discuss the different uses to which laboratory experimentation is being put in economics.

I think that, loosely speaking, many of the experiments that have been conducted to date fall on an imaginary continuum somewhere between experiments associated with testing and modifying formal economic theories (which I shall call "Speaking to Theorists"), and those associated with having a direct input into the policy-making process ("Whispering into the Ears of Princes"[1]). Somewhere in between lie experiments designed to collect data on interesting phenomena and important institutions, in the hope of detecting unanticipated regularities ("Searching for Facts"). Most experimental investigations contain elements from more than one of these categories.

I have had helpful correspondence and discussion on this subject with Jack Ochs, Paul Milgrom, and Charles Plott. This work has been supported by grants from the National Science Foundation and the Office of Naval Research, and by a Fellowship from the Alfred P. Sloan Foundation. Charles Plott and Charles Holt graciously gave me permission on behalf of themselves and their colleagues to reproduce figures from their experiments.
[1] This latter kind of laboratory experiment is in some respects close kin to field experiments [see, e.g., Ferber and Hirsch (1982) or Hausman and Wise (1985)].

In the following sections I briefly describe examples of each of these activities, and how they interact with and contribute to other parts of economic research. I like to think of economists who do experiments as being involved in three kinds of (overlapping) dialogues, which the examples are designed to illustrate. Material discussed under the heading "Speaking to Theorists" illustrates the kind of dialogue that can exist between experimenters and theorists, whereas the material in "Searching for Facts" illustrates the kind of dialogue that experimenters can engage in with one another. The section entitled "Whispering in the Ears of Princes" deals of course with the kind of dialogue that experimenters can have with policy makers.

One sign of how experimental economics has grown in recent years is that it would be impossible, in the space available here, even to attempt a comprehensive survey of the great variety of experimental investigations that have been undertaken. My aim here will be only to briefly describe some work exemplifying each of the activities and dialogues mentioned. There are many other examples I could have chosen.[2]

2   Speaking to theorists

The experiments discussed first, in which I have been personally involved [for a fuller discussion, see Roth (forthcoming)], are concerned with two-person bargaining under the following rules. The two agents may allocate some valuable resource between themselves in any way they like, provided they both agree. If they fail to agree on how to allocate the resource, they each receive nothing. This is an example of what is sometimes called a "pure" bargaining game, which can be thought of as the opposite of the idealized case of "perfect" competition: Whereas individual agents have negligible influence under perfect competition, in a pure bargaining game each agent has an absolute veto over every division of the resource between the bargainers.

At least since the time of Edgeworth (1881) it has been argued by some economists that pure bargaining games are fundamentally indeterminate. In the language of cooperative game theory, the problem is that the core of such a game is the large set of outcomes corresponding to the entire set

---

[2] One important topic I will not cover (because it is the subject of another presentation in this symposium) is experimental studies of individual choice behavior. Some provocative discussion of the implications of these studies for economics is found in Thaler (in press) and Knez and Smith (in press), which are contained in a collection of papers [Roth (in press a)] presenting the different points of view of a number of economic experimenters.

of agreements that leave no part of the resource unallocated.[3] The prediction that observed outcomes will be in the core is therefore a fairly weak (although not an empty) prediction. There has thus been considerable sustained interest in developing theories that attempt to predict specific outcomes in the core. Such theories attempt to make use of information concerning some measure of the *intensity* of the agents' preferences, and most often do so by using the kind of information contained in a von Neumann–Morgenstern expected-utility function representing those preferences.[4] That is, these theories attempt to predict the outcome of bargaining on the basis of information about each bargainer's willingness to tolerate risk.

In the theoretical literature concerned with such matters, these theories were regarded primarily as offering predictions about bargaining conducted under conditions of complete information, in which bargainers were assumed to know the information about one another's preferences contained in their expected utility functions. The formal requirements of the complete-information condition were often regarded as an idealization, incapable of a concrete realization. Furthermore, it was sometimes argued that basing a theoretical model of bargaining on the complete information contained in the agents' utility functions was somehow overdetermining the problem; that is, the actual phenomena being modeled would be sensitive only to a subset of this information. In any event, because an agent's willingness to tolerate risk cannot be readily observed in uncontrolled, naturally occurring environments, theories of this kind proved unusually difficult to test with field data.

Laboratory experimentation offers (at least) two promising approaches for testing theories whose predictions are sensitive to difficult-to-observe attributes of the agents, such as their risk posture and information. The first of these is to design experiments that control for individual differences on the relevant dimensions, using the extensive possibilities for control inherent in setting up economic environments in the laboratory [in contrast to (nonexperimental) field studies, where the environment must be taken as given]. The second is to measure directly the relevant attri-

---

[3] And this same set of outcomes can be achieved as the equilibria of the game in strategic form.

[4] The most influential single theory of this sort is one due to John Nash (1950), whose work led to the development of a family of related theories in the tradition of cooperative game theory [see Roth (1979) for a full account]. More recently, there has been a growing body of work on theories of bargaining in the tradition of noncooperative game theory [see Roth (1985a) for a collection of representative work]. Some of this work uses information about time preference rather than risk preference in the preferences of the bargainers, in a manner exemplified by Rubinstein (1982).

butes of agents, taking advantage of the relatively unrestricted access to agents that is available in the laboratory (again, in contrast to field studies). My colleagues and I found it convenient to use the first of these approaches to test theoretical predictions concerning what information possessed by the agents would influence the outcome of bargaining, and to use the second approach to test predictions concerning the effects of differences in the bargainers' risk postures.

For the experiments designed to test predictions about the distribution of information on the outcome of bargaining, an experimental design was developed [see Roth and Malouf (1979)] that controlled for the risk preferences of the bargainers. Bargainers play binary lottery games in which each agent i can eventually win only one of two monetary prizes, a large prize λ_i or a small prize σ_i ($\lambda_i > \sigma_i$). The players bargain over the distribution of lottery tickets that determine the probability of receiving the large prize: For instance, an agent i who receives 70 percent of the lottery tickets has a 70 percent chance of receiving the amount λ_i and a 30 percent chance of receiving the amount σ_i. Players who do not reach agreement in the alloted time each receive σ_i. Because the information about preferences conveyed by an expected utility function is meaningfully represented only up to the arbitrary choice of origin and scale, there is no loss of generality in normalizing each agent's utility so that $u_i(\lambda_i) = 1$ and $u_i(\sigma_i) = 0$. The utility of agent i for any agreement is then precisely equal to his probability of receiving the amount λ_i, that is, equal to the percentage of lottery tickets he receives.[5]

Note that restricting each agent to an environment in which all choices involve lotteries over only two ultimate payoffs (receiving his large prize or his small prize) controls out the effects of risk aversion or risk preference, phenomena that arise in making tradeoffs among three or more outcomes. That is, on the restricted choice domain of a binary lottery game, the differences in risk posture that individuals bring to the bargaining table are controlled away; that is, they have no scope for expression. Consequently, theories such as Nash's (and a broad class of related axiomatic

[5] Of course, we have not addressed here the (empirical) question of whether a given individual's choice behavior can indeed be summarized by a preference relation exhibiting the regularity conditions needed for it to be accurately represented by an expected-utility function. In fact, a substantial body of empirical work has recorded a number of systematic ways in which individual preferences often fail to exhibit these regularities. However, virtually all of these departures from expected-utility maximization involve the way tradeoffs are made among three or more riskless alternatives [see Machina (1983)]. Consequently, these kinds of departures cannot occur when only two such alternatives are feasible, as in a binary lottery game. Some methodological innovations that make clear how to extend the use of binary lottery games to experimentally explore a wide variety of economic environments have been described by Berg et al. (1986).

and strategic theories), which distinguish between individual bargainers only on the basis of their expected utility payoffs, treat all bargainers in binary lottery games symmetrically. One prediction of such theories is that resulting agreements will give each bargainer 50 percent of the lottery tickets. This is so independently of the value of the monetary prizes and (specifically) independently of whether the prizes of one bargainer are equal to those of the other.

Note further that bargaining under this design meets the requirement for being a game of complete information, because the information determining each agent's utility for any outcome is his percentage of lottery tickets at that outcome (which is common knowledge). The design thus provides the opportunity to test the predictions of various economic theories of bargaining precisely on the domain to which they are intended to apply. Since the bargainers have complete information whether or not they know the value of one another's prizes, a second prediction made by theories of bargaining that use as data only this information is that the outcome of bargaining will be the same when bargainers know one another's prizes as when they do not.

The experiment of Roth and Malouf (1979) was designed in part to test these predictions, and to determine whether or not changes in the sizes of the prizes, and whether the bargainers knew one another's prizes, influenced the outcome. Each bargainer played games with different prizes[6] against different opponents in one of two information conditions. In the "full-information" condition, each bargainer knew both his own prize and that of the other bargainer; bargainers who were assigned to the "partial-information" condition knew only their own prize value.

The results of the experiment were that – in the partial-information condition, and also in those full-information games where the two bargainers had equal prizes – agreements were observed to cluster, with very low variance, around the equal-probability agreement giving each bargainer 50 percent of the lottery tickets. In full-information games where the bargainers' prizes were not equal, agreements tended to be distributed between two focal points: the equal-probability agreement and the equal-expected-value agreement giving each bargainer the same expected value. That is, in these games the bargainer with the lower prize tended to receive a higher share of the lottery tickets. Contrary to the prediction of the theory, the monetary value of the bargainers' prizes and whether each bargainer knew his opponent's prize were both clearly observed to influence the outcome.

My first inclination on seeing these results was that they would be ex-

---

[6] In these games the small prize was always equal to zero for both bargainers.

plainable within the framework of traditional noncooperative (strategic) game-theoretic models, by modeling the game in greater detail so as to take into account the larger strategy sets that more information gives to the bargainers. However, an experiment utilizing a strategically equivalent bargaining environment in which bargainers knew the value of one another's prizes in terms of an artificial intermediate commodity (rather than in terms of their monetary value) showed that this was not the case [Roth, Malouf, and Murnighan (1981)]. Information about the artificial commodity did not affect the outcomes in the same way as did strategically equivalent information about money. The results of this experiment supported the hypothesis that there is a *social* aspect to the focal-point phenomenon that depends on something like the players' shared perceptions of the credibility of any bargaining position.

Although it is still not clear what theoretical tools can fruitfully be brought to bear on the task of explaining this class of unpredicted phenomena, it was not too difficult to design experiments to explore it further. The experiment of Roth and Murnighan (1982) was designed to separate the observed effect of information into components that could be attributed to the possession of specific information by specific individuals.

Each game of that experiment was a binary lottery game where one player had a $20 prize and the other a $5 prize. In all eight conditions of the experiment, each player knew at least his own prize. The experiment used a 4 (information) × 2 (common knowledge) factorial design. The information conditions were: (1) neither knows his opponent's prize; (2) the $20 player knows both prizes but the $5 player knows only his own prize; (3) the $5 player knows both prizes but the $20 player knows only his own prize; and (4) both players know both prizes. The second factor made this information common knowledge for half the bargaining pairs, but not common knowledge for the other half.[7] Note that the two conditions making it common knowledge that neither player knew both prizes or that both players knew both prizes provide a replication of the experiment of Roth and Malouf (1979).

The results of this experiment permitted three principal conclusions. First, the equal-expected-value agreement becomes a focal point if and

---

[7] For example, when the $20 player is the only one who knows both prizes then the (common) instructions to both players in the common-knowledge condition reveal that both players are reading the same instructions, and that after the instructions are presented one player will be informed of only his own prize while the other will be informed of both prizes. In the noncommon-knowledge condition, the instructions simply state that each player will be informed of his own prize and may or may not be informed of the other prize.

only if the player with the smaller prize knows both prizes. When the $5 player knew that the other player's prize was $20, this was reflected not only in his messages and proposals, but also in the mean agreements (when agreement was reached) and in the shape of the distribution of agreements (see Figure 1). Note that, in the four conditions where the $5 player does not know his opponent's prize, the distribution of agreements has a single mode corresponding to the 50:50 equal-probability agreement. However, in the four conditions where the $5 player *does* know that the other player has a $20 prize, the distribution of agreements is bimodal, with a second mode corresponding to the 20:80 equal-expected-value agreement. The mean agreements that are reached when neither player knows both prizes and when both players know both prizes replicate the results of Roth and Malouf (1979), both in direction and magnitude.

Second, the frequency of disagreement is influenced by whether or not the information possessed by the bargainers is common knowledge. The frequency of disagreement in the two noncommon-knowledge conditions where the $5 player knew both prizes is significantly higher than in the other conditions. The highest frequency of disagreement (33%) occurs when the $5 player knows both prizes, the $20 player does not, but the $5 player is unaware that the $20 player does not know both prizes. [In this situation, the $5 player cannot accurately assess whether or not the $20 player's (honest) skepticism that his opponent's prize is only $5 is just a bargaining ploy.]

Third, in the noncommon-knowledge conditions, the relationship among the outcomes is consistent with the hypothesis that the bargainers are rational utility maximizers who correctly assess the tradeoffs involved in the negotiations. That is, in the noncommon-knowledge conditions there is a tradeoff between the higher payoffs demanded by the $5 player when he knows both prizes (as reflected in the mean agreements reached), and the number of agreements actually reached (as reflected in the frequency of disagreement). One could imagine that, when $5 players knew both prizes, as a group they might have tended to persist in unrealistic ambitions about how high a percentage of lottery tickets they could expect to get. The mean overall payoffs (which include both agreements and disagreements) indicate that this is not the case. The increase in the number of disagreements just offsets the improvement in the terms of agreement when the $5 players know both prizes, so that the overall expected payoff to the $5 players does not change. This means that the behavior that $5 players were observed to employ in any one of these conditions could not profitably have been substituted for the behavior observed in any other condition. The same is true of the $20 players: In particular, the expected

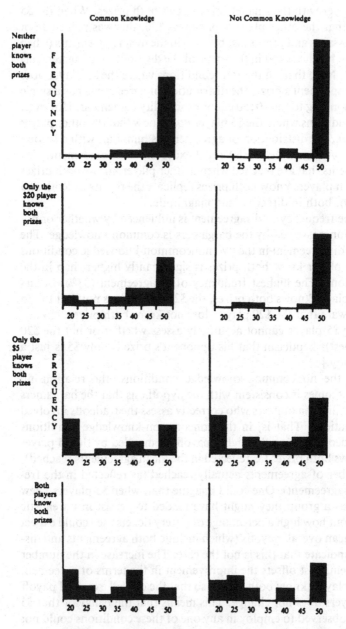

Figure 1. Frequency of agreements in terms of the percentage of lottery tickets obtained by the $20 player.

payoff of $20 players who knew both prizes does not differ from that of those who knew only their own prize (although it is significantly affected by what the $5 player knows), so that a $20 player who knew both prizes, for example, could not have profited from behaving as he would have if he knew only his own prize.

Thus, although the effect of information and the bimodal distribution of agreements between focal points observed in all of these experiments are unpredicted by existing theory, the data nevertheless exhibits observable regularities that resemble other phenomena for which theoretical models exist, such as equilibrium behavior in certain games of incomplete information. It is common in incomplete-information models to observe a "screening" effect, in which a bargainer whose (private) attributes put him in an unusually strong bargaining position must distinguish himself from weaker bargainers by demonstrating a willingness to accept some higher cost, such as a higher probability of disagreement [see, e.g., Chatterjee (1985)]. Although these models will not be directly applicable (since the experimental observations discussed here occur under conditions of complete information), the pattern of observable regularities suggests that theories capable of describing these phenomena may not necessarily have to be radical departures from existing theories.

However, the evidence also suggests that descriptive theories of bargaining will have to take account of some information beyond the traditional game-theoretic specification of what constitutes complete information. [Recall that the experiment of Roth, Malouf, and Murnighan (1981) identified a social component to the observed effect of information about prize values.] A subsequent experiment [Roth and Schoumaker (1983)] lends support to the hypothesis that the effect of information about the cash value of prizes is attributable to its effect on the *expectations* of the bargainers about what constitutes a credible bargaining position. Such information may help bargainers (and theorists) to select from among the multiplicity of equilibria that are found in bargaining games [cf. Rubinstein (1985)].

So far, the bargaining experiments discussed here have focused on observable effects due to experimental manipulations that existing theory predicts should have no effect. Such manipulations are a powerful experimental device for exploring the underlying assumptions of a given theory or class of theories.[8] However, the significance of these unpredicted effects for our evaluation of the overall state of the theory cannot

---

[8] Compare this to the research strategy followed by, e.g., Kahneman and Tversky on utility theory and "framing effects" in individual choice. [See Kahneman and Tversky (1984), Tversky and Kahneman (1981), Thaler (in press).]

be evaluated in isolation. We must also consider the descriptive power of the theory's *predicted* effects, and conduct experiments that will permit us to evaluate how well the theory predicts the effects of manipulating those factors that it designates as important.

Risk posture is obviously an important factor in the predictions of theories that are stated in terms of the von Neumann–Morgenstern utilities of the bargainers. In turned out, however, that the predictions of these theories about the specific effects of risk aversion had not been developed in a way that yielded experimentally testable hypotheses. (One indirect virtue of experimentation is that it can provide a discipline to theoretical work and suggest directions in which theory ought to be explored.) To this end, therefore, a systematic study of the predictions of these models relating to risk posture of the bargainers was carried out in Roth (1979), Kihlstrom, Roth, and Schmeidler (1981), Roth and Rothblum (1982), and Roth (1985b). Rather surprisingly, a very broad class of apparently quite different models, including all the standard axiomatic models[9] and the strategic model of Rubinstein (1982),[10] yield a common prediction regarding risk aversion. Loosely speaking, these models all predict that risk aversion is disadvantageous in bargaining, except when the bargaining concerns potential agreements that have a positive probability of yielding an outcome that is worse than disagreement. That is, these models all predict that a personal attribute of the bargainers – specifically, their risk aversion – will have a decisive influence on the outcome of the bargaining. This prediction concerning risk aversion is important to test because it connects the theory of bargaining with what has proved to be one of the most powerful explanatory hypotheses in a number of other areas of economics – for example, in explanations of investment behavior, futures markets, and insurance.

Three studies exploring the predicted effects of risk aversion on the outcome of bargaining are reported in Murnighan, Roth, and Schoumaker (1985). Whereas binary lottery games were employed in the earlier experiments precisely in order to control out the individual variation due to differences in risk posture, these studies employed ternary lottery games with *three* possible payoffs for each bargainer i. These are large and small prizes λ_i and σ_i obtained by lottery when agreement is reached, and a disagreement price δ_i obtained when no agreement is reached in the allotted time. (In binary lottery games, $\sigma_i = \delta_i$.)

---

[9] These models include those of Nash (1950), Kalai and Smorodinsky (1975), and Perles and Maschler (1982).

[10] But see Binmore, Rubinstein, and Wollinsky (1985) for an alternative theoretical interpretation.

The bargainers' risk postures were first measured by having them make a set of risky choices. Significant differences in risk aversion were found among the population of participants, even on the relatively modest range of prizes available in these studies (where typical gambles involved choosing between receiving $5 for certain or participating in a lottery with prizes of $\lambda_i = \$16$ and $\sigma_i = \$4$).

Those bargainers with relatively high risk aversion bargained against those with relatively low risk aversion in pairs of games such that $\delta_i > \sigma_i$ in one game and $\delta_i < \sigma_i$ in the other. The prediction of game-theoretic models such as Nash's is that agreements reached in the first game should be more favorable to the more risk-averse of the two bargainers than agreements reached in the second game.

The results of these experiments support the predictions of the game-theoretic models, but suggest that – in the (relatively modest) range of payoffs studied here – the effects due to risk aversion are smaller than some of the focal-point effects observed in previous experiments. The significance of this is that the classical models of bargaining attribute the entire variability in bargaining outcomes to the difference in bargainers' risk posture, and predict no influence for the information (about prizes) that allows a second focal point to come into play. Our observations here are that the predicted cause of variability has less effect in this range of prizes than the unpredicted cause. Even if subsequent experiments should show an increased effect due to risk aversion when the prizes are larger, these results give ample reason for devoting additional effort to theoretical and experimental study of the focal-point phenomenon.

Taken together, these experiments do several things. First, they disconfirm some important aspects of the received theory of bargaining, chief among which is what constitutes a "complete" specification of the information available to bargainers. This is particularly notable in light of the fact that much of the theoretical criticism of the complete-information assumption is founded on the assumption that bargaining is better modeled by assuming that the bargainers have strictly less than complete information. The experimental evidence suggests that although bargainers may certainly be expected in general to have less of *some kinds* of information, the outcome of bargaining is also highly sensitive to information the bargainers may have about each other *in addition* to what is included in complete information about utility functions. These experiments also provide preliminary support for some of the subtle but robust predictions of these bargaining theories about the effect of risk aversion. They also serve to illustrate what I suspect will prove to be fairly typical interactions between formal theories and experiments designed to explore them. But this last point will be easier to discuss once we have looked at some other uses of experimentation.

3   Searching for facts

The set of experiments I discuss next involve markets where buyers and sellers seek to trade with one another under one of a variety of rules of market organization.[11] In each market, sellers were told how many units of a good they could produce and were given a schedule of unit costs – that is, a seller might be told that he may sell up to two units, the first of which will cost him $1.00 to produce and the second $1.25. At the conclusion of the experiment, each seller is paid the sale price of any unit he has sold minus its cost; that is, if the above seller sells only one unit at a price of $1.10, he will receive (a profit of) $0.10 for the transaction. Similarly, buyers are told how many units they can consume, and what the value to them of each unit is. That is, a buyer might be told he can only consume one unit, and it is worth $1.00 to him. At the conclusion of the experiment, each buyer is paid the value to him of any units he has purchased, minus the purchase price. Thus if the above buyer makes a purchase at a price of $0.75, he will receive $0.25 for the transaction.[12] Each agent knows only his own costs or values. All goods are indivisible and homogeneous.

Various rules for making transactions were compared in these experiments. In a *double auction* sellers may make offers and buyers may make bids. Sellers and buyers may make new offers and bids whenever they like; the lowest outstanding offer is the "market asked price" and the highest outstanding bid is the "market bid price." If any seller offers the market bid price or if any buyer bids the market asked price, a transaction is consummated between the seller and buyer whose prices coincide.

In a *single auction* only one side of the market is allowed to suggest prices. There are thus two kinds of single auctions: the *bid* auction, in which buyers may make bids; and the *offer* auction, in which sellers may make offers. Agents on the passive side of the market may merely accept the current market (bid or asked) price, or remain silent. Agents on the active side of the market may revise their prices whenever they wish.

[11] See Smith (1964, 1976, 1982a); Plott and Smith (1978), and Plott (1982). Here I will be concerned with the general design and results of these experiments, and will not discuss details of the procedure.

[12] In the experiments discussed here, agents were effectively forbidden to make trades that would bring them a negative return. In some of these experiments, agents were also credited with a small "commission" for each trade they made.

A transaction occurs when an agent on the passive side of the market accepts the market price.

In a *posted-price market,* as in the single auction, only one side is allowed to suggest prices. However, each agent on the active side of the market must "post" his price when the market opens, and is thereafter not free to change it. There are of course two kinds of posted-price markets, depending on whether sellers are posting offers or buyers are posting bids.

In each of these experiments, some small numbers of buyers and sellers (typically from 4 to 12 of each) engaged in some moderate number of repetitions of such a market (typically 5 to 25 "trading days") under one of the market institutions described above. Each trading day constitutes a new market, with the same agents and parameters. (Thus in the various auctions agents could revise their prices as often as they wished each trading day, but in the posted-price markets prices could be posted only at the beginning of each trading day.) The final payment that subjects received was equal to their total profit on all transactions in all trading days.

In all of the experiments, transaction prices in the final period were observed to be substantially closer to the competitive price than in the first period. This was most clearly observed in the double-auction markets, where many transactions in the final periods occurred precisely at the competitive price and where the quantity traded was virtually always within a single unit of the competitive quantity.

Although other market institutions also exhibited a tendency to converge toward the competitive price and quantity, Plott and Smith (1978) observed that, as compared with results of the double-auction markets, single auctions and posted-price markets each exhibited a bias toward one or the other side of the market. Curiously, the bias in the single auctions is in favor of the passive side of the market, while the bias in the posted-price markets is in favor of the active side. That is, compared to the prices observed in the double auction (and to the competitive price), a single auction yields a higher price when buyers can make bids and a lower price when sellers can make offers, whereas the posted-price market yields a higher price when sellers can post offers and a lower price when buyers can post bids. Thus it is an advantage to be on the active side of a posted-price market rather than on the passive side, and an advantage to be on the passive side of a single auction rather than on the active side.[13]

[13] A considerable amount of subsequent data gathered on experimental posted-price markets largely replicate this result. As far as I know, much less additional data has been gathered on single auctions of this kind, so that the conclusions regarding single auctions must be regarded as being of a more tentative nature.

As far as I know, no presently available theory is able to account for these results, which are a good example of the kind of unanticipated regularity that can arise from using experimental methods to search for facts. [However, recent theoretical advances concerning games of incomplete information have made important progress in elucidating some similar phenomena – see, e.g., Wilson, Chapter 2 this volume.] It is difficult to imagine how empirical support for such a proposition might have been gathered without using experimentation, because (in naturally occurring economic environments) we normally observe different market institutions in operation only in quite different markets. In the laboratory, however, it is possible to conduct an experiment designed so as to hold constant all other market features – such as the number of buyers and sellers, the distribution of supply and demand – and compare the outcomes of otherwise identical markets under these different institutions.[14]

Turning back to the double-auction institution, the fact that the experimental markets conducted under these rules were often observed to converge precisely to the competitive equilibrium is rather surprising, in view of the small numbers of traders involved and the active role played by each in determining the price. This is clearly not an environment that approximates perfect competition as it has traditionally been formulated. What seems to be happening is that a great deal of information is conveyed to the agents in this kind of market, not merely by the transactions that take place but also by the bids and offers that are not accepted and do not lead to transactions. For example, if the first few trades that take place on the first trading day happen to occur at a price far above the competitive price, then some potential buyers will be priced out of the market. As the trading day progresses, sellers who have units left to sell lower their asking prices a little, hoping to transact with some of these buyers. Every buyer learns from these lower asking prices that some units are available at a lower price than previous transactions, and this influences the bids made on the next trading day.[15]

---

[14] To avoid confusion, a note on terminology is in order here. I use the term "experiment" to denote a set of experimental observations (e.g., of auction markets) that permit some comparisons to be made, and the term "experimental design" to denote the relationship among the parameters and procedures used to make the different observations. In some of the literature discussed here, the term "experiment" is used to denote a single observation of a multiperiod market while "experimental design" is used to denote the parameter settings in each market.

[15] Recall that information about supply and demand obtained from offers and transactions in one trading day is highly germane to the next trading day because these experiments were conducted so that the market starts over again each trading day, with supply and demand unchanged by the trades that occurred on the previous trading day.

There remains a spectrum of opinion on how robust is the convergence to competitive equilibrium in double auctions – that is, on the extent to which such convergence is due to the double-auction institution itself, as opposed to other features of the way the experiments were conducted. Smith (1982b) states:

> The double auction . . . is a remarkably robust trading institution for yielding outcomes that converge to the C.E. It achieves these results with a small number of agents, under widely different supply and demand conditions, with each individual agent having strict privacy, that is, the agent only knows his/her own value or cost conditions. Several sets of experiments have been conducted to test the boundary of application of these conditions. One set of experiments [Smith 1981, Smith and Williams 1981] used only one or two sellers. . . . Only in the one-seller experiments is there a failure to arrive consistently at C.E. outcomes, thus establishing "one" as the limiting number of sellers at which competitive price theory fails under double auction trading.

This is a strong and simply stated conclusion. One of the virtues of the experimental method is that, if a conclusion drawn from experimental data appears to other investigators to be too strong or too simple, further experiments can be designed and data gathered to reopen the question. Two experiments with a bearing on the above conclusion are briefly discussed below.

Holt, Langan, and Villamil (1984) considered whether convergence to competitive equilibrium in double auctions might be influenced by the parameters determining the supply and demand curves. They considered, for example, a double auction examined by Smith, which he reported [Smith (1982a, p. 172)] ". . . provides the most stringent of all reported tests of the equilibrating tendency in double auction trading," because the competitive equilibrium gave all of the exchange surplus[16] to one side of the market. They observed that although in this dimension the test is indeed stringent, nevertheless the supply and demand is such that "[t]he lack of market power is so severe in this design that even if one buyer unilaterally withholds demand for all four of his units, he has no effect on market price." They proposed to examine double-auction markets that differed from those previously examined, in that agents on one side of the market had market power – that is, by forgoing some trades such agents could move the competitive price sufficiently in their favor to earn a larger profit on their remaining transactions than if they had made all trades that originally would have been profitable for them.

---

[16] Except for the "commissions" that were paid for each transaction.

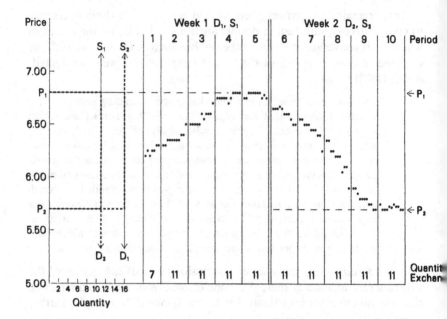

Figure 2

Holt et al. first replicated the results of the double auction discussed by Smith, confirming the tendency of the market to converge to competitive equilibrium (see Figure 2). They then conducted seven multiperiod double auctions, each involving five buyers and five sellers, using the procedures of previously published experiments but with parameters that gave market power either to some of the buyers or to some of the sellers. Three of their double auctions used experienced subjects. Contrary to the convergence to competitive equilibrium uniformly observed in earlier experiments [Smith (1982b)], four of the seven auctions observed here (including all of those with experienced subjects) failed to converge to the competitive price and converged instead to a price reflecting the distribution of market power (see, e.g., Figure 3). The results of this experiment thus support the hypothesis that parameters of the market may influence the convergence to competitive equilibrium previously observed in double-auction markets, particularly when experienced subjects are involved. [For closely related results, see also the subsequent paper by Holt and Villamil (1984).]

In most of the multiperiod repeated-auction experiments conducted to date, the number of periods was determined fairly arbitrarily, typically

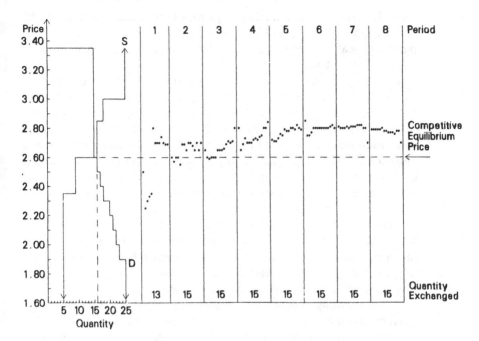

Figure 3

with an eye toward the time constraints of running the experiment. Alger (1984) noted that this left it impossible to tell whether or not these markets had stabilized; that is, whether they would continue to behave much as in the final periods of observation if they were allowed to continue operating. He designed an experiment, using posted-price markets, to see if behavior in the number of periods typically examined in previous experiments resembled the market behavior when it had been in operation long enough to fully settle down. His operational definition was to terminate each market only after there had been no deviation in seller profits for "at least five periods (usually ten periods) or if an obvious cyclic pattern developed." In order to allow market periods to be run very quickly (in order to accommodate a potentially large number of periods), Alger simulated the buyer side of the market by having buyers behave competitively. Therefore, the only active agents in his markets were sellers. He examined the two-seller case.

His results are thought-provoking. First, he observed that markets often took many more periods to stabilize than were allowed in previous experiments, and that while the initial periods of his markets looked a great deal like the same number of periods in the earlier literature,[17] the final periods – when the market had stabilized – did not. In particular, a pattern typically observed was that prices initially fell to somewhere near the competitive level but later rose to near the monopolistic price, as the sellers succeeded in signaling to each other their willingness to cooperate by raising their posted prices. The striking thing about these results is not merely that markets finally settle down near the monopolistic price when previous experiments involving posted-price markets had supported the conclusion that they tended to settle near the competitive price. What is particularly interesting is that, if only the same number of (initial) periods of this experiment were examined as were observed in previous posted-price markets, the conclusion in this experiment too would be that prices tend to converge to the competitive price.

Alger quite properly emphasizes that it would be premature to try to draw direct conclusions about previous experiments from the results of this one, because of the many design differences other than the number of periods observed. However, the time pattern of his results raises questions that will likely stimulate further experimental study.

A striking thing to note about this whole group of experiments is that it has been conducted without reference to a well-articulated body of formal theory. Instead, what we are seeing is a series of experiments – inspired by previous experiments – that seek to isolate, identify, and delimit experimentally observed empirical regularities. These experiments have shown that competitive equilibrium outcomes can be observed with very few buyers and sellers. This simple fact seems to provide a powerful challenge and stimulus to developing new theories of competitive behavior. And, because there is evidence supporting a diversity of opinion about how robust this observation is likely to prove, it would be surprising if these results do not stimulate further experimental work as well.

4   Whispering in the ears of princes

The next set of experiments I discuss have been motivated by questions of policy, questions of the kind raised by government regulatory agencies, typically about the effect of changes in the rules by which some market is organized. These investigations offer the possibility of bringing scientific methods to bear on one of the traditional nonscientific vocations of economists, which is whispering in the ears of princes who require advice about pressing practical questions whose answers lie beyond the reliable scientific knowledge of the profession.

---

[17] In particular, he compares his data to the posted-price markets discussed by Ketcham, Smith, and Williams (1984) and Fouraker and Siegal (1963).

One of the studies I discuss [Hong and Plott (1982)] arose in a matter of concern to the Interstate Commerce Commission; the other [Grether and Plott (1984)] in a case before the Federal Trade Commission. Both cases had to do with complex posted-price markets, and in both cases an attempt was made to mirror as closely as possible in the laboratory the industrial structure of the market in question [see also Plott (1985; in press)].

The ICC case concerned whether barge operators should be required to post their prices and to announce price changes in advance. The existing market allowed rates to be set by individual negotiations between barge operators and their customers, so that the terms of each contract were private information. Plott (in press) reports that the question arose because railroad companies were lobbying to require such price posting. The reasons offered by the railroads were that "the public information feature of posted rates would make the industry more competitive, allow the railroads to compete better, and aid the small barge owners who were allegedly secretly being undersold by the large barge companies."

In their introductory comments, Hong and Plott (1982) say the following about their use of laboratory experimentation to illuminate the issues raised by the proposed change.

> The full consequences of a rate filing policy are unknown. Plausible theoretical arguments can be made on both sides of the policy argument. When existing theory does not yield a definitive answer, one can usually turn to previous experiences with policies, but in this case we are aware of no industrial case study that would provide direct evidence on either side of the controversy.

They go on to note that it would be difficult to draw any compelling policy conclusions regarding the barge industry from previous laboratory experiments concerning posted-price markets, because

> [a]ny extrapolation from published experimental results to the barge industry itself is open to two potential criticisms, the reasonableness of which this study was designed to assess. First, the barge industry has several prominent economic features that are not incorporated in existing laboratory market studies. Examples include the relative sizes of buyers and sellers, the demand and supply elasticities, and the cyclical nature of demand. Naturally, we can never be certain that all the important features have been included in the present design. If something important has been misspecified or omitted, then the observed behavior of the laboratory market may not extend to the barge industry, and additional appropriately modified experiments can be conducted as checks on our conclusions. The second potential criticism is that the effects of price posting in laboratory studies have only been measured relative to the

performance of oral auction markets. Since auction markets differ from the negotiated price markets of the industry, the relevance of the comparison can be questioned.

Hong and Plott proceeded to design their experiment around a laboratory market scaled to resemble, in the features mentioned above, the market for transporting grain along the upper Mississippi River and Illinois Waterway during the Fall of 1970. (This market was chosen because it was believed to be representative of a significant portion of the dry bulk barge traffic in the United States, and because adequate data about the market parameters were available.) Aggregate supply and demand functions for the laboratory market were scaled to estimates available for the target market, as was the distribution of large and small firms on each side of the market. The laboratory market was divided into periods representing two weeks of the target market, and the seasonal aspects of the target market were modeled by having demand in the laboratory market scaled to resemble two months of normal demand followed by two months of high demand, followed by two months of normal demand. The experimental design involved running the market under both posted-price and negotiated-price policies.

In presenting the data from this experiment, Hong and Plott report that

> [t]he results are easy to summarize. The posted price policy causes higher prices, reduced volume, and efficiency losses. Furthermore, the posted price policy works to the disadvantage of most market participants, especially the small ones, and helps only the large sellers.

They also conclude that the posted-price markets react more slowly to the seasonal change in demand than do the negotiated-price markets.[18]

We will consider the relationship of these experimental results to policy conclusions after briefly discussing the experiment of Grether and Plott, which was motivated by an FTC complaint that also involved (among other things) posted prices.

The FTC case involved a complaint by the FTC against the pricing practices of the Ethyl Corporation, E.I. du Pont de Nemours and Company, PPG Industries, Inc., and Nalco Chemical Corporation – the four domestic producers of tetraethyl and tetramethyl lead, the additives in leaded gasoline that raise its octane level. The FTC sought to have the producers cease and desist from a number of unusual pricing practices

---

[18] Plott (in press) reports that this experimental evidence helped to deter the lobbying of the railroads on this matter, and that the price-posting policy they had advocated was not pursued.

used for these additives, practices that (according to the FTC) had the effect of reducing price competition.

One of these pricing practices was that suppliers agreed to give at least a thirty-day notice of all proposed price increases, and usually such announcements were made with even more than the contractual thirty-day warning. Another practice was that "most-favored nation" clauses were commonly included in contracts, by which a buyer was assured that he would receive the best terms being offered by the seller to any customer. (Apparently "meet-or-release" clauses were sometimes also used, which assured a buyer that the seller would meet the price offered by any other seller, or else release the buyer from any contractual obligation to buy from that seller.) In addition, all prices were quoted in terms of "delivered prices," for goods delivered to the purchaser regardless of his location.

Some of these practices might appear to favor the buyers, but the FTC theory was that together they worked to allow the producers to cooperate in raising prices. One way to explain this idea is as follows. If a producer thought that a price increase was desirable, he could announce, with somewhat more warning than the required thirty days, his intention to raise his price. This would not cause a customer with a meet-or-release clause to start searching for a supplier with a better price, because such a customer is assured that, in any event, he will only be charged the lowest price. (The lowest price is known because prices are announced, and it is unambiguously defined because only delivered prices are quoted, so there can be no hidden discounts in transportation costs.) If the other producers agree that this price increase is desirable then they can also announce it; otherwise, it will be rescinded by the initial producer. So a producer faces little cost in exploring the possibility of a price rise and at the same time has little incentive to explore a price cut, because he will not be able to increase his market share (again, due to advance announcements and meet-or-release clauses).

In its defense, the industry advanced the competing theory that price levels were determined entirely by the concentrated structure of the industry, and that in such a concentrated industry prices were unaffected by the pricing practices described.

Expert testimony by economists was available in support of both positions. The experiment of Grether and Plott was intended to be a possible source of evidence for rebuttal of the industry theory that the indicated pricing policies could not be affecting the price in such a concentrated industry. A scaled-down model of the industry was implemented in the laboratory, with careful attention paid to preserving the relative costs, capacities, and numbers of participants. The experimental design involved a number of multiperiod repeated markets, each one of which would be

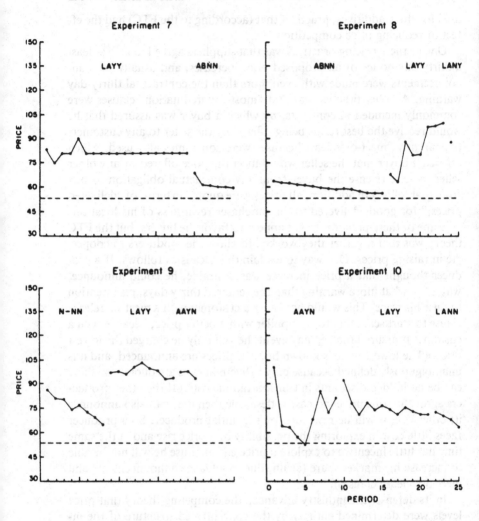

Figure 4

examined both with and without (some or all of) the pricing practices in question. The results were fairly clear - when all the practices are in force, the observed prices are above those that are observed when none of the practices are employed (see Figure 4).[19]

---

[19] Plott (in press) reports that this experimental evidence was ultimately not used in court testimony. The government won the case, but was reversed on appeal. For some subsequent theoretical work that supports the general conclusions of the experiment, see Holt and Scheffman (1985).

Looking at these two experiments together, it is apparent that one of the differences between these experiments and those described previously has to do with the complexity of the economic environment being studied. There is some tension between the goal of designing an experimental market to resemble a particular naturally occurring market, and the goal of designing an experiment whose results will be likely to support some fairly general conclusion.

On the other hand, it should also be apparent that these policy-oriented experiments have something in common with the theory-testing experiments described in Section 2: Both involve testing of hypotheses, whether those hypotheses arise from formal economic theories or from the arguments of lawyers, lobbyists, and expert witnesses. However, in contrast to hypotheses drawn from general economic theories that are presumably applicable to any market in which the conditions of the theory are met, the hypotheses of interest in this case are explicitly concerned with the target market and not with the experimental market. Therefore, the bearing that the experimental evidence has on the hypotheses is different in these policy-oriented experiments than in the theory-testing experiments discussed in Section 2.

Plott (in press) aptly describes the role of experimental evidence in policy debates of this kind as serving to "shift the burden of proof." Hong and Plott (1982), speaking of the experiments modeled on the barge industry, put it this way:

> From a scientific point of view, we have solid evidence only that price posting markets do not necessarily operate better than negotiated price markets under the parametric conditions we considered. From a policy point of view, the evidence presumably shifts the burden of proof to the price posting advocates, who must now identify the specific features of the barge industry which, if incorporated in the experiment, would reverse the conclusions.

5   Some important omissions

While any survey of this sort must inevitably have more omissions than inclusions, there are two bodies of work that I shall mention here in order to briefly highlight some different aspects of experimental work.

Recall that the section on theory-oriented experiments discussed a research program that started with a body of formal theory, proceeding to develop a set of experiments that allowed some conclusions to be drawn about the theory. This is by no means the only direction that the dialogue between experimenters and theorists can take. A good example of a complementary approach is given by the work of Selten on coalition formation. [See particularly Selten (in press); but also Selten (1972, 1982) and Selten and Krischker (1982).] Selten considers the formation of coalitions in three-person games presented in what game theorists call "characteristic function form." He starts not with a theory of coalition formation that he wishes to test in the laboratory, but rather with a body of data from a number of experiments involving three-person games that were conducted under varying experimental conditions by a variety of experimenters and motivated by differing theoretical considerations.

Selten identifies some empirical regularities in this diverse set of experimental data, and constructs a formal theory of "equal division payoff bounds" to describe and explain them. He proposes statistical tests that allow the descriptive accuracy of his theory to be compared to that of previously existing theories applicable to this data, and shows that these measures support the hypothesis that his theory may have superior predictive power for experiments of this kind. There are two points that I would like to make concerning how this work exemplifies different aspects of the dialogue that can occur between experimenters and theorists.

The first point is that, whereas the next step of the work described in Section 2 is to construct new theory that is able to describe the observed data, the logical next step of Selten's work is to conduct new experiments specifically designed to test the predictive value of the proposed theory. In general, this back-and-forth process between conducting experiments and constructing theories can be expected to keep iterating, with experimental data motivating new theory, which in turn can motivate new experiments, and so forth.

The second point is that the demands on theory made by experimental data can be quite different than those imposed by traditional deductive considerations. In this respect, Selten conducts something of a dialogue with himself. As a theorist he is well known for his seminal work on perfect equilibria, which forms the basis for much of the current theoretical work on rational and "hyper-rational" behavior [see, e.g., Rubinstein (Chapter 5, this volume)]. But on the basis of his reading of the experimental data, he finds himself constructing a theory of a radically different sort. Indeed, he writes [Selten (in press)]: "The success of the theory of equal division payoff bounds confirms the methodological point of view that the *limited rationality* of human decision behavior *must be taken seriously*" (emphasis added); and "[t]he optimization approach fails to do justice to the structure of human decision processes." It is the mark of a committed scientist to be able to adjust his theoretical ideas in the face of compelling evidence, and I think that a characteristic of experimental evidence is that it will often have the power to compel such adjustments in economic theories.

The other body of experimental work that I wish to mention in this section addresses the fact that powerful general theories may often have application on unexpected domains. Specifically, a number of experiments have now been conducted to test the applicability of economic theories of consumption and labor supply to the behavior of laboratory animals, namely pigeons and rats. [See particularly Kagel (in press); Kagel, Battalio, and Green (1981).] In these experiments, the laboratory animals are observed in controlled environments where they may perform specific tasks (such as pecking a key for pigeons, or pressing a lever for rats) to obtain food or water. By changing the number of key pecks required to obtain a given amount of food or a given amount of water, the relative prices of food and water can be changed, and observations about changes in the consumption of food and water (and leisure) can be compared to the prediction of economic theories. There is a large body of theory and experimental evidence on animal behavior in the behavioral psychology literature, and it appears that economic theories of behavior compete quite effectively in terms of their predictive and explanatory power.

However, economic theories also suggest a host of questions not likely to have been raised by psychologists studying animal behavior. Kagel (in press) discusses a number of such questions. For example, the "welfare-trap hypothesis" is that agents who receive unearned income will become "hooked on leisure" and subsequently reduce their labor supply. Kagel observed a significant but quantitatively small effect in this direction among pigeons who had in earlier periods been given unearned income in the form of free access to food and water.[20] Similar experiments were motivated by the "cycle-of-poverty hypothesis" that low-income agents will tend to discount the future more heavily than high-income agents. Kagel observed the opposite effect among liquid-deprived rats who were able to choose (by pressing one of two levers) between small immediate payoffs of saccharin water or larger delayed payoffs. In another experiment, rats were observed to exhibit violations of the independence axiom of expected-utility theory, similar to violations by human subjects observed in choice situations like the Allais paradox [see Machina (1983)]. Kagel (in press) presents a very clear and provocative discussion of the interplay between economic theories and animal experimentation, both from the point of view of better understanding animal behavior and from the (somewhat more controversial) point of view of understanding fundamental biological components of human economic behavior.

---

[20] Needless to say, some of the technical questions of experimental design that arise in experiments with animal subjects (such as controlling for subjects' body weight) are quite different than those that arise in experiments with human subjects.

6   Discussion

In evaluating a new method of research such as laboratory experimentation in economics, two different kinds of question are important. The first is, "What new economic phenomena have been elucidated so far? What facts have been established through experimentation? What new avenues of research have been opened?" The second is, "How do these new methods relate to the other approaches available to economists?"

I believe it is fair to say that there already exists a body of successful experimental economic research so large as to make a comprehensive answer to the first kind of question impractical in an essay of this scope. At the same time, the experimental approach is still too new to allow a definitive answer to the second kind of question. But we have considered some examples of what has been learned from experimental studies, and I hope that the organization of this chapter gives some perspective on the way experimentation is related to other things that economists do.

One thing that should now be clear is that when we think of what we have learned from a particular experimental study, we need to think not only of what we now know but also of what we now know that we do *not* know. Good experimental research is in this regard like good research of other kinds: It raises new questions even as it provides answers to others. But the kinds of questions raised by experiments may be novel in some respects.

This is in part because the process of designing an experiment requires a very detailed specification of all aspects of the economic environment in question. In fact, perhaps the most important conclusion supported by most experimental studies of economic issues, and one of the first things one notices when setting out to do economic experiments, is that many of the factors that must be considered in setting up an experiment are not spoken of in theoretical papers, nor specified in conventional descriptive accounts of economic institutions. Furthermore, many of these factors have an important influence on the behavior observed.[21] There is nevertheless no easy way to summarize how economic theory in general fares when tested experimentally, because the results of some experiments falsify the predictions of the theory they are designed to test while the results of other experiments support them.[22]

---

[21] In this sense, simply designing an experiment is an exercise in model building akin to specifying a game in extensive form. But whereas factors that are left out of a theoretical model can subsequently have no influence on its behavior, factors overlooked in designing an experiment have a way of showing up in unanticipated ways when the experiment is conducted.

[22] For those for whom a little philosophy of science is a dangerous thing, I should probably

As economists further explore the uses of laboratory experimentation in economics, new uses are sure to emerge. For example, it seems to me that there is considerable potential for using laboratory experiments in conjunction with more traditional kinds of empirical research. Although it is not yet clear what shape this might take, I think it is reasonable to expect that, in addition to the dialogues discussed here, a fruitful interaction can develop between experimenters and applied economists concerned with a variety of empirical questions.

I am often asked to explain how (or whether) I think experimental methods can have a bearing on the explanation and understanding of naturally occurring economic phenomena involving large-scale and highly complex systems. I think that a useful parallel can be drawn with the experience of evolutionary biology, which (like economics) is a science that deals largely with historical data. Although experiments cannot be conducted on the fossil record, biologists obtain much of their present understanding of selection and evolution from controlled experiments in molecular biology, genetics, and plant breeding. While it is probably impossible to draw precise analogies between economics and other sciences, I think that experimental methods have the potential to play a role in economics that is roughly similar to their role in evolutionary biology. Experiments give us a way of learning the answers to certain kinds of questions that we have no other way of answering.

That being the case, I think it is a promising sign that experimental economics appears to have secured a solid foothold in economic discourse. Not only is it becoming more commonplace to find experiments reported in the major journals of the profession, a wider circle of economists are now conducting experiments.[23] Looking into the future, which (if any) of the experimental results discussed here will remain important depends both on how future experimental results refine our understanding of what has been observed to date, and also on what kinds of questions remain or become important in light of new theoretical developments. But if I were to try my hand at prophecy, I would say there is a good chance that one of the things that will be remembered about science in the latter part of

---

not say that the evidence ever "supports" a theory; please feel free to understand me as saying that the evidence fails to falsify the theory.

[23] In this respect, the development of laboratory experimentation in economics may parallel in some ways the growth of game theory as a major tool of economic theory. Not so long ago, game theory was done almost exclusively by "game theorists," whereas today it provides tools that are used as needed by a broad spectrum of economic theorists. Similarly, we are beginning to see experiments conducted not just by a small group of "experimentalists," but by a broader group of economists who turn to experimental methods when they seem appropriate. [For example, in addition to the experiments discussed in Section 2, see Binmore, Shaked, and Sutton (1985, 1986).]

the twentieth century is that laboratory experimentation entered the portfolio of tools that economists use to study the world.

References

Alger, Dan. 1984. "Equilibria in the Laboratory: Experiments with Oligopoly Markets Where Goods Are Made-To-Order." Working Paper No. 121, Bureau of Economics, Federal Trade Commission.

Berg, Joyce E., Lane A. Daley, John W. Dickhaut, and John R. O'Brien. 1986. "Controlling Preferences for Lotteries on Units of Experimental Exchange." *Quarterly Journal of Economics* 101: 281-306.

Binmore, Ken, Ariel Rubinstein, and Asher Wollinsky. 1985. "The Nash Bargaining Solution in Economic Modelling." Theoretical Economics Discussion Paper Series, London School of Economics.

Binmore, Ken, Avner Shaked, and John Sutton. 1985. "Testing Noncooperative Bargaining Theory: A Preliminary Study." *American Economic Review* 75: 1178-80.

1986. "An Outside Option Experiment." Mimeo, London School of Economics.

Chatterjee, Kalyan. 1985. "Disagreement in Bargaining: Models with Incomplete Information." In A. E. Roth (ed.), *Game-Theoretic Models of Bargaining*, pp. 9-26. Cambridge: Cambridge University Press.

Edgeworth, F. Y. 1881. *Mathematical Psychics*. London: Kegan Paul.

Ferber, Robert, and Werner Z. Hirsch. 1982. *Social Experimentation and Economic Policy* (Cambridge Surveys of Economic Literature). Cambridge: Cambridge University Press.

Fouraker, L. E., and Siegal, S. 1963. *Bargaining Behavior*. New York: McGraw-Hill.

Grether, David M., and Charles R. Plott. 1984. "The Effects of Market Practices in Oligopolistic Markets: An Experimental Examination of the Ethyl Case." *Economic Inquiry* 22: 479-507.

Hausman, Jerry A., and David A. Wise (eds.). 1985. *Social Experimentation*. National Bureau of Economic Research.

Holt, Charles A., Loren Langan, and Anne P. Villamil. 1984. "Market Power in Oral Double Auctions: Convergence to Competitive Equilibrium Prices Reconsidered." Working Paper, University of Minnesota.

Holt, Charles A., and David T. Scheffman. 1985. "The Effects of Advance Notice and Best-Price Policies: Theory, with Applications to *Ethyl*." Working Paper, University of Virginia.

Holt, Charles A., and Anne P. Villamil. 1984. "The Effect of Market Power on the Direction of Convergence in Oral Double Auctions." Working Paper, University of Virginia, University of Minnesota.

Hong, James T., and Charles R. Plott. 1982. "Rate Filing Policies for Inland Water Transportation: An Experimental Approach." *Bell Journal of Economics* 13: 1-19.

Kagel, John H. In press. "Economics According to the Rats (and Pigeons Too):

What Have We Learned, and What Can We Hope to Learn." In Alvin E. Roth (ed.), *Laboratory Experimentation in Economics: Six Points of View*. Cambridge: Cambridge University Press.

Kagel, John H., Raymond C. Battalio, and Leonard Green. 1981. "Income-Leisure Tradeoffs of Animal Workers." *American Economic Review* 71: 621-32.

Kahneman, Daniel, and Amos Tversky. 1984. "Choices, Values, and Frames." *American Psychologist* 39: 341-50.

Kalai, Ehud, and Meir Smorodinsky. 1975. "Other Solutions to Nash's Bargaining Problem." *Econometrica* 43: 513-18.

Ketcham, J., V. L. Smith, and A. Williams. 1984. "A Comparison of Posted-Offer and Double-Auction Pricing Institutions." *Review of Economic Studies* 51: 595-614.

Kihlstrom, R., A. E. Roth, and D. Schmeidler. 1981. "Risk Aversion and Solutions to Nash's Bargaining Problem." In O. Moeschlin and D. Pallaschke (eds.), *Game Theory and Mathematical Economics*, pp. 65-71. Amsterdam: North-Holland.

Knez, Mark, and Vernon L. Smith. In press. "Hypothetical Valuations and Preference Reversals in the Context of Asset Trading." In Alvin E. Roth (ed.), *Laboratory Experimentation in Economics: Six Points of View*. Cambridge: Cambridge University Press.

Machina, Mark J. 1983. "The Economic Theory of Individual Behavior Toward Risk: Theory, Evidence, and New Directions." Technical Report #433, Institute for Mathematical Studies in the Social Sciences, Stanford University.

Murnighan, J. Keith, Alvin E. Roth, and Francoise Schoumaker. 1985. "Risk Aversion in Bargaining: an Experimental Study." Working Paper, University of Montreal.

Nash, John. 1950. "The Bargaining Problem." *Econometrica* 28: 155-62.

Perles, M. A., and M. Maschler. 1981. "The Super-Additive Solution for the Nash Bargaining Game." *International Journal of Game Theory* 10: 163-93.

Plott, Charles R. 1982. "Industrial Organization Theory and Experimental Economics." *Journal of Economic Literature* 20: 1485-1527.

  1985. "Laboratory Experiments in Economics: The Implications of Posted Price Institutions." Mimeo, California Institute of Technology.

  In press. "Dimensions of Parallelism: Some Policy Applications of Experimental Methods." In Alvin E. Roth (ed.), *Laboratory Experimentation in Economics: Six Points of View*. Cambridge: Cambridge University Press.

Plott, Charles R., and Vernon L. Smith. 1978. "An Experimental Examination of Two Exchange Institutions." *Review of Economic Studies* 45: 133-53.

Roth, Alvin E. 1979. *Axiomatic Models of Bargaining*. Berlin: Springer-Verlag.

  1983. "Toward a Theory of Bargaining: An Experimental Study in Economics." *Science* 220: 687-91.

  1985a (ed.). *Game-Theoretic Models of Bargaining*. Cambridge: Cambridge University Press.

  1985b. "A Note on Risk Aversion in a Perfect Equilibrium Model of Bargaining." *Econometrica* 53: 207-11.

In press a. "Bargaining Phenomena and Bargaining Theory." In Alvin E. Roth (ed.), *Laboratory Experimentation in Economics: Six Points of View*. Cambridge: Cambridge University Press.

In press b (ed.). *Laboratory Experimentation in Economics: Six Points of View*. Cambridge: Cambridge University Press.

Roth, Alvin E., and Michael W. K. Malouf. 1979. "Game-Theoretic Models and the Role of Information in Bargaining." *Psychological Review* 86: 574-94.

Roth, Alvin E., Michael W. K. Malouf, and J. Keith Murnighan. 1981. "Sociological Versus Strategic Factors in Bargaining." *Journal of Economic Behavior and Organization* 2: 153-77.

Roth, Alvin E., and J. Keith Murnighan. 1982. "The Role of Information in Bargaining: An Experimental Study." *Econometrica* 50: 1123-42.

Roth, Alvin E., and Uriel G. Rothblum. 1982. "Risk Aversion and Nash's Solution for Bargaining Games With Risky Outcomes." *Econometrica* 50: 639-47.

Roth, Alvin E., and Francoise Schoumaker. 1983. "Expectations and Reputations in Bargaining: An Experimental Study." *American Economic Review* 73: 362-72.

Rubinstein, Ariel. 1982. "Perfect Equilibrium in a Bargaining Model." *Econometrica* 50: 97-109.

1985. "Choice of Conjectures in a Bargaining Game with Incomplete Information." In Alvin E. Roth (ed.), *Game-Theoretic Models of Bargaining*, pp. 99-114. Cambridge: Cambridge University Press.

Selten, Reinhard. 1972. "Equal Share Analysis of Characteristic Function Experiments." In H. Sauermann (ed.), *Contributions to Experimental Economics III*, pp. 130-65. Tübingen, West Germany: Mohr.

1982. "Equal Division Payoff Bounds for 3-Person Characteristic Function Experiments." In R. Tietz (ed.), *Aspiration Levels in Bargaining and Economic Decision Making*, pp. 265-75. Berlin: Springer-Verlag.

In press. "Equity and Coalition Bargaining in Experimental 3-Person Games." In Alvin E. Roth (ed.), *Laboratory Experimentation in Economics: Six Points of View*. Cambridge: Cambridge University Press.

Selten, Reinhard, and Wilhelm Krischker. 1982. "Comparison of Two Theories for Characteristic Function Experiments." In R. Tietz (ed.), *Aspiration Levels in Bargaining and Economic Decision Making*, pp. 259-64. Berlin: Springer-Verlag.

Smith, Vernon L. 1964. "Effect of Market Organization on Competitive Equilibrium." *Quarterly Journal of Economics* 78: 181-201.

1976. "Bidding and Auctioning Institutions: Experimental Results." In Y. Amihud (ed.), *Bidding and Auctioning for Procurement and Allocation*. New York: New York University Press.

1981. "An Empirical Study of Decentralized Institutions of Monopoly Restraint." In G. Horwich and J. Quirk (eds.), *Essays in Contemporary Fields of Economics*. West Lafayette: Purdue University Press.

1982a. "Markets as Economizers of Information: Experimental Examination of the 'Hayek Hypothesis'." *Economic Inquiry* 20: 165-79.

1982b. "Microeconomic Systems as an Experimental Science." *American Economic Review* 72: 923–55.

Smith, Vernon L., and Arlington W. Williams. 1981. "The Boundaries of Competitive Price Theory: Convergence, Expectations and Transaction Cost." Presented at the Public Choice Society Meetings, New Orleans, Louisiana.

Thaler, Richard. In press. "The Psychology of Choice and the Assumptions of Economics." In Alvin E. Roth (ed.), *Laboratory Experimentation in Economics: Six Points of View.* Cambridge: Cambridge University Press.

Tversky, Amos, and Daniel Kahneman. 1981. "The Framing of Decisions and the Psychology of Choice." *Science* 211: 453–8.

CHAPTER 8

Increasing returns and the theory of international trade

Paul R. Krugman

Abstract: Increasing returns are as fundamental a cause of international trade as comparative advantage, but their role has until recently been neglected because of the problem of modeling market structure. Recently, substantial theoretical progress has been made using three different approaches. These are the Marshallian approach, where economies are assumed external to firms; the Chamberlinian approach, where imperfect competition takes the relatively tractable form of monopolistic competition; and the Cournot approach of noncooperative quantity-setting firms. This chapter surveys the basic concepts and results of each approach. It shows that some basic insights are not too sensitive to the particular model of market structure. Although much remains to be done, we have made more progress toward a general analysis of increasing returns and trade than anyone would have thought possible even a few years ago.

Since the beginnings of analytical economics, the concept of comparative advantage has been the starting point for virtually all theoretical discussion of international trade. Comparative advantage is a marvelous insight: simple yet profound, indisputable yet still (more than ever?) misunderstood by most people, lending itself both to theoretical elaboration and practical policy analysis. What international economist, finding himself in yet another confused debate about U.S. "competitiveness," has not wondered whether anything useful has been said since Ricardo?

Yet it has long been clear that comparative advantage – which I will here interpret loosely to mean a view that countries trade in order to take advantage of their differences – is not the only possible explanation of international specialization and exchange. As Ricardo doubtless knew, and as modern theorists from Ohlin on have reemphasized, countries may also trade because there are inherent advantages in specialization, arising from the existence of economies of scale. At a logical level a theory of trade based on increasing returns is as fundamental as one based on comparative advantage; at a practical level it is reasonable to argue that economies of scale, if perhaps not as important as national differences as a motive for trade, are at least of the same order of magnitude.

Increasing returns as an explanation of trade has, however, until recently received only a tiny fraction of the theoretical attention lavished upon comparative advantage. Again, the reasons are not hard to find. Where the concept of trade based on comparative advantage has opened up broad avenues of research, the attempt to formalize trade based on increasing returns seemed until recently to lead to an impenetrable jungle of complexity. Economics understandably and inevitably follows the line of least mathematical resistance, and so until about ten years ago the role of scale economies was at best a point to be mentioned in passing within most discussions of international trade.

During the last decade, however, several paths through the wilderness have been found. The new literature on increasing returns and trade does not yet have the generality and unity of traditional trade theory, and it may never be tied up in quite as neat a package. We can, however, now provide a far more systematic account of the role of increasing returns in international trade – and of the way this role interacts with that of comparative advantage – than would have seemed possible not long ago. The purpose of this chapter is to review the new concepts that have made this progress possible.

The central problem in theoretical analysis of economies of scale has always been, of course, the problem of market structure. Unexhausted scale economies are inconsistent with the standard competitive model; the problem of introducing them into trade theory is thus one of finding departures from that model which are both tractable and capable of accommodating increasing returns. Progress in recent years has been based on three such departures, and this chapter deals with each type of market structure in turn.

The first departure from the standard competitive model is the oldest. This is the Marshallian approach, in which increasing returns are assumed to be wholly external to the firm, allowing perfect competition to remain. Marshallian analyses of increasing returns and trade go back to the early postwar period. The early literature on the Marshallian approach, however, seemed discouraging in that even with the simplest assumptions it seemed to lead to a welter of multiple equilibria. Only in the last few years has it become clear that under certain circumstances it is possible to bring order to this complexity.

The second departure is a more recent creation. Less than ten years ago, several trade theorists independently applied formal models of Chamberlinian monopolistic competition to trade. The Chamberlinian approach has proved extremely fruitful, providing a simple tool for thinking about a variety of issues in international economics.

Finally, the Cournot approach to oligopoly has begun to be widely used in international trade theory. Much of this use is in normative analyses of trade policy, which are not the subject of this chapter, but some positive analysis of trade has also been based on this approach.

The plan of this chapter, then, is to discuss in succession recent developments in trade theory based on Marshallian, Chamberlinian, and Cournot approaches to the problem of market structure. A final section concludes with some issues for future research.

The limitations of the chapter should be made clear at the outset. The work discussed here is theoretical work aimed at understanding the causes and effects of trade, rather than at providing guidance to trade policy. That is, I am concerned here with why trade happens and what difference it makes, not with what we should do about it. Allowing for the importance of imperfect competition may have major implications for the analysis of trade policy as well, but I leave discussion of these implications to Avinash Dixit (Chapter 9, this volume). Also, no attempt is made to discuss empirical work, which in any case has so far been quite scarce in this area.

1   The Marshallian approach

In a sense, the Marshallian approach to the analysis of trade under increasing returns goes back to Frank Graham's famous argument for protection [Graham (1923)]. Explicit general-equilibrium analysis of trade in the presence of external economies began with Matthews (1949), and was continued in a number of papers, including Kemp and Negishi (1970), Melvin (1969), Chacholiades (1978), and Panagariya (1981). For the most part, however, this literature was not successful in bringing increasing returns into trade theory in a way that generated useful insights or attracted additional research. In particular, the literature did not seem to offer the possibility of a fruitful marriage of increasing returns and comparative advantage as explanations of trade. Ironically, this failure may been been in part because of an excessive loyalty to the *techniques* of conventional models – production possibility curves, offer curves, and so forth. As it turns out, it is possible to have models in which comparative advantage and Marshallian economies interact in a clear way, but the development of such models depends crucially on the introduction of new techniques.

The key innovation here was the work of Ethier (1979, 1982a), who showed that the analysis of trade in the presence of Marshallian external economies is greatly clarified if we work from the allocation of resources to production and trade rather than the other way around. This may seem like a minor change, but it leads to a thorough revamping of modeling strategy. As we will see, a synthesis of Marshallian increasing returns and comparative advantage comes easily only if we focus on factor prices and the factor content of trade, rather than on goods prices and goods trade.

In this section, then, we will focus on the new version of the Marshallian approach, distinguished from the older approach by the way it works from resource allocation to trade. In addition to its direct usefulness, we will see that this approach provides us with techniques and insights that are directly relevant to the Chamberlinian approach as well.

A   *The simplest model*

There is a family resemblance between the simplest model of trade based on increasing returns and the basic Ricardian model. In both cases a fundamental principle of international trade can be derived from studying an imaginary world of two countries, two goods, and one factor of production. If the increasing returns model has not had anything like the same influence, it is because there seem to be too many things that can happen. The task of the theorist is to find restrictions that narrow the set of possibilities in an interesting way.

Suppose, then, following the formulation of Ethier (1982a), that the world consists of two countries, each with only one factor of production: labor. To strip the problem down to bare essentials, we assume that the two countries possess identical technology with which to produce two goods. One of these goods – call it Chips – is produced at constant returns at the level of the firm, but is subject to positive external economies so that at the level of the indusry there are increasing returns. These external economies are assumed to be country-specific; it is each country's domestic industry rather than the world industry as a whole that is subject to increasing returns. The other good – call it Fish – is produced at constant returns to scale at the level of both the firm and the industry. We will assume that both Fish and Chips can be traded costlessly.

Now it is immediately apparent that even though both countries start with the same technological possibilities, the existence of economies of scale makes it inevitable that there will be international specialization. To see this, suppose that both countries were to produce both goods. The fact that both were producing Fish would imply equal wage rates. But this would mean that whichever country had the larger Chips industry would have lower cost in that industry; this would presumably lead that industry's relative size to increase still further, reinforcing the cost advantage; and we will have a cumulative process of differentiation between the countries that continues until at least one of the countries has specialized.

And as long as one country has specialized, we will have international trade. So the model tells us that increasing returns will, as expected, lead to specialization and trade.

The problem, of course, is that while the outcome must involve specialization and trade, this still allows a number of possible equilibria. A little thought will suggest that there are three different kinds of equilibrium that can result. First, one country might produce both Chips and Fish while the other produces only Fish. Second, both countries might specialize, one in Chips and one in Fish. Third, one country might specialize in Chips while the other produces both goods. Since it is also possible that either country may take on either role, we have as many as six possible equilibria even in this simplest model.

To sort out this complexity, it is useful to begin by noticing that our first kind of equilibrium, where both countries produce Fish, is quite different from the other two in its implications for factor prices and welfare. As long as both countries end up producing the constant-returns good they will have equal wages, something that will not be true in the other types of equilibrium. Because the countries will have equal wages, it does not matter to their welfare which country the good is produced in. Suppose that we could assure ourselves that the international equilibrium was in fact going to be of this type, where common production of a constant-returns good ensures equal wage rates. Then we might still have two equilibria, in that either country could produce Chips, but these equilibria would have a good deal in common. In each, the world output of Chips would be concentrated in a single country; and the volume both of that output and the world output of Fish would be the same across the two equilibria. Further, welfare – not only for the world as a whole but for each individual – would be the same regardless of which country ends up with the Chips industry. Thus the indeterminacy of the model, while not eliminated, would be sharply circumscribed.

Welfare in this case does not depend on which country produces Chips; how does it compare with autarky? A further appealing feature of the equal-wage equilibrium is that it yields a very simple condition for gains from trade. This is that each country gains from trade provided that the scale of the world Chips industry after trade is larger than the scale of the national industry before trade. The reason is that this implies a lower unit labor cost and therefore a lower price in terms of the (common) wage rate. The important points to notice about this criterion are (first) that it does not depend on which country actually produces Chips, and (second) that it is a very mild condition, likely to be satisfied. Thus we have in a quite simple way captured the idea that it is to everyone's advantage to be part of a larger market.

The relative simplicity of the analysis when wage rates are equalized might lead us to ask whether there is some common ground between this case and the case of factor price equalization in the Heckscher–Ohlin model. In fact there is a common aspect, pinpointed in Helpman and Krugman (1985). In both the Heckscher–Ohlin and external economy models, factor price equalization is a symptom of a deeper aspect of the trading equilibrium, namely that "trade reproduces the integrated economy." By this we mean that the output and resource allocation of the world economy as a whole are the same as they would have been if all factors of production had been located in a single country. Or to put it another way, equalization of factor prices occurs when the fact that the world's productive factors are geographically dispersed turns out not to matter.

Once we realize that wage equalization amounts to saying that the integrated economy is reproduced, a technique for analyzing the prospects for wage equalization readily follows. First, construct the integrated economy – that is, from tastes, technology, and factor endowments calculate what the allocation of labor between the Fish and Chips industries would have been if labor had been able to move freely between the two countries. Now, in order to reproduce the integrated economy, the trading world must be able to achieve the same scale of Chips production. Because external economies are assumed to be country-specific, this means that the world Chips industry of the integrated economy must now fit into one of the national economies with some room to spare.

The implications of this condition are illustrated in Figures 1 and 2. In each diagram the line OO^* represents the world endowment of labor. The division of that endowment between the two countries can be represented by a point on that line. Also, in each figure the distance $OQ = Q'O^*$ represents the labor force devoted to Chips production in the integrated economy. The difference between the figures is that in Figure 1 the Chips industry is assumed to employ less than half the world's labor force, while in Figure 2 it is assumed to employ more than half.

It is now straightforward to see what is necessary to allow reproduction of the integrated economy. In Figure 1, splitting the world to the left of Q allows the Chips industry to fit into Foreign at integrated economy scale; splitting it between Q and Q' allows it to fit into either; splitting it to the right of Q' allows it to fit into Home. Thus there is always a trading equilibrium in which wages are equalized. In Figure 2, if the two countries are too nearly equal in size – the endowment lies in $Q'Q$ – the integrated equilibrium cannot be reproduced, but otherwise it can.

What this analysis shows is that an equal-wage equilibrium in which both countries produce Fish is not unlikely to exist. Indeed, such an equilibrium always exists unless the share of the world labor forced devoted

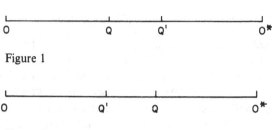

Figure 1

Figure 2

to Chips exceeds one-half, and even then it will frequently exist. So concentrating on the equal-wage case does not mean focusing on a rare event.

Unfortunately, the fact that an equal-wage equilibrium exists need not mean that it is the only equilibrium. Suppose, for example, that Foreign is substantially smaller than Home, so that the endowment point in Figure 1 lies to the right of Q'. Then there is an equal-wage equilibrium with the Chips industry concentrated in Home, but there might also be an equilibrium in which Foreign specializes in Chips and has higher wages. We can only rule this out if Figure 1 is the relevant figure and the endowment division lies between Q and Q' – in effect, if the increasing returns sector is not too large and the countries are not too unequal in size.

An equal-wage equilibrium in which trade reproduces the integrated economy, then, is not the only possible outcome even in this simplest model. It is however a plausible outcome and one which yields appealingly simple results. Thus there is some justification for stressing this sort of outcome. Further, the idea of reproducing the integrated economy through trade provides a natural way to integrate the analysis of scale economies with that of comparative advantage, as we will see shortly.

Before proceeding to the next section, however, we need to ask what has happened to the traditional argument that increasing-returns sectors are desirable property, and that the possibility that they will contract as a result of trade is a source of doubt about the gains from trade. The answer is of course that this argument depends on the integrated economy *not* being reproduced, so that wages end up unequal. Suppose that Figure 2 is the relevant diagram, and that the countries have equal labor forces. Then wages cannot be equal; we will clearly have one country that specializes in Chips and has a higher wage than the other country, which might lose from trade and in any case will not be happy about the outcome. One can argue about whether this situation is more or less realistic than an equal-wage equilibrium; I would argue that it is less realistic, but the main reason for focusing on the case of factor price equalization, here as elsewhere, is of course that it is so much simpler to work with.

B   *Increasing returns and comparative advantage*

The model presented above is one in which increasing returns is the only source of trade and gains from trade. This is of course an extreme and unrealistic case, just as is the Heckscher–Ohlin model in which differences in relative factor endowments are the only source. What we would like is a model in which both types of motive are able to operate.

There is a considerable literature on what happens in the 2×2 model when one sector is subject to increasing returns. Contributions to that literature include in particular Kemp and Negishi (1970), Melvin (1969), and Panagariya (1981).

Our discussion of a one-factor model suggests, however, that 2×2 may not be the most productive or even the easiest model to study. The simplifying device we found useful there was a focus on trading equilibria that reproduce a hypothetical integrated economy. We also noted that factor price equalization in constant-returns models is also equivalent to reproducing the integrated economy through trade. This makes it natural to look for assumptions that allow reproduction of an integrated economy when there are both increasing returns and differences in national factor endowments.

Suppose that there are some goods produced with country-specific external economies, and that there are others produced with constant returns. Suppose also that there are two or more factors of production. Then a little thought will show that in order to reproduce the integrated economy we must be able to do the following: We must be able to distribute the integrated economy's industrial output among countries, *using the integrated economy techniques of production,* in such a way as to employ fully each country's factors of production; and when we do this each industry subject to country-specific external economies must be concentrated in a single country.

It is immediately apparent that we are very unlikely to be able to distribute industries so as to fully employ all factors of production in each country, unless there are at least as many industries to distribute as there are factors. Furthermore, increasing returns sectors are not really "fungible"; because they must be concentrated in a single country, they can be reallocated among countries only in a discrete fashion. So to reproduce the integrated economy we need to have as many constant-returns sectors as there are factors of production. The minimal model with this property is 2×3: two factors of production and three goods, only one of which is produced subject to increasing returns.

Imagine, then, that we have a world in which there are at least as many constant-returns industries as there are factors, plus some increasing-returns industries, and that trade reproduces the integrated economy. Then we of course have factor price equalization. What else can we say about trade?

The first thing we can say is that there will be specialization due to economies of scale: Every increasing-returns sector will be concentrated in a single country. Thus, even if every country had the same factor endowment, there would still be specialization and trade due to scale economies. As in the case of the one-factor model, this specialization will in general have an arbitrary component: Each increasing-returns industry must be concentrated in a single country, but which country it is concentrated in may be indeterminate.

Despite this indeterminacy, in an average sense there will be a relationship between factor endowments and the pattern of production and trade. A country with a high relative endowment of capital must on average produce a capital-intensive mix of goods, although it may produce some relatively labor-intensive ones. That is, the factor content of a country's production must match its factor endowment. On the other hand, if countries spend their income in the same way, all countries will consume the same mix of goods, and thus the same mix of factor services embodied in those goods. It follows that countries will be net exporters of the services of factors in which they are abundantly endowed, and thus that in an average sense the factor proportions theory of trade will hold.

The next question is that of gains from trade. Clearly there are now two sources of potential gains from trade: specialization to take advantage of differences in relative factor endowments, and specialization to achieve larger scale of production. The usual analysis of gains from trade, with its discussion of the enlargement of each nation's consumption possibilities, does not carry over easily into an increasing-returns world where the pattern of production and trade may well be indeterminate. We have just argued, however, that factor prices and the pattern of trade in factor services will still be determinate if we have factor price equalization, so we might suppose that the issue of gains from trade might also be resolvable if we focus on factors rather than goods. And this is in fact the case.

What we can establish is the following: After trade a country will be able to afford its pre-trade consumption provided that the world scale of production of increasing-returns goods is larger than that country's national scale of production before trade. [The scale need not be larger in all industries; roughly what is needed is that on average world industries be larger than pre-trade national industries would have been. For an exact statement see Helpman and Krugman (1985).] Thus our criterion for gains from trade in the simplest model has now become a sufficient – not necessary – condition for gains in a more elaborate model. The reason it

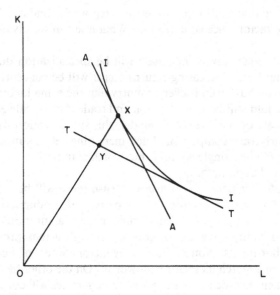

Figure 3

is only a sufficient condition is, of course, that there are now additional gains from comparative advantage which will occur even if scale gains should somehow fail to materialize.

To understand this condition, consider a country that uses two inputs, capital and labor. Let us first imagine that all industries operate under constant returns. In Figure 3 we show the unit isoquant for some industry as *II*. The line *AA* represents pre-trade factor prices. Thus *OX* is the vector of pre-trade inputs per unit of the good. Now suppose trade is opened, and that factor prices are equalized across countries. Then the new factor prices will be different from before, say *TT*. This change in factor prices is immediately a source of gains from trade. The reason is as follows. Before trade, the economy used *OX* to produce each unit of the good. After trade, however, the income of a smaller vector of resources, *OY*, is now sufficient to buy one unit of the good. Because this must be true for every good, the economy can now earn enough to purchase its pre-trade consumption and still have resources to spare.

Suppose now that some goods are produced with economies of scale. Provided that the scale of an industry after trade is larger than in the country before trade, the effect will be – as in Figure 4 – to shift the unit isoquant inward. This will add to the gains from trade. If there were no scale change, *OY* resources would be needed to purchase a unit of the

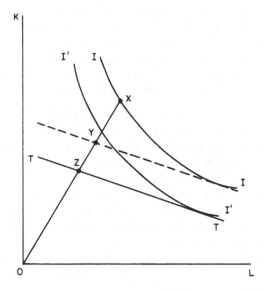

Figure 4

output; so $OX - OY$ can be thought of as the comparative advantage component of the gains from trade. Scale effects, however, will generally shift the isoquant inward (not necessarily for our country, but for the country where the good is produced, which is all that matters). The result will be to lower the resources needed to purchase the good still further, to OZ, so that $OY - OZ$ can be thought of as the scale economy component of the gains from trade.

Obviously, if scale effects run the wrong way (so that isoquants shift outward) the effect will be to offset the comparative advantage gains and perhaps produce losses from trade. However, because the scale comparison is one of national scale before trade with world scale after trade, there is a strong presumption that scale effects will generally be a source of gains over and above those from comparative advantage.

C   *The external economy approach: summary*

Recent work has shown that when the Marshallian external economy approach to increasing returns is looked at in the right way with the right assumptions, a clear and appealing story about trade emerges. The essential requirements to get this story are the willingness to assume that a trading world reproduces the aggregate outcomes of a hypothetical perfectly integrated economy – with factor price equalization as one of the consequences; and a willingness to focus on net trade in factor services rather than on trade in goods, which is typically indeterminate. Given these concessions, we are able to describe a world economy in which both factor proportions and scale economies contribute to international trade, and in which both are sources of gains from trade. In particular:

(i) Although there is typically some indeterminacy in the precise pattern of trade, factor proportions theory continues to hold in an average sense. Countries will be net exporters of the services of factors with which they are abundantly endowed.

(ii) At the same time, the trading economy will be characterized by geographical concentration of each industry subject to country-specific increasing returns. This concentration will be an independent source of trade, and would require trade even if factor endowments were identical.

(iii) The opportunity to exchange factor services at prices different from those that would prevail in the absence of trade will lead to gains from trade for all countries.

(iv) These gains will be supplemented by additional gains if the world scale of production in increasing-returns industries – wherever they may be located – exceeds the national scale that would prevail in the absence of trade.

2   The Chamberlinian approach

The 1970s were marked by substantial progress in the theoretical modeling of imperfect competition. Among the approaches developed by industrial organization theorists was a revival of Chamberlin's "large group" analysis of competition between similar firms producing differentiated products. This analysis, once put in the form of fully specified general equilibrium models, could be applied in a straightforward way to international trade, where it has proved a flexible tool of analysis.

The basic Chamberlinian idea is that one can think of at least some industries as being characterized by a process of entry in which new firms are able to differentiate their products from existing firms. Each firm will then retain some monopoly power – that is, will face a downward-sloping demand curve. Given economies of scale, however, this is not inconsistent with a situation in which entry drives economic profits to zero. Thus Chamberlin's vision was of an industry consisting of many little monopolists who have crowded the field sufficiently to eliminate any monopoly profits.

The limitation that prevented much use of this approach in international trade theory before the 1970s was the absence of any rigorous treatment of the process of product differentiation. In the 1970s, however, two approaches to this problem were developed. The first, identified with the work of Dixit and Stiglitz (1977) and Spence (1976), imposed the assumption that each consumer has a taste for many different varieties of a product. Product differentiation then simply takes the form of producing a variety not yet being produced. The alternative approach, developed by Lancaster (1979), posited a primary demand not for varieties per se but for attributes of varieties, with consumers differing in their preferred mix of attributes. Product differentiation in this case takes the form of offering a variety having attributes that differ from those of varieties already available.

For some purposes the differences between these approaches are important. For international trade theory, however, it does not much matter which approach is used. The important point is that both approaches end with an equilibrium in which a number of differentiated products are produced by firms that possess monopoly power but earn no monopoly profits. This is all we need to develop a remarkably simple model of international trade.

A   *The basic model*

Chamberlinian trade models that are essentially very similar can be found in papers by Dixit and Norman (1980), Ethier (1982b), Helpman (1981), Krugman (1979, 1981), and Lancaster (1980). A synthesis approach is given in Helpman and Krugman (1985), and I follow that approach here.

Consider a world consisting of two countries, Home and Foreign, endowed with two factors of production, capital and labor, and using the same technology to produce two goods, Food and Manufactures. Food is simply a homogeneous product produced under constant returns to scale. Manufactures, however, is a differentiated product, consisting of many potential varieties, each produced under conditions of increasing returns. We assume that the specification of tastes and technology in the Manufactures sector is such that it ends up being monopolistically competitive; beyond this the details do not matter.

As in our analysis of the Marshallian approach, the trick in analyzing this model is to start by constructing a reference point, the "integrated economy." That is, given tastes and technology, we find the equilibrium of a hypothetical closed economy endowed with the total world supplies of capital and labor. The key information we need from this calculation is the allocation of resources to each industry and relative factor prices.

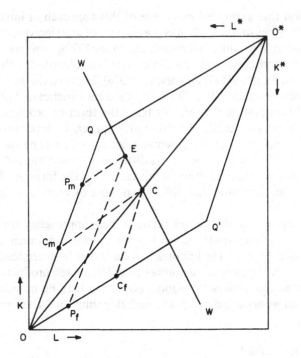

Figure 5

This information is shown in Figure 5. The sides of the box represent the total world supplies of capital and labor. The vector $OQ = O^*Q'$ is the allocation of resources to Manufactures production in the integrated economy; $QO^* = Q'O$ is the allocation of resources to Food; the slope of WW is relative factor prices. As drawn, Manufactures is more capital-intensive than Food, but this is not important.

The next step is to ask whether a trading economy will reproduce this integrated economy. Let us measure Home's endowment starting from O, and Foreign's endowment starting from O^*. Then the division of the world into countries can be represented by a point in the box, such as E. If we assume that the varieties of Manufactures are so numerous that we can ignore integer constraints, then it is immediately apparent that trade reproduces the integrated economy as long as the endowment point lies inside the parallelogram OQO^*Q'.

Once we have ascertained that the integrated economy's resource allocation is reproduced, we can determine the resource allocation within each country by completing parallelograms. If the endowment is E then Home must devote resources OP_m to Manufactures and OP_f to Food;

the balance of the integrated economy's production of each good must be produced in Foreign. Because there are economies of scale in production of Manufactures, each country will produce different varieties of manufactured goods; which country produces which varieties is indeterminate but also unimportant.

We have now determined the pattern of production; to determine consumption and trade we now make use of factor prices. The line WW has a slope equal to relative factor prices, and thus can be seen as a line along which the shares of Home and Foreign in world income are constant. This means in particular that resources OC receive the same share of world income as OE, and thus that OC/OO^* is the Home country's share of world income. Let us now add the assumption of identical spending patterns, and we know that each country will consume embodied factor services in the same proportion as the world supplies. It follows that OC is also Home consumption of factor services, and thus that EC is net trade in factor services. As in the Marshallian case analyzed above, the precise pattern of trade is indeterminate but the factor content of trade reflects factor endowments.

We can say more, however. Since OC is Home consumption of factor services, it must consume OC_m of these services embodied in Manufactures and OC_f embodied in Food. This tells us that Home must be a net exporter of Manufactures and a net importer of Food.

Home is a net exporter of Manufactures; however, we have already noted that each country will be producing a different set of varieties. Because each country is assumed to demand all varieties, this means that Home will still demand some varieties produced in Foreign. The result will be a pattern of trade looking like that illustrated in Figure 6. Home will import Food and be a net exporter of Manufactures, but it will also import Manufactures, so that there will be "intra-industry" trade. This intra-industry trade is essentially caused by scale economies; if there were no scale economies, each country would be able to produce all varieties of Manufactures itself. Because intra-industry trade arises from scale economies rather than differences between countries, it does not vanish as countries become more similar; indeed, it is apparent that if we shift E toward C then the volume of intra-industry trade will rise both absolutely and relatively to inter-industry trade. In the limit, if countries have identical relative factor endowments they will still trade, but all their trade will be intra-industry trade based on scale economies.

The interesting point about this analysis of the trade pattern under monopolistic competition, as it has emerged from a number of years of clarifying analysis, is how little it seems to depend on the details. At a minor level, the differences between alternative formulations of product

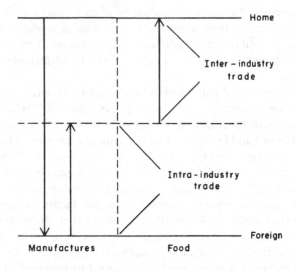

Figure 6

differentiation clearly make no difference. More important, in a broad sense the analysis is essentially the same as the one we have seen emerging from the assumption that economies of scale are external to firms. The precise pattern of trade is indeterminate, but factor proportions continue to determine trade in an average sense; scale economies lead to concentration of production and to a persistence of trade even when countries have identical factor endowments. As we will argue in a moment, the analysis of gains from trade is also quite similar.

What this suggests is that it is a mistake to lay too much stress on the Chamberlinian assumption per se. The models in this literature make extensive use of product differentiation and are often related to the empirical phenomenon of intra-industry trade, but the issues should be seen as broader. The importance of increasing returns in trade does not stand or fall on the validity of particular interpretations of product differentiation or of two-way trade within statistical classifications.

B   *Applications and extensions*

Once we move away from the central issue of trade pattern, the conclusions of the Chamberlinian approach become a bit more dependent on particular assumptions. Several areas have, however, yielded results that either look fairly general or are of particular interest. We consider four such areas: the gains from trade, trade and income distribution, intermediate goods, and transport costs.

Gains from trade

At first sight it might seem that the analysis of gains from trade in the external economies approach would carry over directly to the Chamberlinian approach as well. In fact, however, the translation is not direct, for two related reasons. First, the relevant scale variable is not the scale of the industry but the scale of production of individual firms, and with entry the effects of trade on this scale are not immediately obvious. Second, trade may lead to extra gains due to an increase in the variety of products available.

What we can certainly say is that a country will gain from trade if after trade both the number of available varieties and the scale of production of each variety are at least as large as before trade. Further, there is a strong presumption that the diversity of products will be larger after trade than before. The problem is one of pinning down what happens to scale.

Here the nature of product differentiation does make a difference. What happens to the scale of production depends (for homothetic production functions – otherwise still more complications arise) on what happens to the elasticity of demand for individual varieties. With Dixit–Stiglitz preferences, this elasticity is constant; trade offers greater variety but not greater scale [Dixit and Norman (1980); Krugman (1980, 1981)]. With Lancaster preferences, trade is likely, though not certain, to lead to more elastic demand, forcing firms to move further down their average cost curves, so that the advantages of a larger market are reflected both in greater diversity and lower average cost [Helpman (1981)].

Again, however, we should not make too much of the details. Both increased scale of production and increased diversity of available products can be seen as gains from scale, broadly defined. This insight is given a more concrete form by Helpman and Krugman (1985), where it is shown that under some assumptions both scale and diversity will move monotonically with gross industry output. This leads to the following criterion for gains from trade: Trade is beneficial if the world output of Manufactures is larger than our national output would have been in the absence of trade. The similarity to the criterion for the external economy case should be obvious.

Trade and income distribution

We have argued for a presumption that scale economies lead to additional gains from trade above and beyond those resulting from comparative advantage. This seems to be only a quantitative difference. However, it can lead to a qualitative difference in the effects of trade on particular groups within countries. Constant-returns trade models predict very strong income-distribution effects from changes in relative prices, so that even though trade is beneficial in the aggregate, individuals who draw their income mostly from factors that are relatively scarce end up worse off as a result of trade. Once we add gains from larger scale, however, it seems possible that everyone may gain from trade.

What makes this an interesting possibility is that it suggests that the effects of trade may depend on its character. If trade is mostly Heckscher–Ohlin in motivation – which we would expect if countries are quite different in relative factor endowments and there are weak economies of scale – then the conventional result that scarce factors lose from trade may be expected to hold. If trade is mostly motivated by scale economies – which would happen if countries are similar and scale is important, and would be associated with a prevalence of intra-industry trade – we might expect to find that even scarce factors gain.

This insight sounds fairly general. To demonstrate it in any rigorous way is not easy, however. Krugman (1981) develops an example in which there are natural indices of both similarity of countries and the importance of scale economies, and shows that one can in fact establish a boundary in terms of these two indices between the case where scarce factors lose and the case where they gain. It is possible to establish as a more general proposition that gains for all factors are more likely the more similar is a country's endowment to that of the world as a whole, and the smaller is the country; this is shown in Krugman (1984).

Intermediate goods

Ethier (1979, 1982b) has suggested that scale-based international trade is more likely to be important in intermediate goods than in final goods. He argues forcefully that the scope for productive differentiation of products – and the extent to which even the world market is likely to be too small to allow exhaustion of scale gains – is greatest for highly specialized components, capital goods, and so forth, rather than for consumer products.

What difference does this make? The answer is that as long as trade reproduces the integrated economy, as it does in the models of Ethier (1979, 1982b) and Helpman (1985), having trade in intermediate goods rather than final goods does not make much difference at all. The main difference is one of emphasis: It now becomes very clear that the right scale variable to emphasize, when we consider the role of scale in producing gains from trade, is the size of the world industry after trade versus the national industry before trade. We have seen that this is probably the right way to think about the issue even with consumer goods trade, but here the point becomes indisputable. The related nuance is that the doubts that occasionally surface, about whether an increase in the diversity of consumer goods really increases welfare, seem much less reasonable when it is the diversity of lathes or robots that is at issue.

We may also note a point raised by Helpman and Krugman (1985): If intermediate goods produced with economies of scale are *not* tradeable, the result will be to induce the formation of "industrial complexes" – groups of industries tied together by the need to concentrate all users of a nontradeable intermediate in the same country. In this case the pattern of specialization and trade in the Chamberlinian world will actually come to resemble the pattern in the Marshallian world described previously.

Transport costs

The exposition that we have presented of the Chamberlinian approach to trade is based heavily on the assumption that trade reproduces the integrated economy, with zero transport costs a key element in this assumption. For some purposes this is clearly an annoying limitation. No general integration of transport costs into the Chamberlinian trade model has been achieved, but some work has been done on special cases, with interesting results.

One way to allow for transport costs with a minimum of complexity is to assume that these costs are either zero or prohibitive, so that we get a strict division of industries into tradeables and nontradeables. If we then assume that there are enough tradeable sectors and that countries are sufficiently similar in their factor endowments, we can still have factor price equalization. In this case, however, factor price equalization need not mean that the integrated economy is reproduced; if differentiated products are included in the set of nontraded goods, the fragmentation of the world economy reduces the scale at which these products are produced as well as the number of varieties available to consumers.

This is a useful observation in itself; it becomes especially interesting when we combine it with some consideration of factor mobility. For if there are nontraded goods produced with increasing returns, this provides an incentive for migration to large economies, a process that will in turn reinforce these economies' size advantage. This point was noted by Helpman and Razin (1984) and elaborated upon in Helpman and Krugman (1985), where it is also noted that the incentive is actually for a change in the location of consumption, not production.

The more realistic case – where transport costs matter, but are not prohibitive – is much harder to analyze, except under very specific assumptions about tastes and technology. A very special model is considered by Krugman (1980) and elaborated upon by Venables (1985). This model generates a result that, upon reflection, looks as though it ought to be more general than the particularity of the assumptions might lead one to believe. The result is this: Other things being equal, countries will tend to be net exporters of goods for which they have relatively large domestic markets.

The logic of this result is quite simple. Suppose there is a product that is sold to two locations and can be produced in either one at equal cost. Suppose further that there are transport costs between the two locations, but that economies of scale are strong enough to assure that nonetheless the product will be produced in only one place. Then the location of production will be chosen to minimize transport costs, and this clearly means producing in the location with the larger market and exporting to the smaller market.

C   Multinationals and trade in technology

In addition to allowing a very concise treatment of the role of economies of scale in international trade, the Chamberlinian approach has proved useful as a way to organize thinking about two related issues that do not fit at all well into perfect-competition trade models. These are the role of trade in technology and the role of multinational firms.

The reason why trade in technology cannot be treated in conventional models is that investment in knowledge is hard to model except as a kind of fixed cost, which inevitably leads to a breakdown of perfect competition. Once we have a Chamberlinian setup, however, the issue is straightforward. One simply has firms in one country develop products and then sell the knowledge of how to produce these products to firms in another country, who set themselves up as monopolistic competitors. A model along these lines was developed by Feenstra and Judd (1982); their analysis makes clear the point that trade in technology need not be much different in its effects from any trade in which fixed costs play a significant role.

A natural extension of this analysis is to imagine that for some reason licensing or sale of technology is not possible, so that technology can only be transferred within firms. In this case the model of technology transfer can then be reinterpreted as one of multinational firms. A simple model of this type is set forth in Krugman (1980); like the Feenstra–Judd analysis, it suggests that multinational enterprise is more like ordinary trade than one might have supposed.

The identification of direct foreign investment with technology transfer is too narrow, however. A more general approach was suggested by Helpman (1984) and in turn simplified and generalized in Helpman and Krugman (1985). This approach essentially argues that multinational enterprise occurs whenever there exist related activities for which the following is true: there are simultaneously transaction-cost incentives to integrate these activities within a single firm and factor-cost or other incentives to separate the activities geographically. Suppose, for example, there is a two-stage production process consisting of a capital-intensive upstream activity and a labor-intensive downstream activity, and that (for any of the usual causes) there are compelling reasons to combine these activities inside vertically integrated firms. Suppose further that countries are sufficiently different in factor endowments that unless these activities are geographically separated there will be unequal factor prices. Then the result will clearly be the emergence of firms that extend across national boundaries.

Probably the main contribution of the new literature on multinational enterprise has been to clear away some confusions about what multinationals do. What the new models make clear, above all, is that multinational enterprise is not a type of factor mobility. It represents an extension of control, not necessarily a movement of capital. The key lesson is that direct foreign investment is not investment.

D *Summary*

When it was first introduced, the Chamberlinian approach to trade analysis represented a breakthrough. For the first time it became possible to discuss trade issues involving scale economies and imperfect competition intelligibly. At the same time, however, it was difficult to assess how general were the insights gained from the very special models first presented.

Subsequent work has removed some of this uncertainty. Many of the conclusions of the monopolistic competition approach have proved to be independent of the details of the specification. In fact, as we have suggested, in a broad sense many of the insights carry over to other market structures as well. This realization in a way devalues the Chamberlinian approach – it should now be seen as one of several useful analytical devices rather than as *the* alternative to constant-returns trade theory. But the simplicity and clarity of monopolistic competition models of trade ensures that they will remain a valuable part of the toolbox for a long time.

3 The Cournot approach

Our first two approaches to trade under conditions of increasing returns may be viewed as being driven by the desire to focus on decreasing costs as a motive for trade, while avoiding as much as possible being bogged down in issues of market structure. The Marshallian approach preserves perfect competition despite the presence of scale economies by assuming that these economies are wholly external. The Chamberlinian approach abandons perfect competition but turns instead to the opposite pole of a world of little monopolists, avoiding the awkward middle ground of oligopoly. As a research strategy, this artful theoretical dodging is wholly defensible, especially given our continuing lack of anything like a general theory of competition among small numbers of firms. Yet we cannot completely ignore the oligopoly issue, especially if we suspect that the interaction of imperfect competition with trade may give rise to important effects missed by these approaches.

There is no general analysis of oligopoly; but even a special analysis is better than none. Some important insights into international trade have been gained by adopting the admittedly unsatisfactory Cournot assumption that imperfectly competitive firms take each others' outputs as given. Much of the usefulness of this approach has come in the analysis of trade policy, discussed by Dixit (Chapter 9, this volume); but two themes deserve discussion in this chapter. The first is the role of trade in reducing monopoly power and increasing competition. The second is the possibility that market segmentation and price discrimination can serve as a cause of seemingly pointless trade.

A   *Trade and market power*

Suppose there is some industry that in each of two countries contains only a few firms. Suppose also that these firms compete in a Cournot fashion, so that (in equilibrium) price will be above marginal cost by a markup that depends on the perceived elasticity of per-firm demand. Finally, suppose that in the absence of trade in this industry the price of the good it produces would be the same in both countries.

Under perfect competition, allowing trade in this industry would have no effect. With Cournot competition, however, this is no longer the case. If trade is opened, each firm will become part of a larger, more competitive market. It will see itself as facing a higher elasticity of demand, leading it to expand output. Thus industry output will expand, and the price will fall. If the countries are, as described, symmetric then welfare will rise in both, due to the reduction on the monopoly distortion. Interestingly, this effect need not be associated with any actual trade in either direction. It is potential foreign trade (which changes the slope of the demand curve), rather than the actual trade flows, that exerts the pro-competitive effect.

The possibility of gains from trade due to increased competition has been understood for a long time. It was emphasized in particular by Caves (1974). However, early analyses usually assumed that the move was from pure monopoly to perfect competition; only with the work of Dixit and Norman (1980) was the more reasonable case – of movement from more to less imperfect competition – formally considered.

Why should there be only a limited number of firms in the industry? The obvious answer is the presence of some form of economies of scale internal to firms. Once we allow this, however, it becomes an obvious possibility that the increase in competition due to trade may leave firms unable to charge a markup on marginal cost sufficient to cover their average cost. The result will be exit. Dixit and Norman develop a simple example in which they show that the effect of opening trade in a Cournot market is to lead to a world industry that has fewer, larger firms than the sum of national industries before trade, but where competition is nonetheless increased. Thus the opening of trade leads not only to a reduction in the monopoly distortion but also to an increase in productive efficiency. Once again, it is the potential for trade (rather than the trade flows themselves) that does the good work.

The pro-competitive effect of trade is not exactly a scale economy story. It goes naturally with such a story, however, precisely because decreasing costs are the most natural explanation of imperfect competition.

B   Market segmentation and price discrimination

At the beginning of this chapter we suggested that trade can always be explained as being due to the combined effects of two motives for specialization, differences between countries and economies of scale. Remarkably, the Cournot approach has actually led to the discovery of a third possible explanation for trade – although arguably not of equal importance in practice. This is the possibility that trade may arise purely because imperfectly competitive firms have an incentive to try to gain incremental sales by "dumping" in each others' home markets.

The seminal paper is by Brander (1981). The model envisages an industry consisting of two firms, each in a different country. These firms are assumed to be able to choose separately their deliveries to each national market, and to take the other firm's deliveries to each market as given. Suppose that initially there were no trade in this industry. Then each firm would act as a monopolist, restricting market deliveries to sustain the price. There would, however, then be an incentive for each firm to sell a little bit in the other's home market as long as the price there exceeds the marginal cost. This process will continue until, with symmetric firms, each firm has a 50 percent share of each market.

If the markets are separated by transport costs, the outcome will not be so extreme. Nonetheless, it is shown in Brander and Krugman (1983) that even with transport costs there may be "cross-hauling" – two-way trade in the same product. What sustains this trade is the fact that each firm sees itself as facing a higher elasticity of demand on its exports than it does on domestic sales, because it has a smaller share of the foreign than the domestic market. This means that the firm is willing to sell abroad at a smaller markup over marginal cost than at home, making it willing to absorb the transport cost on foreign sales. Indeed, it is this difference in perceived demand elasticity that drives the determination of the volume of trade: The equilibrium market share of imports is precisely that which makes exporters just willing to absorb transport costs.

This theory of seemingly pointless trade, which is described in Brander and Krugman as "reciprocal dumping," is related in important ways to the traditional industrial organization literature on basing point pricing and cross-hauling [Smithies (1942)]. What the new models make clear, however, is that despite the waste involved in transporting the same good in two directions, trade can still be beneficial. Against pointless transport costs must be set the increase in competition. Indeed, if there is free entry and exit of firms, it can be shown that the gains from "rationalizing" the industry and increasing the scale of production always outweigh the waste of transport.

C   *Summary*

The application of Cournot-type models to trade theory leads to new and important insights about international trade. Papers using the Cournot approach have had a fundamentally different orientation from those using the Marshallian or Chamberlinian approaches. Instead of focusing on economies of scale and treating market structure as (at best) a supporting player, this literature has treated imperfect competition as the protagonist and used economies of scale mostly as an explanation of the existence of oligopoly.

The payoff from this shift in emphasis is substantial. A new source of potential gains from trade is identified – namely, the effect of trade in increasing competition (and, if it induces exit, in rationalizing production). More surprisingly, a new cause of trade is also identified: interpenetration of markets because oligopolists perceive a higher elasticity of demand on exports than on domestic sales.

The major importance of the Cournot approach, however, lies outside the scope of this chapter. This is its versatility and flexibility for the discussion of trade policy. The models we have described under the headings of Marshallian and Chamberlinian approaches depend – as a way to make the analysis tractable – mostly on the assumption that trade reproduces an integrated economy. Tariffs, quotas, and subsidies inevitably break this perfect integration, rendering these models unsuitable. The Cournot approach, however, does not have this problem, and has led to a rapidly growing literature on trade and industrial policy under imperfect competition.

4 Conclusions

A *What we have learned*

Intellectual progress is often hard to perceive. Once new ideas have become absorbed they can seem obvious, and one begins to believe that one always understood them. The ideas that trade can be caused by increasing returns, and that increased scale is a source of gains from trade, are sufficiently simple that the memory of how little these ideas were appreciated even five years ago is fading fast. Thus it is probably worth restating what we have learned.

It is probably fair to say that a few years ago, if international economists thought at all about the role of increasing returns in trade, they implicitly thought in terms of a 2×2 model in which one sector is subject to external economies. In this approach, economies appear as a modification or distortion of comparative advantage, rather than an independent source of trade. The effect of increasing returns is to make it likely, other things being equal, that large countries will export goods subject to scale economies. One can find many writings in which the view is taken that this effect is the only possible role of increasing returns in international trade.

What we have now moved to is a far more satisfactory view, where increasing returns are fully integrated into the trade model rather than grafted on to the Heckscher–Ohlin model as an afterthought. The new approaches allow us to understand clearly that decreasing costs are an independent source of both trade and gains from trade, and to have a clear vision of a trading world in which both increasing returns and differences in factor endowments drive the pattern of specialization and trade.

This shift in view was initially brought about largely by the introduction of new models of imperfect competition into trade theory. With some perspective, however, we can now see that the details of these models are less important than might have appeared at first. What is really crucial for the new view of trade is not so much the particular model of market structure but a change in modeling strategy. The key breakthrough has been a willingness to ask different questions, and to be satisfied with a somewhat different answer than we were used to.

Traditionally, trade models have given us a precise description of the pattern of trade in goods. In models where there are important increasing returns, however, a characteristic feature is the existence of multiple equilibria. What we have learned to do is essentially to live with multiple equilibria, by focusing on models where a good deal can be said without requiring that we know the precise pattern of specialization and trade. By concentrating on resource allocation rather than goods production; by looking at trade in embodied factor services rather than in the precise goods in which these factor services are embodied; by noting that it may be more important to be able to show that production will be concentrated somewhere than to say where it will be concentrated – thus are we able to bypass the complexities that for many years led trade theory to avoid discussion of increasing returns.

To answer a question by changing it is not something to everyone's taste. However, the payoff here has been remarkable: By what (in retrospect) seems a minor shift in emphasis, we have greatly enlarged the range of phenomena that our theory can encompass.

B   *What needs to be done*

The theory of trade under increasing returns is not a finished product. Much work still needs to be done, especially in the three following areas.

(i) *Dynamic models.* In the real world, many of the advantages of large scale probably take the form of dynamic economies, either in the form of learning effects or fixed-cost-like R&D. The problem is that dynamic competition in oligopolistic markets may be quite different in character from what static models would suggest; such competition needs further study.

(ii) *More realistic models of competition.* Not much need be said here. The external economy approach is clearly unrealistic in assuming perfect competition; the Chamberlinian approach relies on fundamentally peculiar cross-restrictions on technology and utility; the Cournot approach is surely far too crude.

(iii) *The unreproduced integrated economy.* Assuming that trade reproduces the integrated economy does wonders for simplifying the analysis. Now we must edge back toward considering what happens when – especially because of trade barriers and transport costs – trade does not reproduce the integrated economy.

These theoretical extensions are important and needed. What we need even more, however, is to go from qualitative theory to numerical applications. This has always been difficult in international trade. The new work on trade makes it even harder, because once we are no longer assuming perfect competition and constant returns we need far more information to model behavior. In fact, we probably need a whole new methodology for empirical work, possibly mixing case-study evidence and even interview results with econometrics and simulation techniques. Still, now that we have an elegant theory, this is the obvious next step.

References

Brander, J. 1981. "Intra-industry Trade in Identical Commodities." *Journal of International Economics* 11: 1–14.

Brander, J., and P. Krugman. 1983. "A 'Reciprocal Dumping' Model of International Trade." *Journal of International Economics* 15: 313–21.

Caves, R. E. 1974. *International Trade, International Investment, and Imperfect Markets.* Princeton Special Papers in International Economics No. 10. Princeton University.

Chacholiades, M. 1978. *International Trade Theory and Policy.* New York: McGraw-Hill.

Dixit, A. K., and V. Norman. 1980. *Theory of International Trade.* Cambridge: Cambridge University Press.

Dixit, A. K., and J. Stiglitz. 1977. "Monopolistic Competition and Optimum Product Diversity." *American Economic Review* 67: 297–308.

Ethier, W. 1979. "Internationally Decreasing Costs and World Trade." *Journal of International Economics* 9: 1–24.

1982a. "Decreasing Costs in International Trade and Frank Graham's Argument for Protection." *Econometrica* 50: 1243–68.

1982b. "National and International Returns to Scale in the Modern Theory of International Trade." *American Economic Review* 72: 389–405.

Feenstra, R., and K. Judd. 1982. "Tariffs, Technology Transfer, and Welfare." *Journal of Political Economy* 90: 1142–65.

Graham, F. 1923. "Some Aspects of Protection Further Considered." *Quarterly Journal of Economics* 37: 199–227.

Helpman, E. 1981. "International Trade in the Presence of Product Differentiation, Economies of Scale, and Monopolistic Competition – A Chamberlinian-Heckscher-Ohlin Approach." *Journal of International Economics* 11: 305–40.

1984. "A Simple Theory of Trade with Multinational Corporations." *Journal of Political Economy* 92: 451–72.

1985. "International Trade in Differentiated Middle Products." In D. Hague and K. G. Jungenfeldt (eds.), *Structural Adjustment in Developed Open Economies.* New York: Macmillan.

Helpman, E., and P. Krugman. 1985. *Market Structure and Foreign Trade: Increasing Returns, Imperfect Competition, and the International Economy.* Cambridge, Mass.: MIT Press.

Helpman, E., and A. Razin. 1984. "Increasing Returns, Monopolistic Competition and Factor Movements: A Welfare Analysis." In H. Kierzkowski (ed.),

Monopolistic Competition and International Trade. New York: Oxford University Press.

Kemp, M., and T. Negishi. 1970. "Variable Returns to Scale, Commodity Taxes, Factor Market Distortions, and Their Implications for Trade Gains." *Swedish Journal of Economics* 72: 1–11.

Krugman, P. 1979. "Increasing Returns, Monopolistic Competition, and International Trade." *Journal of International Economics* 9: 469–79.

———. 1980. "Scale Economies, Product Differentiation, and the Pattern of Trade." *American Economic Review* 70: 950–9.

———. 1981. "Intraindustry Specialization and the Gains from Trade." *Journal of Political Economy* 89: 959–73.

———. 1982. "The New Theories of International Trade and the Multinational Corporation." In. D. Audretsch and C. Kindleberger (eds.), *The Multinational Corporation in the 1980s.* Cambridge, Mass.: MIT Press.

———. 1984. "Growth, Trade, and Income Distribution under Increasing Returns." Mimeo.

Lancaster, K. 1979. *Variety, Equity, and Efficiency.* New York: Columbia University Press.

———. 1980. "Intra-industry Trade Under Perfect Monopolistic Competition." *Journal of International Economics* 10: 151–75.

Matthews, R. C. O. 1949. "Reciprocal Demand and Increasing Returns." *Review of Economic Studies* 37: 149–58.

Melvin, J. 1969. "Increasing Returns to Scale as a Determinant of Trade." *Canadian Journal of Economics* 2: 389–402.

Panagariya, A. 1981. "Variable Returns to Scale in Production and Patterns of Specialization." *American Economic Review* 71: 221–30.

Smithies, A. 1942. "An Economic Analysis of the Basing-Point System." *American Economic Review* 32: 705–19.

Spence, A. M. 1976. "Product Selection, Fixed Costs, and Monopolistic Competition." *Review of Economic Studies* 43: 217–36.

Venables, A. 1985. "Trade and Trade Policy with Differentiated Products: A Chamberlinian–Ricardo Model." Mimeo.

CHAPTER 9

Strategic aspects of trade policy

Avinash Dixit

1 Introduction

To most non-economists, and to some economists, the word "strategic" in the title will have either military connotations (securing our supplies of essential materials, denying such materials or sensitive technology to our adversaries) or industrial policy connotations (identification and promotion of sectors that are of special importance to our economy). The role of trade policy in such situations is indeed an interesting question; for recent analyses see Cooper (1987, pp. 305–15) and Krugman (1987), respectively.

However, it has become customary in international trade theory to use the word "strategic" in a different sense – namely, that of game theory.[1] In the working of trade and trade policy, there is the usual structural interaction among the firms and governments: The outcome for each depends on the actions of all. The added element of strategic interaction arises when each decision maker is aware that he faces an environment that is not passive, but composed of other rational decision makers, who in turn are similarly aware, and so forth.

One expects such strategic interactions to arise when there is a small number of large buyers, sellers, or policy makers. During the last four decades, such conditions have arisen due to the growth of large and multinational firms, of public enterprises in major industries, and of large

I thank Wilfred Ethier, Gene Grossman, Kala Krishna, Paul Krugman, Raymond Riezman, Ariel Rubinstein, and T. N. Srinivasan for helpful comments on earlier drafts, and the National Science Foundation for research support under grant SES-8509536.
[1] Readers unfamiliar with the elements of game theory will find a simple account in Bacharach (1976); Chapters 4 and 5 are particularly relevant to our concerns. Many concepts and techniques from oligopoly theory will also be useful; Henderson and Quandt (1980, Chapter 8) and Friedman (1983, Chapters 2, 5, and 9) give the necessary background.

countries and blocks with considerable economic power. Until recently, trade theory neglected these developments. The standard model assumed perfect competition among firms, and allowed only one government to be active in policy making. The only exception was the analysis of optimum tariffs and retaliation, reviewed in Section 2. The main conclusion of this theory was that interference with free trade was justified only for the case of a large country seeking to improve its terms of trade, and even then it was harmful to the world as a whole. This model and its result were increasingly seen as irrelevant by practical people, who advocated more interventionist trade policies.

In the last few years, trade theorists have turned their attention to issues of imperfect competition and strategic policies. They have produced a much richer understanding of the problems as well as policy prescriptions that modify the conventional wisdom of free trade, but offer little comfort to its practical mercantilist critics. This chapter is a selective survey of these developments.

Strategic interactions can arise in international trade in several different ways, and they can be classified along many dimensions for the purpose of analysis. Consider first the distinction between one-off or static interactions, and repeated or sequential dynamic ones. In a static setting, we can have simultaneous-move games; this is the way the familiar analysis of optimum tariffs with retaliation was modeled. Dynamics introduces richer possibilities. When a game is played repeatedly, it becomes possible to achieve new cooperative or coercive outcomes sustained by an appropriate structure of future rewards and punishments. Some recent work on the optimum tariff problem has taken this approach. If moves are sequential – for example, if governments fix their trade policy rules before firms choose their outputs or prices – we find other new possibilities, such as commitments and threats. The use of such devices for capturing pure profits, deterring entry, and so forth has been studied in several contexts.

Another aspect to consider is whether the players choose their actions in coordination; that is (in technical terms) whether the game is cooperative. Most of the work on trade policy takes the noncooperative approach, and with good reason. The enforcement mechanisms at the international level for any explicitly cooperative arrangements are very feeble. Contract laws and tort laws are virtually non-existent; sovereign immunity handicaps firms in their dealings with foreign governments; the GATT has loopholes or is bypassed. Therefore it is usual to stipulate that the players act independently and that any cooperation to emerge is tacit, being sustained by the players' self-interest. This may include the rationally foreseen prospect of the collapse of the arrangement, or of punishments that are in the other countries' interest to inflict, but not actions directed by any supranational body.

There is yet another dimension of classification, one that provides the basis for the organization of this chapter: It considers the *types* of strategic decision makers involved. First we have the case where all firms are price takers, and only the governments are game players. This is the familiar problem of optimum tariffs with retaliation, which is examined in Section 2. Then we have oligopolistic firms interacting among themselves while government policies interact at another level or stage of a sequential game; this is the subject of Section 3. Finally, there are confrontations of large firms with governments. These occur most often in contexts of direct investment; Section 4 examines some of the issues involved.

In all of this work, consumers are presumed to be nonstrategic price takers. This is often reasonable, but there is a lot of trade in intermediate products, where the buyers are other firms with some monopsony power. This situation remains unexplored in the literature.

I shall omit two important categories of interactions for reasons of space. The first is cooperative pursuit of policies by coalitions of countries – that is, customs union theory. The survey by Lipsey (1960) remains useful; some recent developments can be found in Ethier and Horn (1984) and Riezman (1984). The second topic is the strategy that goes into the formation of trade policy within a country – that is, the positive theory of protectionism, including rent seeking. Baldwin (1982) offers a good overview, and Bhagwati (1982) presents a synthesis of the theory.

2 Trade strategies with competitive markets

Even if individual consumers and producers everywhere are small enough to be price takers, countries can be so large as to have some monopoly power in world trade. Their governments can use trade restrictions to exploit it. When two or more governments attempt to do so at the same time, their strategies interact.

The first formal model of this game is due to Johnson (1953/54). He considered a two-good, two-country world in which the policy instruments were import tariffs and the game was of the static, simultaneous-move kind. Mayer (1981) cast the model in a more modern framework, gave some algebraic details, and extended the analysis. I shall begin by outlining this work, and then examine some extensions and modifications. The exposition will be confined to the two-good, two-country case. There is no difficulty in extending the noncooperative model and interpreting the results for the case of more goods and countries; see Kuga (1973) for a formal statement. In the cooperative mode, there arise new possibilities

Avinash Dixit

of coalition formation, which lead to customs union theory. That is too large a subject to cover here.

Call the countries "home" and "foreign," and call the goods x and y. Choose the labels so that the home country imports good x, and let t denote its ad valorem tariff rate.[2] Let t^* be the tariff rate of the foreign country on its imports of y. In terms of a common numeraire, let (p_x, p_y) and (p_x^*, p_y^*) be the prices in the two countries, so that

$$p_x = p_x^*(1+t) \quad \text{and} \quad p_y^* = p_y(1+t^*).$$

Let $\pi = p_x^*/p_y$ be the relative price of x in "no-man's land," that is, with neither tariff applied. Then π measures the terms of trade. A decrease in π cheapens the home country's imports; this improves its terms of trade and worsens those of the foreign country.

In this model, intra-country distributional issues are neglected. Thus each country has an indifference map representing the tastes of a single consumer or a Samuelsonian social welfare function. Given t and π, we can determine the home country's import demand $M(\pi, t)$ and welfare level $U(\pi, t)$. Similarly, for the foreign country we have $M^*(\pi, t^*)$ and $U^*(\pi, t^*)$. Next, the trade balance condition,

$$\pi M(\pi, t) = M^*(\pi, t^*),$$

determines π as a function of t and t^*. Substituting this into the earlier expressions for the welfare levels, we can express them also as functions of t and t^*; let W and W^* denote these new functions, so that

$$W(t, t^*) = U(\pi(t, t^*), t) \quad \text{and} \quad W^*(t, t^*) = U^*(\pi(t, t^*), t^*).$$

Assuming the Marshall–Lerner stability condition (the sum of the elasticities of import demands exceeds 1), we find that each country's tariff improves its terms of trade; that is, $\partial \pi/\partial t < 0$ and $\partial \pi/\partial t^* > 0$. Then each country's tariff harms the other; that is, $\partial W/\partial t^* < 0$ and $\partial W^*/\partial t < 0$. We also have $\partial W/\partial t > 0$ when $t = 0$; that is, the home country gains by restricting trade slightly if it is initially not doing so, for any given value of t^*. Similarly, $\partial W^*/\partial t^* > 0$ when $t^* = 0$ for the foreign country.

Further results require special assumptions. The case that is commonly regarded as central in this analysis is shown in Figure 1. In (t, t^*) space, we have the contours of W and W^*, and some further information derived from them. Vertically lower W contours correspond to higher home-country welfare. (i) It is assumed that W has a unique maximum with respect to t for each given t^*. The locus of these maxima, or the curve

[2] Negative values of t correspond to import subsidies; the lower bound on t is -1.

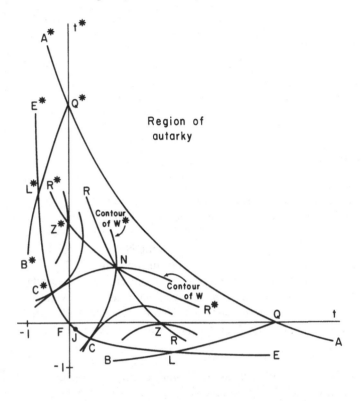

Figure 1

RR defined by $\partial W/\partial t = 0$, is the home country's reaction or best-response curve.[3] This is shown negatively sloped. Such need not be the case, but for our present purpose that does not matter.[4] Similarly, we have R^*R^* for the foreign country. Note that $t > 0$ along RR and $t^* > 0$ along R^*R^*. (ii) It is assumed that RR and R^*R^* have a unique intersection point N. This is the Nash equilibrium of the noncooperative tariff game. Neither country acting independently would want to change its tariff rate away from N. Note that N must lie in the first quadrant. The central case under consideration assumes that the free-trade point F is preferred to N by

[3] It should be said that in a static game there is no rigorous sense of response or reaction. These curves should be thought of as steps in the construction of the Nash equilibrium.

[4] We can transform $\partial W/\partial t = 0$ into the usual optimum tariff formula, $t = 1/\epsilon^*$, where ϵ^* is the elasticity of the foreign country's supply of exports of x with respect to the terms of trade π. There is no general economic reason why ϵ^* should have any monotonicity as t^* changes.

both countries. This need not be the case; one (but not both) may prefer N.[5] From time to time, I shall depart from the central case to cover this possibility.

Figure 1 shows two other loci that prove useful. The first, EE^*, gives the Pareto efficient combinations of tariff policies. Because this requires the relative price of x to be the same in the two countries, we have

$$\pi(1+t) = \pi/(1+t^*),$$

or

$$(1+t)(1+t^*) = 1. \tag{1}$$

The free-trade point is of course on EE^*, but there is a continuum of other efficient policies where one country or the other subsidizes imports. The welfare of the home country falls steadily, and that of the foreign country rises, as we move from E to E^* along the locus. Points on the portion CC^* are preferred by both countries to the Nash equilibrium N. In our central case, the free-trade point F lies in the range CC^*.

The other locus is that of tariff combinations that eliminate all trade. Define p_a, the home country's autarkic relative price of x, as that value of $\pi(1+t)$ that reduces M to zero. Similarly, define $p_a^* = \pi/(1+t^*)$ when $M^* = 0$ for the foreign country. Eliminating π between the two, we have

$$(1+t)(1+t^*) = p_a/p_a^*. \tag{2}$$

The right-hand side exceeds 1 because the home country imports good x; this is just the principle of comparative advantage. Then the autarky locus AA^* defined by (2) lies above the efficient locus EE^*. All along and everywhere above AA^*, each country's welfare is constant at the autarkic level.[6]

Suppose AA^* meets the axes at $Q = (t_a, 0)$ and $Q^* = (0, t_a^*)$ respectively. The figure shows two other curves, QB and Q^*B^*, meeting EE^* at L and L^* respectively. In the region $A^*Q^*B^*$, the home country is worse off than it would be in autarky. This is because it is subsidizing imports too heavily; see Dixit and Norman (1980, pp. 72–3) for details. Similarly, the foreign country is worse off in the region AQB than in autarky.

---

[5] As Figure 1 suggests, our central case will obtain when there is reasonable symmetry between the countries. Parameterizing the relevant functions and examining asymmetric cases, Johnson (1953/54) finds that the country with the more elastic import demand is the one more likely to prefer the Nash equilibrium of tariffs to free trade. Kennan and Riezman (1984) find that it is likely to be the larger country.

[6] I interpret a tariff as a tax on an imported good, with neither tax nor subsidy if the same good comes to be exported. An alternative is to think of it as a wedge that maintains the home price above the foreign price, thus acting as a tax if the good is imported and as a subsidy if it is exported. With this interpretation, the region above AA^* would have trade with the reverse pattern. I shall leave it to the reader to develop this case.

Now consider any tariff rates (t, t^*) with $t \geq t_a$ and $t^* \geq t_a^*$. This is a Nash equilibrium of the tariff game. Each country's tariff is so high that no trade occurs even if the other country sets a zero tariff. Therefore the two are helplessly locked into autarky. Recall that we already have a Nash equilibrium at N with positive volume of trade. Thus there is an inherent non-uniqueness of equilibrium.

This does not appear to have been recognized in the literature.[7] One can argue that in a single play of the game, the non-uniqueness is not a problem, and that the point N with positive trade will emerge. First, because N is preferred by both countries, one can be reasonably confident that, even without any explicit communication, it will serve as a focal point. That is, the countries will have an intuitive understanding to choose the tariffs appropriate to N rather than the autarkic ones. There is also a stability argument. If a choice happens to be made in the region of autarky, chance deviations or shifts in the economic conditions will eventually push it on or across the border of this region. Then a conventional adjustment process will take us to N. Neither of these arguments is logically watertight, but together they carry some force. For the most part, when I speak of the static Nash equilibrium I shall refer to N.

However, in dynamic contexts, the existence of another equilibrium with autarky offers some benefits. In a repeated game, the two countries can try to sustain tacit cooperation by invoking the threat of a costly outcome if either country defects from the mutually beneficial policies. In such a situation, reversion to A is a more potent threat than N, and it pays the countries to achieve an intuitive understanding that A will be the fallback. We will see the effects of this soon.

Figure 2 translates some of the results of the above analysis to the welfare space. The notation is preserved; for example, A is the autarky point and Z is the point where t is optimized given $t^* = 0$. Of the various special features of Figure 1, only two have a significant impact on Figure 2. The first is the assumption of uniqueness of the Nash equilibrium; this will be maintained throughout. The other is the assumption that the free-trade point F lies on the portion CC^* of the efficient locus; this will be reexamined from time to time.

The most important thing to note from these figures is that the Nash equilibrium is not efficient. There are several other joint policy choices that will leave both countries better off. At all of these points, tariff rates must be lower in both countries than at N. In our central case, free trade is one such point, and an efficient one. However, the countries disagree in their ranking of the efficient alternatives. In the static game, their inde-

---

[7] Under the alternative interpretation of a tariff mentioned in note 6, autarky is not a possible Nash equilibrium.

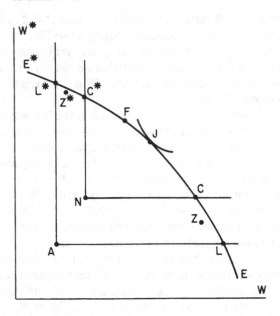

Figure 2

pendent pursuit of self-interest takes them to the inefficient Nash out-come. This is an instance of the familiar Prisoners' Dilemma. Mutual benefit requires explicit or tacit coordination to reduce tariffs. The question is whether some alternative mechanism can achieve this.

Mayer (1981) considers a coordinated reform scheme like the ones used in the Kennedy and Tokyo Rounds of GATT. Taking the initial tariffs as given, a formula for reducing them is determined. This can be a proportional cut, replacing t by t/α and t^* by t^*/α for some number α greater than 1. Or it can be more complex, like the Swiss formula of the Tokyo Round, replacing t by $t/(1+\alpha t)$ and t^* by $t^*/(1+\alpha t^*)$. The magnitude of the cut is governed by the size of α; this can be chosen to achieve the largest cut compatible with leaving both countries better off than the status quo. The new point can become the status quo in the next round of negotiation. However, the procedure does not eliminate conflict. One country does better under one formula, and the other does better under another. Thus the focus of bargaining shifts to the choice of the formula. There are other problems, too. With many countries and goods, the determination of simple formulas capable of benefiting all of them is by no means easy. Despite these difficulties, the method is noteworthy because of the previous attempts to use it in practice.

Riezman (1982) considers a different cooperative method – namely, the arbitration scheme (often called the bargaining solution) proposed by Nash. He allows only two basic choices of trade strategies to each country: either free trade under all circumstances or the optimal response to the other's tariff; that is, to operate on the appropriate locus RR or R^*R^*. Correspondingly, there are four basic outcomes, namely F, N, Z, and Z^*. Mixed strategies are also allowed. Thus the feasible region is the quadrilateral $NZFZ^*$ (not shown explicitly). We can be more general and allow all points on or below EE^*.

The next step is to look for the threat point – that is, the outcome if there is no agreement. The natural candidates for this are the Nash equilibria N and A. Choose the former for definiteness; its welfare levels are (W_N, W_N^*). Then the cooperative scheme splits the gains above this by choosing (W, W^*) from the feasible set to maximize $(W - W_N)(W^* - W_N^*)$. This is done finding a tangency between EE^* and a rectangular hyperbola based on N. The result is the point J in the figure.

It can be argued that A is the better choice for the threat point than N. Each choice will lead to a final outcome on EE^*. Because both are Pareto efficient, the countries cannot be unanimous: One must prefer the outcome based on the threat point N and the other that based on A. The latter country can take unilateral action to bring about its preferred threat – namely, levy its prohibitive tariff – whereas the former cannot. Therefore A is the more natural threat point.

The main problem with this solution is its implementation. Unless the final efficient point to be implemented on EE^* happens to be the free-trade point F, one of the countries must subsidize imports, a most uncommon and politically difficult policy. An external agency may be needed to force the countries to follow the policies corresponding to the arbitration solution. In a world of sovereign countries, this is politically and administratively very difficult.

Let us therefore turn to self-enforcing or tacit coordination. This theory exploits the close formal analogy between our problem and that of Cournot duopoly. For tariff rates of the two countries read output levels of two firms, and for welfare levels read profits. Then our Figures 1 and 2 become the standard pictures of industrial organization theory.[8] The question of how two countries might cooperate tacitly to reduce tariffs for mutual benefit becomes that of how two firms might collude to restrict output to raise prices and profits. A great deal is known about the latter question, and we can translate that to our context.

---

[8] Figure 1 is a more elaborate form of Figure 8.1 in Henderson and Quandt (1980) or Figure 4.1 in Bacharach (1976); Figure 2 is Figure 5.2 of Friedman (1983) and related to Figure 5.2 of Bacharach. See also Figure 3 below.

The simplest and the best-known approach stems from the recognition that in reality such relationships are long-lived; that is to say, the game is played repeatedly.[9] First suppose the repetition is infinite or indefinite. Call the whole game consisting of all the repetitions a supergame, and each iteration a play. Let r be the discount rate between two successive plays. In the case of indefinite repetitions, this can capture the probability of the game ending at the next iteration.

In the supergame each country chooses a strategy, which is a complete plan specifying the action to be taken at each play. Each such choice can depend on the history, consisting of observations of the other's choices and the memory of one's own choices in prior plays. We then look for a Nash equilibrium of such complete strategies.

The simple pair of strategies where each country makes the static Nash choice in each play is always such an equilibrium. When the other country is acting thus, one cannot do any better by acting differently. Thus repetition need not lead to tacit cooperation. It may do so, however, because there may be other equilibria.

Consider some point $P = (W_0, W_0^*)$ that lies within the realm of technical possibilities – that is, on or below the efficient frontier EE^* of Figure 2 – and is strictly Pareto superior to the Nash point N. Suppose (t_0, t_0^*) are the tariff rates that give rise to P. Consider the following strategy for the home country: At each play, choose t_0 so long as the history is one of adherence to P; otherwise make the static Nash choice. Define a strategy for the foreign country analogously. Let us see when such a pair of strategies can constitute an equilibrium.

At each play, the home country has the temptation to switch to a tariff rate t' that is the best response to t_0^*; that is, so that the point (t', t_0^*) lies on the reaction function RR. This catches the foreign country off guard, and gives the home country a welfare level $W' > W_0$ for this period. However, at the next play this defection will be a part of the history, and the outcome will revert to the static Nash point with welfare $W_N < W_0$. The home country will not find this switch of strategy attractive if the short-run gain is more than offset by the discounted present value of the subsequent loss; that is, if

$$(W' - W_0) < (W_0 - W_N)/r. \tag{3}$$

This will be true if r is sufficiently small. There will be a similar inequality for the foreign country. If both of them are satisfied, then neither country will attempt a defection from P, and that point can be sustained as a tacitly cooperative outcome that gives both countries a permanently higher welfare level than the static Nash point.

[9] For a discussion of this in the oligopoly context, see Friedman (1983, pp. 123–34).

One point remains to be clarified. What keeps each country from yielding to the temptation of the short-run gain is the implicit threat that doing so will cause the arrangement to collapse. Is this threat credible? That is to say, if the matter were put to the test would it be in the other country's interest to carry out the stated strategy of reverting to static Nash choices? If such is not the case, the equilibrium becomes less reliable as a guide to reality; in technical terms, it is not a subgame-perfect equilibrium.

What helps us here is the fact that the strategies of always choosing the static Nash actions constitute an equilibrium of the supergame. Therefore, if the countries start out on the path of tacit coordination at P, and by mischance or miscalculation a defection occurs, the strategies of reverting to the static Nash point become optimal responses to each other, and therefore credible.

However, the story is not free of conceptual difficulties. The most serious is that of non-uniqueness. This should be evident from the fact that we allowed P to be any technically feasible point that was Pareto superior to N. In fact, if the interest rate is zero, the "folk theorem" of repeated games [see Aumann (1985)] tells us that any point in the region NCC^* of Figure 2 can be achieved as a perfect equilibrium of the supergame. Faced with such a multiplicity, countries will find it difficult to coordinate on any one point, especially since their interests diverge in this matter. If the free-trade point lies in the range CC^*, and if it satisfies condition (3) and the corresponding one for the foreign country, then its prominence may give it the role of a focal point at which their expectations might converge [Schelling (1960, pp. 99–115)]. Otherwise, the outcome seems unclear.

There is another kind of non-uniqueness that is less serious: One outcome might be sustained by different underlying strategies. For example, if (3) is satisfied with some slack, then the threat of reversion to static Nash choices for a finite but large enough number of plays will be sufficient to remove the temptation to defect. The best-known strategy of this kind is "tit-for-tat"; see the recent discussion by Axelrod (1983). Although its perfectness is problematic, its simplicity may have much practical value.

We have so far interpreted (3) as giving a bound on the discount rate to sustain a given degree of cooperation. We can also look at it from another angle, showing the extent of cooperation that is possible for a given discount rate. Typically, as W_0 increases, the gain from defection rises faster than the loss from reversion to static Nash. Therefore, for given r, (3) defines an upper bound on W_0. There is a similar bound for the other country. These limits may preclude the attainment of efficiency; then we must look for alternative ways of sustaining greater tacit coordination. What is needed is a more severe threat – that is, a larger cost of defection. The question is whether such more severe threats are credible in the sense explained above. We are fortunate here, because the most severe threat (i.e., autarky) is one possible equilibrium of the static game. In the static context, we expect that the countries' intuitive understanding will serve to avoid such an outcome. But in the supergame, it pays them to develop an intuitive understanding that will invoke the more dire equilibrium as a more potent threat. Then they will be able to deter cheating that much more effectively, and therefore sustain greater tacit coordination.

Even if this mechanism is thought to be unreliable,[10] it is possible to make credible threats somewhat more severe than those of reversion to N. The problem to be overcome is that each country has the ex post incentive to back off. However, this can be checked by a threat to punish such a backslider with a second-round penalty, and so on. With no definite termination date, the whole code of punishments can be held together by its own bootstraps. For a formal model of this and an application to oligopoly, see Abreu (1984).

It is also necessary to point out a practical difficulty. All such schemes of tacit coordination depend on the discount rate being small enough. However, there is much evidence that governments, especially democratic ones, have very short time horizons and correspondingly high discount rates. Their ability to sustain cooperation is therefore very doubtful.

Next consider repetitions with a fixed and finite termination. The usual argument is that in this case there can be no tacit cooperation. At the last play, neither country has any consideration that countervails its temptation to defect. The outcome of that play is therefore going to be the static Nash point. Then the repeated game unravels by backward induction.

However, this argument is invalid if the static game has multiple equilibria. In our case, the outcome at the last play must be a Nash equilibrium, but this could be either N or A. Consider the play before the last one, and ask if a point (such as P) that is mutually preferred to N can be achieved. Suppose the common understanding is that adherence to P will be followed by N in the last play, but that any defection will be punished by the selection of A. Given this, each country can do no better than to go along. Let W_A be the home country's autarkic welfare level, and let the rest of the notation be as in (3). Then the home country will find it undesirable to defect at the penultimate play if

$$W' + W_A/(1+r) < W_0 + W_N/(1+r),$$

or

$$(W' - W_0) < (W_N - W_A)/(1+r). \tag{4}$$

---

[10] Or unavailable under the alternative interpretation of tariff policies mentioned previously in notes 6 and 7.

Note how the possibility depends crucially on the existence of two distinct static equilibria with $W_N > W_A$. Now we can work backwards to find that ever greater cooperation can be sustained in earlier plays of a longer sequence. For a general theory of this, see Benoit and Krishna (1985).

There are some other factors conducive to the emergence of tacit coordination with a finite and fixed horizon, two of which are considered by Jensen and Thursby (1984). The first way is to consider a different equilibrium concept. For a given positive number ϵ, a pair of strategies constitutes an ϵ-Nash equilibrium if neither country can make a unilateral change of strategy to increase its discounted welfare sum by more than ϵ. The idea is that there are costs of calculation, and small gains are not worth pursuing. Now consider a supergame with T repetitions. For simplicity, let each country have a binary choice at each play between free trade and the static Nash choice of tariff. Consider strategies of the following form: Choose free trade until K periods have elapsed, or there has been a defection, whichever comes sooner; then switch to the static Nash choice. If K is large enough, and the discount rate is small enough, then the gain from defecting a little sooner will be less than ϵ. Therefore the strategies can yield an ϵ-Nash equilibrium, and tacit coordination can persist for K periods.

The other approach is to introduce incomplete information. This is most easily done using the model of Kreps et al. (1982). Suppose each country attaches a small positive probability ϵ to the event that the other country is "nice," and will try to establish an understanding to follow free trade. Then it becomes a rational strategic ploy for each to foster such a belief about itself in the other country, by actually pursuing free trade for an initial phase of the supergame. The strategy includes a sneak defection after a while; this is usually brought about by resorting to randomized or mixed actions for a middle phase of plays. The feature of greatest interest to us is the fact that the first (free-trade) phase lasts for all but a few terminal plays whose exact number depends on ϵ. Jensen and Thursby (1984) have a somewhat different model of incomplete information, and tacit coordination emerges in the form of mixed strategies in equilibrium.

Both of these ideas have some merit, but neither is free from difficulties. Both suffer from non-uniqueness. The outcome with no coordination is a possible ϵ-equilibrium; there are several with some coordination corresponding to different values of K. The model of incomplete information has a multiplicity similar to that ensured by the folk theorem; almost any outcome can be made into an equilibrium by assuming just the right kind of information structure. The problem then becomes one of judging whether the particular assumption is reasonable, and that is not easy.

One other approach to tacit coordination tries to capture the dynamics of reaction in a static model. This is done using conjectural variations; see Thursby and Jensen (1983). The home country is assumed to believe that t^* is linked to t, with a conjectural derivative $(dt^*/dt)_c$ governing the response. Then the first-order condition for maximizing the home country's welfare is

$$(\partial W/\partial t) + (\partial W/\partial t^*)(dt^*/dt)_c = 0,$$

or

$$(dt^*/dt)_{W\,\text{constant}} = -(\partial W/\partial t)/(\partial W/\partial t^*) = (dt^*/dt)_c.$$

For example, if it is supposed that the conjectural derivative is 1/2, then the condition is satisfied at all points where the W contours have the slope 1/2. This defines a locus in (t, t^*) space that is the analogue of the Nash best-response curve RR in Figure 1. In fact, that model can be considered a special case of this one, where the conjectural variation is zero. Now we can construct a similar locus for the foreign country. The conjectural-variations equilibrium is defined by the point of intersection of the two loci.

If each country believes in a positive conjectural derivative – that is, if each thinks the other will retaliate against any tariff increase and reciprocate a tariff cut to some extent – then these loci will be closer to the axes than RR and R^*R^*. In a reasonably symmetric case, the resulting conjectural-variations equilibrium will have lower tariff rates than the Nash equilibrium. In this sense, it can be said to show tacit coordination.

It is hard to defend such a model on the basis of rational decision making. In a static single-play game, there is no sense in which t^* can be functionally linked to t, and the home country would be foolish to believe otherwise. Even if one accepts such beliefs, the logical conclusion of the mode of analysis raises new difficulties. Instead of taking the conjectural derivatives to be exogenous, we can require each to be consistent with the other country's actual best-response locus defined by its first-order condition. Because the problem is formally similar to the conjectural-variations model for oligopoly [Bresnahan (1981)], the consistent conjectures will normally turn out to be negative. The resulting tariff will then be higher than those at the Nash equilibrium.

For a trenchant critique of the conjectural-variations approach, see Friedman (1983, Chapter 4). However, the model has the merit of simplicity, and pending the arrival of equally usable but more rigorous dynamic models, it will continue to find applications.

Finally, mention should be made of an interesting attempt by Baldwin and Clarke (1985) to examine the Tokyo Round of GATT from a game-theoretic perspective. They do not use the standard economic welfare function, but construct ones that take into account some political considerations and are roughly compatible with the countries' expressed views on the alternative proposals offered during the negotiations. They compute the noncooperative Nash equilibrium as well as two cooperative Nash arbitration solutions, one using the status quo as the threat point and the other using the noncooperative equilibrium. They find that the actual outcome was worse for major participants (U.S. and EEC) than any of the game-theoretic solutions. They believe that the blame lies with the mercantilist maneuvers that took place in later stages of the negotiations and led to several exceptions from (and withdrawals of) tariff cuts.

All of the above discussions assumed that tariffs were the instruments of policy. If we allow quotas instead, the picture changes in one important respect: The only static Nash equilibrium of the noncooperative game is complete autarky [Tower (1975)]. Then the set of mutually beneficial alternatives in Figure 2 is enlarged to include all points in the region *ALL**. The free-trade point *F* is always Pareto superior to *A*, and is available to serve a focal role in negotiations. Unlike the tariff case, no special central case restrictions need be imposed.

As a practical matter, the availability of alternative instruments can reduce the prospects of an effective cooperative arrangement. Given an agreement about tariffs, explicit or tacit, the countries retain an incentive to cheat. If cheating through tariffs is effectively deterred, they can switch to other instruments that are not covered by the arrangement but serve as good or partial substitutes for tariffs. Policies that are less easy to detect or punish come into play – for example, voluntary export restraints or bureaucratic barriers. These indirect instruments usually have greater efficiency costs. Therefore such "increasing opaqueness" in trade policy is a cause for concern.

3   Oligopoly and profit shifting

When the firms in an international industry are large enough for strategic interaction with their rivals, the world market will be imperfectly competitive. This introduces some new aspects of trade, and of trade policy. The former are discussed by Paul Krugman (Chapter 8, this volume); the latter are the subject of this section and the next.

The most important new feature is the existence of supernormal profits. Each country's real income includes such profits accruing to its residents or (to a reasonable first approximation) those made by its firms. Therefore each country stands to gain, other things being equal, by shifting excess profits away from other countries' firms and toward its own. Of course, firms have a parallel interest in their own profits, and the desirability of profit shifting translates into an argument for policy activism only if governments have additional strategic instruments for this purpose. This possibility arises if there is a sequential structure to the game – governments choose their policies first and irreversibly, and the industry equilibrium is determined at a second stage of action. Then the governments can use this power of commitment to a policy and alter the industry equilibrium, which the firms could not do on their own. This is the approach adopted almost uniformly in this line of research.

There are two broad aspects of a country's profit-shifting policies. One is to improve the strategic position of domestic firms vis-à-vis foreign ones; the second is to avoid excessive competition among domestic firms. For an exporting country, the latter is similar to the optimum tariff problem considered in Section 2, but the former raises some interesting new issues. For an importing country, the profit-shifting motive interacts with the concern for domestic consumer surplus. All of this is made even more complicated by the fact that in oligopoly there can be two-way trade; that is, a country may simultaneously export and import the same good.

Research in the last five years has produced an abundance of models that explore various aspects of this issue, and some surveys have also appeared [e.g., Dixit (1984); Grossman and Richardson (1985)]. Here I begin with an exposition of the simplest profit-shifting model, and point out its relation to some recent work in industrial organization. Then I outline some extensions that qualify or change the results of the simple model. I conclude the section by summing up the policy implications.

The essence of profit shifting can be brought out in the simplest way by leaving out many other aspects. This was done in the pioneering work by Brander and Spencer (1984, 1985). An important extension by Eaton and Grossman (1986) shows the role of oligopolistic conduct, and this is the form in which I shall discuss it.

The simplifying assumptions of the basic model are as follows. There are just two firms in this industry, and they are located in different countries. Label the firms and the corresponding countries 1 and 2. Think of 1 as the home country and 2 as the foreign. In each country's economy, the firm is small enough that its activities do not affect factor prices. The marginal costs of production are constant and equal to c_1 and c_2 respectively. Initially, suppose neither country consumes the products of the industry; that is, the market is entirely in third countries. This removes consumer surplus from welfare calculations, and the focus is squarely on profits. The firms' interaction is modeled as a conjectural-variations Nash equilibrium. We saw the logical difficulties of such a construct, but the practical merit is that by varying the conjectural-variation parameters we can capture different degrees of implicit collusion in the duopoly and see the difference this makes for the profit-shifting policies.

Let x_1 and x_2 be the respective output quantities[11] of the two firms, and $R_1(x_1, x_2)$, $R_2(x_1, x_2)$ their revenues. The goods need not be perfect substitutes. Denoting the profit of firm i by π_i, we have

$$\pi_i = R_i(x_1, x_2) - c_i x_i.$$

Let firm 1 entertain the conjectural variation v_1 about firm 2's output response; that is,

$$v_1 = (dx_2/dx_1)_c$$

in the notation used before, and similarly write v_2 for firm 2's conjectural-variation parameter.[12] Denote partial derivatives of the revenue functions by the appropriate subscripts, and use a comma to separate the function label from the differentiation subscript – for example, $\partial R_1/\partial x_2 = R_{1,2}$. Then first-order conditions for profit maximization by the two firms are

$$R_{1,1} + v_1 R_{1,2} = c_1 \tag{5}$$

and

$$R_{2,2} + v_2 R_{2,1} = c_2. \tag{6}$$

Each defines a locus in (x_1, x_2) space. These can be called the firms' respective best-response or reaction functions.

Soon we will alter this equilibrium through tax or subsidy policies. We can set the stage for that by examining the comparative statics of the system with respect to changes in the costs. We have

$$\begin{bmatrix} R_{1,11} + v_1 R_{1,21} & R_{1,12} + v_1 R_{1,22} \\ R_{2,21} + v_2 R_{2,11} & R_{2,22} + v_2 R_{2,12} \end{bmatrix} \begin{bmatrix} dx_1 \\ dx_2 \end{bmatrix} = \begin{bmatrix} dc_1 \\ dc_2 \end{bmatrix}. \tag{7}$$

If c_1 alone changes, the reaction function of firm 1 shifts, and the equilibrium moves along the reaction function of firm 2. Then we can find r_2, the slope of the reaction function of firm 2, by setting dc_2 equal to zero in (7); this yields

$$r_2 = -(R_{2,21} + v_2 R_{2,11})/(R_{2,22} + v_2 R_{2,12}). \tag{8}$$

The expression for the slope of firm 1's reaction function r_1 is similar.

Letting Δ denote the determinant of the matrix on the left-hand side of (7), the solution is

---

[11] There is no loss of generality in assuming that firms choose quantities rather than prices in conjectural variations models, because there is a one-to-one correspondence between the two formulations. See Kamien and Schwartz (1983).

[12] I am treating the quantity conjectures as exogenous parameters. The correspondence between price- and quantity-choice models mentioned in note 11 requires the two kinds of conjectures to be appropriately related functions. This can be handled at the cost of some complication in algebra.

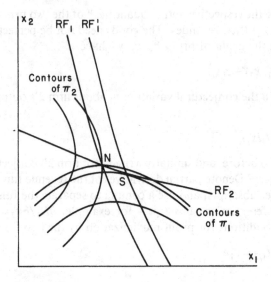

Figure 3

$$\begin{bmatrix} dx_1 \\ dx_2 \end{bmatrix} = \Delta^{-1} \begin{bmatrix} R_{2,22} + v_2 R_{2,12} & -(R_{1,12} + v_1 R_{1,22}) \\ -(R_{2,21} + v_2 R_{2,11}) & R_{1,11} + v_1 R_{1,21} \end{bmatrix} \begin{bmatrix} dc_1 \\ dc_2 \end{bmatrix}. \quad (9)$$

It can be shown [e.g., Dixit (1986a)] that for stability of the equilibrium with respect to the natural adjustment process, Δ must be positive and the diagonal entries of the matrix must be negative. Then $\partial x_i / \partial c_i < 0$ for $i = 1$ and 2. The signs of the cross-derivatives depend on the slopes of the reaction functions; thus $\partial x_2 / \partial c_1 > 0$ if $r_2 < 0$. The familiar Figure 3 shows many of these results for the Cournot case, where $v_1 = v_2 = 0$. The iso-profit loci of the two firms are shown as contours of π_i, and the reaction functions are RF_i. The shift from RF_1 to RF_1' occurs when c_1 decreases.

Now suppose the home country offers its firm an export subsidy of e_1 per unit. This reduces the marginal cost to $c_1 - e_1$. We can carry out the comparative statics exactly as above, and find $\partial x_1 / \partial e_1 > 0$ and so forth. The home country's welfare is its firm's profit minus the cost of the subsidy; that is,

$$W_1 = [R_1(x_1, x_2) - (c_1 - e_1)x_1] - e_1 x_1 = R_1(x_1, x_2) - c_1 x_1. \quad (10)$$

Then

$$dW_1 = R_{1,1} dx_1 + R_{1,2} dx_2 - c_1 dx_1.$$

Using firm 1's first-order condition (4), this becomes

$$dW_1 = (-e_1 - v_1 R_{1,2}) dx_1 + R_{1,2} dx_2.$$

Because firm 2's cost is not changing, the equilibrium moves along its reaction function – that is, $dx_2 = r_2 dx_1$. Therefore, we finally have

$$\partial W_1 / \partial e_1 = [-e_1 + R_{1,2}(r_2 - v_1)](\partial x_1 / \partial e_1). \tag{11}$$

By evaluating this expression at $e_1 = 0$, we obtain an idea of the kind of policy the home country will find desirable. The sign is determined by the sign of $r_2 - v_1$; that is, by the relation between the slope of firm 2's actual reaction function and firm 1's conjecture about this response.

In the Cournot case, $v_1 = 0$ and the normal sign of r_2 is negative. Since the products of the two firms are assumed to be substitutes, $R_{1,2} < 0$. Then $\partial W_1 / \partial e_1 > 0$ at $e_1 = 0$; that is, the home country will benefit from an export subsidy. The optimal subsidy can be found by setting the right-hand side of (11) equal to zero. This is the basic model of Brander and Spencer (1985); its effect can be seen from Figure 3. The subsidy lowers the marginal cost to firm 1, and shifts its reaction function to the right. The equilibrium moves along the reaction function of firm 2. The contours of π_1 in Figure 3 did not include the export subsidy, so by (10) they can be reinterpreted as the contours of W_1. Then the welfare of country 1 increases up to the point S of tangency of the iso-profit curve with firm 2's reaction function. The result is as if firm 1 becomes the Stackelberg leader in the game. It would do so by its own actions if it could, but the rules of the Cournot game do not allow it any such strategy. The export subsidy generates a credible shift in its reaction function.

We can capture the familiar Bertrand model of price setting in this framework by defining the conjectures appropriately. It turns out, in the normal case here, that $v_1 < 0$ and $r_1 - v_1 > 0$. Then $\partial W_1 / \partial e_1 < 0$ at $e_1 = 0$; that is, the desired policy is an export *tax*. Thus we see that the correct policy for profit shifting depends sensitively on the nature of the duopoly equilibrium. This was the finding of Eaton and Grossman (1986). The transition point is where $r_2 = v_1$; that is, when firm 2's actual reaction is locally correctly conjectured by firm 1. In this case of a consistent-conjectures equilibrium [e.g., Bresnahan (1981)], the home country finds free trade optimal.

To understand these differences in the results, we should examine what is signified by a difference between r_2 and v_1. If $r_2 - v_1$ is negative, which is the normal Cournot result, then firm 1 conjectures that a unit increase in x_1 will lead to a smaller decrease in x_2 (i.e., that firm 2 will be less accommodating) than is actually the case. Given this belief, firm 1 will be less aggressive than is optimal for its profit. The cost reduction it obtains from the export subsidy induces it to expand output and thus become more aggressive in the duopoly, which is what is desired. If $r_2 - v_1$ is positive then the argument goes the opposite way: Firm 1 is too sanguine about firm 2's reaction, and acts too aggressively. An export tax will hold it back, and that will be right direction for its profits to increase. With consistent conjectures, firm 1 is locally correct about firm 2's response, and there is no profit shifting at the margin by inducing it to behave differently.

This is all very similar to recent work on two-stage oligopoly [e.g., Fudenberg and Tirole (1984); Bulow, Geanakoplos, and Klemperer (1985)]. In those models, the firms themselves choose the first-stage variables – for example, capacity levels. But these choices are irreversible, and therefore have the same commitment value as the tax or subsidy choices made by the governments here. A firm setting its capacity at stage 1 will look ahead to the effect on the price or quantity duopoly equilibrium to come. In the Cournot case, the strategic consideration will entail a higher level of capacity than the choice that would be made in a one-stage game without the strategic effect; in the Bertrand case, a lower level will be required. Using the analogy and adopting the picturesque terminology of Fudenberg and Tirole, the home country's government wants to make its firm a top dog if the competition is Cournot and a puppy dog if it is Bertrand.

If there are several home firms then it becomes desirable to increase their tacit collusion with one another – that is, to make them produce less than they would in a Nash equilibrium. This works in favor of an export tax. In the Cournot case, for example, the optimum policy switches from subsidizing to taxing exports as the number n_1 of home firms rises from 1 to a large level [Dixit (1984); Salant (1984)]. With consistent conjectures, an export tax becomes optimal as soon as $n_1 \geq 2$.

What happens if both countries are pursuing profit-shifting policies? We have a two-stage game with the governments and the firms as players. The policies are chosen at stage 1, taking into account the effect on the Nash equilibrium of the duopoly at stage 2. Then we look for a Nash equilibrium of the policies, and the total result is a subgame-perfect Nash equilibrium of the two-stage game. Let us consider the cases of Cournot and Bertrand duopolies separately.

With Cournot behavior, each government uses an export subsidy. In a reasonably symmetric case, the result is a larger output for both firms than in free trade, and lower welfare levels for both countries. The rivalry in export promotion hurts both exporting countries, and the gainers are the consumers in the importing third country. The formal structure of the problem is of a Prisoners' Dilemma exactly like that examined in Section 2 for optimum tariffs. Readers can therefore readily construct further details (e.g., the use of repetition in achieving tacit policy coordination). An interesting practical example of such attempts at coordination, and of the difficulties they encounter, can be found in the multilateral efforts to curtail export credit subsidies. With sufficient asymmetry, one of the exporting countries might gain despite retaliation by the other.

With Bertrand behavior, an export tax is levied by both governments, who thereby exert market power over the consumers in the third country. In a symmetric situation, the welfare of both exporting countries rises. However, the restraint of output by one country has a spillover benefit for the other; these are not included in the first country's noncooperative calculation of its own welfare. Therefore the export taxes in such an equilibrium will be below the joint welfare-maximizing levels. Once again, repetition can secure greater tacit cooperation.

Next consider the interaction with consumer interests in one of the countries. For simplicity, suppose the entire market for the products is in the home country. Now the relevant policies are the home country's import tariff, t_1 per unit quantity of import, and the foreign firm's export subsidy, e_2 per unit quantity of its export. Let us consider these one at a time, beginning with the tariff. Suppose the aggregate utility function in the usual industry analysis (partial equilibrium) form is $U(x_1, x_2)$. The inverse demand functions are $p_i = \partial U / \partial x_i = U_i$, and the revenues are $R_i = p_i x_i$. Home country welfare is the sum of the consumer surplus, the home firm's profit, and the tariff revenue; that is,

$$W_1 = [U(x_1, x_2) - p_1 x_1 - p_2 x_2] + (p_1 - c_1)x_1 + t_1 x_2.$$

Differentiating totally,

$$dW_1 = -x_1 dp_1 - x_2 dp_2 + x_1 dp_1 + (p_1 - c_1)dx_1 + t_1 dx_2 + x_2 dt_1.$$

Then

$$\partial W_1 / \partial t_1 = (p_1 - c_1)(\partial x_1 / \partial t_1) - x_2(\partial p_2 / \partial t_1 - 1) + t_1(\partial x_2 / \partial t_1). \tag{12}$$

The comparative static effects of the tariff on the quantities are found by the same method as that used for export subsidies above. We have $\partial x_1 / \partial t_1 > 0$, and if the reaction function of firm 1 is downward-sloping in quantity space (as is usually assumed) then $\partial x_2 / \partial t_1 < 0$. This enables us to sign and interpret two of the terms on the right-hand side of (11).

The first term is the effect of the home consumption distortion. In equilibrium p_1 exceeds c_1, so it is desirable to expand the output of x_1. A tariff does so. In the process it normally increases p_1 and so reduces consumer surplus, but that is more than offset by the increase in the home firm's profit.

The third term is a similar distortion in trade. When $t_1 > 0$, the price of imports exceeds their opportunity cost. An increase in the tariff, by reducing x_2, worsens this distortion.

The second term multiplies the quantity of imports x_2 by the change in the net price received by the foreign country, $p_2 - t_1$; it is therefore the terms-of-trade effect. Unlike the competitive case of Section 2, its sign is ambiguous. In oligopoly, the incidence of a tax can easily exceed 100 percent [Seade (in press)]. If this occurs (i.e., if $\partial p_2 / \partial t_1 > 1$) then an increase in the tariff will worsen the home country's terms of trade. If demand functions are not too convex, however, the problem does not arise, and this term yields a benefit from the tariff.

The optimum tariff will balance these considerations, and the first-order condition will be found by setting the right-hand side of (11) equal to zero.

Brander and Spencer (1981) consider a special case where the foreign firm uses limit pricing to deter entry of home country firms. This fixes p_2 independently of t_1. Then $\partial p_2/\partial t_1 = 0$, and the tariff has a particularly favorable terms-of-trade effect. Another way to express this is to say that the tariff captures all of the foreign monopolist's profit with no loss of home consumer surplus, so long as limit pricing to deter entry remains the foreign firm's optimal strategy. However, in this instance there are no home firms, so the first term in (11) is zero. The tariff does not increase the home firms' profit.

Turning to the foreign government's export promotion, we have

$$\partial W_1/\partial e_2 = (p_1 - c_1)(\partial x_1/\partial e_2) - x_2(\partial p_2/\partial e_2).$$

The second term helps the home country by lowering the price of its imports in the usual way, but the new first term can hurt it by worsening the domestic consumption distortion. In the homogeneous product case, Dixit (1984) found that the net effect at the margin was harmful for small subsidies but beneficial for large ones.

The home country can always use a fully countervailing duty ($t_1 = e_2$). This leaves the equilibrium quantities and prices unchanged, and merely transfers revenue from the foreign government to the home one. However, this is not the optimal response. With linear demand curves and Cournot behavior, it is optimal to countervail half the subsidy – that is, to set $t_1 = e_2/2$. With isoelastic demands, or with more competitive conduct, less countervailing is indicated.

The next question to address is that of simultaneous oligopoly in several markets. The most interesting instance is that of two countries exporting to each other.[13] The firms' production and sale decisions can be linked across the markets for several reasons. Marginal costs can depend on total outputs. Arbitrage can unify the markets on the demand side, within limits imposed by the tariff policies. If there is a fixed cost, the requirement that a firm's profits be nonnegative applies jointly to its markets. Finally, the firms' conjectural variations can in principle have very general links across the markets. The last point leads us into a mess of taxonomy with doubtful significance, but each of the others has some interesting implications.

---

[13] In Chapter 8 of this volume, Krugman discusses how such two-way trade arises under imperfect competition, and examines its effects on welfare.

The case of cost interactions is examined by Krugman (1984) for the case of falling marginal costs. Now protection of the home market has the initial effect of shifting the home market equilibrium in favor of the home firm. This lowers the home firm's marginal cost and raises that of the foreign firm. Then the equilibrium in the foreign market also shifts in favor of the home firm. Thus, in contrast with the perfectly competitive paradigm, import restriction can act as export promotion.

A similar effect arises in a different way in the model of Venables (1985). He introduces a fixed cost, so average cost is decreasing. Free entry ensures zero profit for each firm in equilibrium. The active firms behave in a Cournot fashion in both markets. Transport costs, or product differentiation, impart an own-market bias to each country's firms. Now let the home country impose a tariff. Each foreign firm that was making zero profit on its worldwide operations under free trade is now disadvantaged in the home-country market, and so suffers a loss. Some foreign firms exit until zero profit is restored. Conversely, some new home firms enter. The result is that the price at home falls and the price abroad rises. This benefits the home country at the other's expense.

Both these models (and most others in this area) assume that the markets in different countries are segmented. There is no third-party arbitrage, and firms can practice price discrimination across countries constrained only by the oligopolistic competition of other firms. If arbitrage is allowed, such strategies are much more severely constrained. For example, if a good has price p_1 at home and p_2 abroad, and the home country has an ad valorem tariff t_1, then we must have $p_1 \leq p_2(1 + t_1)$. Suppose this constraint is binding. A firm that sells to both markets cannot divide a marginal unit of output arbitrarily across them, but must choose the allocation that maintains $p_1 = p_2(1 + t_1)$.

The difference this makes is dramatically illustrated by contrasting Venables's model with that of Horstmann and Markusen (1986). The two are very similar, and can be made identical except that Horstmann and Markusen allow arbitrage while Venables maintains market segmentation. In the Horstmann–Markusen model, a home-country tariff induces entry of home firms. But this cannot selectively reduce the price at home. On the contrary, the entry process can result in home firms of a smaller size, raising average costs and prices. This effect can outweigh any benefit from a terms-of-trade improvement. Recall that in Venables's model, the tariff was beneficial to the country imposing it. The results for an export subsidy are in even more striking contrast: A small subsidy gives a clear welfare improvement to the country using it in the Venables model, and a clear loss in the Horstmann–Markusen model.

More generally, with free entry there are some important cases where the equilibrium yields zero profit, thereby removing the profit-shifting motive for policy activism. One such case arises if entry costs are small and there are numerous identical potential entrants. The market structure is not perfectly competitive; there might be Cournot competition with large numbers, or Chamberlinian monopolistic competition. There remains a domestic distortion because prices exceed marginal costs, and there remain unexhausted economies of scale. These can provide arguments for strategic use of trade policy, but they are more subtle and specific to the details of each model. The second context is that of a race to develop a new product or process. The winner will acquire a temporary monopoly and earn large profits. But there will be several losers, and industrywide profit will be zero if there is free entry into the race. For more discussion of this point, see Dixit (1986b).

However, if the costs of entry are large and there is only a small group of identifiable firms involved, then there can be substantial positive profits in equilibrium. This opens up the possibility of entry-promoting or entry-deterring strategies to ensure that the successful firms are from one's own country. Dixit and Kyle (1985) have analyzed such a situation and classified the possibilities, a few of which can be mentioned here. The stylized picture is of the game where the EEC tries to promote the entry of Airbus into the medium-range commercial jet aircraft market while the United States tries to deter it. Consider a case where the entry cost is so large that Airbus cannot be profitable unless it has a protected home market *and* access to the U.S. market. Suppose the EEC contemplates closing its market to Boeing in its attempt to promote the entry of Airbus. The United States can deter this by threatening to close its market to Airbus should it enter. With access to the U.S. market no longer available, it is pointless for the EEC to provide protection alone. Then Boeing has a worldwide monopoly, and the United States benefits from the large profit. Now suppose the EEC has available the additional instrument of subsidizing the entry costs for Airbus. It no longer need rely on access to the U.S. market, and the U.S. threat is ineffective. Dixit and Kyle find that threats of retaliatory protection are generally less powerful against foreigners' subsidies than against their protection.

Many important modifications of the basic profit-shifting model have been considered in the literature, and I shall briefly discuss some of them. The first departure is to introduce factor markets. All of the work discussed so far took the industry's cost curves to be exogenous. If its activities can significantly affect factor prices, either because the industry is large or because it uses some specific factor, then its interaction with factor markets must be considered.

Helpman and Krugman (1985, Chapter 5) construct such a model to examine the trade patterns and factor prices in oligopolistic general equilibrium. The policy implications in a particular context of interest are studied by Dixit and Grossman (1986). The idea is that support to one home industry for purposes of profit shifting will raise the prices of the inputs it uses and thereby handicap other home industries that use the same inputs. To the extent that these other industries are zero-profit ones, this may not be of great concern. But if they are also oligopolistic, then profit shifting in one industry must come at the expense of profit shifting in another. A case in point is a whole sector of high-technology industries competing for the scarce input of specialized scientific labor. In such a situation, a much more refined calculation is necessary to determine the relative merits of the industries. Dixit and Grossman obtain the theoretical criteria for this, but point out that these are so demanding of information as to be quite impractical.

Krishna (1984a) considers quotas and voluntary export restraints as policy instruments. These change the oligopolistic game in very significant ways. Consider an international duopoly that would be in Bertrand competition under free trade. With quotas, such competition is quantity-constrained, and an equilibrium in pure strategies often does not exist. Krishna considers the mixed-strategy equilibrium and the use of a quota to alter it. She finds that a suitable quota can increase the profits of both firms. The intuition is that the quota acts like a credible promise of restraint by the foreign firm, and therefore serves as a device to facilitate collusion between the firms. Of course, the domestic consumers lose. A similar effect would arise in a Cournot duopoly if the trade restrictions pertained to the market share of the foreign firm.[14]

An even greater departure from the usual rules of the profit-shifting game is considered by Carmichael (1984). He argues that in some practical applications, such as the working of the Ex-Im Bank in the United States, the order of moves between the government and the firms should be reversed: The firms set the prices before the government determines the export credit subsidy. The firms make their choices knowing the policy rules and the extent of ex post discretion. Carmichael finds that in equilibrium the subsidy is captured fully by the firms. There is no change in the price charged to the buyers, and the effect is simply a transfer from our government to our firms.

Finally, let us introduce some dynamics to the oligopoly. Having seen the dynamics of tariff policy interaction in Section 2, readers can easily construct what will happen. I shall mention a few examples. Davidson (1984) considers an oligopoly of home and foreign firms selling in the home market. In free trade, they sustain some collusion using the threat of reversion to a noncooperative static Nash point in future iterations.

---

[14] The effect of quotas on the upgrading of the quality of imports is well known under perfect competition. For similar analyses under imperfect competition, see Krishna (1984b) and Das and Donnenfeld (1985).

A tariff changes the calculation of the costs and benefits of defection from this arrangement. For home firms, the threat point gives greater profits than before, so the cost of defection is reduced. To avoid their cheating, the allocation of cartel output must be changed in their favor. But this reduces the foreign firms' collusive profit, and makes it harder to keep them in line. For large tariffs, it becomes impossible to find an arrangement that keeps both kinds of firms from cheating. Then the cartel collapses, the price falls, and the tariff paradoxically benefits home consumers. This is an interesting theoretical possibility, but I doubt its practical significance. The more common effect of tariffs is to increase the collusion of home firms. Pinto (1985) considers the case of two-way trade. The firms involved can benefit (at the expense of the consumers) by agreeing not to invade each other's market. In a repeated game, such an arrangement can be sustained tacitly in the usual way. Baldwin and Krugman (in press) extend the model of scale economies to the dynamic setting of learning curves. There is corresponding gain for each country in supporting its firms in such an industry, and presumably equal scope for mutually damaging competition when they both try such policies.

One might hazard a guess that research on static models of oligopolistic trade and trade policy has more or less run its course. But dynamics remains a rich area for research. As our ability to solve dynamic games increases, we are sure to have a flood – or a cornucopia, depending on one's point of view – of work on dynamic oligopolies in trade and trade policy.

It is premature to draw confident or firm policy implications from such an unfinished and ongoing body of research. Nevertheless, it is important to take stock of what has been learned and suggest what needs still to be done; this I shall attempt in concluding the section.

The early work on trade policy in oligopolistic industries had a distinctly neo-mercantilist flavor. Brander and Spence (1984, 1985) found arguments for tariffs and export subsidies in the national interest; Krugman (1984) argued that protection and export promotion might be jointly achievable and desirable. Subsequent research has qualified or subdued such claims. Changes in the assumptions about oligopolistic conduct, general equilibrium effects working through factor markets, restoration of competition through entry or its threat – all are known to reduce or reverse the force of the mercantilist policy prescriptions. The current median view of the profession in this matter can be fairly characterized as (i) a recognition that the existence of imperfect competition does modify or overturn some conventional beliefs about trade policy, and (ii) an awareness that the design of policy to fit each situation requires close attention to its specific details. This suggests that research should be directed toward improving our understanding of the realities of some industries that are likely candidates for strategic trade policies. Some tentative beginnings are being made [e.g., Dixit (in press) and Baldwin and Krugman (in press)], but much more work is needed.

4   Investment and expropriation

Thus far, I have considered trade in goods and services only. However, there are other international transactions that in reality have a large and growing quantitative importance, and also raise strategic issues of equal interest. I refer to international investment, both direct (ownership and management of productive capital assets in another country, undertaken mostly by multinational corporations) and portfolio (ownership of financial assets abroad, undertaken by financial institutions and individuals).

There are two new strategic aspects that arise when we consider investment. First, the problem is inherently dynamic. The costs are incurred before the benefits arise. The parties to the transaction have opportunities to alter the course of events at different times, and therefore face different constraints and expectations. Although repetitions or sequential moves could bring similar complications for trade in goods and services, we could (and did) model a static transaction where – all at once – production occurred, prices were determined, and payments made. That is not a reasonable way to treat investment. Second, when we considered oligopolistic trade and issues of policy in that context, the strategic games that occurred were between firms at one level and between governments at another. Now we shall find one country's firms pitted directly against another country's government.

The problem arises in the following way. Any investment involves various risks (e.g., changes of taste or technology, or exchange rate movements) that will affect the returns to the investor. International investments entail a different kind of risk as well, one arising from the lack of an effective structure of contract law. Seizure of assets or repudiation of debts by private parties in other countries is difficult enough to counter. There is even less recourse against expropriation or repudiation by foreign governments who are protected by the doctrine of sovereign immunity. Such actions may be indirect – for example, an increase in the tax rate on the investor's profits, or the imposition of exchange controls that prevent their repatriation to the home country. It may be partial – for example, nationalization with inadequate compensation, or rescheduling of a loan under easier terms.

Expropriation or repudiation may occur for non-economic reasons – for example, the coming to power of a government with a nationalist or socialist philosophy. From the point of view of economic analysis, these would be regarded as exogenous risks. However, the actions may also be the result of a strategic rational calculation of their costs and benefits. We should be able to incorporate this possibility in our analysis. This is the theme of many recent contributions, the most comprehensive of which is probably Eaton and Gersovitz (1983). I shall give a brief review of the issues based on this work. My focus will be on direct investment, but financial investment and international debt raise many similar problems.

The simplest setting to indicate the nature of the problem is a two-period model. A home-country firm contemplates making an investment in the foreign (or host) country. This means a sunk commitment of capital in period 1; the returns are obtained in period 2. Once the firm makes this commitment, it is a hostage to fortune. The foreign government may expropriate it and collect all the returns. In the simple model, this action would be rational for the government. The firm would anticipate it, and therefore not make the investment at all. In technical terms, this would be the only possible subgame-perfect equilibrium; interested readers can easily construct the game tree and verify this assertion. In simple words, if the foreign government is unable to make a credible promise not to expropriate, it will be unable to attract any investments from home-country firms. The problem is a very general one, and was recognized as early as 1651 by Thomas Hobbes: [15] "If a Covenant be made, wherein neither of the parties performe presently, but trust one another; . . . upon any reasonable suspition, it is Voyd: . . . For he that performeth first, has no assurance that the other will performe after; because the bonds of words are too weak to bridle mens . . . avarice."

The outcome is undesirable for both the home-country firm and the foreign government. If the investment is economically sound, there is always a way of dividing the returns so that they can both gain. The question is whether the government can attain the credibility necessary to induce the firm to invest. Hobbes's answer was that "there are in mans nature, but two imaginable helps to strengthen [their Covenants]. And those are either a Feare of the consequence of breaking their word; or a Glory, or Pride in appearing not to need to breake it." Some such mechanisms must operate sufficiently well in practice, because we observe a large volume of international investment and relatively little expropriation. Recent theoretical work has brought to light several such possibilities.

First consider what the firm can do on its own. If it can change the form of the investment in such a way that the foreign government will

---

[15] *Leviathan,* Chapter 14.

neither be able to operate the project nor obtain any profits after expropriation, this will remove the temptation from the foreign government and make it attractive for the firm to invest. One such device is to increase the capital intensity or the level of technology of the project. This may work particularly well against less developed countries (LDCs) lacking the skilled personnel needed to operate such industries. It would work less well to the extent that necessary training can easily be obtained by sending their nationals to the home country for training, or by hiring "mercenary" workers from there. Some casual observations are in accordance with the idea of strategic use of technology in this way. Many observers of investment in LDCs have complained about its excessive capital intensity in relation to the factor prices in those countries, and have offered numerous explanations ranging from non-existence of appropriate technologies to monopoly power of multinational corporations [see Lall and Streeten (1977, p. 72)]. The strategic requirement of making the investment less susceptible to expropriation offers an alternative explanation that seems better grounded in rational behavior. One also observes the governments in LDCs, and international organizations that represent them, complain that foreign investment does not bring them any benefits of technology transfer. Once an investment has been made it is rational for the foreign governments to want the technology, but – in the absence of other credible means of forswearing expropriation – they may not be able to attract investments at all if they insist on technology transfer.

Another device that may be available to some multinationals is control over some vertically related industry – for example, the supply of an essential input or the channels of distribution. If the firm can make a credible threat of barring an expropriating government from access to these industries, then it can make the investment with the assurance that it will not be expropriated.

Next consider what the firm and the host government can do together. The first (and best known) of these devices is to split the transaction into several stages. The firm increases its commitment to the project gradually, and the returns also accrue gradually. At the beginning, the government does not want to expropriate and terminate the process, because there is much more investment to come. This check gradually weakens, and eventually expropriation will occur. But by then the firm will have obtained returns that are large enough to make the investment attractive. This concept is called an "obsolescing bargain." A delicate balancing over time of the firm's and the government's incentives is required in the design of such a scheme. In technical terms, what we want is a perfect equilibrium of the sequential game. An example linking the firm's investment and the government's tax policy is constructed by Doyle and van Wijn-bergen (1984). The tax rate is initially low to allow the firm sufficiently large early returns, and then gradually rises over time. Such "tax holidays" are often observed in early phases of transnational investments.

A related phenomenon arises if the investment is not an isolated act, but rather is likely to be one of a sequence of opportunities in that country. Then the government will have an incentive to establish a reputation for honor. Readers can easily guess the line of reasoning that follows. With infinite or indefinite repetitions, one can construct a supergame with perfect equilibria that involve investment and no expropriation if the foreign government's discount rate is low enough. With finite repetitions, such a mutually beneficial arrangement can occur for a long initial phase if an ϵ-equilibrium concept is relevant, or if there is some incomplete information. For example,[16] suppose countries come in two kinds: those that will expropriate if it is economically rational for them to do so, and those that will never expropriate (on account of the kind of Glory or Pride mentioned by Hobbes). Firms do not know what kind of country they face, but have in mind a small probability ϵ that it is honorable. Then, in the early phase of the game, an economically rational country has the incentive to appear honorable by not expropriating. In the second phase such a country follows a randomized strategy, where the probability of expropriation gradually increases over time. In a terminal phase, it always expropriates. The length of the last two phases can be bounded above by a number that behaves like $-(\log \epsilon)$: rising very slowly as ϵ goes to zero. Therefore a very small prior probability of honor ensures the mutually beneficial outcome of investment and no expropriation for most of the time, if the time horizon is sufficiently long (albeit finite).

Finally, consider some arrangements that rely on third-party enforcement. The investing firm can get its home government involved as a player by persuading it to retaliate against the foreign government's expropriation. There are some statutory provisions of this kind, but their practical effectiveness is doubtful. For example, the Hickenlooper Amendment stipulates a cutoff of aid to a government that expropriates assets of a U.S. firm. However, larger considerations of foreign policy usually intervene, and the provision is rarely invoked [Dunn (1983, p. 154)].

The reputation mechanism described above can fail if a government faces different firms over time, and knowledge or belief about its honor or lack thereof is not easily transmissible between firms. Then a third party can act as an agent for all the firms, thus unifying and restoring

---

[16] The following is based on unpublished joint work with Henrik Horn of Stockholm University. The formal model is very similar to Kreps and Wilson (1982).

reputation effects. The World Bank may have such a role to play with regard to direct investments, and the International Monetary Fund for financial ones.

5 Concluding remark

In the last decade, advances in the theory of sequential and dynamic games (and improvements in their applicability) have had a dramatic effect on industrial organization. The effect on the theory of international trade and trade policy, while somewhat more recent, is proving to be equally dramatic. The work has enriched our understanding of many real-world phenomena that were beyond the scope of the traditional theory based on perfect competition. However, empirical work has lagged behind, and it needs to be improved greatly in both quality and quantity if we are to have a better idea of the scope and significance of these theoretical advances. Such empirical implementation and testing of theory should be the top research priority in this area for the immediate future.

References

Abreu, D. 1984. "Infinitely Repeated Games with Discounting: A General Theory." Discussion Paper No. 1083, Institute of Economic Research, Harvard University.

Aumann, R. J. 1985. "Repeated Games." In G. R. Feiwel (ed.), *Issues in Contemporary Microeconomics and Welfare.* Albany: SUNY Press.

Axelrod, R. 1983. *The Evolution of Cooperation.* New York: Basic Books.

Bacharach, M. 1976. *Economics and the Theory of Games.* London: Macmillan.

Baldwin, R., and P. Krugman. In press. "Market Access and International Competition: A Simulation Study of 16K Random Access Memories." In R. Feenstra (ed.), *Empirical Methods for International Trade.* Cambridge, Mass.: MIT Press.

Baldwin, R. E. 1982. "The Political Economy of Protectionism." In J. Bhagwati (ed.), *Import Competition and Response.* Chicago: University of Chicago Press.

Baldwin, R. E., and R. N. Clarke. 1985. "Game Modelling of the Tokyo Round of Tariff Negotiations." Discussion Paper No. 85-3, Economic Policy Office, U.S. Department of Justice.

Benoit, J-P., and V. Krishna. 1985. "Finitely Repeated Games." *Econometrica* 53: 905–22.

Bhagwati, J. N. 1982. "Directly Unproductive, Profit-Seeking Activities." *Journal of Political Economy* 90: 988–1002.

Brander, J. A., and B. J. Spencer. 1981. "Tariffs and the Extraction of Foreign Monopoly Rents under Potential Entry." *Canadian Journal of Economics* 14: 371–89.

360   **Avinash Dixit**

1984. "Tariff Protection and Imperfect Competition." In. H. Kierzkowski (ed.), *Monopolistic Competition and International Trade*. New York: Oxford University Press.

1985. "Export Subsidies and International Market Share Rivalry." *Journal of International Economics* 18: 83–100.

Bresnahan, T. F. 1981. "Duopoly Models with Consistent Conjectures." *American Economic Review* 71: 934–45.

Bulow, J. I., J. D. Geanakoplos, and P. D. Klemperer. 1985. "Multimarket Oligopoly: Strategic Substitutes and Complements." *Journal of Political Economy* 93: 488–511.

Carmichael, C. M. 1984. "The Control of Export Credit Subsidies and Its Welfare Consequences." Working Paper, Princeton University.

Cooper, R. N. 1987. "Trade Policy and Foreign Policy." In R. M. Stern (ed.), *U.S. Trade Policies in a Changing World Economy*. Cambridge, Mass.: MIT Press.

Das, S. P., and S. Donnenfeld. 1985. "Oligopolistic Competition and International Trade: Quantity and Quality Restrictions." Working Paper, University of Wisconsin–Milwaukee.

Davidson, C. 1984. "Cartel Stability and Trade Policy." *Journal of International Economics* 17: 219–37.

Dixit, A. 1984. "International Trade Policy for Oligopolistic Industries." *Economic Journal* 94 (Supplement): 1–16.

1986a. "Comparative Statics for Oligopoly." *International Economic Review* 27: 107–22.

1986b. "Trade Policy: An Agenda for Research." In P. R. Krugman (ed.), *Strategic Trade Policy and the New International Economics*. Cambridge, Mass.: MIT Press.

In press. "Optimal Trade and Industrial Policies for the U.S. Automobile Industry." In R. Feenstra (ed.), *Empirical Methods for International Trade*. Cambridge, Mass.: MIT Press.

Dixit, A. K., and G. Grossman. 1986. "Targeted Export Promotion with Several Oligopolistic Industries." *Journal of International Economics* 21: 233–49.

Dixit, A. K., and A. S. Kyle. 1985. "The Use of Protection and Subsidies for Entry Promotion and Deterrence." *American Economic Review* 75: 139–52.

Dixit, A., and V. Norman. 1980. *Theory of International Trade*. Welwyn, U.K.: Nisbets.

Doyle, C., and S. van Wijnbergen. 1984. "Taxation of Foreign Multinationals: A Sequential Bargaining Approach to Tax Holidays." Discussion Paper No. 25, Centre for Economic Policy Research, London School of Economics.

Dunn, J. 1983. "Country Risk: Social and Cultural Aspects." In R. J. Herring (ed.), *Managing International Risk*. Cambridge: Cambridge University Press.

Eaton, J., and M. Gersovitz. 1983. "Country Risk: Economic Analysis." In R. J. Herring (ed.), *Managing International Risk*. Cambridge: Cambridge University Press.

Eaton, J., and G. M. Grossman. 1986. "Optimal Trade and Industrial Policy Under Oligopoly." *Quarterly Journal of Economics* 101: 383–406.

Ethier, W., and H. Horn. 1984. "A New Look at Economic Integration." In H. Kierzkowski (ed.), *Monopolistic Competition and International Trade.* New York: Oxford University Press.

Friedman, J. 1983. *Oligopoly Theory.* Cambridge: Cambridge University Press.

Fudenberg, D., and J. Tirole. 1984. "The Fat-Cat Effect, the Puppy-Dog Ploy, and the Lean and Hungry Look." *American Economic Review, Papers and Proceedings* 74: 361-6.

Grossman, G. M., and J. D. Richardson. 1985. "Strategic U.S. Trade Policy: A Survey of Issues and Early Analyses." Special Paper No. 15, International Finance Section, Princeton University.

Helpman, E., and P. Krugman. 1985. *Market Structure and Foreign Trade.* Cambridge, Mass.: MIT Press.

Henderson, J. M., and R. E. Quandt. 1980. *Microeconomic Theory,* 3rd ed. New York: McGraw-Hill.

Horstmann, I., and J. R. Markusen. 1986. "Up the Average Cost Curve: Inefficient Entry and the New Protectionism." *Journal of International Economics* 20: 225-47.

Jensen, R., and M. Thursby. 1984. "Free Trade: Two Non-cooperative Approaches." Working Paper, Ohio State University.

Johnson, H. G. 1953/54. "Optimum Tariffs and Retaliation." *Review of Economic Studies* 21: 142-53.

Kamien, M. I., and N. L. Schwartz. 1983. "Conjectural Variations." *Canadian Journal of Economics* 16: 191-211.

Kennan, J., and R. Riezman. 1984. "Do Big Countries Win Tariff Wars?" Working Paper No. 84-33, College of Business Administration, University of Iowa.

Kreps, D., and R. Wilson. 1982. "Reputation and Imperfect Information." *Journal of Economic Theory* 27: 253-79.

Kreps, D., P. Milgrom, J. Roberts, and R. Wilson. 1982. "Rational Cooperation in the Finitely Repeated Prisoners' Dilemma." *Journal of Economic Theory* 27: 245-52.

Krishna, K. 1984a. "Trade Restrictions as Facilitating Practices." Discussion Paper No. 1119, Institute of Economic Research, Harvard University.

1984b. "Tariffs vs. Quotas with Endogenous Quality." Working Paper, Harvard University.

Krugman, P. R. 1984. "Import Protection as Export Promotion: International Competition in the Presence of Oligopoly and Economies of Scale." In H. Kierzkowski (ed.), *Monopolistic Competition and International Trade.* New York: Oxford University Press.

1987. "Strategic Sectors and International Competition." In R. M. Stern (ed.), *U.S. Trade Policies in a Changing World Economy.* Cambridge, Mass.: MIT Press.

Kuga, K. 1973. "Tariff Retaliation and Policy Equilibrium." *Journal of International Economics* 3: 351-66.

Lall, S., and P. Streeten. 1977. *Foreign Investment, Transnationals and Developing Countries.* London: Macmillan.

362   Avinash Dixit

Lipsey, R. 1960. "The Theory of Customs Unions: A General Survey." *Economic Journal* 70: 496–513.

Mayer, W. 1981. "Theoretical Considerations on Negotiated Tariff Adjustments." *Oxford Economic Papers* 33: 135–53.

Pinto, B. 1985. "Repeated Games and the Reciprocal Dumping Model of Trade." Working Paper, The World Bank.

Riezman, R. 1982. "Tariff Retaliation from a Strategic Viewpoint." *Southern Economic Journal* 48: 583–93.

———. 1984. "Customs Unions and the Core." Working Paper No. 84-32, University of Iowa.

Salant, S. W. 1984. "Export Subsidies as Instruments of Economic and Foreign Policy." Working Paper N-2120-USDP, Rand Corporation.

Schelling, T. C. 1960. *The Strategy of Conflict.* Cambridge, Mass.: Harvard University Press.

Seade, J. K. In press. "Profitable Cost Increases and the Shifting of Taxation: Equilibrium Responses of Markets in Oligopoly." *Journal of Public Economics.*

Thursby, M., and R. Jensen. 1983. "A Conjectural Variations Approach to Strategic Tariff Equilibria." *Journal of International Economics* 14: 145–61.

Tower, E. 1975. "The Optimum Quota and Retaliation." *Review of Economic Studies* 42: 623–30.

Venables, A. J. 1985. "International Trade in Identical Commodities: Cournot Equilibrium with Free Entry." *Journal of International Economics* 19: 1–20.

CHAPTER 10

Equilibrium without an auctioneer

Peter Diamond

The development of the microfoundation of macroeconomics has been slow going; very interesting, but slow going. I want to begin with an elaboration of why this subject is hard (for me). I will then discuss two lines of research that explore what happens when economies are modeled without a Walrasian auctioneer – search theory (Section 1) and the theory of bank runs (Section 2). Of course, this is only a piece of the literature that identifies itself as the microfoundations of macroeconomics. I will concentrate on the flavor of results, rather than on the technical problems of constructing tractable macro-oriented models within the micro rules of model construction.

Microanalysis

The fundamental theorem of welfare economics makes possible straightforward use of the competitive general equilibrium model for the analysis of distortions in the economy. Because the economy would be Pareto optimal otherwise, it is easy to see the welfare implications of altering one of the assumptions of the Arrow–Debreu model. Observing pollution, one changes the assumption that production decisions do not affect individual utilities directly. One can then analyze the utility implications of pollution (compared with a different production technology or a different production decision), calculate socially optimal production decisions (for different criteria and different accompanying income redistribution tools), and design price and tax policies to improve or optimize resource allocation. A parallel literature analyzes congestion.

Observing sales taxes, income taxes, tariffs, and import quotas, one contrasts equilibrium involving these government actions with that arising

I am grateful to Bernard Saffran and Sidney Winter for helpful discussion and to the National Science Foundation for research support.

from some different level (perhaps zero) of these government variables. In these examples, the relationship is clear between some easily observed phenomenon and the assumptions underlying the fundamental welfare theorem. Naturally, economists differ on the quantitative importance of these deviations, which depend on the value of nontraded interactions as well as on demand and supply elasticities.

Changing a second assumption of the fundamental welfare theorem can alter the welfare analysis of a previous assumption change. One example is the Coase theorem, where costless direct negotiations imply that pollution and congestion do not interfere with the Pareto optimality of equilibrium. Another example is optimal tax theory, where the absence of lump-sum redistribution of income allows the equity gains from distorting taxes to outweigh their efficiency losses. In both cases, it is reasonably clear which observations are sufficient to select the appropriate theory for application to a particular case.

This introduction on the standard style of microeconomic analysis is meant to highlight the ways in which the microfoundations of macroeconomics are different. There is the obvious difference with some microanalyses that macroeconomics attempts to address phenomena that are economywide (or nearly so), rather than phenomena occurring in a single industry or group of industries, or whose important effects can be analyzed in the context of a single industry even though similar phenomena occur in many industries. My focus here is on another difference. Macroeconomics starts with data on outcomes of the allocation process – data on unemployment, output, and capacity utilization – not with data on the assumptions of the Arrow–Debreu model. It is not clear which of the many inaccurate assumptions of the Walrasian model are important for macroeconomic phenomena. The key word here is "important," for all models are false. The choice of assumptions to change is important because welfare implications may vary over the combinations of changed assumptions that yield similar aggregate data.

Focusing (as I shall) on real variables, not price levels, there are the basic stylized facts of macroeconomics; these can be divided into three categories. There are static facts of equilibria with low levels of output and factor usage. There are dynamic facts of the tendency of the economy to have prolonged movements up and down over time with fairly distinct turning points. And there are individual longitudinal facts on the pattern of unemployment. A satisfactory theory would address all three categories. However, the important factors explaining how the economy can have a prolonged period of low output may be different from the factors that are important for determining turning points. In turn, these two categories are conceptually separable from the individual incidence pattern of unemployment. Thus, it may entail enormous complexity to address all the stylized facts at one time. However, the models addressing the separate pieces of these stylized facts should be compatible with each other, not mutually exclusive. These observations suggest that there is something wrong in the Arrow–Debreu model, but they do not point to any particular single assumption as the one that should be changed. And that is what makes macroeconomics so hard for microeconomists. Judgment on choice of assumptions is as important as analysis of particular assumptions. Moreover, it is likely that the behavior of the economy depends in important ways on many of the deviations from the assumptions of the fundamental welfare theorem, and not just on one or two such deviations.

Paralleling the usual microeconomic strategy, the microfoundations of macroeconomics proceed by altering just one or two assumptions of the Walrasian model. Such a small change can be made in the belief that a satisfactory model can be built with only a few changes. This I take to be the basic stance of equilibrium business cycle analysis, with missing markets and limited information as the critical changed assumptions. Or one can believe (as I do) that it will be necessary to alter many of the assumptions of the Walrasian model, and yet choose to begin by altering just one or two assumptions rather than building a more radically new model. I consider a single leap to a totally different model too unlikely of success to consider pursuing.

When envisioning a research strategy that involves exploring many assumption changes, a researcher faces the problems of deciding which step to take next and of evaluating how well the project is going. Evaluation involves an even more selective use of empirical facts than usual, because an adaptation of the theory in its present state (in order to fit some fact best approached in a later variant of the model) can worsen the development of the project. For example, it may be better research strategy to pursue aggregate demand issues in a model without involuntary unemployment, rather than complicating the model with the many reasons that combine to yield this phenomenon. I certainly hope so.

Walrasian theory is based on three premises: rationality, large numbers, and trade coordination by the auctioneer. The standard premise of rationality, including a correct understanding of the economic environment, is obviously not a universal trait. Individual behavior that differs from the standard – particularly in the form of poor predictions or of wage and price stickiness – are probably central elements in the actual behavior of the economy. Similarly, many industries are dominated by small numbers of firms or unions, which means that price taking is not a universal trait.

With both of these assumptions (rationality and large numbers), I believe the U.S. economy is significantly different from standard assumptions. However, it does not seem likely that the deviations from these two assumptions will be sufficient for a satisfactory macroeconomic theory. If it is necessary to model differently the coordination of trade, then the most rapid progress may follow from performing the analysis in the familiar setting of large numbers of conventionally rational agents. Therefore, I will focus on the third assumption – coordination by the Walrasian auctioneer.

Walrasian auctioneer

The Walrasian model assumes a very special trade coordination mechanism, in sharp contrast to the generality allowed in preferences and production technology. In other words, from the perspective of issues of trade coordination the Arrow–Debreu model is a very special example, not a general model. The Walrasian auctioneer makes everyone aware of prices and trading opportunities in the economy, at no cost to anyone. By coordinating would-be traders (including selecting particular points in offer correspondences), the auctioneer makes trivial the problem of pairwise matching of buyers and sellers. Moreover, by coordinating all trade simultaneously the auctioneer gives each trader a single budget constraint. It is obvious that life is not like this. It takes time to learn about particular trading opportunities for goods, for labor, and for credit. (Depending on one's feelings about shopping, this may be unpleasant or – up to some limit – pleasant.) It is not easy to form a judgment about the stochastic properties of the attempt to trade, especially since the economic environment is not stationary. Moreover, each individual trade must be completed with some form of purchasing power – barter, money, or credit. Because of the sequential nature of trade, one only learns of one's (ex post) budget constraint over time.

Paralleling traditional microanalysis, we have identified the assumption of the Walrasian model we wish to change. The logical next step is to construct an alternative model to see if it fits data on resource allocation better than the Walrasian model, and to see if it has significantly different implications for important policy actions. The trouble is that the modeling problem is hard. Generalizing the trade coordination mechanism in interesting ways has, thus far, required severe restrictions on preferences and production technologies. In addition, the generalizations of trade coordination have been extremely narrow and unrealistic. As narrow and unrealistic as these mechanisms have been, most trade coordination technologies that have been analyzed include the Walrasian auctioneer as a special case when the coordination process becomes infinitely rapid. These models are therefore more general than the Arrow–Debreu model in this dimension, while being less general in the dimension of preferences and production technologies.

To proceed, we need three new descriptions, along with the familiar preferences and production opportunities:

(i) how people learn about the distribution of trading opportunities;
(ii) how the individual pairwise trades are organized, which involves both matching and bargaining; and
(iii) how budget constraints evolve.

In terms of (i), it is probably significant for the shape of business cycles that at least some people do not accurately perceive the (time-dependent) stochastic structure of trading opportunities. I suspect that excessive entry in very good times tends to lengthen both booms and recessions. Nevertheless, the current literature has focused on the rational-expectations special case. This choice reflects (at least) three factors. One is the lack of well-documented alternative hypotheses (combined with diverse views on the extent and importance of error). A second is the complication from evolving perceptions (as opposed to the fixed-point argument needed for rational expectations). A third is the desire to understand the workings of non-Walrasian allocation mechanisms in a rational-expectations setting, so as to isolate the implications of the change in allocation mechanism. I will stay within the rational-expectations framework in the discussion below, and assume that in equilibrium people know the stochastic structure of trading opportunities.

To see aspects of the two remaining issues [(ii) and (iii)], I will consider output search models without credit and then credit models without search. Both are models without an auctioneer. In the absence of a Walrasian auctioneer (even with the usual assumptions about commodities), an economy will have unrealized mutually advantageous trading opportunities. That is, costly trade coordination will naturally yield lower economic activity levels than would occur with costless coordination. In addition, the extent to which mutually advantageous opportunities are not realized will have partly endogenous determinants and endogenous dynamics. This gives the potential of explaining why output is particularly low at some times and why it tends to fluctuate. This is the heart of my approach to the microfoundations of macroeconomics.

I will proceed by first summarizing the simplest barter-search model that brings out an example of the mechanism. Then I will ask whether money, pricing behavior, or credit are likely to change the results. This will be followed by a fresh start, indicating how the lack of an auctioneer in credit markets yields macroeconomic problems even when all other markets are Walrasian.

1   Search models

In the Walrasian model, all contracting comes first. Production and the delivery of goods are then spread out in time. Although some goods are contracted for before production, much of commodity production is for inventory, in the hope of a quick sale at a good price. (I ignore for present purposes the perhaps important time structure of production labor, wage payment, and sale of goods.) The ease and profitability of trade from inventory depends on the level of demand, with the dependence varying with the specification of the trade coordination mechanism. Consider a barter economy with a single good produced by individuals who must trade before they can consume. Artificially keeping all traders in symmetric positions, we get one-for-one trade. With no money or credit, the level of demand depends on the distribution of stocks of inventories of others that are available for trade, as well (in more general models) as expectations about future production and trade opportunities. The greater the stocks of inventories of others, the greater the expected profitability of producing for inventory. Thus there is a trading externality that has a character similar to technological (not pecuniary) externalities in the Arrow–Debreu model. Moreover, this externality involves a positive feedback that greater inventories make production for inventory more profitable. Whether set up as a single-period model or as a stochastic stationary state, the equilibrium in such an economy (with a plausible trading technology) is marked by two features – inefficiency of equilibrium due to trading externalities, and possible multiple equilibria due to the positive feedback. Both features come from the feedback mechanism that greater production for inventory makes production for inventory more profitable. Prices are set in bilateral trade. With a symmetric structure, prices have no reason to respond to overall low output. Since I have discussed this structure at length previously (Diamond 1984), I will not spell out such a model here. Rather, I move on to the questions raised by this result: the three R's of realism, relevance, and robustness.

1.   Realism

When considered in the context of such prolonged periods of low output as the 1930s, it really is the case that production is more profitable when output levels are high, although simultaneity problems would make testing difficult. (Around turning points there probably is no static monotone profitability–output relationship.) That is, I believe the model is capturing a real phenomenon. However, leading to this high profitability are many factors, of which the model captures only one – and not necessarily the most important one. There are distributional effects from the payment of wages before goods are sold; at a time of high output there is likely to be the old-fashioned accelerator effect; there may be reasons due to long-term contracts. No doubt there are others. Moreover, there are alternative ways of modeling the economy that will give a similar mathematical result [see Cooper and John (1985)] – for example, monopolistic competition and suitable demand functions, especially with only approximately optimal pricing.

As further model development depends on the interpretation given to the mathematical structure, one needs to choose the form of interpretation most likely to be helpful, as well as a mathematical structure yielding the type of results one believes (or has checked) to be empirically correct. I doubt one could claim that this model captures an overwhelming fraction of the reasons that production is more profitable over a period when others are producing at a high level. The most that can reasonably be hoped is that this mechanism is an adequate surrogate for these other features that would require additional modeling complexity because of the need for more detail. In other words, perhaps this is a model that can be built upon. It certainly is a model that is firmly in the microeconomic tradition.

2.   Relevance

The purpose of the microfoundations of macroeconomics is to help with macroeconomic policy, which conventionally means open-market operations or cyclically sensitive tax or expenditure policies. In addition, macroeconomic policy may include institutional reform. The class of models described so far do not have an adequate representation of either money or bonds to permit direct analysis of monetary policy. The most that can be gleaned from such models is the relevance of aggregate demand analysis for welfare economics and so the possibility of a consistent micro-based model for countercyclical monetary policy. A useful monetary policy must of course affect aggregate demand – but all that this requires is for the policy not to be equivalent to a change in monetary units, which is clearly the case for the full range of conventional monetary policy tools.

A similar conclusion can be reached for fiscal policy. The inadequacy of the model in this case arises from the complication of addressing lag structures, which are the most serious limitation for fiscal policies. The lack of institutional detail of the models makes them unlikely candidates for analysis of institutional reform. In the face of the rational-expectations attack, we are left with a partial legitimation of conventional aggregate demand-based approaches to macroeconomic policy, plus the hope of further model development.

Another sense of relevance is whether the model captures enough macroeconomic problems to be relevant. In particular, with the labor market clearing, can a too low level of output be a satisfactory proxy for a low level of employment? It is surely relevant for the shape of business fluctuations that low levels of aggregate demand result in high levels of (conventionally measured) unemployment rather than low wages or work sharing. This set of microeconomic phenomena, partially explored in the contracts literature, belongs in an eventual model of the microfoundations of macroeconomics. It is surely relevant for actual macroeconomic policy. However, there is no reason to think it undercuts the (limited) policy inferences that come from the models under discussion. One would expect that replacing a perfect labor market by a more complicated imperfect allocation mechanism would enhance the welfare relevance of aggregate demand policy despite the possible presence of "offsetting effects." Moreover, similar models can be built focusing on search in the labor market with perfect output markets. [See, e.g., Howitt and McAfee (1984).]

A third sense of relevance is whether the model is about important or unimportant effects. In the United States, wholesale and retail trade value added is about 15 percent of GNP. This is a much larger figure than would occur with a costless allocation mechanism. The problem of trade coordination is not trivial.

3.   *Robustness*

The simplest models have limited pricing policies and credit markets. Is it possible that the conclusions of the simplest search models will be removed by the functioning of price or interest-rate determination? After all, the simplest Keynesian model ignores prices; yet the role of prices is precisely to clear markets. I believe that this case is different. Implicit in a search model is decentralized (non-auctioneer) price determination. This can come about by bargaining or (with suitable institutional structure) by prices set on a take-it-or-leave-it basis. In both pricing situations, a fall in aggregate demand may well have the effect of lowering prices in a monetary model. (That the effect may be absent in a barter model is not relevant.) Is there reason to believe, however, that such a mechanism will keep the economy on an even keel in the presence of a tendency either to endogenous fluctuations or macroeconomic shocks? (The fact that a pricing overreaction to monetary policy reverses the map of what is expansionary and what is contractionary does not contradict the possibility of successful policy.) Such a conclusion seems unlikely. The simplest monetary version of the barter-search model described above has similar properties to the barter version. More fully fleshed-out models seem quite likely to preserve the twin features of generally inefficient equilibrium and possible multiple equilibria. The determinants of trading prices in a search setting offer little reason to expect price determination to approximate market-clearing levels or offset inappropriate aggregate demand levels.

This is not the place to catalog the reasons why some trading prices are not at competitive levels in search models. Nonetheless, I find the arguments persuasive.

Multiple equilibria

The presence of multiple equilibria is a sign of an incomplete theory. Yet it is a commonplace in the microfoundations literature to take multiple equilibria as a virtue. A cursory literature search turned up no defense of this view, so I want to indicate why I share it. There is a mathematical basis for this view and an economic one. The mathematical basis is that static or steady-state models with multiple equilibria often have dynamic versions with stationary or stochastic (sunspot) cycles [Diamond and Fudenberg (in press), Grandmont (1985), Woodford (1984)]. This seems to fit with the persistence of movements in modern economies. Although I believe it is important to understand a wide range of the mathematical properties of the models one uses, I suspect that the expectation coordination mechanism of these rational-expectations cycles is a small part of the range of causes of cyclic movements and probably not an adequate surrogate for missing factors requiring a rich sectoral structure to model adequately. This basis of cycles focuses attention on educating the public (to choose the right equilibrium) and on credibility issues, rather than pushing toward more realistic analyses of what is, in fact, a very complicated decentralized allocation mechanism. Although expectations about the economy's general stability matter greatly, we need to know much more about the effects of monetary and fiscal policy on individual transactions.

The economic basis for the view that multiple equilibria may be a virtue comes from a suspicion of how a richer class of models may work. For tractability, we generally work with static or stationary models that are meant to approximate some portion of a richer nonstationary intertemporal model. In terms of the static view of some year in the 1930s, it is natural to think that there was a high-employment equilibrium that might have been reached as well as the low-employment equilibrium that actually was. The intertemporal links that select the particular equilibrium from the set of static equilibria are missing in the static model. Having a static model with multiple equilibria is consistent with the perspective that something led the economy to a poor outcome when it might have been led to a good one with a relatively small change in some actions (private or governmental). Another way of saying more or less the same thing is that monetary and fiscal policies seem to affect the real economy more than a Walrasian model suggests they should. The concept of pump priming is based on the idea of a large long-lasting response to a small temporary policy. In a complete model with a unique equilibrium, a large sensitivity of equilibrium to macroeconomic policy may come from the same factors that give an incomplete model multiple equilibria. The self-reinforcing nature of different expectations in a model considering only rational expectations may make induced expectation change a powerful lever in an expectation-formation model.

Finance constraint

Before proceeding to a discussion of credit, it will be useful to recast the discussion above in terms of budgets. Whether set up in a single period or as a steady state, the model described above has purchasing power determined by previous production decisions. In a search setting, the level and distribution of purchasing power are then relevant for the level of trade in the economy, however trading prices are determined. I believe that one could greatly complicate the description of goods and preferences without altering the basic results of the model. The interesting direction of development, however, is the determination of purchasing power – does the underlying problem of too little purchasing power change with the introduction of money or credit in the economy?

For simplicity, assume that goods are bought only with money (no barter or credit). The level of trade will depend on the level of inventories on the supply side and the level and distribution of real money holdings on the demand side. Nominal money holdings are determined by past actions. Real money holdings depend on nominal money holdings and price setting behavior. In a search setting, prices are set to optimize or are bargained over. There is no mechanism to assure an efficient level of aggregate demand, although it is not necessarily too low. There is also no assurance of an efficient level of production for inventories. There are rampant externalities. Monetary policy in the form of a helicopter drop will alter equilibrium by altering the distribution of real money holdings unless the helicopter drop is precisely proportional to existing holdings.

With money and no credit, aggregate demand depends on past behavior determining the distribution of money holdings and current pricing behavior; production decisions are irrelevant. To bring back the relevance of production decisions for demand, we could add collateralized borrowing of money at a zero interest rate (for tractability). Although such a model has not been worked out, it seems likely that the availability of such credit makes production for inventory more attractive, both privately and socially. This is in contrast to a production-unrelated and universally available line of credit that merely adds to the stock of purchasing power and is neutral in steady state.

Production with inputs owned by others directly affects the distribution of purchasing power. Another link between current production and purchasing power is through possibly changed expectations about future trading in the economy, and thus also a change in credit made available in the expectation of repayment from future trading. This suggests that credit availability is highly relevant for the workings of the economy, and leaves open the role of interest rates as smoother or amplifier of macroeconomic difficulties.

2 Credit models

When the resource allocation process is costly and/or time-consuming, intermediation matters for the workings of the allocation process. In contrast to frictionless allocation models, models with friction do not give rise to Modigliani–Miller-style irrelevance theorems. Moreover, the credit allocation process itself has the potential of adding to the ways (arising from frictions in the goods and labor markets) in which the economy is sensitive to short-run aggregate demand.

Credit allocation takes resources and time. Costly evaluation of creditworthiness is sufficient for the existence of financial intermediation, provided the rest of the institutional structure is appropriate (large projects calling for pooling or economies of scale in small credit transactions, plus adequate monitoring of the intermediary). For some modeling purposes, however, it matters that the allocation process takes place in real time, rather than all transactions taking place at once. Here is where the absence of an auctioneer matters.

I start with all-at-once trading. Consider a Fisherian two-period economy. Each person is endowed with a production possibility set defined over output-today and output-tomorrow. With a Walrasian coordination mechanism we have each person choosing a production and consumption pair, both of which lie on the same budget line, tangent to the production possibility set and an indifference curve. Projects with particularly large investments (relative to the endowment of the owner of the production possibility) will involve negative levels of output-today as part of the production plan. Because negative consumption is not possible, borrowing is necessary to carry out such a plan. In this sense, the availability of credit enlarges individual production possibility sets as well as permitting a more efficient aggregate production plan.

If this story is altered – by replacing the Walrasian auctioneer by some other mechanism that involves either transactions costs or some degree of market power for some agents – then, in general, we have a different final allocation. With changes in either the underlying production possibilities or the credit allocation mechanism, the difference between the allocation and the Walrasian allocation can change. That is, a shock to the production technology can widen the gap between Walrasian and non-Walrasian outcomes. Also, a shock to the credit allocation mechanism can have a similar widening effect [Bernanke and Gertler (1985)]. Bernanke (1983) has argued that, through such a mechanism, the bank difficulties of the 1930s resulted in a lower level of production. It is particularly the sunk cost of gathering information about individual debtors that makes the system sensitive to the intermediation structure. Troubled banks affect the production plans of the economy.

In a repeating discrete-time model of this type, banks will find themselves in trouble if they make bad investments. This can happen because of corrupt bank management, or poor selection of investments, or calculated gambles that come out badly. The latter may arise from interest-rate changes, in a model richer than one with certainty and a single pair of periods.

Once we recognize that the allocation process takes place over time and that many transactions are financed by money holdings, there is the opportunity for intermediaries to borrow by providing liquidity services. That is, there is a niche in the set of intermediaries for one that makes purchasing power available on demand or very short notice, on terms involving little risk, and with the convenience of checking. This possibility naturally depends on a suitable transactions cost structure plus the uncertain evolution of purchasing-power needs of individuals.

Given the existence of such intermediaries, the fact that the allocation process is spread out in time implies the possibility of bank runs. This has been modeled by Diamond and Dybvig (1983) as multiple equilibria in a discrete-time model, with bank action restricted to limited observation of what is happening in a period. This artificial restriction in a discrete-time model is a natural way to capture aspects of a more realistic continuous-time model. The critical ingredient here is that the value of an asset portfolio depends on the speed with which it must be sold. This can arise from the cost of evaluation of individual assets (rather than waiting for them to mature), the difficulty of quickly finding eager buyers for idiosyncratic assets, and the market power of hard-to-find eager buyers. Such problems can arise for individual banks. They can also arise for entire banking systems. The implied drop in perceived wealth is relevant for aggregate demand.

In contrast to the Diamond–Dybvig approach of modeling bank runs as one of (at least) two equilibria, Chari and Jagannathan (1984) and Postlewaite and Vives (1984) have constructed models with a unique equilibrium in which there is a bank run in some states of nature, with accompanying inefficiencies.

The flavor of these results can be brought out in a continuous-time Poisson model. Consider an individual with wealth W at time zero. There are two available investments. The illiquid investment opportunity yields a random return r (with mean $\bar{r}$) at time one. If this investment is undertaken, consumption occurs at time one and utility is equal to wealth consumed (i.e., risk neutrality). Thus expected utility from this investment strategy is $W(1+\bar{r})$. Alternatively, the wealth can be held in liquid form giving zero financial return. However, during the time between zero and one there is a flow probability that a good consumption opportunity will arrive. If one arrives, it costs precisely W and yields utility $W(1+b)$. The opportunity is only available fleetingly, so that someone without liquid wealth cannot take advantage of it. In addition, whether a consumption opportunity is ordinary or "good" is not observable to others. [This will be recognized as a variant of Goldman preferences. For consideration of the Diamond–Dybvig model with more general preferences, see Jacklin (1985).] If no opportunity arrives by time one, the wealth W is consumed. Thus, expected utility for someone holding the liquid investment is $W(F(1+b)+(1-F))=W(1+Fb)$, where F is the probability of the arrival of a consumption opportunity before time one.

Assume that with the underlying technology, the liquid investment strategy is optimal for an isolated individual:

$$\bar{r} < Fb. \tag{1}$$

We will add other conditions as we go along.

Now assume two individuals with identical and independent consumption opportunities and perfectly correlated illiquid investment opportunities. Because of the independence of their abilities to profitably use resources early, there is a pooling opportunity. Together, they can hold 0, 1, or 2 times W in liquid form. With full information, total expected utilities for these levels of liquid holdings are then

$$2W(1+\bar{r}), \quad W(2+\bar{r}+(2F-F^2)b), \quad \text{and} \quad 2W(1+Fb).$$

Assume that the aggregate mixed portfolio is optimal:

$$F^2b < \bar{r} < bF. \tag{2}$$

We have repeated (1) as well as giving the new condition. Thus pooling can raise expected utilities.

We now consider the difficulties of implementing this strategy under various information and observation technologies. We have assumed that arrival of a good consumption opportunity is not observable. Remember that such an opportunity is only fleetingly available at some time in the continuous interval between zero and one. The natural symmetric rules are that the first of the pair to try to withdraw the liquid wealth W may do so. The other depositor then receives the illiquid investment at time one. If neither withdraw, they share equally the total wealth available at time one. By our Poisson assumption they don't both attempt to withdraw at the same time. If each one attempts to withdraw only when there is a genuine consumption opportunity, expected utility for each is half the total return from the mixed portfolio with full information. From the assumptions in (2), this is a perfect Nash equilibrium.

There are a variety of ways of creating difficulty for this equilibrium. Following Diamond and Dybvig we can simply consider the situation if each one begins to think that the other might soon withdraw funds regardless of whether an opportunity arrives. This consideration occurs after funds have been committed to the investments. (It would be more realistic to consider a continuous overlapping-generations model.) Rushing to withdraw before the other yields $W(1 + Fb)$, assuming that none of the probability of consumption opportunity has passed. If the other person withdraws first, expected utility is $W(1 + \bar{r})$. Thus we have a classic case of two Pareto comparable Nash equilibria, once funds have been committed. The story can be enriched by adding depositors and adding assets that can be sold off at a loss. This lowers further the return to late withdrawals in the event of a bank run and reinforces the conditions that give rise to the multiple equilibria. Diamond and Dybvig argue that deposit insurance has the potential to ease this difficulty.

Following Chari and Jagannathan as well as Postlewaite and Vives, one can now add signals to the model. These arrive early in time and (for mathematical convenience) not simultaneously to both depositors. Signals could contain information about the random return on the illiquid asset or the arrival rate of consumption opportunities. For some signals, immediate attempted withdrawal is the unique Nash equilibrium response. Examples are signals of a sufficiently low illiquid return or sufficiently high probability of either one's own good consumption opportunity or of the other person's. For low-probability signals, this can occur as part of a perfect equilibrium with the investment behavior described above.

The indivisibilities assumed in this example severely limit the set of interesting contracts. An overlapping-generations model (without observability of age) would also limit contracts. Bounded rationality and transactions cost also limit contracts. So I do not find this limitation to be a telling one against the model.

A cornerstone of these models is the limited technology available to banks (as well as an allocation process spread out in time). The existing literature has taken the degree of liquidity in the investment technology as given. Even with this limited perspective on the scope for intervention, deposit insurance is potentially useful to prevent harmful scrambles for liquidity. But this form of modeling misses the additional role for a central bank associated with open-market operations. Since liquidity comes primarily from borrowing and from the sale of assets to others (rather than from early realization of physical investments), the menu of liquidity-return tradeoffs is endogenous. By acting at the macroeconomic level on the available tradeoff as well as on the microeconomic level on run behavior, a central bank can seriously affect resource allocation. However, the problem of modeling the endogenous determination of the liquidity technology is a major one on which I have seen no work.

Although bank runs are the most visible phenomenon involving multiple equilibria of this sort, I believe similar phenomena occur elsewhere in the credit allocation process. Wherever there are multiple creditors and an expectation of credit rollover, there is a similar situation. Willingness to lend depends on beliefs about the abilities of both borrower and lender to borrow in the future. This can yield multiple equilibria in credit extension without the special circumstance of demand deposits or even intermediation of any kind. That is, the positive feedback of beliefs about easy credit or the easy availability of credit has the potential of generating both easy-credit and tight-credit equilibria. This possibility parallels the work of Pagano (1985) that a stock market can have thin and thick equilibria (i.e., equilibria with few and many traders) because of the dependence of volatility on the thickness of the market.

Credit and search

Output-search models yield multiple equilibria and inefficiency. Credit-intermediation models have similar properties. This naturally raises the question of interactions. The credit market may well amplify fluctuations from the goods market as credit availability depends on perceptions of future output levels. This raises the natural question of whether interest-rate variations won't offset this feedback and (returning to the theme of robustness) possibly alter the findings of the simplest model. An interest-rate increase affects the likelihood of failure to repay a loan by requiring a different future payment (as well as having adverse selection and moral hazard implications that are familiar from the credit literature). This limited ability of interest rates to clear the credit market is a fundamental difference between static and intertemporal trade.

Concluding remarks

In a Walrasian system, the evolution of aggregate demand (either endogenously or in response to shocks) is of no consequence for efficiency. In a search-mediated economy (as in one with existing incomplete lagged contracts) the evolution of aggregate demand matters. This raises three questions – how aggregate demand affects the static efficiency of the economy, how government policies affect aggregate demand, and how systematic manipulation of aggregate demand affects the evolution of the economy. To pursue these questions, we need a richer set of tractable models of allocation processes that are more realistic than the Walrasian auctioneer. Staying within microeconomic rules of model construction, it has been hard to construct even special models (much less general models) encompassing the set of institutions needed to answer these questions. Nevertheless, the existing models point up the likelihood that macroeconomic policy can be used constructively, and make the case that this is potentially a very valuable research agenda, as well as one that is fun.

References

Bernanke, B. 1983. "Nonmonetary Effects of the Financial Crisis in the Propagation of the Great Depression." *American Economic Review* 73: 257–76.

Bernanke, B., and M. Gertler. 1985. "Banking in General Equilibrium." Presented at the Conference on New Approaches to Monetary Economics, Austin, Texas.

Chari, V., and R. Jagannathan. 1984. "Banking Panics, Information and Rational Expectations Equilibrium." BRC Working Paper #112, J. L. Kellogg School of Management, Northwestern University.

Cooper, R., and A. John. 1985. "Coordinating Coordination Failures in Keynesian Models." Cowles Foundation Discussion Paper No. 745, Yale University.

Diamond, D., and P. Dybvig. 1983. "Bank Runs, Deposit Insurance, and Liquidity." *Journal of Political Economy* 91: 401–19.

Diamond, P. 1984. *A Search-Equilibrium Approach to the Micro Foundations of Macroeconomics.* Cambridge, Mass.: MIT Press.

Diamond, P., and D. Fudenberg. In press. "An Example of Rational-Expectations Business Cycles in Search Equilibrium." *Journal of Political Economy*.

Grandmont, J-M. 1985. "On Endogenous Competitive Business Cycles." *Econometrica* 53: 995–1045.

Howitt, P., and R. McAfee. 1984. "Stable Low-Level Equilibrium." Research Report 8403, Department of Economics, University of Western Ontario.

Jacklin, C. 1985. "Essays in Banking." Ph.D. thesis, Stanford University.

Pagano, M. 1985. "Market Size and Asset Liquidity in Stock Exchange Economies." Ph.D. thesis, Massachusetts Institute of Technology.

Postlewaite, A., and X. Vives. 1984. "Bank Runs as an Equilibrium Phenomenon." Unpublished manuscript, University of Pennsylvania.

Woodford, M. 1984. "Indeterminacy of Equilibrium in the Overlapping Generations Model: A Survey." Unpublished manuscript, Columbia University.

CHAPTER 11

Arrow–Debreu programs as microfoundations of macroeconomics

Robert M. Townsend

1   Introduction

The class of general equilibrium models of Arrow (1964), Debreu (1959), McKenzie (1959), and others is an excellent starting point for the study of actual economies. On the positive side, this class of models can be used to address the standard macroeconomic concerns of inflation, growth, and unemployment, and also more general phenomena such as the objects and institutions of trade, the absence of insurance arrangements of some kinds, or the dispersion of consumption in a population. On the normative side, this class of models can be used to study stabilization policy and optimal monetary arrangements.

Contrary views are often expressed in professional conversations and in the literature. Indeed, the Arrow–Debreu model is often said to be operational only under such unrealistic assumptions as full information, complete markets, and no diversity. Here, however, an alternative view is argued. The Arrow–Debreu model can accommodate not only diversity in preferences and endowments but also private information, indivisibilities, spatial separation, limited communication, and limited commitment. That is, standard results on the existence of Pareto optimal allocations and on the existence and optimality of competitive equilibrium allocations can be shown to apply to a large class of environments with these elements. Further, stylized but suggestive models with these elements can be constructed and made operational so that Pareto optimal and/or competitive equilibrium allocations can be characterized. On the positive side,

Helpful comments from V. V. Chari, Peter Diamond, Gary Hansen, Lars Hansen, Robert E. Lucas, Jr., Allen Meltzer, William Rogerson - as well as research support from the National Science Foundation under grant #8406771 and the Alfred P. Sloan Foundation - are all gratefully acknowledged. The author assumes full responsibility for any errors and for the views expressed herein.

these models deliver implications for the methods of interaction of economic agents and for the outcomes from that interaction. On the normative side, the Pareto optimal or core allocations of these models allow scope for activist policy.

To sharpen the argument, a terminological point should be resolved immediately. Here an Arrow–Debreu model or (better put) an Arrow–Debreu environment is one specified at the level of the primitives of, say, Debreu (1959): households $j = 1, 2, ..., n$; linear commodity space L; consumption set X^j in space L for each household j; preferences represented by a utility function u^j on set X^j for each household j; an endowment point w^j in space L for each household j; firms $k = 1, 2, ..., m$; and production possibility set Y^k in space L for each firm k. (Here, moreover, household j will be said to have direct access to production technology Y^j, so that reference to firms as entities apart from households will be suppressed.) Thus, given an Arrow–Debreu environment, one can deliver (under specified assumptions) Pareto optimal allocations as solutions to the problems of maximizing weighted sums of the utilities of the households, subject to the constraints implied by endowments and technology. That is, maximize the objective function

$$\sum_{j=1}^{n} \lambda^j u^j(x^j)$$

subject to the constraints

$$x^j \in X^j \quad j = 1, 2, ..., n \quad \text{(feasible consumption)},$$

$$y^j \in Y^j \quad j = 1, 2, ..., n \quad \text{(feasible production)},$$

$$\sum_{j=1}^{n} x^j = \sum_{j=1}^{n} w^j + \sum_{j=1}^{n} y^j \quad \text{(resource feasibility)},$$

with values for the weights λ^j satisfying

$$0 \leq \lambda^j \leq 1, \quad \sum_{j=1}^{n} \lambda^j = 1.$$

Such programming problems are referred to in this chapter as Arrow–Debreu programs, and hence our title: Arrow–Debreu programs are the microfoundations for the broad positive and normative view of macroeconomics outlined above.

Of course, the outcome of an Arrow–Debreu program – a Pareto optimal allocation – may or may not be decentralizable under a price system, and in that sense the standard competitive-markets hypothesis intimately associated with the general equilibrium models of Arrow, Debreu, McKenzie, and others need not be imposed. That is, one may not necessarily worry about whether there exist a price system p^* and allocations x^{j^*} and y^{j^*}, $j = 1, 2, \ldots, n$, such that:

(i) for every household j, x^{j^*} solves

$$\underset{x^j \in X^j}{\text{maximize}} \; u^j(x^j)$$

subject to $p^* x^j \le p^* w^j + p^* y^{j^*}$;

(ii) for every "firm" j, y^{j^*} solves

$$\underset{y^j \in Y^j}{\text{maximize}} \; p^* y^j;$$

(iii) $\displaystyle\sum_{j=1}^{n} x^{j^*} = \sum_{j=1}^{n} w^j + \sum_{j=1}^{n} y^{j^*}.$

On the other hand, the hypothesis that allocations are those achieved in competitive markets often serves to sharpen the predictions of the model, tightening the mapping from Arrow–Debreu environments into outcomes. And (of course), under the competitive-markets hypothesis, sense can be made empirically of observations on prices. Thus, implications under the competitive-markets hypothesis are also described in many of the environments discussed below, as a useful supplement to the discussion of Pareto optimal allocations. In fact, it is stressed in this chapter that standard theorems on the existence and optimality of competitive equilibria can be shown to apply to a large class of these environments, including environments with diversity and various impediments to trade. The point is that competitive markets need be complete only relative to the natural commodity space for a specified environment. With private information, for example, full indexation is generally neither required nor possible.

An alternative hypothesis to be coupled with Pareto optimality is the idea that allocations must be in the core. That is, an allocation x^{j^*}, y^{j^*}, $j = 1, 2, \ldots, n$, is in the core if it is feasible [i.e., if it satisfies the competitive equilibrium condition (iii) above] and if there does not exist any subset C of households with allocation $\bar{x}^i, \bar{y}^i$, $i \in C$, with the property that the allocation $\bar{x}^i, \bar{y}^i$ is feasible for C, that is,

$$\bar{x}^i \in X^i, \quad \bar{y}^i \in Y^i, \quad \text{and} \quad \sum_{i \in C} \bar{x}^i = \sum_{i \in C} \bar{y}^i + \sum_{i \in C} w^i;$$

and allocation $\bar{x}^i, \bar{y}^i$ improves upon the *-allocation for C, that is,

$$u^i(\bar{x}^i) \ge u^i(x^{i^*})$$

for all $i \in C$, with a strict inequality for at least one $i \in C$.

In many environments the set of core allocations is smaller than the set of Pareto optimal allocations, and so again the mapping from environments into outcomes can be tightened. In fact, core allocations and competitive-equilibrium allocations are sometimes coincident. The core notion is especially nice for an analysis of economies in which production or distribution must be done by groups of agents, as by banks or intermediaries, and should be useful also for analysis of the outcomes of political processes.

To reiterate, then: The class of general equilibrium models of Arrow, Debreu, McKenzie, and others is a useful starting point for the study of actual economies. The idea is to start with a stylized Arrow–Debreu environment; impose Pareto optimality, the competitive-markets hypothesis, or the core hypothesis; and then make predictions about the methods of interaction of economic agents or the outcomes from that interaction. This way of proceeding has theoretical content, insofar as variations in Arrow–Debreu environments do imply variations in outcomes. Indeed, these variations are especially striking when one includes diversity, uncertainty, and various impediments to trade. Furthermore, if we search broadly for observations, we discover variations in environments and in outcomes for actual economies. Thus one can contemplate matching stylized theories with observations in some way. For example, one can try first to match an environment from an actual economy having some apparent impediment to trade with the environment of a theory having a stylized version of that impediment, and then one can try to see if the observed outcome of the actual economy matches up in some way with the outcome predicted by the theory. Alternatively, one can begin with some striking arrangement in an actual economy and ask whether any theoretical environment might yield such an arrangement. Either way, one hopes to match observations with theories without making the theoretical environment too complicated or implausible.

This matching exercise is instructive, but at a relatively early stage. Thus no particular economy is studied here in great detail and no grand cross-economy comparisons are attempted. But observations from actual economies serve at least to motivate the theoretical environments studied in the sections that follow. That is, observations from the typical medieval village studied by economist McCloskey (1976), historian Bennett (1974), and sociologist Homans (1975), from the Pacific island communities studied by anthropologists Malinowski (1953) and Firth (1939), from hill tribe communities in northern Thailand studied by anthropologist van Roy (1971), from villages in southern India studied by economists Binswanger and Rosenzweig (1984), and from African hunter-gatherer tribes studied by anthropologist Lee (1979) all suggest that economywide consumption and labor sharing, the presence or absence of currency, and other forms of social interaction are interesting arrangements to study, and also that uncertainty, private information, indivisibilities, spatial separation, limited communication, and limited commitment may be useful in helping to understand these arrangements.

In summary, then, this chapter proceeds as follows. Section 2 sets up a programming problem for a standard general equilibrium model with uncertainty and some diversity among agents. Solutions to that programming problem are then described, with an emphasis on co-movement implications for consumption. Theorems on the existence and optimality of competitive equilibria are also reviewed. Section 3 extends the analysis to an economy with multiple commodities; Section 4 deals in particular with leisure, deriving implications for leisure sharing, absence of quid pro quo, and monitoring. Section 5 extends the analysis to include capital goods. Existence and optimality theorems are reviewed for the general, extended models of these sections. Aggregation across diverse households facilitates the analysis in these sections and delivers as a special case the standard neoclassical growth model.

Section 6 introduces the possibility of private information, to cope with observations from "primitive" societies that are anomalous relative to full information theory. Section 6 also describes how to handle some nonconvexities in the underlying commodity space induced by this private information, namely by the introduction of lotteries. With these lotteries, existence and optimality results follow by more or less standard arguments. Section 7 introduces the possibility of indivisibilities in consumption and/ or leisure, and asks in a preliminary way whether this might help to account for anomalous observations. Section 8 in turn introduces the possibility of spatial separation. With indivisibilities or spatial separation one must again face a nonconvexity in the underlying commodity space, and Sections 7 and 8 describe how to do this successfully. Again, lotteries are useful and allow one to recover standard optimality and existence theorems. Special cases of these models deliver the macroeconomic neoclassical models of recent literature, seeking to explain anomalous time-series observations.

Section 9 introduces the possibility of limited communication into a model with spatial separation and private information, motivated by an effort to explain the observed use of currency and financial intermediaries in some societies. Again, it is shown how to deliver a programming problem for various possible communication technologies, and an effort is made to interpret these various programming problems and their solutions relative to actual observations. As a byproduct of this discussion, one can discuss optimal currency rules and other normative issues. Finally, Section 10 introduces the possibility of limited commitment, to explain observed and more standard roles for currency and to explain the existence of markets in some societies but not others. Here a kind of sequential core notion is adopted, and it is argued that the outcomes of various competitive spatial models of currency can be interpreted as the outcomes of modified programming problems. This class of models with spatial separation and limited commitment also offers promise as a class of neoclassical macroeconomic models seeking to explain observed fluctuations.

2   Uncertainty and the standard Arrow–Debreu program with cross-household diversity

It is difficult at best to make inferences about risk sharing and co-movements of household consumption from descriptive historical or anthropological material. Still, it seems from the work of Homans (1975) and McCloskey (1976) that the dominant institutional arrangement of the medieval village economy – the so-called strip system – was designed in effect as an economywide insurance arrangement. Fields of a typical village were divided into long narrow strips, and any individual's holdings were dispersed so as to reduce the variability associated with diverse soil, topographical, and meteorological conditions. Even more obvious ex post risk sharing is apparent in the primitive island communities studied by Firth (1939) and Malinowski (1953), where relatively large portions of agricultural output were transferred to local chiefs, followed by some redistribution. In northern Thailand, hill tribe communities apparently engage in extensive intravillage and intervillage sharing of rice. The sharing of produce and equality in consumption of the hunter-gatherer tribes studied by Lee (1979) is renowned.

The theory of risk bearing and the treatment of uncertainty developed by Arrow (1964), Debreu (1959), and others predicts such economywide insurance arrangements, at least under specified assumptions and in the absence of various "frictions." In particular, imagine a stylized pure-exchange economy subject to uncertainty. There are a finite number of households indexed by j, $j = 1, 2, ..., n$, and these will be taken to be the primitive economic units. There are a finite number of consumption dates t, $t = 1, 2, ..., T$ and one planning date, $t = 0$. Thus, for simplicity, identical finite lifetimes of households are assumed. Each household j has a continuous concave date-t utility function $U^j(c_t^j)$ over units of consumption c_t^j of the single underlying consumption good of the model at date t. For each household j, satiation in consumption is impossible; on the other hand, there may be a minimal subsistence level of consumption. Consumption c_t^j must lie in some a priori consumption set X_t^j, and this is assumed to be closed, convex, and bounded from below. The utility of future consumption is discounted at rate β, $0 < \beta < 1$, the same rate for all households. The endowment $e_t^j(\epsilon_t)$ of each household j at date t of the single consumption good is a function of some publicly observed shock ϵ_t at date t and is in the interior of the consumption set X_t^j. The shocks ϵ_t are each presumed to take on at most a finite number of values, say from some common set S. From the point of view of the planning date $t = 0$, shock sequence $(\epsilon_1, ..., \epsilon_t)$ is drawn with probability $\text{prob}(\epsilon_1, ..., \epsilon_t)$. [Extensions to more general stochastic processes are given in Hansen and Richard (in press).] There is presumed to be no storage of any kind, at least not initially. That is, the pure exchange case is studied first, for simplicity.

Following the indexation insight of Arrow (1964) and Debreu (1959), the natural commodity space in this model is the space of state-contingent consumptions, where a state at date t is a specification of the entire history of shocks through date t, namely $(\epsilon_1, \epsilon_2, ..., \epsilon_t)$. That is, let $c_t^j(\epsilon_1, \epsilon_2, ..., \epsilon_t)$ denote the proposed consumption of agent j at date t as a function of the entire history of shocks. Then a consumption point x^j to household j is the obvious vector $x^j = \{c_1^j(\epsilon_1), c_2^j(\epsilon_1, \epsilon_2), ..., c_T^j(\epsilon_1, ..., \epsilon_T)$ with indexes running over all dates t and over all histories $(\epsilon_1, ..., \epsilon_T)\}$. The consumption set X^j of household j is then the obvious cross-product of consumption set X_t^j and is therefore closed, convex, and bounded from below. Similarly, as a linear combination of weakly concave functions, the global utility function as of the planning date $t = 0$ is

$$u^j(x^j) = E \sum_{t=1}^{T} \beta^t U^j[c_t^j(\epsilon_1, ..., \epsilon_t)]$$

and is obviously continuous and concave. Thus we are led to a concave programming problem for the determination of Pareto optimal allocations as follows.

Program 2.1. Maximize by choice of the $c_t^j(\epsilon_1, ..., \epsilon_t)$ in the sets X_t^j the objective function

$$\sum_{j=1}^{n} \lambda^j \left\{ E \sum_{t=1}^{T} \beta^t U^j[c_t^j(\epsilon_1, ..., \epsilon_t)] \right\} \tag{2.1}$$

subject to the resource constraint

$$\sum_{j=1}^{n} c_t^j(\epsilon_1, ..., \epsilon_t) \leq \sum_{j=1}^{n} e_t^j(\epsilon_t) \tag{2.2}$$

for each date t and each history $(\epsilon_1, \epsilon_2, ..., \epsilon_t)$, where again the weights λ^j satisfy $0 \leq \lambda^j \leq 1$, $\sum_j \lambda^j = 1$.

Here expectations are taken as of the initial date $t = 0$, and all expectations are held in common. Of course, resource constraint (2.2) bounds consumptions from above.

The objective function (2.1) is continuous in the choice variables, the constraint set is closed and bounded, and autarky is feasible; therefore, a maximizing solution to Program 2.1 is guaranteed to exist. Further, it can be established that any solution to Program 2.1 is necessarily Pareto optimal. Conversely, any Pareto optimum is associated with some point on the utilities possibilities frontier, and – because the set of utility possibilities is convex – that point can be found as a solution to the program for some weights λ^j. Hereafter, then, solutions to Program 2.1 shall be taken as equivalent to the set of Pareto optimal allocations.

Supposing single-valued interior consumption solutions for all households at all dates and histories leads to first-order conditions

$$\beta^t \lambda^j \operatorname{prob}(\epsilon_1, \ldots, \epsilon_t) U^{j'}[c_t^j(\epsilon_1, \ldots, \epsilon_t)] = \mu(\epsilon_1, \epsilon_2, \ldots, \epsilon_t), \qquad (2.3)$$

where $\mu(\epsilon_1, \ldots, \epsilon_t)$ is the Lagrange multiplier on the resource constraint at date t and history $(\epsilon_1, \ldots, \epsilon_t)$. It becomes apparent, then, that the aggregate endowment is to be distributed across households in such a way that weighted marginal utilities are equated across households. Furthermore, with a common discount rate and common expectations, the terms $\beta^t \operatorname{prob}(\epsilon_1, \ldots, \epsilon_t)$ factor out of these equalities, and the distribution satisfying the equalities is independent of the date and the history of shocks. Thus only the magnitude of the aggregate endowment,

$$\sum_{j=1}^{n} e_t^j(\epsilon_t) \equiv \bar{e}(\epsilon_t), \qquad (2.4)$$

matters in the determination of any household's consumption at any date and any history. That is (with some abuse of notation), each c^j depends only on the aggregate endowment $\bar{e}$, and one writes $c^j(\bar{e})$. Further, this residual "static" one-period risk-allocation problem has been studied by Wilson (1968) and Diamond (1967), among others, yielding

$$\frac{\partial c^j(\bar{e})}{\partial \bar{e}} = \frac{-U^{j'}[c^j(\bar{e})]/U^{j''}[c^j(\bar{e})]}{\sum_k \{-U^{k'}[c^k(\bar{e})]/U^{k''}[c^k(\bar{e})]\}}. \qquad (2.5)$$

The right-hand side of (2.5) is a number between zero and unity, and thus individual household consumption must vary positively with the aggregate endowment. Further, this derivative is shown to depend on measures of risk aversion in the population at an optimal allocation.

Sharing rules generally are not linear, as there is no reason a priori to expect the expression on the right-hand side of (2.5) to be some constant. Two special cases may be noted, however. For the first case, suppose the utility functions themselves display constant absolute risk aversion $1/\gamma_j$ for household j, with inverse γ_j; that is,

$$U^j(c) = -\gamma_j \exp[-c/\gamma_j], \quad c \geq 0. \qquad (2.6)$$

Then for a two-agent economy, for example, the consumption share of the first agent is

$$c^1(\bar{e}) = \left(\sum_j \gamma_j^{-1} \right)^{-1} \log(\lambda^1/\lambda^2) + \bar{e}\frac{\gamma_1}{\gamma_1 + \gamma_2}. \tag{2.7}$$

Again the λ^j are the weights from the programming problem and the coefficient on $\bar{e}$ is as predicted in (2.5). For the second case, suppose

$$U^j(c) = [(d)(1-d)]^{-1}(c-b^j)^d, \tag{2.8}$$

where $0 < d < 1$ with $c \geq b^j$. Then, with $a = (1-d)^{-1}$,

$$c^1(\bar{e}) = \left[\sum_j (\lambda^j)^{-a} \right]^{-1} [(\lambda^1)^{-a}b^1 - (\lambda^2)^{-a}b^2] + \bar{e}\frac{(\lambda^1)^a}{(\lambda^1)^a + (\lambda^2)^a}. \tag{2.9}$$

One can imagine "fitting" versions of (2.2) and (2.3) to actual observations. In fact, Leme (1984) has asked whether such an exercise would be reasonable for aggregate cross-country data, taking advantage of the monotonicity property (2.5) and the fact that monotonicity holds at any level of aggregation. Unfortunately, monotonicity does not hold uniformly in the postwar data. But then, the world as a whole is hardly an Arrow–Debreu economy. Smaller, self-contained economies are more obvious sources of observations.

Unfortunately, though, panel data from such sources are frequently not available; consistent observations on household consumptions are rare, as are observations on actual exchanges among households. On the other hand, there is sometimes reasonable evidence on aggregate output or aggregate consumption and reasonable evidence on prices or interest rates, say (respectively) on land or one-period loans. Thus one can try to use these observations to address the hypothesis of risk aversion – for example, to estimate the free parameter d in equation (2.8).

If one is to use available price data, one must then include as part of the model what role prices are playing. The obvious assumption analytically is that prices are such that allocations are achieved as if in an equilibrium of competitive markets. This assumption is restrictive and ad hoc – nothing in the theory predicts the existence of competitive markets. On the other hand, the competitive-markets hypothesis is clean and analytically powerful. For, in the present context, competitive equilibria can be shown to exist. Further, the usual welfare theorems apply so that competitive equilibria are necessarily Pareto optimal, and all optima can be supported as competitive equilibria.

More specifically, let the consumption set X^j of each household j with typical component x^j be defined as above. Let the endowment point w^j to household j be the vector $w^j = \{e_1^j(\epsilon_1), e_2^j(\epsilon_1, \epsilon_2), \ldots, e_T^j(\epsilon_1, \epsilon_2, \ldots, \epsilon_T)$ with indexes running over all dates t and over all histories $(\epsilon_1, \ldots, \epsilon_T)\}$. A preference ordering $\geq_j$ for household j is induced by the utility function $u^j(x^j)$ as defined above. Then certain assumptions are satisfied: (a.1) X^j is closed; (a.2) X^j is convex; (a.3) X^j has a lower bound; (a.4) there is no satiation consumption in X^j; (a.5) for every point $x' \in X^j$ the upper and lower contour sets $\{x \in X^j : x \geq_j x'\}$ and $\{x \in X^j : x \leq_j x'\}$ are closed in X^j; (a.6) if x' and x'' are two points in X^j and if t is any real number in $(0,1)$, then $x'' \geq_j x'$ implies $tx'' + (1-t)x' \geq_j x'$; (a.7) there is some x^0 in X^j such that $x^0 \ll w^j$. By Theorem 1 of Debreu (1959, §5.7), under assumptions (a.1)–(a.7) there exists a competitive equilibrium as previously defined in Section 1. In particular, there exists a price system p^* specifying $p_t^*(\epsilon_1, \ldots, \epsilon_t)$ for all dates t and all histories $(\epsilon_1, \ldots, \epsilon_t)$ such that, for every household j, allocation x^{j^*} maximizes $u^j(x^j)$ subject to $x^j \in X^j$ and

$$\sum_{t=1}^{T} \sum_{(\epsilon_1, \ldots, \epsilon_T)} [c_t^j(\epsilon_1, \ldots, \epsilon_t) - e_t^j(\epsilon_t)] p_t^*(\epsilon_1, \ldots, \epsilon_t) \leq 0, \qquad (2.10)$$

and the allocations x^{j^*}, $j = 1, 2, \ldots, n$, satisfy market-clearing condition (2.2). Also, by Theorem 6.4 of Debreu, under assumptions (a.2), (a.5), and (a.6) for every optimum x^{j^*}, $j = 1, 2, \ldots, n$, there exists a price system p^* such that x^{j^*} minimizes expenditure $p^* x^j$ on the upper contour set $\{x^j \in X^j : x^j \geq_j x^{j^*}\}$. Further, if the exceptional case

$$p^* x^{j^*} = \min_{x^j \in X^j} p^* x^j \qquad (2.11)$$

does not occur, then x^{j^*} maximizes $u^j(x^j)$ subject to $x^j \in X^j$ and condition (2.10) above, with the endowment w^j replaced by x^{j^*}. Finally, by Theorem 1 of Debreu (1959, §6.3), under assumptions (a.2), (a.4), and (a.6), every competitive equilibrium is an optimum.

Again, under the competitive-equilibrium hypothesis, time series on rents or interest rates can – at least in principle – be used to check on the fit of the theory with the reality of an actual economy. At the level of generality and diversity assumed thus far, however, this still can be a challenging exercise, as it can be difficult to work backward from prices and aggregate quantities to individual demands and hence to individual preferences. More structure is needed.

An extreme but operational assumption that does allow a fitting exercise is that preferences of individual households aggregate in the sense of Gorman (1953); that is, there exists a utility function for a representative consumer which, when evaluated at aggregate quantities, can be used to deliver equilibrium prices. In fact, the asset-pricing literature of Grossman and Shiller (1981), Hall (1981), Eichenbaum, Hansen, and Richard (1987), Hansen and Singleton (1982, 1983), Mankiw, Rotemberg, and Summers (1985), Mehra and Prescott (1985), Shiller (1981), and others can be interpreted as adopting this aggregation hypothesis. It is equivalent, for the pure-exchange single-good economy here, with the supposition that preferences are of the form of (2.6) or (2.8). It must be emphasized, however, that some diversity in preferences and consumption sets as well as some competitive-equilibrium trade can be accommodated. The representative consumer construct does not require that households literally be identical.

3   Programs with multiple commodities and further aggregation possibilities

The theory thus far assumes only one consumption good, yet on the face of it this is unsatisfactory, especially if one tries to match the theory to the reality of any economy. In the medieval village, for example, various crops were grown, including wheat, oats, barley, rye, peas, and beans. And in the island community of Tikopia studied by Firth (1939), yams, fruits, and fish were all part of the regular diet.

Fortunately, formal aspects of the theory are easily modified. If there are m consumption goods, then one need only let $c_t^j(\epsilon_1, \ldots, \epsilon_t)$ and $e_t^j(\epsilon_t)$ denote m-dimensional vectors and continue to make the same assumptions for the consumption sets X_t^j and utility functions $U^j(\cdot)$ as above. Program 2.1 then remains intact and its solutions still correspond with the Pareto optima. In fact, standard theorems on the existence and optimality of competitive equilibria still apply.

Aggregation possibilities in the sense of Gorman (1953) and described by Hansen (in press) are also possible. That is, under specified assumptions, a representative-consumer construct can be used to deliver competitive-equilibrium prices as marginal rates of substitution at aggregate quantities. More specifically, suppose for sake of illustration that there are two underlying commodities, so that $c_t^j = c = (c_1, c_2)$, and that preferences for each household j, $j = 1, 2, \ldots, n$, over bundles c in some consumption set $X_t^j \subset R^2$ at date t are described by a family of indifference curves of the form

$$c^j = \rho^j(d) + \rho_0(d)(U^j). \tag{3.1}$$

Here, d is a 2-dimensional vector (d_1, d_2), and d_1/d_2 is the marginal rate of substitution. Thus, as d_1/d_2 is varied parametrically, one moves along an indifference curve determining bundle c^j for household j. The particular indifference curve for household j is determined by the utility index U^j, where utility number U^j can result from a monotonic transformation of some underlying utility function. The point is that diversity in preferences across households j can be accommodated, namely in the "baseline" indifference curves $\rho^j(d)$. However, the "expansion factor" $\rho_0(d)$ is common.

We may note that at a Pareto optimum with interior consumption solutions, marginal rates of substitution must be equated, so that d would be common across households. Adding up (3.1) over j for fixed d then yields

$$\bar{c} = \bar{\rho}(d) + \rho_0(d)\left[\sum_{j=1}^{n} U^j\right], \tag{3.2}$$

where the over-bar indicates aggregate numbers or functions. Of course, in any optimal allocation resources are not wasted, so $\bar{c} = \bar{e}$, the aggregate endowment. That is, from (3.2),

$$\bar{e} = \bar{\rho}(d) + \rho_0(d)\left[\sum_{j=1}^{n} U^j\right]. \tag{3.3}$$

System (3.3) has two equations in essentially two unknowns, marginal rate of substitution d_1/d_2, and aggregate utility index $\sum_{j=1}^{n} U^j$, and so under specified assumptions both these are determined by (3.3). In particular, then, the marginal rate of substitution at an optimum is pinned down by the aggregate endowment, although the distribution of utilities and hence of consumptions is not. Of course, in a competitive equilibrium this marginal rate of substitution must be the price ratio.

Important also is the fact that if there is any nontrivial choice of "endowment" e, say from some aggregate production possibilities set, then the preferences of the representative consumer with indifference curves represented by (3.2) can also be used to determine a Pareto optimal outcome. For, as in Figure 1, a move from point A to point 0 must necessarily increase the utility indexes $\sum_{j=1}^{n} U^j$. Thus, any distribution of household utilities at point A can be dominated by a suitable distribution at point 0.

The class of preferences that aggregate in the sense of Gorman include the class of utility function studied by Eichenbaum, Hansen, and Richard (1987), namely,

$$\frac{1}{\delta\sigma}\left\{\sum_{i=1}^{m} \theta_i[\delta(c_i^j - b_i^j)]^\alpha\right\}^{\sigma/\alpha}$$

when b_i^j is a subsistence point of household j for commodity i with $\sigma < 1$ and $\alpha < 1$. This includes as a special case $\sigma = \alpha$, so that preferences are separable over consumption goods, with each commodity utility function displaying the same index of relative risk aversion. It also includes as a special case $\theta_i = \delta = \alpha = 1$, but $\sigma < 1$ so that direct aggregation of underlying commodities and risk aversion is allowed.

Such special cases also allow Program 2.1 to deliver strong implications for co-movements of consumption as before. Essentially, separability delivers m separate marginal conditions and eliminates interaction

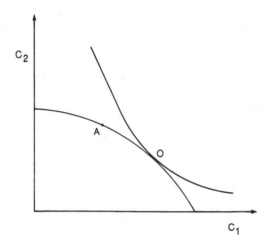

Figure 1

across commodities, something that can overturn the earlier analysis. And
when direct aggregation is possible the analysis can proceed in an obvious way, namely by combining commodities directly into some aggregate.
Unfortunately, strong results for the general case are not going to fall out
easily, as Scheinkman (1984) has emphasized. It can be said, however,
that observations have pushed the theory in an interesting direction.

4   Programs with production and with leisure as another commodity

Labor arrangements are often of interest in primitive economies, in part
because such arrangements seem to differ from those to which we have become accustomed. In the medieval village, for example, virtually all residents participated in *benes,* communal works for the local lord in times of
need. These and other more standard tasks were specified in great detail
and were associated with an elaborate system of monitors. In the primitive island community studied by Firth (1939), there were community-
wide requests for labor for household-specific projects, and this labor
was often supplied without apparent compensation.

To extend the theory to incorporate leisure, let household j have preferences over units of consumption c_t^j and leisure ℓ_t^j respectively, as represented by a date-t utility function $U^j(c_t^j) + V^j(\ell_t^j)$, with each functional
component continuous, weakly concave, and strictly increasing. Separability is assumed here for tractability, as motivated above. The future is

discounted at common rate β, $0 < \beta < 1$. Consumption and leisure must be at least nonnegative, and leisure is bounded from above by the number of hours available to household j per unit time, $\bar{\ell}^j$. In addition, the consumption set X_t^j retains the properties assumed earlier. Aggregate output $\bar{q}_t$ at date t is some function $f(\cdot, \cdot)$ of aggregate hours worked, $a_t = \sum_{j=1}^{n}(\bar{\ell}^j - \ell_t^j)$, and some publicly observed shock ϵ_t. For each shock ϵ_t the function $f(\cdot, \epsilon_t)$ displays constant or decreasing marginal returns to hours worked.

Indexing all commodities by histories $\epsilon_1, \ldots, \epsilon_t$ leads to Program 4.1.

Program 4.1. *Maximize by choice of the $c_t^j(\epsilon_1, \ldots, \epsilon_t)$ and the $\ell_t^j(\epsilon_1, \ldots, \epsilon_t)$ the objective function*

$$\sum_{j=1}^{n} \lambda^j \left\{ E_0 \sum_{t=1}^{T} \beta^t [U^j[c_t^j(\epsilon_1, \ldots, \epsilon_t)] + V^j[\ell_t^j(\epsilon_1, \ldots, \epsilon_t)]] \right\} \tag{4.1}$$

subject to $(c_t^j(\cdot), \ell_t^j(\cdot)) \in X_t^j$,

$$\sum_{j=1}^{n} c_t^j(\epsilon_1, \ldots, \epsilon_t) \le \bar{c}_t(\epsilon_1, \ldots, \epsilon_t), \tag{4.2}$$

$$\sum_{j=1}^{n} \ell_t^j(\epsilon_1, \ldots, \epsilon_t) \le \bar{\ell}_t(\epsilon_1, \ldots, \epsilon_t), \tag{4.3}$$

$$\bar{c}_t(\epsilon_1, \ldots, \epsilon_t) \le f\left[\sum_{j=1}^{n} \bar{\ell}^j - \bar{\ell}_t(\epsilon_1, \ldots, \epsilon_t), \epsilon_t \right]. \tag{4.4}$$

Proceeding as before, one obtains the implication that consumption c_t^j of household j should move monotonically with aggregate consumption $\bar{c}_t$. Here as well, leisure ℓ_t^j of household j should move monotonically with aggregate leisure $\bar{\ell}_t$, at least if boundary constraints are avoided. Both these relationships are invariant as to date and histories. Thus consumption and leisure sharing are delivered, with possibly variable shares determined by preferences and the weights λ^j. Further, the weights λ^j may also have implications for the cross-sectional distribution of consumption and leisure. For example, a household with high consumption on average might also have high leisure on average. On the other hand, there should be no direct contemporaneous link between a household's actual effort and a household's final consumption, because ℓ_t^j depends on $\bar{\ell}_t$ and c_t^j depends on $\bar{c}_t$. For example, high labor effort to avert disaster due to some shock ϵ_t might not be associated with increased communal consumption. A relationship between aggregate consumption and aggregate leisure contingent only on contemporary shock ϵ_t can be delivered, a relationship that can also depend on the weights λ^j. However, if preferences aggregate in the sense of Gorman, this is sufficient for the relationship between aggregate consumption and aggregate leisure to not depend on the weights λ^j, and this relationship can be delivered as if from the preferences of a representative consumer.

Another implication of these Arrow–Debreu economies for labor assignments is evident from the literature on the principal–agent problem of Grossman and Hart (1983), Harris and Raviv (1979), Holmström (1979), Mirrlees (1975), Shavell (1979), and others. For specializing our notation somewhat, let there be two households: household 1 associated with an agent and household 2 associated with a principal. Suppose that the agent alone can supply labor effort a_1. That is, household 1 has preferences over consumption c^1 and leisure ℓ^1; household 2 has preferences over consumption c^2 only. By the analysis above we may consider a static problem and index consumption to aggregate output $\bar{c}$. Thus we are led to Program 4.2.

Program 4.2. *Maximize by choice of $c^1(\bar{c})$, $c^2(\bar{c})$, $\ell(\epsilon)$ the objective function*

$$\lambda^1\{E[U^1[c^1(\bar{c})] + V^1[\ell(\epsilon)]]\} + \lambda^2\{E[U^2[c^2(\bar{c})]]\} \tag{4.5}$$

subject to

$$c^1(\bar{c}) + c^2(\bar{c}) = \bar{c}, \tag{4.6}$$

$$\bar{c} = f[\bar{\ell}^1 - \ell(\epsilon), \epsilon]. \tag{4.7}$$

Solution $c^1(\bar{c})^*$, $c^2(\bar{c})^*$, and $\ell(\epsilon)^*$ to Program 4.2 displays an incentive problem: Given the optimal consumption schedule $c^1(\bar{c})^*$, if household 1 were asked to choose its own level of leisure (effort) $\ell(\epsilon)$ then that choice would in general differ from $\ell(\epsilon)^*$. That is,

$$U^1[c^1(\bar{c})^*] + V^1[\ell(\epsilon)] > U^1[c^1(\bar{c})^*] + V^1[\ell(\epsilon)^*], \tag{4.8}$$

where again $\bar{c}$ on the left-hand side of (4.8) is determined for some other leisure choice $\ell(\epsilon)$. In fact, household 1 would generally want to work less (i.e., consume more leisure) than at the optimum. This idea generalizes to multiagent problems.

One might also ask whether these implications of Program 4.1 survive the obvious decentralization hypothesis, that allocations are achieved as if in competitive markets. To do this, one must distinguish individual choices from aggregate outcomes. Thus suppose each household j, $j = 1, 2, \ldots, n$, has a production function $q^j = f^j(a^j, \epsilon_t)$ displaying constant or diminishing returns to scale with a^j as labor input measured in negative units. That is,

$$q_t^j = f^j\left(\sum_{k=1}^n a_t^{kj}, \epsilon_t\right) \quad j = 1, 2, \ldots, n,$$

where $a_t^{k,j}$, measured in negative units, is labor hours supplied by household k to household j at date t. Of course, individual leisures satisfy

$$\ell_t^j = \bar{\ell}^j + \sum_{k=1}^{n} a_t^{jk},$$

and aggregate consumption satisfies

$$\bar{c}_t \le \sum_{j=1}^{n} q_t^j.$$

Date-t and history $(\epsilon_1, \dots, \epsilon_t)$-contingent production sets can now be defined for household j with the second component for labor input and the first component for commodity output, namely

$$Y_t^j(\epsilon_1, \dots, \epsilon_t) = \{ y_{1t}(\epsilon_1, \dots, \epsilon_t), y_{2t}(\epsilon_1, \dots, \epsilon_t) : y_{1t}(\epsilon_1, \dots, \epsilon_t) \ge 0,$$
$$y_{2t}(\epsilon_1, \dots, \epsilon_t) \le 0, y_{1t}(\epsilon_1, \dots, \epsilon_t) \le f^j[y_{2t}(\epsilon_1, \dots, \epsilon_t), \epsilon_t]\}.$$

Evidently, with set Y^j as the obvious cross-product over all possible dates t and histories $(\epsilon_1, \dots, \epsilon_t)$ and with aggregate set Y as the sum over the Y^j, certain assumptions are satisfied: (d.1) $0 \in Y^j$; (d.2) Y is closed; (d.3) Y is convex; (d.4) $Y \cap (-Y) \subset \{0\}$ or impossibility of free production; and (d.5) $Y \supset (-\Omega)$ or free disposal.

Preferences of each household j can be defined over consumption and labor supply measured in positive and negative units respectively. That is, the utility functions $U^j(\cdot)$ and $V^j(\cdot)$ deliver function $W^j(x_{1t}, x_{2t})$ and hence discounted expected utility function $u^j(x)$ for x in consumption set X, with the latter as the obvious cross-product over the redefined X_t^j. The endowment w^j with a component of zero for labor supply is obviously defined. It facilitates the analysis here to suppose the component for consumption of w^j is strictly positive.

Proceeding as before, define – over all dates and histories – a price system $p_t(\epsilon_1, \dots, \epsilon_t)$ and $w_t(\epsilon_1, \dots, \epsilon_t)$ for the consumption good and for labor effort, respectively. There follows the standard definition of a competitive equilibrium with production as given in Section 1. The existence of a competitive equilibrium follows under the previous assumptions on consumers and assumptions (d.1)–(d.5) on firms. That a competitive equilibrium is an optimum follows as before under the previous assumptions. That any optimum can be supported as a valuation equilibrium follows as before with additional assumption (d.3).

The implication of leisure sharing is robust to the decentralization by competitive markets, as leisure sharing holds for all weights λ^j; the competitive hypothesis just picks out particular weights. Absence of quid pro quo of consumption for labor supply is problematical, however. Under the decentralization hypothesis, each household j perceives itself as being free to vary labor supply, by (say) reducing $\ell_t^j(\epsilon_1, \ldots, \epsilon_t)$ and receiving $w_t^j(\epsilon_1, \ldots, \epsilon_t)$ in compensation. In this sense there is quid pro quo. In fact, if the substitution effect dominates, higher wages could effect higher effort. However, this increased purchasing power could be spent on *all* consumptions $c_\tau^j(\epsilon_1, \ldots, \epsilon_\tau)$, $\tau = 1, 2, \ldots, T$ and thus absence of movement in contemporary consumption is possible in equilibrium. Observationally, matters are subtle because one must distinguish quid pro quo in accounting credits from changes in actual consumption. That is, in an economy with diversity and trade it is a tricky business to distinguish compensation intended for *final consumption* from compensation as an accounting payment. Of course, if preferences aggregate in the sense of Gorman then the relative wage can be determined as the obvious marginal rate of substitution of a representative consumer at aggregate leisure and consumption, and thus time series on wages, aggregate consumption, and aggregate labor effort can be delivered. Thus, one can ask whether there would be quid pro quo in these data.

Under the decentralization hypothesis, household j chooses a contract specifying consumptions and labor supplies under all possible contingencies subject only to the budget constraint. In this sense, then, labor is not assigned. However, once a contract is entered into, the $\ell_t^j(\epsilon_1, \ldots, \epsilon_t)^*$ plan must be carried out, and this requires that leisure and labor effort be observed. Monitoring would still be necessary for enforcement of the competitive-equilibrium outcome.

5   Programs with capital goods and storage

A study of various primitive economies reveals the existence of storage possibilities and various capital assets. The magnitude of within-period consumption risk in the medieval village, and therefore the need for insurance and the strip system, would seem to turn on the possibility of intertemporal storage. Similarly, oxen for ploughing in the medieval village and canoes in the island economy studied by Firth represent important capital assets and seem positively associated with the owner's economic position.

To begin thinking about storage and capital assets and their implications for risk and for compensation, imagine that aggregate output $\bar{q}_t$ at date t is some function of aggregate labor supply, aggregate capital or storage, and the contemporaneous shock; that is,

$$\bar{q}_t = f\left(\sum_{j=1}^{n} \bar{\ell}^j - \bar{\ell}_t, K_t, \epsilon_t \right),$$

and consider the following program.

Program 5.1. *Maximize by choice of* $c_t^j(\epsilon_1, ..., \epsilon_t)$, $\ell_t^j(\epsilon_1, ..., \epsilon_t)$, *and* $\bar{i}_t(\epsilon_1, ..., \epsilon_t)$ *the objective function*

$$\sum_{j=1}^{n} \lambda^j \left\{ E_0 \sum_{t=1}^{T} \beta^t [U^j[c_t^j(\epsilon_1, ..., \epsilon_t)] + V^j[\ell_t^j(\epsilon_1, ..., \epsilon_t)]] \right\} \tag{5.1}$$

subject to

$$\sum_{j=1}^{n} c_t^j(\epsilon_1, ..., \epsilon_t) \leq \bar{c}_t(\epsilon_1, ..., \epsilon_t), \tag{5.2}$$

$$\sum_{j=1}^{n} \ell_t^j(\epsilon_1, ..., \epsilon_t) \leq \bar{\ell}(\epsilon_1, ..., \epsilon_t), \tag{5.3}$$

$$\bar{c}_t(\epsilon_1, ..., \epsilon_t) + \bar{i}_t(\epsilon_1, ..., \epsilon_t)$$

$$\leq f\left[\sum_{j=1}^{n} \bar{\ell}^j - \bar{\ell}_t(\epsilon_1, ..., \epsilon_t), \bar{K}_t(\epsilon_1, ..., \epsilon_t), \epsilon_t \right] \tag{5.4}$$

$$\bar{K}_{t+1}(\epsilon_1, ..., \epsilon_t) = (1-\delta)[\bar{K}_t(\epsilon_1, ..., \epsilon_{t-1}) + \bar{i}_t(\epsilon_1, ..., \epsilon_t)], \tag{5.5}$$

with $[c_t^j(\epsilon_1, ..., \epsilon_t), \ell_t^j(\epsilon_1, ..., \epsilon_t)] \in X_t^j$.

Here $\bar{c}_t$, $\bar{i}_t$, $\bar{\ell}_t$, and $\bar{K}_t$ are aggregate consumption, investment, leisure, and beginning-of-period capital (or storage), respectively, at date t. Inequality (5.4) divides output into consumption and investment (additions to storage), and equation (5.5) is the law of motion on aggregate capital (or storage) with δ as the rate of depreciation.

The aggregate function here, $f(\cdot, \cdot, \cdot)$, is derived from individual production functions

$$q_t^j = f^j\left(\sum_{k=1}^{n} a_t^{kj}, \sum_{k=1}^{n} K_t^{kj}, \epsilon_t \right) \tag{5.6}$$

for each household j, where a_t^{kj} is as before (in Section 4) and K_t^{kj}, measured in negative units, is capital supplied by household k to household j at date t. Further, let i_t^j, measured in negative units, denote additions to household j's capital at the end of date t from current production. The aggregate resource constraint may now be written

$$\sum_{j=1}^{n} (-i_t^j) + \sum_{j=1}^{n} c_t^j \leq \sum_{j=1}^{n} q_t^j. \tag{5.7}$$

Despite this appearance of individual ownership, capital in Program 5.1 can be viewed as common property, allocated across projects at each date, helping to deliver aggregate output. No household should receive increased compensation for the act of supplying a capital good to anyone else's project. Consumption is determined still by aggregate consumption, and so on as before. Of course, the weights λ^j could be related to initial capital holdings, and if so this invariance result could be weakened. More generally, one might consider whether versions of this economy with capital can be decentralized and what interpretations follow.

To do this, let the generic commodity point be a 5-tuple: the first component for consumption, the second for investment, the third for beginning-of-period capital, the fourth for end-of-period capital, and the fifth for labor–leisure. Then imagine household j has two production technologies, the first for production of the consumption-investment good of the form

$$Y_t^{1j}(\epsilon_1,\ldots,\epsilon_t) = \{y_t(\epsilon_1,\ldots,\epsilon_t) \in \Re^5 : \underset{+}{y_{1t}}(\epsilon_1,\ldots,\epsilon_t) + \underset{+}{y_{2t}}(\epsilon_1,\ldots,\epsilon_t)$$

$$\leq f^j[\underset{-}{y_{5t}}(\epsilon_1,\ldots,\epsilon_t), \underset{-}{y_{3t}}(\epsilon_1,\ldots,\epsilon_t), \epsilon_t]$$

$$\text{and } \underset{+}{y_{4t}}(\epsilon_1,\ldots,\epsilon_t) \leq -\underset{-}{y_{3t}}(\epsilon_1,\ldots,\epsilon_t)\}$$

and the second for capital accumulation of the form

$$Y_t^{2j}(\epsilon_1,\ldots,\epsilon_t) = \{y_t(\epsilon_1,\ldots,\epsilon_t) \in \Re^5 : y_{3,t+1}(\epsilon_1,\ldots,\epsilon_{t+1})$$

$$\leq -\{(1-\delta)[y_{4t}(\epsilon_1,\ldots,\epsilon_t) + y_{2t}(\epsilon_1,\ldots,\epsilon_t)]\}\}.$$

Here the $\pm$ notation below the variables indicates $+$ for output and $-$ for input, and indicates as well the ranges of the indicated variables; otherwise variables must be zero. As before, let profit shares in both technologies be $\theta^{kj} = 0$ for $k \neq j$ and $\theta^{jj} = 1$. Evidently, assumptions (d.1)–(d.5) are satisfied with Y^{1j} and Y^{2j} as the obvious cross-products over dates t and histories $(\epsilon_1,\ldots,\epsilon_t)$, Y^j as the sum of Y^{1j} and Y^{2j}, and Y as the sum over j. Households' endowment vectors in this space are all zero. But note that production technology Y^{2j} is defined relative to some fixed initial assignment of capital, $y_{3,t=1}$, and this may yield some profit to household j. Household j has preferences over consumption and labor supply,

$$\underset{+}{x_{1t}}(\epsilon_1,\ldots,\epsilon_t) \quad \text{and} \quad \underset{-}{x_{5t}}(\epsilon_1,\ldots,\epsilon_t)$$

at date t under history $(\epsilon_1,\ldots,\epsilon_t)$.

The standard definition of a competitive equilibrium follows as before with price system $p_t(\epsilon_1,\ldots,\epsilon_t) \in \Re^5$ having components for consumption, investment, beginning-of-period capital, end-of-period capital, and labor. And as above, competitive equilibria can be shown to exist and to satisfy the two welfare theorems.

In a standard competitive equilibrium, household j acting under technology Y^{1j} makes a "rental" payment $p_{3t}(\epsilon_1,\ldots,\epsilon_t) - p_{4t}(\epsilon_1,\ldots,\epsilon_t)$ per unit capital used during period t under history $(\epsilon_1, \ldots, \epsilon_t)$, and thus it would appear to offer explicit compensation for capital supplied to it. In this sense there is quid pro quo. However, as before, recipients of these payments – say, household h – may purchase consumption goods over the entire horizon and all contingencies. Thus consumption $c_t^h(\epsilon_1, \ldots, \epsilon_t)$ need not increase with increases in capital supplied. Thus there need be no explicit quid pro quo of contemporary capital for contemporary consumption in equilibrium. On the other hand, as noted above, there may be a more subtle relationship between capital, consumption, and leisure that would be apparent from Program 5.1: A competitive equilibrium is associated with particular Pareto weights λ^j, and initial capital holdings $y_{3, t=1}$ determine the income helping to deliver the competitive equilibrium. Thus, roughly, the higher is household j's initial capital, the higher is j's weight λ^j, and the higher (on average) might be consumption and leisure.

Of course, to follow this through one must determine the competitive equilibrium relationship among consumptions, capital (inventory) holdings, and rentals across households over time and over shocks. Unfortunately, though, with the level of diversity allowed thus far, this is not a trivial endeavor. Of course, with the aggregation hypothesis one *can* generate time series on aggregates from the maximization problem of a representative consumer, for then Program 5.1 reduces to the standard neoclassical growth model.

The standard neoclassical growth model studied by Brock and Mirman (1972), Cass (1965), Danthine and Donaldson (1981), Koopmans (1965), and Sargent (1979), among others, is often maligned as being unrealistic and a poor choice for the study of fluctuations and economywide phenomena. Yet we see now how one is led to it in an attempt to understand dynamic phenomena, starting from a natural base and getting rid of some (but not all!) of the diversity across agents. In fact, recent papers of Lucas (1985, 1987), Kydland and Prescott (1982), and Altug (1984) illustrate how little we know about dynamics induced by optimizing agents, in particular how time series of aggregate variables can depend critically on assumptions about technology and preferences. As Lucas (1987) notes, for example, solutions of the Kydland–Prescott (1982) version of Program 5.1 display too little variability in hours worked and investment and too much variability in consumption, at least relative to postwar U.S. time-series data. Yet a combination of intertemporal substitution of leisure, gestation lags, and lags in the resolution of uncertainty can at least partially overcome the deficiency. Further, the work of Altug (1984) indicates there is a tradeoff between intertemporal substitution of leisure and multiple capital goods. And it is unclear whether some reasonable combination of costly physical storage, productive planting of seed, variable weather, and risk aversion can be reconciled with the observations of low carryovers and periodic starvation in typical medieval villages. Again it seems that dynamic phenomena consistent with the neoclassical growth model are not sufficiently well understood, and are naturally the subject of continuing research.

6 Programs with private information

As noted earlier, primitive societies can generate observations that are anomalous relative to standard Arrow–Debreu theory. In the rice-sharing scheme of northern Thailand, for example, it is apparent that track is kept of households' rice "deficits" *over time*. In particular, it seems that a given deficit cannot be indefinitely large or sustained on an indefinite basis – at some critical point, reciprocity in terms of labor is required. And, in the absence of that, the deficit-ridden household may be kicked out of its village. Again, these kinds of intertemporal tie-ins are not consistent with solutions to standard programming problems of the type considered thus far. Of course, in the case of northern Thailand it is plausible that unobserved labor effort is the neglected element. One also suspects that anomalous consumption and leisure patterns abound in villages of southern India, where apparently there is no explicit monitoring of labor effort on sharecropped fields. Thus one might again suppose that private information is a neglected element.

Fortunately, the programming methods under discussion thus far can be modified to incorporate explicit private information, delivering yet another class of Arrow–Debreu programs. Moreover, the solutions to these modified programs can differ in substantial and systematic ways from the solutions to full-information, standard Arrow–Debreu programs. This section will elaborate on both these points.

To begin, it will prove instructive to return to the pure-exchange economy of Sections 2 and 3 and incorporate a minimal amount of private information. Thus, consider an essentially static pure-exchange economy with two agents, a and b, each endowed with an m-dimensional vector of consumption goods dependent on some shock ϵ. In fact, suppose realizations of agent a's endowment $e^a(\epsilon)$ are seen by agent a alone taking on (say) at most two values, θ' and θ'', with generic element θ, in some consumption period. And suppose for simplicity that realizations of agent b's endowment $e^b(\epsilon)$ are public, say some constant W. Were we to solve Program 2.1 for this special case, ignoring the private information, we would deduce the fact (with risk aversion) that consumptions of agents a and b should be functions of the aggregate endowment $W + \theta$ or (for simplicity) just θ, and we would write $c^a(\theta)$ and $c^b(\theta)$.

But now a potential problem emerges. For let $f^a(\theta)$ denote the effective net transfer that agent a is to receive when his endowment is θ; that is, $f^a(\theta) \equiv c^a(\theta) - \theta$. It is possible that

$$U^a[\theta' + f^a(\theta')] < U^a[\theta' + f^a(\theta'')], \tag{6.1}$$

so that if agent a's endowment were actually θ' and he were asked to name a value for it, he would choose to name θ'', and the allocation to him would be $\theta' + f^a(\theta'')$ rather than $\theta' + f^a(\theta')$.

As is apparent, this problem might be remedied by the imposition of (6.1) with the inequality reversed; that is,

$$U^a[\theta' + f^a(\theta')] \geq U^a[\theta' + f^a(\theta'')] \tag{6.2}$$

and similarly, for $\theta = \theta''$,

$$U^a[\theta'' + f^a(\theta'')] \geq U^a[\theta'' + f^a(\theta')]. \tag{6.3}$$

That is, one might be tempted to impose constraints (6.2)–(6.3) directly onto Program 2.1 before deriving a solution. In fact, it is the implication of the work of Myerson (1979) and of Harris and Townsend (1981) that such a procedure can be rigorously justified. In economies with private information there is essentially no loss of generality in imposing such constraints; such constraints capture all the additional restrictions associated with private information.

Of course, these restrictions can be substantial. Private-information optimal allocations often differ substantially from full-information optimal allocations – the point to be made in this section. With only one good for the economy just described, for example, the solution with private information would be autarkic.

Two qualifications to this discussion should be noted, however. First, when there is private information on quantities, as in the economy just described, constraints like (6.2) and (6.3) sometimes can be weakened. In effect, agent a could be asked both to name a value for his endowment *and* to display the endowment (if necessary) as evidence of his claim. This can be captured formally by allowing agent a to transfer some amount of his consumption good to some center, as a "tax," before receiving any compensation, as a "subsidy." Second, even without this modification, constraints (6.2) and (6.3) do not necessarily leave the space of allocations $[f^a(\theta'), f^a(\theta'')]$ convex. That is, problems such as Program 2.1 with (6.2) and (6.3) appended as constraints are not necessarily concave problems. But Prescott and Townsend (1984a, b), among others, have shown that this problem can be remedied with the use of lotteries, and beneficial exchange is made possible as well. Intuitively, the risk aversion of agent a can vary across distinct deterministic allocations, and thus lotteries can help to weaken the effect of the incentive constraints, leading to a Pareto improvement. (An explicit example of this will be given momentarily.)

More formally for the environment at hand, let $T(\theta)$ denote the set of all feasible displays or "taxes" $\tau = (\tau^a, \tau^b)$ on agents a and b respectively, satisfying constraints $0 \le \tau^a \le \theta$ and $0 \le \tau^b \le W$. Similarly, let $S(\tau)$ denote the set of all second-round conditional "subsidies" $s = (s^a, s^b)$ on agents a and b respectively, satisfying the constraints $s^a \ge 0$, $s^b \ge 0$, and $s^a + s^b \le \tau^a + \tau^b$, so that the sum of the subsidies is bounded by the sum of the taxes or displays. Next, let $\pi^\tau(\theta)$ be a lottery on taxes in the space $T(\theta)$, let $\pi^s(\theta, \tau)$ be a lottery on subsidies in the space $S(\tau)$ conditioned on tax τ, and let $\pi(\tau, s, \theta)$ be the joint lottery on taxes τ and subsidies s. Agent a is then imagined to effect lotteries $\pi^\tau(\theta)$ and $\pi^s(\theta, \tau)$ or (more directly) $\pi(\tau, s, \theta)$, by his announcement of θ. Program 2.1 is thus reduced to the following.

Program 6.1. *Maximize by choice of the lotteries* $\pi(\tau, s, \theta)$ *the objective function*

$$\lambda^a \left\{ E_\theta \iint U^a[\theta - \tau^a + s^a]\, \pi(d\tau, ds, \theta) \right\}$$

$$+ \lambda^b \left\{ E_\theta \iint U^b[W - \tau^b + s^b]\, \pi(d\tau, ds, \theta) \right\} \tag{6.4}$$

and given endowment $\theta = \theta'$ *subject either to*

$$\pi^\tau(\theta'') \text{ is not a lottery on the space } T(\theta'), \tag{6.5}$$

so that some realization of the tax lottery or display is not feasible given $\theta = \theta'$, *or to*

$$\iint U^a[\theta' - \tau^a + s^a]\, \pi(d\tau, ds, \theta')$$

$$\ge \iint U^a[\theta' - \tau^a + s^a]\, \pi(d\tau, ds, \theta''), \tag{6.6}$$

so that agent a *has no incentive to lie, announcing* θ'' *given the endowment is* $\theta = \theta'$, *and subject to*

constraints analogous to (6.5) *and* (6.6)
when the endowment is $\theta = \theta''$. $\tag{6.7}$

In the absence of qualifications like (6.5), at least, Program 6.1 can be converted to a program that is linear in unconditional probabilities $\pi(\tau, s, \theta)$.

Techniques like this turn out to be surprisingly robust, that is, able to handle a wide range of private-information problems. First, of course, one can handle situations with private information on actions, as in the standard principal–agent problem; see Myerson (1982). Essentially, one need only reverse the strict inequality in (4.8) to a weak inequality in the other direction and place the resulting constraint into Program 4.2. Second, one can handle situations in which private information can be made public at some cost, as with (potentially random) audits or monitoring technologies, triggered by announcements of agents with private information; see Baiman and Demski (1980) and Townsend (1979). Third, one can handle multiperiod problems, even with period-by-period private information, as in W. Rogerson (1985) or Townsend (1982). And, finally, one can handle multilateral private information, as in Moore (1984), Myerson (1986), and Townsend (1986b), even in multiperiod contexts, provided there is sufficient commitment or technology to enforce internal randomization devices. These set-ups, as well as those in Section 9, allow for difficulties in processing and communicating information and for endogenous information systems.

This is not to say that the outcomes of arbitrary programming problems are necessarily sharp or well understand. It turns out to be difficult to characterize optimal consumption schedules in the classic principal-agent problem; without demanding assumptions, these schedules need not be even weakly monotone increasing. The problem of when to monitor or audit and acquire otherwise private information is also difficult analytically. Multiperiod private information problems deliver history dependence and intertemporal tie-ins, but the exact nature of these tie-ins and the extent of dependence remain open questions, especially for relatively long horizons with discounting of the future. Finally, little is known about the solutions to multilateral private-information problems, especially in multiperiod contexts. Generally, then, the solutions of many private-information programs are not neatly characterized and are sensitive to the nature of preferences, technology, and uncertainty.

Still, the potential of private-information programs to deliver interesting outcomes and interesting institutions cannot be ignored. The remainder of this section tries to establish this by consideration of three models from recent literature.

Private-information economy 6.1

First, imagine with Prescott and Townsend (1984b) an economy in which each of a continuum of households can supply its own labor to a household-specific production function, its own unobserved "back-yard technology," yielding output of an idiosyncratic nontraded consumption good contingent on some production shock $\theta \in \{1, 2\}$. Each household can also supply labor to the public production of an observed transferable consumption good, and each household has its own linear technology for this production of the form $q = ba$, where variable a is market labor supply to its project and coefficient b is positive. Thus each household has an induced or indirect shock-contingent utility function over units of consumption of the publicly produced good c and units of its own market labor assignment a of the form $U_\theta(c, a) = U(c) - W_\theta(a)$, where (for simplicity) $0 \le c$ and $0 \le a \le \bar{\ell}$. Fraction ω_θ of agents in the population receive the household production shock θ, while in the planning period each household views shock θ as occurring with probability ω_θ.

Suppose now that, in the planning period, households enter into an agreement to receive the market consumption good in amount c and supply labor in amount a contingent on some announced value of the privately observed shock θ. That is, households can enter into a contract with individually effected options θ. Further, suppose for simplicity that consumption c and labor supply a can take on at most a finite number of values, and that these can be determined at random, so that whether or not a household works (and how much it works) are determined under a well-specified lottery. Thus, let $\pi_\theta(c, a)$ denote the probability of getting market consumption bundle c and supplying labor to the market in amount a. Then, the appropriate programming problem for the representative consumer in the planning period is the following.

Program 6.2. *Maximize by choice of the $\pi_\theta(c, a)$ the objective function*

$$\sum_\theta \omega_\theta \sum_{(c, a)} \pi_\theta(c, a) U_\theta(c, a), \tag{6.8}$$

subject to the resource constraints

$$\sum_\theta \omega_\theta \sum_{(c, a)} \pi_\theta(c, a) ba \ge \sum_\theta \omega_\theta \sum_{(c, a)} \pi_\theta(c, a) c; \tag{6.9}$$

subject to the incentive constraints

$$\sum_{(c, a)} \pi_1(c, a) U_1(c, a) \ge \sum_{(c, a)} \pi_2(c, a) U_1(c, a), \tag{6.10}$$

$$\sum_{(c, a)} \pi_2(c, a) U_2(c, a) \ge \sum_{(c, a)} \pi_1(c, a) U_2(c, a); \tag{6.11}$$

and subject to the obvious constraints on probabilities

$$\sum_{(c, a)} \pi_\theta(c, a) = 1, \quad \pi_\theta(c, a) \ge 0, \quad \theta \in \{1, 2\}. \tag{6.12}$$

Note that here the objects $\pi_\theta(c, a)$ enter into the objective function (6.8) as probabilities of bundle (c, a) if θ is announced, and appear in the resource constraint (6.9) as fractions of type-θ agents obtaining bundle (c, a), so that average output is no less than average consumption.

Solutions to Program 6.2 can be striking. To see this, imagine an extreme case with $U(c) = \ln(c)$, $W_1(a) = a$, and $W_2(a) = a^2/3$, so that households of type $\theta = 1$ are ex post neutral in labor supply although households of type $\theta = 2$ are not. The full-information solution to the programming problem for the determination of Pareto optimal allocations – that is, the solution with constraints (6.10) and (6.11) deleted – is $c_1 = c_2 = b$, $a_1 = 1/2$, and $a_2 = 3/2$ if $\omega_1 = \omega_2 = 1/2$. Of course, with private information this is not obtainable because consumptions are equated while type-2 households work harder. But randomness can be introduced into the labor supply of type 1, preventing type-2 households from claiming to be type 1, with no effect on the ex ante utility of type-1 households. In fact, set $c_1 = c_2 = b$ as before; set $a_1 = \bar{\ell}$, the upper bound, with probability α; and set $a_1 = 0$, the lower bound, with probability $(1 - \alpha)$, so that expected labor supply satisfies $\alpha\bar{\ell} + (1 - \alpha)0 = 1/2$. This satisfies all incentive constraints for $\bar{\ell}$ sufficiently large. Less dramatic examples with lotteries can be constructed with all agents risk-averse, but with a loss of ex ante expected utility relative to the full-information solution.

Indeed, we are reminded – in this discussion of lotteries and diverse employment experience for otherwise identical households – of what might happen in a market economy with excess labor supply and sticky wages. For this and other reasons, it is interesting to ask if the private-information economy just described can be decentralized; that is: Is there a market that would support the optimum? The affirmative answer given in Prescott and Townsend (1985b) is summarized here.

Suppose that, prior to the resolution of uncertainty (i.e., in the planning-period market), each household as a firm or intermediary can make commitments to the market to supply any number of (c, a) pairs. More formally, let $y_\theta(c, a)$, if positive, denote the number of commitments to provide c units of output for and to hire a units of labor from the group of households who announce they are of type θ (such announcements are public). Each firm–intermediary is constrained by a production-intermediation set

$$Y = \left\{ y = \{y_\theta(c, a)\} : \sum_\theta \omega_\theta \sum_{(c, a)} y_\theta(c, a)(ba - c) \geq 0 \right\},$$

which states in effect that the firm–intermediary cannot plan to distribute more of the consumption good than it provides on average. The coefficients in set Y are taken as given. Also, because this production set is the same over all households and displays constant returns to scale, there is no loss in simply positing set Y as the aggregate production–intermediation set.

Each firm–intermediary acts to maximize profits from competitive markets, taking prices as given. Thus, let $p_\theta(c, a)$ be the per-unit price of a $y_\theta(c, a)$ commitment in terms of some abstract unit of account. Then the firm–intermediary acts to maximize

$$\sum_\theta \sum_{(c,a)} y_\theta(c, a) p_\theta(c, a)$$

subject to $y \in Y$.

Households also make market commitments over output labor pairs, but with a different interpretation. Households are imagined to choose ex ante in the planning-period market a contract with options, indexed by $\theta \in \Theta$. Each option is a (possibly degenerate) lottery over consumption and labor-supply pairs, and the household can choose the terms of the lottery as well. But the options are such that a household of type θ ex post will choose ex post the option indexed by θ if indeed it suffers shock θ. Finally, of course, all the contracts are priced in a competitive market. More formally, motivated by the discussion above, let the common consumption set be

$$X = \left\{ \{x_\theta(c, a)\} : x_\theta(c, a) \geq 0, \sum_{c,a} x_\theta(c, a) = 1, \right.$$
$$\left. \sum_{c,a} x_\theta(c, a) U_\theta(c, a) \geq \sum_{c,a} x_\phi(c, a) U_\theta(c, a), \; \theta, \psi \in \Theta \right\}.$$

Let the endowment w be the element $w_\theta(c, a) = 0$ unless $(c, a) = (0, 0)$ for each $\theta \in \Theta$; that is, w puts all mass on the zero point of the underlying commodity space. Then the objective of the representative consumer is to maximize ex ante expected utility

$$\sum_\theta \omega_\theta \sum_{(c,a)} x_\theta(c, a) U_\theta(c, a)$$

by choosing $x \in X$ in the budget set

$$\sum_\theta \sum_{(c,a)} p_\theta(c, a) x_\theta(c, a) \leq \sum_\theta \sum_{(c,a)} p_\theta(c, a) w_\theta(c, a).$$

To reiterate, each household purchases a contract as a package and does not purchase the components separately. But the valuation of a contract is determined by the valuation of its individual components. In particular, with constant returns to scale in production, individual components in equilibrium must satisfy

$$p_\theta^*(c, a) = \omega_\theta(c - ba) \quad \forall \theta \in \Theta, \text{ all } (c, a) \text{ pairs.}$$

To ensure consistency of actions taken by households and the firm–intermediaries, the usual market clearing condition is needed:

$$x_\theta(c, a) = y_\theta(c, a) + w_\theta(c, a).$$

This condition, when substituted into the production-intermediation set Y, yields the resource constraint (6.9).

A standard competitive equilibrium (as defined in Section 1) can be shown to exist and to be Pareto optimal. Here, in fact, the representative-consumer construct facilitates the argument. But the argument can be generalized considerably, as in Prescott and Townsend (1984b), for – as is now apparent – preferences are linear in lotteries, the consumption set and production set are defined by a finite set of linear inequality constraints, and so on. The set of sufficient assumptions is drawn from Debreu (1962), and the argument is given explicitly in Section 7 in an extension to indivisibilities. Further, the discrete commodity space can be filled into a continuum, following arguments like those of Bewley (1972) and Mas-Colell (1975) as well as Prescott and Townsend (1984b). The general class of private-information environments that allows standard existence and optimality theorems is given in Prescott and Townsend (1984a). Of course, not every private-information environment can be decentralized in the standard way, as might well be anticipated from the earlier work of Rothschild and Stiglitz (1976), Spence (1974), and Wilson (1978).

Private-information economy 6.2

As a second private-information economy, imagine with Ito (1984) that each of a continuum of households can supply one unit of labor either to an unobserved back-yard technology or to a publicly observed central technology. In particular, each agent of type j can produce $a_j + \epsilon$ units of the single consumption good of the model from one unit of labor supplied to its back-yard production technology, where a_j is private information to agent j and ϵ is a privately observed random variable uniformly distributed on some closed interval. Alternatively, each agent of type j can produce $m(g)$ or $m(b)$ units of the single transferable consumption good in the central public technology, depending on the state of nature s: either good, $s = g$; or bad, $s = b$. Public production $m(s)$ occurs with probability $p(s)$, $s = g, b$. Virtually all households are risk-averse, with a common strictly concave utility function $U(c)$ over units of consumption c. Labor is supplied inelastically. The fraction of agents of type j is ω_j, and there are n agent types, so that $j = 1, 2, \ldots, n$. Further, households are ordered in private productivities so that $a_1 < a_2 < \cdots < a_n$. The exception is one household with mass ω_0, say of type 0, who is risk-neutral and who supplies no labor to any technology.

All households are imagined to be gathered initially at the central public technology, and all decide on a common resource allocation scheme. Next, all households make declarations of their type. Next, all observe the public technology shock s. Then a decision is made in some way, perhaps in accord with prior plans, as to whether or not each agent of (declared) type j is to discover the ϵ-draw in its back-yard technology. The cost of this search to each agent is $z > 0$ units of consumption. Finally, with state s public and a_j and ϵ private, each household of type j is allocated in some way to one of the two available technologies.

To simplify the presentation of a programming problem, suppose initially that the ϵ-draws are all degenerate at zero and that this is common knowledge. Then the only issue is whether a type-j agent does or does not go to his back-yard technology in states s, since there is no point in returning to the public technology. Thus, let $w_j(s)$ denote the units of consumption wage for agent j from the public technology in state s, if indeed agent j is assigned to that technology; let $c_j(s)$ denote the compensation from the public technology (gross of search costs) in the event that agent j is assigned to his back-yard technology in state s; and let $\chi_j(s)$ denote an assignment function that is either one or zero depending on whether agent j is or is not assigned to the public technology in state s. [More generally, $\chi_j(s)$ could be interpreted as a population fraction for the resource constraint.] For simplicity in notation, let $w_0(s)$ denote the consumption of agent 0 with $\chi_0(s) \equiv 1$.

With this notation, the planning-period problem for the determination of a Pareto optimal allocation, with weights λ^j to agents of type j, is equivalent to the following.

Program 6.3. *Maximize by choice of the $w_j(s)$, $c_j(s)$, and $\chi_j(s)$ the objective function*

$$\sum_{j=0}^{n} \lambda^j \left\{ \sum_s p(s)[\chi_j(s) U[w_j(s)] + (1 - \chi_j(s)) U[c_j(s) + a_j - z]] \right\}$$

(6.13)

subject to the resource constraints

$$\sum_{j=1}^{n} \chi_j(s) m(s) \omega_j \geq \sum_{j=1}^{n} (1 - \chi_j(s)) c_j(s) \omega_j$$

$$+ \sum_{j=1}^{n} \chi_j(s) w_j(s) \omega_j + \omega_0 w_0(s),$$

$$s = g, b \quad (6.14)$$

and subject to the incentive constraints

$$\sum_s p(s)[\chi_j(s)U[w_j(s)] + (1-\chi_j(s))U[c_j(s)+a_j-z]]$$

$$\geq \sum_s p(s)[\chi_i(s)U[w_i(s)] + (1-\chi_i(s))U[c_i(s)+a_j-z]]. \quad (6.15)$$

Ito (1984) examines a particular but intuitively appealing solution to this programming problem. In particular, suppose the risk-neutral agent is to receive zero (expected) consumption; suppose we ignore momentarily the incentive constraints; and suppose the economy is such that no one is to leave the public technology in the good state $s = g$. Then, for type-j agents who are to stay with the public technology in the bad state $s = b$, $w(g) = w(b)$ where for these agents $w(\cdot)$ is independent of j. Similarly, for those type-j agents who are to leave the public technology in the bad state $s = b$, $w_j(g) = c_j(b) + a_j - z$. Thus there is full insurance (constant consumption) over states s ($s = g, b$) for each agent type, although there may be nontrivial variation over types j for j types who leave. Further, as one might hope with the presence of a risk-neutral agent, production assignments are efficient in the sense that agents leave the public project when they are relatively inefficient there; that is, $\chi_j(b) = 0$ if $m(b) < a_j - z$. Indeed, individual productivities are supposed to be such that there exists some nontrivial critical value of the private production parameter a, say a^*, with $\chi_j(b) = 0$ for all $a_j > a^*$ and $\chi_j(b) = 1$ for $a_k \leq a^*$ (a^* nontrivial in that such a k exists). Finally, the incentive constraints can be satisfied by making the wage schedule in the good state, $w_j(g)$, monotone increasing in j and by making the compensation schedule in the bad state, $c_j(b)$, monotone decreasing in j for all j such that $\chi_j(b) = 0$. The idea here is that for agent j to pretend to be a type i rather than type j with $i > j$, there is relatively higher consumption when $s = g$ [by the monotonicity of $w_j(g)$] but relatively lower compensation and hence lower consumption when $s = b$; that is, $c_i(b) + a_j - z < c_j(b) + a_j - z$. The consequent risk keeps agent j from pretending to be a type i, $i > j$. And a similar argument applies for type i, $i < j$. Indeed, Ito finds consumption and compensation schedules by decentralizing the economy, letting agents choose actuarially fair insurance ex ante, and letting agents make their own state-contingent decisions about whether or not to search and therefore what compensation to claim given their choice of an insurance package.

Ito goes on to consider an even more interesting case. Suppose in particular that the ϵ distribution is not degenerate. Then, upon seeing $a_j + \epsilon$ at cost z, agent j must decide whether or not to return to the public technology. Of course, with low ϵ's there may be a return and with high ϵ's not. But a returning agent cannot effectively claim a *particular* ϵ value, and nonreturning agents are similarly uninsured. Indeed, under his decentralization hypothesis, this lack of insurance delivers for Ito an allocation $w_j(g)$ on state $s = g$ greater than the compensation for returning workers of type j on state $s = b$. Thus there is no longer full insurance. More dramatically, relative to the case where ϵ-draws are fully observed by everyone, there are fewer agent types searching their back-yard technologies (the critical a^* is higher), and also those who search more are likely to return to the public technology. Indeed, this effect is reinforced if agents can pretend to search, returning to the public technology to receive a wage different from the one they would have received had they not "searched" at all. Ito terms the latter "phantom" search, in contrast to the case where the act of search is public.

It remains to be seen if solutions like these emerge generally for alternative weights λ^j in the programming problem. And some check should be made to see if the assumed decentralization of decisions is innocuous, especially when search is public and can be imposed or assigned. However, based on Ito's results thus far, it seems that private information can generate some kind of persistence.

Private-information economy 6.3

A third private-information economy helps make the point that private information can be an important determinant of institutions and economywide arrangements. Thus, consider with Boyd and Prescott (1986) an economy with a countable infinity of agents, each of whom lives two periods. In the first period, each agent has one unit of time and one investment project. In the second period, agents eat the single consumption good of the model. Time can be used in the first period in some investment project to help produce the consumption good for the second period, or time can be used in the first period to evaluate one project. Preferences are ordered in the first period by expected second-period consumption. The per-unit return r on an investment project if funded is either good (i.e., $r = g$) or bad (i.e., $r = b$), where of course $g > b$. The maximal investment per project is χ. Evaluation e of a project in the first period generates signal $e = g$ or $e = b$ in the first period, and these are (imperfectly) predictive of future return r on the project. Agents are ordered initially by types i, $i = g$ or $i = b$, and an agent's type i is also (imperfectly) predictive of the future returns r on his project. Here, then, $\pi(i, e, r)$ denotes the fraction of agents of type i who would receive signal e if their projects were evaluated and obtain return r if their projects were funded, and $\pi(i, e, r)$ also determines the conditional probability of the event (e, r) from the viewpoint of an individual agent of type i. Each agent's type is

410 Robert M. Townsend

presumed to be private to the individual. On the other hand, the acts of evaluating and investing are supposed to be publicly observed, as are the returns r, evaluations e, and consumptions c. Finally, the return r on a project is supposed to be known ex post even if the project is not funded.

To write down a programming problem for the determination of Pareto optimal arrangements, one needs a little additional notation. Thus, let z_i denote the fraction of (declared) type-i projects evaluated, as well as the probability of an evaluation for an agent of (declared) type i; x_i the amount of time invested in a (declared) type-i project if not evaluated; x_{ie} the amount of time invested in a (declared) type-i project with evaluation e; c_{ir} the amount of consumption to a (declared) type-i agent when his own project is not evaluated and the return on it is r; and c_{ier} the amount of consumption to a (declared) type-i agent with evaluation e and return r on his project. Finally, let z, x, and c denote the associated vectors with components specifying these objects. Then, given z, x, and c, the expected utility of a type-i agent who reports to be of type j is

$$U_i(c, z, j) = z_j E_{e,r}\{c_{jer} \mid i\} + (1 - z_j) E_r\{c_{jr} \mid i\}, \tag{6.16}$$

where expectations are over evaluations e and returns r given actual agent type i, and again the probabilities are determined by the $\pi(i, e, r)$. The programming problem with weights λ^j, $j = g, b$, can then be written as follows.

Program 6.4. Maximize by choice of z, x, and c the objective function

$$\lambda^g U_{i=g}(c, z, j = g) + \lambda^b U_{i=b}(c, z, j = b), \tag{6.17}$$

subject to the time constraint for investing and evaluating in per-capita terms,

$$E_{i,e}\{(1 - z_i)x_i + z_i(x_{ie} + 1)\} \le 1; \tag{6.18}$$

the resource constraint for distribution of the consumption good,

$$E_i\{z_i E_{e,r}\{c_{ier} \mid i\} + (1 - z_i)E_r\{c_{ir} \mid i\}\}$$
$$\le E_i\{z_i E_{e,r}\{rx_{ie} \mid i\} + (1 - z_i)E_r\{rx_i \mid i\}\}; \tag{6.19}$$

the incentive constraints,

$$U_i(c, z, j = i) \ge U_i(c, z, j \ne i) \quad \text{all } i, j; \tag{6.20}$$

individual rationality constraints on participation,

$$U_i(c, z, j = i) \ge E_r\{r \mid i\}; \tag{6.21}$$

and the constraint that

$$0 \le z_i \le 1 \quad all \ i,$$
$$0 \le x_i, x_{ie} < \chi \quad all \ i, e.$$

(6.22)

Boyd and Prescott (1986) go on to define a core allocation as an allocation that cannot be blocked by a coalition. They also assume that the specification of parameters χ, g, b, and π are such that: (1) if agent types were fully known there would be evaluations of good projects; (2) there would not be evaluations of bad projects; (3) investing in $i = b$ projects dominates investing in $i = g$ projects with $e = b$; and (4) if all types of $i = g$ projects are evaluated and are funded or not at maximum level χ under the above rule then some time would remain, so that bad projects are the marginal projects. Under these assumptions there exists an (essentially) unique core allocation, one that is weighted in favor of the agents of type $i = g$.

Boyd and Prescott (1986) characterize this core allocation. They show, for example, that if evaluations e are uninformative but agent types i are private information then there can be nontrivial evaluations. Of course, these evaluations are dissipative in the sense that with full information no evaluations would take place. Even more impressive, though, are results characterizing the arrangements themselves. In particular, Boyd and Prescott show that – under their definitions – core allocations can be achieved by nontrivial coalitions of agents, whereas core allocations cannot be supported in a decentralized security market arrangement, at least not if there is private information on initial agent types and if evaluations are possible. In this sense, then, their paper delivers some kind of collective or centralized institutions, which Boyd and Prescott interpret as banks, adding to our understanding of such institutions and to the related papers of Diamond (1984) and Townsend (1978, 1983), for example.

Though they may seem alien at first, various kinds of collective or restrictive resource-allocation schemes have been observed in practice. In the Pacific island economies studied by anthropologist Malinowski, for example, only the chief was allowed to store many essential commodities, though storage displays were themselves public. Similarly, in the centralized societies of the Egyptian pharaohs there seemed to have been extensive restrictions on trade and retrade. The private-information theories described in this section are at least suggestive of these kinds of institutions.

Thus far, little has been directly said about how to tie this section's private-information programs to time-series observations and more standard macroeconomic concerns. The problem, again, is that multiperiod private-information programs are difficult to solve generally. However, progress is being made. Indeed, Green (1985) has solved an explicit infinite-horizon version of a multiperiod private-information model, at least with the assumptions of constant absolute risk aversion and unbounded negative consumption. Such contributions provide important links from the microeconomic contract-theoretic literature to the macroeconomic literature on growth and fluctuations, and support the broad view of macroeconomics adopted in this chapter.

7   Programs with indivisibilities

Observations from primitive economies suggest that certain indivisibilities may be crucial. The oxen of the medieval village can be utilized only in discrete units, and the canoes of the Polynesian islands come only in minimal sizes. Similarly, a migrant worker either does or does not labor at a specified location or project. Fortunately, an Arrow–Debreu environment with such indivisibilities can be analyzed along the lines of Prescott and Townsend (1984a, b) and the general equilibrium literature described above, so that standard existence and optimality theorems apply. Further, environments with indivisibilities can be shown in this way to have interesting dynamic properties.

For purposes of exposition we shall consider here an extended, generalized version of the environment considered by G. Hansen (1985). That environment is much like the one that underlies the neoclassical growth model (Program 5.1), but with the following modifications. First, there is a continuum of type-j households, fraction ω^j of the total set of households, with the latter being the set of households whose names lie on the unit interval. Names will be ignored in what follows, however, and type-j households will be treated identically ex ante, as if there were one type-j agent with weight ω^j. More relevant for the present discussion of indivisibilities, pair (c, a) of consumption c and labor supply a can take on at most a finite number of values for each and every household, and (for simplicity) consumption sets X_t^j are identical across households j. Thus, from the point of view of household j as consumer, the commodity point will be a specification of the probability $x^j(c, a)$ of the pair (c, a) over all pairs (c, a) in some set $\bar{X}$.

With these modifications, and the obvious adjustments for converting leisure to labor, Program 5.1 becomes the following.

Program 7.1. *Maximize by choice of the* $x_t^j(c, a, \epsilon_1, ..., \epsilon_t)$ *and the* $\bar{l}_t(\epsilon_1, ..., \epsilon_t)$ *the objective function*

$$\sum_{j=1}^{n} \lambda^j \left\{ E_0 \sum_{t=1}^{T} \beta^t \left\{ \sum_{(c, a)} x_t^j(c, a, \epsilon_1, ..., \epsilon_t)[U^j(c) - W^j(a)] \right\} \right\} \quad (7.1)$$

subject to

$$\sum_{j=1}^{n} \omega^j \sum_{(c,a)} cx_t^j(c, a, \epsilon_1, \ldots, \epsilon_t) \le \bar{c}_t(\epsilon_1, \ldots, \epsilon_t), \tag{7.2}$$

$$\sum_{j=1}^{n} \omega^j \sum_{(c,a)} ax_t^j(c, a, \epsilon_1, \ldots, \epsilon_t) \le \bar{a}_t(\epsilon_1, \ldots, \epsilon_t), \tag{7.3}$$

$$\bar{l}_t(\epsilon_1, \ldots, \epsilon_t) + \bar{c}_t(\epsilon_1, \ldots, \epsilon_t)$$
$$\le f[\bar{a}_t(\epsilon_1, \ldots, \epsilon_t), \bar{K}_t(\epsilon_1, \ldots, \epsilon_t), \epsilon_t], \tag{7.4}$$

$$\bar{K}_{t+1}(\epsilon_1, \ldots, \epsilon_t) = (1 - \delta)[\bar{K}_t(\epsilon_1, \ldots, \epsilon_{t-1}) + \bar{l}_t(\epsilon_1, \ldots, \epsilon_t)], \tag{7.5}$$

$$0 \le x_t^j(c, a, \epsilon_1, \ldots, \epsilon_t) \le 1 \quad \sum_{c,a} x_t^j(c, a, \epsilon_1, \ldots, \epsilon_t) = 1. \tag{7.6}$$

This is a concave program despite the indivisibilities. Further, it can be solved analytically. Hansen does so by assuming one type of consumer, so that the j notation can be suppressed; labor supply a taking on only two values, (say) $a = 0$ and $a = \bar{a}$; and consumption taking on a continuum of values. In this case, one is reduced to the representative-consumer problem of the standard neoclassical growth model, with the exception here that (say) $\alpha_t(\epsilon_1, \ldots, \epsilon_t)$, the fraction of agents who work $\bar{a}$ hours, replaces $\bar{l}_t(\epsilon_1, \ldots, \epsilon_t)$ in Program 5.1 as the obvious labor choice variable at date t under history $(\epsilon_1, \ldots, \epsilon_t)$.

We might note in passing that Hansen's model is designed to address the anomalies raised in the earlier work of Kydland and Prescott (1982) – that Program 5.1 delivers too little variability of hours worked relative to U.S. postwar time-series data. And Hansen is successful, inasmuch as his version of Program 7.1 delivers too much variability in hours. That is, Hansen does seem to have selected a key aspect of the model to modify. It might also be stressed that the variability is induced by the indivisibility, a "real rigidity," and that nominal rigidities so often believed to be necessary are, in fact, not needed (which is not to say that nominal rigidities are unimportant). Similarly, lotteries transform the underlying preferences of consumers to some mongrel objective function (7.1), and measured risk aversion for the mongrel may bear little relation to actual risk aversion for underlying preferences.

It should be stressed also that existence and optimality results follow as in Prescott and Townsend (1984b), despite the indivisibilities. The common consumption set of type-j households is the set of possible lotteries over consumption c (measured in positive units) and labor supply a (measured in negative units) in underlying consumption set $\bar{X}$ over all dates and histories; that is,

$$X = \left\{ \{x_t(c, a, \epsilon_1, \ldots, \epsilon_t)\} : \right.$$
$$\left. 0 \le x_t(c, a, \epsilon_1, \ldots, \epsilon_t) \le 1, \sum_{c, a} x_t(c, a, \epsilon_1, \ldots, \epsilon_t) = 1 \right\}.$$

Underlying consumption set $\bar{X}$ is presumed to contain the point $(0, -\bar{\ell})$ of zero consumption and maximal labor supply for each household j. Set $\bar{X}$ also contains the endowment point of each household, the point $(0, 0)$. Further, as is apparent from Program 7.1, one can trace out the path of maximal aggregate feasible consumption – say, $\bar{e}_t(\epsilon_1, \ldots, \epsilon_t)$ at date t and contingent on history $(\epsilon_1, \ldots, \epsilon_t)$ – by supposing that aggregate labor supply is at a maximum at each date, investment is arranged to support maximal carryover earlier, and so on. Next, define

$$\bar{e}_t^*(\epsilon_1, \ldots, \epsilon_t) = \max_i \left[\frac{\bar{e}_t(\epsilon_1, \ldots, \epsilon_t)}{\omega^i} \right]$$

and

$$\bar{e}^{**} = \max_{t, (\epsilon_1, \ldots, \epsilon_t)} [\bar{e}_t^*(\epsilon_1, \ldots, \epsilon_t)].$$

Then some consumption number $c^{**} > \bar{e}^{**}$ along with zero labor supply is supposed also to be in underlying consumption set $\bar{X}$. This will ensure that no household j is ever satiated in its attainable consumption set $\hat{X}$; that is, there is always a dominating element in consumption set X even though set X itself is bounded.

Preferences $u^j(x^j)$ over set X are defined in the obvious way, as is the endowment w^j, the latter putting all mass on the underlying endowment bundle $(c, a) = (0, 0)$ uniformly for all dates and histories. Household j as producer makes $y_t(c, a, \epsilon_1, \ldots, \epsilon_t)$ commitments if positive to deliver c units of output for consumption (measured in positive units), and to hire a units of labor (measured in negative units) at date t, contingent on history $(\epsilon_1, \ldots, \epsilon_t)$, as well as deciding as before on components $y_{2t}(\epsilon_1, \ldots, \epsilon_t)$, $y_{3t}(\epsilon_1, \ldots, \epsilon_t)$, and $y_{4t}(\epsilon_1, \ldots, \epsilon_t)$ for investment, beginning-of-period capital, and end-of-period capital. That is,

$$Y_t^{1j}(\epsilon_1, \ldots, \epsilon_t) = \left\{ y_t(\epsilon_1, \ldots, \epsilon_t) : \sum_{c, a} y(c, a, \epsilon_1, \ldots, \epsilon_t) c + y_{2t}(\epsilon_1, \ldots, \epsilon_t) \right.$$
$$\le f^j \left[\sum_{c, a} y(c, a, \epsilon_1, \ldots, \epsilon_t) a, y_{3t}(\epsilon_1, \ldots, \epsilon_t), \epsilon_t \right] \text{ and}$$
$$\left. y_{4t}(\epsilon_1, \ldots, \epsilon_t) \le -y_{3t}(\epsilon_1, \ldots, \epsilon_t) \right\}$$

with $Y_t^{2j}(\epsilon_1, \ldots, \epsilon_t)$ exactly as before in Section 5. Finally, it may be supposed that each of the fractions ω^j is a rational number, so that some integer m may be taken to be a least common denominator. Then the continuum-agent economy is equivalent to a finite-agent economy with number $\omega^j m$ agents of type j.

One can now make use of the theorem in Debreu (1962): The finite-agent economy has a quasi-equilibrium (defined below) if (a.1) $A(mX) \cap (-A(mX)) = \{0\}$; (a.2) X is closed and convex; (b.1) for every j and for every consumption x' in $\hat{X}$, there is a consumption in X preferred by j to x'; (b.2) for every $x' \in X$ the sets $\{x^j \in X : u^j(x^j) \geq u^j(x')\}$ and $\{x^j \in X : u^j(x^j) \leq u^j(x')\}$ are closed in X; (b.3) for every x' in X, the set $\{x^j \in X : u^j(x^j) \geq u^j(x')\}$ is convex; (c.1) $(\{mw^j\} + mY) \cap mX \neq \varnothing$; (c.2) $(\{w^j\} + A(Y)) \cap X \neq 0$; (d.1) $0 \in Y^j$; and (d.2) $A(mX) \cap A(Y) = \{0\}$. Here $A(S)$ denotes the asymptotic cone of set S. Each of these conditions can be verified to hold for the economy with indivisibilities under consideration, just as in Prescott and Townsend (1984b). One key, of course, is that the consumption set is defined by a set of linear inequalities and that preferences are linear in lotteries.

Here a *quasi-equilibrium* is a state $[(x^{j^*})(y^{j^*})]$ and a price system p^* such that

(α) for every j, x^{j^*} is a greatest element in
$\{x \in X : p^* \cdot x \leq p^* \cdot w^j + p^* \cdot y^{j^*}\}$ under $u^j(x)$
and/or $p^* \cdot x^{j^*} = p^* \cdot w^j + p^* \cdot y^{j^*} = \text{Min } p^* \cdot X$;

(β) $p^* \cdot y^{j^*} = \text{Max } p^* \cdot Y^j$;

(γ) $\sum_j m\omega^j x^{j^*} = \sum_j m\omega^j y^{j^*} + \sum_j m\omega^j w^j$; and

(δ) $p^* \neq 0$.

Thus a quasi-equilibrium can differ from a standard competitive equilibrium in condition (α). Here, however, the configuration of equilibrium prices p^* can be delivered from profit-maximization condition (β) on the aggregate production set Y; in particular, the price $p_t^*(c, a, \epsilon_1, \ldots, \epsilon_t)$ for the (c, a) component at date t under history $(\epsilon_1, \ldots, \epsilon_t)$ satisfies

$$p_t^*(c, a, \epsilon_1, \ldots, \epsilon_t) = \psi_t^1(\epsilon_1, \ldots, \epsilon_t) \left[c - \frac{\partial f(\cdot, \cdot, \epsilon_t)}{\partial a} a \right],$$

where $\psi_t^1(\epsilon_1, \ldots, \epsilon_t)$ is the Lagrange multiplier of the aggregate production constraint $Y_t^1(\epsilon_1, \ldots, \epsilon_t)$ and its associated aggregate production function $f(\cdot, \cdot, \epsilon)$. If all the $\psi_t^1(\epsilon_1, \ldots, \epsilon_t)$ were zero then all $p_t^*(c, a, \epsilon_1, \ldots, \epsilon_t)$ would be zero, and this would imply from condition (β) that $p^* = 0$, in contradiction to condition (δ). Thus at least one $\psi_t^1(\epsilon_1, \ldots, \epsilon_t)$ is positive and this makes $p^* w^j + p^* \cdot y^{j^*} > \text{Min } p^* \cdot X$ because the point $x \in X$, putting mass unity on point $(0, -\bar{\ell})$ for all t and $(\epsilon_1, \ldots, \epsilon_t)$, has negative valuation. Thus the first part of conditions (α) must prevail, and there exists a standard competitive equilibrium.

That competitive equilibria are necessarily Pareto optimal and that Pareto optima can be supported as competitive equilibria also follow directly from the arguments in Prescott and Townsend (1984b) and in Debreu (1954).

In summary, then, lotteries facilitate the analysis of economies with some underlying nonconvexity, here delivering existence and optimality theorems. And they help in this regard even when they are not needed – that is, even when lotteries are not actually used at an optimum or in equilibrium.

8   Programs with spatial separation

The Polynesian economy studied by Firth (1939) and the hill tribe communities studied by Van Roy (1971) have prominent aspects of spatial separation, with clusters of population separated by nontrivial distances. Still, these clusters are not isolated from one another. In the island economy studied by Firth (1939), agents occasionally migrate in order to engage in group canoe-building projects or to work in dispersed orchards. And in the economy studied by Van Roy (1971), there is (as noted earlier) sharing of rice across villages and occasional migration of some laborers from one village to another. For these environments, then, we might not want to look at individual consumption relative to aggregate consumption or individual leisure relative to aggregate leisure, at least not without taking into account some aspects of this spatial separation.

But how are we to do this? It would seem natural and instructive to answer this question first in the context of a simple pure-exchange economy of the type described at the beginning of previous sections, but modified here to accommodate a minimal amount of movement of agents across space.

Thus consider an economy with two locations, two dates, and four agents, as described in Table 1. Here agents a and a' reside in locations 1 and 2 (respectively) for both dates, while agents b and b' reside in locations 1 and 2 (respectively) at the first date, and for unspecified exogenous reasons switch locations at the beginning of the second date. Agents are presumed to have endowments and preferences over consumption goods in each location where they happen to be.

One could write down a concave programming problem for the determination of a Pareto optimum for this spatial economy, much like Program 2.1 except that here there would be a resource constraint not only for each date and history but also for each location. Thus one would distribute the consumption good at each particular location among all participants at that location in such a way as to equate weighted marginal utilities. Individual consumptions thus would vary positively (weakly)

Table 1. *Agent pairings in a spatial economy*

	loc 1	loc 2
$t=1$	(a,b)	(a',b')
$t=2$	(a,b')	(a',b)

with location-specific aggregates at a point in time over shock realizations, and – to the extent that a population remained unaltered over subsets of dates at any location – individual consumptions would vary positively (weakly) with location-specific aggregates over time. But the distribution of the consumption good would be sensitive, generally, to the population mix at any given location, making the implications of the theory more difficult to test. (Of course, conclusions like this would hold even if entire groups of a given population were to move about exogenously.)

A still more elaborate treatment of spatial separation (required in a serious application) would recognize that location choices are endogenous, that individuals are capable of supplying labor in any location they might choose, and that consumption may be transferable. This raises a potential nonconvexity problem, but fortunately the problem can be solved. This is illustrated well by a model of R. Rogerson (1985), and it will be described in this section.

So, imagine with Rogerson (1985) an economy with two sectors or locations. In each location i, $i=1,2$, production can take place according to the familiar neoclassical production function

$$q_{it} = f_i(a_{it}, K_i, \epsilon_t). \tag{8.1}$$

Here a_{it} is aggregate man-hours supplied in location i at date t measured in positive units; K_i is the stock of an immobile capital in location i, the same at any date t; ϵ_t is a common date-t shock; and so on. However, capital K_i plays no role in the analysis, and it is hereby suppressed from the notation. There is a continuum of workers, again with names on $[0,1]$, and each worker has an endowment of $\bar{\ell}$ units of leisure at each date. If a representative worker were to supply a_{1t} hours in location 1 at date t and a_{2t} hours in location 2 at date t, as well as to receive c_t units of consumption, then his utility (with the exception noted below) would be

$$U[c_t, a_{1t}, a_{2t}] = c_t + V[\bar{\ell} - (a_{1t} + a_{2t})]. \tag{8.2}$$

However, only one of either a_{1t} or a_{2t} can be positive, and this is the nonconvexity. Further, there is an assumed psychic cost to moving, so that if a worker in location 1_{t-1} at date $t-1$ is allocated to sector 1_t at date t with

$1_{t-1} \neq 1_t$, then a positive term m is subtracted from the utility function in (8.2). This induces a location-contingent utility function

$$\bar{U}(c_t, a_t, 1_t \mid 1_{t-1}) = \begin{cases} c_t + V[\bar{\ell} - a_t] & \text{if } 1_t = 1_{t-1}, \\ c_t + V[\bar{\ell} - a_t] - m & \text{if } 1_t \neq 1_{t-1}, \end{cases} \quad (8.3)$$

where it is understood that consumption c_t and labor a_t take place at location 1_t at date t, that consumption is transferable across locations, but that labor supply is not transferable. Finally, at the first date $t = 1$ the upper branch of the utility function applies, and the previous location conditioning element is suppressed from the notation.

Rogerson overcomes the nonconvexity problem by letting the location assignment of each individual be determined in a lottery. In particular, adopting notation different from Rogerson's, let $\pi_1(c_1, a_1, k, \epsilon_1)$ be the probability that an individual at date 1 and contingent on shock ϵ_1 is assigned location k, $k = 1, 2$, receives consumption in amount c_1, and supplies labor in amount a_1. Here, for simplicity of notation and analysis, both c_1 and a_1 are assumed to take on at most a finite number of values, though it may be noted that, in a Pareto optimum with a continuum of values, lotteries on c_1 and a_1 would be degenerate; that is, c_1 and a_1 would be deterministic up to ϵ_1. Indeed, c would be independent of location k. Of course, $\pi_1(c_1, a_1, k, \epsilon_1)$ also denotes the fraction of agents in the population who are assigned at date 1 and contingent on ϵ_1 the location k and the bundle (c_1, a_1). Also let $\pi_2(c_2, a_2, i, \epsilon_1, \epsilon_2 \mid k)$ be the probability that an individual is assigned at date 2 and contingent on history (ϵ_1, ϵ_2) the location i and the bundle (c_2, a_2), given the date-1 assignment to location k. Of course, $\pi_2(c_2, a_2, i, \epsilon_1, \epsilon_2 \mid k)$ also denotes the fraction of agents in the population who experience the latter event.

To further facilitate the analysis, the numbers $\pi_1(c_1, a_1, k, \epsilon_1)$ and $\pi_2(c_2, a_2, i, \epsilon_1, \epsilon_2 \mid k)$ are combined by multiplication; that is, let

$$\pi(c_1, a_1, k, c_2, a_2, i, \epsilon_1, \epsilon_2) = \pi_2(c_2, a_2, i, \epsilon_1, \epsilon_2 \mid k)\pi_1(c_1, a_1, k, \epsilon_1) \quad (8.4)$$

so that $\pi(\cdot)$ on the left-hand side of (8.4) is the obvious joint probability over the event in parentheses, indexed by (ϵ_1, ϵ_2). Further, let

$$\pi(c_1, a_1, k, \epsilon_1, \epsilon_2) = \sum_{c_2} \sum_{a_2} \sum_i \pi(c_1, a_1, k, c_2, a_2, i, \epsilon_2, \epsilon_2) \quad (8.5)$$

so that $\pi(\cdot)$ on the left-hand side of (8.5) is the marginal probability of the event in parentheses, indexed by (ϵ_1, ϵ_2). Finally, because ϵ_2 is not known at date 1, require

$$\pi(c_1, a_1, k, \epsilon_1, \epsilon_2) = \pi(c_1, a_1, k, \epsilon_1, \epsilon_2') \quad \forall \epsilon_2, \epsilon_2', \quad (8.6)$$

so that the argument ϵ_2 is not present. This thus yields the $\pi_1(c_1, a_1, k, \epsilon_1)$ specified initially.

With this notation, the determination of a social optimum in a two-period world reduces to the following.

Program 8.1. *Maximize by choice of*

$$\pi(c_1, a_1, k, \epsilon_1) \quad and \quad \pi(c_1, a_1, k, c_2, a_2, i, \epsilon_1, \epsilon_2)$$

the objective function

$$E_0 \left\{ \sum_{c_1} \sum_{a_1} \sum_{k} \bar{U}(c_1, a_1, k) \pi(c_1, a_1, k, \epsilon_1) \right.$$

$$+ \sum_{c_1} \sum_{a_1} \sum_{k} \sum_{c_2} \sum_{a_2} \sum_{i} \bar{U}(c_2, a_2, i \mid k)$$

$$\left. \cdot \pi(c_1, a_1, k, c_2, a_2, i, \epsilon_1, \epsilon_2) \right\} \tag{8.7}$$

subject to the resource constraints at date $t = 1$, contingent on ϵ_1,

$$\sum_{c_1} \sum_{a_1} \sum_{k} c_1 \pi(c_1, a_1, k, \epsilon_1)$$

$$\leq \sum_{k} f_k \left[\sum_{c_1} \sum_{a_1} a_1 \pi(c_1, a_1, k, \epsilon_1), \epsilon_1 \right]; \tag{8.8}$$

subject to the resource constraints at date $t = 2$, contingent on (ϵ_1, ϵ_2),

$$\sum_{c_1} \sum_{a_1} \sum_{k} \sum_{c_2} \sum_{a_2} \sum_{i} c_2 \pi(c_1, a_1, k, c_2, a_2, i, \epsilon_1, \epsilon_2)$$

$$\leq \sum_{i} f_i \left[\sum_{c_1} \sum_{a_1} \sum_{k} \sum_{c_2} \sum_{a_2} a_2 \pi(c_1, a_1, k, c_2, a_2, i, \epsilon_1, \epsilon_2), \epsilon_2 \right]; \tag{8.9}$$

and subject to constraints (8.5) and (8.6) on π's.

Now one can let a common-date $t = 0$ consumption set X be determined by probabilities $x(c_1, a_1, k, \epsilon_1)$ and $x(c_1, a_1, k, c_2, a_2, i, \epsilon_1, \epsilon_2)$ between zero and one, summing to one for each shock ϵ_1 and history (ϵ_1, ϵ_2), respectively, with restrictions like (8.5) and (8.6) for the $x(\cdot)$. And one can let production set Y be determined by the elements $y(c_1, a_1, k, \epsilon_1)$ as units of commitments to hand out c_1 units of output at location k and hire a_1 units of labor at location k, both contingent on ϵ_1; and by the elements $y(c_1, a_1, k, c_2, a_2, i, \epsilon_1, \epsilon_2)$ as units of commitments to hand out c_1 units of output at location k and hire a_1 units of labor at location k, to hand out c_2 units of output at location i and hire a_2 units of labor at location i, all contingent on (ϵ_1, ϵ_2) with $y(\cdot)$ replacing $\pi(\cdot)$ in (8.5), (8.6), (8.8), and (8.9). Thus theorems on the existence and optimality of competitive equilibrium follow by standard arguments. In fact, the argument is virtually immediate because everyone is alike in the planning date $t = 0$, so there is (in effect) a representative consumer.

R. Rogerson (1985) apparently solves Program 8.1 indirectly, by use of recursive methods. In fact, Rogerson has computed recursive equilibria to his model for example environments (though initial location assignments appear to be given, potentially inconsistent with the formulation of the optimum problem given here). In these examples, with some reluctance to move ($m > 0$), changes in hours per worker lead changes in employment, employment displays some persistence, and hours per worker are more highly correlated with real wages than is employment. The point is that Rogerson's model seems to offer a rich variety of time series dynamics, and so again models motivated (as here) by a study of primitive economies seem useful in addressing standard macroeconomic concerns.

9   Programs with limited communication

We have argued thus far that programs with private information and spatial separation are rich in implications and at least suggestive of actual arrangements. Still, it is a striking fact that none of these programs can explain commonly observed arrangements such as the use of currency and financial instruments. One way to remedy this failure is to incorporate limited communication, as in Townsend (1987b) and the related work of Brunner and Meltzer (1971), Gale (1980), Ostroy (1973), and Ostroy and Starr (1974). (A second way – the incorporation of limited commitment – is discussed in Section 10.)

To begin the discussion, then, it is useful to merge the private information economy generating Program 6.1 with the spatial model depicted in Table 1. In particular, agents a and a' move between two locations according to the pattern in Table 1 (i.e., do not actually move at all), and have random privately observed endowments θ_{1t}^a and $\theta_{2t}^{a'}$ (respectively) observed at the beginning of date t, $t = 1, 2$, at locations 1 and 2 (respectively). Agents b and b' move according to the specified pattern of Table 1 and have public endowments w_{it}^b and $w_{it}^{b'}$ (respectively) at location i and date t. Each agent j has preferences over consumption bundles c at each date t and at his assigned location i as represented by the utility function $U^j(c_{it}^j)$. Also, for simplicity, suppose there is only one underlying consumption good; that agents a and a' are identical in preferences and in the distribution of endowments; and that agents b and b' are identical to one another as well.

Now suppose the most primitive of communication technologies is in effect; that is, suppose there are no telecommunications, no recording devices, no portable but otherwise worthless tokens, and no storage possibilities for the consumption good. At each location and date agents can make announcements of their contemporary but privately observed endowments, and can make announcements as well of their histories of privately observed endowments, announcements, and trades. Thus, one can consider allocation rules $\pi_{it}^{r}(\cdot)$ and $\pi_{it}^{s}(\cdot)$ at location i and date t which have as arguments these announcements, and it is possible to write down a programming problem for the determination of Pareto optimal outcomes, much like Program 6.1, keeping track of the 4 agents and 2 locations. However, announcements of past histories have no force in any incentive-compatible arrangement. Given the imposed communication technology, there is no way to achieve bona fide intertemporal tie-ins, as agents will always make the best possible announcement given the contemporary state. Thus, the programming problem would reduce to four separate versions of Program 6.1. With only one commodity, then, the solution is necessarily autarkic, at least if utility functions display decreasing absolute risk aversion; see Townsend (1985b).

This dismal outcome can be avoided if the spatial itinerary of agents is altered or if the communication technology is slightly improved. Taking the first suggestion, suppose agents b and b' do not move in the above model. Then, as in W. Rogerson (1985) and Townsend (1982), intertemporal links and beneficial trade is possible. Indeed, more elaborate set-ups in which agents return periodically to some go-between allow beneficial trade and suggest a model of an intermediary.

Taking the second suggestion, while still precluding telecommunications and commodity storage, suppose the existence of portable concealable artificial tokens – objects that do not enter into anyone's utility function or into any production technology but that can be carried about and redistributed at any location where agents meet under the prespecified rules of a resource allocation process. Then, in the model considered above, beginning-of-second-period token holdings are an endogenously determined and privately observed endowment, an extra state variable that can be announced by the agents, triggering taxes and subsidies both of tokens and actual commodities. Indeed, with the symmetry assumptions, one can write down an (apparent) two-agent, two-period programming problem, much like Program 6.1 with the following exceptions: There are token as well as commodity taxes and subsidies at the first date, contingent on a's (or a''s) endowment announcement at the first date, say θ_1; there are token as well as commodity taxes and subsidies at the second date, contingent on a's (or a''s) endowment announcement at the second date, say θ_2, *and* on a's (or a''s) announced beginning-of-period token holdings, say m_2; and there are incentive constraints in both the first and second periods, to ensure truthful revelations. It can be shown that these portable concealable tokens allow beneficial multilateral trade.

These results can be extended in several directions. The first is by considering alternative communication technologies. For example, if one considers storage and bona fide commodity tokens, the intertemporal incentive constraints generally are more binding and the solutions generally are Pareto inferior; essentially, commodity storage confounds the use of objects as signals of past events. Alternatively, systems with multiple artificial tokens can dominate systems with single artificial tokens; that is, multiple tokens allow more intertemporal tie-ins and hence weakened or less binding incentive constraints. Written message systems generally do even better, in the sense that more history becomes a matter of reliable record and not subject to the requirements of incentive-compatible reporting. Finally, centralized electronic interspatial telecommunication systems represent an endpoint in the spectrum of communication technologies, removing limited communication as a constraint on the outcomes of programming problems.

These private-information, spatial-separation, limited-communication set-ups can be taken to observations from actual economies. For example, the role for intermediaries described above is not inconsistent with the role played by medieval bankers in twelfth-century Italy, as described by Townsend (1985). There, bankers were essentially person-specific oral assignment systems. Similarly, as is argued in Townsend (1987b), observations by anthropologists on the strange use of noninterchangeable multiple commodity currencies and ceremonial objects in various close-knit societies are not inconsistent with the use made (in the theory) of multiple portable tokens. There is also some evidence that financial instruments emerged in Europe in the fifteenth century as written messages sent among partners in long-term trading relationships; see Townsend (1985).

Another direction for this work is the study of optimal monetary policy, as in Townsend (1987a). For example, in writing down a programming problem for the determination of optimal arrangements in the token/currency set-up described above, one is naturally poised to ask questions concerning the optimal social use of currency in the face of various private and economywide shocks. One can use as a base the banking model of Diamond and Dybvig (1983), where groups of agents suffer from privately observed shocks determining their urgency to consume. The more urgent is consumption, the more goods an agent wishes to withdraw from an otherwise productive investment project. As for the model of Diamond and Dybvig, a Pareto optimal consumption allocation can be determined as some solution to a programming problem, as in Section 6. On this base, then, one can impose some spatial separation (say, two spatially separated investment projects) and suppose that groups of agents are exogenously shifted over time, much like single agents b and b' above.

Tokens then serve as concealable records of deferred consumption for patient movers, and it can be shown that both the level of tokens and the mix of tokens relative to location-specific "bank credits" should be responsive to economywide shocks determining the relative number of patient consumers and the relative number of movers. Thus Arrow–Debreu optimum problems allow considerable scope for activist monetary policy.

10 Programs with limited commitment

If the interpretation of currency given above seems somewhat unusual, perhaps that is because one does not tend to think of currency as an efficient communication device in the context of a social planning problem. Rather, one may view currency as an object that preserves value and facilitates trade in a decentralized market economy, an economy in which agents meet anonymously or infrequently and have little commitment to one another. Indeed, in Europe from the tenth to the fifteenth centuries, for example, gold coins circulated largely among international traders, facilitating interregional trade in occasional periodic meetings [see Townsend (1985)]. More generally, circulating currency emerged at roughly the same time as market exchange. This use of currency, then, has not yet been explained by the theory.

For that matter, markets themselves have not yet been explained by the theory. As emphasized, many of the programming problems described above can be decentralized with a price system, and in that sense an optimum is not inconsistent with the existence of markets. And price observations have been used to fit various of the economies described to data; see especially the work of Eichenbaum, Hansen, and Richard (1987). But the theory itself does not explain markets as an efficient institutional arrangement.

What the theory is missing, apparently, is some lack of commitment. That is, in the programming problems described above, it is as if agents agree at some initial date to allocation rules for future dates, contingencies, and locations – rules that are costlessly enforced and maintained despite possible time inconsistencies and incentives to renege. In fact, it may be difficult to enforce such rules and prevent reneging, and this can be an important determinant of actual arrangements.

A natural way to introduce limited commitment is to suppose that planning problems must be solved successively, period by period, perhaps for particular and potentially variable weights λ^j across agent types j. Thus there would be no precommitment to a social rule, and agents would do what is best for themselves at the moment looking forward to the future. Indeed, this leads logically to the notion of a *sequential core*, something akin to a notion suggested earlier by Gale (1980). In some last period (if there is one), the allocation of consumption goods must be in the core, not blocked by a coalition of agents. With the prespecified direct utility functions for consumption, this core outcome then induces indirect utility functions for all agents up to state variables such as beginning-of-period capital holdings or currency. Then, in the next-to-last period, the allocation of consumption goods and capital or currency must be in the core – given the current state, the contemporary direct utility functions for consumption, and the last-period value functions derived above. Continuing in this way, perhaps indefinitely (so as to be rid of sensitivity to initial conditions), one can generate sequential core outcomes.

An equivalence between core allocations and competitive-equilibrium allocations then helps to make the connection to models with sequential competitive markets. In the models of currency with spatially separated agents described in Townsend (1980), for example, agents move about exogenously from location to location, trade commodities against paper currency in competitive markets when they meet, and then continue on, perhaps never to meet again. Thus one can conjecture that the noninterventionist monetary equilibria of Townsend (1980) – equilibria with valued currency – are (essentially) equivalent to sequential core outcomes, and the role played by currency when commitment is limited would be explained. Again, this theory would be consistent with the observations given above on the emergence and use of currency.

Thus spatial models of currency, and some of the so-called Clower constraint models of currency [e.g., Lucas and Stokey (1984), Townsend (1987d)], appear to be within the Arrow–Debreu tradition described in this chapter: They seem to yield outcomes that are solutions to programming problems with limited commitment. Further, these currency models promise to be an interesting base for the study of more traditional macroeconomic phenomena, addressing observations that are anomalous relative to the standard neoclassical growth model. Finally, in better matching the environment of the theory with the environments of actual economies, this class of spatial limited-commitment models promises to be an interesting study in its own right.

References

Altug, S. J. 1984. "Gestation Lags and the Business Cycle: An Empirical Analysis." Ph.D. dissertation, Carnegie-Mellon University.

Arrow, K. 1964. "The Role of Securities in the Optimal Allocation of Risk Bearing." *Review of Economic Studies* 31: 91–6.

Baiman, S., and J. Demski. 1980. "Economically Optimal Performance Evaluations and Control Systems." *Journal of Accounting Research* (supplement): 184–220.

Bewley, T. F. 1972. "Existence of Equilibria in Economies with Infinitely Many Commodities." *Journal of Economic Theory* 4: 514–40.

Bennett, H. S. 1974. *Life on the English Manor.* Cambridge: Cambridge University Press.

Binswanger, Hans, and Mark R. Rosenzweig. 1984. *Contractual Arrangements, Employment, and Wages in Rural Labor Markets in Asia.* New Haven: Yale University Press.

Boyd, J., and E. Prescott. 1986. "Financial Intermediary Coalitions." *Journal of Economic Theory* 38: 211–32.

Brock, W. A., and L. Mirman. 1972. "Optimal Economic Growth and Uncertainty: The Discounted Case." *Journal of Economic Theory* 4: 479–513.

Brunner, K., and A. H. Meltzer. 1971. "The Uses of Money: Money in the Theory of an Exchange Economy." *American Economic Review* 61: 784–805.

Cass, D. 1965. "Optimal Growth in Aggregate Model of Capital Accumulation." *Review of Economic Studies* 32: 233–40.

Danthine, J. P., and J. B. Donaldson. 1981. "Stochastic Properties of Fast vs. Slow Growing Economies." *Econometrica* 49: 1007–33.

Debreu, G. 1954. "Valuation Equilibrium and Pareto Optimum." *Proceedings of the National Academy of Science* 40: 588–92.

1959. *The Theory of Value.* New York: Wiley.

1962. "New Concepts and Techniques for Equilibrium Analysis." *International Economic Review* 3: 257–73.

Diamond, Douglas. 1984. "Financial Intermediaries and Delegated Monitoring." *Review of Economic Studies* 51: 393–414.

Diamond, D., and P. Dybvig. 1983. "Bank Runs, Deposit Insurance, and Liquidity." *Journal of Political Economy* 91: 401–10.

Diamond, Peter. 1967. "The Role of Stock Markets in a General Equilibrium Model with Technological Uncertainty." *American Economic Review* 57: 759–76.

Eichenbaum, M. S., and L. P. Hansen. 1987. "Estimating Models with Intertemporal Substitution using Aggregate Time Series Data." NBER Working Paper No. 2181.

Eichenbaum, M. S., L. P. Hansen, and S. Richard. 1987. "Aggregation, Durable Goods, and Nonseparable Preferences in an Equilibrium Asset Pricing Model." Unpublished manuscript.

Firth, Raymond. 1939. *Primitive Polynesian Economy.* London: Stephen Austin and Sons.

Gale, D. 1980. "Money, Information and Equilibrium in Large Economies." *Journal of Economic Theory* 23: 28–65.

Gorman, W. M. 1953. "Community Preference Fields." *Econometrica* 21: 63–80.

Green, Edward J. 1985. "Lending and the Smoothing of Uninsurable Income." Unpublished manuscript.

426   Robert M. Townsend

Grossman, S., and O. Hart. 1983. "An Analysis of the Principal Agent Problem." *Econometrica* 51: 7–46.

Grossman, S., and R. Shiller. 1981. "The Determinants of the Variability of Stock Market Prices." *American Economic Review, Papers and Proceedings* 71: 222–7.

Hall, R. E. 1981. "Intertemporal Substitution in Consumption." Mimeo, Hoover Institution, Department of Economics, Stanford University.

Hansen, Gary. 1985. "Indivisible Labor and the Business Cycle." *Journal of Monetary Economics* 16: 309–27.

Hansen, Lars P. In press. "Calculating Asset Prices in Three Example Economies." In T. F. Bewley (ed.), *Advances in Economic Theory – Fifth World Congress*, Vol. I. Cambridge: Cambridge University Press.

Hansen, L. P., and S. Richard. In press. "The Role of Conditioning Information in Deducing Testable Restrictions Implied by Dynamic Asset Pricing Models." *Econometrica*.

Hansen, L. P., and K. J. Singleton. 1982. "Generalized Instrumental Variables Estimation of Nonlinear Rational Expectations Models." *Econometrica* 50: 1269–86.

  1983. "Stochastic Consumption, Risk Aversion, and the Temporal Behavior of Stock Market Returns." *Journal of Political Economy* 91: 249–65.

Harris, M., and A. Raviv. 1979. "Optimal Incentive Contracts with Imperfect Information." *Journal of Economic Theory* 20: 231–59.

Harris, M., and R. M. Townsend. 1981. "Resource Allocation under Asymmetric Information." *Econometrica* 49: 33–64.

Holmström, Bengt. 1979. "Moral Hazard and Observability." *Bell Journal of Economics* 10: 74–91.

  1982. "Moral Hazard in Teams." *Bell Journal of Economics* 13: 324–40.

Homans, George C. 1975. *English Villagers of the Thirteenth Century*. New York: Norton.

Ito, Takatoshi. 1984. "Self-Selection and Moral Hazard in Implicit Contracts with Asymmetric Information on Workers' Search." Unpublished manuscript.

Koopmans, T. 1965. "On the Concept of Optimal Economic Growth." *Academic Science* 28: 225–300.

Kydland, F. E., and E. C. Prescott. 1982. "Time to Build and Aggregate Fluctuations." *Econometrica* 50: 1345–70.

Lee, Richard. 1979. *The !Kung San*. Cambridge: Cambridge University Press.

Leme, Paulo. 1984. "Integration of International Capital Markets." Unpublished manuscript, University of Chicago.

Lucas, Robert E. 1985. "On the Mechanics of Economic Development." Unpublished manuscript.

  1987. *Models of Business Cycles*. YRJO Jahnsson Lectures. Oxford: Blackwell.

Lucas, R. E., and N. L. Stokey. 1984. "Optimal Fiscal and Monetary Policy in an Economy without Capital." *Journal of Monetary Economics* 12: 55–93.

McCloskey, Donald. 1976. "English Open Fields as Behavior Towards Risk." *Research in Economic History* pp. 124–71.

McKenzie, L. W. 1959. "On the Existence of General Economic Equilibrium for a Competitive Market." *Econometrica* 27: 54–71.

Malinowski, Bronislaw. 1953. *Argonauts of the Western Pacific,* Chapter 3. New York: Dutton.

Mankiw, N., G. and J. Rotemberg, and L. H. Summers. 1985. "Intertemporal Substitution in Macro-Economics." *Quarterly Journal of Economics* 100: 225–52.

Mas-Colell, Andreu. 1975. "A Model of Equilibrium with Differentiated Commodities." *Journal of Mathematical Economics* 2: 263–95.

Mehra, R., and E. C. Prescott. 1985. "The Equity Premium: A Puzzle." *Journal of Monetary Economics* 15: 145–61.

Mirrlees, J. A. 1975. "The Theory of Moral Hazard and Unobservable Behavior, Part 1." Oxford Mimeos, Nuffield College.

Moore, John. 1984. "Contracting Between Two Parties with Private Information." Unpublished manuscript.

Myerson, Roger B. 1979. "Incentive Compatibility and the Bargaining Problem." *Econometrica* 47: 61–74.

   1982. "Optimal Coordination Mechanisms in Generalized Principal–Agent Problems." *Journal of Mathematical Economics* 10: 67–81.

   1986. "Multistage Games with Communication." *Econometrica* 54: 323–58.

Ostroy, J. M. 1973. "The Informational Efficiency of Monetary Exchange." *American Economic Review* 63: 597–610.

Ostroy, J. M., and R. M. Starr. 1974. "Money and the Decentralization of Exchange." *Econometrica* 52: 1093–1113.

Prescott, E., and R. Townsend. 1984a. "Pareto Optima and Competitive Equilibria with Adverse Selection and Moral Hazard." *Econometrica* 52: 21–45.

   1984b. "General Competitive Analysis in an Economy with Private Information." *International Economic Review* 25: 1–20.

Rogerson, Richard. 1985. "Nonconvexities and the Aggregate Labor Market." Working Paper.

Rogerson, William. 1985. "Repeated Moral Hazard." *Econometrica* 53: 69–76.

Rothschild, Michael, and Joseph Stiglitz. 1976. "Equilibrium in Competitive Insurance Market." *Quarterly Journal of Economics* 90: 629–49.

Sargent, T. J. 1979. "Tobin's *q'* and the Rate of Investment in General Equilibrium." In K. Brunner and A. Meltzer (eds.), *On the State of Macroeconomics.* Amsterdam: North-Holland.

Scheinkman, Jose A. 1984. "General Equilibrium Models of Economic Fluctuations: A Survey of Theory." Unpublished manuscript, University of Chicago.

Shavell, S. 1979. "Risk Sharing and Incentives in the Principal and Agent Relationship." *Bell Journal of Economics* 10: 55–73.

Shiller, R. J. 1981. "Do Stock Prices Move too Much to be Justified by Subsequent Changes in Dividends." *American Economic Review* 71: 421–36.

Spence, Michael. 1974. *Market Signaling.* Cambridge, Mass.: Harvard University Press.

Townsend, Robert. 1978. "Intermediation with Costly Bilateral Exchange." *Review of Economic Studies* 45: 417–25.

1979. "Optimal Contracts and Competitive Markets with Costly State Verification." *Journal of Economic Theory* 21: 265–93.

1980. "Models of Money with Spatially Separated Agents." In Neil Wallace and John Kareken (eds.), *Models of Monetary Economies.* Federal Reserve Bank of Minneapolis.

1982. "Optimal Multiperiod Contracts and the Gain from Enduring Relationships under Private Information." *Journal of Political Economy* 90: 1166–86.

1983. "Theories of Intermediated Structures." *Carnegie-Rochester Conference Series on Public Policy* 18: 221–72.

1985. "Taking Theory to History: Explaining Financial Structure and Economic Organization." Unpublished manuscript.

1987a. "An Optimal Activist Currency Rule." Unpublished manuscript.

1987b. "Economic Organization with Limited Communication." Unpublished manuscript.

1987c. "Private Information, Volatility, and Economic Welfare." Unpublished manuscript.

1987d. "Asset Return Anomalies in a Monetary Economy." *Journal of Economic Theory* 41: 219–47.

Van Roy, Edward. 1971. *Economic Systems of Northern Thailand: Structure and Change.* Ithaca, N.Y.: Cornell University Press.

Wilson, C. 1977. "A Model of Insurance Markets with Incomplete Information." *Journal of Economic Theory* 16: 167–207.

Wilson, Robert. 1968. "The Theory of Syndicates." *Econometrica* 36: 119–293.

Printed in the United States
By Bookmasters